COMMITTEES AND COMMISSIONS IN INDIA

Details of Published Volumes

COMMITTEES AND COMMISSIONS IN INDIA 1947-80

(In 18 Vols.)

Vol. 1	1947-54	Rs. 1500
Vol. 2	1955-57	Rs. 1500
Vol. 3	1958-59	Rs. 1500
Vol. 4	1960-61	Rs. 1500
Vol. 5	1962-63	Rs. 1500
Vol. 6	1964-65	Rs. 1500
Vol. 7	1966	Rs. 1500
Vol. 8	1967	Rs. 1500
Vol. 9	1968-69	Rs. 1500
Vol. 10	1970	Rs. 1500
Vol. 11	1971-73	Rs. 1500
Vol. 12	1974	Rs. 750
Vol. 13	1975	Rs. 750
Vol. 14	1976	Rs. 750
Vol. 15A	1977	Rs. 750
Vol. 15B	1977	Rs. 750
Vol. 15C	1977	Rs. 750
Vol. 15D	1977	Rs. 750
Vol. 16A	1978	Rs. 750
Vol. 16B	1978	Rs. 750
Vol. 17A	1979	Rs. 750
Vol. 17B	1979	Rs. 750
Vol. 18A	1980	Rs. 750
Vol. 18B	1980	Rs. 750

COMMITTEES AND COMMISSIONS IN INDIA 1947-1973

Volume X : 1970

Virendra Kumar

CONCEPT PUBLISHING COMPANY, PVT. LTD. NEW DELHI-110059

ISBN : 81-7022-217-2 (Vol. X)

First Published 1983
Reprinted 2011

Virendra Kumar *(b. 1933-)*

Published and Printed by
Ashok Kumar Mittal
Concept Publishing Company Pvt. Ltd.
A/15-16, Commercial Block, Mohan Garden
NEW DELHI-110059 (India)

Phones : 25351460, 25351794
Fax : 091-11-25357109
Email : publishing@conceptpub.com
Website : www.conceptpub.com

INTRODUCTION

The Tenth Volume attempts to understand and analyse the activities of the various "Committees and Commissions" during the period 1970 which have received, as far as the previous Volumes are concerned, scant attention from even bibliographies and documentation experts. It is known that governments all over the world largely rely on Committees and Commissions for their decisions on particular subjects. Governments make extensive use of the Instrument of Public Enquiries which ultimately help in lessening managerial tensions as well as in quietening the allegations of misrule. According to John Stuart Mill, "A man seldom judges right, even in his own concerns, still less in those of the public, when he makes habitual use of knowledge but his own or that of some single adviser". Thus the "Committee System" greatly helps the proper functioning of a democratic set-up.

A Commission is a "Governmental Agency created to perform a particular function such as a special investigation or on governmental regulations of business". It is appointed mainly when it is thought that a matter involves some financial questions. There are other reasons for which a Commission is appointed, e.g., in matters pertaining to the welfare of the State and its citizens and for improving the efficiency in an administration. The status of a Committee is the same as that of a Commission, but it does not possess powers as wide as are enjoyed by a Commission and has to limit itself in relation to specific work assigned to it under its term of reference. While arriving at decisions in the form of recommendations, a Committee or Commission ensures that such decisions are representative of the interests of various types of people and also a safeguard against abuse of power.

Committees and Commissions always advise a Government offering valuable suggestions and recommendations for smooth operation and efficiency in administration for the welfare of the people.

A Committee or a Commission comprises a Chairman, the Members and the Member-Secretary (sometimes there is also a Vice-Chairman and an Assistant Secretary). In some cases there are even One-Man Commissions and enquiries conducted by such Commissions are entrusted to an Official-on-Special Duty or a Judge of the High Court.

The Chairman of a Commission is a person well versed in legal affairs and is often a retired Judge of a High Court or the Supreme Court of India. Occasionally, a Member of Parliament is also appointed to the post of Chairman of a Commission. Regarding Committees, the Chairman is usually a specialist in the subject of the Committee. He can be a Leader or a Convener also if he heads a Panel, Study Group, Working Group or a Delegation, etc.

The Members of a Commission, Committee, Panel, Study Group, Working Group etc., are specialists in their respective fields and provide valuable guidance to the Commission in making recommendations.

The Member-Secretary or Secretary is nominated from among the experienced officials who have the requisite competent knowledge of the subject on which the Commission or the Committee is appointed.

The Study of the "Committees and Commissions" is divided into two main parts :

(I) **Pre-Independence :** From 1772 to August 1947; and

(II) **Post-Independence** : From August 1947 to 1973.

The First Volume covers the period from August 1947 to 1954, the Second Volume covers the period from 1955 to 1957, the Third Volume covers the period from 1958 to 1959; the Fourth Volume covers the period from 1960 to 1961; the Fifth Volume covers the period from 1962 to 1963; the Sixth Volume covers the period from 1964 to 1965; the Seventh Volume covers the period from 1966. The Eighth Volume covers the period from 1967; the Ninth Volume covers the period from 1968 to 1969. The present Volume, Volume Ten in the Series covers the year 1970.

The work provides information on subjects like **Bibliographical Data** of the Committees and Commissions, the **Chairman, Leader, Convener,** etc., **Appointments, Terms of Reference, Contents** and **Recommendations.**

Arrangements : The arrangements in the "Committees and Commissions" are chronological and items have been arranged according to their dates of appointment and not according to their dates of publication.

I am sure, that this reference work will continue into a number of volumes, for it is unique in nature. I have spared no efforts to make it a comprehensive reference work and it will be of great use to research scholars, sociologists, historians, economists, students of political science, as well as to all those connected with the study of administration and legal affairs. I have tried my level best to rectify all errors of commission and omission that I noticed in the previous Volumes. It will be my effort to go on improving these Volumes. The introductory part in Volume I deals with the **why, what** and **how** of the "Committees & Commissions".

In the end, I must express my gratitude to the Press that reviewed and appreciated the work. I am also indebted to my wife and children who have sacrificed their personal comforts by providing me with every facility to make this Volume ready for publication within a reasonably short time.

VIRENDRA KUMAR

NEW DELHI
Makar Sankranti
14 January 1983

CONTENTS

1970

BANKING COMMISSION, STUDY GROUP ON BANK PROCEDURES, 1970—REPORT

Delhi, Manager of Publications, 1971. 182p.

Chairman : Shri D.R. Joshi.
Members : Shri T.N. Ramamurthi; Shri N.K. Randeria; Shri V. Mahadevan; Shri S.P. Chandavarkar; Shri Krishan Murari; Shri J.B. Kamath.
Convener : Shri K.B. Chore.

APPOINTMENT

According to one of its Terms of Reference, the Banking Commission set up by the Government of India is required to make recommendations for improving and modernising the operating methods and procedures and the management policies of Commercial Banks. The Commission appointed the Study Group in February 1970 to go into the matter and to make suitable recommendations.

TERMS OF REFERENCE

(i) To review the operating methods and procedures prevalent in the banking system in the country and to make suitable recommendations for their improvement, keeping in view the need for rendering speedy and efficient service to various types of constituents as also the safety of banking transactions.

(ii) To make recommendations on any other related subject matter which the Study Group may consider germane to the subject of enquiry or any related matter which may specifically be referred to the Group by the Commission.

CONTENTS

Introduction; Background and Formulation of Approach; Deposits; Clearing; Collection of Outstation Cheques, Bills and Other Instruments; Remittances; Advances—General; Financing of Agriculture; Financing of Small Scale Industries; Financing of Exports; Financing of Other Small Borrowers; Inter-Branch Account; Internal Audit and Inspection; Periodical Returns; Miscellaneous; Summary of Recommendations; Annexures from I to V; Appendices from I to III.

RECOMMENDATIONS

Various recommendations made by us in earlier chapters are summarised below. Figures in brackets indicate the chapter number and paragraph number in which the relative recommendation has been incorporated.

Deposits

The statements of account and pass books should be written neatly, legibly and accurately and furnished to the customers promptly. Adequate arrangements should also be made to ensure prompt compliance with the customers' stop payment and standing instructions.

The teller system should be adopted in all banks at all important branches for encashment of cheques and receipt of cash for credit to accounts. Banks may use their discretion as regards the type of the teller system, the nature of accounts to which it should be made applicable as well as in regard to the maximum limit for receipt and payment of cash under the system.

First line supervisors should be permitted to pass cheques for payment in cash upto at least Rs. 5000. Ledger keepers should also be given powers to pass cheques for small amounts depending upoh the size of the branch and the experience of the concerned staff. They should be entrusted with authority to issue cheque books against production of requisition slips to the depositors who call at the bank personally.

Whenever necessary, supervising officers should go to ledger keepers for passing cheques instead of waiting for the papers, ledgers or registers to be brought to them by messengers.

The system of maintaining accounts in an alphabetical order should be replaced by a numerical system. The number allotted to each account holder may be so devised as to indicate some information about him e.g. profession, constitution (individual, firm, company) etc., by adding suitable prefix to his account number. To facilitate location of accounts, card indices should be maintained both in alphabetical as well as numerical order and where necessary, rotating equipment should be used for tracing accounts.

Mechanisation should be introduced by banks, especially at larger branches, by adopting a phased programme on a planned basis and by taking the employees' unions into confidence. This will enable the staff doing work involving a lot of drudgery to do work of a higher order and enable their abilities to be used for more faithful purpose. The Government on its part should also take positive steps to help the banks in getting over the difficulties such as non-availability of machines and opposition, if any, of the staff.

Banks should exercise adequate care and take concerted action while buying machines to avoid their underutilisation and their becoming obsolete due to change in procedures and other reasons. Indigenous manufacturers should be encouraged to produce machines to suit the requirements of Indian banking. Each bank should devise a system of data processing to serve both the operational requirements and the requirements in respect of economic information of the bank itself as also of the Reserve Bank and the Government.

Issue of pass books should be discontinued in respect of savings bank account holders who are allowed to make withdrawals by cheques and instead statements of account should be supplied to them, say at bimonthly intervals. The banks which still issue pass books to the current account depositors should switch over to the system of furnishing statements of account.

The practice of obtaining balance confirmations for credit balances in deposit accounts should be discontinued. The statements of account furnished to the depositors should contain a stipulation that the items and the balances shown therein should be verified by the concerned depositor and the bank notified of any discrepancy within a specified time, failing which the last balances shown would be presumed as correct. The branch agent should, however, be allowed discretion to obtain confirmations in particular accounts where he considers them necessary in the light of his personal knowledge about the depositor and operations in their accounts. Besides, the Internal Auditor, during the course of audit should request a few depositors, selected at random, to confirm their balances, and send the confirmations direct to him.

Banks should issue cheque books with crossing printed thereon to the customers who require them. Such customers should be provided with two cheque books simultaneously—a crossed one and an open one—printed in different colours for easy identification.

A similar system should be followed in respect of bank drafts.

Banks may consider the feasibility of making payment of interest on fixed deposits on the expiry of every six months from the date of deposit instead of paying it at the end of each calendar half year.

Intricate and detailed calculations may not be resorted to for arriving at the exact amount of interest payable on various types of deposits at the end of each month for the purpose of making provision therefor. An approximate provision may be made on the basis of average rate of interest paid during the previous half year applied on the daily balances in the General ledger.

Banks should take expeditious steps to encourage the members of the staff and officers to learn local languages and for dispensing with the practice of obtaining letters of idemnity for vernacular signatures of the depositors and of transcribing and attesting such signatures.

Banks should make arrangements for keeping on record photographs of illiterate depositors for facilitating their identification. The branches at places where the facility for obtaining photographs is not available, should be provided with cameras and the branch officials given some training in taking photographs.

Banks may adopt the system of balancing the current account ledgers at monthly intervals instead of at weekly or fortnightly intervals. While summations should be worked out on ledger folios in order to verify the correctness of the balance in the account, their periodical balancing may be dispensed with.

Clearing

The feasibility of opening clearing houses at places with population of more than 50,000 which are served by more than 3 or 4 banks should be examined keeping in view the factors such as the expenses involved, the problem of space and personnel. The number of bank accounts and the average number of instruments that would pass through clearing, the State Bank of India should take a lead in the matter as it or its subsidiaries manage the clearing houses at places where the Reserve Bank of India has no office. At centres where the State Bank of India is not established but other banks or their customers feel a need for establishment of a clearing house, the initiative should be taken by the banks themselves, preferably by the lead bank.

In order to reduce the work-load on the clearing houses and main offices of banks in metropolitan cities and with a view to ensuring quicker clearance of cheques the feasibility of opening sub-clearing houses should be expeditiously considered by the Indian Banks' Association. The location of sub-clearing houses should depend upon the concentration of branches, the communication facilities and volume and pattern of payment flows. Banks which have not so far introduced the system of 'home' clearing in metropolitan cities should do so, so that cheques tendered by an account holder for credit of his account and drawn on another local branch of the same bank are realised expeditiously.

The question of admitting non-scheduled banks and co-operative banks as full-fledged members of clearing houses as also liberalising the clearing house rules regarding the number of instruments and banks, the terms and conditions of membership etc., should be examined by the Reserve Bank of India and the State Bank of India.

The measures relating to the simplification of clearing procedures are being considered by the Indian Banks' Association with particular reference to the city of Bombay. Special problems relating to the clearing of cheques in other large centres should also receive similar attention.

Steps should be taken to gradually discontinue the Outward Clearing Register. Customers should be required to note the details, now entered in the register, on the reverse of the pay-in-slips.

In order to facilitate tracing of credits and debits and matching them at a later stage, cheques and pay-in-slips should be appropriately numbered and the numbers of the accounts to which credits are being given should be recorded on the reverse of the cheques.

The feasibility of introducing the system of "Flying Squad" for collecting the cheques for the day's clearing may be considered by banks having a large number of branches in big cities.

Use of cheque sorting machines should be made at major branches of banks for expediting clearing work and minimising the occurrence of clearing differences.

Collection of Outstation Cheques, Bills and other Instruments

The Indian Banks' Association should take expeditious steps to introduce courier system for transmitting outstation bills, cheques, etc., on behalf of member banks from one centre to another by night air mail. Government should also render such help, as may be necessary, in resolving the legal and technical difficulties which the Association might encounter. After the scheme proves successful, the feasibility of extending it to other cities connected by air should be examined by the Association. Alternatively, the Postal Department itself may consider organising a courier system by making appropriate arrangements. It may recover from the banks the costs incurred by it on the basis of an agreed formula.

Banks should issue instructions to their branches that the cheques and drafts sent by them to outstation branches for collection, through the courier system, should be considered as realised and proceeds credited to the customers' accounts if they are not returned unpaid or information regarding their dishonour is not received from the collecting branches within seven clear working days. In order to minimise the risk involved, non-payment advices should be sent through the courier system and in the case of instruments for large amounts non-payment may also be advised by telegram telex.

Even as regards the cheques and drafts sent for collection to outstation centres which are not covered by the courier system, credit to the relative customers' accounts should be afforded after lapse of specified periods even if the information regarding the fate of the instrument is not received from the collecting branch. Further, banks may progressively adopt the system of purchase/discount of cheques and bills in replacement of the collection system. At large towns where the collection business is sizable, banks may consider opening 'collection branches' in suitable localities exclusively for this business.

Banks should introduce manifold system for collection of bills in order to avoid duplication of work involved in writing the same particulars in the bills registers, covering schedules, advices to parties, etc.

The Despatch Department should work, where necessary, on a shift basis so that covering schedules of bills, realisation advices, etc., which are ready for despatch in the afternoon can be sorted out and sent in the evening on the same day. The documents to be sent by registered post should be positively despatched at least on the next day. Branches doing sizable business should use addressograph, auto-weigh and franking machines in order to save labour and time involved in manual work.

Particulars of inward bills, cheques, etc., received for collection need not be entered in the Dak Receipt Register. After the covering schedules and the attached documents are sorted by the official receiving the dak, they should be handed over against acknowledgement to the official of the Bills Department/Deposit Accounts Departments by entering their total number in a pass book.

Toning up of the Bills and Despatch Departments so as to eliminate the errors in preparing covering schedules, realisation advices, writing the addresses, etc., will go a long way in minimising the complaints and rendering expeditious and satisfactory service to customers.

The practice of passing contra entries daily in the books in respect of bills under collection may be discontinued.

Remittances

First line supervisors, who are normally promoted to that position after adequate experience in the capacity of a clerk or a trainee officer, should be allowed to sign drafts singly at least upto Rs. 5,000. Manifold draft requisition form with carbon attached should be introduced in order to reduce the waiting time of customers. In order to popularise the drafts as a mode of remittances as also to inculcate the cheque habit amongst the public, it is necessary to dispense with the formality of identification in respect of instruments for small amounts, except in cases where there are reasonable grounds to suspect that the presenter is not entitled to receive payment. The legal aspects of the question should, therefore, be examined carefully and the provisions of law suitably amended, if necessary.

Such of the non-nationalised banks as are willing to participate in the scheme for inter-bank drawings and inter-bank collections (which is being considered by the Public Sector Banks) may be permitted to do so to the extent possible.

An independent agency with the collaboration of banks, embodying the principles of Giro, may be created to clear the transactions relating to transfer of funds within the metropolitan cities of Bombay, Calcutta, Delhi and Madras and in between these cities in the first instance. The agency may also undertake issue of travellers' cheques and drafts and clearance of transactions relating to remittance of funds by a non-account holder to an account holder and vice versa.

Advances—General

In order to expedite decision making and to exercise effective supervision and control over the working of the branches, regional offices should be created or reorganised by banks. The number of branches under the jurisdiction of a regional office in the mofussil may be 25 to 50 depending upon communication facilities, nature and volume of business conducted, contemplated expansion in the network of branches etc. In the metropolitan areas it may be possible for a regional office to handle a larger number of branches. The region should comprise a contiguous area, no branch being very far away from the regional office.

To ensure that regional offices do not become one-more tier in the administrative set up, they should be granted adequate powers not only for sanction of advances but also in regard to administrative matters. They should be placed under the charge of experienced and capable senior officers.

Regional offices should maintain specialised cells on functional basis with adequate trained staff for assessment of advance proposals from priority sectors and for supervision and review of advances granted to them. They should also conduct and arrange for surveys, research and pilot projects for development activities in respect of deposit mobilisation, geographical expansion and grant of credit of priority sectors. They should further maintain a close contact with the branches and review their working periodically.

The regional manager should not be over burdened with routine work so that he may be able to discharge his supervisory functions effectively as also to pay visits to the branches under his charge at least once in a quarter.

The head office should arrange to carry out periodically thorough inspections of the regional offices in order to ensure that they are discharging their functions effectively and efficiently.

Delegation of discretionary powers to agents and regional offices to sanction advances to small borrowers should be liberalised. While vesting such powers the head office should, however, prescribe overall ceiling on the total amount of credit that could be advanced at each of the branches to various categories of borrowers, in order to ensure equitable distribution of credit in relation to the bank's total available resources and in the context of liquidity requirements. Delegation of authority should be reviewed at least once in two to three years and discretionary powers should be varied, if necessary, according to requirements.

The provisions of Section 292 of the Companies Act, 1956 may be suitably amended so that in the case of banking companies, the Board of Directors is enabled to authorise the Chief Executive Officer or a committee of directors to exercise the powers of the Board in regard to specifying the total amount upto which loans may be made by the delegates, the purposes for which the loans may be made and the maximum amount of loan which may be made for each such purpose in individual cases.

A quarterly scrutiny of the advances to priority sectors granted by branch agents should be carried out by a set of roving officers attached to the functional cells at regional offices. After some time, when the agents have gained sufficient experience, the frequency of the scrutiny may be suitably reduced. Branches should be required to maintain a register recording the receipt of loan applications (whether made orally or in writing) and their disposal. The roving officers should examine this register in order to find out whether there has been any delay or wrongful refusal of credit facilities.

While exemplary punishment should be awarded to the agents who are found guilty of deliberate misuse of powers, gross negligence, dishonesty or favouritism in order to curb any tendency to abuse the powers vested in them, the agents should be protected even though an advance becomes difficult of recovery if it was granted in the normal course without mala fide intent.

The application form in respect of advances to borrowers may be bifurcated into two parts—(i) application form to be filled in and signed by the borrower containing essential information of a simple nature relating to his bio-data and credit requirements, and (ii) interview form in which additional information obtained by questioning the applicant and perusing his books of account and other relevant papers may be recorded by the bank's officer.

While the application form may be common for all small advances, separate interview forms may be prescribed for different types of borrowers such as small scale industries, agriculturists, road transport operators, service unit owners, retail traders, etc.

Detailed credit reports need not be maintained on borrowers who have been sanctioned the following types of advances :—

(i) temporary overdrafts granted under the discretionary powers of the branch agent;

(ii) advances against deposits with the bank and surrender value of life insurance policies;

(iii) advances upto Rs 5 lakhs against government and other trustee securities;

(iv) advances upto Rs. 50,000 against readily marketable shares and debentures; and

(v) secured advances to agriculturists upto Rs. 10,000, to small scale industries upto Rs. 25,000 and to other small borrowers upto Rs. 10,000.

Banks should, however, ensure that the borrowers are properly introduced and also satisfy themselves regarding the viability of the project, purpose of the advance and need-based requirements before sanctioning the credit limits to them.

At the time of renewal of an advance, a fresh credit report may be prepared only if there have been any significant changes in the means and standing of the borrowers; in other cases a dated remark may merely be recorded on the earlier credit report stating that the information has been verified and the party's position substantially remains unchanged or briefly indicating the minor changes that have occurred. A suitable remark to the same effect should also be made on the renewal proposal sent to the regional/head office. However, a fresh credit report should be prepared at least once in two years.

Branches should not be required to send copies of credit reports to the head/regional office on borrowers to whom advances have been sanctioned under the agent's discretionary powers. The personal liabilities and assets of proprietors and partners of business concerns should be taken into consideration while assessing their credit-worthiness.

The Reserve Bank of India may examine the feasibility of establishing a Credit Intelligence Bureau for compiling and furnishing credit information to various financial institutions in the country by enlarging the functions of the Credit Information Bureau or by establishing a separate agency for the purpose.

Banks should, where necessary, suitably revise the advance proposal form which should contain adequate information regarding the volume and turnover of the borrower's business, sales and purchases on cash and credit basis, current assets and liabilities, extent of his own resources, seasonal trends and other relevant details justifying his credit requirements from the bank under different facilities.

The credit facilities to a borrower should be so arranged that the cycle of business from the purchase of raw materials to the receipt of sale proceeds is not hindered for lack of finance. The head office/regional office should also give discretion, to some extent, to the branch agent to interchange the limits according to requirements from time to time.

If a constituent has been borrowing from other sources for his business purposes, the bank should endeavour to persuade him to repay such borrowings and deal exclusively with it for all his credit requirements. If necessary, finance to repay existing borrowings from other sources should be made available, provided such borrowings are availed of for business purposes. Where the requirements of a borrower are large, the principle of one bank one borrower can, however, be modified by a consortium of banks entering into participation arrangements or by mutual arrangement between banks. Exception to the principle of one bank one borrower may also be allowed in the case of advances availed of from term financing institutions, factories of the same concern situated at different places, etc.

The Agent and/or other senior officials should pay frequent visits to the place of business of the borrowers accommodated for manufacturing, production or trading activities, for discussion with them on matters such as trend of business, difficulties encountered in dealing with the branch and measures to solve them.

Financing of Agriculture

The Agents of the rural branches should be vested with discretionary powers to sanction advances upto Rs. 3000 per borrower. The bulk of advances in excess of this amount should be allowed to be granted by regional offices and reference to the head office should be restricted to the proposals in regard to plantations, large scale farming, land development and irrigation schemes, etc.

Regional offices of banks should issue guidelines to branches in their respective areas indicating the scale of finance applicable to different types of crops by collecting information from the studies already made by other institutions, and also after consulting officials who have expert knowledge of the subject. They may also consider financing such studies by local universities, colleges or other expert bodies.

The total amount sanctioned to the farmers should be disbursed in instalments in accordance with their needs for various agricultural operations. The number of instalments should not, however, be too many (generally not exceeding three) as the agriculturist is busy during the season and he would find it difficult to visit the bank often to collect the loan instalments.

As far as possible, banks should disburse credit by making direct payments to the suppliers of inputs, taking care to see that finance in respect of a particular input is commensurate with the need-based requirements of the farmer. To avoid wide spread misuse of the facility, any instance of wrongful utilisation which comes to notice during the scrutiny of roving officers or branch officials or as a result of investigation of complaints received should be strictly dealt with by taking appropriate action against the relative dealer and the borrower.

Expeditious steps should be taken, in the light of the suggestions made by the Talwar Committee, to ensure that Commercial Banks are not made to suffer from any direct or indirect legal disabilities which Co-operative Banks are not subjected to and also to ensure that all the privileges and concessions enjoyed by these banks are extended to commercial banks.

Frequent visits should be paid to the farmers or borrowers by the branch officials as well as by the officers attached to the agricultural cells at regional offices. The purpose of the visit should be to ascertain the progress of cultivation, verification of security charged to the bank and of implements purchased with the use of bank's finance and to find out whether the finance already granted has been properly utilised as also to assess the quantum of finance needed for further agricultural operations. The branch agent should, as far as possible, ensure that such verification has been carried out before making available to the borrowers further drawings from their accounts in accordance with the phased programme for grant of credit. The branch officials have also to keep a watch on the marketing arrangements made by the farmer for disposal of his goods in order to ensure that the advance is repaid when the crop, for raising of which finance was made available by the bank, is sold by him.

The area served by a village branch should normally be restricted to a radius of about 15 to 20 kilometers from the branch depending upon the nature of available communication and conveyance facilities. Exceptions may, however, have to be made to this general rule in suitable cases, particularly in respect of underbanked regions until banking facilities are adequately spread out.

As far as possible, local persons with requisite minimum qualifications should be recruited at the rural branches. Further, to the extent possible, part time, temporary or seasonal staff may be employed at such branches.

The branches of banks at rural and mandi centres should be kept open in the evening, if necessary, by suitably reducing the working hours in the day time to provide convenience to the villagers. The extension of the facility of mobile banks can also be helpful in this regard.

Financing of Small Scale Industries

Branch agents of small urban branches should be vested with discretionary powers to sanction working capital advances to small scale industries at least to the extent of Rs. 10,000 against hypothecation of stocks; Rs. 25,000 against pledge of stocks, Rs. 2,500 on a clean basis and Rs. 10,000 against documentary bills. Powers of branch agents at bigger branches should be fixed suitably, taking into account the type of business at the branch and the experience and ability of the concerned officials. The bulk of the credit limits in excess of the discretionary powers of branch agents should be sanctioned by regional offices.

Relaxations from usual formalities such as grant of hypothecation advances or mandi type advances in place of factory type advances, release of pledged goods against trust receipts, low margins on the basis of the ability of the borrowing concerns to provide them and valuation of goods on a realistic basis should be extended to deserving small scale industries.

Financial guarantees to a reasonable extent may be given on behalf of small scale industries to enable them to secure contracts for supply of goods, carry out works undertaken etc.

In respect of working capital advances to small scale industries technical reports from consultancy firms or institutions need not be insisted upon as a matter of course.

Banks need not insist upon, as a matter of course, mortgage of immovable property and hypothecation of machinery as collateral security for working capital advances to small scale industries.

Visits to the factories of the barrowing concerns should be paid by the branch officials at least once a month and, besides, the technical staff at the regional offices should visit the factories at periodical intervals. As the Agents or the Accountants of branches having a large number of small scale industries accounts will not have sufficient time at their disposal to pay monthly visits, banks should appoint supervisors for the purpose at such branches.

A separate supplementary agency, as envisaged by the Thakkar Committee, should be created for giving guidance and rendering technical and management consultancy services to the borrowers rather than the banks themselves undertaking this function. Banks may, however, make available the service of their technical staff in their spare time to the borrowing units—on their request and on an informal basis for consultation on urgent problems.

Financing of Exports

The number of centres where banks provide intensive export finance facilities are limited and should, therefore, be increased.

Whenever documents (drawn under a letter of credit), tendered by the exporter for discounting, are sent by an inland branch to a branch authorised to transact foreign exchange business, the former branch should obtain idemnity from the exporter against any discrepancies in order to avoid protracted correspondence between the two branches.

To eliminate the delay involved in sending bills of exchange to the stamp office for being stamped before execution, banks should be allowed to stock stamps and instal special franking machines in larger offices, if necessary, by amending the Stamp Acts suitably. There is apparently a need for expansion of clean packing credit facilities. The grant of such facilities should depend upon the credit worthiness of the exporter, his past dealings and past export performance. Constant and strict vigilance would also be necessary to ensure proper end-use of such packing credit facilities.

An Inter-Bank Export Information Centre may be set up to collect and disseminate up-to-date export information which would be of general and practical interest to all banks and would benefit small exporters who have neither contacts nor financial means to explore foreign markets. In order to provide facilities to the customers and guidance to the branch agents, banks should post at least one officer with adequate knowledge of foreign exchange procedures at the regional offices which do not have fullfledged foreign exchange departments. These officers, whenever necessary, visit the branches within the region for guiding the agents and other staff in handling foreign exchange business as well as for attending to developmental activities and for giving assistance to the customers in respect of their foreign trade problems.

Financing of other Small Borrowers

Branch agents of small branches should be authorised to grant advances to small borrowers upto at least Rs. 5,000 on secured and Rs. 2,500 on clean basis without reference to the regional office or the head office. The powers of the agents of bigger branches should be suitably fixed at higher levels. The feasibility of creating a suitable machinery for registration of charge on movables, with a simple and inexpensive procedure for its verification, should be examined from legal as well as practical angles.

Banks may insist upon guarantees of third parties in respect of advances to small borrowers only when there are reasonable doubts about the repaying capacity of the borrower.

Branch officials should pay a visit to the borrowers' place of business, even in cases where clean advances have been granted, at least once a quarter, in order to keep a constant watch on the condition of their business. It should be ensured that the formalities prescribed regarding the submission of stock statements, maintenance of stock registers, etc., do not become irksome to small borrowers who are not in a position to maintain adequate staff for the purpose.

Banks may introduce night safe facility at suitable centres to enable small borrowers to deposit their daily cash collections for credit to their accounts on the following purpose.

Inter-Branch Accounts

Of the three inter-branch accounting systems, viz., mutual accounting system, centralised-cum-regional accounting system and centralised accounting system, the last named appears to be the most suitable as, besides ensuring effective control, it is also more amenable to mechanisation. However, inter-branch transactions between branches situated in the same city may be passed through the accounts maintained by them with the local main office instead of through the head office account. In order to avoid passing of incorrect entries at the responding branch, the originating branch should take care to ensure that the covering schedules, remittance or realisation advices and daily statements of head office account are neat, clear and accurate and are despatched promptly.

To eliminate the confusion caused by the similarity in names, code numbers should be allotted to branches which should be required to write the number, in addition to the name of the branch, on all advices, daily statements of head office account, remittance schedules etc.

The number of entries in inter-branch account can be reduced considerably by passing consolidated debit and credit entries in respect of each branch according to the categories of transactions instead of passing separate entries for each draft issued or each bill realised or for other similar transactions.

In order to facilitate matching of entries at the Central Accounts Section, daily transactions relating to inter branch account should be grouped at branches under specified categories and schedules of different colours should be prepared for each category of entries, using the same colour for schedules of debit and credit transactions of similar type. The schedules should be sent to head office together with the statement of head office account which should contain totals of debit and credit entries detailed in the schedules, besides the opening and closing balances.

Telegram and postage charges, etc., incurred in connection with the collection of bills should be borne by the branch which actually incurs them. To avoid protracted correspondence and disputes, such charges should not be debited to the branch from which the bill was received for collection.

The outstanding entries should be promptly followed up and the reasons for their remaining outstanding should be ascertained. The form used by the Central Accounts Section for obtaining comments of a branch in respect of outstanding entries, besides detailing the particulars of relative entries, should contain alternative replies expected from the branch in the lower portion separated by perforation.

The reasons for which the originating debit entries and reversal entries have been passed should be suitably explained by the branches while reporting them to the Central Accounts Section in the daily statements. The latter should examine the entries carefully.

The long outstanding entries for large amounts say

above Rs. 10,000, should be immediately brought to the notice of a senior executive who should decide whether any special probe is necessary in regard to any particular transaction.

The Internal Auditor should scrutinize the long outstanding entries pertaining to the branch during the course of his audit. Besides, he should make a sample check to the entries in the head office account at the branch. It may be useful in the case of banks having a large number of branches to select a few branches, on the basis of a properly devised sample, for examination of all transactions pertaining to say week or a fortnight.

Internal Audit and Inspection

Inspection staff should normally consist of Internal Auditors, Branch Inspectors and Godown Inspectors. However, as it may not be convenient for small banks to maintain inspection staff of three categories, the Branch Inspectors appointed by them may also carry out internal audit and godown inspection.

While the Internal Auditors may examine documents, operations, etc., in respect of all advances to agriculturists, they may verify securities only in respect of selected accounts on random sampling basis. It would, however, be desirable to verify all securities held in accounts which are grossly out of order or in respect of which complaints have been received. The Inspection and Audit Department should be directly responsible to the Chief Executive Officer of the bank. For the sake of convenience and in the interest of economy members of the inspection staff may be posted at different regional offices but they should be under the direct administrative charge of the head office and the regional managers should have no control over their promotions, transfers, increments, leave, etc., during the period they are entrusted with inspection duty.

In view of the nature of their duties, Internal Auditors should have a thorough knowledge of the procedures and at least five years' experience of handling different types of work in responsible capacities. Banks should institute suitable recruitment policies and training programmes to achieve this objective.

Branch Inspectors should be senior and experienced enough to be in a position to critically comment on and assess the quality of business conducted by the branch officials. The internal audit/inspection should ordinarily be conducted once every year on surprise basis. The verification of stocks pledged/hypothecated to the bank (which should also be on a surprise basis) should be carried out once in each quarter, one of the quarterly visits of the Godown Inspector should synchronize with the annual audit/inspection.

While drawing the inspection programme it should be ensured that an official does not visit the same branch consecutively. To facilitate chalking of inpection programme, Cards for each branch containing history of previous inspections may be maintained by the Inspection and Audit Department. The Cards should be arranged in a chronological order on the basis of the dates of last inspections.

As far as possible, the inspection should be taken up when the internal audit is nearing completion or soon after its completion. However, in the case of large branches, the audit and inspection may be taken up simultaneously and one or more Internal Auditors may be deputed to assist the Inspector. Continued presence of inspection staff at a branch for a long time disturbs its day-to-day working and, therefore, the size of the team should be sufficiently large so as to complete the audit/inspection expeditiously. Banks may carry out concurrent audit of their main offices in the metropolitan cities.

Branch inspection should not merely be a routine check of the books and records of the branch but an intelligent examination of the assets and liabilities and overall review of the branch's working.

Apart from the examination of various assets and liabilities of a branch outstanding at the time of audit a test check of some of the transactions effected since the date of last audit on random sampling basis, and a percentage check (say 5 to 10 percent) of the account opening forms, specimen signature cards, notings in respect of cheque books issued, recording of stop payment instructions, compliance with standing instructions, etc., should be made by the Internal Auditor.

In order to ensure that audit/inspection is thorough and exhaustive, a check list on the lines of the "Hand Book for Bank Inspector" prepared by the Bankers Training College should be supplied to the inspection staff. The approach of the Inspector should not be merely critical but should be constructive. He should not only bring out the irregularities observed but also make suggestions for improvement in the working of the branch. He should discuss the findings of the audit/inspection with the branch officials and should arrange with the branch agent to have minor irregularities rectified, to the extent possible, during the course of inspection. A list of such irregularities should be supplied to the branch agent and a copy thereof, together with the agent's comments, should be appended to the inspection report.

Major irregularities observed in the working of the branch which require specific action, including comments on advances which are grossly out of order, should be highlighted by incorporating them in an appendix to the report. Similarly, the suggestions for improving the working of the branch should also be given in another appendix. Inspection staff should make efforts not only to detect frauds committed by employees and/or others but also to find out laxity or loopholes in the procedures relating to accounting, checking, custody of valuables, security arrangements, etc., at the branch. On the basis of the findings of audit and inspection of a branch, the Inspector should arrive at an overall assessment of the working of the branch and classify it according to its standard of efficiency. In order to avoid personal bias and to eliminate subjective assessment, rating should be on a scientific basis. A representative body like the National Institute of Bank Management may compile a suitable scheme for this purpose for adoption by banks.

One copy of the audit report may be submitted by the Internal Auditor to the Inspection and Audit Department at the head office while another copy may be given to the branch for forwarding its comments to the head office. One copy should also be sent to the regional office. If the Internal Auditor observes any serious irregularity during the course of the audit, he should report it to the head office immediately by means of a separate communication. A copy of the inspection report should be sent to the regional office and the head office but not to the branch. The head office should examine the report and take up the matters on which action is necessary with the branch and the regional office.

Any serious irregularity reported to the head office by the Internal Auditor or the Inspector should be immediately brought to the notice of the Chief Executive Officer of the bank, who may, if considered necessary, refer it also to the Board of Directors/ Executive Committee. The irregularities should be followed up vigorously till they are rectified.

At the end of the each quarter, the Inspection and Audit Department should prepare a memorandum on the basis of the inspection/audit reports received during the quarter for submission to the Board of Directors, bringing out, inter alia, major irregularities observed and action taken or proposed to be taken to rectify them.

A Committee may be appointed under the auspices of the Reserve Bank of India or the National Institute of Bank Management to consider in detail the question of creation of a comman agency for inspection of the offices of all banks in the Public Sector and to formulate standard forms and procedures, keeping in view the need for progressive mechanisation on a planned basis for rendering better customer service.

Periodical Returns

Statistical returns (excepting those required to be sent by branches direct to the Reserve Bank of India) should be submitted to the regional office, which should send consolidated statements to the head office. However, where the head office has automation facilities, returns may be submitted direct to that office for consolidation and feed back of information to regional offices. Also, in cases where information is required for submission to the Government of India or the Reserve Bank of India urgently (e.g., weekly statement under Section 42 of the Reserve Bank of India Act 1934), it may continue to be collected by head offices. Considering the importance of analysis and processing of statistical information as an aid in formulation of policies in regard to operations, organisation, development and planning, it is necessary that banks should establish and/or strengthen Statistical/Economic Departments.

Branches should not be required to submit statements of all outstanding advances (other than U.B.B. returns) at frequent intervals and it will be adequate if such statements are called for once every year at the time of the annual closing.

Branches should not normally be required tn submit periodical returns giving details of advances sanctioned by officials within thier discretionary powers.

The control of the head office over advances through periodical returns should relate only to irregular advances, the position of the other advances being examined during the course of the annual inspection of branches. Branches should send returns of irregular advances (including bills purchased and discounted) to the regional office/head office at monthly intervals. Separate statements of irregular advances may be prepared for different types of advances, i.e., cash credits, fixed loans, over drafts, bills purchased, etc., and sent on different dates of the month so as to stagger the work at the branch and facilitate scrutiny at the head office. As regards the advances involved in litigation, a return may be sent at quarterly intervals.

The control returns should be scrutinised at the head office by the supervising staff and, where necessary, prompt follow-up action should be taken through the regional offices. All advances having serious irregularities, which are likely to jeopardise the bank's interests, should be immediately brought to the notice of the top management.

Internal Auditors, during their visits to branches, should make a test check of the statements sent to the head office/regional office in order to find out whether all relevant advances had been included in the concerned return and whether the various particulars had been mentioned therein correctly and fully.

Miscellaneous

At the branches where the teller system has not been introduced the waiting time of the customers paying in cash should be reduced by authorising the cashier to issue the counterfoil, without its being countersigned by another official. In order to maintain an independent record of cash receipts, Scroll Book may be maintained by a member of the Accounts Department who should sit near the cash counter.

Cash registering machines may be intorduced at bigger branches. Use of counting machines will also be helpful in expediting cash transactions. Cheques and other instruments tendered for collection should be allowed to be received by the bills clerk who should be authorised to sign the counterfoils singly after verifying that the instruments tendered are in accordance with the particulars noted in the pay-in-slip. Customers should, however, be notified to cross all instruments before tendering them for collection.

The practice of maintaining a record of denominations of currency notes in the Cash Receipt and Cash Payment books involves duplication and should be dispensed with. Further, for the sake of convenience, the particulars of currency notes may be noted on the face of the pay-in-slips instead of on the back by changing the form suitably.

Receipt and payment cashiers may be required to maintain cash boxes which may be locked by them at the close of business every day and deposited in the vault without their contents being checked by the Head Cashier. The locked boxes should be delivered to the cashiers next morning. Cashiers should certify every day the amount of cash contained in the locked boxes and proper record of it should be maintained. Where considered necessary, a maximum limit may be fixed for cash thus kept in the cashiers' boxes. The contents of the boxes should be verified at periodical intervals on a surprise visit by the head cashier/agent.

Increased use of ultra-violet ray equipment should be made by banks at their urban branches and they should also supply protectograph machines to all branches which are authorised to issue drafts. A planned programme for use of regional languages for account opening forms, pay-in-slips, cheque books, pass books, statements of account, etc., should be adopted and implemented by banks, so that within a period of three years or so dealings with customers are carried out entirely in the languages they fully understand. In order to make banking easily understood by the public, audio-visual publicity through exhibition of documentaries and publicity through pamphlets in regional languages, portraying the advantages of carrying out monetary transactions through the medium of banks, would be immensely helpful.

Government departments, local bodies, educational institutions, public utility concerns, public sector undertakings, etc., should encourage the use of cheques in their financial transactions with the public where necessary, by suitably amending their rules and regulations.

Banks may discontinue the practice of half-yearly closing of accounts at the end of June each year as it entails considerable labour without commensurate benefits.

The question of standardising the form of import letter of credit may be considered by the Exchange Central Department of the Reserve Bank of India in consultation with the Foreign Exchange Dealers' Association and in keeping with the requirements of importers. The Reserve Bank of India may also consider the feasibility of the suggestion that banks be allowed to send copies of letters of credit opened, with a covering list indicating only the distinctive numbers of letters of credit and their amounts, instead of the prescribed monthly statements of import letters of credit opened.

The Foreign Exchange Dealers' Association may consider standardising the form of mail transfer receipts.

Indian banks which have not so far established a separate O & M Department may establish it as early as possible. However, in case any of the small banks finds it difficult to establish a full-fledged department for the purpose, in view of the cost involved, it should train one or two of its officials in O & M work. These officials will be able to attend to O & M aspects of the bank's working, in addition to other normal duties, where necessary. The heads of O & M Department of different banks should meet periodically, say once every half-year, for exchanging the information regarding the studies made by them. The Reserve Bank of India may take the initiative in the matter. The banks which have not so far introduced a suggestion scheme should do so at an early date.

Complaint-cum-suggestions boxes should be provided at all branches of banks for use of the public. Regional Managers and Development Officers attached to regional offices, on their visit to the branches, should spare some time to hear the grievances and suggestions of the local constituents. Whenever possible, banks should try to shift a portion of the work at a very big branch to new premises in the same locality by opening another branch. For housing new branches, particularly in the rural areas where suitable premises on rent are not available, it would be preferable for banks to encourage construction of buildings by advancing money to persons owning suitable land instead of constructing the buildings themselves which would result in locking up of their funds. Adequate attention to matters such as lay out, colour scheme, construction of modern counters, pleasing lighting arrangements, decor, staff and customer amenities should be paid while planning new buildings. While designing a bank building, the problems of special categories of customers such as pensioners and women should be kept in view and discussed with the architects. The security aspect should of course be borne in mind.

The question of making a suitable legal provision permitting banks to destroy cheques, ledgers and other records after lapse of specified periods should be examined. Banks may also consider the feasibility of micro filming important records before their destruction, taking into account the cost aspect.

Banks should take steps to inprove the lay out in their offices, in order to enhance the efficiency of the staff as also for improving customer service, after conducting studies of office routine from time and motion and flow angles.

To begin with and on an experimental basis, administrative offices of banks may remain fully closed on Saturdays and, to compensate for the loss of man-hours, the working hours on other week days should be suitably enhanced. The question of introducing similar change in the bank offices dealing with the public may be considered later.

Wherever feasible, working hours in residential areas of urban centres may be in the mornings and evenings to suit the convenience of the clientele.

REVIEW COMMITTEE ON NATIONAL AKADEMIES AND INDIAN COUNCIL FOR CULTURAL RELATIONS, 1970—REPORT

New Delhi, Ministry of Education and Social Welfare, 1972. 221p.

Chairman : Shri Justice G.D. Khosla

Members : Shri Amrit Nahata; Prof. Hirendra Nath Mukherjee; Shri D.N. Tiwari; Shri Lok Nath Misra; Prof. Saiyid Nurul Hasan (resigned); Dr. Narayana Menon; Shri Sham Lal; Prof. A.K. Narain (resigned); Dr. Umashankar Joshi.

Coopted Members : Prof. Rasheeduddin Khan; Smt. Girija Devi; Smt. Rukmini Devi Arundale; Shri M.F. Hussain.

APPOINTMENT

The Review Committee on National Akademies and Indian Council for Cultural Relations was constituted under the Ministry of Education and Social Welfare vide their Resolution No. F. 16-35/69-C.A. II (3) dated 2 February 1970.

TERMS OF REFERENCE

(a) To review the working of the three National Akademies and the Indian Council for Cultural Relations with reference to their overall objectives and the recommendations made by the Bhabha Committee;

(b) To suggest measures for improving the working of these bodies and strengthening their activities in relation to broad priorities; and

(c) To recommend a suitable pattern of organisation and suggest changes as may be necessary in the articles of association (rules and regulations) consistent with the requirements of autonomy and public accountability.

CONTENTS

Introductory; Historical; Cultural Policies of Some Foreign States; Cultural Patterns and Responses in States; Achievements and Failings; Recommendations; Summary of Conclusions and Recommendations; Appendices; Note.

RECOMMENDATIONS

Two broad objectives of the Akademies may be

summarised as:

(a) to promote the growth and development of the creative arts, and

(b) to create conditions for the better dissemination of the arts.

The General Council of the Sahitya Akademi should be reorganised and consist of (i) the President, (ii) the Financial Adviser, (iii) five persons nominated by the Government of India of whom one shall be a representative of the Ministry of Information & Broadcasting, and one of the National Book Trust and two persons eminent in the fields of letters, (iv) one representative of each of the State Sahitya Akademies, or where there is no State Sahitya Akademi, a member elected by the recognised literary bodies in the State, (v) one representative each of the Sangeet Natak Akademi and Lalit Kala Akademi, (vi) twenty representatives of the Universities chosen from a panel consisting of three nominees of each university. No university can have more than one representative and each of the languages recognised by the National Sahitya Akademi must have at least one representative, (vii) Eight persons eminent in the field of letters coopted by the General Council.

The Lalit Kala Akademi should consist of (i) the Chairman, (ii) the Financial Adviser, (iii) the Director, National Museum or his nominee, (iv) the Curator, National Gallery of Modern Art, (v) Five persons nominated by the Government including a representative of the Ministry of Culture and four persons who are prominent art critics, art historians, or persons interested in the creative arts, (vi) one representative of each State Lalit Kala Akademi, (vii) Fifteen persons elected by a college of 200 persons formed by the common nominees of the Lalit Kala Akademi and the protesting artists and coopting further members, (viii) nine eminent artists appointed by the General Council, (ix) one representative each of the Sangeet Natak Akademi and Sahitya Akademi, (x) three persons well-known as art critics, art historians or Heads of Faculties of Arts and Archaeology, (xi) two representatives of the All India Board of Technical Studies in Applied Art, and (xii) four eminent architects.

The General Council of the Sangeet Natak Akademi should consist of (i) the Chairman, (ii) the Financial Adviser, (iii) five persons, not civil servants, nominated by the Government of India, (iv) one representative each of the State Sangeet Natak Akademies, (v) one representative of the Ministry of Information & Broadcasting, (vi) twenty persons to be coopted, of which six must represent the main schools of Indian classical dancing and folk dance and music, (vii) eight should represent music of which not less than three should have adequate knowledge of Hindustani music and not less than three of Karnataka music, the remaining six must represent drama, (viii) eight persons in the fields of music, dance and drama from different regions.

The Vice-Chairman will be elected by the General Council at its first meeting.

The Executive Board of each Akademi should consist of nine members, namely, the President, the Vice-President, the Financial Adviser, a representative of the Ministry of Culture and five persons elected by the General Council.

The Chairman, the Secretary and the senior officers in each Akademi must be either practising artists or have sufficient knowledge of the particular field of art in which they are called upon to work.

The Chairman of each Akademi should be appointed by the President of India out of a panel of three names selected by the General Council of the Akademi.

The General Council should meet at least twice a year and the Executive Board four or five times each year and devote more time to administrative matters.

The term of the President, the General Council and the Executive Board should be only four years and not be renewable more than once.

The number of Fellows should be 60 for the Sangeet Natak Akademi and the Sahitya Akademi and 30 for the Lalit Kala Akademi.

Each year's programme of all the Akademies should be published in a joint booklet by April 1.

Long term planning is essential. Ad hoc grants stand in the way of planning and programming.

The Akademies should remian distinct autonomous bodies, but there should be greater coordination between them and the Chairmen and Secretaries of the three Akademies should meet atleast once a quarter every year to exchange information and make joint plans. There should be one telephone exchange, one canteen, common lecture rooms, a common pool of photographers, designers and layout men for the three Akademies.

The States should set up Akademies on the pattern of National Akademies. These should be housed in Cultural Centres, the expenses being borne jointly by the State and the Centre. Each Centre must have an auditorium, a library, conference rooms, an exhibition gallery, rest rooms, green rooms, etc.

There should be constant report and discussion between the National Akademies and the State Akademies.

The Akademies should cease direct publication of all books.

The quality of translations must improve and there

should be more vigilant scrutiny of the quality of the translations.

The procedure for the award for books may remain unaltered, but the names of the judges and the reasons upon which their choice was based must be made public as soon as the awards are announced.

The Sangeet Natak Akademi may continue to sponsor recitals and performances. The State Akademies should concern themselves more enthusiastically in the development of folk art, music and dance.

The Sangeet Natak Akademi should hold a drama festival every year, and every second or third year an arts festival which should include the plastic and the performing arts.

Small sub-committees to deal with specific projects and programmes should be appointed by the Akademies.

The Akademies should prepare a comprehensive inventory of the cultural institutions in the country, giving essential information about the institutions, such as the date when it was established, the nature of the work done by it, the number of students being taught, the number of exhibitions held, the annual budget, etc. This inventory will facilitate the task of choosing deserving institutions for grants.

The Akademies should draw up a scheme for assisting old masters of music, dance and drama, indigent artists and retired writers.

The National School of Drama should be established as an independent institution with increased funds. A National Repertory Theatre should also be instituted.

The Kathak Kendra should not be administered by the Sangeet Nataka Akademi and should be allowed to resume its independent existence.

A travelling art exhibition will stimulate interest in the arts. National exhibition may be held in circulation at important artistic centres.

The Akademies should be consulted whenever cultural delegations are to be sent abroad and their advice should not normally be disregarded.

An attempt should be made to improve the quality of indigenous artists' materials.

There should be a scheme for the purchase of works of arts. Schools and colleges should be asked to buy the work of artists. A relief in income-tax should be given to persons who present works of art to the nation.

The journals published by the Akademies should be revitalised and improved in quality.

A thorough-going assessment of the people's artistic needs should be undertaken.

More money should be provided to the Akademies. A funding system should be adopted.

The Indian Council for Cultural Relations should pay more attention to neighbouring countries and countries which, though not openly hostile, have taken up attitudes which are not friendly. The Council should depend more on its own resources than on the uninformed advice of Cultural Attaches in the Embassies.

STUDY GROUP ON BANK PROCEDURES 1970—REPORT

Delhi, Manager of Publications, 1972. 182p+ixp.

Chairman : Shri D.R. Joshi.
Members : Shri T.N. Ramamurthi; Shri N.K. Randeria; Shri V. Mahadevan; Shri S.P. Chandavarkar; Shri Krishan Murari.
Convener : Shri K.B. Chore.

APPOINTMENT

According to one of its Terms of Reference, the Banking Commission set up by the Government of India is required to make recommendations for improving and modernising the operating methods and procedures and the management policies of commercial banks. The Commission appointed the Study Group vide their Office Order No. BCS/BP/1/70 dated February 14, 1970 to go into the matter and to make suitable recommendations.

TERMS OF REFERENCE

(i) To review the operating methods and procedures prevalent in the banking system in the country and to make suitable recommendations for their improvement, keeping in view the need for rendering speedy and efficient service to various types of constituents as also the safety of banking transactions;

(ii) To make recommendations on any other related subject matter which the Study Group may consider germane to the subject of enquiry or any related matter which may specifically be referred to the Group by the Commission.

CONTENTS

Introduction (Constitution of the Study Group; Composition of the Study Group; Terms of Reference; The Scope of Study; Procedure of Enquiry and Methodology Followed; Meetings of the Study Group; Preparation and Finalisation of the Report; Outline of the Report; Acknowledgements); Background and Formulation of Approach (A Brief Review of the Changes in Bank Procedures in India and Need for their Modernisation; Factors Governing the Bank Procedures; Studies Already Made Elsewhere in Regard to Improvement in Bank Procedures; the Study Group's Approach to the Subject); Deposits (Teller System; Simplification of Procedures for Passing of Cheques; Numerical System of Maintaining Ledger Accounts; Mechanisation; Statements of Account and Pass Books; Balance Confirmation Letters; Printing of Crossing on Cheques; Payment of Interest on Fixed Deposits; Accrued Interest on Deposits; Letter of Indemnity for Vernacular Signatures; Photographs of Illiterate Depositors; Balancing of Current Account Ledgers); Clearing (Extension of Clearing House Facilities; Relaxation of Clearing House Rules; Simplification of Clearing House Procedures; Use of Cheque Sorting Machines); Collection of Outstation Cheques, Bills and Other Instruments (Courier System; Manifold System for Collection of Bills and Cheques; Receipt and Despatch of Bills; Passing of Contra Entries in Respect of Outward and Inward Bills); Remittances (Procedure Relating to Issue of Drafts; Delegation of Authority to Sign Drafts; Use of Manifold Draft Application Form; Payment of Drafts—Identification of the Payee; Inter-Bank Collection and Transfer System; Introduction of Giro System in India); Advances—General (Creation of Regional Offices, Their Functions, Duties and Responsibilities; Delegation of Discretionary Powers to Sanction Advances; Application Forms for Advances to Small Borrowers; Credit Reports on Borrowers; Exchange of Credit Information; Proposals Recommending Sanction of Credit Limits; Follow-up of Advances at the Branch Level); Financing of Agriculture (Delegation of Powers to Sanction Advances; Guidelines Relating to Scale of Finance; Disbursement of Crop Loan to the Farmer; Extension to Commercial Banks of the Privileges and Concessions Enjoyed by Cooperative Banks; Supervision over Advances; Rural Branch—Area of Operation, Recruitment of Staff and Working Hours); Financing of Small Scale Industries (Delegation of Powers; Terms and Conditions of Advances; Technical Reports; Collateral Security; Supervision over Advances; Technical and Management Consultancy Services); Financing of Exports (Extension of Export Finance Facilities to Inland Centres; Handling of Export Documents; Packing Credits; Inter-Bank Export Information Centre; Posting of Officers with Foreign Exchange Expertise at the Regional Offices); Financing of Other Small Borrowers (Delegation of Powers to Branch Agents; Registration of Hypothecation Charge; Third Party Guarantees; Supervision of Advances; Night-safe Facility); Inter-Branch Accounts (Accounting Systems; Allotment of Code Numbers to Branches; Passing of Consolidated Entries; Use of Schedules of Different Colours; Entries Relating to Telegrams, Postage Charges, etc.; Follow-up of Unmatched Entries; Frauds in Inter-Branch Accounts); Internal Audit and Inspection (Types of Inspections; Organisation of Inspection and Audit Department; Frequency of Audit; Inspection and Formulation of Programmes; Guidelines for Inspection Staff; Detection of Frauds; Rating of Branches; Follow-up Action; Common Inspection Agency for Public Sector Banks); Periodical Returns (Statistical Returns; Returns Relating to Advances for the Purpose of Control; Scrutiny of Periodical Returns; Test Check of Returns by Internal Auditors); Miscellaneous (Receipt of Cash and Cheques etc., for Collection at the Counter; Record of Denomination of Currency Notes; Deposit of Cash Boxes in the Vault; Safeguards Against Wrongful Alterations in Cheques, Drafts, etc.; Use of Regional Languages; Half-yearly Closing of Accounts; Forms of Import Letter of Credit and Mail Transfer Receipt; Review of Procedures; Complaints from Public; Premises and Lay Out; Working Hours of Banks); Summary of Recommendations; Annexures.

RECOIMMENDATIONS

Deposts

The statements of account and pass books should be written neatly, legibly and accurately and furnished to the customers promptly. Adequate managements should also be made to ensure prompt compliance with the customers' stop payment and standing instructions.

The teller system should be adopted in all banks at all important branches for encashment of cheques and receipt of cash for credit to accounts. Banks may use their discretion as regards the type of the teller system, the nature of accounts to which it should be made applicable as well as in regard to the maximum limit for receipt and payment of cash under the system.

First line supervisors should be permitted to pass cheques for payment in cash upto at least Rs. 5,000. Ledger keepers should also be given powers to pass cheques for small amounts depending upon the size of the branch and the experience of the concerned staff.

They should be entrusted with authority to issue cheque books against production of requisition slips to the depositors who calls at the bank personally.

Whenever necessary, supervising officers should go to ledger keepers for passing cheques instead of waiting for the papers, ledgers or registers to be brought to them by messengers.

The system of maintaining accounts in an alphabetical order should be replaced by a numerical system. The number allotted to each account holder may be so devised as to indicate some information about him, e.g., profession, constitution (individual, firm, company) etc., by adding suitable prefix to his account number. To facilitate location of accounts, card indices should be maintained both in alphabetical as well as numerical order, and, where necessary, rotating equipment should be used for tracing accounts.

Mechanisation should be introduced by banks, especially at larger branches, by adopting a phased programme on a planned basis and by taking the employees' unions into confidence. This will enable the staff doing work involving a lot of drudgery to do work of a higher order and enable their abilities to be used for more fruitful purpose. The Government on its part should also take positive steps to help the banks in getting over the difficulties such as non-availability of machines and opposition, if any, of the staff.

Banks should exercise adequate care and take concerted action while buying machines to avoid their underutilization and their becoming obsolete due to change in procedures and other reasons. Indigenous manufacturers should be encouraged to produce machines to suit the requirements of Indian banking.

Each bank should devise a system of data processing to serve both the operational requirements and the requirements in respect of economic information of the bank itself as also of the Reserve Bank and the Government.

Issue of pass books should be discontinued in respect of savings bank account holders who are allowed to make withdrawals by cheques and instead statements of account should be supplied to them, say at bimonthly intervals. The banks which will issue pass books to the current account depositors should switch over to the system of furnishing statements of account.

The practice of obtaining balance confirmations for credit balances in deposit accounts should be discontinued. The statements of account furnished to the depositors should contain a stipulation that the items and the balances shown therein should be verified by the concerned depositor and the bank notified of any discrepancy within a specified time, failing which the last balances shown would be presumed as correct. The branch agent should, however, be allowed discretion to obtain confirmations in particular accounts where he considers them necessary in the light of his personal knowledge about the depositors and operations in their accounts. Besides, the Internal Auditor, during the course of audit, should request a few depositors, selected at random, to confirm their balances and send the confirmations direct to him.

Banks should issue cheque books with crossing printed thereon to the customers who require them. Such customers should be provided with two cheque books simultaneously—a crossed one and an open one—printed in different colours for easy identification. A similar system should be followed in respect of bank drafts.

Banks may consider the feasibility of making payment of interest on fixed deposits on the expiry of every six months from the date of deposit instead of paying it at the end of each calendar half-year.

Intricate and detailed calculations may not be resorted to for arriving at the exact amount of interest payable on various types of deposits at the end of each month for the purpose of making provision therefor. An approximate provision may be made on the basis of average rate of interest paid during the previous half-year applied on the daily balances in the general ledger.

Banks should take expeditious steps to encourage the members of the staff and officers to learn local languages and for dispensing with the practice of obtaining letters of indemnity for vernacular signatures of the depositors and of transcribing and attesting such signatures.

Banks should make arrangements for keeping on record photographs of illiterate depositors for facilitating their identification. The branches at places where the facility for obtaining photographs is not available, should be provided with cameras and the branch officials given some training in taking photographs.

Banks may adopt the system of balancing the current account ledgers at monthly intervals instead of at weekly or fortnightly intervals.

While summations should be worked out on ledger folios in order to verify the correctness of the balance in the account, their periodical balancing may be dispensed with.

Clearing

The feasibility of opening clearing houses at places with population of more than 50,000 which are served by more than 3 or 4 banks should be examined keeping in view the factors such as the expenses involved, the problem of space and personnel, the number of bank accounts and the average number of instruments that would pass through clearing. The State Bank of India should take a lead in the matter as it or its subsidiaries manage the clearing houses at places where the Reserve Bank of India has no office. At centres where the State Bank of India is not established but other banks or their customers feel a need for establishment of a clearing house, the initiative should be taken by the banks themselves, preferably by the lead bank.

In order to reduce the work-load on the clearing houses and main offices of banks in metropolitan cities and with a view to ensuring quicker clearance of cheques, the feasibility of opening sub-clearing houses should be expeditiously considered by the Indian Banks' Association. The location of sub-clearing houses should depend upon the concentration of branches, the communication facilities and volume and pattern of payment flows.

Banks which have not so far introduced the system of 'home' clearing in metropolitan cities should do so, so that cheques tendered by an account holder for credit of his account and drawn on another local branch of the same bank are realised expeditiously.

The question of admitting non-scheduled banks and cooperative banks as full-fledged members of clearing houses as also liberalising the clearing house rules regarding the nnmber of instruments and banks, the terms and conditions of membership etc., should be examined by the Reserve Bank of India and the State Bank of India.

The measures relating to the simplification of clearing procedures are being considered by the Indian Banks' Association with particular reference to the city of Bombay. Special problems relating to the clearing of cheques in other large centres should also receive similar attention.

Steps should be taken to gradually discontinue the Outward Clearing Register. Customers should be required to note the details, now entered in the register, on the reverse of the pay-in-slips.

In order to facilitate tracing of credits and debits and matching them at a later stage, cheques and pay-in-slips should be appropriately numbered and the numbers of the accounts to which credits are being given should be recorded on the reverse of the cheques.

The feasibility of introducing the system of 'Flying Squad' for collecting the cheques for the day's clearing may be considered by banks having a large number of branches in big cities.

Use of cheque sorting machines should be made at major branches of banks for expediting clearing work and minimising the occurrence of clearing differences.

Collection of Outstation Cheques, Bills and Other Instruments

The Indian Banks' Association should take expeditious steps to introduce courier system for transmitting outstation bills, cheques, etc., on behalf of member banks from one centre to another by night air mail. Government should also render such help, as may be necessary, in resolving the legal and technical difficulties which the Association might encounter. After the scheme proves successful, the feasibility of extending it to other cities connected by air should be examined by the Association. Alternatively, the Postal Department itself may consider organising a courier system by making appropriate arrangements. It may recover from the banks the costs incurred by it on the basis of an agreed formula.

Banks should issue instuctions to their branches that the cheques and drafts sent by them to outstation branches for collection, through the courier system, should be considered as realised and proceeds credited to the customers' accounts if they are not returned unpaid or information regarding their dishonour is not received from the collecting branches within seven clear working days. In order to minimise the risk involved, non-payment advices should be sent through the courier system and in the case of instruments for large amounts non-payment may also be advised by telegram/telex.

Even as regards the cheques and drafts sent for collection to outstation centres which are not covered by the courier system, credit to the relative customers' accounts should be afforded after lapse of specified periods even if the information regarding the fate of the instrument is not received from the collecting branch. Further, banks may progressively adopt the system of purchase/discount of cheques and bills in replacement of the collection system. At large towns where the collection business is sizable, banks may consider opening 'collection branches' in suitable localities exclusively for this business.

Banks should introduce manifold system for collection of bills in order to avoid duplication of work involved in writing the same particulars in the bills registers, covering schedules, advices to parties, etc.

The Despatch Department should work, where necessary, on a shift basis so that covering schedules of bills, realisation advices, etc., which are ready for despatch in the afternoon can be sorted out and sent in the evening on the same day. The documents to be sent by registered post should be positively despatched atleast on the next day. Branches doing sizable business should use addressograph, auto-weigh and franking machines in order to save labour and time involved in manual work.

Particulars of inward bills, cheques, etc., received for collection need not be entered in the Dak Receipt Register. After the covering schedules and the attached documents are sorted by the official receiving the dak, they should be handed over against acknowledgement to the official of the Bills Department/ Deposit Accounts Department by entering their total number in a pass book.

Toning up of the Bills and Despatch Departments so as to eliminate the errors in preparing covering schedules, realisation advices, writing the addresses, etc., will go a long way in minimising the complaints and rendering expeditious and satisfactory service to customers.

The practice of passing contra entries daily in the books in respect of bills under collection may be discontinued.

Remittances

First line supervisors, who are normally promoted to that position after adequate experience in the capacity of a clerk or a trainee officer, should be allowed to sign drafts singly atleast upto Rs. 5,000.

Manifold draft requisition form with carbon attached should be introduced in order to reduce the waiting time of customers.

In order to popularise the drafts as a mode of remittances as also to inculcate the cheque habit amongst the public, it is necessary to dispense with the formality of identification in respect of instruments for small amounts, except in cases where there are reasonable grounds to suspect that the presenter is not entitled to receive payment. The legal aspects of the question should, therefore, be examined carefully and the provisions of law suitably amended, if necessary.

Such of the non-nationalised banks as are willing to participate in the scheme for inter-bank drawings and inter-bank collections (which is being considered by the Public Sector banks) may be permitted to do so to the entext possible.

An independent agency with the collaboration of banks, embodying the principles of Giro, may be created to clear the transactions relating to transfer of funds within the metropolitan cities of Bombay, Calcutta, Delhi and Madras and in between these cities in the first instance. The agency may also undertake issue of travellers' cheques and drafts and clearance of transactions relating to remittance of funds by a non-account holder to an account holder and *vice versa*.

Advances—General

In order to expedite decision making and to exercise effective supervision and control over the working of the branches, regional offices should be created or reorganised by banks. The number of branches under the jurisdiction of a regional office in the mofussil may be 25 to 50 depending upon communication facilities, nature and volume of business conducted, contemplated expansion in the network of branches, etc. In the metropolitan areas it may be possible for a regional office to handle a larger number of branches. The region should comprise a contiguous area, no branch being very far away from the regional office.

To ensure that regional offices do not become one more tier in the administrative set up, they should be granted adequate powers not only for sanction of advances but also in regard to administrative matters. They should be placed under the charge of experienced and capable senior officers.

Regional offices should maintain specialised cells on functional basis with adequate trained staff for assessment of advance proposals from priority sectors and for supervision and review of advances granted to them. They should also conduct and arrange for surveys, research and pilot projects for developmental activities in respect of deposit mobilisation, geographical expansion and grant of credit to priority sectors. They should further maintain a close contact with the branches and review their working periodically.

The regional manager should not be overburdened with routine work so that he may be able to discharge his supervisory functions effectively as also to pay visits to the branches under his charge at least once in a quarter.

The head office should arrange to carry out periodically thorough inspections of the regional offices in order to ensure that they are discharging their functions effectively and efficiently.

Delegation of discretionary powers to branch agents and regional offices to sanction advances to small borrowers should be liberalised. While vesting such powers, the head office should, however, prescrible overall ceiling on the total amount of credit that could be advanced at each of the branches to various categories of borrowers, in order to ensure equitable distribution of credit in relation to the bank's total available resources and in the context of liquidity requirements. Delegation of authority should be reviewed at least once in two to three years and discretionary powers should be varied, if necessary, according to requirements.

The provisions of Section 292 of the Companies Act, 1956 may be suitably amended so that in the case of banking companies, the Board of Directors is enabled to authorise the Chief Executive Officer or a committee of directors to exercise the powers of the Board in regard to specifying the total amount upto which loans may be made by the delegates, the purposes for which the loans may be made and the maximum amount of loan which may be made for each such purpose in individual cases.

A quarterly scrutiny of the advances to priority sectors granted by branch agents should be carried out by a set of roving officers attached to the functional cells at regional offices. After some time, when the agents have gained sufficient experience, the frequency of the scrutiny may be suitably reduced. Branches should be required to maintain a register recording the receipt of loan applications (whether made orally or in writing) and their disposal. The roving officers should examine this register in order to find out whether there has been any undre delay or wrongful refusal of credit facilities.

While exemplary punishment should be awarded to the agents who are found guilty of deliberate misuse of powers, gross negligence, dishonesty or favouritism in order to curb any tendency to abuse the powers vested in them, the agents should be protected even though an advance becomes difficult of recovery if it was granted in the normal course without *mala fide* intent.

The application form in respect of advances to small borrowers may be bifurcated into two parts—

(i) application form to be filled in and signed by the borrower containing essential information of a simple nature relating to his biodata and credit requirements, and

(ii) interview form in which additional information obtained by questioning the applicant and perusing his books of account and other relevant papers may be recorded by the bank's officer.

While the application form may be common for all small advances, separate interview forms may be prescribed for different types of borrowers such as small scale industries, agriculturists, road transport operators, service unit owners, retail traders, etc.

Detailed credit reports need not be maintained on borrowers who have been sanctioned the following types of advances—

(i) temporary overdrafts granted under the discretionary powers of the branch agent;

(ii) advances against deposits with the bank and surrender value of life insurance policies;

(iii) advances upto Rs. 5 lakhs against Government and other trustee securities;

(iv) advances upto Rs. 50,000 against readily marketable shares and debenture; and

(v) secured advances to agriculturists upto Rs. 10,000, to small scale industries upto Rs. 25,000 and to other small borrowers upto Rs. 10,000.

Banks should, however, ensure that the borrowers are properly introduced and also satisfy themselves regarding the viability of the project, purpose of the advance and need-based requirements before sanctioning the credit limits to them.

At the time of renewal of an advance, a fresh credit report may be prepared only if there have been any significant changes in the means and standing of of borrower; in other cases a dated remark may merely be recorded on the earlier credit report stating that the information has been verified and the party's position substantially remains unchanged or briefly indicating the minor changes that have occurred. A suitable remark to the same effect should also be made on the renewal proposal sent to the regional/head office. However, a fresh credit report should be prepared atleast once in two years.

Branches should not be required to send copies of credit reports to the head/regional office on borrowers to whom advances have been sanctioned under the agent's discretionary powers.

The personal liabilities and assets of proprietors and partners of business concerns should be taken into consideration while assessing their credit-worthiness.

The Reserve Bank of India may examine the feasibility of establishing a Credit Intelligence Bureau for compiling and furnishing credit information to various financial institutions in the country by enlarging the functions of the Credit Information Bureau or by establishing a separate agency for the purpose.

Banks should, where necessary, suitably revise the advance proposal form which should contain adequate information regarding the volume and turnover of the borrower's business, sales and purchases on cash and credit basis, current assets and liabilities, extent of his own resources, seasonal trends and other relevant details justifying his credit requirements from the bank under different facilities.

The credit facilities to a borrower should be so arranged that the cycle of business from the purchase of raw materials to the receipt of sale proceeds is not hindered for lack of finance. The head office/regional office should also give discretion, to some extent, to the branch agent to interchange the limits according to requirements from time to time.

If a constituent has been borrowing from other sources for his business purposes, the bank should endeavour to persuade him to repay such borrowings and deal exclusively with it for all his credit requirements. If necessary, finance to repay existing borrowings from other sources should be made available, provided such borrowings were availed of for business purposes. Where the requirements of a borrower are large, the principle of one bank one borrower can, however, be modified by a consortium of banks entering into participation arrangements or by mutual arrangement between banks. Exception to the principle of one bank one borrower may also be allowed in the case of advances availed of from term financing institutions, factories of the same concern situated at different places, etc.

The agent and/or other senior officials should pay frequent visits to the place of business of the borrowers accommodated for manufacturing, production or trading activities, for discussion with them on matters such as trend of business, difficulties encountered in dealing with the branch and measures to solve them.

Financing of Agriculture

The agents of the rural branches should be vested with discretionary powers to sanction advances upto Rs. 3,000 per borrower. The bulk of advances in excess of this amount should be allowed to be granted by regional offices and reference to the head office should be restricted to the proposals in regard to plantations,large scale farming, land development and irrigation schemes, etc.

Regional offices of banks should issue guidelines to branches in their respective areas indicating the scale of finance applicable to different types of crops by collecting information from the studies already made by other institutions and also after consulting officials who have expert knowledge of the subject. They may also consider financing such studies by local universities, colleges or other expert bodies.

The total amount sanctioned to the farmers should be disbursed in instalments in accordance with their needs for various agricultural operations. The number of instalments should not, however, be too many (generally not exceeding three) as the agriculturist is busy during the season and he would find it difficult to visit the bank often to collect the loan instalments.

As far as possible, banks should disburse credit by making direct payments to the suppliers of inputs, taking care to see the finance in respect of a particular input is commensurate with the need-based requirements of the farmer. To avoid widespread misuse of the facility, any instance of wrongful utilisation which comes to notice during the scruting of roving officers or branch officials or as a result of investigation of complaints received should be strictly dealt with by taking appropriate action against the relative dealer and the borrower.

Expeditious steps should be taken, in the light of of the suggestions made by the Talwar Committee, to ensure that commercial banks are not made to suffer from any direct or indirect legal disabilities which cooperative banks are not subjected to and also to ensure that all the privileges and concessions enjoyed by these banks are extended to commercial banks.

Frequent visits should be paid to the farms of borrowers by the branch officials as well as by the officers attached to the agricultural cells at regional offices. The purpose of the visit should be to ascertain the progress of cultivation, verification of security charged to the bank and of implements purchased with the use of bank's finance and to find out whether the finance already granted has been properly utilised as also to assess the quantum of finance needed for further agricultural operations. The branch agent should, as far as possible, ensure that such verification has been carried out before making available to the borrowers further drawings from their accounts in accordance with the phased programme for grant of credit. The branch officials have also to keep a watch on the marketing arrangements made by the farmers for disposal of his goods in order to ensure that the advance is repaid when the crop, for raising of which finance was made available by the bank, is sold by him.

The area served by a village branch should normally be restricted to a radius of about 15 to 20 kilometres from the branch depending upon the nature of available communication and conveyance facilities. Exceptions may, however, have to be made to this general rule in suitable cases, particularly in respect of under banked regions until banking facilities are adequately spread out.

As far as possible, local persons with requisite minimum qualifications should be recruited at the rural branches. Further, to the extent possible, part-time, temporary or seasonal staff may be employed at such branches.

The branches of banks at rural and mandi centres should be kept open in the evening, if necessary by suitably reducing the working hours in the day time, to provide convenience to the villagers. The extension of the facility of mobile banks can also be helpful in this regard.

Financing of Small Scale Industries

Branch agents of small urban branches should be vested with discretionary power to sanction working capital advances to small scale industries atleast to the extent of Rs. 10,000 against hypothecation of stocks, Rs. 25,000 against pledge of stocks, Rs. 2,500 on a clean basis and Rs. 10,000 against documentary bills. Powers of branch agents at bigger branches should be fixed suitably, taking into account the type of business at the branch and the experience and ability of the concerned officials. The bulk of the credit limits in excess of the discretionary powers of branch agents should be sanctioned by regional offices.

Relaxations from unsal formalities, such as grant of hypothecation advances or *mandi* type advances in place of factory type advances, release of pledged goods against trust receipts, low margins on the basis of the ability of the borrowing concerns to provide them and valuation of goods on a realistic basis should be extended to deserving small scale industries. Financial guarantees to a reasonable extent may be given on behalf of small scale industries to enable them to secure contracts for supply of goods, carry out works undertaken, etc.

In respect of working capital advances to small scale industries technical reports from consultancy firms or institutions need not be insisted upon as a matter of course.

Banks need not insist upon, as a matter of course, mortgage of immovable property and hypothecation of machinery as collateral security for working capital advances to small scale industries.

Visits to the factories of the borrowing concerns should be paid by the branch officials at least once a month and, besides, the technical staff at the regional offices should visit the factories at periodical intervals. As the Agents or the Accountants of branches having a large number of small scale industries accounts will not have sufficient time at their disposal to pay monthly visits, banks should appoint supervisors for the purpose at such branches.

A separate supplementary agency as envisaged by the Thakkar Committee, should be created for giving guidance and rendering techincal and management consultancy services to the borrowers rather than the banks themselves undertaking this function. Banks may, however, make available the services of their technical staff in their spare time to the borrowing units—on their request and on an informal basis—for consultation on urgent problems.

Financing of Exports

The number of centres where banks provide intensive export finance facilities are limited and should, therefore, be increased.

Whenever documents (drawn under a letter of credit), tendered by the exporter for discounting, are sent by an inland branch to a branch authorised to transact foreign exchange business, the former branch should obtain indemnity from the exporter against any discrepancies in order to avoid protracted correspondence between the two branches.

To eliminate the delay involved in sending bills of exchange to the stamp office for being stamped before execution, banks should be allowed to stock stamps and instal special franking machines in large offices, if necessary, by amending the Stamp Acts suitably.

There is apparently a need for expansion of clean packing credit facilities. The grant of such facilities should depend upon the credit-worthiness of the exporter, his past dealings and past export performance. Constant and strict vigilance would also be necessary to ensure proper end-use of such packing credit facilities.

An Inter-Bank Export Information Centre may be set up to collect and disseminate upto-date export information which would be of general and practical interest to all banks and would benefit small exporters who have neither contacts nor financial means to explore foreign markets.

In order to provide facilities to the customers and guidance to the branch agents, banks should post at least one officer with adequate knowledge of foreign exchange procedures at the regional offices which do not have full-fledged foreign exchange departments. These officers should, whenever necessary, visit the branches within the region for guiding the agents and other staff in handling foreign exchange business as well as for attending to developmental activities and for giving assistance to the customers in respect of their foreign trade problems.

Financing of Other Small Borrowers

Branch agents of small branches should be authorised to grant advances to small borrowers upto at least Rs. 5,000 on secured and Rs. 2,500 on clean basis without reference to the regional office or the head office. The powers of the agents of bigger branches should be suitably fixed at higer levels.

The feasibility of creating a suitable machinery for registration of charge on movables, with a simple and inexpensive procedure for its verification, should be examined from legal as well as practical angles.

Banks may insist upon guarantees of third parties in respect of advances to small borrowers only when there are reasonable doubts about the repaying capacity of the borrower.

Branch officials should pay a visit to the borrowers' place of business, even in cases where clean advances have been granted, at least once a quarter, in order to keep a constant watch on the condition of their business.

It should be ensured that the formalities prescribed regarding the submission of stock statements, maintenance of stock registers, etc., do not become irksome to small borrowers who are not in a position to maintain adequate staff for the purpose.

Banks may introduce night safe facility at suitable centres to enable small borrowers to deposit their daily cash collections for credit to their accounts on the following day.

Inter-Branch Accounts

Of the three inter-branch accounting systems, viz., mutual accounting system, centralised-cum-regional accounting system and centralised accounting system, the last named appears to be the most suitable as, besides ensuring effective control, it is also more amenable to mechanisation. However, inter-branch transactions between branches situated in the same city may be passed through the accounts maintained by them with the local main office instead of through the head office account.

In order to avoid passing of incorrect entries at the responding branch, the originating branch should take care to ensure that the covering schedules, remittance or realisation advices and daily statement of head office account are neat, clear and accurate and are despatched promptly.

To eliminate the confusion caused by the similarity in names, code numbers should be allotted to branches which should be required to write the number, in addition to the name of the branch, on all advices, daily statements of head office account, remittance schedules, etc.

The number of entries in inter-branch account can be reduced considerably by passing consolidated debit and credit entries in respect of each branch according to the categories of transactions instead of passing separate entries for each draft issued or each bill realised or for other similar transactions.

In order to facilitate matching of entries at the Central Accounts Section, daily transactions relating to inter-branch account should be grouped at branches under specified categories and schedules of different colours should be prepared for each category of entries, using the same colour for schedules of debit and credit transactions of similar type. The schedules should be sent to head office together with the statement of head office account which should contain totals of debit and credit entries detailed in schedules, besides the opening and closing balances.

Telegram and postage charges, etc., incurred in connection with the collection of billes should be borne by the branch which actually incurs them. To avoid protracted correspondence and disputes, such charges should not be debited to the branch from which the bill was received for collection.

The outstanding entries should be promptly followed up and the reasons for their remaining outstanding should be ascertained. The form used by the Central Accounts Section for obtaining comments of a branch in respect of long outstanding entries, besides detailing the particulars of relative entries, should contain alternative replies expected from the branch in the lower portion separated by perforation.

The reasons for which the originating debit entries and reversal entries have been passed should be suitably explained by the branches while reporting them to the Central Accounts Section in the daily statements. The latter should examine the entries carefully.

The long outstanding entries for large amounts, say above Rs. 10,000, should be immediately brought to the notice of a senior executive who should decide whether any special probe is necessary in regard to any particular transaction.

The Internal Auditor should scrutinize the long outstanding entries pertaining to the branch during the course of his audit. Besides, he should make a sample check of the entries in the head office account at the branch. It may be useful in the case of banks having a large number of branches to select a few branches, on the basis of a properly devised sample, for examination of all transactions pertaining to say a week or a fortnight.

Internal Audit and Inspection

Inspection staff should normally consist of Internal Auditors, Branch Inspectors and Godown Inspectors. However, as it may not be convenient for small banks to maintain inspection staff of three categories, the Branch Inspectors appointed by them may also carry out internal audit and godown inspection.

While the Internal Auditors may examine documents, operations, etc., in respect of all advances to agriculturists, they may verify securities only in respect of selected accounts on random sampling basis. It would, however, be desirable to verify all securities held in accounts which are grossly out of order or in respect of which complaints have been received.

The Inspection and Audit Department should be directly responsible to the Chief Executive Officer of the bank. For the sake of convenience and in the interest of economy, members of the inspection staff may be posted at different regional offices but they should be under the direct administrative charge of the head office and the Regional Managers should have no control over their promotions, transfers, increments, leave, etc., during the period they are entrusted with inspection duty.

In view of the nature of their duties, Internal Auditors should have a thorough knowledge of the procedures and at least five years' experience of handling different types of work in responsible capacities. Banks should institute suitable recruitment policies and training programmes to achieve this objective.

Branch Inspectors should be senior and experienced enough to be in a position to critically comment on and assess the quality of business conducted by the branch officials.

The internal audit/inspection should ordinarily be conducted once every year on a surprise basis. The verification of stocks pledged/hypothecated to the bank (which should also be on a surprise basis) should be carried out once in each quarter. One of the quarterly visits of the Godown Inspector should synchronize with the annual audit/inspection.

While drawing the inspection programme it should be ensured that an official does not visit the same branch consecutively. To facilitate chalking of inspection programme, cards for each branch containing history of previous inspections may be maintained by the Inspection and Audit Department. The cards should be arranged in a chronological order on the basis of the dates of last inspections.

As far as possible, the inspection should be taken up when the internal audit is nearing completion or soon after its completion. However, in the case of large branches, the audit and inspection may be taken up simultaneously and one or more Internal Auditors may be deputed to assist the Inspector. Continued presence of inspection staff at a branch for a long time disturbs its day-to-day working and, therefore, the size of the team should be sufficiently large so as to complete the audit/inspection expeditiously.

Banks may carry out concurrent audit of their main offices in the metropolitan cities.

Branch inspection should not merely be a routine check of the books and records of the branch but an intelligent examination of the assets and liabilities and overall review of the branch's working.

Apart from the examination of various assets and liabilities of a branch outstanding at the time of audit, a test check of some of the transactions effected since the date of last audit on random sampling basis and a percentage check (say 5 to 10 per cent) of the account opening forms, specimen signature cards, notings in respect of cheque books issued, recording of stop payment instructions, compliance with standing instructions, etc., should be made by the Internal Auditor.

In order to ensure that audit/inspection is thorough and exhaustive, a check list on the lines of the 'Hand Book for Bank Inspectors' prepared by the Bankers Training College should be supplied to the inspection staff.

The approach of the Inspector should not be merely critical but should be constructive. He should not only bring out the irregularities observed but also make suggestions for improvement in the working of the branch. He should discuss the findings of the audit/inspection with the branch officials and should arrange with the branch agent to have minor irregularities rectified, to the extent possible, during the course of inspection. A list of such irregularities should be supplied to the branch agent and a copy thereof, together with the agent's comments, should be appended to the inspection report.

Major irregularities observed in the working of the branch which require specific action, including comments on advances which are grossly out of order, should be highlighted by incorporating them in an appendix to the report. Similarly, for suggestions for improving the working of the branch should also be given in another appendix.

Inspection staff should make efforts not only to detect frauds committed by employees and/or others but also to find out laxity or loopholes in the procedures relating to accounting, checking, custody of valuables, security arrangements, etc., at the branch.

On the basis of the findings of audit and inspection of a branch, the Inspector should arrive at an overall assessment of the working of the branch and classify it according to its standard of efficiency. In order to avoid personal bias and to eliminate subjective assessment, rating should be on a scientific basis. A representative body like the National Institute of Bank Management may compile a siutable scheme for this purpose for adoption by banks.

One copy of the audit report may be submitted by the Internal Auditor to the Inspection and Audit Department at the head office while another copy may be given to the branch for forwarding its comments to the head office. One copy should also be sent to the regional office. If the Internal Auditor observes any serious irregularity during the course of the audit, he should report it to the head office immediately by means of a separate communication. A copy each of the inspection report should be sent to the regional office and the head office but not to the branch. The head office should examine and report and take up the matters on which action is necessary with the branch and the regional office.

Any serious irregularity reported to the head office by the Internal Auditor or the Inspector should be immediately brought to the notice of the Chief Executive Officer of the bank, who may, if considered necessary, refer it also to the Board of Directors/ Executive Committee. The irregularities should be followed up vigorously till they are rectified.

At the end of each quarter, the Inspection and Audit Department should prepare a memorandum on the basis of the inspection/audit reports received during the quarter for submission to the Board of Directors bringing out, *inter alia*, major irregularities observed and action taken or proposed to be taken to rectify them.

A committee may be appointed under the auspices of the Reserve Bank of India or the National Institute of Bank Management to consider in detail the question of creation of a common agency for inspection of the offices of all banks in the Public Sector and to formulate standand forms and procedures, keeping in view the need for progressive mechanisation on a planned basis for rendering better customer service.

Periodical Returns

Statistical returns (excepting those required to be sent by branches direct to the Reserve Bank of India) should be submitted to the regional offices, which should send consolidated statements to the head office. However, where the head office has automation facilities, returns may be submitted direct to that office for consolidation and feed back of information to regional offices. Also, in cases where information is required for submission to the Goverment of India or the Reserve Bank of India urgently (e.g., weekly statement under section 42 of the Reserve Bank of India Act 1934), it may continue to be collected by head offices direct to avoid time lag involved in its being routed through regional offices. Considering the importance of analysis and processing of statisical information as an aid in formation of policies in regard to operations, organisation, development and planning, it is necessary that banks should establish and/or strengthen Statistical/ Economic Departments.

Branches should not be required to submit statements of all outstanding advances (other than U.B.B. returns) at frequent intervals and it will be adequate if such statements are called for once every year at the time of the annual closing.

Branches should not normally be required to submit periodical returns giving details of advances sanctioned by officials within their discretionary powers.

The control of the head office over advances through periodical returns should relate only to irregular advances, the position of the other advances being examined during the course of the annual inspection of branches. Branches should send returns of irregular advances (including bills purchased and discounted) to the regional office/head office at monthly intervals. Separate statements of irregular advances may be prepared for different types of advances, i.e., cash credits, fixed loans, overdrafts, bills purchased, etc., and sent on different dates of the month so as to stagger the work at the branch and facilitate scrutiny at the head office. As regards the advances involved in litigation, a return may be sent at quarterly intervals.

The control returns should be scrutinised at the head office by the supervising staff and, where necessary, prompt follow up action should be taken through the regional offices. All advances having serious irregularities, which are likely to jeopardise the bank's interests, should be immediately brought to the notice of the top management.

Internal Auditors, during their visits to branches, should make a test check of the statements sent to the head office/regional office in order to find out whether all relevant advances had been included in the concerned return and whether the various particulars had been mentioned therein correctly and fully.

Miscellaneous

At the branches where the teller system has not been introduced, the waiting time of the customers paying in cash should be reduced by authorising the cashier to issue the counterfoil, without its being counter-signed by another official. In order to maintain an independent record of cash receipts, Scroll Book may be maintained by a member of the Accounts Department who should sit near the cash counter.

Cash registering machines may be introduced at bigger branches. Use of counting machines will also be helpful in expediting cash transactions.

Cheques and other instruments tendered for collection should be allowed to be received by the bills clerk who should be authorised to sign the counterfoils singly after verifying that the instruments tendered are in accordance with the particulars noted in the pay-in-slip. Customers should, however, be notified to cross all instruments before tendering them for collection.

The practice of maintaining a record of denominations of currency notes in the Cash Receipt and Cash Payment books involves duplication and should be dispensed with. Further, for the sake of convenience, the particulars of currency notes may be noted on the face of the pay-in-slips instead of on the back by changing the form suitably.

Receipt and payment cashiers may be required to maintain cash boxes which may be locked by them at the close of business every day and deposited in the vault without their contents being checked by the head cashier. The locked boxes should be delivered to the cashiers next morning. Cashiers should certify every day the amount of cash contained in the locked boxes and proper record of it should be maintained. Where considered necessary, a maximum limit may be fixed for cash thus kept in the cashier's boxes. The contents of the boxes should be verified at periodical intervals on a surprise basis by the head cashier/agent.

Increased use of ultra-violet ray equipment should be made by banks at their urban branches and they should also supply protectograph machines to all branches which are authorised to issue drafts.

A planned programme for use of regional languages for account opening forms, pay-in-slips, cheque books, pass books, statements of account, etc., should be adopted and implemented by banks, so that within a period of three years or so dealings with customers are carried out entirely in the languages they fully understand.

In order to make banking easily understood by the publics audio-visual publicity through exhibition of documentaries and publicity through pamphlets in regional languages, portraying the advantages of carrying out monetary transactions through the medium of banks, would be immensely helpful.

Government departments, local bodies, educational institutions, public utility concerns, public sector undertakings, etc., should encourage the use of cheques in their financial transactions with the public, where necessary, by suitably amending their rules and regulations.

Banks may discontinue the practice of half-yearly closing of accounts at the end of June each year as it entails considerable labour without commensurate benefits.

The question of standardising the form of import letter of credit may be considered by the Exchange Control Department of the Reserve Bank of India in consultation with the Foreign Exchange Dealers' Association and in keeping with the requirements of importers. The Reserve Bank of India may also consider the feasibility of the suggestion that banks be allowed to send copies of letters of credit opened, with a covering list indicating only the distinctive numbers of letters of credit and their amounts, instead of the prescribed monthly statement of import letters of credit opened.

The Foreign Exchange Dealers' Association may consider standardising the form of mail transfer receipts.

Indian banks which have not so far established a separate O & M Department may establish it as early as possible. However, in case any of the small banks finds it difficult to establish a full-fledged department for the purpose, in view of the cost involved, it should train one or two of its officials in O & M work. These officials will be able to attend to O & M aspects of the bank's working, in addition to other normal duties, where necessary. The heads of O & M Department of different banks should meet periodically, say once every half-year, for exchanging the information regarding the studies made by them. The Reserve Bank of India may take the initiative in the matter. The banks which have not so far introduced a suggestion scheme should do so at an early date.

Complaint-cum-suggestion boxes should be provided at all branches of banks for use of the public. Regional managers and development officers attached to regional offices, on their visit to the branches, should spare some time to hear the grievances and suggestions of the local constituents.

Whenever possible, banks should try to shift a portion of the work at a very big branch to new premises in the same locality by opening another branch. For housing new branches, particularly in the rural areas where suitable premises on rent are not available, it would be preferable for banks to encourage construction of buildings by advancing money to persons owning suitable land instead of constructing the buildings themselves which would result in locking up of their funds. Adequate attention to matters such as lay out, colour scheme, construction of modern counters, pleasing lighting arrangement, decor, staff and customer amenities should be paid while planning new buildings. While designing a bank building, the problems of special categories of customers such as pensioners and women should be kept in view and discussed with the architects. The security aspect should of course be borne in mind.

The question of making a suitable legal provision permitting banks to destroy cheques, ledgers and other records after lapse of specified periods should be examined. Banks may also consider the feasibility of micro filming important records before their destruction, taking into account the cost aspect.

Banks should take steps to improve the lay out in their offices, in order to enhance the efficiency of the staff as also for improving the customer service, after conducting studies of office routine from time and motion and flow angles.

To begin with and on an experimental basis, administrative offices of banks may remain fully closed on Saturdays and, to compensate for the loss of man-hours, the working hours on other week days should be suitably enhanced. The question of introducing similar change in the bank offices dealing with the public may be considered later.

Wherever feasible, working hours in residential areas of urban centres may be in the mornings and evenings to suit the convenience of the clientele.

STUDY TEAM ON DESIGN ORGANISATIONS IN SELECTED PUBLIC UNDERTAKINGS, 1970—REPORT

Delhi, Controller of Publications, 1974. 144p+vp.

Chairman : Shri Y.P. Passi (replaced by Shri Ajit Singh).

Members : Dr. B.N. Bhargava (replaced by Shri Kan. D. Mariwalla) ; Shri A.B. Malik ; Shri T.M. Varughese (replaced by Er. A.P. Paracer) ; Shri B.R. Singh ; Shri B.M. Sen.

APPOINTMENT

The A.R.C. in its "Report on Public Sector Undertakings" had recommended that these undertakings should be encouraged and assisted to set up adequate design and consultancy organisation. This recommendation was accepted by Government and as a result the Bureau of Public Enterprises constituted a Study Team in March 1970 to carry out field studies of design organisations in selected public enterprises with a view to identify areas in which they needed assistance.

TERMS OF REFERENCE

To cover the following specific areas :

(i) To assess the adequacy or otherwise of organisations for product designing in the context of the requirements of the undertakings ;

(ii) to find out the extent to which these have helped to establish indigenous capability in the field of product designing ;

(iii) the extent to which collaboration agreements have been made use of in making further improvements on imported designs and developing new ones ;

(iv) to identify gaps in the field of product design capacity and suggest ways to bridge them ;

(v) to lay down guidelines for manning design organisations; and

(vi) to assess the adequacy or otherwise of the policy relating to research and design development activities and training of design engineers.

CONTENTS

Introduction; Role and Importance of Design Organisations; Objectives of Design Organisations; Structure of Design Organisations; Design Development—Capabilities; Product Design—Gaps; Personnel Problems; Applied Research; Foreign Collaboration and R & D; Financing R & D; Government and R & D; Summary of Conclusions and Recommendations; Annexures I to VII.

RECOMMENDATIONS

Role and Importance of Design Organisations

There is possibility of the technological gap between India and the advanced countries widening because of our inability to invest resources in research and design on a scale comparable with those of the advanced countries. The Indian context differs significantly from the advanced countries which have comparatively abundant capital resources and shortage of manpower. Their approach to evolving plant-product designs and technologies has largely been conditioned by these two factors. In our case, while capital resources are either absent or limited, the abundance of cheap labour may not provide the comparable driving force to innovate with a view to reduce labour costs. Despite this, there is a peculiar challenge in a situation like ours in which scarce capital resources have to be conserved with a view to reduce costs. This challenge has not been fully met.

The need to innovate varies from industry to industry. It is intense in rapidly changing fields where products become technically obsolescent within a few years. This is so in young industries like Petrochemicals, Electricals/Electronics etc. Complete independence in the matter of designs/technology, however, is virtually impossible to achieve. Nor can it become even an object of pursuit.

Selective approach : The time has now been reached when we should take stock of the skills developed with a view to plan further development based on a selective approach. A state of technological take-off in design capability could be considered to have been reached once a high level of technological capability is achieved in selected keyfields even though there may be a number of areas where dependence on foreign collaboration may remain inevitable for some time to come. Adequate design organisations have, therefore, to be built to meet these requirements.

Objectives of Design Organisation

Broadly, the short and long term objectives of the Design Organisations studies are as follows :—

Short term objectives : (1) To get familiar with imported designs and know-how.

(2) To develop capability to cary out modifications to foreign designs with a view to utilize indigenous materials.

(3) To achieve standardisation of components.

(4) To achieve maximum productivity.

(5) To keep up-to-date the designs acquired.

(6) To draw up commissioning and testing instructions.

(7) To evaluate the performance of equipment manufactured in order to improving the designs, solving engineering problems etc.

(8) To solve technical problems of diversification of production connected with projects.

Long term objectives : (1) To be independent from foreign design and consultancy service.

(2) To keep abreast of developments made by leading manufacturers and evolve more efficient designs, reduce cost, improve reliability and performance.

(3) To build sound research and development activity to provide backing for introduction of new and sophisticated products.

(4) To project the technical image of the organisation.

These objectives are not, by and large, time-bound. Also, they do not provide any quantified yardsticks with reference to which performance of the Design Organisations in terms of achieving design development targets can be measured. There is also no concrete plan of action formulated to achieve the specified goals.

Each enterprise should draw up concrete, quantified and time-bound objectives in terms of its projected production and a detailed schedule of programme directed to meet those objectives. The programme should also provide a system for its periodic evaluation in terms of its objectives.

Staff Strength of Design Unit

The criteria adopted by the undertakings for fixing the staff strength of the design organisations were generally based on the recommendations of the collaborators as modified by the plant authorities to suit conditions obtaining in the country. Some of these are :—

(a) Type and quantity of products/equipments.

(b) Frequency of repetitive orders.

(c) Experience of the foreign collaborator in his own country, modified to suit Indian conditions.

(d) Requirements of development work.

The lack of clarity about the criteria for fixing staff strength of design organisations is partly due to lack of specifity in the objectives of these organisations.

Position of Design Unit in the Organisational Hierarchy

There is diversity in the pattern of organisation of design units. Some are product-centred while others are unit-based, in the case of multi-unit enterprises. Similarly, the level of reporting also shows variations. The function of the Chief of Design Organisation in some plants has become increasingly administrative and managerial. In order to allow him to contribute his best to a field which he has specialised in, it is necessary that he should be divested of the day-to-day administrative and managerial work. Both working conditions and organisational procedures should be such as to allow him time to think, to observe production and allied operations, to discuss with experts in the various levels of other functions (IE, OR production, materials management, accounting etc.) in his own plant and outside. Simultaneously, there is a case for inducting specialists in these functions in the Design Teams as regular members.

There is considerable gap between the sanctioned strength of staff and the actuals in position in the middle and lower categories. While no reasons have been given for this gap, it is obvious that the personnel with the requisite educational qualifications and experience required by the undertakings in these categories are not easily available.

Functions of Design Unit

Bulk of staff in design organisation is mainly engaged in product design. An important point to be borne in mind here is that the role of design cells of large public sector undertakings shoud be limited to improving the evolving Product-Designs only, so that the cost of production could be brought down and the product improved to keep pace with technological progress and development. The scope of work relating to plant engineering/design is best allotted to separate public sector consultancy agencies. A limited portion of power station and industrial projects engineering work in the case of heavy electricals plants has, however, to be undertaken necessarily by the equipment-manufacturers themselves.

Design Organisation : Product or Functional Basis

Whether a centralised design organisation working on a functional basis would suit the requirements of a particular undertaking or a decentralised design function distributed product-wise would be more appropriate would have to be decided by the undertakings themselves taking into account their individual requirements, the stage of their development and the experience of organisations referred to above. In a multi-unit organisation, with each unit specialising in a particular area of production, the design and development effort would have to be decentralised. In the areas of "advance design" and where specialised skills are scarce, the advantage would lie in building up centralised design development facilities.

Applied Research Orientation of Staff

While the building up of self-reliance in design capability at the earliest remains the long term objective of these undertakings, the present disposition of design staff is biased towards adaptation of product-designs and design of tools and other means of production. In order to achieve the long term objective, there is need to reorient the staffing pattern towards applied industrial research. The setting up of a separate Advanced Design Unit as part of the Design Organisation as in the case of HMT would go a long way in development of requisite techincal skills.

Design Development Capabilities

Design capabilities built up by the enterprises fall into three distinct categories.

Absorption of imported know-how : (a) The HEIL and the BHEL are, by and large, no longer dependent on Collaborators for Switchgear, Controlgear, Transformers, 60-120 MW boilers, 60-100 MW turbosets.

Cost Reduction : (b) Inprovements on imported designs and Cost reductions/import substitution. The enterprises have been able to modify/adapt foreign specifications of components/raw materials to suit indigenous availabilities. These efforts have resulted in considerable savings in cost, though in many cases it is difficult to assess the total quantum of savings. In BHEL substitution of arsenical brasss tubes for Admiralty brass tubes, aluminium brass tubes for Cupronickel tubes and mild steel for

Muntz metal has resulted in considerable economies.

Material substitution : The undertakings have been successful in economic substitution of easily available material e.g., resinglass tapes in transformer cores (HEIL).

Foreign Exchange Savings : Considerable progress has been made in indigenisation of raw materials/components in certain undertakings resulting in sizable savings in foreign exchange. HEIL have saved Rs. 760 lakhs till July 1968, Tiruchi Boiler Plant of BHEL has achieved an indigenous content of 60-65 per cent, depending on imports only for boiler quality plates, seamless steel tubes, specialised value fittings etc. This unit has saved Rs. 3.18 crores so far. Import content of HMT products is as low as 8 per cent, needed for specialised equipment like quality bearings etc.

Incorporation of new features : The two Electrical Units and the HMT have distinguished themselves by introducing several new features into existing designs e.g.. Thyristors which dispense with motor generator sets in industrial drive designs, criurped teminals and aluminium busbars for heavy currents, hydrostatic lubrication of thrust bearings (HEIL); HMT have developed new products like, lapping machines, Progmato Electrical Programming unit etc.

Material and component standardisation : The HEIL are the only undertaking who have attempted standardisation for almost all the materials used by them. As regards components, divisional and company standardisations have been introduced.

New designs : The HEIL, BHEL and MAMC claim to have designed independently a large number of equipments to suit the specification of customers. No technological innovation in design development has been reported by HEC as the accent has been on build up of production based on current designs. It would be possible to break loose from the apron strings of the collaborators only when the second generation cycle starts.

Since design efforts have an important bearing on the profitability of the organisations, specifiic studies should be carried out by the undertakings to assess the cost benefit relationship in the design efforts, as a regular part of the Management Control Systems.

In the earlier stages, because of the emphasis on production to meet current demands, the undertakings have paid less attention to applied Research and Development. The design organisations were engaged generally in absorption and assimilation of borrowed designs of products/equipment and carrying out minor modifications, and evolving substitute materials to suit Indian conditions. This does not help in bridging the technological gap between India and the advanced countries, whose success can be traced to the high pitch of development activity. Their programmes are oriented to provide answers to the problems of the future, to evolving entirely new products and equipment etc. In contrast ours is of the 'absorptive' and not of the 'innovative' type. Design organisations should keep their horizons and visions broader.

As a number of products are custom-built to unique specifications, it has to be brought home to the undertakings in sufficient force that the design effort has a very large part to play in improving the profitability of the company.

Production of specialised equipments like quality bearings, high quality steel and quality hydraulic equipment should be undertaken indigenously after working out their economics and their impact on the promotion of indigenous technological advancement.

Project planning : Some undertakings, besides the direct work concerning design of equipment/products, have ventured into the field of project design and allied activities. MAMC have designed the ore and coal handling plant for the Haldia Dock Project. HEC's Project and Development Division undertake turn-key jobs, e.g., pig casting machine at Durgapur.

An important point to be borne in mind is that the role of design cells of large public sector undertakings, should be limited to improving and evolving product designs only so that cost of production could be brought down and the products improved to keep pace with technological progress and improvement. The scope of work relating to plant engineering/design is best allotted to separate public sector consultancy agencies. A limited portion of power station and industrial projects engineering work in the case of heavy electricals has, however, to be undertaken by the equipment manufacturers themselves.

Performance standards and goals : No specific performance standards in terms of design output are laid down by the enterprises. In the absence of these specific goals, the recruitment of design engineers is not related to specific design 'task' but is oriented towards general strengthening of the organisation. Design organisation should be, as far as possible, product-based with time-bound and quantified goals. The recruitment of engineers should also be with reference to specific individual design 'tasks'.

Design gaps

In the Heavy Electricals Sector, there are a

number of areas where wide gaps still exist between the needs of their production programmes and the design capabilities. The HEIL continues to depend on foreign design know-how for steam turbines for pump storage schemes, nuclear and gas turbines. BHEL depend on foreign consultants for designing boilers of parameters higher than 120 MW, turbo-blowers and compressors for the chemical and fertiliser industry.

For ship building dependence on foreign design is almost total. For sophisticated semi-container cargo vessels and modern dredgers, bullons/Ram type Bows Hindustan Shipyard needs foreign consultancy.

In the Heavy Engineering area also, dependence upon foreign designs is substantial. HEC depends heavily on foreign know-how for heavy steel plant equipment and heavy machine tools. For coal washing and quik handling equipment MAMC relies on foreign assistance.

In the machine building area, some achievements have been made but these are areas where foreign collaboration is necessary. HMT is self-reliant except in respect of certain complicated and sophisticated machines, e.g., hydraulics and numerical controls.

Value analysis and maintainability : By and large the concepts of 'Value Analysis' and 'Maintainability' have not had full implementation and no adequate control systems have been built to assess the cost-benefit of design efforts. It is highly necessary that these concepts should be given practical shape and necessary machinery set up in each undertaking for this purpose. In this connection, we would recommend setting up of Product Development Committee in the plants involving functions such as production, sales, purchase as well as value engineers and maintenance engineers. A suitable control system for receipt of feed-back information on maintenance problems with a view to identify improvements required should also be built. Regular studies should be carried out by the undertakings to assess the cost-benefit relationship of design efforts as part of their management control systems.

Use of computers : The use of computers for purposes of design calculations is yet in the initial stages. HEIL and BHEL use the computer for algebraic, matrix and differential equations, flexibility calculations, dynamic modelling etc. Hindustan Shipyard have made use of the computer for obtaining Banjean's curves, hydro-static particulars and moment of inertia data and have reported considerable saving in time. HMT have utilised the computer for optimisation of machine tool drives etc. MAMC have not made use of computers for design work. Computer application has important bearing on design development and will increase as undertakings' capabilities for independent design development increase. The team recommend that the undertakings should be given full assistance to utilise computer facilities.

Dearth of design personnel : As the areas of operation of the selected undertakings were new to the country at the time these undertakings were set up, experienced personnel to man the design department were not available. The procedure generally adopted by the undertakings in recruiting the required staff was (i) to draw upon experienced persons in allied industry and (ii) to recruit raw engineering graduates and train them in the collaborator's works or in the training schools attached to the undertakings.

Flight of personnel : Apart from the difficulties in obtaining suitable persons, the undertakings were also experiencing considerable difficulty in retaining qualified technical personnel as job opportunities both within the country and abroad have increased. The major attraction of job security in Government undertakings no longer holds good, in the context of better emoluments and benefits offered by the private sector to the design personnel who have gained experience in the public undertakings. In fact, there appears to be a deliberate attempt by the private enterprises to 'steal' them away from these undertakings as it is cheaper to do so rather than train up fresh design engineers from the raw.

It has been revealed by a separate study made recently by the Bureau that the incidence of flight of technical personnel is highest among graduate engineers. The undertaking stricken most by this problem is the MAMC. The study has found that this corporation lost 27 out of 57 engineers trained by them in the fields of design and technology development. The study has also found that the loss has been greater among design engineers as compared to other technical personnel.

The reasons for resignation of these persons were (i) for going abroad either for study or for employment or for improving career prospects, (ii) more congenial work environments elsewhere, (iii) to join another enterprise for bettering prospects, (iv) the tendency of management to concentrate more attention on manufacturing activities and less on the areas such as designs, research and development etc., which are slow in yielding results and which also keep the Design Bureaus consequently under-loaded resulting in the designers spending their time in looking for better prospects outside.

In some cases, for want of promotion opportunities within the Design Organisations, experienced Chiefs of Designs have gone over to higher managerial or administrative posts, thereby, denying the Design Organisation, the benefits of their rich experience.

The flight of highly qualified and experienced design engineers not only represents a substantial loss to the undertakings who have invested large sums in their training but is a serious reflection on our present policies and proof that the incentives to retain them are not sufficiently attractive.

Measures to Retain and Motivate Design Personnel

The problem of flight of design engineers to other organisations or even outside the country is inevitable as it is impossible to ensure that conditions of service and prospects for promotion in a particular undertaking would always be better than those available elsewhere. Despite this, it is necessary that undertakings should take all possible steps to retain experienced design engineers within the organisation. For this, a number of steps would be necessary. We would recommend the following :

(i) Adequate opportunities for advancement should be provided within the Design Organisations by creating intermediary and special grades.

(ii) After an engineer has put in five to six years of service in a particular grade he should be provided a higher grade instead of allowing him to stagnate in that grade for a long time.

(iii) The Chiefs of Design Organisations, at least in large undertakings, should be equated with the post of General Manager or Deputy General Manager. The officer in design organisation should enjoy a status equal, if not higher, to those holding managerial posts. This would minimise, if not altogether remove, the possibilities of their seeking jobs in other departments within the organisation.

(iv) Design engineers with aptitude for managerial functions should not, however, be debarred from moving to such positions.

(v) The present requirement that a trainee has to sign a bond that he will not leave the organisation for certain number of years after completion of his training should be raised to 8 or 10 years.

(vi) One of the measures necessary to fill the gaps resulting from inevitable departures from the organisation would be to have a regular minimum number of trainees in the 'pipe line' throughout.

Sometimes there is a lack of opportunities for career development owing to the following factors :

(a) Recruitment of a large number of engineers in the earlier stages of the project at almost the same period either for foreign training or for training in India.

(b) As such officers are in the age group of 28 to 45 there is not likely to be any significant retirement during the next 6-10 years in the higher posts.

(c) Limited scope for expansion of activities which could provide adequate openings in the future.

Some of the steps suggested to meet this situation are :

(a) Intermediary stages in the pay scales, providing for special pay be introduced so as to provide incentive. Deserving officers in the scale of Rs. 775-1375 be provided incentive through "promotion" to those stages carrying special pay of Rs. 100 and Rs. 200 p.m. A special pay of Rs. 90 be introduced between the scale of Rs. 450-1075 and Rs. 775-1375. Similarly officers in the grade of Rs. 1375-1735 be given incentives on the basis of their merit and accomplishment in the form of a special pay of Rs. 150/-.

(b) Review of the sanctioned strength in the cadre from time to time in order to provide for the needs of the organisation as well as career advancement for the engineers.

(c) The intake from outside be regulated.

(d) Deployment of some personnel at the senior levels in other organisations either by deputation, transfer or absorption so as to avoid their stagnation and to provide scope for chain promotions.

(e) In specialised organisations, the need for a longer grade especially at the lower levels appears inescapable. In the longer grade itself, there should be room for promotion by selection.

The question of undertaking applied research work connected with development by the undertakings raised two questions, viz. (a) whether such work, in view of the large resources required, should be left exclusively to separate research organisations/laboratories outside the undertakings; and (b) whether in a multi-unit organisation (if part of such work has to be with the undertakings), this work should be centralised or left to the units concerned. Different views have been expressed on this; some hold that in view of their immediate objective to achieve rated production levels, this work should be entrusted to ouside organisations. Others are of the veiw that this is an integral part of their work and facilities should be created for carrying it out effectively within their own plants.

Some of the enterprises have suggested that a percentage of their turnover should be spent on R & D activity.

The cost of undertaking R & D work, arising from the requirements of design development, would be obviously quite large. The undertaking would naturally be reluctant at the present stage of their development to take up this work, even if it may legitimately be part of their product development effort. Some of the undertakings are quite positive than R & D work connected with product development should be an integral part of their activities and it is only this close and continuous relationship between the two areas, within the manufacturing plant, that will be effective and yield satisfactory results. The same practice is followed in some of the large manufacturing companies abroad.

Facilities for Applied Research

It would be in the interests of product development, if some applied research facilities are set up at the plant level itself. This would also help to provide the necessary climate and motivation for carrying out improvements/innovations in designing the products they are manufacturing. Since design innovation has a major bearing on profitability of the organisation, the motivation for carrying out problem oriented research can be provided by the organisation itself. In the area of product improvement, facilities for such work can be organised under their own umbrella, possibly under a separate functional wing.

In view of the need to interlink design and production effort closely, it would be advantageous to locate the design development effort at the unit level in the case of units of a multi-unit organisation producing different products. Research problems having a wider bearing and affecting a number of other products, will inevitably have to be entrusted to national or regional research organisation.

The present set up of the design organisations seriously lacks research base. The creation of such a base should be the long term objective of undertakings for which planned measures will have to be initiated even from now.

Liaison with Research Organisations

One of the essential requisites of successful design and development effort is that whatever capability is available in related research and production organisation is fully made use of. This requires close liaison between the production units and the national laboratories.

HEIL and BHEL maintain close liaison with each other and technological institution like MACT, Bhopal, IIT, Kanpur, Electronic Research Institute, Pilani and Power Research Institute, Bangalore. Even so they feel the liaison needs further strengthening.

HEC keep in close touch with CMTI, CMERI, etc. HMT co-operate with the CMTI and other Government research organisations and laboratories. As machine tool development requires continuous research backing, they would like Government help to establish contact with research institutions in Europe and America.

It is likely that the national laboratories do not find industrially oriented projects sufficiently challenging in terms of technical achievements. The Team are, therefore, of the view that as the benefits from industry-oriented projects could be very great in terms of import savings, 25 per cent of the programmes (in monetary terms) of the national laboratories should be set apart for such projects. Individuals actively participating in such projects may also be rewarded suitably.

Measures for Better Liaison with Research Bodies

To facilitate direct dialogue and more dynamic and committed efforts for indigenous development of industrial products and processes, each undertaking should have direct understanding with one national R & D institute specifically and a few others in general. Senior board members of such industry should be associated in the policy/ project formulation level of the institute.

Periodic industry-wise seminars should be organised to consider design and technological problems of different industries to enable transfer of know-how between industy and research institutions.

A Co-ordination Committee should be set up in the D.G.T.D. to consolidate information relating to available indigenous knowhow in various fields.

A permanent cell may be created in the BPE to coordinate and pool the equipments of the undertakings in the fields of developing design capability and procuring necessary facilities.

Common chairmanship of the undertaking and the associated research body will help the flow of design data between them within the contractual obligations imposed on the production units by their collaborators.

Deputation of personnel on an exchange basis will help flow of information from one organisation to another under the present constraints of secrecy of collaboration agreements. This is a field where Government's present policy in regard to deputationists needs a small change.

By and large, very little resources are devoted to problems of advance design. HEIL have an advance design centre for steam turbines only. Their forward plan pays attention to new developments. The Tiruchi plant of the BHEL has drawn up a list of projects calling for concentrated attention. HEC have stressed the need for an advance design institute for steel industry. The Hindustan Shipyard will rely on the work of the Central Marine Design & Research Organisation, when it is established. The undertaking has prepared a feasibility report of this organisation. The HMT have a well organised R & D Department engaged in a number of developments whose products are to be released for commercial production. MAMC has not felt the need for a separate Advance Design Centre.

The design organisations have generally grown in an unplanned manner. There is need to organise them on sound footing to meet the current operational requirements and also to meet the future needs of the undertaking and the concerned industry group. This wider aspect of R & D activity has to be kept in mind by public undertakings in the larger interests of the country as, in most cases they would be the biggest units in the respective industries. Consequently, the Design Organisation in each undertaking should be so organised as to be able to do forward planning based on market research to develop new products continuously. It should be the responsibility of a cell in the design organisation to "look ahead" and adopt a futuristic approach. "Advanced Design Cells" should be set up in all undertakings to build up capabilities for designing proto-types of new advanced machines. It is necessary to lay much greater emphasis on this aspect of development work in view of the avowed policy of the Government and objectives of the undertakings to develop indigenous technology.

Technical image : The role of the design organisation in projecting the technical image of the undertaking to which it belongs needs more attention.

The Team support the suggestion of HEC to set up an institute for research problems of designing equipment etc. for Steel Industry.

Perspective plan : It is necessary that the design organisation should have a perspective plan for a reasonable period, say 10 to 15 years. Based on the manufacturing or production programme, the Design Department should draw up a perspective plan of action for developing product designs.

The Team supports the proposal of Hindustan Shipyard for setting up a Central Marine Design and Research Organisation with financial support from the Government.

Foreign Collaborations

Achievements of the design organisations have been possible largely through purchase of technical know-how, design documentation, etc. A number of difficulties/problems have been experienced by the undertakings in respect of the collaboration agreements. Certain HEIL agreements provided only for supply of manufacturing information and not design know-how. HEC have felt the lack of provision for up-dating the designs. Basic documents and calculations are not also made available to help initiate applied design work. Hindustan Shipyard felt the need for providing for training of design personnel on a continuous basis. In the case of tailor-made equipment, MAMC have experienced difficulties relating to Indian Standards, use of indigenous materials, etc.

Some of the deficiencies noticed in the collaboration agreements are given below :

(a) Some of the collaboration agreements entered into in the past provide for only supply of documentation without the supporting basic calculations.

(b) There has generally been no provision making it obligatory on the collaborator to transfer information regarding improvements/developments to equipments/processes.

(c) Entering into collaboration agreements for total project know-how on a total turn-key basis is a very costly manner of acquiring design know-how.

(d) The provision prohibiting the disclosure of know-how to third parties often leads to repetitive import of the same know-how by different agencies.

(e) In some cases, provision relating to training of Indian personnel in the collaborators' works did not include the requirement for acquainting the engineers with design knowhow but only with the manufacturing processes.

While considerable advances have been made in building up technical knowhow in certain areas, dependence on imported technology will have to continue in certain areas till requisite skills are built up within the country. Since it would not be profitable to attempt to master all the design and technological practices being developed abroad, it would be more profitable to concentrate the scarce technical talents in limited areas and to buy the technical know-how and designs from abroad in sophisticated areas in the short run.

Collaboration Agreements : Need for Care

Greater care should be taken in drawing collaboration agreements to ensure that :

(a) the transfer and assimilation of technical knowledge, design know-how and other facilities are brought about in the most advantageous manner;

(b) collaboration agreements provide for supply

of not only documentation but also of detailed design sheets, specifications and calculations. Such details as quality of raw materials, substitute material and alternative processes to suit different working conditions should also be invariably incorporated;

(c) collaboration agreements also ensure that knowhow/further developments, adaptations and improvements effected by the collaborator to the design/processes/equipment supplied by him are made available to the contracting Indian parties;

(d) in some spheres knowhow could be imported through national Institute and sub-licensed to the industry. Close association of public undertakings with the National Institutes and setting up of working arrangements between them for better assimilation of knowhow would enable comparative analysis of knowledge/processes available in the world and selection of the best available;

(e) for better assimilation of basic concepts, data and information and to ensure fuller utilisation, improvement and diversification within a reasonable period, each undertaking should have a R and D cell working from the very beginning;

(f) care should be taken to break down the project into various sub-elements to ensure that designs and processes are obtained from the most capable manufacturers in the world for each of these elements instead of entering into blanket agreements;

(g) training of personnel by the collaborators should also cover training of the engineers at their R & D organisation. Refresher courses to enable the teams to absorb knowledge about latest improvements should also be provided for;

(h) in the case of collaboration for tailor-made items of equipment, a liaison officer shoud be kept at the collaborator's works, while the designs are prepared to guide them with regard to indigenous availability of raw materials, implementation of Indian Standards, safety and other requirements;

(i) restrictions placed by the 'disclosure' clause can be overcome by adopting one of the following measures :

- (i) The clause should be so worded as to permit the use of information obtained by one undertaking in other Government undertakings.
- (ii) Government should directly acquire design knowhow.
- (iii) If holding company type of organisation would make the transfer of the imported knowhow to its subsidiaries easier and enable its better utilisation and assimilation, it may be desirable to set up such companies in different sectors.
- (iv) In certain spheres, knowhow could be imported through national Institutes and then sub-licensed.

(j) Imports of sophisticated equipments/components/spares should be accompanied by acquisition of their design knowhow specifications etc.

(k) In view of the scarcity of technical talent in the country, it would be profitable to concentrate the personnel in limited areas in the short-run and buy the technical knowhow and designs from abroad in sophisticated areas. As the case of R & D widens, it would be possible gradually to eliminate dependence on foreign sources; and

(l) Technical teams should be sent out to different countries at regular intervals to scout for information relating to designs and latest technologies.

Financing R & D

One of the major constraints with regard to undertaking R & D work by the undertakings is finance.

Finance for R & D effort could be found by the following methods :

(a) Setting apart a fixed budget provision varying the type and size of industry. This may be made as a statutory obligation.

(b) Provision of separate equity capital or interest-free loans by Government.

(c) Allowing the enterprises to add a certain percentage to the manufacturing cost on a cost-plus basis. Enterprises in the competitive sector devote a certain percentage of income for R & D.

(d) Government should give outright subsidies to enterprises with long gestation period and low profitability rate for carrying out R & D work.

(e) Development work in respect of large products should be financed by Government e.g. development work in respect of generators should be financed by the Ministry of Irrigation and Power.

(f) While R & D efforts in the field of advance design should be centralised, such effort as is connected with the production carried on by the individual plant should be located in that plant.

(g) The activities of the Design & Development work could be financed by charging the factory for the services rendered by it and by maintaining a separate profit and loss account.

(h) As part of its exercise to fix economic, financial and social objectives for the undertakings, Government should lay down in consultation with enterprises specific design development goals for each undertaking, indicating the ways and means of financing them.

(i) In view of the high cost involved, R & D work in some important and strategic areas should be sponsored by the Government at its own cost as is being done in some of the advanced countries.

Procedural Bottle-necks

The undertakings stated that they face several procedural difficulties in obtaining Government clearance/approval for technical collaborations, import licences for equipment, critical components and raw materials needed for research and analytical tests. The team, therefore, suggest that release of foreign exchange, clearance by DGTD, and issue of import licences by CCI and E to R & D institutions should receive better consideration. There is need to identify bottle-necks in this regard with a view to eliminate such delays. The team, therefore, recommend allocation of special foreign exchange and issue of blanket import licences for R & D purposes.

Design Archives

Closer association of the undertakings with research institutions should be supplemented by the establishment of a national Design Archives which will store all design information available in the country both in the private and public sectors. A beginning could be made by setting up archives on a regional/sectoral basis or by pooling the available information in R & D organisations of the public sector. This could possibly be made part of the Data Bank being set up in the BPE.

WORKING GROUP ON RESOURCE MOBILISATION, PROFITABILITY, ETC., OF STATE FINANCIAL CORPORATION 1970—REPORT

Bombay, Reserve Bank of India ; 1972. 160p.

Chairman : Shri K.N.R. Ramanujam.
Members : Shri Brahma Swarup; Shri V.G. Hegde; Shri J.R. Joshi; Shri M.S. Palnitkar; Shri M.R. Roy; Shri S.P. Sen-Gupta; Shri C.S. Seshadri; Shri Sundar Singh; Shri A.N. Vij.
Member-Secretary : Shri P.R. Rajaratnam.

APPOINTMENT

The Reserve Bank of India set up in April 1970 a Working Group to examine certain aspects of the operations of State Financial Corporations (SFCs) in pursuance of the decision taken at the Fourteenth Conference of representatives of SFCs held at Bombay in March 1970.

TERMS OF REFERENCE

(i) To review the position of resources of SFCs and the cost of raising them and to suggest measures for augmenting the resources, having regard to the need for increasing and diversifying their business particularly for undertaking underwriting obligations and participating in equity;

(ii) To examine and suggest modifications, if necessary, to statutory provisions governing mobilisation of resources by SFCs;

(iii) To study the profitability of SFCs with particular reference to their liability for payment of subvention, for payment of minimum dividend, taxes, stamp duty, registration charges on documents, etc. and make suggestions for improving their profits and reserves;

(iv) To examine the statutory provisions regarding SFC's operations and suggest changes required, if any; and

(v) To consider and make recommendations on other incidental matters.

CONTENTS

Introductory; General Background to the Operations of SFCs; A Perspective of the Performance of the SFCs During the Fourth Plan Period; The Scope for Expanding Functionally and Geographically the Assistance of SFCs; The Statutory Framework of SFCs Working—the Scope for its Modification; Management and Organisational Issues; Miscellaneous Matters; Summary of Recommendations; Acknowledgements; Appendices from I to XVII.

RECOMMENDATIONS

The more important recommendations made in the previous chapters are summarised below :—

The Reserve Bank may take up with the Kerala State Government the question of extending the jurisdiction of the Kerala SFC to the Laccadive group of islands.

Six SFCs with working funds below Rs. 4 crores as on 31 March 1970 should take urgent steps to increase their business expeditiously if they are to reach the minimum size for viability.

The SFCs may make arrangements to obtain up-to-date lists of functioning small industrial units in the non-corporate sector from the appropriate departments of the respective State Governments.

SFCs may arrange for periodical surveys and/or seminars at selected growth centres in every district and arrange for periodical contacts with all existing and potential entrepreneurs.

SFCs should be enabled to extend financial assistance to certain additional lines of activity besides those covered at present.

SFCs may not finance concerns engaged in film production, construction of cinema theatres, medical units and service units like laundering and advertising.

In view of the magnitude of assistance to the small-scale industries envisaged in Fourth Plan period, there is a case for larger coordination and participation between SFCs and commercial banks.

Where a bank's credit-deposit ratio is on the high side and it has also granted sizable term loans to small and medium industries without entering into participation arrangements with SFCs, the Reserve Bank may consider the question of advising it to evolve suitable arrangements.

The SFCs may be authorised to issue guarantees in favour of scheduled banks and State Co-operative banks in respect of not only loans but also other types of credit facilities.

In order to be of effective assistance to small and medium industries for import of plant and machinery, the SFCs may be enabled to issue guarantee in favour of ICICI.

In cases where an engineer or a technically qualified person has just enough resources to meet the initial pre-construction expenses and margin for working capital, SFCs may grant loans with very low margins of 5 per cent to 10 per cent on the value of fixed assets and postpone the collection of the interest accruing during the first two or three years i.e. till such time as the borrowing concerns are able to make satisfactory gross profit. The refinance scheme of IDBI could also be modified to suit instances of this nature.

In view of the restricted transferability of the shares of a private company it may not be prudent for an SFC to subscribe to its equity shares.

Where a private company has or is likely to have sufficient fixed assets to offer as security, loans alone may be provided either carrying on interest during the first two or three years and slightly higher than normal rate during the later years or a progressively increasing rate. Where the company has potentialities for growth but promoters do not have sufficient funds for the initial capital, the SFC might subscribe to redeemable cumulative preference shares subject to certain safeguards.

SFCs may subscribe both to equity and preference capital of a public company subject to certain safeguards.

In order to undertake financial assistance to industrial units in the form of loans with no or low rates of interest in the initial years, or participation in preference or equity shares, SFCs may be allowed to create a special class of capital bearing no minimum dividend obligation to be contributed entirely by the State Governments and the Reserve Bank/IDBI in agreed proportions.

It might be prudent for SFCs to restrict investments in shares in each year to the amount of special capital which the SFC might be able to raise and the total of outstanding portfolio of share investments to not more than 15 per cent of its outstanding loans and advances. An overall ceiling on the extent of investment in shares and outstanding underwriting obligations may be set at an amount equivalent to the amount of special capital plus 50 per cent of the normal paid-up capital and reserves of an SFC.

SFCs should build up at least in their head-offices an appropriate machinery for financial and technical appraisal of projects and for advising assisted units on their problems.

SFCs may devise means of supplementing the efforts at State Governments and the IDBI in order to achieve a more balanced territorial distribution of SFCs' assistance and also to ensure a reasonable coverage of all the districts.

Each SFC, as far as possible, should aim at having

at least one office in each region. The State Government or the Reserve Bank may subsidise the cost of branch expansion programmes of SFCs deserving support in this regard for an initial period of 3 years.

Industrial surveys which are to be jointly conducted by the Reserve Bank, IDBI, ICICI and IFCI in certain developing States might cover not only the establishment of large and medium industries but also small industries. In addition, arrangements should be made whereby, where necessary, individual industry profiles or project reports should be prepared and furnished to prospective entrepreneurs.

The responsibility for formulating policy measures governing the growth of small industries should be fixed on the Industrial Finance Department of the Reserve Bank.

The contingent liability may be excluded from the purview of the ceiling prescribed in Section 7(5) of the SFCs Act.

A ratio of 5:3 may be observed as between bonds issued by an SFC and the amount of refinance obtained by it from IDBI. This ratio may be relaxed to 5:4 in deserving cases for short periods.

There is no case at present for enhancing the existing ceiling limits on loans and advances to individual borrowers. However, the ceiling on assistance to private companies may be raised to Rs. 20 lakhs.

The assistance that may be provided by an SFC to a single concern in the form of deferred payments guarantees, underwriting agreements and capital participation, along with loans and loan guarantees may not exceed Rs. 30 lakhs in the case of a company or a co-operative society and Rs. 15 lakhs in the case of other types of concerns.

In order to ensure that the SFCs confine their dealings to the small and medium scale units in the lower brackets, the Reserve Bank may prescribe a suitable ceiling on the size of an industrial concern eligible for financial assistance from an SFC.

IDBI may be specifically mentioned as a separate class of shareholder in the same way as the State Government and the Reserve Bank in sub-section (3) of Section 4 of the SFCs Act.

SFCs may increase their capital by making private issues to be subscribed to by the State Governments and the Reserve Bank of the IDBI carrying a minimum dividend liability of 3 per cent or 3½ per cent.

The State Governments may allow the SFCs to convert the subvention liability into special capital bearing no minimum dividend obligation.

The statute may be amended to enable IDBI also to forgo the dividend on its shareholdings in SFCs for credit to the Special Research Funds of the SFCs. The existing ceiling of 10 per cent of paid-up capital on the total amount that may be credited to the Special Reserve Fund may be raised to 25 per cent of paid-up capital. The SFCs may be allowed to utilise the balances in the Fund towards expenses for developmental purposes approved by the Reserve Bank and the State Government.

The existing ceiling limit at 60 per cent of the paid-up capital on borrowings under Section 7(2) (b) of the SFCs Act from the Reserve Bank may be raised to 90 per cent of the paid-up capital.

The Reserve Bank may extend accommodation under Section 7(2)(b) against an agreement executed by each SFC Act from the Reserve Bank may be raised to 90 per cent of the paid-up capital.

The Reserve Bank may extend accommodation under Section 7(2)(b) against an agreement executed by each SFC instead of an ad hoc bond. The State Government's guarantee for such advances should be automatic under the statute as in the case of deposits accepted at present by SFCs.

While settling the annual market programme of SFCs the Reserve Bank may take into account the utilisation of alternate avenues of raising resources such as refinance.

The SFCs may be allowed to raise a part of their resources through issue of bonds of shorter maturity, say, 7 years.

In order to enable SFCs to utilise the refinance facilities on a liberal scale, the IDBI may allow some relaxations and make some adjustments in its procedures subject to the SFCs complying with certain minimum requirements.

IDBI may sanction refinance normally up to three times and in special circumstances up to four times the paid-up capital and reserves of an SFC.

Any accommodation that the SFCs may obtain from the State Government should be after obtaining the prior approval of the Reserve Bank as regards the quantum and the terms and conditions.

It is not in the interest of SFCs to change the existing ceiling limit on deposits that may be accepted by an SFC.

SFCs may be compelled by statute to transfer 40 per cent of their profits each year to a reserve fund, the amount so transferred being eligible for income-tax concession under Section 36(1)(viii) of the Income Tax Act. The State Governments should make a matching concession by waiving at least 50 per cent of the stamp duty and registration charges on the documents that may be executed in favour of the SFCs by borrowers in the small-scale industrial sector. The existing ceiling of Rs. 3 crores on paid-up capital for eligibility for the maximum concession under Section 36(1) (viii) of the Income-tax Act may be raised to Rs. 5 crores.

The bonds to be issued by the SFCs may be exempted from stamp duty through appropriate changes in the relevant statutes.

An SFC which has temporarily surplus funds, may lend to the call money market provided they do not at that time remain indebted to the Reserve Bank, or purchase participation certificates recently introduced by some commercial banks.

In the interests of orderly development of the business of the SFCs and for better co-ordination of the activities of IDBI and the SFCs, the Reserve Bank should have the power to issue directives to the SFCs.

A provision may be made for the IDBI's nominee on the Board of Directors of each SFC in place of the IFCI's nominee.

No elected director should continue to hold that post beyond a maximum period of eight years.

An elected director may resign from that office by giving notice of resignation to the Chairman of the Board of Directors of the SFC (instead of the State Government as at present).

As in the case of commercial banks, an SFC should be precluded from granting loans and advances or any other accommodation to a concern in which any of its directors is having substantial interest.

A State Government may, while appointing the Chairman of the Board of Directors of the SFC, choose him from among prominent industrialists in the region or retired civil servants with appropriate background and experience in industry or industrial finance.

The appointment of the Managing Director should be for a minimum period of four years subject to the State Government, on the recommendation of the Board of Directors, having the power of removing him from the post at any time. The appointment should not also be made for an unduly long period.

The Reserve Bank may in consultation with the State Government, prepare a panel of suitable candidates for appointment as the Managing Director of each SFC and the State Government make the appointment on the advice of the Reserve Bank.

The Boad of Directors of an SFC may take decisions on purely administrative matters relating to its Staff Regulations without reference to the Reserve Bank or the State Government.

The Indian Partnership Act may be amended to provide for partnership on limited liability basis.

The Chief Presidency Magistrate or the District Magistrate may be empowered to assist an SFC in taking over the management, or, as the case may be, realising the property of the defaulting concern.

The Comptroller and Auditor General may prepare a panel of auditors acceptable to the State Government. The other class of shareholders may choose one of the auditors in the panel to avoid multiplicity of audits.

There should be a statutory ban on the use of the words "Finance Corporation" or 'Financial Corporation' as part of the name of any concern unless approved by the Reserve Bank.

While making the annual appropriations to the National Industrial Credit (Long Term Operations) Fund, the Reserve Bank may take into account the likely demand that may arise from the various sectors—small-scale, large-scale and public—and earmark the amount specially intended for small industries.

There appears to be no need for the Central Government to make any separate allocation of large funds to the State Governments for enabling the latter to extend financial assistance, except for small amounts, to industrial units under the State Aid to Industries Act.

The SFCs should not extend accommodation solely on the guarantee of State Government. Such guarantee may be accepted only as additional or collateral security, where warranted.

To avoid overlapping of functions, the Development Corporations may render financial assistance of any kind only to units which cannot be assisted by SFCs and a provision may be made for the appointment of the Managing Director of the Development Corporation as a director of the SFC and vice versa.

SFCs may put up the lending rates on loans by ½ per cent.

WORKING GROUP ON METROPOLITAN TRANSPORT SERVICES, 1970—REPORT

Delhi, Manager of Publications, 1970. 108p.

Chairman : Shri G.C. Baveja
Members : Shri K.K. Nambiar; Shri K.A. Khan; Shri R.V. Subramanian; Shri T.V. Joseph; Shri G.H. Lalvani; Shri Rajinder Singh; Shri P.M. Belliappa; Shri B. Mukhopadhyay; Shri A.K. Datta; Shri J.H. Shukla; Shri K.C. Joshi; Shri S. Sundaresan; Shri J.N. Gupta; Shri R.B. Mathur.
Secretary : Shri S.B. Saharya.

APPOINTMENT

In order to make life of the workers and middle classes in urban areas easier the Prime Minister had indicated that it was necessary to evolve urgently an integrated approach to the problems of public transport and that a time-bound programme should be drawn up to improve public transport services in metropolitan cities. It was desired that the study for the present be confined to metropolitan cities, such as Calcutta, Bombay, Delhi and Madras where the problem was most acute and should cover such matters. So the Working Group on Metropolitan Transport Services was set up by the Planning Commission at the suggestion of the Prime Minister in March 1970.

TERMS OF REFERENCE

(i) Increase in production of public transport vehicles coupled with reduction in prices;

(ii) Pattern of taxation of passenger services in urban areas;

(iii) Provision of adequate finance for augmentation of transport facilities; and

(iv) Improvement in operational efficiency of metropolitan transport undertakings including improvements in suburban train services.

CONTENTS

Introduction; Metropolitan Growth and Transport Problems; Calcutta State Transport Corporation; Bombay Electric Supply and Transport Undertaking; Delhi Transport Undertaking; Madras City Transport Services; Design and Availability of Buses; Financial Requirements of the Undertakings; Pattern of Taxation of Passenger Road Transport Services; Organisational and Financial Structure; Operational Efficiency Measures; Undertakings of the Calcutta Tramways Company Ltd.; Suburban Railway Services; Conclusion; Summary of Observations and Recommendations.

RECOMMENDATIONS

Metropolitan Growth and Transportation Problems

1. Traffic studies conducted in the metropolitan cities indicate that between 45 to 50 per cent of the total daily passenger trips are performed during the peak hours of the day, about 60 to 70 per cent of which are for journey to work and back. Such acute 'peak' traffic conditions are caused by the concentration of large employment centres improperly located in relation to residential areas, coupled with increasing distances between work places and dwellings.

2. During the peak hours, the suburban trains in Bombay are packed to 'crush load'. The location of the suburban terminals, particularly in Calcutta and Bombay is such that the majority of the detraining passengers at the terminals have to depend on road transport for completing their journey to destination in the central area of the city, with the result that an additional burden is imposed on road traffic.

3. The road transport undertakings in metropolitan cities have not been able to cope with the increasing volume of passengers for providing comfortable and convenient travel at time and places of major demand because they could not augment their capacities. Moreover, the existing fleet consists of a large number of overage and uneconomic-to-repair buses.

Calcutta State Transport Corporation

4. To meet the city's growing demand for transport services, the CSTC had increased its fleet to 1093 (as on March 31, 1970), from its initial fleet of 670. In spite of the large increase in fleet, the number of effective buses on road on an average was 561 during 1969-70. This was mainly due to a number of overage buses in the fleet and frequent

breakdowns.

5. Out of the total fleet of 1093 buses about 72.3 per cent buses were over 5 years old and 47.3 per cent buses were over 10 years old. The overage fleet is a very serious problem for the CSTC.

6. The Corporation has been facing serious difficulties in procuring imported spare parts so essential for overhauling and maintenance of heavy duty buses. The number of buses held up in the workshop for want of imported spares was 298 as on 31st March, 1970. Due to limited fleet strength the Corporation has been obliged to put such buses on the road resulting in frequent breakdowns, interruption in service schedules and increased cost of operation.

7. The CSTC has been running at a loss since 1962-63 and the gap between the income and expenditure is widening every year. The loss incurred by the CSTC during 1969-70 was Rs. 355 lakhs. The present position is such that the Corporation cannot even meet its operational cost, not to speak of payment of interest on the capital or contribution to the depreciation fund.

Bombay Electric Supply and Transport Undertaking

8. Out of the BEST fleet of 1307 buses as on 31st March, 1970, 45.1 per cent (589) buses were over 5 years old and 17.4 per cent (228) buses over 10 years old and 3 per cent (39) over 15 years old. The overage fleet is one of the serious problems for the Undertaking.

9. The Undertaking has at present only one major workshop at Kingsway which was originally designed in 1948 to cater to the needs of 1000 buses only. The present workshop facilities are inadequate to meet the needs of efficient maintenance and heavy repairs. In view of the increasing operational area, it may be necessary to examine the strengthening/decentralisation of its workshop facilities.

10. Out of the 119 bus routes operated by the BEST Undertaking, over 74 routes fail to cover the operational costs due to low occupation ratio. It is hoped that the management will be able to introduce the desired re-routing plan shortly which will meet the requirements.

11. At present, there are three major bus stations in the city viz., at Colaba, Sion and Mahim and two in the suburbs viz., at Mulund and Juhu. At least two more bus stations would require to be constructed in the city preferably, at Museum and Kings Circle.

12. The financial position of the BEST has been steadily deteriorating since 1963-64. The losses have increased from Rs. 43.9 lakhs in 1963-64 to Rs. 155.1 lakhs in 1969-70.

Delhi Transport Undertaking

13. The overage fleet is one of the serious problems for the DTU. Out of a fleet of 1193 as on 31st March, 1970, 679 buses (i.e. 56.9 per cent) were over 5 years old, 469 buses (i.e. 39.3 per cent) were over 8 years old and 290 (i.e. 24.3 per cent) buses over 10 years old.

14. On the basis of generally accepted yardstick of eight years of life a single deck bus, the DTU needs to replace 469 buses immediately. Another 210 buses (over 8 years) will become due for replacement by March 1973. The DTU would, therefore, need 679 buses in all to be replaced during the Fourth Plan.

15. For economic operation and efficient working a depot should be medium-sized with a stabling capacity of 100 to 125 buses. The DTU therefore, needs at least 2 additional depots and 4 sub-depots, suitably located for garaging and maintenance facilities in order to reduce dead kilometrage to the minimum.

16. To cope with the increased workload of maintenance and heavy repairs of the anticipated large number of buses and in view of the large operational area, it will be necessary for the DTU to decentralise its workshop facilities.

17. The DTU has been experiencing difficulties in getting spare parts in time. At present the bulk supply of the spares are being obtained directly from the manufacturers who do not have their sales depots at Delhi. M/s Ashok Leyland & TELCO have since agreed to open their sales depots at Delhi. This would not only be economical to the Undertaking but also reduce the procurement-lead time.

18. Almost all the routes operated by the DTU fail to cover even operational costs. Taking into consideration the traffic pattern and with a view to making them economically viable and improving efficiency, it is necessary for the Undertaking to reorganise its routes on scientific basis.

19. The Undertaking has been incurring losses since 1963-64. During 1969-70 the losses were estimated to be Rs. 212.35 lakhs. Due to its difficult financial position, the Undertaking has not been able to repay any of the loan instalment and interest charges thereon to the Central Government since Ist October, 1965.

Madras City Transport Services

20. During the peak hours there is overcrowding in the buses. While the capacity of a bus is 61 passengers it carries about 90 passengers during peak period. To meet peak hour rush the Department needs large carrying capacity buses.

21. Out of the fleet of 1022 as on 31-3-1970, only 11.7 per cent (120) buses were 5 years old and 2.9 per cent (30) buses were over 8 years old. Thus overage fleet is not much of a problem in Madras city as the Tamil Nadu State Transport Department has been following a policy of timely replacement of its overage fleet, which is 6 years or 3.5 lakhs kms. in case of Leyland Comet and 5 years or 2.75 lakhs kms in case of TMB buses.

Design and Availability of Buses

22. To meet the peak hour demand the city transport undertakings should introduce large capacity buses, preferably double deckers.

23. Taking into account the production programme of the manufacturers it is recommended that the requirements of the bus chassis for city transport may be standardised to the following three categories :

(1) Cometised Titan Double Deck Chassis;

(2) Semi-articulated vehicle with a Leyland Comet Tractor and a suitable trailer chassis to mount a single or double deck bogie;

(3) Leyland Comet AI-GOP-311 passenger chassis with a wheel base of 210", or TMB chassis LP-1210/52 with a wheel base of 205".

24. The Working Group is also of the view that in case any manufacturer is able to develop chassis conforming to the above requirements, these can also be considered for purpose of standardisation for use in city operation.

25. The fleet in Calcutta and Bombay mostly consists of imported double deckers and heavy duty single deckers. It would be economical to bring back to road some of the old imported buses through reconditioning. The Working Group recommends that the Ministry of Industrial Development should allot an ad hoc foreign exchange to the extent of Rs. 17.80 lakhs to the CSTC to bring back 150 double deckers into service. As regards the BEST, the requirement of foreign exchange for procuring imported spares is Rs. 30 lakhs for reconditioning of 200 old imported buses.

26. Till 1967-68 the basis for allocation of foreign exchange for imported spares was Rs. 1000 per bus per annum. It has recently been reduced to Rs. 600. This amount is just adequate for meeting the needs of the Indian made medium duty vehicles. Treating imported buses on the same footing as the buses manufactured in India is not justified. The Working Group, therefore, recommends that the allotment for existing heavy duty buses which were imported from U.K. should be at least Rs. 2500 per year. The double deckers manufactured in India should also be treated at par with the imported buses. It is recommended that the Ministry of Industrial Development may adopt the above basis for allocation of foreign exchange for imported spares and also ensure clearance of licences expeditiously.

Financial Requirements of the Undertakings

27. In view of the difficult financial position of the city transport undertakings and to render satisfactory service to the travelling public the Working Group recommends that necessary financial arrangements should be made for replacement of overage buses and also reasonable augmentation of their fleet. The requirements of the CSTC during the remaining period of the Fourth Five Year Plan are Rs. 5 crores and for the BEST and DTU is Rs. 8.4 crores. The DTU would, therefore, need additional provision of Rs. 3.6 crores during the Fouth Plan. The Madras City Transport Service needs Rs. 2.4 crores over and above the cost of replacement programme to be met out of depreciation fund already provided by the Department.

28. The provision for the current year for the Calcutta State Transport Corporation should be augmented by Rs. 60 lakhs and that for the DTU by Rs. 1 crore.

Pattern of Taxation of Passenger Road Transport Services

29. Passenger road transport services in cities are subject to direct and indirect taxes. During 1969-70 the percentage share of direct taxes in the total expenditure was 11.9 in the case of Madras City and Suburban Services as compared with 3.6 for DTU, 7.1 for BEST and 3.3 for CSTC.

30. The percentage share of indirect taxes levied by the Central and State Governments in the total expenditure per vehicle in 1969-70 amounted to 25.7 for DTU, 21.3 in case of BEST and 25.4 for Madras City and Suburban Services.

31. It is recommended that the principle of lower rates of taxes for city services should be accepted by the Central and all State Governments concerned in view of the difficult financial position of the city transport undertakings.

32. It is further recommended that the rates of taxes levied by the Governments on passenger vehicles plying in metropolitan areas should not be raised further.

Organisational and Financial Structure

33. The present organisational structure of the BEST and the DTU is not a satisfactory arrangement

for efficient running of the undertaking. It is recommended that the present organisational set up should be replaced by a Statutory Corporation. This would be in keeping with the general policy of the Government of India that passenger road transport services should be run through corporations.

34. The Board of Directors of the Corporation should be appointed strictly on the basis of skills and experience useful to a transport undertaking and should be capable of reviewing operations and recommending improvements.

35. The Chief Executive should be a person responsible for management of the Corporation at the top level and he should be a member of the Board of Directors.

36. The Working Group recommends that there should be larger delegation of powers for the Chief Executive and other managerial staff so as to ensure optimum performance. Even pending the formation of Corporation, it is necessary to delegate more powers to the General Managers of the Undertakings.

37. There have been more than five changes in the post of General Manager of the DTU during the last 12 years, although under the Delhi Municipal Corporation Act the tenure of a General Manager is normally for five years. In Madras too, no Director continued in his post for more than a year during the last three years. The Working Group strongly urges upon the concerned authorities that frequent changes in top management personnel should be avoided.

38. The Working Group recommends that each transport undertaking should set up a Planning Group of competent people to undertake necessary studies to improve the efficiency of the service. This Group should assist the General Manager in planning improvement of the projects and should report to him regularly.

39. The transport undertaking also needs a special group to make cost studies with a view to achieving economies in all departments. It would be of advantage to have costing personnel in the various depots so that performance of a depot or maintenance/operations unit could be compared with one another.

40. It is recommended that capital contribution to the city transport undertakings should be in the form of share capital. At present the Central and State Governments contribution to the capital of State Road Transport Corporations through the Railway Board is in the ratio of 1:2. The same ratio can be adopted in the case of city undertakings if they are converted into Corporations and contributions by the Central Government made through the Ministry of Shipping and Transport. A beginning in this regard can be made with Calcutta where a Corporation is already running the city road transport services.

41. The loans so far advanced to the undertakings should be treated as share capital contribution and should not carry interest.

42. The Working Group feels that the Undertakings should at least cover the operating expenses.

43. The Working Group recommends that the undertakings should have freedom to determine their fares to meet at least the increases in the operating expenses which may be beyond their control.

Operational Efficiency Measures

44. It is suggested that measures, such as scientific Inventory Management, rationalisation and streamlining of purchase procedure, proper quality control and inspection of the materials purchased, route planning on scientific basis, adequate workshop and depot facilities, should be adopted by the undertakings to improve their operational efficiency.

45. The Undertaking should reduce leakage in revenue with greater alertness on the part of the supervisory staff. Arrangements for advance booking should be intensified on the routes on which passenger load is high.

46. It is recommended that the highest priority should be given to replacement of level crossings by overbridges or subways.

47. Priority should be given to explore the possibility of further staggering working hours for Government offices as well as educational institutions and commercial establishments, if necessary on statutory basis.

48. The Working Group is of the view that the tendency towards urban concentration must be effectively restricted. The Working Group hopes that the Maharashtra Government would stop further reclamation of the Back Bay area as the Railways and the BEST are much concerned with this development.

Undertaking of the Calcutta Tramways

49. The number of trams up for want of spares has been rising from year to year. The Tramways find it difficult to get import licence to procure some essential materials and components like traction motors, insulated copper wire, switches, rails, tyres etc. which are not manufactured in the country.

50. The derailment of trams increased from 30 in 1963 to 2403 in 1969 due to heavy wear and tear of the tracks as well as the inability of the Tramways to procure rolled steel tyres for a number of years.

51. The financial position of the Tramways has been deteriorating since 1967 and the loss incurred

by the Undertaking during 1969 amounted to Rs. 85.11 lakhs.

52. For improving the operational efficiency of the Tramways, it is recommended that an additional provision of Rs. 3 crores should be made during the Fourth Plan to meet the cost of maintenance of tracks, rolling stock, overhead insta lations etc.

53. The Heavy Electricals Ltd., Bhopal should be persuaded to take up the manufacture of traction motors required by the Tramways.

54. A sum of only Rs. 10 lakhs has been provided in the Annual Plan for 1970-71. It is recommended that the Plan provision for the current year should be suitably enhanced so as to make available Rs. 225.90 lakhs during the two years 1970-71 and 1971-72.

55. The Tramway Undertaking need special allotment of foreign exchange for imports of switch points, grooved rails, traction motors and circuit breakers amounting to Rs. 123.63 lakhs during 1970-72. It is recommended that ad hoc allocation of foreign exchange for the above amount should be made to the Undertaking to meet its requirements.

56. Increasing foreign exchange difficulties had forced the Tramways to use locally made soft cast steel tyres in place of rolled steel tyres. Since Railways had booked the entire rolling capacity of the TISCO, the supply to tyres to the Company through this source has ceased. It is, therefore, necessary that Railways should allow the TISCO to resume rolling of these tyres for the Undertaking. In case it is not feasible, the Working Group recommends that foreign exchange to the extent of Rs. 4 lakhs per annum for importing them should be allocated to the Undertaking.

57. The Undertaking is unable to get grooved rails causing heavy financial loss and increased cost for renewal programme. The requirement of grooved rails will be of the order of about 1200 tonnes per annum for the next five years and thereafter 600 tonnes per annum for normal replacement. The Hindustan Steel Plant at Bhilai may by persuaded to take up this order.

58. The Tramways have to pay Rs. 4 lakhs per month for consumption of electricity. Under the provision of a Statute the Railways are exempted from payment of electricity duty. The Working Group suggests that the State Government should consider exempting the Tramway Undertaking from payment of electricity duty on the pattern of Railways.

59. The tariff structure for electricity supply is governed by successive agreements with Calcutta Electricity Supply Corporation. Under the agreement of 1950 the Undertaking has been given a flat rate and thus deprived of getting the advantage of su mmated maximum demand on the ground that it received supply through eleven sub-stations owned and operated by it. The Working Group is of the view that the agreement with Calcutta Electricity Supply Corporation may be re-examined with a view to determining a reasonable tariff structure for the Tramways.

Suburban Railway Services

60. The Railways constitute the most expedient and effective means of mass transportation in the metropolitan areas. About 7.44 lakh commuters in Calcutta, 22 lakh in Bombay and 2.4 lakh in Madras are being carried daily by the suburban railways.

61. The Final Location Survey for the Suburban Dispersal Line in Calcutta is under progress and is scheduled to be completed by April, 1971 when the construction of the project could be taken in hand. The Planning Commission has already provided a sum of Rs. 30 crores in the Development Plan of the Railways during the Fourth Plan for the construction of the above line. It is recommended that the survey should be completed as early as possible.

62. The Railways have already initiated the techno-economic feasibility studies for the mass rapid transit system in Calcutta. According to the Railways the studies are expected to be completed by December, 1971. It is recommended that all possible efforts should be made to complete these studies in time and commence construction on this Project as early as possible.

63. The preliminary engineering feasibility study for their terminal at Ballard Estate (Bombay) which is already in progress is expected to be completed by December, 1970. The Working Group is of the view that the construction of the new terminal if found feasible, would relieve congestion on the existing two terminals—V.T. and Churchgate.

64. The Traffic Cell set up by the Government of Maharashtra to undertake studies for preparing a long-term transportation plan for Bombay has submitted its report to the Metropolitan Transport Team. As soon as the corridors for the rapid transit are finalised, the Railways would be in a position to undertake the techno-economic feasibility studies for system selection.

65. The traffic and transportation studies for preparing long-term transportation plans for Madras and Delhi are under progress. It is expected that the reports will be available to the Metropolitan Transport Team by March, 1971. The Team would then finalise the corridors and give its report so as to enable the Railways to carry out the techno-economic

feasibility studies for system selection for rapid transit system in Madras and Delhi. No time should be lost in finalising these studies.

66. Steps should be taken to find out ways and means for meeting the demand of the Western and the Central Railways for DC E.M.U. stock. Efforts should be made to further increase annual capacity of I.C.F. for this purpose. Also total foreign exchange required for the purchase of spare parts for the repairs and rehabilitation of old EMU stock should be released expeditiously.

67. The proposal of running 12 coach trains in Bombay is expected to cost on a rough estimate about Rs. 40 crores and take about 5 years for implementation. Before a decision on this Project is taken, a techno-economic study should be undertaken by the Railways.

68. During monsoon, dislocation of suburban services in Bombay is caused due to flooding of tracks. The Railways should provide adequate drainage outlets for such sections of the tracks which are liable to flooding.

69. Trespassing of the tracks is a menace to the smooth running of trains. Immediate steps should be taken to provide foot over-bridges where colonies have sprung up on either side of the track or where the industrial areas have developed. At present the entire cost of the foot over-bridges is being met by the Municipal bodies. The Working Group is of the view that such over-bridges should be financed on the same pattern as the replacement of level crossings by grade/separated arrangements.

70. There are innumerable thefts of track materials and signalling equipment which cause dislocation in services and heavy losses to the Railways. Measures should be taken to check lawlessness by better coordination between the Railway Police, the State Police and the Railway Protection Force.

71. All the important level crossings within the metropolitan area should be replaced by grade-separated arrangements on priority basis. The Railways may consider sharing the cost equally with the local bodies for the construction of over/under bridge, including approaches, upto the width of 60 ft. instead of 36 ft. as at present.

DIRECT TAXES ENQUIRY COMMITTEE, 1970—REPORT

Delhi, Manager of Publications, 1971. 315p.

Chairman : Shri Justice K.N. Wanchoo.

Members : Shri M.P. Chitable; Shri S. Prakash Chopra; Shri P.C. Padhi; Shri D.K. Rangnekar.

Secretary : Shri S. Narayan.

APPOINTMENT

On 19th December, 1969, Shri Lok Nath Misra, M.P. moved the following resolution in the Rajya Sabha on behalf of Shri Sundar Mani Patel, M.P.

"This house is of opinion that Government should constitute a Committee consisting of experts and Members of Parliament to go into the failure of the Central Board of Direct Taxes, Ministry of Finance, in the timely collection of taxes and to suggest remedial measures for improving the collection system".

Replying to the resolution Shri R.K. Khadilkar, Minister of State in the Ministry of Finance announced the Government's decision to appoint a Committee of experts to suggest means for tackling problems of black money, tax-evasion and tax arrears. Accordingly, this Committee was constituted by a Resolution dated 2nd March 1970. "The Government of India have decided to appoint a Committee of experts to examine and suggest legal and administrative measures for countering evasion and avoidance of direct taxes".

TERMS OF REFERENCE

Following is the term of reference :—

(a) The Committee will recommend concrete and effective measures;

(i) to unearth black money and prevent its

proliferation through further evasion;

(ii) to check avoidance of tax through various legal devices, including the formation of trusts; and

(iii) to reduce tax arrears.

(b) Examine various exemptions allowed by the Tax Laws with a view to their modification, curtailment or withdrawal;

(c) indicate the manner in which tax assessment and administration may be improved for giving effect to all its recommendations.

The Committee will function in the Department of Revenue and Insurance of the Ministry of Finance.

The Committee will submit its report to the Ministry of Finance.

CONTENTS

Introduction; Black Money and Tax Evasion; Tax Avoidance; Tax Arrears; Exemption and Deductions; Tax Administration; Summary of Observations and Recommendations, Minutes of Dissent; Appendices.

RECOMMENDATIONS

Basic Considerations

The richest one-tenth of the households in the country account for about 25 per cent of the total private consumption, over 40 per cent of the total household incomes, and not less than two-thirds of privately-owned wealth. The major share of the additional resources has to come from this stratum.

Indirect taxes have an important role in the fiscal system. It would also be possible to achieve a degree of progression through indirect taxation by levying it on commodities and services consumed by the richer sections of the population. Nevertheless, commodity taxation has serious limitations as an instrument of resource mobilization, since it is more easily shifted and very often leads to unintended cost escalations. For equitable distribution of the burden it is essential to use direct taxation to the maximum extent possible for resource mobilization.

The incidence of direct taxation should be broadly the same on comparable income and wealth groups irrespective of the sources of income and the forms in which wealth is held. This does not necessarily mean that the forms of direct taxation adopted for application to different categories of income and wealth should be identical.

Direct taxes on agriculture levied by the States (viz., land revenue, cesses and surcharges based on land revenue, crop cesses and agricultural income-tax) account for barely 1 per cent of the net Domestic Product from agriculture, and the proportion varies widely from State to State; it is about 0.24 per cent in Orissa and Punjab and 1.34 per cent in Rajasthan.

In devising a system of direct taxation of agriculture, it is necessary to ensure that the relatively better-off sections pay proportionately more out of their income and wealth so that there is a reasonable degree of progression in the tax.

The principle of progression has not governed the land revenue—the largest element of direct taxation of agriculture. Since there is no perceptible progression in the incidence of surcharges on land revenue and since other taxes levied on agriculture are relatively light, income-earners belonging to the higher strata pay less than those in comparable strata deriving their income from non-agricultural sources.

The proposed ceilings on land holdings have greatly reduced the scope for progressive taxation in agriculture. Even so, there will be incomes earned from agriculture large enough to come within the purview of progressive tax. The size of operational ceilings would not necessarily be limited by the proposed ceilings. Further, with technological improvement, productivity of land is likely to increase in future.

For purposes of direct taxation the family—consisting of husband, wife and minor children—should be the basic unit of assessment. This is required also for preventing large-scale avoidance. If direct taxation is to become a major instrument of resource mobilization on an equitable basis, it is also necessary to close the loopholes offered by the various exemptions and deductions.

With a ceiling on land holdings, a growing percentage of the agricultural population particularly in the higher strata is likely to turn increasingly to non-agricultural sources of income. There has to be, therefore, a mechanism to ensure that incomes whether derived from agricultural or non-agricultural activities are taken into account for progressive direct taxation.

In looking for a suitable system of direct taxation of agriculture the facts of a federal polity and of the distribution of functions and powers between the Centre and the federating States have to be borne in mind.

Alternative Approaches to Direct Taxation of Agriculture

One alternative which is readily available for the direct taxation of agriculture is integrated taxation of agricultural and non-agricultural wealth. There is no constitutional impediment to the levy of such a tax by the Centre, if the coverage of the tax is widened by adopting the family as the basic unit or by reducing the basic exemption limit or by cutting down the exemptions wealth-tax can be a useful instrument of direct taxation. But if the exemption limit is lowered several difficulties will arise including problems of indentifying potential assessees, the taxable assets and valuation of assets etc. In the conditions of Indian agriculture this will inevitably give rise to considerable harassment and possibly lead to savings being increasingly held in forms that are more easily concealed such as gold and currency hoards. Hence caution has to be exercised in the use of wealth-tax as the principal instrument of resource mobilization from the agricultural population.

An alternative recommended by many is a completely integrated system of taxation of agricultural and non-agricultural incomes. This would require a major constitutional amendment to empower the Centre to levy tax on agricultural incomes. Such a course of action is not favoured by the States. Besides, since proper assessment of agricultural incomes requires a degree of knowledge of local conditions, in any practical system of taxation of agricultural incomes the primary responsibility for the levy and collection of the tax will have to be with the States. Apart from these considerations, taxation of agriculturists, according to actual incomes assessed from year to year poses various problems. The computation of actual income from farming with any degree of precision is extremely difficult. Few among the farmers keep detailed accounts. Hence the risk of harassment by tax officials and equally the opportunities for understanding incomes are likely to be considerable if the tax is based on the 'actual income' concept.

An alternative often suggested is a progressive surcharge on the existing land revenue. But there is no uniformity in the principle and procedures followed in land-revenue assessments in different States and in different areas within the same State. The existing land revenue therefore does not offer a satisfactory basis for a system of progressive surcharge.

A rational system of direct taxation of agriculture (i) should take account of the differences in productivity of land depending upon the particular crops grown in a region, (ii) its incidence should be uniform in different parts of the country, and (iii) it should reflect changes in productivity and prices over a period of time. Moreover, it should be possible to build into the tax an element of progression.

Agricultural Holdings Tax

The major factors underlying differences in the productivity of land are, (i) soil-climatic differences; (ii) conditions of water supply; and (iii) crops grown. An Agricultural Holdings Tax (AHT) needs to be devised to adequately take account of the factors making for such variations in the productivity of land.

The salient features of the proposed scheme of AHT are as under :—

(a) The country should be divided into a sufficiently large number of soil-climatically homogeneous districts/tracts so that differences having any significant influence on productivity are taken into account;

(b) For each such district/tract norms of output of different crops per hectare for each year should be worked out on the basis of estimates of yield for the previous 10 years; these should be valued at the relevant average harvest prices of the preceding three years. The State Governments should notify the markets and post-harvest prices of the preceding three years. The State Governments should notify the markets and post-harvest marketing periods relating to each crop in each district/tract and arrange to collect, record and publish the relevant prices on a regular basis;

(c) The norms so derived would provide the norms of the value of output per hectare of different crops of different districts/tracts;

(d) From the value of the gross output of the crops arrived at as above allowance should be made for the paid out costs of cultivation other than expenses of irrigation and also for depreciation of assets (other than livestock) along the lines indicated.

(e) The norms arrived at in the above manner would form the ratable value of a hectare of land growing different crops in different districts/tracts.

(f) If in a given year, the average output of a crop in a district is less than half the average output of earlier 10 years, the ratable value of land under such a crop should be taken at zero. Relief may be allowed for crop failures in part or parts of a district/tract after enquiry by an appropriate authority.

(g) To simplify the computation crops under a district/tract may be suitably grouped under a few crop-groups.

(h) For each district/tract there will be a schedule of ratable value of land per hectare under different crops/crop-groups. The schedule should be revised every year taking into account, the crop yields of the preceding 10 years, the harvest prices of the preceding 3 years and any revision that may be made from time to time in the scale of deduction to be made on account of the costs of cultivation of different crops. The schedule of ratable value of lands under different crops in each district/tract should be prepared on this basis every year and included in the legislation of the year in question. The construction of the schedule for each district/tract in a State will be primarily the responsibility of the State Government concerned.

(i) The ratable value of an assessable land holdings will be computed from the ratable values of land under the crops actually grown (harvested) on it during the year of assessment after deducting the expenses of irrigation in the manner indicated.

To provide for the costs of development, a development allowance should be given to all agricultural holdings at the rate of 20 per cent of the ratable value subject to a maximum of Rs. 1000.

The actual tax liability under the Agricultural Holdings Tax would be arrived at by applying a simple formula to the ratable value of the holdings minus the development allowance; if the ratable value of a holding (minus the development allowance) is 'X' thousand rupees the AHT should form X/2 per cent of this amount. Thus for example, if the ratable value of a holding is Rs. 10,000 the AHT would be 9.0/2 or 4.5 per cent of Rs. 9000 (i.e. Rs. 10,000 minus Rs. 1000 deductible as development allowance), which is equal to Rs. 405.

As the incidence of the AHT decreases progressively on small holdings, the formula should be applied to ratable values upto Rs. 600. For holdings of ratable value below Rs. 600 AHT may be fixed at a flat rate of Re. 1 per holding.

Tax on agricultural holdings should be levied on operational holdings and on a family basis (family consisting of husband, wife and minor children). Adoption of the operational holding as the basis for the AHT will discourage illegal or concealed leases and thus help protect the rights of the tenants.

The implementation of the AHT may be made in two phases. In the first phase the present land revenue should be replaced by the AHT on all operational holdings with ratable value of Rs. 5000 or more. Suitable steps would need to be taken in the first phase for identification of all operational holdings likely to have ratable value of Rs. 5000 and for aggregation of holdings of all family members. Holdings lying in different States should be treated as separate holdings and assessed as such. In the second phase the system may be extended to operational holdings of ratable value below Rs. 5000 according to the convenience of each State Government.

To facilitate the determination of ratable values of holdings a system of crop inspection and recording of crop acreages should be evolved. Recording of crop acreages on assessable holdings must be done expeditiously so that the ratable value is ascertained well within the year of assessment. Reasonable opportunity should be given to each assessee where records of land holdings are incorrect. A regular procedure will have to be laid down for the purpose. It would be convenient if a separate 'Agricultural Holding Book' is issued to each assessable landholder in which are entered details relating to members of the family, details of operational holdings, changes in the area covered by the holding from time to time and crops grown in different seasons each year. The ratable value of the holding, the AHT assessment and the recovery of instalments as also all loan transactions related to the land holdings should be entered in this book. The book should be permanently with the land holder.

The assessment year should be uniformly from Ist July to 30th June. Every year on the basis of the recorded crop groups the ratable value of each holding should be worked out, the AHT computed at the prescribed rates and a notice of demand presented to each assessee before 30th June of the assessment year. The recovery of the tax may be made in suitable instalments in the following year.

The AHT should replace land revenue for all operational holdings of ratable value of Rs. 5000 and more. Extension of the AHT of holdings of smaller ratable value may be made at the discretion of State Governments in the following phases :

(i) All operational holdings with ratable value of Rs. 2500 and above may be covered;

(ii) On the remaining holdings a census of land utilisation and recording of crop acreage may be done once in 5 years. Their ratable value may be ascertained on this basis, the AHT assessed and kept fixed for the next 5 years. All agricultural holdings with the ratable value of less than Rs. 600 may be required to pay AHT at a flat rate of Re. 1 per holding.

Whether an operational holding stands in the name of a trust, the holding should be notionally apportioned among the beneficiaries in the proportion in which the income of the trust is enjoyed by them and the respective shares aggregated with the holdings of the families to which the beneficiaries belong. Where the share of the beneficiaries is indeterminate, the agricultural holdings of the trust should be assessed to AHT at a minimum rate of 20 per cent of the ratable value. There should be no concessional treatment for charitable or religious trusts.

In the case of cooperatives, in so far as a part or the whole of the operational agricultural holding of a cooperative society consists of lands identifiable as legally belonging to individual members such lands should be treated as part of the agricultural holdings of the family to which these members belong. Where such lands are not so identifiable they may be deemed to be operated by the members in equal parts and each such part treated as a component of the agricultural holdings of the respective members.

Holdings of agricultural companies may be assessed for AHT on the same basis as family holdings subject to a minimum of 20 per cent of the ratable value of their operational holdings. As regards holdings of plantation companies, the present system of agricultural income taxation on plantation companies may continue. However, to the extent the area operated by them is used for growing non-plantation crops, these companies should be subjected to AHT like any other agricultural company.

After the notice of demand is served an opportunity should be given to the tax-payer to challenge the correctness of the computation of the tax-liability.

While framing the scheme of the AHT the requirement that a tax statute like any other statute must respect the principle of equality enshrined in the Constitution has been kept in view.

To ensure uniform and objective application of the AHT all over the country there should be a standing All-India Committee on Agricultural Holdings Tax. This Committee should be appointed by the Planning Commission and it should consist of three members :

(i) A non-official economist;

(ii) An official with experience of Revenue Administration at the State level; and

(iii) A technical officer who is or has been a Director of Agriculture in a State.

The Committee should undertake every year a post facto review of the operation of the AHT in all the States and consult the State Government where significant departures are found from the desired uniformity and objectivity in the application of the AHT. The Committee should submit an Annual Review to the Planning Commission and the Review should be placed before the National Development Council.

On the basis of available data the Agricultural Holdings Tax may be expected to yield about Rs. 200 crores per annum, if applied to all holdings with ratable value of Rs. 5000 and above. If this tax replaces land revenue and related surcharges and cesses, the net additional revenue that may be collected from this tax would be around Rs. 150 crores. If extended to all holdings of ratable value of Rs. 2500 or more, the additional resources may be around Rs. 200 crores.

Partially integrated Taxation of Non-agricultural Income with Income derived from Agriculture

There should be some arrangement to ensure that the tax burden on assessees with similar incomes does not differ sharply merely because of the fact that part of it is derived from agriculture. This can be achieved without bringing agricultural incomes under the charge of Central income-tax if such incomes are taken into account in determining the rate of tax applicable to non-agricultural incomes. This would also help check evasion through the device of camouflaging taxable income as gains from agriculture.

A suitable provision should therefore be made in the Income Tax Act, 1961 whereby both agricultural and non-agricultural components of a tax-payer's income are aggregated and the tax on the non-agricultural portion is levied as if the latter were placed in the top slabs of the aggregate income. Integration of agricultural and non-agricultural incomes should take effect only if an assessee has taxable income exceeding the minimum exemption limit laid down for the levy of the Central income-tax. In determining the rate of tax on non-agricultural income, the agricultural income and non-agricultural income should be combined in the following manner and order: (i) the initial exemption allowed out of non-agricultural income (Rs. 5000 at present), (ii) agricultural income, and (iii) the balance of non-agricultural income.

Since the proposal does not envisage levy of any tax on agricultural income by the Centre it would not require any constitutional amendment.

The suggestion to achieve partial integration by allowing the States to levy tax on agricultural income at the rates appropriate to the total income comprising both agricultural and non-agricultural income is not practicable.

In computing net income from agriculture for the purpose of partial integration, all items of expenditure allowed under the Income-tax Act in the computation of income from business or profession, including depreciation of machinery and tools used in agriculture, should be deducted from gross receipts. To avoid harassment to assessees however, rules should be framed by the Central Government in consultation with the State Government and the proposed All-

India Committee on Agricultural Holdings Tax prescribing the maximum scale of expenses allowable under the major heads in computation of agricultural income in different districts/tracts.

The liability on account of the proposed Agricultural Holdings Tax should not be allowed as deductible expenditure while computing agricultural income.

Losses incurred in agriculture should be allowed to be set-off only against gains from agriculture.

Administrative arrangements should be made for certification of the extent of the aggregate agricultural holding of assessees, the nature of crops grown and the ratable value of the holdings by an appropriate revenue authority designated by the State Governments in each district.

The additional revenue realised as a result of the partial integration of agricultural with non-agricultural income in the above manner should go entirely to the State of origin of the agricultural income so aggregated.

Integrated Taxation of Agricultural Property through Wealth-tax and of Capital Gains on Agricultural Assets through Income-tax

The AHT should be supplemented with a tax on agricultural property and a tax on capital gains arising out of transactions in such property.

It is now well settled that Parliament can legislate for the levy of tax on net wealth including the value of agricultural land. At present, however, the wealth-tax in general has a number of limitations due to numerous exemptions allowed. Many of the exemptions now allowed are regressive in effect. If it is considered necessary to stimulate saving or to promote saving in particular forms, the financial institutions concerned may be enabled to offer higher rates of return to all investors.

Wealth tax should be levied on a family basis. The basic exemption limit may be raised to Rs. 1.5 lakhs and all other exemptions done away with as far as possible. If the exemption limit is so fixed few families in agriculture would be required to pay any wealth-tax on their own agricultural holdings, unless they have substantial assets in other forms as well. With the removal of all exemptions other than that provided by the basic exemption limit, there would be a case for lowering the rates of tax in order that assessees on the margin of the exempted limit are not too heavily burdened.

Value of shares in companies and cooperatives should be included in full in the taxable wealth of the share holders and their market worth determined rigorously. No concession should be given to religious and charitable trusts in the matter of wealth-tax.

Valuation of farm lands for wealth-tax purposes should, generally, be made through the method of income-capitalization. A simple and adequate method would be to take 4 to 6 times the ratable value of a holding averaged over a period of years. Guidelines may be issued to the assessing officers regarding factors to be kept in view while taking a decision about the figure of the multiplier to be adopted for income-capitalization.

The definition of capital asset should be so widened as to permit taxation of capital gains from transfer of all agricultural lands irrespective of their location. Gains from transaction in assets held for not more than a year should be treated as ordinary income and taxed accordingly. To mitigate the inequity involved in the taxation of capital gains derived from sale of assets held for more than a year at progressive rates a method of prorating the long-term capital gains over a number of years, without reopening any back year's assessment may be followed. Treatment of losses on long-term capital assets might continue as at present. The exemption of long-term capital gains from tax currently allowed (when a non-corporate assessee's income does not exceed Rs. 10,000 or when the gains are less than Rs. 5000) should go once the prorating method is adopted.

As capital gains are not taxable until an asset is sold, other alternatives have to be looked for in order to recoup a part of the cost of development projects within a reasonable period.

The additional revenue likely to be realised if the tax on agricultural wealth and on capital gains on agricultural assets is operated on an integrated basis on the lines suggested would be arround Rs. 100-150 crores.

Related Matters

As has been suggested for the AHT the basic unit of the assessment for income-tax and wealth-tax also should be the family consisting of the husband, wife and minor children being the unit of income-receipt, of consumption and all related decision making. However, when the family is made the tax unit, a deduction may be allowed from salary income at the rate of 10 per cent of the joint income of the spouses when both are employed outside the household (and 20 per cent of the income of a surviving spouse with minor children to maintain), subject to a maximum of Rs. 2000.

While the adoption of the family as the basic tax

unit, the recognition of the Hindu Undivided Family as a tax entity should be withdrawn.

Income from livestock-breeding and poultry and dairy farming, which is now exempt from taxation should be subjected to income tax.

Irrigation water should be viewed as an input and should be priced to cover the cost of providing it. Under pricing of inputs like water is undesirable except in the initial stages. The betterment levy is unsuitable as an instrument for recovering capital cost of projects. In the case of certain kinds of public investment, such as those involved in urban development, the capital costs may be recouped by setting up a Land Commission and vesting it with power to "acquire, manage and pricing of inputs like water is, undesirable except in the initial dispose of land". The Land Commissions can play a useful role in framing and securing the financial support for development programmes.

REVIEWING COMMITTEE FOR INDIAN INSTITUTE OF TECHNOLOGY MADRAS, 1970—REPORT

New Delhi, Manager of Publications; 1971. 148p.

Chairman : Prof. P.L. Bhatnagar.
Members : Prof. G.S. Ramaswamy; Prof. G.R. Damodaran: Dr. G.S. Laddha; Shri M.V. Arunachalam.
Secretary : Shri M.S. Srinivasan.

APPOINTMENT

The President of India, in his capacity as Visitor of the Indian Institute of Technology, Madras, in exercise of the powers vested in him under sub-section (2) of Section (9) of the Indian Institute of Technology (Madras) Act, 1956 (51 of 1956) appointed the Committee vide Government of India, Ministry of Education and Youth Services, Notification No. F. 5-11/68-T6 dated March 30, 1970 to review the work and progress of the Indian Institute of Technology, Madras, since its inception in 1959.

TERMS OF REFERENCE

(i) To review the present progress of the Institute of Technology in the fulfilment of its broad objective as a centre of advanced studies and research in science, engineering and technology ;

(ii) To examine how far the Institute has interacted with other technical institutions with particular reference to courses of study, programme of research and faculty development;

(iii) To assess the overall impact of the Institute on the training of higher grade engineers for the technological development of the country;

(iv) To recommend the lines along which the Institute should be further developed for advanced study and research, taking into account the developments that have taken place or are projected at the other Institutes of Technology and the Indian Institute of Science, Bangalore; and

(v) To report on any other aspect or aspects that are relevant to the overall functioning of the Institute.

CONTENTS

Introduction and Project Report; General Recommendations; Department-wise Review and Recommendations of the Reviewing Committee; Central Service Facilities; Inter-Disciplinary Projects; Staff and Students Amenities in the Campus; Industrial Experimentation and Design Engineering Centre and Centre for Advanced Studies; Financial Review; Appendices I and II.

RECOMMENDATIONS

Emphasis on Post-graduate Education

When the Institute was started, it was envisaged that the ratio of under-graduate students to post-graduate students should be 2:1. Since then, a large number of Regional Engineering Colleges and other engineering institutions have come into existence. Moreover, the Indian Institutes of Technology have resources which are of high order both in terms of academic personnel and laboratory equipment. It was thought necessary by the Reviewing Committee to examine the question why should the Indian Institute of Technology not concentrate to a much larger extent on the post-graduate training than at present. This problem was also raised and discussed with the Committee by many eminent persons as well as the faculty of the Institute, and the general concensus of opinion was that it is high time for the Institute to devote its attention to a greater extent to the post-graduate training and research than to under-graduate training. The Committee, after examining the facilities available at the Institute is of the definite opinion that to make full use of these facilities, the Institute should concentrate more on post-graduate training and research. It is hoped that at the end of the plan period, the Institute will be able to bring parity in the levels of undergraduates and post-graduates. The following student enrolment is now suggested.

DEPARTMENTS	B. Tech.	M. Tech.	DIIT	M.Sc.	Post M.Sc.	M.S.	Ph.D.	Post Doctoral
1	2	3	4	5	6	7	8	9
1. Aeronautical Engineering	18×5=90	15×2=30	—	———	—	8	10	1
2. Applied Mechanics	———	15×2=30	—	———	—	8	10	1
3. Chemical Engineering	30×5=150	25×2=50	15	———	—	8	10	1
4. Civil Engineering	30×5=150	30×2=60	—	———	—	8	10	1
5. Electrical Engineering	60×5=300	50×2=100	—	———	—	1	15	2
6. Mechanical Engineering	60×5=300	50×2=100	—	———	—	15	15	2
7. Metallurgy	30×5=150	20×2=40	—	———	—	8	10	—
8. Mathematics	———	———	—	25×2=50	10	—	30	2
9. Physics	———	———	—	25×2=50	10	—	30	2
10. Chemistry	———	———	—	25×2=50	10	—	30	2
11. Humanities and Social Sciences	———	25×2=50	—	———	—	—	10	—
12. Inter-Disciplinary (3-Year Course)	20×3=60	———	—	———	—	—	35	—
TOTAL	1,200	440	15	150	30	65	215	14

Under Graduate Students : 1,200   Post-graduate Students : 930

It is felt that a reduced number of under-graduate students in each discipline of the engineering science should be accepted every year. Only those specialisations (at under-graduate level) should be taught, which reflect the facilities and achievements of the Institute, keeping in view the national needs and the facilities available elsewhere.

Generally, it will be advisable that the students who have undergone intensive under-graduate training at the Institute in these specialisations be admitted to the post-graduate courses, as it will ensure higher quality of student material in post-graduate classes. The Committee recommends taking all the facts into consideration, a reduced enrolment at under-graduate level.

It is further suggested that at the under-graduate level only those specialities may be included which are usually not taught in other institutions and for which the Institute possesses high expertise. The Committee suggests inclusion of the courses on topics like Transportation Technology, Coastal Engineering, Ship Building, which are relevant to this part of the country.

Research Programmes

While choosing the problems for research and project work, priority should be given to those topics which could be identified as problems of national importance and which can be tackled more effectively at the Institute than at other places by utilising the existing facilities both in respect of the academic personnel and equipment.

It should be the aim of the Institute to take up only those problems which will give material benefit to the society and which will fully utilise the resources that exist or that will be created in future at the Institute. The problem was discussed at length with the teaching and research faculty of the Institute and they were of the definite opinion that the Institute is capable of tackling a number of problems of inter-disciplinary nature of national importance.

With the restriction on diversification of research projects, it will be possible for the Institute with the existing resources, to explore the important areas of knowledge intensively and to develop expertise in the areas of research which are of national importance. It is only by such a concentrated effort that the Institute can make effective and significant contribution to knowledge.

M. Tech. Project Work

Even at the M. Tech. level it will be advisable to choose live problems from industry for project work. Generally, each such problem will be a complex one and it will be necessary to break it into smaller bits, each bit relating to some specific discipline. These bits may form the subject matter for the project reports for the students in the disciplines. The main advantage of choosing such problems is that the students will be introduced to the complexity of the problems which they have to face in their future career. Moreover, the successful completion of the problems will go a long way to create confidence in them for tackling real problems of industry. The synthesis of these various investigations by experts may, in general, provide a satisfactory solution to an important problem raised by the Industry.

The following are some of such suggestive problems of immediate interest which could be tackled at various levels at the Institute :

1. Low cost housing both for urban and rural areas.
2. Treatment of brackish water for purposes of drinking and other uses by the community.
3. Design and construction of silos for proper storage of grain and other food material.

Inter-Disciplinary Projects

The Institute with its strong faculty and excellent equipment in various disciplines is a suitable place for undertaking inter-disciplinary projects of national importance.

The Faculty and the Director are very anxious to make a good beginning in this direction. They have suggested the following :

(a) Desalination,

(b) Air and Water Pollution, and

(c) Bio-Medical Engineering.

The Committee is of the view that a small beginning may be made in each of the above areas and progress watched to test the capability and urge to take up these projects. In course of time they may be developed into their fullness.

The first two projects are important on account of geographical situation of the Institute. As far as the Bio-Medical project is concerned a small start has already been made with the assistance of the Medical Faculty of the University of Madras. The Committee surmises that these inter-disciplinary projects will create new channels of investigation. Moreover, initiation of such inter-disciplinary projects will bring the faculties in different departments together in a collaborative effort to solve problems which defy solution by an individual department.

Liaison with Industry

As suggested earlier, the Institute should take up live problems of Industry. For isolating and recognising these problems, it is essential that the Institute and its faculty establishes an effective liaison with the Industry. Such a liaision is also essential to give realistic form to engineering education in this Institute. This liaison with industry can be achieved in the following ways :

(i) the students and the faculty of the Institute visit the industries and have detailed discussions about their requirements, and

(ii) the industry itself contacts the experts at the Institute for helping them in developing their processes or solving their problems.

A beginning has already been made in this direction by the Institute, but it needs further strengthening. The Committee recommends that special facilities may be afforded for this purpose. To acquaint the students with the live problems of the industry and to create in them the spirit of research, some of the outstanding students with the post-graduate and research level may be associated with the projects undertaken by the faculty on behalf of the industry formally by giving them appropriate remuneration. The Industry might not be unwilling to support such association of the students.

Establishment of Engineering Experimental Centre

(I) Necessity of Engineering Experimental Centre : The present growth of industry in the country will be maintained and further upgraded only if their developmental problems are tackled expeditiously. This sets an important task for technological institutes. These institutes should be willing to take up the challenge of tackling the problems relating to development of new products and new processes and of designing sophisticated machinery and equipment required for the purpose. At present there are very few places, where such assistance can be sought for by the industry. The Committee feels that the Indian Institute of

Technology, Madras, can effectively take up this challenge with its trained personnel in diversified engineering disciplines and excellent laboratory facilities. However, with the preoccupation of the faculty in instructional and research work of the department, it will not be able to divert work of the department, it will not be able to divert any attention and resource for this purpose. The Committee, therefore, recommends establishment of an Engineering Experimentation Centre, where developmental projects emanating from the industry could be tackled on both short-term and long-term basis. The creation of such an experimental centre will prove to be extremely useful for the growth of the industries for it will be possible to develop indigenous know-how which will make the country soon self-reliant.

(ii) Structure of Engineering Experimental Centre : The proposed Engineering Experimental Centre should have broadly two divisions—one dealing with process development and another dealing with design development. It is recommended that, for effective functioning of the Centre, in addition to the existing faculty, it will also be necessary to attract specialised personnel from industry or other institutions in the country or deputed to work at the Centre for short periods if the available resources of the Centre are not adequate to deal with some specific problems. While recruiting the staff for the Centre, it will be necessary to lay special emphasis on industrial experience.

(iii) Functioning of the Centre : It should be the responsibility of this Centre to work out in detail the schemes that may be taken up and indicate the financial requirements and the expected time for completion of the projects.

It is envisaged that the expenditure incurred by the Centre in any specific project will come from the agency which sponsors it. It is expected that if this practice is followed, then, in course of time, this Centre will become self-supporting, provided the revenue earned by the Centre is credited to the fund created for its functioning and not to the general funds of the Institute. This is necessary to encourage research and development activities of the Centre without having to make incoordinate grants for its activities. However, to begin with, it is recommended that some sizable grant is made available for establishing the Centre.

Courses of Study and Instruction

(i) Special type of courses : It is necessary that the Institute does not confine itself to conventional courses. With the expertise available at the Institute, it should be possible to offer some courses in specialised areas and in depth. The choice of these courses should be geared to the ultimate goal of the students to make significant contribution to the national effort for development. Such courses may be thrown open to all students irrespective of their department for promoting inter-disciplinary activity which is essential for solution of many complex technological problems of to-day. Some of these courses may also be made compulsory for students going for Ph. D. programmes.

(ii) Courses for self-employment : Our national priorities envisage the setting up of small scale industries and it is essential that some among the alumni of this Institute should be enabled to look to this field for their future career. The content of the courses at the Institute should, therefore, be so oriented as to cater to this need. Moreover, it will be necessary for the Institute to offer Industrial and Management Courses to an adequate extent for creating this ability among such alumni. Agencies like the Small Industies Service Institute, National Productivity Council and All India Management Association may perhaps be consulted in framing of these courses.

It must be regarded as an important duty of the faculty in each department to recognise the students, who have intentions of starting small industrial units and who have aptitude and ability for this and to encourage them. Institution of awards on successful completion of projects of this nature will go a long way to encourage them.

(iii) Development of teaching material : It will be necessary for the departments to develop teaching material for such non-conventional courses in the form of monographs. After running these courses for a couple of years and modifying them in the light of the experience thus gained, this material may be brought out as publications in the book form by the Institute itself.

Since the commercial publishing houses will not be interested in undertaking the publication of these advanced monographs and books, it is recommended that an adequate provision is made for establishing a publication unit. This unit may undertake publication of such textbooks which the staff of the Institute may be able to write. Such publication will be useful not only to the students of the Institute but also to the students of other Universities and institutions.

With this facility, the Institute will be able to take up publication of some of the outstanding project reports and Ph.D. theses, which may be judged to be of wider interest.

(iv) Printing Press : For printing of technical

journals, monographs and teaching material, the Institute is at present depending on outside agencies. High level technical printing is an expensive job as the commercial printers charge exhorbitantly for printing technical matter. It is, therefore, necessary that the Institute owns a modern printing press with facilities for block making.

It is further suggested that the Institute procures a Zerox machine for multiple duplication of research material to be made available to workers at the Institute. This is necessary to keep the research journals in the library for consultation.

Central Instrumentation and Servicing Facility

(i) Housing of costly instruments : Some of the modern techniques of analysis require sophisticated and costly equipments and generally such instruments are required by more than one department for their own research activity. Due to heavy cost and maintenance charges, it would not be possible for the Institute to multiply such facilities in various departments. It is, therefore, suggested that such equipment may be treated as a Central facility, looked after by properly trained maintenance staff and its use may be made available to scientific workers of the Institute as and when requested. The Committee recommends a creation of a Central Instrumentation and Servicing Laboratory for housing such equipment.

(ii) Computer : The Reviewing Committee was told that the Institute is shortly to acquire a good size Computer, which will be of use not only to the Institute but will also cater to the needs of the industry and other educational institutions in the region. It is suggested that this Computer should also be housed in this Central Instrumentation and Servicing Laboratory and not attached to any particular department. However, it will be necessary to have a Committee consisting of experts, among others, from the departments, such as Mathematics, Electrical Engineering, Electronics Engineering and Physics, which will assist the Director in the running of the Computer Centre.

(iii) Programming courses : For the fuller and intelligent use of the Computer, it is necessary that the faculty and the students in the Institute learn how to programme their problems and how to operate the instrument. For this, it is suggested that the Department of Mathematics organise regularly every term a course on 'Programming and Numerical Methods'. For checking the programmes prepared by an individual user, it will be desirable to have a few well-trained programmers attached to the Computer arrives. It is also suggested that as soon as the make of the Computer is decided for the Institute, the corresponding punching machines might be purchased in advance, so that the programmes may be punched on them locally and these punched cards be sent to the Computer Centre where the programme has to be run. This will reduce considerably the cost of computation.

Students

The students at the technological institutes are selected on an All-India basis and generally they belong to the group of well-qualified and well-motivated students. It is necessary to sustain this motivation by providing adequate facilities for the all round development of their personality and character by providing the academical leadership by the staff. In the absence of such an intimate contact with the faculty, the feeling of frustration and disillusionment is bound to grow in them.

(i) Association of the senior staff with undergraduate classes : In discussions with the students' representatives, it was brought out that generally the under-graduate classes are handled by the junior staff members and the students, in their earlier classes, do not get the benefit of instruction by the senior members in sufficient measure. The Committee is of a firm opinion that it is necessary for the senior members of the faculty of participate in undergraduate teaching, as it is necessary to provide adequate inspiration to the young students for acquiring scholarship and to provide correct orientation and philosophy of the course content.

(ii) Assessment of students' performance : The fulfilment of any educational system in developing the thinking processes and in preparing the young people for life rather than in scoring high scores at the examinations. The assessment system must take care of this fact.

(iii) Students' activities : The Institute, with the selection of students on all-India basis, provides a fertile situation for developing a sense of national integration. What is necessary is to generate cultural and extra-curricular activities, in which the students from various parts of the country present programmes based on their cultural patterns for the information of the others. This is necessary to create an attitude of understanding of other man's culture and to learn to live together in harmony. Another worthwhile item in these programmes is the visits to various parts of the country under the guidance of the faculty on subsidised and concessional basis. There is some provision for students' activities both co-curricular and extra-curricular on the campus. In the opinion of the Committee, this facility requires considerable augmentation. The Committee, therefore, recommends that an adequate provision be made for a good modern functional gymkhana building for indoor games, dramas, debates, hobby workshop and the like.

(iv) Students' guidance and counselling : It is necessary for an Institute of this type to have a complete record of the products of the Institute, not merely for the purpose of feed-back but also to keep track of the alumni for the better employment by various agencies in a co-ordinated manner. For this purpose, the Committee suggests a Department of Placement for Training and Employment, headed by a person competent for the task with sufficient industrial contacts. In the initial stages, the department will also provide counselling to individual students in selecting their courses according to their ability, attainment and aptitude. It will also make known to the students, the opportunities which are available in the country for their employment. It is well recognised that the training of a student is not complete by the formal instruction alone, and to develop a wholesome personality, he must be made fully aware of the professional ettiquette and develop a sense of responsibility and integrity. With this point in view, the Committee recommends the opening of various Students' Chapters at the Institute to provide opportunities to the students to associate themselves with people who have attained eminence in their discipline and get acquainted with their problems and aspirations.

Staff

As the Institute is growing in age, more and more of the middle level staff would have reached the maximum of their grades. To provide some motivation and incentive for their growth, it is necessary to provide some incentive to them. The Committee feels that instead of making a rigid allocation of the staff in various cadres in each department, the numbers in various cadres may be kept floating, so that a person of outstanding ability may be promoted from one cadre to the higher cadre after appropriate evaluation of the merit of such a person by the Director.

For the high quality specialised work that the Institute is supposed to do, it is necessary that a constant effort is made to attract highly qualified staff and to devise ways and means to retain them. The Committee recommends the institution of some suitable incentive scheme.

Sometimes, when highly qualified person is available, the Institute finds it helpless in appointing him on account of the non-availability of the vacancy. In such cases, the person may be given some suitable position against any vacancy if the Institute is convinced that his services are very essential for the good work of the Institute, he may be absorbed in the permanent cadre.

When some posts in the departments fall vacant, before advertising them, the job requirements of these posts should be subjected to review and as far as possible these should be filled with people of inter-disciplinary qualifications, so as to ensure dynamic growth of the Institute in the coming years. This provision will enable the Director of the Institute to bring in new talent in the fields of specialisation which deserve development and growth.

In fact, all the above suggestions can be achieved if a certain change in the concept of the department is brought about. The appointments may be made against specialities and a person may belong to more than one department for the purposes of teaching.

Laboratory System

The system of laboratories prevalent at the Institute is good and it has served the Institute very well indeed. However, the Committee feels that each laboratory be governed by a Committee, whose members are drawn from those departments who use it and for the maintenance and development of this laboratory, a separate cadre of technical staff is made available. For example, there may be an engineer in-charge of the laboratory supported by senior and junior technical officers. The job of this maintenance and development staff will be solely to keep the laboratory in a trim condition and to develop and fabricate the instruments which are needed from time to time both for instruction and research by the scientific worker at the Institute. If this suggestion is implemented, academic staff in engineering disciplines will be freed from the burden of servicing and maintenance of the laboratories and will be able to attend to the needs of developmental work in the laboratory.

Indo-German Agreement

It is necessary that even after the present Indo-German Agreement comes to an end, sufficient assistance both by way of hardware and technical personnel will be required to continue the work of the Institute already started. Similarly, provision has to be made for the supply of spare parts for the specialised equipment already supplied by the Federal Republic of Germany. Possibilities of further sisterhood programmes in counter part German Universities should also be explored.

However, it is felt that for the maintenance and servicing of the sophisticated equipment supplied by the Federal Republic of Germany, technical personnel may be trained at the Institute. This will ensure proper functioning of the equipment on a continuing basis even when the German technical staff is withdrawn. It is also suggested that the scientific personnel thus trained may form a separate cadre from the academic staff, so that the maintenance and servicing of this equipment and the development of instruments becomes their primary duty.

I. Aeronautical Engineering Department

The Aeronautical Engineering Department is the youngest department of the Indian Institute of Technology, even though started in the year 1965 as part of Applied Mechanics Department, it was given independent status in the year 1969. The first batch of 12 B.Tech. students in Aeronautical Engineering graduated in the year 1968. M.Tech. programme with 12 students as well as M.S. programme and Ph.D. programmes were started in the year 1968. This department has not received any aid from the German Aid Programme and as such the Institute had formulated programmes of the department and procured equipment from indigenous sources. The following 4 laboratories have been developed in the department :

1. Aerodynamics Laboratory.
2. Aircraft Design and Systems Laboratory.
3. Propulsion Laboratory, and
4. Structural Mechanics Laboratory.

The Department has good contacts with National Aeronautical Laboratory, Hindusthan Aeronautics Limited, Bangalore and Space Science Technology Centre at Thumba.

The output of the Department since 1964 is : 44 candidates for B.Tech., 10 for M.Tech. The department has contributed 13 departmental reports and a few research papers in technical journals. The proposals for development of the department are detailed below :

1. Completion of Aircraft Structures Laboratory.
2. Building up of a Composite Structures Laboratory.
3. Development of a Jet-Propulsion-cum-Supersonic Aerodynamics Laboratory.
4. Setting up of a small Hypersonic test facility which may be the first of its kind in India.
5. Setting up of a Research-team in the area of Shell Structures.
6. Preparation of an Air-Craft Design Manual and an Aircraft Structures Laboratory Manual.

The proposals also include :

Non-Recurring

	Existing	*Addl. required*
Building	29,250 sq. ft.	6,600 sq. ft.
Equipment	Rs. 1.1 lakh	Rs. 25.00 lakhs

Recurring

Maintenance	Rs. 0.41 lakh	Rs. 0.35 lakh
Staff	Rs. 2.13 lakhs	Rs. 3.43 lakhs

Staff

Professors	3	5
Asst. Professors	4	6
Lecturers	5	—
Others	24	22

Review and Recommendations

In the context of very rapid development in the field of missiles and space science it is necessary that the department develops its facilities in the following research areas :

(i) Hypersonics,
(ii) Propulsion and
(iii) Aircraft Structures.

The Committee also suggests that in this connection duplication of efforts that are carried out at the Indian Institute of Science, Bangalore, National Aeronautical Laboratory and in the Research Laboratory of Hindusthan Aeronautics Limited, Bangalore, should be avoided in the departmental programmes. It is, however, necessary that the study in Fluid Mechanics with facilities of Wind Tunnels should be intensified with collaboration with Department of Applied Mechanics to train proper personnel at an advanced level in the field of Aeronautics. Care must be taken that unnecessary heavy expenditure is avoided in developing these facilities. In the light of these observations and taking into account the future development of the Institute in this department, the Reviewing Committee recommends the following facilities :

Non-Recurring

Equipment Rs. 25.00 lakhs

Recurring : (Additional) :

Staff

Professors	2
Asst. Professors	6

Supporting Staff — As required, to the extent of 40 per cent of the expenditure on the above academic staff.

Working Expenses ... Rs. 0.90 lakh p.a.

II. Applied Mechanics Department

The Department of Applied Mechanics was started in the year 1961. The Applied Mechanics Department has well equipped laboratories in :

(i) Elasticity.
(ii) Fluid Mechanics.
(iii) Machine Dynamics.

In the year 1963 Aeronautics was added as an additional section but was separated in the year 1969, when it was given a status of full-fledged department. The department offers certain courses both at undergraduate and post-graduate levels which are of inter-disciplinary nature and in addition conducts M.Tech. programmes in Engineering Mechanics with specialisation in Structural Mechanics, which was started in the year 1967. Most of the equipment in Fluid Mechanics and Machine Dynamics were obtained from German aid and almost all the items in the Elasticity Laboratory have been acquired from indigenous sources. The Elasticity Laboratory has necessary conventional facilities for testing including the specialised items such as (i) Net Work Analyser, (ii) a Membrane Analogy apparatus, (iii) Photoelastic equipment etc. The Fluid Mechanics Laboratory is well equipped with close circuits and open circuit wind tunnels. Machine Dynamics Laboratory has specialised equipment for studies of Vibration and Mechanisms and Tribology.

The out-put of candidates from this department since 1961 is indicated below :

Ph. D.	M. Tech.	B. Tech.	No. of Publications
—	14	—	92

At present 6 candidates are working for their Ph. D. degree in the department and 10 for M. Tech.

The department proposes to set up five major laboratories as follows :

(i) Analogue Laboratory.
(ii) Bio-Mechanics Laboratory.
(iii) Structural Dynamics Laboratory.
(iv) Fracture Mechanics Laboratory.
(v) Statics and Dynamics Model Room.

For the proposed future programmes the department has requested the following facilities :

Non-Recurring

	Existing	*Addl. required*
Buildings	30,000 sq. ft.	33,000 sq. ft.
Equipment	Rs. 25.89 lakhs	Rs. 10.00 lakhs

Recurring

Staff

Professors	3	6
Asst. Professors	4	6
Lecturers	10	6
Other academic and technical staff	41	39

The department has assisted many industries and other agencies in carrying out projects of industrial importance.

The department proposes to develop a specialised laboratory for Elasticity and organise refresher courses in (i) Vibration Studies, (ii) Elasticity, and (iii) Wind Tunnel Techniques.

Review and Recommendations

The Committee has carefully considered the present contribution and the development proposals of the department of Applied Mechanics and had had discussions with the Professors and staff of the Institute in connection with the future activity of the department. The Committee observed that most of the work done in this department is of inter-disciplinary nature. For example, even though this department has a Fluid Mechanics Laboratory comprising of close circuit and open circuit Wind Tunnels, this subject is of great importance to Aeronautics in particular, and departments of Mechanical Engineering, Chemical Engineering etc., in general. The subjects of specialised studies in the department in the field of Elasticity and Machine Dynamics are of equal importance to the Department of Mechanical Engineering for regulating proper growth of research activity in the fields of Fluid Mechanics, Elasticity and Machine Dynamics. It is, therefore, imperative that these laboratories do not isolate themselves from inter-departmental activity, but work with inter-departmental cooperation. The present proposals from the Applied Mechanics Department to start a laboratory of Elasticity are considered essential in the light of the work done in the department. The Committee recommends additional grants for the laboratories as follows :

Non-Recurring

Buildings	Rs. 6.00 lakhs.
Equipment	Rs. 8.00 lakhs.

Recurring (Additional) :

Since at present there are 3 main laboratories and there is already a sanction of 3 Professors in the department for augmenting the activity in the shape of a new laboratory proposed, the Committee recommends additional staff of

Professor	—	2
Asst. Professors	—	6
Lecturers	—	6
Academic and non-academic other staff		To the extent of 40 per cent of the recurring expenditure on addl. staff recommended
Working Expenses	—	Rs. 0.15 lakh p.a.

III. Chemistry Department

The Department of Chemistry was established in June 1961. The department offers the following courses :

1. First and Second year students of all branches of engineering : Lecture and laboratory courses in fundamental aspects of physical chemistry, inorganic chemistry and organic chemistry.

2. Integrated course in physical chemistry, instrumental methods of analysis and inorganic chemistry with laboratory practicals (3rd year B. Tech. students).

3. Post-graduate course in Chemistry leading to the degree of Master of Science. The department also has facilities for post-graduate research work.

Research laboratories have developed the following areas of specialisation listed below :

1. Physical Chemistry — Catalysis, Reaction Kinetics, Thermo-dynamics.
2. Theoretical Chemistry — Molecular Structures, Statistical Mechanics.
3. Inorganic Chemistry — Coordination Chemistry, Bio-inorganic Chemistry, Solid State Inorganic Chemistry.
4. Organic Chemistry — Physical aspects, Reaction Mechanisms.
5. Nuclear Chemistry — Tracer Techniques, Radio-isotope methodology technical applications.

Special Instruments Laboratory is being set up to house the sophisticated equipment like I.R., U.V., NMR., EPR and Mass Spectro-meter, X-Ray Diffraction Unit etc. These facilities will strengthen research activity in the existing fields like Photochemistry, Polymer Chemistry, Electro-Chemistry and Bio-Inorganic Chemistry. The department, under the German aid, is also setting up a modern High Pressure Laboratory and a Nuclear Chemistry Laboratory.

The research programmes of the department had received support with a grant of US $ 17,000 from the Petroleum Research Fund from U.S.A.

Since 1959 upto the year 1970 the department has trained 51 candidates for M.Sc. and 13 for Ph.D. Programmes. At present 30 candidates (24 full-time and 6 part-time) are working for the Ph.D. degree of the Institute. In addition there is also one Post-doctoral fellow working in the department. The department has to its credit 73 research publications from 1959 to 1970.

The department proposes to introduce 1-year post-diploma course in M.Sc. in the following areas :

1. Industrial Catalysis.
2. Industrial Analytical Chemistry.
3. Technical Inorganic Chemistry.
4. Radio Isotope methodology, and
5. Bio-Inorganic Chemistry.

The department wishes to have also the facilities in setting up the following laboratories :

1. Analytical Service Centre.
2. Catalyst Research Laboratory.
3. High Pressure Laboratory.
4. Special Instruments Laboratory, and
5. Nuclear Service Centre.

To meet these objectives the following facilities have been requested :

Non-Recurring

	Existing	*Addl. required*
Buildings	85,000 sq. ft.	NIL
Equipment	Rs. 14.44 lakhs	Rs. 10.00 lakhs

Recurring

Staff

Professors and Associate Professors	3	3
Asst. Professors	5	7
Lecturers	11	3
Non-Academic staff	41	36
Staff salary	Rs. 3.71 lakhs	Rs. 3.59 lakhs
Working Expenses	Rs. 0.91 lakh	Rs. 0.30 lakh p.a.

Review and Recommendations

Taking into account the interest and the specialisations of the present members of staff and also the facilities available, the Reviewing Committee is of the opinion that the courses in Radio Isotope methodology and Bio-Inorganic Chemistry need not be started. However, since a Laboratory for Nuclear Chemistry is being set up under the German aid, it would be desirable for the department to have research projects in Nuclear Chemistry as part of Doctoral or Post-doctoral programmes. It is also felt that the proposed diploma course in Technical Inorganic Chemistry is also not desirable inasmuch as such an activity is a part of the activities of the department of Chemical Engineering which is better equipped for instruction and research facilities in connection with manufacture and production of inorganic chemicals.

The Committee is of the opinion that development of Analytical Laboratory and Analytical Service Centre may be taken up as it will be possible to train personnel who would be useful to the industry which now has many sophisticated analytical apparatus for control of industrial processes. It is, however, felt that this laboratory should not duplicate instruments and apparatus which are already available in the Institute as a whole.

What is required is re-grouping of some of the sophisticated equipments and this could act as a Cell where sophisticated analysis can be done around the clock for the benefit of research projects in the entire Institute. This Cell should be provided with proper maintenance and operative staff. The Reviewing Committee is in favour of starting a post-M.Sc. diploma course in Industrial Analytical Chemistry.

The Committee observes that the department's research programme so far has been in the field of Industrial Catalysis and the department's contribution in Heterogeneous Catalysis are regarded as quite significant for use in Chemical industry. The department had also undertaken a scheme of comprehensive study of Transition Metal oxides as a part of Catalysis development activity with the support of PL-480 scheme made available to the department. In the opinion of the Committee the field of Industrial Catalysis is regarded as important because of the possibilities of its application in developing country like India. The Committee is, therefore, of the view that the research effort of the department should continue in this specialised area Concentrated effort should be made to study Reaction Mechanisms and the effect of Catalyst structure on the Mechanism of reactions. The research on Catalysis in the department should include structural aspects of the inorganic solids that are used as catalysis and of the transfomations in such solids in various environmental conditions. As an adjunct to this activity the Committee is also of the view that it is necessary for the department to have a well equipped laboratory for high pressure and high temperature reactions. The department should also have suitable facilities for the use of Radio Isotope techniques which are of use in the study of reaction kinetics. In the light of these observations, the Committee favours offering of Post-M.Sc. diploma course in field of "Industrial Catalysis".

To achieve the above developments the Committee recommends the following facilities :

Non-Recurring

Equipment	Rs. 4.00 lakhs

Recurring (Additional)

Staff

Professors	2 (One each for Analytical Catalysis and Analytical Chemistry)
Asst. Professors	5
Lecturers	4
Technical and non-technical (academic staff).	To the extent of 40 per cent of the expenditure on additional staff recommended.
Working Expenses	Rs. 0.59 lakh p.a.

IV. Chemical Engineering Department

The Department of Chemical Engineering statrted functioning in June 1959. Excellent facilities are available for undergraduate and post-graduate programmes with special emphasis on :-

(i) Transfer and Mechanical Operations;
(ii) Chemical Reaction Engineering;
(iii) Process Dynamics and Control; and
(iv) High Polymer Engineering.

and for conduction research in :-

(i) Fluid Particle Systems;
(ii) Particle Technology;
(iii) Heat and Mass Transfer;
(iv) Applied Thermo Dynamics;
(v) Reaction Process Dynamics; and
(vi) Control in certain areas of Chemical Engineering/Technology.

The various instructional programmes lead to

B.Tech., M.Tech., and Ph.D. degrees and a diploma in Chemical Engineering Practice. The following table gives the number of students trained by the department from its inception in 1959 to 1970 :

B.Tech.	M.Tech.	D.I.I.T.	No. of publications
280	69	15	135

The department has conducted seminars or symposia in the following fields during the period under review :

(1) Utilisation of Chlorine;

(2) Development in Chemical Engineering;

(3) Development and Design of Chemical Process Equipment;

(4) Particle Technology.

During the next few years the department proposes to develop the following divisions of specialised studies :

(i) Particle Technology;

(ii) Transfer Operations;

(iii) Chemical Reaction Engineering;

(iv) Process Dynamics and Control;

(v) Chemical Engineering Plant Design and Management;

(vi) High Polymer Engineering;

and desires to establish a Practical School in Chemical Engineering.

To achieve these objectives, the department has requested for the following facilities :-

Non-Recurring

	Existing	*Addl. required*
Building	50,000 sq. ft.	30,000 sq. ft.
Equipment	Rs. 35.63 lakhs	Rs. 45.00 lakhs

Recurring

Staff

Professors	2	4
Asst. Professors	7	5
Associate Lecturers	16	4
Others	49	22
Working Expenses	Rs. 0.73 lakh	Rs. 1.12 lakh
Library (Additional grant for books)		Rs. 0.50 lakh p.a.

Review and Recommendations

(a) Teaching Programmes : (i) The department has good facilities for work in Particle Technology and it is to the credit of the department that excellent contributions have been made in this specialised field. It is recommended that this activity of the department be consolidated and suitably augmented for developing excellence in this area at the post-graduate and research level. It is also suggested that further work in this field be not confined only to the behaviour of solid particles but gradually extended to Particulate Technology.

(ii) The division of Transfer Operations has competent staff. For the fuller utilisation of the expertise of the academic staff, it is recommended that a further stimulus be given to this area to ensure greater contribution from the department. In the opinion of the Reviewing Committee, there is considerable potentiality for good work in this area.

(iii) Most of the Chemical Engineering industries require the knowledge of Reaction Kinetics on the process know-how. In the light of this statement, a two-year M.Tech. programme with elective in Chemical Reaction Engineering is recommended. The institution of such a programme will help in the growth of Indian Chemical Industry.

(iv) The work in the field of Process Dynamics and Control is very important in controlling Reaction Processes in Chemical Engineering industry. It is suggested that the department should organise full-fledged under-graduate and post-graduate laboratories for instruction as well as for research programmes.

Chemical plant design and management : (v) The organisation of programmes of designing of Chemical Engineering Plants, their erection and commissioning is quite complex. It is desirable for the department not to diffuse its energy in this particular field. However, it is recommended that certain courses be developed at the undergraduate as well as at the post-graduate level, in which the topic of Chemical Plant Design can be included. Further consultations about the design of specified epuipment for Chemical industry, in the opinion of the Committee, would better be done by the properly trained personnel in the Engineering Experimentation Centre, that is being recommended. It is also recommended that some specialised staff capable of offering courses in Chemical Plant Design be recruited to strengthen the departmental activity in this area.

(vi) The department has commissioned some good equipment in the field of High Polymer Engineering and the first batch of four M.Tech. students with training in this area has recently come out. It is suggested that the activity of this department should not be confined only to processing of Plastics, but should be extended to a larger area of High Ploymer Science.

Practice School in Chemical Engineering : (vii) The basic idea for collaboration with industry to run such a Practice School meets the general approval of the Reviewing Committee. However, for this School to be effective, many complex problems, like the collaboration with industry on a continuing basis, stationing of Institute's personnel in various industries and giving them plant training, have to be first tackled. These observations should be carefully checked and scrutinised before starting the proposed School and then the performance of this School be evaluated on continuing basis.

(b) Research Programmes : As many technological problems today connected with the development of new products and processes are regarded as quite complex requiring knowledge and expertise of many scientific and technological disciplines, it is imperative that some measure of research in the department should be re-oriented, so as to lay emphasis on such inter-disciplinary research projects. It was gratifying to note that some of the personnel in the department are already engaged in such inter-disciplinary projects. The Committee observes that the department of Chemical Engineering has the potentiality of participating in such inter-disciplinary projects as (i) Bio-Medical Engineering, (ii) Air and Water Pollution, and (iii) Saline Water conversion. It is expected that the research work of the above type will be taken up in greater depth by the department.

To enable to implement these recommendations the following additional assistance is suggested :

Non-Recurring

Buildings	Rs. 6.00 lakhs
Equipment	Rs. 15.00 lakhs

Recurring (Additional)

Staff

Professors	4
Asst. Professors	5
Supporting Staff	To the extent of 40 per cent of the Recurring Expenditure on additional staff recommended.
Working Expenses	Rs. 1.46 lakhs p.a.

V. Civil Engineering Department

The department of Civil Engineering started functioning during the year 1959. The activity of the department is built mainly around the following laboratories :

1. Geology Laboratory,
2. Survey Laboratory,
3. Highways Labortory,
4. Public Health Engineering Laboratory,
5. Soil Mechanics Laboratory,
6. Hydraulics Laboratory,
7. Structures Laboratory,
8. Materials Laboratory, and
9. Building Science Laboratory.

Of these, the first 4 laboratories are equipped for under-graduate teaching and the rest 5 laboratories are planned to be developed for under-graduate and post-graduate study and research. This is one of the departments where German aid is obtained on relatively much smaller scale and most of the conventional equipment have been obtained from indigenous sources. As per the Second Indo-German agreement the Structures and Hydraulics laboratories alone were in receipt of German equipment and staff for training facilities. The out-turn of the students since 1959 has been as follows :

B.Tech.	M.Tech.	M.Sc.	Ph.D.	No. of Publications
235	81	—	5	115

The present student strength of post-graduate courses is as follows :

M.Tech.	17
M.S.	1
Ph.D.	
Full-time	9
Part-time	18

The depeartment has done excellent work in the field of Civil Engineering and more than 30 organisations including Engineering Construction Corporation and Atomic Power Project have been assisted. The department conducted in the year 1966 a short-term course on the Design of Multistoreyed Buildings in collaboration with National Buildings Organisation and conducted seminars on "Problem of prestressing" and "Foundation Problems in and around Madras" in collaboration with other institutions and organisations.

The department has close collaboration with agencies like Highways Research Station, Madras Public Works Depratment the C.P.W.D. and Army Engineers.

The following are the facilities existing in the department :

Non-Recurring

Buildings	1,11,000 sq. ft.
Equipment	Rs. 44.41 lakhs

Recurring

Staff

Professors	3
Asst. Professors	5
Lecturers	20
Others	65
Staff Salaries	Rs. 5.52 lakhs
Working Expenses	Rs. 0.84 lakh

A laboratory for Building Science is in the planning stage. The development plans comprises the following:

(i) Organising a One-year post-graduate diploma course in "Building Technology".

(ii) Conducting short-term intesive courses for the benefit of University teachers and practising engineers in Shell Construction, Prestressed Concrete Construction etc.

(iii) To institute a programme of study for improvement in the methods of teaching and research techniques.

(iv) To augment the industrial liaison activity in areas of Soil Mechanics, Structures and Building Technology.

(v) To institute one-year post-diploma course in Ship Model Technique.

To achieve the objectives stated above the following facilities have been requested for by the department:

Non-Recurring (additional)

Building

Building approximately 30,000 sq.ft.	Rs. 3,00,000
Covered shed for curing tank etc.	Rs. 1,00,000
Space for Hydraulic Model Test.	Rs. 1,00,000
Total	Rs. 5,00,000

Equipment

Soil Mechanics Laboratory	Rs. 10.00 lakhs
Building Sciences	Rs. 5.00 lakhs
Materials Laboratory	Rs. 2.00 lakhs
Hydraulics Laboratory	Rs. 1.00 lakh
Indigenous equipment for Structures Laboratory	Rs. 2.00 lakhs
Total	Rs. 20.00 lakhs

Recurring (additional)

Staff

Professors/Associate Professors	6
Assistant Professors	9
Lecturers	6
Other academic staff	6
Non-academic staff	28

Books

Additional books for each section	Rs. 0.50 lakh p.a.
Block grant for each post-graduate courses at Rs. 50,000/- per annum	Rs. 2.00 lakhs p.a.

Review and Recommendations

The Reviewing Committee is of the opinion that the department of Civil Engineering is well equipped in the divisions of Soil Mechanics, Structural Engineering, Hydraulics and Building Technology. The activities of these laboratories are regarded satisfactory. Since it is the aim of the department to improve the teaching and research aids it would be worthwhile to explore the possibility of having collaboration with the Technical Teachers' Training Institute which is located very near the Institute. The department should also explore the possibility of closer liaison not only with engineering industries but also with Structural Engineering Research Centre of C.S.I.R. closer to the Indian Institute of Technology campus. It is also suggested that the department may conduct intensive study and research programme in the fields of Ground Water Engineering, Transportation Engineering, Coastal Engineering as part of a broader programme of Ocean Engineering and Bridge Engineering. The Reviewing Committee suggests introduction of the two post-graduate courses; one in Ocean Engineering and the other in Building Technology. It is desirable that the number of post-graduate students are increased specially for M.Tech. degree level. In order to consolidate the present activities of the department and the proposals of the department to start two diploma courses in Ocean Engineering and Building Technology, the following additional facilities are recommended:

Non-Recurring (Additional)

Buildings

Soil Mechanics Laboratory Covered Shed for curing Tank etc. Space for Hydraulic Model Test.	Rs. 5.00 lakhs

Equipment

Soil Mechanics Building Science Materials Laboratory Hydraulics Structures	Rs. 15.00 lakhs

Recurring (Additional)

Staff

Professors	3
Asst. Professors	6
Technical and non-technical supporting staff	To the extent of 40 per cent of the expenditure on above addl. staff.
Working Expenses (additional)	Rs. 1.28 lakhs p.a.

VI. Electrical Engineering Department

The Department of Electrical Engineering commenced its activities in the year 1959. This is one of the departments of the Institute which has received considerable assistance from German Aid programme. Under the first consignment arrived from Germany, the total equipment so far received is worth of Rs. 12.00 million. In addition to this supplemental equipment worth about Rs. 1.00 million were indigenously purchased. Each major item was necessary for instructional purposes. Under Indo-German collaboration programme so far 5 German Professors have served the department in organising the laboratories and courses of instruction.

The first batch of students in B.Tech. graduated in 1964. Post-graduate course leading to M.Tech. was started in the year 1963. The first batch of M.Tech. took their degrees in 1965. The first batch of Ph.D. degrees awarded was in 1967.

The activities of the department are built around the following major laboratories :

1. Fundamentals and Measurements Section.
2. Machinery and Control Section.
3. Power Engineering Section.
4. Electronics and Communication Section.
5. Common Facilities.

Among the specialised equipment the department has, mention may be made about :

1. Analog Computer and 800 KV high Voltage equipment with operational amplifiers;
2. High Voltage and conventional electrical and electronics equipment needed for undergrauate and post-graduate study.
3. Net work analyser and close circuit television unit for undergraduate and post-graduate programmes.

These laboratories may be regarded as some of the best in the country. The following data gives an idea of the facilities in the department :

Non-Recurring

Buildings	...	96,875 sq. ft.
Equipment	...	Rs. 91.88 lakhs

Recurring

Staff

Professors	...	4
Asst. Professors	...	10
Lecturers	...	22
Others	...	86
Working Expenses	...	Rs. 0.56 lakh p.a.

The out-turn of the department since its inception is as follows :

B. Tech.	M. Tech.	Ph.D.	No. of Publications
409	84	5	113

Research activities in the Fundamentals and Measurements Laboratory include :

1. Studies on Earthing Schemes.
2. Studies on Current Transformers.
3. Energy Meter Testing.
4. Digital Measurements.
5. Electrical and Electronics means of Power and Energy.
6. Electronic Measurements and Instruments.

Electronic Measurements and Instrument Laboratory have reported research contribution in Analog Dividers, Photo electric circuits, Electrnoic measurements etc.

Similarly the net work and systems laboratory have ambitious research programmes. Machinery and Control Engineering Laboratory have taken research programmes connected with electrical machinery and controls. The Department has reported data on Semi Conductors, Electronic circuits and Communication Engineering.

The department has maintained close liaison with outside organisations and industries and has participated in consultaticn work with agencies like Madras

Refineries Project, Orthopaedic and Cardiographic department of General Hospital, Madras etc. The department has organised sequential summer schools in Electric Engineering in cooperation with U.S.A.I.D. and other institutions in India. Under the Indo-German collaboration programme, German Professors have been invited to visit the Institute and give lectures on specialised topics in the field of Electrical Engineering.

The department has rendered assistance to a number of industries through tests on energy meters, instrument transformers and protective relays.

At present the department offers the following programmes of study and research :

(i) 5-year integrated programme for the B. Tech. degree in Electrical Engineering with specialisation in

(a) Power and

(b) Electronics.

(ii) 2-Year M. Tech. programme in Electrical Engineering with specialisation in

(a) Control System.

(b) Electronics.

(c) Power Systems.

(d) Measurements.

(e) Radar Technology and

(f) Electrical Traction and Drives.

In addition to the above, the department has a research programme leading to Master's degree in Electrical Engineering and facilities are available for Ph.D. programmes.

Development proposals are envisaged for :

(a) B. Tech. degree programme in Instrumentation and Control in collaboration with Mechanical Engineering, Chemical Engineering and Aeronautical Engineering.

(b) 2-Year M. Tech. programme in Computer Science.

(c) 2-Year M. Tech. programme in Television Engineering.

It is also proposed to initiate new research programmes in the specialised areas of Computers and Correlators, Dialectrics, Semi Conductors, solid state devices for Micro-wave transmission, digital techniques, Computer aided net work and System design, Computer Technology and Bio-Medical Engineering.

To achieve the objectives of the future development the following grants have been requested :

Non-Recurring

Buildings (to augment the existing area of 11,000 sq. mr.)	3,000 sq. mr.	At a cost of Rs. 6.00 lakhs
Equipment.		Rs. 50.00 lakhs

Recurring

Staff

	Existing	*Addl. required*
Professors	4	4
Asst. Professors	10	18
Lecturers	22	4
Non-Academic staff	75	25
Working expenses-- consumables including sundry equipment	Rs. 1.10 lakh	Rs. 1.5 lakh

Review and Recommendations

The members of the Reviewing Committee were satisfied with the way the various laboratories of the department of Electrical Engineering have been organised and with the research programmes conducted. Since these laboratories are regarded as some of the best in the country, it is suggested that industrial liaison activity and collaboration with Electrical Engineering industry should be continued with greater vigour so that the department may be able to play a very active role at the national level in the fields of Electrical Engineering and Electronics. The Committee supports the B.Tech. degree programme in Instrumentation and Control taking into account the industrial development that is taking place in the country. As far as the M. Tech. degree in Computer Science is concerned the Committee is of the opinion that this should be offered at the Computer Centre which is recommended to be a central facility for the Institute. The Electrical Engineering department should, however, play an active role in running this programme.

The Committee also approves starting of M.Tech. programme in Television Engineering in view of the proposed expansion by the Government for television facility in the country, specially in view of the fact that a television broadcasting centre may soon be established in Madras.

Since the department has very sophisticated equipment for testing and measurements it is anticipated that many industries and industrial units will continue to avail of such facilities from the department. In order that such measurements and testing work should not interfere with the academic programmes it is suggested that a separate Cell be formed to attend to such type of industrial liaison work. This will facilitate better efficiency and quickness which are very essential in the promotion of Industrial liaison.

Taking into account the 4 specialised laboratories existing at present and the proposals for participating in the Computer Science programmes and 2 M. Tech. programmes, the Committee is of the view that the present position of professorial appointment be increased from 4 to 8 and the supporting staff is also deemed to be necessary for the proper development of the laboratories.

Additional Non-Recurring

Buildings	...	Rs. 6.00 lakhs
Equipment	...	Rs. 25.00 lakhs

Additional Recurring

Staff

Professors	...	3
Asst. Professors	...	4
Supporting staff	...	Expenditure upto 40 per cent of the above staff salaries.
Working Expenses	...	Rs. 2.89 lakhs p.a.

VII. Humanities and Social Sciences Department

The department of Humanities and Social Sciences came into being in the year 1959 primarily with the object of offering courses in English and foreign languages in Humanities and Social Sciences, and Management as an integral part of the 5-year B. Tech. programmes of the Institute. The broad break-up of the courses offered by the department as part of the 5-year B. Tech. degree course is as follows:

1. English language.	Ist Year of B. Tech.
2. German language and English literature.	2nd Year of B. Tech.
3. History and Culture.	3rd Year of B. Tech,
4. Principles of Economics.	4th Year of B. Tech.
5. Industrial Economics & Industrial Management.	5th Year of B. Tech.

From the year 1967 the post-graduate diploma (D.I.I.T.) course of one year duration in Industrial Engineering was started and so far 57 students have graduated with this diploma. This diploma course was up-graded as Master's degree course of two years' duration in Industrial Engineering and Management from the year 1969-70. There are at present 14 candidates taking this course and 4 staff members working for the Ph.D. degree of the Institute. The department has four laboratories:

(i) Industrial Engineering Laboratory.
(ii) Social Sciences Laboratory.
(iii) Language Laboratory.
(iv) Computation Room.

Nearly 40 research papers have been published and presented at various conferences. More than 80 project studies were undertaken for Government departments and industrial organisations. The departmental staff have also published a number of books.

The main lines of development proposed by the department are indicated below:

1. Facilities for offering instruction in one or more foreign languages, besides German.

2. Facilities for the translation of papers into English from several foreign languages.

3. Establishment of facilities for research in Industrial Engineering & Management and Social Sciences.

The following facilities have been requested by the department for development:

Non-Recurring

	Existing	*Addl. required*
Buildings	30,380 sq. ft.	38,346 sq. ft.
Equipment	Rs. 1.32 lakh	Rs. 5.00 lakhs

Recurring

Staff

Professors	3	12
Asst. Professors	5	24
Lecturers	7	22
Other Staff	19	22
Staff salary	Rs. 2.13 lakhs	Rs. 9.58 lakhs
Working Expenses.	Rs. 0.05 lakh	Rs. 0.20 lakh

The department proposes to have (20×2) 40 students for M.Tech., and 5 students for Ph.D. programmes.

Review and Recommendations

The Reviewing Committee is of the opinion that facilities for translation of papers from foreign languages should form the activity of the Central Library rather than the department of Humanities and Social Sciences. The departmental staff may, however, assist in giving the required assistance for such facilities. It is also necessary that the department consolidates its activities in connection with M.Tech. programmes in Industrial Engineering and Management.

It is suggested that the department should not dissipate its activities in undertaking courses like Philosophy, Arts etc., which are available elsewhere in many institutions and Universities and the primary objective of the department should be to help in providing the engineering graduates with knowledge in industrial engineering and management.

For proper development of the department it is also necessary that the existing facilities for M. Tech. programmes and facilities for research be augmented.

It might also be indicated that facilities for teaching more foreign languages should be made on a gradual basis taking into account the need for such courses for the Institute's growth and development. The following additional facilities are, therefore, recommended :

Non-Recurring

Equipment	—	Rs. 3.00 lakhs

Recurring

Staff

Professors	—	2
Asst. Professors	—	4
Lecturers	—	3
Supporting staff :		To the extent of 40 per cent of the expenditure on staff salaries recommended above.
Working Expenses		Rs. 0.90 lakh p.a.

The Reviewing Committee suggests that the designation of the department be changed as the "Department of Industrial Engineering and Management." This will aptly emphasise the main functions of the department. A division of instruction may form a part of the department.

A block grant of Rs. 2.00 lakhs for books for this department has been separately recommended in the provision made for the Central Library.

VIII. Mathematics Department

The department of Mathematics was started in 1959, and from its very inception it was charged with the duties of teaching mathematics to the students enrolled in various engineering departments of the Institute and of conducting post-graduate studies and research of its own. The department has effectively collaborated in research with the departments of Civil, Mechanical and Chemical Engineering.

The department undertakes teaching of all B.Tech. students and first two semester students of M.Tech.

The M.Sc. courses run by the department lay emphasis both on pure and applied mathematics. Among the optional courses included in M.Sc. syllabus mention may be made of the subjects like Celestial mechanics, Continuum mechanics and theory of Differential equations.

The research activities of the department embrace the following areas :

1. Continuum Mechanics.
2. Differential Equations.
3. Stochastic Processes including Operations Research and Mathematical Biology.
4. Quantum Mechanics, Fields and Graph Theory.
5. Cosmic Rays.
6. Statistical Physics.

The department has published 146 research papers and trained during the years from 1964 to 1970 the following number of students :

M.Sc.	Ph.D.
46	18

In addition to the research papers, the following two monographs and a text-book have been written by the members of the department :

Monographs : 1. Stochastic theory and Cascade Processes by Sri S.K. Srinivasan (Elsevier Publishing Co., 1969).

2. Introduction to Random Differential Equations and their applications by Sri S.K. Srinivasan (Elsevier Publishing Co., 1970).

Text-Books : 1. Computer Programming with Engineering and Industrial application by Sri N.V. Koteswara Rao in collaboration with Sri S. Ramani and Sri R. Nagarajan (Modern Management Council, Bombay, 1970).

The department has—

(i) conducted a summer institute in Mathematics for teachers of Kendriya Vidyalaya in 1969, and

(ii) organised in 1965 the 9th Congress of the Indian Society of Theoretical and Applied Mechanics at the Institute.

The department publishes a quarterly journal under the title 'Journal of Mathematical and Physical Sciences' with Editorial Board of international character consisting of eminent scientists drawn from a number of countries. The first three volumes have already come out.

Departmental Proposals : (a) With a view to be able to interact with the other disciplines in the Institute, the department during the next ten years propose to develop the following specialised research areas :—

(i) Continuum Mechanics
(ii) Stochastic Processes and their applications including Operations Research and Bio-Engineering
(iii) Differential Equations
(iv) Computer Science

(b) The department has also proposed one-year Post-M.Sc. courses in the above topics with a view to re-orient the students in a particular subject, so as to take him to the research level. Each course will comprise of four subjects in each of the two semesters and a dissertation.

To achieve these objectives, the department has requested for the following additional facilities :

	Existing	Additional requested for
Non-Recurring		
Accommodation	13,000 sq.ft.	11,563 sq.ft.
Equipment	Rs. 0.97 lakhs	Rs. 1.00 lakh
	Existing	Requested
Recurring		
Academic staff :		
Professors	2	4
Assistant Professors	5	9
Lecturers	5	5
Others	15	24
Working Fxpenses	Rs. 2,000/-	Rs. 20,000/-

Review and Recommendations

(a) Teaching Programme : (i) The M.Sc. courses are good, but the intake of the students is rather low. This is perhaps due to the nearness of the Institute to the University of Madras with a number of local colleges offering M.A. and M.Sc. courses in Mathematics and due to the fact that the students are required to be in residence. In view of the above, the Committee suggests, to fully utilise the teaching effort on M.Sc. students, the intake of students should not be less than 15 (say). To attract good students in required numbers, it would perhaps be necessary to offer some stipends to them to meet the hostel expenses.

(ii) As regards starting of the one-year Post-M.Sc. diploma courses, the Committee is of the view that the beginning may be made with Continuum Mechanics and Computer Science. After seeing the popularity and effectiveness of these diploma courses, the other two diploma courses may be started. It is suggested that, for teaching the recommended diploma courses, the resources of the other departments may also be tapped. For example, in the course in Continuum Mechanics, a certain amount of practical work may be included to give the real feel for the subject. This part of the instruction can be best done by the departments of Civil Engineering (incompressible fluids) and Aeronautics (Compressible fluids and Solid Mechanics). Similarly, for giving a good course in Computer Science, the collaboration of Electrical and Electronics Engineering will be utmost necessary and this may be done at the Computer Centre.

(iii) As pointed out in general recommendations, it is suggested for the teaching of mathematics courses, more than any other courses, that the higher cadre staff should take part in the instruction of undergraduate classes. This is necessary to convey the abstract mathematical concepts accurately to the students from the very beginning.

(iv) The inclusion of the subjects like Celestial Mechanics and Orbital Theory in the departmental courses will enable the department to do some collaboration work with Space Centre at Thumba.

(b) Research Programmes : The department has made a good name in the following areas of research :

(i) Fluid Mechanics

(ii) Stochastic Processes and their application

and has trained a good number of Ph.D. students. This activity must be strengthened. The department has just made a beginning in Differential Equations and Bio-Mechanics. These research areas have their own significance. The former subject is an important part of the broader heading of 'Mathematical Methods' and is of great importance for the work of the Institute. The latter subject is in the nature of inter-disciplinary subject and the local medical faculty is willing to co-operate in this effort. The Committee is of the view that these areas of research receive encouragement and support of the Institute.

Summary of Recommendations

Additional accommodation

	Carpet area
(i) Laboratory, Library, Lecture Hall	2,000 sq.ft.
(ii) Sitting place for staff	3,500 sq.ft.
Total	5,500 sq.ft.

This accommodation will be made available to the department by adjustment of the accommodation in the buildings with other departments. No grant is therefore recommended.

Equipment

Rs. 1.40 lakhs for Electronic desk calculators, etc.

Staff

Professors	2
Assistant Professors	5
Lecturers	5
and	

Appropriate supporting Staff	Upto 40 per cent of the expenditure incurred on the above.
Working Expenses	Rs. 20,000/- p.a.

A block grant of Rs. 2.00 lakhs for books for this department has been separately recommended in the provision made for the Central Library.

IX. Mechanical Engineering Department

The department of Mechanical Engineering commenced its activities in July 1959 and has the following laboratories :

1. Machine Elements and Mechanical Handling.
2. Production Engineering, Machine Tools and Metrology.
3. Fine Techniques
4. Heat Transfer and Thermal Power
5. Internal Combustion Engines
6. Thermo-Dynamics and Combustion
7. Turbo-Machines
8. Refrigeration and Air-conditioning

The section of Machine Elements and Mechanical Handling was planned with the association of Prof. O. Lutz of the Technical University, Braunschweig, Prof. Kollmann of University of Karlsruhe and Prof. Vie ling of the Technical University of Hannover.

Planning of the Production Engineering and Machine Tools Laboratories was done with association of Prof. Pahlitzsch and Prof. Spur and the Metrology Laboratory in association with Prof. Weingraber of Technical University, Braunschweig.

Fine Techniques Laboratory was planned with the assistance of Prof. A. Kuhlenkanp of Technical University, Braunschweig.

Heat Transfer and Thermal Power Laboratory was planned with the association of University of Stuttgart. Prof. Heitland of Aachen and Prof. Lutz of Stuttgart were associated with the installation and commissioning of the Plant in the Steam Power Laboratory.

The facilities for Internal Combustion Engines Laboratory were planned in association with Prof. Lohner of Braunschweig University, assisted by Prof. G. Stahl.

The Thermo-dynamics and Combustion Engineering Laboratory was planned by Prof. Heitland of University of Aachen and was commissioned in early part of 1966 and this was formally inaugurated by Prof. Sohmissier, Aachen, in 1967.

The specialised Turbo-Machines Laboratory was planned with the association of Prof. Metermann of the Pfleiderer Institute, University of Braunschweig and the installation and commissioning of the equipment was done in 1963.

The Refrigeration and Air-conditioning Laboratory started functioning in January 1969 and is one of the youngest in the Department of Mechanical Engineering.

The laboratories in the Department of Mechanical Engineering have received considerable assistance from German aid and are well-equipped for under-graduate and post-graduate research work. The department offers at present :

1. 5-year Integrated course leading to B.Tech. degree in Mechanical Engineering.
2. 2-year Post-graduate course leading to M.Tech. degree in Mechanical Engineering with the following option in the areas :
   - (i) Machine Design
   - (ii) Machine Tools
   - (iii) Mechanical Handling
   - (iv) *Tharmal Sciences* :
     - (a) Heat Transfer and Thermal Power,
     - (b) Internal Combustion Engines,
     - (c) Combustion and Propulsion,
     - (d) Turbo-Machines and Hydraulic Machines

and facilities for research leading to M.Sc. and Ph.D. degrees in Mechanical Engineering are available.

The following is the summary of the facilities available in the department now :

Accommodation	1,35,072 sq.ft.
Equipment	Rs. 154.62 lakhs

Staff

Professors	4
Assistant Professors	11
Lecturers	26
Others	132
Working expenses	Rs. 1.32 lakhs

The department has so far trained since 1959, 483 candidates for B.Tech. degree, 86 for M.Tech. degree and 5 candidates for Ph.D. degree.

Many research contributions in various specialised fields have been published. The department has also maintained close liaison with local industries and successfully completed the industrial problems and have tried to keep the laboratories in tune with the latest contributions. Many visiting Scientists have been invited to give specialised lectures in various fields of Mechanical Engineering. The department has also organised seminars and symposia of interest for Mechanical Engineers.

Proposals for development of the department in the next decade are detailed below :

1. Consolidation of B.Tech. and M.Tech. degree programmes.
2. Offering of courses in Instrumentation Techniques, and Environmental Engineering as specialised areas for M.Tech. programmes.
3. To augment research activity in specialised fields.
4. To participate in inter-disciplinary activities.

To achieve the above objectives, the following facilities have been requested :

Non-recurring (Additional)

Buildings	6,000 sq.m.	Rs. 15.24 lakhs

Equipment

1. Equipment and instrumentation for strengthening current research and development activity.	Rs. 40.17 lakhs
2. Equipment for laboratory shop units.	Rs. 8.35 lakhs
3. Equipment and instrumentation for the introduction of the two new M.Tech. streams.	Rs. 10.00 lakhs
4. Equipment for Central Air Supply Unit for the Air-Thermal Turbo-machine laboratory.	Rs. 7.02 lakhs
5. Equipment for Physical machining and numerically controlled machine tools for the Production Engg., Machine Tool and Metrology Laboratories.	Rs. 15.00 lakhs
Total	Rs. 80.00 lakhs
Block grant for additional books, periodicals in the newer areas of development.	Rs. 3.00 lakhs

Recurring

Annual grant to the Department	Rs. 0.30 lakhs

Staff

	Addl. required
Professors	18
Assistant Professors	40
Lecturers	45
Associate Lecturers	20
Senior Techincal Assistants	45
Other supporting staff	237

Review and Recommendations

The laboratories of the Mechanical Engineering department are among the best in the country and have great potentialities for work.

The Committee is of the view that the specialised areas in the department of Mechanical Engineering may be classified for the purpose of recruitment of staff as follows:

1. Machine Elements and Mechanical Handling Laboratory.
2. Production Engineering, Machine Tool and Metrology Laboratory.
3. Fine Techniques Laboratory.
4. Internal Combustion Engines Laboratory.
5. Heat Transfer and Thermal Power Laboratory.
6. Thermo-dynamics and Combustion Engineering Laboratory.
7. Thermo-machines Laboratory (Air and Water).
8. Refrigeration and Air-conditioning Laboratory.

Non-Recurring

Buildings : As 2 new M.Tech. laboratories are to be envisaged and facilities for the additional programmes are required, the Committee recommends 20,000 sq ft. at a cost of Rs. 6.00 lakhs towards buildings.

Equipment : In the opinion of the Reviewing Committee the laboratories are well-equipped. However, for strengthening the research and developmental activities, the Committee recommends additional equipment as follows for the various laboratories :

1. Fine Techniques Laboratory. 2. Heat Transfer and Thermal Power Laboratory. 3. I.C.I. Engines Laboratory. 4. Thermo-Dynamics and Combustion Laboratory. 5. Turbo-Machines Laboratory. 6. Refrigeration and Airconditioning Laboratory, 7. Production Engineering, Machine Tools and Metrology Laboratory Auxiliary facilities like Air equipment, etc.	Rs. 30.00 lakhs
Introduction of two M.Tech. schemes	Rs. 10.00 lakhs
Total	Rs. 40.00 lakhs

Recurring (Additional)

Staff

Professors	...	6 (4 as replacement to the German staff as and when the latter returns to Germany)
Assistant Professors	...	9
Supporting Staff	...	to the extent of 40 per cent of the recurring expenditure involved.
Working expenses (additional)	...	Rs. 2.5 lakhs p.a.

X. Metallurgy Department

The department of Metallurgy came into existence in the year 1959 with the starting of the Institute. However, the first instructional course was offered by the department in 1961-62. The department commenced its work in 1961 when the first member of the staff was appointed. The first batch of under-graduate students came out in 1964. The first batch of post-graduate students was admitted in July 1968. The department offers specialisation in two fields (i) Physical Metallurgy and (ii) Industrial Metallurgy. The first research degree is expected to be awarded during the current year.

The activities of the department are centred around the following main laboratories :

1. Metal Joining.
2. Metal Forming.
3. Metal Casting.
4. Metallography.
5. Metallurgical Analysis.
6. Refractories.
7. Electro-Metallurgy and Corrosion.
8. Mechanical Testing and Strain Measurements.
9. Extrative Metallurgy.
10. Electron Microscopy.
11. X-Ray Diffraction.
12. Non-destructive Testing.
13. Heat Treatment.

The value of the equipment provided for these laboratories upto March 1970 totals about Rs. 34.54 lakhs, of which equipment worth of Rs. 30.9 lakhs have come from German aid. Under German aid, specialised equipments in Metallurgy including Metal Joining, Hot and Cold Working of metals have been provided.

The department offers courses in B.Tech., M.Tech. and has facilities for research work leading to M.S., and Ph.D. degrees. M.Tech. course now offered at present permits specialisation in the field of Physical and Industrial Metallurgy (Metal Joining, Metal Forming and Metal Casting) and places considerable emphasis on modern experimental techniques like X-Ray and Electron Metallography.

A large number of tests regarding the composition, quality and mechanical and physical properties of metallic materials and products and orders have been carried out for industrial establishments, and government organisations. Development work has also been undertaken for replacement of imported material, and for improvement of design of specific interest to industry.

The following is the summary of the facilities available at present :

Accommodation	33,125 sq.ft.
Equipment	Rs. 34.54 lakhs

Staff

Professors	3
Assistant Professors	3
Lecturers	7
Others	48
Working expenses	Rs. 0.77 lakhs p.a.

Until March 1970, the out-turn of the department is as follows :

B.Tech.	M.Tech.	No. of Publications
164	5	60

The proposals for development include starting of 2-year programmes for M.Tech. degree in Metallurgy in the field of :

(i) Ceramic Engineering
(ii) Extraction Metallurgy
(iii) Strengthening and consolidating of existing B.Tech. and M.Tech. courses and also continuing short-term courses in selected topics like :
 (a) Alloy Steel Technology and
 (b) Non-Destructive Testing.

To achieve these objectives, the department has requested the following facilities :

Non-recurring :

Building 6,000 sq.ft. at Rs. 40/- per sq.ft.	Rs. 2.40 lakhs
Equipment (details of equipment not given for assessment)	Rs. 40.00 lakhs

Recurring

Books

Block Grant	Rs. 0.20 lakhs
Books	Rs. 0.75 lakhs p.a.

Staff

	Addl. required
Senior Professors/Professors and Associate Professors	5
Assistant Professors	3
Lecturers	2
Other academic and non-academic Staff	25

Review and Recommendations

Metallurgy being a very important discipline at the national level in the country, it is necessary in the opinion of the Reviewing Committee, that the existing department of Metallurgy be organised in such a way that the post-graduate programme will exhibit excellence in contribution to national products/problems. The laboratories in Metal Forming and Metal Joining appears to be one of the best in the country with German aid in the form of specialised equipment and expertise. This Laboratory, to give the desired output in the form of national problems being tackled, has to be associated with Physical Metallurgists on one side as well as the Department of Mechanical Engineering. For developing excellence and contribution to industry, it is recommended that the existing laboratories of the Institute in Metal Casting, Metal Joining, Metal Forming along with the laboratories of Machine Tools and Metrology at present forming part of the department of Mechanical Engineering be re-organised and grouped to be nucleus of the formation of the Department of Production Engineering.

In the opinion of the Committee, the Department of Metallurgy could form a nucleus for Material Science programme activity at the inter-disciplinary level in the Institute and as such it is suggested that proper working group be formed for Material Science activity, which in conjunction with the existing staff of Metallurgy division of the Institute may offer teaching programmes and research projects to tackle problems of national importance and inter-disciplinary work in the Institute. It is also suggested that the department be designated as the 'Department of Metallurgy and Material Science'.

The Committee feels that time is not opportune for starting of M.Tech. programme in Ceramic Engineering, as expertise in this field will have to be developed. However, it is suggested that aid be given to form research nucleus in this area. In view of Steel Plants coming up in the southern region, it would be necessary to augment the activity of the present Department of Metallurgy and in the field of Alloy Steel Technology and High temperature alloys. The Committee is of the view that special elective subjects in Alloy Steel Technology and Non-destructive Testing be offered in B.Tech. and M.Tech. programmes. To achieve these objectives, the Committee recommends the following additional facilities :

Non-Recurring

Buildings	Rs. 4.4 lakhs
Equipment	Rs. 15.00 lakhs

Additional Recurring

Staff

Professors	3
Assistant Professors	9
Other academic and non-academic staff	To the extent of 40 per cent of the recurring expenditure towards additional staff recommended.
Working expenses (additional)	Rs. 1.00 lakh p.a.

XI. Physics Department

The Department of Physics came into existence on May 10, 1959. The department, from its very inception, apart from teaching Physics courses to the various engineering departments of the Institute, has been engaging itself in post-graduate research work of its own. The department lay emphasis on the following :—

1. To develop the laboratory courses in Physics as a Science of Measurement.

2. To develop good methods of teaching of Physics through demonstration experiments during lectures.

3. To organise post-graduate teaching and research in the fields of Defect Solid State and Transistor Physics and Technology.

The department has adequate laboratory facilities to teach Physics to B.Tech. students upto the usual B.Sc. level. The list of experiments is periodically reviewed to inject new and more instructive experiments. The department offers a special laboratory programme on Vacuum Technology to the Metallurgy students in the sixth semester.

M.Sc. laboratories provide facilities for experiments on Modern Physics, Solid State Physics and Electronics.

Research laboratories are broadly classified as :

1. Dialectrics.
2. Colour Centres.
3. Electrical Conduction.
4. Thermo-luminescence.
5. Nuclear quadrupole Resonance.
6. Stress-Optics.
7. Magneto-Optics.
8. Semiconductor Research.
9. X-ray Crystallography/Spectrocopy.
10. Nuclear Tracer Methods.

The nomenclature of these laboratories indicate broadly the research activities of the department.

A summary of the facilities available at the deprtment is as follows :—

Accommodation	64,771 sq.ft.
Equipment	Rs. 15.00 lakhs

Staff

Professors	2
Assistant Professors	4
Lecturers	10
Others	50
Working expenses	Rs. 0.47 lakhs

The out-turn of the department so far is as follows :—

M.Sc.	Ph.D.	No. of Publications
67	12	113

Besides the usual academic activities, the department has helped some industrial concerns in the matter of testing and precision physical measurements, for example, intensity measurement of light-house lamps; high vacuum testing and determination of specific heats of rock samples for the Kalpakkam Atomic Power Project.

During the course of research work in the laboratories of the department, several measuring units have been developed. Most of these are fabricated using indigenous materials and components. The following are among those designed and constructed by the staff of the department :—

1. Electrical conductivity measuring unit for insulating crystals down to 10 ohm cm for temperature upto 1000°C using a low leakage circuit.

2. A cryostat which enables measurements of optical absorption and photo-conductivity of crystals down to liquid nitrogen temperatures.

3. A thermo luminescence measuring system has been assembled and is being used.

4. A dielectric cell is designed and constructed and a new method is developed to measure the complex permitivity of liquids at microwave frequencies.

5. A new method is developed to determine the dielectric constant of solids at radio and audic frequencies as a function of temperature. This method avoids the errors in resetting for the equivalent air condenser of the conventional methods.

6. Apparatus for imbedding platinum wire in single crystals of alkali halides.

7. Crystal puller for growing alkali halides.

8. A field effect measuring unit has been constructed and used to study surface states of semiconductors.

9. A proton resonance meter for monitoring radio frequencies.

10. A semi-micro balance is modified and used for measuring minute changes of magnetic susceptibility of crystals (.01 mg.).

11. A goniometer for X-ray diffraction analysis. This uses a special mechanism to obtain a 1:2 ratio between the angular velocities of the crystal and detector without using gears, thus avoiding back-lash errors.

12. A low temperature attachment for a Weisenberg Camera : This incorporates a Dewar with a thermally insulated communicating tube for supplying boiling nitrogen.

13. A cooling attachment to grow crystals in situ on the Weisenberg goniometer for substances cystallizing below room temperature.

14. An apparatus for measuring stress-optic coefficients of crystals has been constructed.

15. A high power oscillator (80 watts working at a frequency of 10 mc/s) has been designed and constructed for exciting molecular spectra.

16. A nuclear quadrupole resonance-Spectrometer has been designed and constructed to study chlorine resonances.

17. An ultrasonic composite oscillator method of determining elastic constants.

18. A scintillation counter has been assembled and used to measure low level alpha activity of rocks.

The department has conducted a short course on High Vacuum Technology in 1968 in collaboration with Bhabha Atomic Research Centre and helped the latter to organise the twelfth annual Nuclear Physics and Solid State Physics Symposium in the same year.

The department has organised the 'Physics

Association', which arranges lectures by distinguished visitors, the staff and post-graduate students of the department.

The following major equipment is expected as German Aid during 1971—It will be used for research, post-graduate teaching and industrial liaison :—

1. Electron spin resonance spectrometers for both X and Q bands attachments : Liquid helium Dewar, Optical resonant vacity, frequency measuring unit, magnetic field monitoring unit. Spare electromagnet and microwave components for the wavelength region 10 cm to 0.5 cm.

2. Helium liquifier, liquid nitrogen plant, storage tanks for liquid nitrogen; cryostats with pumping systems and temperature measuring accessories.

3. Crystal growing unit, thin film coating unit with thickness monitors and special furnaces for heating annealing and drying. Vacuum and ultra high vacuum equipment.

4. X-ray generators with current stabilisation, demountable microfocus X-ray unit for diffraction work, different types of cameras.

5. Cary double beam spectrophotometer, micro-densitmeters, atomic absorption spectrophotometer, helium neon and ruby laser systems, special lamps of xenon hydrogen and mercury.

6. Electronic measuring instruments like high speed oscillographs, dielectric measuring bridge, wave analyser, low current measuring amplifiers, wave form generators, phase sensitive detector special power supplies, electronic desk calculator.

Departmental Proposals

New Courses : 1. The department proposes to start one-year post-M.Sc. course in Materials Science and Technology and

2. A five-year integrated M.Sc. course.

Research and Development : With arrival of the new equipment from Germany, the department proposes to intensify the existing research activities and to start work on :

(i) Low Temperature Thermal Properties of Crystals.

(ii) Electron Spin Resonance of Crystals with Defects.

(iii) Spectroscopic studies in Infra-red and Visible Regions.

(iv) Stimulated Raman and Brillouin Scattering.

(v) Growth and Purification of Semi-conducting crystals and an intensive study of their electric magnetic and optical properties.

The department also proposes to increase the number of research scholars by 24.

To achieve these objectives, the department has requested the following additional facilities :—

Non-Recurring

Additional accommodation	1,000 sq.ft. (carpet area)
Equipment	Rs. 10.00 lakhs (spread over five to ten years).

Recurring

Academic Staff

Professors	4
Assistant Professors	13
Lecturers	6
Associate Lecturers	3
Senior Research Assistants (lecturer's grade)	10
Research Associates	10
Post-Doctoral Fellows	10
Research Scholars	24
Total	80

Technical Staff

Technical Assistants	7
Foremen	2
Supervisors	3
Total	12

Supporting Staff

Mechanic 'A'	4
Mechanic 'B'	7
Mechanic 'C'	6
Laboratory Attendant	5
Total	22

The above additions will involve the following expenditure per annum :

Academic staff	Rs. 5,45,500/-
Teaching staff	Rs. 93,900/-
Supporting staff	Rs. 90,600/-
Scholarships	Rs. 72,000/-
Total	Rs. 8,02,000/-

Working Expenses

Consumables and others	Rs. 1,28,000/-
Equipment	Rs. 1,50,000/-
Books, etc.	Rs. 10,000/-
Total	Rs. 2,88,000/-

Review and Recommendations

(a) **Teaching** : (i) The present two-year M.Sc. course includes the following topics :

1. Classical Mechanics,
2. Quantum Mechanics,
3. Electromagnetic Theory,
4. Mathematical Physics,
5. Statistical Mechanics,
6. Experimental Techniques,
7. Spectroscopy with one elective course from :
   (i) Transistor Physics,
   (ii) Instrumentation and Automatic Control,
   (iii) Microwaves, and
   (iv) X-ray Crystallography.

The department has developed a very good M.Sc. course well-balanced between theoretical and experimental studies. This should continue with further innovation of new experiments.

(ii) As regards starting the new post-M.Sc. course in Material Science and Technology, the Committee is of the view that in order to avoid duplication of this course, the representatives of all Indian Institutes of Technology and Indian Institute of Science should meet together and take a decision.

(iii) As suggested in the general recommendations, the Institute consistent with the aim of starting it should develop in post-graduate teaching and research in technological areas which are vital in the context of the national development. Moreover, there are a large number of Universities which teach M.Sc. Physics courses and it would be difficult to convince oneself about the advisability of awarding M.Sc. degree after P.U.C., or Higher Secondary. The Committee does not favour this proposal.

(b) **Research** : (i) The department has produced good research work in some areas of Solid State Physics and has competence to extend this activity. The Committee views the proposals for expansion of research with favour. The department is receiving a big list of equipment from the Federal Republic of Germany and it will be advisable to first take up the areas which can be investigated with them. After fully consolidating this activity, new problems may be taken up.

(ii) The Reviewing Committee whole heartedly supports the proposal of the department about collaboration with the Electrical Engineering Department on Semiconductor Devices.

Summary of Recommendations

Non-Recurring (Additional)

Equipment	Rs. 5.00 lakhs

Recurring (Additional)

Staff

Professors	3
Assistant Professors	6
Lecturers	3
Non-academic supporting staff	Upto 40 per cent of the expenditure of the academic staff is recommended.
Working Expenses (additional)	Rs. 1.00 lakh

XII. Central Library

With the starting of about 4,000 volumes in the year 1959-60, the Central Library has at present about 90,000 volumes. A separate building was completed in 1967. About 350 journals are now being obtained as part of the activity of this Institute. Till to-day, approximately Rs. 34.00 lakhs have been spent for the development of the Library. The Library also has a large number of micro-films of technical literature and looks after different tasks of circulation, reference work, translation and reprography. A catalogue of periodical holdings and a fortnightly library bulletin are also available. A separate Bindery Service, Microfilming Unit and a Telex Service with other libraries have also been planned. The proposal for development includes :

1. Development of a Union Catalogue to facilitate inter-library loan system.
2. Improvement and expansion of Readers' services and translation service.
3. Reprint service for the departments.
4. Technical Information Clearance Centre.
5. Documentation of Micro Films.

The Reviewing Committee approves the following financial requirements of the development of Central Library as follows :

Non-Recurring

Buildings and Equipment

Library equipment and extension of the present building, air-conditioning of stack and reading rooms	Rs. 5.00 lakhs

Block grant

Block grant inclusive of purchase of periodicals and books	Rs. 20.00 lakhs (*)

(*) of this, Rs. 2.00 lakhs each should be earmarked for books for the departments of Mathematics and Industrial Engineering and Management.

Recurring (additional)

Staff	Rs. 0.81 lakhs p.a.
Purchases of periodicals and books.	Rs. 2.00 lakhs p.a.

Review and Recommendations

Establishment of a Computer Centre in the Institute is expected to generate the dynamic outlook in the research activity and the computing facilities will be a great asset to the development of new and sophisticated research programmes. It is expected that the major part of the establishment of the Computer Centre will be coming through the German aid and as such the cost of Computer has not been taken into account by the Reviewing Committee excepting the maintenance expenditure with operating staff that has been indicated by the Institute.

The Reviewing Committee is of the view that as far as possible the sophisticated and costly instruments in the Institute should be a central facility for the departmental activities and as far as possible these should not be housed in the departments, since the departments normally tend to restrict the use of equipment to those working in the department only. It is also necessary that these units be run by trained technical personnel and maintained well for better output. It is expected that the Central Services Unit will be more competent to maintain and repair these instruments and keep them working around the clock for the benefit of the various departments in the Institute. Establishment of such a Unit will also help in generating new ideas in building new prototype and new instructional equipment, and this activity should be encouraged in the national interest. The working of such a Central Services Unit will, however, has to face many complex problems. It is, therefore, suggested that proper divisions to take charge of these activities be created and if necessary Committees may be constituted with academic experts from the departments to plan day to day activity of this Unit under the guidance of the Director of the Institute.

Based on the above, the following facilities are recommended :

S. No.	Particulars	Recurring: Staff	Recurring: Working expenses	Recurring: Total p.a.	Non-Recurring Expenditure
(1)	(2)	(3)	(4)	(5)	(6)
			(Rupees in lakhs)		
1.	Computer Centre	2.68	3.00	5.68	*
2.	Central Workshops	4.22	1.81	6.03	18.50**
3.	Special Instruments Laboratory	1.34	0.20	1.54	25.00 (Block grant)
4.	Electron Microscope	0.53	0.10	0.63	
5.	Electronic Instruments Servicing & Development Centre	0.93	0.25	1.18	
6.	Central Photographic Section	0.20	0.05	0.25	
7.	Central Glass Blowing Shop	0.43	0.10	0.53	
8.	Air-conditioning Maintenance Unit	0.53	0.30	0.83	
9.	Printing Press	0.50	0.04	0.54	5.00
	Total	11.36	5.85	17.21	48.50

* Capital grant for the Computer is expected to be made available from other sources.
** Building—Rs. 6.00 lakhs and Equipment Indigenous—Rs. 12.50 lakhs.

Review and Recommendations

The Reviewing Committee is of the opinion that the Institute should foster inter-disciplinary projects to tackle problems of national importance. Most of the major technological problems of the present age require participation of experts from many scientific and engineering disciplines and also require the teamwork of these experts working together with inter-disciplinary cooperation. It is, therefore, necessary to clearly define such inter-disciplinary problems of national importance and one should bear in mind the broad base that has been built up for such activity in the Institute.

As far as the project on Bio-Medical Engineering is concerned we note the Institute with the well known physicians and surgeons and some progress in the area of Bio-Medical instrumentation has been attained as a result of the activity in the departments of Electrical Engineering, Chemistry and Central Workshop. The Reviewing Committee is, therefore, in favour of concentrating in this major area of inter-disciplinary work, as far as this Institute is concerned. The work on the other two inter-disciplinary projects viz., (i) Desalination and (ii) Air and Water Pollution are in the stage of infancy in the Institute and as such the Reviewing Committee recommends that a base for greater contribution in these areas is yet to be developed. In the light of this, it is suggested that the Institute might continue to build up activities in these areas and a major project in these areas should be deferred to a later stage. The Committee, therefore, recommends the following grants for development of Inter-Disciplinary Projects :

(a) For Bio-Medical Engineering

Non-Recurring

Buildings	Rs. 3.00 lakhs
Equipment	Rs. 6.00 lakhs
Total	Rs. 9.00 lakhs

Recurring

Staff	Rs. 2.47 lakhs p.a.
Working Expenses	Rs. 0.80 lakhs p.a.
Total	Rs. 3.27 lakhs p.a.

(b) To initiate activity in the projects of (i) Air and Water Pollution and (ii) Desalination :

Non-Recurring

Equipment for both the Projects	Rs. 5.00 lakhs

Recurring

Staff	Rs. 0.53 lakh
Working Expenses	Rs. 0.70 lakh
Total	Rs. 6.23 lakhs p.a.

Since the establishment and development of these projects in the Institute will entail coordination and the solution of many complex problems arising out of inter-disciplinary nature of these projects, it is desirable that the Institute should form a Committee under the chairmanship of the Director to organise and evaluate the work of these projects from time to time and it would also be desirable that these projects are organised as far as possible not in the department, but in the Engineering Experimentation Centre that has been proposed for the Institute.

It is also necessary that these project works which are to be undertaken at the Institute, are properly examined by apropriately constituted Screening Committees.

A summary of the additional financial recommendations for the amenities on the campus is given below :

1.	Dispensary building	Rs. 0.70 lakh
2.	Ambulance	Rs. 0.60 lakh
3.	Hospital Equipment including Beds	Rs. 0.70 lakh
4.	Gymkhana buildings, Swimming pool, Cafeteria and Shopping Centre	Rs. 21.16 lakhs
5.	Staff Club	Rs. 1.00 lakh
6.	Staff Housing	Rs. 75.00 lakhs.
7.	Extension to Women Students' Hostel and family accommodation (flat-lets) for married Research scholars	Rs. 4.68 lakhs
8.	Primary School	Rs. 0.25 lakhs
9.	Auditorium	Rs. 30.00 lakhs
10.	Transport Vehicles	Rs. 3.00 lakhs
	Total	Rs. 137.09 lakhs

To this end, the Committee suggests the following financial support to the Institute for this Centre :

Non-Recurring

Buildings	Rs. 25.00 lakhs
Equipment	Rs. 50.00 ,,

Recurring :

Staff	Rs. 3.00 lakhs p.a.
Supporting Staff	Rs. 1.20 ,, ,,
Working expenses	Rs. 2.00 ,, ,,

The Centre will have minimum workshop facilities for each of the divisions also. However, when bigger projects are undertaken and/or tasks are to be performed the same might be done in the Institute's departmental workshop. The Central Servicing facilities are also expected in course of time, to be located in this Centre itself.

Centre for Advanced Studies

The Committee also suggests that the Institute should be enabled to get benefit of the experience and learning of well-known industrialists and academic people in the respective fields. Engineers and Scientists who are of high standing even if they could be persuaded to spend short periods in the campus will not only tone up the faculty from time to time but also enable new ideas to emerge and new processes of projects to be developed in the Institute. The association of such visiting Scientists and Engineers with the Institute departments and Engineering Experimentation Centre will generate excellence in departmental research programmes and will also help in inspiring the young student body for creative ability and greater tasks of national interest. To enable the Institute to attract such people of standing it has been proposed that fellowships of the value of Rs. 2,000/- p.m. might be offered (irrespective of and in addition to their remuneration that they might be getting from their parent organisations) to such outstanding invitees. The invitations to be issued might be decided by the Institutional authorities i.e., Director and the Board of Governors. Though normally it is expected that such invitees will spend a period of a year or so at the Institute it is possible that in many cases the invitees may not be able to spare more than a couple of months at the Institute since they cannot take themselves away completely from their primary commitments. It is, therefore, recommended that this provision of 12 fellowship of Rs. 2,000/- p.m. should be taken as equivalent to 144 man-months and the period of stay of such invitees will have to be by mutual consent by the person concerned and the institutional authorities. The Institute should also provide for such invitees other perquisites which will help them to devote themselves completely to their work for the duration of their stay at the Institute such as free furnished accommodation (in case of invitees who are accompanied by their wives, family quarters are recommended to be kept at their disposal) and transport. It is expected that these invitees will work both in the departments of Metallurgy and in the Engineering Experimentation and Design Centre. The following financial provision is thus recommended for this purpose :

Fellowships	Rs. 3.00 lakhs

It is also suggested that the Coordinator incharge of the Engineering Experimentation and Design Centre will also be incharge of the Centre of Advanced Studies, to enable fruitful interaction between the various activities of the Institute and the visiting Scientists/Engineers.

The Reviewing Committee understands that the Institute has been forced to keep many of the earlier sanctioned posts unfilled because of financial stringency. Expenditure during the last three years is given in Annexure-IV. Even so, this expenditure enabled the institution just to sustain itself by postponing payment of certain major pending bills to the next year and by not resulting in depleting the faculty, as also every year the department's work goes on at a low efficiency because of the reduced working expenses. The Committee is strongly of the opinion that before the present recommendations are accepted, by the year 1973-74 the Institute should be enabled to fill up all the vacant posts. Starting therefore, from this point of projection of implemention of the earlier sanctions for staff and the present recommendations of the Reviewing Committee the projected expenditure for the Institute for 5 years is indicated below :

Total Recurring expenditure during the year 1970-71 (Annexure-V).	Rs. 142.58 lakhs
Additional amount required for filling up of the sanctioned posts now kept vacant because of lack of funds.	Rs. 39.94 lakhs
Total Expenditure for 1970-71	Rs. 182.52 lakhs
Total projection of expenditure at the present rate of staff for 1973-74.	Rs. 195.13 lakhs
Additional requirements for 1973-74 for implementing the recommendations of Reviewing Committee.	Rs. 120.04 lakhs
Total projection of expenditure for 1973-74 (staff salaries and allowances plus working expenses)	Rs. 315.17 lakhs
Total Projection for 1974-75	Rs. 325.89 lakhs
Total Projection for 1975-76	Rs. 337.04 lakhs
Total Projection for 1976-77	Rs. 348.63 lakhs
Total Projection for 1977-78	Rs. 360.69 lakhs

While calculating the above projections the usual growth rate of 3 per cent for staff salaries and 5 per cent for other working expenditure has been taken into account (Annexure-VI). The Committee also noted that the Indian Institute of Technology, Madras has been at a slight disadvantage, in that, the non-plan expenditure has been permitted for the Institute, has not been sufficiently taken care of for the commitments of the

Institute. The Reviewing Committee suggests strongly that the above expenditure details are taken into account and sufficient plan and non-plan provisions be made to allow proper growth and development of the Institute. It is also suggested that the provision for capital expenditure is made separately on a continuing basis for the whole period to be granted to the Institute as and when the expenditure figures justify the same, keeping the recurring commitments separate as is done in all the other institutions.

ANNEXURE-I

Buildings (Academic)

1. Aeronautical Engg. Dept.	Rs. NIL.
2. Applied Mechanics Dept.	Rs. 6.00 lakhs
3. Chemistry Department	Rs. NIL
4. Chemical Engg. Dept.	Rs. 6.00 lakhs
5. Civil Engineering Dept.	Rs. 5.00 ,,
6. Electrical Engg. Dept.	Rs. 6.00 ,,
7. Humanities & Social Sciences (Industrial Engg. and Management)	Rs......
8. Mathematics Department	Rs......
9. Mechanical Engg. Dept.	Rs. 6.00 ,,
10. Metallurgy Department	Rs. 4.40 ,,
11. Physics Department	Rs......
12. Central Library	Rs. 5.00 ,,
13. Central Services	Rs......*
14. Central Workshop	Rs......*
15. Industrial Experimentation & Design Engineering Centre	Rs. 25.00 lakhs
16. Inter-disciplinary Projects	Rs. 3.00 ,,
Total	Rs. 66.40 lakhs

Equipment

1. Aeronautical Engg. Dept.	Rs. 25.00 lakhs
2. Applied Mechanics Dept.	Rs. 8.00 lakhs
3. Chemistry Department	Rs. 4.00 ,,
4. Chemical Engg. Dept.	Rs. 15.00 ,,
5. Civil Engg. Department	Rs. 15.00 ,,
6. Electrical Engg. Dept.	Rs. 25.00 ,,
7. Humanities & Social Sciences (Industrial Engg. & Management)	Rs. 3.00 ,,
8. Mathematics Department	Rs. 1.40 ,,
9. Mechanical Engg. Dept.	Rs. 40.00 ,,
10. Metallurgy Department	Rs. 15.00 ,,
11. Physics Department	Rs. 5.00 ,,
12. Central Library	Rs. 20.00 ,,**
13. Central Services	Rs. 25.00 ,,*
14. Central Workshop	Rs. 18.50 ,,*
15. Industrial Experimentation & Design Engineering Centre	Rs. 50.00 ,,
16. Inter-disciplinary Projects	Rs. 11.00 ,,
17. Printing Press	Rs. 5.00 ,,
Total	Rs. 285.90 lakhs

Student and Staff amenities

1. Dispensary Building	Rs. 0.70 lakh
2. Ambulance	Rs. 0.60 ,,
3. Hospital equipment	Rs. 0.70 ,,
4. Fixtures (Beds)	
5. Gymkhana Building, Swimming pool, Cafteria and Shopping Centre	Rs. 21.16 lakhs
6. Staff Club	Rs. 1.00 lakh
7. Staff Housing	Rs. 75.00 lakhs
8. Extension to Women students' hostel and family accommodation (flat-lets) for married research scholars	Rs. 4.68 lakhs
	Rs. 352.30 lakhs
9. Primary School	Rs. 0.25 lakh
10. Auditorium	Rs. 30.00 lakhs
11. Transport Vehicles	Rs. 3.00 lakhs
	Rs. 137.09 lakhs

Campus Development

1. Compound Wall	Rs. 0.55 lakh
2. Extension to roads	Rs. 3.47 lakhs
3. Augmentation of water supply and sewage disposal	Rs. 13.60 ,,
4. Electrical Power wiring and distribution system	Rs. 29.55
5. Furniture fittings etc.	Rs. 8.00 ,,
6. Customs duty on German equipment	Rs. 39.00 ,,

* Includes provision for additional buildings for Central Services and Central Workshop.

**Includes Books and Equipment for Library.

7. Other needs such as telephones, typewriters, duplicators, fire fighting equipment etc. Rs. 1.50 lakhs

Rs. 95.67 ,,

Total Rs. 585.06 lakhs

ANNEXURE-II

Additional Academic Staff Recommended

S. No.	Department	Professor	Asst.-Professor	Lecturer
1.	Aeronautics	2	6	—
2.	Applied Mechanics	2	6	6
3.	Chemistry	2	5	4
4.	Chemical Engineering	4	5	—
5.	Civil Engineering	3	6	—
6.	Electrical Engineering	3	4	—
7.	Humanities & Social Sciences (Industrial Engg. & Management)	2	4	3
8.	Mathematics Department	2	5	5
9.	Mechanical Engineering	6	9	—
10.	Metallurgy Department	3	9	—
11.	Physics	3	6	3
	Total	32	65	21

ANNEXURE-III

Additional Recurring Expenditure Recommended

S. No.	Items	Amount
1.	Maintenance & Services	Rs. 3.00 lakhs
2.	Power & water	Rs. 2.00 ,,
3.	Telephones	Rs. 0.50 ,,
4.	Gardens	Rs. 0.10 ,,
5.	Property tax	Rs. 0.30 ,,
6.	Security	Rs. 0.15 ,,
7.	Oil & Petrol etc.	Rs. 0.30 ,,
8.	Duty, Insurance etc.	Rs. 0.05 ,,
9.	General Stores	Rs. 0.20 ,,
10.	Liveries	Rs. 0.20 ,,
11.	Postage	Rs. 0.40 ,,
12.	Stationery & Printing	Rs. 1.00 ,,
13.	Advertisements	Rs. 0.30 ,,
14.	Typewriters	Rs. 0.03 ,,
15.	Audit charges	Rs. 0.07 ,,
16.	Legal expenses	Rs. 0.02 ,,
17.	Contingent expenditure on Electricity, Water, Insurance, dispensary etc.	Rs. 1.00 ,,
18.	Miscellaneous	Rs. 0.50 ,,
19.	Gymkhana	Rs. 0.30 ,,
20.	Primary School	Rs. 0.05 ,,
21.	Academic & Research activities	Rs. 6.00 ,,
22.	Other general miscellaneous provisions such as entrance exam., examiners' fee, convocation, advances etc.	Rs. 3.00 ,,
	Total	Rs. 19.47 ,,

ANNEXURE—IV

Expenditure Incurred During the Last Three Years

Year	Amount (Rupees in lakhs)
1968-69	115.024
1969-70	133.349
1970-71	142.580

ANNEXURE—V

Recurring Expenditure 1970-71

1. Staff salaries Rs. 73.40 lakhs
2. Scholarships Rs. 13.48 ,,
3. Working expenses Rs. 55.70 ,,

Recurring expenditure 1970-71 (at present) Rs. 142.58 lakhs

Recurring Expenditure At Present (1970-71) Rs. 142.58 lakhs

Additional amount required to fill up the vacancies Rs. 39.94 ,,

Total 182.52 ,,

Annual Projection with increase of 3% on staff salaries and 5% on working expenses

Year	Staff Salaries	Scholarships	Working expenses	Total
(1)	(2)	(3)	(4)	(5)
			(Rupees in	*lakhs)*
1971-72	113.4	13.48	55.70	182.52
1972-73	116.74	13.48	58.49	188.71
1973-74	120.24	13.48	61.41	195.13
Additional funds recommended by the Reviewing Committee	60.54	15.00	44.50	120.04
Total Recurring expenditure for implementing Reviewing Committee's recommendations	180.78	28.48	105.91	315.17
1974-75	186.20	28.48	111.21	325.89
1975-76	191.89	28.48	116.77	337.04
1976-77	197.54	28.48	122.61	348.63
1977-78	203.47	28.48	128.74	360.69

SPECIAL COMMITTEE ON REORGANISATION AND DEVELOPMENT OF POLYTECHNIC EDUCATION IN INDIA 1970-71—REPORT

New Delhi, Ministry of Education and Social Welfare, 1971. 245p. (2 parts bound in one)

Chairman : Prof. G.R. Damodaran

Members: Prof. S.K. Das; Dr. S.M. Dasgupta; Shri K.C. Lall; Shri A.L. Narayan; Dr. Pranlal Patel; Shri Y. Saran; Prof. B. Sengupta; Shri S.G. Somani.

Member-Secretary : Shri Biman Sen; Shri D.V. Narasimham

The Committee coopted the following members : Shri K.R. Sivaramakrishnan; Col. S.G. Pendse; Shri M.V.V. Raman; Prof. H.C. Guha.

The following foreign experts were associated with the work of the Committee :

Prof. Ross Henninger—U.S.A.; Mr.E. Houghton—Britain; Prof. W.D. Kurz—West Germany; Dean Minoru Shimosaka—Japan.

APPOINTMENT

On the advice of the All India Council for Technical Education, the Government of India constituted the Special Committee for Reorganisation and Development of Polytechnic Education. The first meeting of the Committee which was held at New Delhi on 4th April, 1970 and was inaugurated by Prof. V.K.R.V.

Rao, Union Minister for Education and Youth Services broadly indicated the guidelines for the work of the Committee.

TERMS OF REFERENCE

The terms of reference of the Committee were as follows:—

(a) to examine the whole system of polytechnic education vis-a-vis the needs of industry for middle level technicians and to prepare a ten year plan for its reorganisation and development;

(b) to recommend measures for improving the practical content of diploma courses through co-operation between polytechnics and industry with particular reference to sandwich courses, apprenticeship training and diversification of subject fields; and

(c) to report on all other aspects of polytechnic education.

CONTENTS

Introduction; A Review of the Development of Polytechnic Education; Concept of Technician and his Education; Survey of Industry; Reorganisation of Polytechnic Education; Faculty Students; Assessment of Education; Training and Employment; Partnership with Industry and Commerce; Status and Professional Development of Techinician; Administration, Finance Control and Inspection; Plan for action; Summary of Recommendations; Appendix II to VI.

RECOMMENDATIONS

A Review of the Development of Polytechnic Education

Polytechnic education should be coordinated with the state of industrial and commercial development and the economic resources of the country as a whole.

Over the next 10 years, higher priority in technician education development should be accorded to the qualitative improvement of courses and consolidation of existing institutions rather than to quantitative expansion.

At least for the next five years, there would be no need to consider the establishment of new polytechnics. As for the intake capacity of existing polytechnics, the position may be reviewed after three years and any changes necessary be made so as to meet the actual needs.

Efforts should be made to prepare realistic estimates of the demand for technicians for the fifth and subsequent plans, region-wise and by specialities and types of technician functions in industry, commerce, services and public utilities, so that appropriate programmes of educational development could be formulated and included in the fifth Five Year Plan.

Concept of Technician and his Education

In industrial organisations there is a broad spectrum of occupations lying between the craftsmen at the one end and the professional engineer at the other. Within this spectrum there are wide differences, both in specialities and degrees of expertise, which must be taken into account when planning educational and training programmes, but the whole band represents a separate and distinct group of people, who can be classified as technicians whatever their specific functions may be. Polytechnics, in association with industry and business, should have the responsibility of educating and training persons for technician functions.

The purpose of polytechnic education is to lay the foundation for the future technicians and for the persons who play a comparable role in business and commercial activities by way of a sound, broad-based theoretical knowledge of the chosen field that helps them to understand the basic principles underlying their activities together with training in the actual practice thereof.

Technician education should not lose sight of the human and social aspects of the work and life of technicians. The confidence and competence needed for self-employment should also be developed.

Programmes of technician education and training should be properly drawn up in an integrated manner with the cooperation of industry.

Reorganisation of Polytechnic Education

The major concern of polytechnics should be to run regular diploma courses designed to meet the educational requirements of the technician positions near the professional level. At the same time, it should be the endeavour of polytechnics to extend their institutional facilities to cater to the needs of the other category of technician positions by organising a variety of short-term and/or part-time courses for technicians and craftsmen in service.

Apart from these courses, polytechnics should organise special refresher and training courses as well as advanced diploma courses for technicians already employed.

Certain selected polytechnicians should be authorised to offer part-time degree courses.

Part-time diploma courses should be started at the initiative and with the co-operation of industry in selected subject fields so as to benefit a large number of skilled persons working in the local industrial and business firms.

Within the broad framework of certain general guidelines as regards the standards, objectives and scope of technician courses, there should be a great deal of flexibility in course planning to permit local variations in their structure, contents and organisation.

Where two or more polytechnics are situated in a centre, co-ordination should be brought about in order that they may avoid duplicating their efforts in the kinds of courses they offer.

Technician courses should aim to prepare the student for entrance into a technician function and at the same time facilitate mobility and future occupational advancement.

At present, narrow specialization should not be the aim of technician courses at the first diploma level. The courses should be designed to be broad-based with provision for diversification.

Diversified courses should be started in those institutions where the need for such course is fully established and may be introduced, in the initial stages, by means of elective subjects within the broad-based diploma courses.

In order to correlate the polytechnic educational programmes with the diverse needs of technicians from time to time, well-organised units should be set up in the departments in charge of technical education at the Centre and in the States for the estimation of future technician needs, speciality-wise on the basis of analysis of occupations.

A technician who emerges from a diploma course should be in a position to tackle most jobs that he may be confronted with. Hence there is need for planning education and training programmes on the basis of analysis of occupations by functions. However, the education should look beyond the boundaries of such occupation-analysis because, in developing countries like India, the technician may have to deal with activities related to, but not necessarily part of his basic functions.

Sandwich courses should be started only after specific study in depth about the adequacy of the industrial co-operation available at any proposed location. They should be so organised that the industrial training is effectively supervised, coordinated and evaluated by the polytechnics and the industry.

Educational programmes in engineering fields should be given a design and production orientation appropriate to the level of technician functions.

Polytechnics should also offer courses in fields such as commerce, business administration etc. which are closely related to industrial activities.

A variety of courses suitable to the temperament and special aptitudes of girls should be organised in Girls Polytechnics. In particular, diploma courses in Home Science and Home Economics options should be introduced in all Girls' Polytechnics.

In respect of polytechnics situated in non-industrial areas, a careful study may be made of the types of courses required for those regions and in the light of such study suitable courses may be organised. However these institutions may concentrate on offering generalised courses. Efforts should be made to set up Industrial Training Institutes in their vicinity to stimulate their growth.

Polytechnics in rural areas may offer courses in agricultural engineering and courses applicable to agro-industries. In such areas, the possibility of setting up Industrial Training Institutes in the proximity of the polytechnics may be considered with a view to augmenting the training facilities for students.

The duration of polytechnic courses should be determined with reference to the nature and requirements of each course. The following normal durations are recommended :

(i) Full-time Institutional courses at first diploma level : 3 years;

(ii) Full-time Sandwich courses at first diploma level : 3-1/2 years;

(iii) Part-time evening courses at first diploma level : not exceeding 4 years (Actual duration should be governed by the subject unit requirements);

(iv) Advanced diploma courses: one year;

(v) Short terms/and special courses : Duration should depend on the subject matter requirements of the course.

The minimum academic qualification for admission to a course at the first diploma level should be a pass in the Pre-University course or Higher Secondary course or its equivalent. Students who have passed only the SSLC or matriculation should undergo successfully a preparatory technical course of one year in the polytechnics.

The curriculum of technician courses should be based on a clear definition of the objectives of each course—both the specific objectives of technician specialities and the general objectives of technician education.

The curriculum should be flexible enough to permit addition or deletion of subjects and alteration in their levels depending upon the pre-entry preparation, the varying needs of industry and direction of technological changes.

The syllabi of polytechnic courses should be

regularly reviewed and revised to meet the changing requirements.

Syllabi should not merely specify the topics but should indicate the depth of their treatment.

Whenever changes are to be effected in the curriculum it is desirable to take into account the views and suggestions of students.

Curricula should be designed to enable a study in depth of the subjects of specialisation and a broad coverage of other related subjects.

The study of basic sciences should be properly oriented to suit the needs of each course and should not only enable the student to understand and learn the technical subjects that follow but also lay the foundation for future adaptability and further studies. They should be taught subjects interwoven into the other subjects.

The study of English language should be emphasized and developed as a tool of effective communication for technical purposes.

As and where relevant to the needs of technician courses, study in appropriate depth, of topics from Industrial Organisation, Human Relations, Factory Laws and Labour Laws, Materials Management, Industial Safety and Concepts of Systems Engineering should be included.

Polytechnic education should develop in the students practical skills and the attitude to understand, appreciate and apply concepts to practice situations through carefully planned laboratory work, workshop practice and project work.

Practical work must form a substantial part of technician courses, particularly of the full regular courses. It should reflect similar work in industry, commerce or other field as closely as possible, within the limitations of institutional facilities.

Project work requiring design and/or fabrication should find an important place in the final year of the diploma programmes and in the advanced diploma courses. Project work must be based on real problems involving industrial/commercial practice and procedures.

Through co-curricular and extra curricular activities and seminars and project work, polytechnics should endeavour to develop in their students the confidence and competence needed for self-employment.

The main criteria in planning laboratory work and practical/field work should be (1) to further a clear understanding of the scientific principles taught, (2) to foster innovation and original thinking, (3) to help develop the ability in the creative use of knowledge and critical appraisal of test results, (4) to develop an appreciation of, and a facility in, the use of the experimental and approach to problem solving and (5) to encourage the fabrication and assembly of simple types of instruments and scientific apparatus and set-ups.

The main objective of workshop practice should be to give the basic training so as to lay the foundation for later shopfloor experience. Workshop practices should aim at helping students to understand, apply and use the basic principles, skills, tools and processes.

The equipping of laboratories and workshops should be governed by a careful consideration of the needs of the courses, the teaching approach of the polytechnics and availability of equipments in collaborating industry and the Industrial Training Institutes situated in the neighbourhood.

The present practice of rigidly following "Standard" lists of equipment should be discontinued although they could serve as guides of minimum requirements. Each Polytechnic should determine the requirements of laboratory and workshop equipment, having regard to the nature of the courses offered from time to time.

Provision should be made for appointing competent laboratory technicians in each laboratory for the proper maintenance and upkeep of laboratories and equipment.

The faculty of polytechnics should be encouraged to develop and fabricate items of laboratory equipment needed for the courses. Deserving proposals in this regard should receive financial support.

Technical Teacher Training Institutes should collect details of equipment devised and fabricated polytechnics and circulate the details to all polytechnics in the country.

In addition to the regular teaching methods, the more modern and effective methods including the tutorial method, the problem-solving method, the project-method and seminar method should be used in polytechnics.

Wherever possible, lectures should be supplemented by audio-visual aids such as slides, filmstrips, blow-ups, charts, films, class room demonstration models and instruction sheets.

A concentrated effort is required to develop teaching aids. Polytechnics should be provided with audio-visual equipment such as over-head projectors, film and slide projectors, epidioscopes etc.

Technical Teacher Training Institutes should develop and produce proto-types of all kinds of teaching aids. They should also keep in touch with polytechnics, other institutions and firms engaged in the development and production of teaching aids and disseminate information about them to all polytechnics in the country.

Case-studies of actual industrial and field problems should be collected by teachers for use in the class-room. The Technical Teacher Training Institutes should compile these problems and bring out case-books and catalogues of case-studies. These should be made available to all polytechnics.

Incentives should be provided to teachers and experienced persons in industry to write textbooks and other supplementary course materials suitable for the different courses and publish them at reasonably low prices.

Textbooks in use should be scrutinised from time to time and brought uptodate.

The use of the library by teachers and students for reference, information and self-development must be encouraged and fostered. The teaching should be so organised as to require and encourage a great deal of self-study and use of library facilities by the students.

All polytechnics should have well-stocked, well-staffed and attractive libraries, with reading room facilities for at least 10 per cent of the student body. Necessary provision should be made for creating and maintaining adequate library facilities and services and for the periodic addition of books and journals.

The library should be in the charge of a well-qualified, competent and well-paid librarian with adequate staff to assist him. The librarian should be given a grade at least equal to that of a lecturer and granted the status of the Head of Department.

Separate text-book libraries should be set up in the polytechnic and, if possible, in the Halls of Residence, for the benefit of students.

For the proper development and growth of technician education and its improvement in quality, autonomy for polytechnics is essential, polytechnics should have complete freedom to experiment with much-needed reforms, restructure their region in training and employing technicians develop the new curricula suited for such courses, evolve their own methodology for education and training and assess and evaluate their students.

A beginning must be made by selecting at least one, but not more than two, polytechnics in each State and Union Territory for the immediate grant of autonomy. These polytechnics must be selected on the basis of the sustained excellence of their standards, facilities, faculty and performance. Based on the experience gained with the working of the autonomous polytechnics initially selected, other polytechnics must be given such freedom as and when they are ripe enough to take up such responsibilities. For this purpose the polytechnics must be assisted to attain the required standards and levels, through a phased programme of development over the next 10 years.

In addition to academic freedom, the autonomous polytechnic should have a Government Council and an Academic Board.

The Government Council of an autonomous polytechnic will be responsible to guide and control the planning, development and administration of the polytechnic and should consist of teachers' representatives of the State Council of Technical Awards (recommended later) the State Board of Technical Education, the All India Council for Technical Education and the State and Central Governments. The Principal of the polytechnic should be the member-Secretary of the Council.

The Academic Board of an autonomous polytechnic will deal with such matters as assessment and evaluation course development, relations with industry, research, and other academic matters. The proposals of the Academic Board should be placed before the Government Council for ratification. The Academic Board should consist of representatives of the faculty, experts from industry and eminent educationists in the fields of technical and secondary education. The Principal of the polytechnic should be the chairman of the Board.

A State Council of Technical Awards (SCTA) should be set up in each State as an independent and autonomous organisation to coordinate and safeguard the necessary standards with respect to technician education and to award diploma.

In respect of the autonomous polytechnics, the SCTA should set and assess standards not by framing and imposing courses and curricula and conducting examinations but inspecting and approving the institutions, scrutinizing and approving new courses and curricula, and schemes of assessment and evaluation, framed by the polytechnics themselves.

The SCTA will lay down the standards by way of facilities and faculty and the general guidelines and requirements for courses.

In respect of the non-autonomous polytechnics, the SCTA should help them to frame and improve their courses and curricula, conduct the external examinations and suggest the methods of internal assessment.

The SCTA should assist the non-autonomous polytechnics to develop the standards of facilities, performance and expertise needed to gain autonomy.

The State Government should determine the manner and method of setting up the SCTA and specify its relationship to the State Board of Technical

Education. The SCTA should consist of representatives of industry, trade and commerce, technical experts from government departments, representatives of the professional bodies, progressive educationists, polytechnic and college teachers and principals etc.

Faculty

The normal pattern of teaching staff categories in a polytechnic should be as follows :

Professor or Head of the Department;
Assistant Professor; and
Lecturer/Associate Lecturer.

The ratio between senior position and junior positions i.e. Professors/Assistant Professors and Lecturers/Associate Lecturers should be of the order of 1:2.

The teacher-students ratio should be not less than 1:10. In counting this ratio only teaching posts of Associate Lecturers and above should be taken into account.

For every diversified course in an institution, at least one professor assisted by an assistant professor or lecturer should be provided, supplemented by part-time lecturers from industry.

Principals and Heads of Departments of polytechnics should be provided with suitable administrative staff. Provision should be made for clerical and laboratory assistance to teachers.

The designations and scales of pay of teaching posts in polytechnics should be the same as in engineering colleges.

The minimum qualification for the post of Associate Lecturer should be a degree in engineering or technology with at least two years of industrial experience. However, a diploma holder with not less than 5 years of industrial experience may be considered subject to his suitability to teaching and improvement of his academic background.

The minimum qualification for posts of lecturers and above should be a degree in engineering or technology, or AMIE with at least 3 years of industrial experience or a TTTI diploma with five years of industrial experience.

For teachers of other professional courses like commerce and business, the minimum qualification should be a degree in the appropriate field with 2 years of professional experience in the relevant field.

For teachers in science, humanities and arts, a post-graduate degree is essential, preference being given to persons with industrial experience.

Training of at least one year in the art and techniques of teaching is desirable for all polytechnic teachers.

All teachers of similar categories whether in engineering, business and commerce, or humanities, arts and science should be allowed the same scales of pay and benefits.

For all teachers from the Associate Lecturer to the Assistant Professor, there should be a composite scale of pay with suitable starting stage for each category.

In view of the industry/application orientation of teaching in polytechnics the practice of transferring teachers between polytechnics and arts and science colleges, wherever it exists, should be discontinued.

Suitable incentives should be provided for teachers to improve their academic qualifications and gain experience.

Teachers deputed for training etc. should be paid their full salary in addition to travelling and other allowances and stipends.

Subject to certain conditions, polytechnic teachers should be given the freedom to take up consultancy work.

Polytechnic teachers may be allowed to take sabbatical leave to pursue research or undertake writing of books or to work in other institutions or industry.

Industry must be willing to accept, encourage and assist the transfer of experienced staff to part-time or full-time teaching work. There must be a much higher interchange of staff between industry and technics.

Opportunities should be made available to teachers for acquiring the needed industrial experience, in the art and techniques of technical teaching higher academic qualifications through seminars, perform courses of various kinds, summer institutes, science training programmes, deputation to Teach-training Institutes during vacation or during the academic year and secondment to industries. Teachers must be required to attend such courses and acquire such training several times during their career to facilitate continuous development and to remain uptodate in their field of knowledge.

Specially designed short-term courses should be organised for providing industrial training to workshop instructors. The cooperation of the Central Training Institutes should be secured for providing training to workshop instructors of polytechnics in respect of skill appreciation.

A crash programme should be implemented for retraining at least 25 per cent of the existing polytechnic teachers within a period of two years. The programme should consist of several courses of short duration on such subjects as assessment and evaluation technique, curriculum development, laboratory work and industrial orientation in teaching.

This crash programme should be followed by a second stage of comprehensive industrial training especially for teachers in certain subjects which are highly practice-oriented or industry-oriented.

A third stage of training of longer duration should cover training in communication skills.

A crash programme should be organised at selected centres in India for Principals of polytechnics to familiarize them with the different aspects of polytechnic education and management and its reorganisation as recommended in this Report.

Teachers of languages, mathematics and the physical sciences should be given special maintation courses in the application-based teaching of these subjects.

Each State should (a) assess the total number of teachers to be trained annually in the first ten years, (b) indicate the type of training programme relevant to Instructors, Associate Lecturers, Lecturers and Heads of Departments to be planned for, (c) work out financial estimates and (d) implement phased programmes of training.

The main functions of the Technical Teacher Training Institutes should be :

(a) organising courses on the art and techniques of teaching and special subject-teaching courses.

(b) Research and training in teaching methods and development and production of teaching aids, charts and publications.

(c) Collecting and disseminating to all polytechnics in the country, information on curricula, examination systems, equipments, teaching aids, technical literature, teaching methods etc.

Close liaison should be established and maintained between the Technical Teacher Training Institutes on the one hand and the principals and senior faculty members of polytechnics on the other.

In order that the Technical Teacher Training Institutes could be successful and effective in their function of training polytechnic teachers, the TTTIs should maintain close relations with industry. The faculty of TTTIs should be encouraged to return periodically to polytechnic teaching and industry.

TTTIs should organise short-term courses for lecturers and instructors on the fabrication and use of teaching aids.

The Technical Teacher Training Institutes should concentrate their energy on the several aspects of teacher training rather than on organising post-graduate courses in subject specialisations.

Students

Information about technician courses and careers should be collected by the Directorates or Departments in charge of Technical Education and transmitted to the educational authorities concerned with institutions conducting pre-university or Higher Secondary courses for due circulation and publicity.

While the performance in an aptitude test should be one of the criteria for admission to polytechnics, its wholesome adoption at the present stage is not favoured. However, a beginning should be made to develop some standard aptitude tests for admission to polytechnics.

Admission should be made by polytechnics on the basis of merit. Some weightage may be given for participation in extra-curricular activities.

Guidance and Counselling Services are essential in Polytechnics to give direction and purpose to the aspirations and activities of students and to assist them to make decisions and adjustments from time to time in respect of their academic, family, social and vocational-educational problems. To begin with, Guidance and Counselling Centres should be set up on an experimental basis, in the autonomous polytechnics. Depending on the experience, the scheme should be extended to cover all the other polytechnics in the course of the next 10 years.

Each Guidance and Counselling Centre should have a Guidance and Counselling officer of the rank of a professor, assisted by suitable staff. The officer should be professionally qualified with adequate training in educational psychology and vocational guidance. The Centre will need to have library facilities and testing laboratory for assessment and diagnosis of students' abilities and disabilities.

Arrangements should be made in all polytechnics to provide hostel facilities for at least 50 per cent of the students.

Polytechnics should take interest not only in the time students spend in the campus but also in the time they spend outside the campus. Interest to do independent work and study, and in hobbies outside formal study hours, should be cultivated in the students. The required facilities for extra curricular activities such as sports, music, arts, histrionics etc. should be provided to develop and foster healthy community life. Student organisations and activities should be encouraged to enrich campus life.

Assessment and Evaluation (Examinations)

The assessment of a student should be continuous and should ultimately be the responsibility of the teachers themselves.

The overall internal assessment of a student's performance and progress should take into account his achievements in assignments, periodical tests etc.

An immediate and complete changeover to purely internal assessment, even though desirable, may not be feasible in all polytechnics in our present set up. Therefore, to begin with, in respect of the non-autonomous polytechnics, continuous internal assessment should be given equal weightage with the final external examination. Complete switchover to continuous internal assessment should be effected within a period of 10 years.

The State Council of Technical Awards should continuously review the method of assessment and evaluation in each polytechnic and suggest necessary improvements.

Training courses in the methods of assessment, evaluation and grading should be arranged for teachers in the form of short training programmes, summer courses etc.

Training and Employment

Basic training covering the basic skills should normally be provided by the polytechnics themselves. For this purpose, the workshop facilities in polytechnics should be strengthened. Wherever possible, closer links should be established between polytechnic and Industrial Training Institutes.

Secondary training should be organised for practical training in industry and should have as an objective a broadening of technical knowledge and gaining of insight into some of the workings and problems of industry in general. In its later stages, training should be more specifically related to the all work on which the technician student will be entitled when he has completed his training.

The training programme should introduce potential technician to a variety of operational problems obtaining in the practice of his occupation, whether these relate to the selection of operational procedures, manufacturing processes, machines, materials and methods, or to the ensuring of control of protection sequences, quality and cost. It should also compose him to conditions of work involving, among other things, organisational procedure, group activities, human relations and production economics.

The programme of practical training should be carefully drawn up by individual polytechnics in cooperation with the collaborating industrial units to suit the needs of each course and should be properly and jointly supervised by the institution and industry.

Training must be properly assessed and evaluated. It should preferably have adequate weightage in the total evaluation. There is a need to devise adequate scientific methods to assess the results of training and evaluate the degree to which the objectives of training have been realized.

It should be the endeavour of all concerned to make arrangements to provide well-organised and supervised practical training in industry for all students of diploma courses during vacations and/or after the completion of the courses.

Production-cum-training centres may be set up at places wherever two or more polytechnics are situated. The facilities available at these centres should also be used for providing training during vacations or after the diploma courses. The centres could also provide practical training to students of polytechnics in rural areas where industries do not exist.

Since several government departments, such as industries, labour, technical education, are administering several kinds of training programmes, an effective coordination of their efforts should be brought about.

A separate training and placement department should be set up in each polytechnic manned by an experienced training and placement officer of the rank of a professor with suitable assistance.

Training departments must be set up in all organisations offering training facilities manned by capable executives who could work in close collaboration with the principals/heads of departments and training officers of the polytechnics.

Partnership with Industry and Commerce

Industries should be fully involved in the planning and development of polytechnic education and in the training of diploma students at every stage.

At the national, regional and State levels, partnership must be strengthened. Industry must be adequately represented in the policy-making and coordinating bodies at these levels and must be closely related with the proposed State Council of Technical Awards and the autonomous polytechnics. At transit level, conditions must be created which are in the close collaboration of industry in the implementation of the programmes of education and training.

Industries should be requested to extend their fullest cooperation in providing the much needed industrial experience to polytechnic teachers either by short-term or long-term training or through other arrangements.

Industries in the neighbourhood of polytechnics

must be encouraged to refer their search, development and production problems to the polytechnics. Industries may also support other research or development projects undertaken by polytechnics.

Experts from industry should be invited to discuss some typical problems of the shop-floor and explain through special lectures and seminars how they are solved. They may also provide the polytechnics with technical information and details of their design, development and production activities.

Status and Professional Development of Technicians

There should be a rationalization of the manpower structure and a clear identification of technician functions in industry and commerce. Technicians must be accorded a recognisable career structure adequately reflecting the importance of their position. Formal technician qualifications should be insisted upon for recruitment.

Polytechnics should organise a variety of up-dating refresher and extension courses including short-term and advanced-diploma courses and part-time degree courses for technicians in service. Through these courses, technicians should be enabled to qualify for higher positions and promotions.

The image of polytechnics as centres of career education should be developed. For this purpose, polytechnics should have the flexibility and freedom to develop in new directions and explore new horizons.

Technicians should have an organised forum for discussing common problems and articulating their needs and aspirations.

The Government should take the initiative in persuading the professional bodies and other organisations and associations concerned with technical education, training, industrial and commercial interests etc. to set up technician sections/technician education and training sub-committees etc. The teachers of polytechnics should also be involved in these sections and sub-committees.

Administration, Finance, Control and Inspection

While a strong national policy on technician education and training is necessary, such a policy should be flexible enough to permit modification according to the peculiar regional or local needs with reference to the type and level of technicians.

The responsibility for the administration and control of technician education should be shared appropriately by bodies at the Central, Regional, State and Unit levels. The responsibilities at each administrative level should be properly defined.

A separate committee on Technician Education and Training should be constituted under the auspicious of the All India Council for Technical Education to deal with all aspects of technician education and training at the national level.

In order to give efficient secretariat help to the proposed Committee on Technician Education and Training, a separate unit may be created in the Ministry of Education.

The regional committees of the AICTE and the regional organisations of the Central Government may have to be reorganised.

Detailed studies of manpower demands in the State, training in industry, programmes of development, teacher development and administration of polytechnics with respect to financial control and coordination at State level, should be the direct responsibility of the State Government so that programmes and schemes may be effectively implemented.

A State Council of Technical Awards (SCTA) should be set up in each State.

There should be adequate delegation of administrative authority and financial power to the Heads of Polytechnics to function efficiently.

As regards the financing of polytechnic education, the Government has to take the major responsibility both at the Central and State levels but industry should also be a part to the financing as it directly benefits from it.

So far as new experiments and innovations in technician education are concerned, the Government should take the entire financial responsibility by sponsoring pilot projects and other programmes.

At the national level, adequate provision should be made for the evaluation of the entire system to ensure that the money spent is effectively and properly utilised and that proper standards are maintained with regard to the overall national needs.

The annual provision under contingencies, materials etc. should be raised to a minimum of Rs. 300/- per student against the present provision of Rs. 120/- to Rs. 150/. The annual per capita recurring expenditure should be revised to a figure of Rs. 1700/- to Rs. 1800/-.

Acknowledgement

We wish to record our gratitude to the Government of India for giving us the opportunity to study the problems of technicians education in this country.

We also record our gratitude to the representatives of various Industries, Chambers of Commerce, Indian Engineering Association, All India Manufacturers

Organisation, Institution of Engineers (India), State Governments and others for their generous cooperation and advice.

Many principals and teachers of polytechnics and individuals submitted their views in writing or during discussions. We express our gratitude to all of them.

We are happy to record our sincere thanks to the foreign Consultants, whose services were kindly lent to us by US-AID, British Council, West German and Japanese Embassies and to Shri G.K. Chandiramani, Educational Adviser (T) and Dr. L.S. Chandrakant, Joint Educational Adviser to the Government of India for their suggestions and advice.

We owe a special debt to the P.S.G. College of Technology, Coimbatore, the Indian Institute of Science, Bangalore, Indian Institute of Technology, Bombay and Delhi, Institution of Engineers (India), Calcutta and Council of Scientific and Industrial Research for providing us accommodation for holding meetings and for the facilities.

We shall fail in our duty, if we do not thank the staff of the P.S.G. College of Technology, Coimbatore, Technical Teachers Traning Institute, Calcutta and of the Technical Division of Ministry of Education for their selfless and devoted assistance.

We cannot conclude our acknowledgement without expressing our indebtedness to Prof. V.K.R.V. Rao for his encouragement and guidance in all work.

THIRD PAY COMMISSION, 1970-1973—REPORT

New Delhi, Ministry of Finance; 4 Vols. separate pages.

Chairman : Shri Raghubar Dayal
Members : Shri Nihar Ranjan Ray
Shri V.R. Pillai
Shri A.K. Das Gupta
Member-Secretary : Shri H.N. Ray

APPOINTMENT

The Third Pay Commission was set up by the Government of India by Resolution No. F 7(25)-E III (A) 69 dated 23rd April 1970.

TERMS OF REFERENCE

The Commission will be required to enquire into and make recommendations on :

(i) The principles which should govern the structure of emoluments and conditions of service of Central Government employees.

(ii) What changes in the structure of emoluments and conditions of service of different classes of Central Government employees are desirable and feasible.

(iii) Death-cum-retirement benefits of Central Government employees;

(iv) the structure of emoluments and conditions of service, including death-cum-retirement benefits, of personnel belonging to the All India Services.

(v) the structure of emoluments including benefits in cash and kind and death-cum-retirement benefits of personnel belonging to the Armed Forces, having regard to their terms and conditions of service;

(vi) the structure of emoluments and conditions of service, including death-cum-retirement benefits of employees of Union Territories; and

(vii) while enquiring into the level of minimum remuneration, the Commission may examine the Central Government employees' demand for a need based minimum wage having regard to all relevant factors.

The Commission will make its recommendations having regard, among other relevant factors, to the economic conditions in the country, the resources of the Central Government and the demands thereon such as those on account of developmental planning, defence and national security, the repercussions on the finances of all the State Governments, public sector undertakings, local bodies etc.

In case, in veiw of the increase in cost of living the need for consideration of relief of an interim character arises during the course of deliberations of the Commission, the Commission may consider the demand for relief of an interim character and send reports thereon. In the event of the Commission recommending any interim relief, the date from which this relief should take effect will be indicated by the Commission.

The Commission will devise its own procedure and may appoint such advisers as it may consider necessary for any particular purpose. It may call for such information and may take such evidence as it may consider necessary. Ministries and Departments of the Government of India will furnish such information and documents and other assistance as may be required by the Commission. The Government of India trust that the State Governments, service associations and other concerned will extend to the Commission their fullest cooperation and assistance.

The Commission will make its recommendations as soon as practicable.

By a subsequent Resolution dated 4th June 1970 para 2 (vii) and para 4 of our terms of reference were subsituted respectively by the following paragraphs.

"2 (vii) having regard to all relevant factors, the Commission may, while enquiring into the level of minimum remuneration, examine the Central Government employees' demand for a need based minimum wage which is based on the recommendations of the 15th Indian Labour Conference.

In case the need for consideration of relief of an interim character arises during the course of deliberations of the Commission, the Commission may consider the demand for relief of an interim character and send report thereon.

In the event of the Commission recommending any interim relief, the date from which this relief should take effect will be indicated by the Commission."

The changes introduced in our original terms of reference by the resolution of 4th June, 1970, were of a material character. We were asked to consider the demand of the Central Government employees, for a need based minimum wage, specially with reference to the recommendations of the 15th Indian Labour Conference (1957). Further this resolution omitted the restrictive clause "in view of the increase in cost of living".

CONTENTS FOR VOLUMES I TO IV

VOLUME I : PART I—Introductory: Our Terms of Reference and Its Scope; Procedure of Work; Employment under the Central Government.

PART II—General Principles including Economic and Financial Considerations: Economic Situation and Financial Resources; Principles of Pay Determination; Minimum Remuneration; Starting Salary of Class I Services and Maximum Salary under the Govenment.

PART III—Pay Scales : Organised Services and Common Categories: General Recommendations on Pay Structure (including a section on Promotion Policies and Selection Grades); Headquarters Organisation of the Government of India; Office Staff in Non-Secretariat Organisations; All India Services; Central Services, Class I; Class II Services and Posts; Engineering Services; Scientific Services; Medical Services; Economists and Statisticians; Class IV Staff; Workshop Staff; Common Categories:— (I) Teachers and other Educational Staff; (II) Storekeeping Staff; (III) Fire Service Staff; (IV) Drivers of Motor Vehicles; (V) Librarians and other Library Staff; (VI) Telephone/Teleprinter/Telex Operators; (VII) Marine Staff; (VIII) Other Common Categories.

VOLUME II : PART I: Ministry of Agriculture; Ministry of Commerce; Ministry of Communications; Ministry of Defence; Ministry of Education and Social Welfare; Ministry of External Affairs; Ministry of Finance; Ministry of Health and Family Planning; Ministry of Home Affairs; Ministry of Industrial Development; Ministry of Information and Broadcasting; Ministry of Irrigation and Power.

PART II: Ministry of Labour and Rehabilitation; Ministry of Law and Justice; Ministry of Planning; Ministry of Railways; Ministry of Shipping and Transport; Ministry of Steel and Mines; Ministry of Tourism and Civil Aviation; Ministry of Works and Housing; Department of Atomic Energy; Department of Science and Technology; Department of Supply; Cabinet Secretariat; Others:— (I) Petroleum and Chemicals; (II) President's Secretariat; (III) Vice-President's Secretariat; Prime Minister's Secretariat; (IV) Department of Parliamentary Affairs; Union Territories.

VOLUME III—Armed Forces Personnel: Reference and Procedure; Our Approach to Armed Forces Pay; Service Officers Pay; Pay Structure of Personnel below officer rank; Allowances and Benefits of Servicemen; Non-effective Benefits of Servicemen; Fixation of pay in the proposed scales and cost of recommendations.

VOLUME IV—Dearness Allowance: Introductory; Revised Dearness Allowance Scheme; Proposed future rates of Dearness Allowance.

Compensatory Allowances: Compensatory (City) Allowance; House Rent Allowance; Housing Facilities; Rent-Free Quarters; Other Compensatory Allowances; All India Transfer Liability Allowance; Risk Allowance; Transport between place of work and residence.

Travelling Allowance: Travelling Allowance for Civilian Employees; Gradation of Government Employees; Mileage Allowance; ACC Travel; Travel by Air; Road Mileage; Conveyance Allowance; Daily

Allowance; Journey on Transfer; Transfer Grant; Transfer Incidentals Baggage Allowance; Transfer Travelling Allowance on Retirement/Death; Travelling Allowance Rules for Railway Employees; School Travel Concession; Travelling Allowance for Officers and Personnel of the Armed Forces.

Leave Travel Concessions : Railway Employees; Civilian Employees of the Central Government other than the Railway Employees; Armed Forces Personnel.

Educational Facilities and Allowances : Introductory; Children's Education Allowance; Hostel Subsidy.

Death-Cum-Retirement Benefits : Age of Superannuation; Premature Retirement; Voluntary Retirement; Restrictions on Commercial Employment after Retirement; Retirement Benefits; Principles governing grant of pension; Existing position; Emoluments; Rates of Pension; Death-cum-Retirement Gratuity; Death Gratuity; Service Gratuity; State Railway Provident Fund; Family Pension Scheme; Invalid Pension; Temporary Service; Benefit of added years; Extraordinary Pension; Compulsory Insurance; Provident Funds Relief to Pensioners; Personnel belonging to the All India Services; Union Territory Employees.

Hours of Work, Holidays and Overtime Allowance : General; Hours of Work; Weekly Off; Public Holidays; Casual Leave; Overtime Allowance; Weightage for Night Duty.

Leave Entitlements : Existing Position; Industrial employees; Non-Industrial employees; Leave Salary; Commutation of Half-pay Leave; Study Leave; Departmental Leave; Maternity Leave; Other kinds of Leave; Leave Encashment.

Medical Facilities : General; Central Government Health Scheme; Medical Reimbursement Scheme; Medical Allowance; Group Medical Insurance Scheme; Medical facilities for Railway employees; Compulsory Medical Check-up of Government Employees.

Staff Amenities : Uniforms, Protective Clothing and Protective Accessories; Canteen Facilities; Advances to Government Servants; Other Welfare Measures.

Miscellaneous : Classification of Services; Temporary and Quasi-Permanent Status; Industrial and Non-Industrial Employees.

A. Staffing and Efficiency in Government Service : Introductory; Some Suggestions for Economy in Staff Expenditure; Unemployment Problem vis-a-vis Overstaffing.

B. Continuing Machinery for Cadre Reviews and Pay Revision : Need for a permanent machinery for Pay Research; Cadre Review and Management; Use of Job Evaluation Techniques; Allotment of Scales to Posts not covered in the Report; Standing "Body on Pay and Cadre Management".

Date of effect of our Recommendations on Pay and Pension; Fixation of Pay in the Proposed Scales; Cost of our Recommendations : Acknowledgements; Notes of Dissent; Summary of Recommendations, Main Conclusions and Observations.

Annexes : (I) Interim Report; (II) Second Interim Report; (III) Third Interim Report; (IV) Questionnaire; (V) Offices, Establishments, etc. visited by the Pay Commission; (VI) Prominent Public men, Economists, Retired Government officials etc.; (VII) Service Associations and Representatives of Groups of Employees; (VIII) Government Officials.

RECOMMENDATIONS

Principles of Pay Determination

A pay structure, if it is to be sound, should satisfy the tests of 'inclusiveness', 'comprehensibility' and 'adequacy'. It should also be fairly simple and rational.

Beyond the minimum subsistence level, the adequacy or otherwise of the Government's pay structure is to be judged by the level of salaries that obtained in alternative occupations. Considerations of supply and demand necessarily play a part, but are subject to certain over-riding considerations. In the intermediate ranges, the limit is set by what the economy can afford. In the upper ranges, the limit is set by considerations of social acceptability.

The principle of "equal pay for equal works" may be considered in the limited context of Government employment, or it may also be assumed to have general applicability. Almost all memoranda received have drawn attention to the more favourable terms admissible to employees in the organised private sector than those admissible to the Central Government employees doing comparable work. The demand has been for 'fair comparison'.

The present wage and salary structure prevailing in organised industry may not represent the structure that would have evolved as a result of the operation of market forces under conditions of near perfect competition, because of the sheltered position enjoyed by Indian industry. There are many distinguishing gestures, which are peculiar either to Government service, or to private trade and industry, with regard to pay, emoluments, conditions of service etc. in the two sectors.

In fixing scales of pay, whether in public sector undertakings or under the Government, disproportionate importance should not be given to private sector salaries. The uncritical use of comparisons between Government salaries and salaries in organised trade and industry without considering the work content and the totality of the prevailing circumstances, would be unjustified. The Government as the dominant employer will have to take note of its dual role, both employer and as the supreme authority responsible for the governance and development of the country. The Central Government should formulate its pay policy having regard to the profound influence that the pay scales adopted by the Central Government exert on State Governments, quasi-governmental institutions etc.

The Government, however, should not ignore the fact that if the organised private sector is consistently able to offer higher wages and salaries than those offered by the Government for comparable work, then there would be a progressive deterioration in the quality and calibre of persons entering Government service. The first requirement is an efficient administration, and this will not be secured without a reasonable pay system which reflects changes in the pattern of remuneration in the outside world. Government service should attract and retain not only a high proportion of persons of average calibre but also a sufficient number of persons of the highest ability and competence to provide leadership and to strengthen the administrative and technical machinery.

Too large a disparity between wages and salaries in the Governmental sector, and those in organised trade and industry, for broadly comparable work should not be permitted, as it is likely to react adversely on the efficiency of the public service in the long run. At the start of a career, the emoluments and other advantages under the Government should approximate fairly closely to what a person with similar qualifications, aptitude and training can obtain from a good employer in the private sector. A greater degree of divergence, however, between the total emoluments in the private sector and under the Government would be feasible and acceptable later in a person's career.

A common wage policy should be evolved for public sector undertakings, and an effective coordinating machinery should be established, charged with the responsibility of ensuring that pay scales of public sector undertakings should be fixed with due regard to possible repercussions on other public sector undertakings, and on the Government's own scales of pay. It should ensure that no single unit goes seriously out of line. The mechanism should respond flexibly to changes taking place in the economy as a whole.

A cautious adoption of job evaluation techniques over a limited sphere, particularly for industrial and fairly standardised jobs, seems to be indicated as an experimental measure.

There are intractable difficulties in directly relating pay with productivity for the bulk of the Government employees. However, the Government can, and should, forge stronger links than are prevalent now between the performance of a Government employee and the pay he draws.

The concept of model employer is open to such diverse interpretations that no precise guidelines of practical value are provided.

The Government being the dominant employer should formulate its own principles of wage determination as suited to its needs. Accordingly, it has been found advisable to bear in mind several principles and conditions in recommending scales of pay rather than rigidly adhering to a single principle. The true test of any set of principles to be adopted by the Government is whether the Government service is attracting and retaining the persons it needs and they are reasonably satisfied with the pay and other conditions of service taken as a whole.

For the majority of posts, the principle of "equal pay for equal work" taken broadly to cover the range of a time scale is generally unexceptionable, when considering the Central Government alone as a separate entity. In the absence of any distinguishing features, employees of the Central Government in different branches should be paid equally if their work is adjudged to be of equal value according to certain well-established criteria.

The pay of a post should be related to the duties and responsibilities attached to that post, to the difficulty and complexity of the task to be performed, to the degree of supervision exercised, and to the qualifications prescribed.

Simplification and rationalisation of the pay structure has been attempted to the extent possible. In devising a sound pay structure, equitable relativities have been sought to be established not only vertically but also horizontally. There are limitations, however to the extent to which the existing pay structure can be simplified and rationalised, e.g., a drastic reduction in the number of grades may result in curtailment of promotion opportunities, and may prove unduly costly.

When making horizontal comparisons, it will initially be possible only to go by a broad overall assessment of the duties and responsibilities of various posts, and to allocate appropriate pay scales accordingly. Such an approach suffers from possible deficiencies and shortcomings. For this reason, the adoption of job evaluation techniques, first on an experimental basis and later, if found successful, on a continuing basis is being suggested.

The principle of determining the pay of a post

according to the duties and responsibilities, etc. attached to that post can be extended for fixing the pay of the members of a regularly constituted service. In the latter case, it is possible only to take a broad overall view of the duties and responsibilities of the separate posts encadred in the service, and of the difficulty and complexity of the functions required to be performed by its members. The underlying assumption is that the more experienced officers will be assigned the more difficult and complex jobs, so that by and large there is correlation between the stage reached in the time scale and the duties and responsibilities of the posts likely to be held at that stage.

Persons required to possess specified postgraduate qualifications or to undergo highly specialised professional training for the due discharge of their official duties should be adequately remunerated and their pensionary benefits safeguarded keeping in view the additional time and money spent in acquiring these qualifications and the relatively shorter period of their effective service.

Minimum Remuneration

There is much to be said for the view that if additional funds could be made available to the Central Government by various economy measures or by additional taxation and economy in non-Plan expenditure, these should first be used for the amelioration of the lot the people who are unemployed or under-employed rather than for ensuring a minimum wage related to certain norms set by the 15th I.L.C for a section of the community.

Fair comparison with the private sector or with the public sector cannot be accepted as a sound basis for fixing minimum remuneration under the Central Government. If there is to be a comparison with the level of wages outside the Government, it cannot be confined only to the organised private or public sector.

Having regard to the prevailing level of wages in the agricultural sector and the general minimum level in trade and industry, the adoption of the minimum remuneration based on the 15th I.L.C. norms at this stage would be tantamount of a misdirection of resources.

With the development of the country and increase in national income the Government employees should, in the fulness of time, be entitled to the need-based minimum wage according to the norms laid down by the 15th I.L.C. But in the present context the Central Government employees should not be treated as a specially privileged section of the community and guaranteed a need-based minimum wage according to these norms when the Government are not able to provide even the barest essential to millions of their less fortunate compatriots.

The 15th I.L.C. norms need some modifications when applied to Government employees. The vegetarian diet schedules recommended by the Indian Council of Medical Research Expert Group in 1968 should be adopted in respect of food requirements. While the activity status of the employee himself should be treated as 'moderate', that of other members of his family should be treated as sedentary. The cost of the food basket should be evaluated at the average prices for the 12-monthly period ending 31st October, 1972 for the four major cities, viz., Bombay, Calcutta, Delhi and Madras. Since a Class IV Central Government employee at the lowest level of salary has to pay rent for Government accommodation allotted to him, at the rate of 7½ of his pay, this would constitute a reasonable basis for determining the quantum of expenditure on house rent.

Even though the fringe benefits result in some saving of expenditure on the part of the recipients or in mitigating the hardship to which they would otherwise have been exposed, no deduction should be made on account of these from the computations of minimum wage.

Since a Central Government employee at the beginning of his career is not usually expected to be responsible for the maintenance of 3 adult consumption units including himself, the starting salary should be so fixed that at the end of 5 years, he should automatically receive a sum equal to the need-based minimum remuneration, according to the Commission's concept.

Having regard to the low per capita income of the country, the acute unemployment situation, the state of finances of the Central Government and the likely repercussions of a high minimum wage on the finances of the State Governments, it is supremely important that the maximum restraint should be exercised in devising the new pay structure. Accordingly, the minimum remuneration for the whole-time Central Government employee at the start of his career should be fixed at Rs. 185 per mensem at the 12 monthly index average of 200 (1960—100).

The special pay of certain categories of Class IV staff, whose work is exceptionally heavy or involves special risks, health hazards or employment in unpleasant or uncongenial occupations, should be raised from Rs. 3 to Rs. 10 per mensem. Government should take action either to lay down uniform criteria or to prepare illustrative lists of categories for which this special pay should be admissible.

Starting Salary of Class I Services and Maximum Salary under the Government

The starting salary in the Class I services, including the all-India Services, should be Rs. 700 per mensem.

No change need be made in the present ceiling of Rs. 3500 per mensem on the maximum salary under the Government.

General Recommendations on Pay Structure

With the attainment of higher levels of development, marginal differences in skills are of little significance for pay fixation. As a general rule posts in different departments which are broadly comparable and for which equivalent qualifications have been prescribed should be placed on the same scale of pay unless there are over-riding administrative considerations to the contrary. It was, in certain cases, found necessary to let the consideration of internal harmony over-ride the need for external parities.

While recommending the continuance of most of the existing allowances and the abolition of some, no new allowances have been recommended nor any demands for increasing the quantum of the existing allowance have been endorsed except where it was found to be absolutely justifiable on strict and critical scrutiny.

Posts in the various departments which are substantially comparable as regards duties and responsibilities, mode of recruitment and qualification standards have been grouped into common category posts.

The existing system of time scales has generally been retained with provision of fixed pay at certain higher levels.

Long pay scales have generally been recommended for entry career grades, especially where promotion outlets are limited. For posts filled by promotion, relatively shorter pay scales have been considered appropriate.

Except in the case of blind alley categories a solution to the problem of stagnation should be sought in revising cadre structure and reforming cadre management.

Continued progression on long scales running from 15 to 20 years or more should depend on periodic assessment of the employee's performance. One efficiency bar has, therefore, been provided in 10-15 years scales and two efficiency bars in the still longer scales.

There should be a more effective application of efficiency bars than has been done hitherto. Measures should be taken to ensure that crossing the efficiency bar is no longer a routine matter and that those who do not pull their weight are denied futher increments. Government should also make more frequent use than they have done in the past of the grant of advance increments to persons who have done specially good work and deserve recognition.

It is not practicable to adopt any predetermined ratio between the minimum and the maximum or a rigid time span. In recommending the quantum of increments in different scales the following broad principles have been followed :—

(i) The increases in the rates of increment, being proposed on account of the erosion that the value of increments has suffered have necessarily had to taper off with increasing levels of pay,

(ii) As far as possible the same size of increment has been suggested for the same pay range except that wherever in a series the lower scale posts are feeder posts for those in the higher scale an increased rate of increment has generally been suggested in the higher scale in order to provide incentive for promotion,

(iii) A higher rate of increment has been provided not only in a higher scale but even within the same pay scale towards the end,

(iv) The almost universal feature of annual increments in the existing pay structure has not been altered, the only exceptions being the posts at the top levels for which the pattern of fixed pay or of biennial increments has been proposed.

In future, an increment should be granted from the first of the month in which it falls due.

The existing system of overlapping scales has been continued.

In all cases of pay fixation under F.R. 22-C where, an employee is drawing pay at the maximum of the lower scale, he should be allowed a notional increment above the maximum of the lower scale (equivalent to the amount of the last increment in the scale) and the pay be then fixed at the next above stage in the higher scale.

In all cases of promotions from one Class I to another Class I post, the pay in the higher scale irrespective of whether the lower post was held in a substantive, officiating or temporary capacity.

The benefit of concordance tables should be available to all organised Class I Services which have the characteristics of an 'established' service. The benefit may continue in the scientific and technical services where it exists at present. The same arrangement should be adopted for fixing the pay of promotees in services which have a junior and senior scale even though lateral induction takes place at the senior scale level also. The admissibility of this benefit should be widely publicised at the time of inviting applications for recruitment as this is likely to enhance the attractiveness of these services.

The device of special pay should be used as sparingly as possible although it cannot be discarded in the case of posts where persons have to be attracted for a fixed tenure from other cadres and departments. The existing practice of granting special pay to officers brought on deputation to the Secretariat, or to posts at the headquarters of the departments should continue.

The existing rates of special pay in respect of posts in the Central Secretariat should continue. As the nature of work in the headquaters' organisations of the Central Services Class I, is broadly comparable to that performed at the levels of Under Secretaries and Deputy Secretaries in the Central Secretariat, the posts in the headquarters' organisations of these services held by the senior scale officers should carry a special pay of Rs. 200 per mensem and those held by officers in the junior administrative and intermediate administrative grades should carry a special pay of Rs. 300 per mensem.

The field posts in the Central Services, Class I to which special pay is attached should, if held by a senior scale officer, carry a uniform special pay of Rs. 100 per mensem and those held by the junior administrative and intermediate administrative grade officers should carry a special pay of Rs. 200 per mensem.

In the technical and scientific departments also, the grant of special pay for posts at headquarters should be adjudged on the basis of the same criteria as applicable to posts in the headquarters of non-technical departments and special pay granted where it is justified on merits. By and large, the rates of special pay attached to the posts at comparable levels should be uniform in different departments.

The system of special pay be continued in the intelligence agencies and police and security organisations in view of the special requirements of these organisations.

The system of granting deputation (duty) allowance is necessary where personnel have to be attracted to hold posts for a relatively short duration or for undertaking duties which are not similar to those entrusted to them in their regular line of work. No change is necessary in the existing provisions in this regard. The extent of application of the system of deputation allowance should, however, be limited to essential cases of deputation in order to avoid discontent among the staff. They should also keep a check on the number of persons from their departments serving outside on deputation at any point of time so that the needs of the department do not suffer.

Promotion Policies: The existing promotion prospects of the Class III as well as Class IV cadres need further improvement. The specific recommendations in this behalf are as follows :—

(i) Study leave rules may be extended to Class IV staff (and in certain cases Class III staff) to enable them to improve their educational or technical qualifications. Serving employees may be encouraged, by sponsoring their names, if necessary, but subsidising the fees to prosecute the requisite training courses after office hours, either by entering the Industrial Training Institutes or by joining any other duly recognised institute. Those who are willing to undergo approved courses of training may be given suitable bursaries. In all these cases, however, the extension of the concession should be subject to suitability as judged by the department and should not be claimed as a matter of right.

(ii) Employees who add to their qualifications in this manner may be allowed to compete with relaxed age limits, along with the outsiders for higher posts. It may also be desirable for the benefit of such candidates to include in the selection tests, certain papers or tests relevant to the duties of the posts considered, in lieu of certain marginally relevant academic papers or tests.

(iii) There is a sizable amount of routine clerical work which in certain departments is assigned to posts of Record Keepers etc. in the grade of Rs. 105-135. Efforts should be made to identify such work and create similar posts in other departments also. These posts may be set apart for the promotion of Class IV officials.

(iv) Cases of direct recruitment which are now occurring at certain intermediate levels in Class III in some departments should be reviewed to see whether their continuance is justified. In any case the serving employees who possess the requisite qualifications should also be made eligible to compete by relaxing the age limits, if necessary.

For enabling the brighter employees in Class II and Class III to get quicker promotion, it would be advantageous to introduce a larger number of limited competitive examinations. If necessary, the existing promotion quotas should be increased.

Lateral Entry: Persons outside the Government

who have gained experience in the various evocations, or who possess specialised qualifications relevant to the tasks in hand should be inducted into the middle management levels of the civil service. The procedure for such lateral induction may be as follows :—

(a) In all the Class I Services (including the Indian Administrative Service but excluding the Indian Police Service and the Indian Forest Service), 10 to 25 per cent of the vacancies* arising each year in the junior Administrative Grade or its equivalent grade should be filled by direct recruitment.

(b) The actual percentage of vacancies to be filled in each service in this manner should be decided upon after a review of the cadre composition and the requirements of each service.

(c) Suitable age limit for competing at the selection should be laid down in respect of the outside candidates. Similarly appropriate qualification requirements and duration of experience should also be stipulated. The experience referred to should be in positions comparable to posts in the Government just below the Junior Administrative Grade or its equivalent.

(d) In order that suitable serving officers are also considered they should be allowed to compete with the outsiders for the vacancies set apart for being filled by direct recruitment. The number of serving officers who should be permitted to offer themselves for selection should be roughly the same as the number included in the zone of selection for normal promotion through the Departmental Promotion Committees, namely not more than 5 to 6 times the anticipated number of vacancies including the quota set apart for direct recruitment.

(e) These recommendations do not refer to services in respect of which separate recommendations have been made in the relevant chapters.

Selection Grades : Selection Grades serve a useful purpose by moderating the disparities which might exist in promotion prospects for comparable cadres in different departments. In Class IV and Class III cadres, the Selection Grade should generally be introduced on the basis of the following criteria :-

(a) Generally selection grades should be provided for the posts which are filled by direct recruitment where the number of higher posts to which employees in a particular cadre can seek promotion is less than half the strength of that cadre.

(b) The number of selection grade posts should not be less than 10 per cent but should not exceed 20 per cent of the posts for which they serve as the selection grade. For the purpose of calculating the number of selection grade posts, all the posts which have been in existence for three years should be taken into account whether the posts are permanent or temporary. The percentage of selection grade posts should be in inverse proportion to the percentage of higher promotion posts available.

(c) The selection grade should not be granted to an employee until the incumbent has covered three-fourths of the span of the main scale.

(d) The number of selection grade posts as also the need for their continuance in a particular cadre should be reviewed every three years and the selection grade posts varied or discontinued, as the case may be.

Headquarters Organisation of the Government of India

It would not be advantageous on the whole to shut out direct entry to the Section Officer's grade.

The existing quota of 10 per cent of the posts in Grade II of the CSCS reserved for the Class IV personnel should be enhanced to 15 per cent.

A regular opportunity should be provided to the stenographers in the non-Secretariat Organisations for entering the cadre of Secretariat Stentographers working in non-secretarial offices.

In the CSSS, a non-functional selection grade should be provided above the present grade of Rs. 350(500)-900. The proposed selection grade should carry the scale of Rs. 900-40-1100-50-1400 and its strength should be 25 per cent of the strength of the existing grade of Rs. 350(500)-900.

Office Staff in Non-Secretariat Organisations

An early comprehensive review should be carried out in order to remove the anomalies in the existing classification of offices into Attached offices and Subordinate Offices.

Lower Division Clerks should be recruited on the basis of open advertisement and a competitive test instead of through the Employment Exchanges.

The existing quota of 10 per cent of the vacancies in the Lower Divison Clerk's grade reserved for the Class IV personnel should be increased to 15 per cent.

The present system of granting advance increments to direct recruits or promotees to the Upper Division Clerk's grade in the Audit Department on their passing the confirmatory test should be discontinued.

The position regarding Selection Grade Upper Division Clerks in Subordinate Offices should be reviewed and only such posts of Selection Grade Upper Division Clerks should be continued as fulfil

* Subject to Member Secretary's reservations

the conditions existing in the Accounts Offices, viz., substantial direct recruitment to the grade of Upper Division Clerks and having to pass a departmental examination to earn future promotion.

Government should review the need for continuing posts of Assistants in the Subordinate offices after all the offices outside the Secretariat have been reclassified.

Except for very small organisations, there should not be less than two nor more than three clerical supervisory levels. The highest supervisory grade (clerical) should be allowed only in the larger offices.

A selection grade on Rs. 550-750 should be allowed to the Stenographers who are today on the scale of Rs. 210-425.

All India Services

Indian Administrative Service : While it is for the Government to devise in consultation with the U.P.S.C. the scheme of examination to suit the requirements of the different Services, the pay scales cannot be related only to the standards of the recruitment examination.

It would neither be practicable nor desirable to dispense with the long senior scale for the I.A.S.

It would not be a feasible proposition to have identical scales both for the I.A.S. and the Central Class I Services. There is, however, a case for narrowing the existing disparities.

The strength of the selection grade in the I.A.S. should be equal to 20 per cent of the senior posts under the State Government with the provision that no officer should be promoted to the selection grade before he has entered the 14th year of service.

While the existing system of special pays should continue, the number of posts in the I.A.S. carrying special pay should not exceed 75 per cent of the senior posts under the State Government (excluding those in the super-time scale).

The Central Government should lay down guidelines for the rates of special pay for various levels of posts in the State Secretariats. It should not be obligatory to attach a special pay to all posts of Deputy Secretary in the States.

State Governments should review the position and grade the different district charges for the purpose of special pays only.

All posts of Secretary in West Bengal should be upgraded to the super-time scale of pay applicable to Divisional Commissioners.

In each State one or two posts should be given the scale recommended for the Additional Secretary to the Government of India.

The existing equation between the Chief Secretary and the Secretary to the Government of India should continue. In the case of the newly-created smaller States, the equation should be with the Additional Secretary.

The Chief Secretary, Delhi should be equated to an Additional Secretary to the Government of India.

The Central Government should, to the extent possible, relieve promotion blocks in the affected States by selectively drawing in from such States a greater number of officers in the super-time scale to the Centre.

Indian Police Service : The existing relativity between the I.P.S. senior scale and that of the Central Class I Services should be retained.

The strength of the selection grade in the I.P.S. should be increased from 15 per cent to 25 per cent of the total number of senior posts in the State with the stipulation that selection grade will not be admissible earlier than the 14th year of service.

Special pay should be allowed to the Superintendents of Police of those districts which are deemed to be more important and difficult charges. The number of posts in the I.P.S. carrying special pay should not exceed 75 per cent of the senior posts under the State Government (excluding those in the super-time scale).

The Inspector General incharge of the State Police, excluding the Inspector General incharge of the State Police in newly created States, should be granted a special allowance of Rs. 250 per mensem.

The Central Government should take a relatively large number of senior I.P.S. officers on tenure deputation from those State cadres where the promotion to the Deputy Inspector General's rank is relatively slower.

The amount of initial grant for uniforms should be raised from Rs. 1000 to Rs. 1200 and that of the renewal grant, payable after an interval of every 7 years, should be raised from Rs. 800 to Rs. 1000.

A Kit Maintenance Allowance of Rs. 40 per mensem should be provided to all I.P.S. officers irrespective of rank so long as they are working at posts which require them to put on and maintain uniforms.

Indian Forest Service : The scheme of pay scales devised for the Indian Forest Service should broadly conform to the pay structure devised for the Central Class I Engineering Services.

A selection grade of Rs. 2000-2250 should be introduced for the Conservator of Forests on the same principles as recommended for the selection grade in the Central Class I Engineering Services.

The Central Government should examine the system of special pays in the Indian Forest Service and, in consultation with the State Governments, list out certain posts on a uniform basis which should carry special pays in all the States.

Central Services, Class I

The integrated time scale of pay at present applicable to six of the Central Services, Class I, should be broken up into separate Junior and Senior Scales of pay.

Recruitment to all the Central Services, Class I should be so regulated as to enable the officers in the Junior Scale to generally get promoted to the Senior Scale after completion of not more than 5 years of service. Proper cadre management and career planning are essential in all these services.

The Junior Administrative Grade for these services should be in the scale of Rs. 1500 (14th year or under)-2000, the maximum being the same as recommended for the maximum of the Senior Scale of the Indian Administrative Service. This grade should be in replacement of the existing scales of Rs. 1300-1600 and Rs. 1600-1800. If however, any of the departments consider it administratively more expedient to retain the existing two separate levels, the two segments should be Rs. 1500 (14th year or under)-1800 and Rs. 1800-2000.

The pay of officers on promotion to the Junior Administrative Grade in the Central Services, Class I, should be fixed as per a concordance table. If the application of the condition of 14th year or under for promotion to the Junior Administrative Grade creates difficulties or operates harshly in respect of the officers promoted from the respective Class II cadres, Government should examine and adopt a formula which would be equitable and also legally tenable for regulating their pay.

The pay scales of the posts of heads of departments in the Central Services, Class I, deserve to be considerably improved, having regard to the duties, the span of responsibilities etc. On the basis of the accepted criteria of workload as reflected in terms of staff strength, jurisdiction, number of sub-offices and other relevant considerations it should be possible to differentiate between the various charges at this level in the different services and the post upgraded to the level of Joint Secretary on a selective basis.

While the scale of Rs. 2250-2500 should apply to the majority of the posts of heads of departments in these services in replacement of the existing scales of Rs. 1800-2250 and Rs. 2000-2500, a minimum of 33-1/3 per cent of the posts in these grades should be placed in the scale of Rs. 2500-2750. If, for administrative and other considerations, it is thought necessary by any department to place some more posts in the higher grade (subject to the number not exceeding 50 per cent of the posts in the existing Senior Administrative Grade), such proposals should require the prior concurrence of the Ministry of Finance. No special pay should be attached to any of the post of heads of departments in these services in addition to the proposed scales.

The existing restrictions on the pay plus special pay of the officers of the Central Services, Class I, in the posts of Under Secretary and Deputy Secretary in the Central Secretariat do not serve much public purpose, merely act as an irritant, and should be discontinued.

Class II Services and Posts

Having regard to the different roles assigned to the Class I and Class II services, and to the need for building up cadres to man the senior administrative posts, the existing division into Class I and Class II services, should be retained.

The distinction made at present between the Class II and the Junior Class I grades is justified and it is not repugnant to any particular principle. The Class II cadre should, therefore, continue as a separate entity.

On the demand for a larger quantum of reservation for promotion to the Class I cadre, there connot be any common pattern, as the practice differs a great deal depending largely on the needs and organisation of the different services.

As regards weightage for the service rendered in the Class II on the subsequent promotion to Class I some weightage should be accorded at least in those Class I services where promotion from Class II is for all practical purposes, to the senior scale of Class I, and the extent and the conditions governing the weightage should be decided by the departments.

The Class II service should be conceived as primarily providing a promotion avenue for the Class III staff, and from the point of view of improving their promotion chances, it would be desirable to avoid direct recruitment to Class II, wherever possible. The choice should, however, be left to the individual departments since the decision would have to depend on the size of the Class II cadre and the quality of the Class III base from which promotion takes place.

Engineering Services

Class I Services: While an arithmetical equation

between the Engineering and the Indian Administrative Service is not practicable, the salary structure should aim at a broad parity between them. With this in view, the junior scales of the two services have been equated, the existing differential at the start of the senior scale narrowed, the Junior Administrative Grade improved, both by equating the maximum of this scale in all the Engineering Services with the maximum of the Senior Scale of the Indian Administrative Service, and by providing an equivalent Selection Grade above this level. The highest posts have also been upgraded so as to bring them in line with the highest posts available to the Indian Administrative Service. Given the basic differences in the present structure between the two serivces, this is the most that is practicable at the present time.

Since the subject matter with which the Secretariat has to deal, has tended to become increasingly technical, or otherwise specialised, there is more scope than before for greater use being made of specialist officers at all levels. The extent of such in-take will depend upon several factors and cannot be considered solely from the aspect of the avenues of promotion that can be created for a particular cadre or cadres—technical or non-technical. The paramount consideration in deployment of personnel should obviously continue to be the promotion of the public interest, and the suitability of the employee for the task in hand.

The demand for the Engineering Officers for various allowances such as techincal pay, Field Duty allowance, Non-Practising allowance and Post-graduate allowance have been examined, and it is found that these demands are not justified. There is, however, a case for the grant of a suitable special pay to personnel in organisations handling complex problems arising in modern types of construction, new designs etc. The actual quantum of the special pay for the different grades may be decided by the Government in consonance with our general recommendations on special pay. While there would normally be no justification for attaching any special pays for this work in organisations such as the Central Water and Power Commission, whose primary concern is design and engineering planning, there is a case for granting special pay to officers posted to investigation circles set up for conducting basic surveys on river valley, irrigation and power projects etc. prior to detailed planning and the engineering of these projects. The Government may decide on the actual rates.

Non-Gazetted Engineering Staff : The entry grades for posts requiring the three year diploma course in engineering, of whatever speciality, should be generally one of Rs. 425-700.

In many engineering organisations specially in the field of telecommunications, graduates in engineering as well as in science have entered in large numbers to the existing initial grade of either Rs. 210-470, Rs. 210-425 or Rs. 180-380. In the non-gazetted scientific category, a uniform grade of Rs. 550-900 has been provided above the initial grade of Rs. 425-700. The next higher grade above the entry scale of Rs. 425-700 should generally be one of Rs. 550-900 in the non-gazetted engineering cadres also. Where, however, the organisation pattern requires the presence of more than one grade above the initial grade, the range of Rs. 550-900 should be split into two grades, namely, Rs. 550-750 and Rs. 700-900.

Railways : In the engineering departments other than mechanical engineering, the grades of Assistant Inspector and Inspector Level III should be merged into a single grade and designated as Inspector Level III. Above this, there should be two grades of Inspector Level II and Inspector Level I.

With the merger of the grades of Rs. 180-240 with the grade of Rs. 205-280, the major grievance of the Train Examiners has been removed. One or two consequences arise out of this decision. First, the complement in the initial grade of Train Examiners has become very large resulting in an unbalanced cadre structure; and second, there is no middle level of sufficient size between the skilled grade (Rs. 110-180) and the Assistant Train Examiners grade which will be in the scale of Rs. 175-380 (in the existing terms). The Government may examine the implications. Government may also review the grade-wise percentage distribution of posts for this category as 92-94 per cent of the posts will not be in the lower grade.

Posts and Telegraphs : Ten per cent of the posts of Engineering Supervisors should be placed in the Selection Grade of Rs. 550-900.

Wireless Planning and Coordination Wing

It is understood that some difficulty has been experienced in recruitment to Technical Assistant Grade (Rs. 210-425) as compared to the other engineering cadres. The promotion prospects of Technical Assistants Grade II are more limited. There is thus a case for reducing the percentage on direct recruitment to Technical Assistant Grade I considering that there is 100 per cent direct recruitment to Grade II.

Overseas Communications Service : The Junior Technical Assistants in the Overseas Communications

Service is one the same scale (Rs. 210-470) as Engineering Assistants in the All India Radio. This scale happens to be higher than those applicable to similar categories in the Posts and Telegraphs (Rs. 180-380) and in the Wireless Planning and Coordination Wing (Rs. 210-425). There is no need to change the existing relativity.

In some departments six advance increments are being given to engineering graduates who are recruited to posts for which the minimum prescribed qualifications are only an engineering diploma. It is not a healthy arrangement to have a large percentage of graduate engineers in cadres for which a diploma in engineering is all that is considered necessary. This practice is not only an unnecessary burden on the exchequer but also involves under-utilisation of engineering graduates and raising expectations in them which cannot be satisfied. This concession should therefore, be withdrawn.

Ministry of Works and Housing : Ten per cent of the posts of Junior Engineers should be placed in the Selection Grade of Rs. 550-900.

Draftsman : There is no justification for the existence of as many as 30 different pay scales in the range of pay from Rs. 110 to Rs. 575 in a category where the levels of the skills required are fairly well established and could be expected to be homogeneous among the following revised scales and should satisfy the qualification requirements noted against each for purposes of direct recruitment :-

Level	Proposed Scale (Rs.)	Qualifications for direct recruitment
I	260-430	Matric plus one year's experience.
II	330-560	Matric plus 2-year Diploma in Draftsmanship or its equivalent.
III	425-700	Matric plus 3-year Diploma in Engineering or its equivalent.
IV	550-750	Degree in Engineering or its equivalent.
V	700-900	Degree in Engineering or its equivalent with experience.

Ferro Printers : There does not seem to be any need of as many as 11 grades that are now in existence and many of which differ only slightly from one another. The scales which now exist should be broadbanded into five scales.

Scientific Services : A longtime-scale is generally unsuitable for scientific work as there is no demonstrable positive link between pay and performance. A graded structure which facilitates the reward of good work through selective promotions would serve as a powerful incentive to better performance. Adequate flexibility should be built into the structure for permitting the timely creation of higher posts to which the abler scientists could be promoted.

As in most of the organised Class I Services promotions to the Senior Scale in the Scientific Services also should take place around the 6th year of entering the Junior Class I Grade. To ensure this, the number of Junior Scale and Senior Scale posts taken together should be fixed for the establishment and the Departments should be given the freedom to vary the individual numbers in the Junior and Senior Scales.

Flexibility should be permitted so that posts in the grade above the Senior Scale also can be readily created to accommodate able scientists who would otherwise be held up for lack of vacancies. The Departments should be allowed to create additional posts, if necessary, in the grade immediately above the Senior Scale for the promotion of merited scientists. The number of posts in the grade immediately above the Senior Scale should not exceed 30 per cent of the total number of posts in the Junior Scale, Senior Scale, and the next higher grade taken together. Normally this proportion would be well below the stipulated figure, so that there is always room for recognition of the meritorious scientists. While it is not necessary to make a stipulation as to the minimum service period for such a promotion it may be proper that normally a scientist should have worked for about five years in the Senior Scale before he is considered for a further promotion.

The higher posts created as a result of the flexible complementing recommended above will be personal to the incumbents, and on vacancies arising owing to further promotion of their incumbents, or otherwise, these posts will revert to the level at which initially sanctioned.

It is not necessary to have this flexibility for the creation of posts in the still higher grades. However, the Department of Atomic Energy enjoys the flexibility to create higher posts also; this arrangement need not be disturbed. However, in other departments also, as a recognition of the contribution of the outstanding scientists, it should be made possible to promote them to any of the prescribed higher grades, commensurate with their merit, by creating new posts on a personal basis. To distinguish this provision from the 'flexible complementing', these other appointments may be called as 'special merit appointments'. The provision for such appointments should also be used to enable an outstanding scientist, if he so chooses, to stay on in his own particular field rather than move to a higher post outside his field of specialisation or into administration.

For the effective implementation of the scheme of flexible complementing and special merit appointments, it is necessary that promotions in the Scientific Departments should be made on the basis of periodical assessments (say, once or twice a year), by one or more Committees consisting of the Head of the Laboratory or other scientific institution and outside experts in kindred disciplines. The further details may be settled at the highest level, in consultation with the Union Public Service Commission, and the National Committee on Science and Technology.

These recommendations would apply to all the scientific posts except those pertaining to administrative and advisory functions in the Ministries and Departments. These recommendations, if necessary with minor modifications, should be applicable even in the scientific surveys and exploratory organisations like the Anthropological, Geological, Botanical and Zoological Surveys also which today have a hierarchical structure.

The provision that exists in some scientific departments for direct recruitment to the Senior Class I Scale and the Junior Administrative Grade or its equivalent, does not seem to have been used to any appreciable extent. With the flexibility recommended for the creation of posts at these levels, it should be possible to induct experienced scientists from outside without jeopardising the promotion prospects of those already in service. The scales recommended for these two grades are sufficient to attract young and meritorious scientists who may be staying abroad. Further, in fast developing technical and scientific fields it is of supreme importance that persons closely associated with scientific developments in the advanced countries, and with current knowledge of research work there, should be persuaded to enter Government research laboratories, and to impart their knowledge to their colleagues. In all scientific organisations there should be provision for lateral induction, by direct recruitment to a reasonable percentage of these posts.

Contrary to the normal run of posts under the Government, for the top scientific posts it is necessary to take cognizance of the merit and worth of the individual scientist, and the pay of an outstanding scientist should be fixed on the individual's merits.

In regard to the proposed merger of the different grades in the Department of Atomic Energy, the department itself would be in a better position to take a decision in the light of the revised pay structure that has been prescribed for scientific officers as a group. Further, substitutes have not been prescribed for the 'fast track' grades; the department may determine these substitutes with reference to the main scales prescribed.

Class II Services and Posts

There appears to be no justification for the large number of scales that at present exist for this group of posts.

Non-Gazetted Scientific Staff: There is no uniformity in the designations of the non-gazetted scientific staff. In this connection the recommendation made by the Second Pay Commission that it would be useful to adopt standardised designations, is reaffirmed.

The levels of duties (of the non-gazetted scientific staff) do not vary to such a great degree as to justify the large number of pay scales that have come into existence.

There should be only four levels in the non-gazetted category of scientific staff :-

Level I should be that corresponding to the existing grade of Rs. 325-575. There should be direct recruitment to the majority of these posts, for which the qualification should be (a) M.Sc., or (b) B.E., or (c) First Class B.Sc. (Honours) or (d) at least a second Class B.Sc. or Diploma in engineering with about 3 years' experience. There should be a provision for the promotion of merited scientific assistants in the next lower grade (Level II).

Level II would be that corresponding to the existing grade of Rs. 210-425. Recruitment to this level should be confined to those having at least a second class B.Sc. Honours or B.Sc. with not less than 55 per cent marks in the aggregate or a Diploma in engineering. There should be a small provision for promotion from the grade indicated below (Level III) but such promotion should be strictly on merit.

Level III should correspond to the existing grade of Rs. 150-300. At present there is a considerable degree of direct recruitment to this grade from among B.Scs or occasionally B.Scs with experience. For the nature of work performed at this level science graduates of superior calibre would be wasted, and a sense of frustration may develop amongst the qualified persons. This level should, therefore, be normally filled by promotion. However, some organisations do not have a sufficiently large base of laboratory assistants or technicians for filling the posts on Rs. 150-300 and, in that case direct recruitment becomes necessary. Where it is impracticable to do away with direct recruitment may have to be continued; but the qualifications prescribed should be distinctly lower than those which we have indicated for Level II above.

Level IV would correspond to the existing grade of Rs. 110-200. For this level Matriculation or Intermediate qualification with a science background, with or without laboratory experience, should suffice. At present there are some posts at this level but on the higher scales of Rs. 150-250, Rs. 150-240, Rs. 150-205, Rs. 150-200 etc. the posts are normally filled by promotion, though there is direct recruitment in some cases. This level should be retained, but the concerned posts should, in future, be normally filled by promotion.

Posts in all the organisations which are not on the scales referred to in Table XI should be replaced by the substitutes which have been indicated against each. In case the qualifications prescribed for any of the posts do not conform to those indicated, then the position should be reviewed where a higher qualification has been prescribed and if the work content of the post justifies its being placed in the higher level, it should be upgraded to that level. Otherwise, the qualification requirements should be commensurately lowered for the future recruits. The posts on scales other than those referred to above should be fitted into the structure that has been envisaged.

Where the grade of Rs. 425-700 would be the highest in the non-gazetted scientific cadre, 10 per cent of these posts should be placed in the selection grade post of Rs. 550-900. There should be at least one such selection grade post, in the scale of Rs. 550-900 provided the number of posts on Rs. 425-700 is not less than five. The other conditions should be as stipulated in our general recommendations regarding selection grades.

Medical Services

All future recruitment to the Central Health Service at the lowest level should be to the Class I junior scale.

The existing posts of General Duty officers Grade II and Grade I should be placed in the Class I junior and senior time-scales and the complements in the two scales so adjusted as to provide for promotion from the junior to the senior scale in about the sixth year of service as in other Central Class I Services.

The procedure for absorption of existing incumbents in the junior and senior scales should be as indicated in para 8.

A structural reorganisation of existing super-time Grade II of the Service has been suggested. There should be at least one post in the new Specialists' Grade I (Rs. 1800-2250) for every clinical speciality.

A scheme of special merit promotions for officers belonging to super-time Grade I and II and specialists Grade I has been suggested.

Future recruitment to the Railway Medical Service should be in the integrated Class I scale. The method of fitment of the existing Assistant Medical Officers in the new integrated scale has been indicated.

The existing prohibition to provide practice by Government doctors and grant of non-practising allowance instead should continue. A revised system of grant of non-practising allowance at fixed rate for various pay slabs has been suggested in lieu of the existing percentage rate.

A qualification pay of Rs. 100 per mensem for possessing a post-graduate degree and Rs. 50 per mensem for possessing a post-graduate diploma should be admissible to doctors (including Dental Surgeons and Physicians of Indigenous Systems of Medicine and Homecpaths) provided such a qualification is not stipulated as essential for the posts concerned. The qualification pay should be admissible even if the qualification is acquired while in service.

Government should examine the feasibility of including the Class I and Class II medical posts outside the Central Health Service in that service.

Ten per cent of the posts of Dental Surgeons in the Railways in the scale of Rs. 650-1200 may be placed in a Selection Grade of Rs. 900-1400.

A post-graduate degree or diploma or a minimum of five years' experience in addition to a degree or diploma may be specified as an essential qualification of posts of Research Officers belonging to the Indigenous Systems of Medicine and the Homeopathy.

The doctors belonging to the Indigenous Systems of Medicine and the Homeopaths may be allowed the facility of private practice subject to certain restrictions. No non-practising allowance should be given in such cases.

Messing Allowance at present admissible for the nursing staff should be merged in their pay scales and should not be granted separately. Dearness allowance and City Compensatory Allowance (wherever admissible) should be allowed to such staff in full at the same rates as applicable to other employees.

A minimum increase in pay of Rs. 150 per mensem should be provided on promotion as Matron Incharge (in Junior Scale Class I) from the grade of Assistant Matron in the existing scale of Rs. 250-380.

Nurses attached to Operation Theatres and Intensive Care Units should be given a special pay of

Rs. 30 per mensem. Government may devise suitable criteria for the application of this recommendation.

Nursing staff who possess at the time of recruitment or acquire subsequently a degree in Nursing should be granted two advance increments provided they are not required to possess it as a condition of their employment.

The rate of Uniform allowance should be increased to Rs. 150 per annum for Nurses and Rs. 200 per annum for Matrons.

20 per cent of the posts of Health Visitor in the revised scale of Rs. 330-560 should be placed in Selection Grade of Rs. 425-640.

Except in the Ministries of Defence and Railways, 20 per cent of the posts of Health/Sanitary and Malaria Inspectors in the revised scale of Rs. 330-560 should be placed in a Selection Grade of Rs. 425-640.

20 per cent of the posts of Radiographers/X-ray Technicians in the scale of Rs. 330-560 may be placed in a Selection Grade of Rs. 425-640.

Except in the Railways, 20 per cent of the posts of Dressers in the scale of Rs. 200-260 should be placed in a Selection Grade of Rs. 225-308.

Economists and Statisticians

In order to improve the cadres structure of the I.E.S. and the I.S.S., the strength of Grade IV of the two Services should be reduced by converting a substantial number of Grade IV posts which are today in Class I into Class II posts. Further the strength of Grade IV and Grade III of these Services should be so adjusted that a direct recruit to Grade IV should have a reasonable prospect of moving into Grade III in about the 6th year of service.

Direct recruitment to two successive grades should be avoided as far as possible. Direct recruitment to Grade III should be abolished and at the leve of Grade II the 50 per cent proportion of direct recruitment should be reduced to about 25 per cent. Direct recruitment to Grade I of these Services seems necessary.

Posts above Grade I, carrying economic or statistical functions, should be filled after considering the eligible officers of these services.

A Selection Grade above Grade I should be provided in the I.E.S. and the I.S S. on the scale of Rs. 2000-2250.

Class IV Staff

All Daftries in the Railways, including those in the Stores Department, should be placed in the same scale of pays as applicable to Daftries in other Government Departments.

Workshop Staff

Wages paid by the Government to the workshop artisan categories should not differ too greatly from the wages prevailing in public sector undertakings or even in private industry, if the Government establishments are to have a fairly contended work force and to avoid any serious depletion of their skilled manpower.

The present classification of workshop staff into unskilled, semi-skilled, skilled and highly skilled does not appear to call for any basic revision. However, instead of classifying the categories by the levels of 'skill', it would be more satisfactory to classify them numerically i.e., Grade I, Grade II, Grade III etc.

There should be only one level for the unskilled and one for the semi-skilled category. One long scale or two short scales (which are segments of the long scale) should be sufficient to cover the range of skilled category. Two scales are considered essential for the highly skilled category. Thus a maximum of six levels should be adequate to cover all reasonable requirements.

The pay scale of skilled grade and highly skilled grade should be comparable to that of a Lower Division Clerk and Upper Division Clerk respectively. The posts in the existing scales of Rs. 100-130 and Rs. 100-142 should be suitably reclassified into semi-skilled or lower skilled grade after assessment of the job. Similarly posts in the scale of Rs. 130-205 should also be properly classified either into the upper skilled grade, or into highly skilled grade II.

A new grade of Master Craftsman should be created subject to the criteria specified. In order to ensure a uniform approach, an inter-departmental committee should work out further detailed criteria for the allotment of this grade.

Government should have agreed to set up expert bodies for reviewing the existing categorisation of workshop staff in all major employing Ministries except Railways. They have also agreed to set up an Inter departmental co-ordination machinery for ensuring a reasonable measure of uniformity of standards. The fitment of categories into the proposed new scales should be made on the basis of the recommendations of these expert bodies.

(i) The demand of the Railway Federation for inclusion of dearness allowance for the calculation of hourly rates under the incentive bonus scheme does not appear to be justified. With the improvement in pay scales which have been recommended, Government should consider either revising the standards for earning incentive bonus or calculating it on the minimum of the scale instead of the weighted mean.

(ii) The demand for treating the incentive bonus as pay on the analogy of running allowance is not justified.

(iii) For workers under piece rate system in Defence establishments, basic time wage should be guaranteed.

(iv) Incentive workers should not ordinarily be put on over-time except when it is absolutely unavoidable in special circumstances.

Government should introduce a well-conceived bonus scheme for Government of India Press staff to maintain efficiency and productivity in the presses.

In the Railway Workshops only Supervisors upto the level of Chargemen 'A' are entitled to incentive earnings as well as overtime; as a consequence certain distortions have occurred in the pay structure. Apart from the proposed increase in pay scales, it may become necessary also to modify the incentive scheme and the hourly rates within the framework of the revised pay structure, to achieve a more satisfactory solution.

Wherever Mistries are supervising the highly skilled grade I workers, their pay scales should be the same as for highly skilled Grade I.

Generally 2 levels of Chargemen and 2 levels of Foremen should be adequate for meeting the supervisory needs of workshops.

At least 33-1/3 per cent of the posts of Chargemen in the grade of Rs. 425-700 (in the Ordnance Factories and other Defence establishments) should be filled by direct recruitment from amongst diploma holders in the Engineering or Science Graduates. A minimum of 25 per cent of posts of Chargemen in the scale of Rs. 550-700 in these establishments should also be filled by direct recruitment from Engineering Graduates.

There is a need for reviewing the complements in the existing grade of Rs. 370-500 in Ordnance Factories and in the existing grade of Rs. 450-650 in the Director General of Inspection and the Naval establishments.

The current distinction between production shops and repair shops need not be maintained in future.

A special grade of Principal Foreman may be introduced. The posts in this grade should be created on a personal basis as a reward for specially meritorious work and proven efficiency in improving out-turn and maintaining discipline.

With the introduction of the new scales, Assistant Foremen and Foremen in the Defence workshops should not be entitled to overtime allowance. Also the technical supervisors in the Ordnance factories and Base establishment should not be allowed the facility of rent-free accommodation.

Government may examine the feasibility of introducing an intermediate supervisory grade between the Technical Assistants and Assistant Engineers in the Posts and Telegraphs workshops.

Common Categories

Teachers and other Educational Staff : Since selection grades have been granted to the Delhi Administration teachers, similar selection grades should be provided for teachers in the other schools run by the Ministries of the Government of India.

For the other school staff such as Physical education teachers, art and craft teachers and librarians working in the schools, suitable revised scales should be fixed after taking the existing relativities or parities vis-a-vis the teachers into account.

For the posts of different categories of teachers in the schools run by Departments other than Railway and Defence for which the recruitment qualifications are the same, as, and where the duties performed are also comparable to, those of similar categories in the Ministry of Railways and Defence, the appropriate revised scales and selection grades prescribed in respect of such categories under the Railways and the Defence Ministry should be adopted. In other cases, such as vocational training institutes, suitable substitutes may be decided upon keeping in view of the revised scales recommended for other comparable categories in each of the organisations in which the teaching posts exist.

Drivers of Motor Vehicles : Government should consider linking up various organisations, where there are no established cadres of drivers, with the main department or with another major organisation under a Ministry/Department for purposes of providing promotional avenues by placing some posts in a selection grade.

Librarians and Library Staff : It is desirable to adopt uniform and precise qualification criteria for all future recruitment to the different grades of Class III posts. There should be only five levels of Librarians and Library Staff depending on the qualifications to be prescribed. And these will be as follows :

Level I : Where the work is of a simple clerical nature and Matriculation without any formal library qualification is required for direct recruitment or where all the posts are filled by promotion only.

Level II : For Matriculates with a certificate (One year's course after matriculation).

Level III : For Matriculate with a diploma in Library Science (two year's course after matriculation) and for promotees from (I) and (II) above.

Level IV (A & B) : For Graduates with degree or diploma in Library Science (one years' course after graduation) or its equivalent and for promotees from (III) above.

Level V : This should normally be a promotion grade for (IV) above; where direct recruitment is to be made a degree followed by diploma in library science (one year's course after graduation) or its equivalent and by four years' experience or M.A./ M.Sc. followed by a diploma in Library Science or its equivalent without experience may be prescribed.

Marine Staff : The pay scales of the executive and engineering categories of marine staff should be related to the three types of the Certificates of Competency issued under the Inland Steam Vessels Act, 1917.

The messing allowance to marine staff in Fisheries Organisations under the Department of Agriculture should be paid on a per diem basis for the days they remain on board.

Marine staff in receipt of messing allowance should be paid full dearness allowance and full compensatory (city) allowance at the same rates as applicable to other Central Government employees.

Ministry of Agriculture

Government should examine the need for direct recruitment at the three consecutive levels of Market Intelligence Inspector, Senior Market Intelligence Inspector and Market Intelligence Officer in the Directorate of Economics and Statistics.

Government should examine whether the cadres of Locust Technical Officer and Senior Technical Assistant/Technical Assistant (Selection Grade) in the Directorate of Plant Protection, Quarantine and Storage could be integrated to form a promotional cadre for the lower grades.

The percentage of Class II posts in the Directorate of Plant Protection, Quarantine and Storage to be filled by promotion from the cadre of Technical Assistants should be increased from 10 to 25.

The Milk Tanker/Milk Van Drivers and the artisan staff employed in the Cold Storage/Boiler Room in the Delhi Milk Scheme should continue to be paid special pay at the existing rates.

The post of Chief Chemist in the Directorate of Marketing and Inspection should be filled by promotion of Senior Chemist only. Government should also consider whether the designations of Chief Chemist and Senior Chemist should be changed to Senior Chemist and Chemist respectively.

Depending upon the field of specialisation, duties and responsibilities, etc., Government should consider upgrading some of the posts of Research Officers in the Forest Research Institute and Colleges from the Class II to the Junior Class I level. With this upgradation, the remaining posts in Class II should be filled entirely by promotion from the Class III staff.

The posts of Research Officer in the proposed Class I scale of pay should be filled partly by direct recruitment and partly by promotion of the Class II officers in the organisation.

Government should also consider whether the percentage of direct recruitment to the posts of Senior Research Officer (Ordinary Grade) in the Senior Class I scale of pay should continue to be the same as at present.

In the Forest Research Institute and Colleges the cadre of Technical Assistants Grade I and Grade II should be merged. The posts in the merged cadre should be filled from amongst those who have passed the Intermediate or Higher Secondary Examination with Science.

Government should also consider reducing the existing percentage of direct recruitment at the level of Research Assistant Grade II.

The Senior and Junior Pilots engaged on flying duties in the Directorate of Agricultural Aviation should be allowed a flying bounty at the rate of Rs. 375 per mensem.

Ministry of Commerce

The feasibility of encadring the posts in the Directorate of Commercial Publicity in the Central Information Service or alternatively, of drawing officers from that Service on deputation may be explored.

There is a substantial degree of direct recruitment at every level in the Directorates of Production and Development and Chemical Processing in this organisation. The present position appears to call for a review.

Ministry of Communications

The need for direct recruitment at all the four levels in the Wireless, Planning and Coordination Branch and at three levels in the Overseas Communications Service should be reviewed.

Direct recruitment should be introduced at the gazetted level for a percentage of the posts in the Traffic Branch of the Overseas Communications Service so that persons trained and experienced in the traffic side will become available to hold the higher posts.

Posts and Telegraphs Department : The Chairman, P & T Board, should continue in the rank of Secretary to the Government of India and all the Senior Members and Members should have equal rank and pay as for the Additional Secretaries to the Government of India.

The posts of Deputy Directors General in the P & T Directorate should be placed in two scales recommended for the Heads of Departments and Government should decide the posts which should be placed in these two grades.

Whether the posts in the Telecommunication Research Centre should be filled by direct recruitment or deputation is a matter to be decided by the Government. However, the deputation of the departmental officers should be so adjusted as not to adversely affect the promotion prospects of directly recruited officers. There should be no rigidity in regard to the period of deputation so as to ensure continuity in the research work.

The Indian Posts and Telegraphs Traffic Service Class I, which now consists of only 5 posts, may be abolished.

Direct recruitment to the Telegraph Traffic Service Class II should be retained.

Government may examine the need for or advantage in having two parallel Class II Services in the Postal Branch.

The existing age limit of 50 years for promotion to the Postal Superintendents Service Class II should be removed. However, to ensure early promotion of the deserving staff, 25 per cent of the vacancies in this service should be filled on the basis of a departmental competitive examination.

One post of Deputy Presidency Postmaster in each of the Presidency Post Offices, Bombay and Calcutta should be placed in the new grade of Rs. 900-1400.

The Class I cadre in the Civil Engineering Wing being small, the department may be faced with difficulties in regard to recruitment and retention, unless there is proper cadre management and recruitment is regulated keeping in view the opportunities of advancement for the direct recruits.

The posts of Managers, Mail Motor Service, should be upgraded to Class I (Junior Scale) and in deserving cases higher initial start upto three advance increments may be granted.

In regard to isolated posts, distributed in the various departments, Government should consider the feasibility of grouping them for purposes of recruitment and promotion. Alternatively, in preference to direct recruitment, such isolated posts may be filled by officers of the available regular Services.

The classification of the P & T establishment into administrative and operating offices should be made on a functional basis adopting some broad and consistent criteria so that the pay structure of the staff employed in the two types of establishments may conform to the classification.

The ministerial staff in the administrative offices also should be provided access to the gazetted grade, as is available to the staff in the operating offices. Also, a percentage of vacancies in the grade of Assistants in the P & T Directorate should be reserved for promotion of Upper Division Clerks from the field offices on the basis of a competitive examination.

The quota for promotion of the lower grade staff to the grade of Time Scale Clerks should be reduced from 50 per cent to 25 per cent.

Conditions regarding educational qualification and age limit should be laid down for promotion of the lower grade staff to the clerical and allied operating categories in all branches of the P & T Department. Also to ensure efficiency, the standard of departmental test should be improved.

The demand for parity in pay scales between the Postal Clerks and Upper Division Clerks is not justified.

There is scope for improvement in the percentage of LSG and HSG posts for the Time Scale categories in all branches by some liberalisation of the standards for creation of such posts.

Above the LSG there should be two supervisory levels viz. HSG-I in the scale of Rs. 700-900 and HSG-II in the scale of Rs. 550-750, the higher scale being applicable only to certain specified categories. With the improvement in the pay scales and promotion prospects recommended and with a view to improving the efficiency of P & T Services the existing system of promotion to the LSG and HSG posts based solely on seniority should be modified. In all branches, one-third of the vacancies in the LSG and all the posts in the HSG-I should be filled by selection on the basis of merit.

The expedient of granting special pay in lieu of a separate scale of pay certain Time Scale posts, carrying higher responsibilities, may continue as it provides administrative flexibility and enable selection of suitable persons for holding such posts.

The Town Inspectors of Post Offices should be upgraded. If necessary, their selection procedures may be revised and additional duties entrusted to them in view of the improved status.

Special pay should be admissible to the Treasurers and Assistant Treasurers of Post Offices regardless of part-time or whole-time treasury work and should be based on the amount of cash disbursed during a month subject to certain restrictions.

The posts of the Sub Postmasters carrying a special pay should be filled by selection on merit.

The demand for parity between the Lower Selection Grade Staff and the Inspectors in the postal branch is not justified.

Considering the wide range and extent of responsibilities attached to the Lower Selection Grade and Higher Selection Grade Postmaster categories there is need to redefine their charges with the object of placing the posts carrying relatively more onerous responsibilities on higher scales of pay.

A considerable degree of uniformity prevails in the method of recruitment, qualifications, training and promotional prospects of the various Time Scale categories. Even in regard to the working conditions the differences are not such as to warrant disturbance of the existing parity among them which has the sanction of past practice, and it would be desirable not to make any differentiation among them.

The present practice of having annual tests for the RMS Sorters should continue as such posts contribute to efficiency.

The present practice of filling 50 per cent of the general line higher Selection Grade posts and the posts of gazetted Postmasters in the postal branch from the cadre of Inspectors of Post Offices should continue.

25 per cent of the vacancies in the cadre of Inspectors in the Postal and Railway Mail Service branches should be filled by direct recruitment either through the Union Public Service Commission or through the Subordinate Service Selection Board.

The demand for parity between the P & T Telegraphists and the Junior Telegraphists in the Overseas Communication Service is not justified.

There should be direct recruitment to the grade of Telegraph Traffic Supervisors to the extent of 25 per cent of the vacancies.

The proposals regarding provision of transport facilities for women Telephone Operators to and from Telephone Exchanges in the case of night duty at late hours or odd hours, adequate provision of dormitories and creches etc. deserve consideration.

The reorganisation of the engineering cadres of the Telegraph Engineering branch is a matter to be decided by the Government. The existing arrangement under which a significant proportion of posts are filled by direct recruitment at three consecutive levels from candidates possessing somewhat similar entry qualifications should be reviewed. The qualifications should be suited to the range of duties and responsibilities of various categories and of various pay scales.

The number of Selection Grade posts for the Cable Jointers should be computed on a circle basis so as to ensure equitable distribution among all the Divisions.

In the interest of uniformity of pay structure in the P &T Directorate, the Secretariat pattern of posts and pay scales may be introduced in its Air and Surface Mail Accounting section also.

Government may examine the feasibility of having a separate cadre of store keeping staff in the Telecommunication Stores organisation.

There should be direct recruitment for 50 per cent of the vacancies of Sarkars.

Government may consider recruitment of candidates with suitable technical qualifications for the posts of Testers in the testing organisation under the Additional Chief Engineer, Technical and Development Circle.

There is no justification for prescribing a higher scale for the test category than for the non-test category of Class IV staff.

The non-test category staff should be provided all reasonable facilities for acquiring literacy and give due priority for absorption in the test category. Further, they should be eligible for promotion to higher posts in the same way as the test category staff, provided they have passed the literacy test and possess the requisite qualifications.

The claim of the Telegraphmen for parity in scales with postmen, who have higher recruitment qualifications and more onerous and varied responsibilities, is not tenable. Their demand for parity with other semi-skilled categories is also difficult to subtain.

Government may evolve a uniform and simple incentive scheme for the Telegraphmen relating the payment to the output above the standard norm. The proposal for treating the incentive earnings as pay for purposes of leave salary and pension is not acceptable.

The Telegraphmen may be granted a cycle allowance if cycles are not provided to them.

All the Class IV posts in a Division or Sub Division should be pooled together branch-wise for purposes of determining the number of posts of Jamadar and such posts should be created according to a uniform standard by upgrading the existing posts and not by creating additional posts.

There does not appear to be any need for setting up

an Expert Committee, as proposed by the Federation of the National P & T Organisations, to examine the general and special conditions of service of the P & T staff, as the basic issues appear to be fairly clear.

In case an employee is required to work on a holiday on account of operational requirements, he should be compensated by grant of one day's salary at the end of the month.

As a rest day is already in built in the weekly duty pattern of the staff working in the RMS sections, it is not necessary to earmark for them a weekly off day separately in addition. However, the staff working in the RMS section having one or two sets may be required to work every day and they should be entitled to a weekly off. The 'call duty' staff should be allowed a weekly off wherever this can be arranged by pooling of staff located at the station. Where this is not possible, the staff called for duty on such off day should be given compensatory leave on another convenient day. As 'call duty' seems to be irksome and not popular, there should be a system of rotation of such staff between the 'call duty' and 'fixed duty' posts.

No change is advocated in regard to the 'alternate set system' prevailing in the RMS branch. Also the present difference in the working hours of the RMS Transit sections and Sorting sections is justified by the difference in the nature of duties performed in them.

The necessity for split duty should be reviewed and wherever it can be dispensed with, it should be done. Where this is inescapable, priority should be accorded in the matter of allotment and construction of quarters for them near the place of duty.

The rate of outstation allowance of the staff working in the RMS Sections should be fixed as a percentage of the daily allowance taking into account the free facilities provided to them.

The rates of 'night halt allowance' paid to certain categories of staff, who travel constantly within their respective beats or jurisdiction, should be fixed as a percentage of the rates of daily allowance.

Ministry of Education and Social Welfare

Government should re-examine the need for direct recruitment to the posts of Chief Archaeological Engineer and Chief Horticulturist specially since there are no promotion avenues. It is suggested that the former could be filled by deputation from the CPWD and the latter by similar deputation or by promotion of Assistant Superintending Horticulturist.

The special pay of Rs. 100 per month admissible to Superintending Archaeologists incharge of four major circles, Chief Horticulturist, Chief Epigraphist, Chief Archaeological Chemist and Archaeological Engineer should merge with the grade pay and these posts should be placed in the scale of Rs. 1300-1700.

The Class III and Class IV establishments of the Social Welfare and Rehabilitation Directorate consists of a variety of instructors in different trades as well as artisans. In many cases posts on different scales bear the same designations. The Department should evolve distinctive designations for the different grades.

Ministry of External Affairs

It will not be appropriate to disturb the existing parity as between the various grade of IFS(B) and the corresponding services organised under the Central Secretariat Services, Scheme.

Cipher Assistants should be put on the same scale as Assistants of the IFS(B) and the CSS with provision for grant of three advance increments on satisfactory completion of the period of probation.

Research Officers in the Historical Division who are to-day on the scale of Rs. 350-800, should be placed on the revised Class I scale of Rs. 700-40-1100-50-1300 after due screening and those not adjudged suitable for the revised Class I scale should be placed on the standard Class II scale, viz., Rs. 650-1200.

A selection grade should be provided for Interpreters on the Class I Junior Scale. It should carry the scale of 1100-50-1300 and its strength should be upto a maximum of 25 per cent of the posts on the scale of Rs. 400-950.

The Additional Foreign Allowance given to the officers of the Ministry of External Affairs on their posting in Missions abroad should be abolished and the rates of Foreign Allowance revised taking this into account.

The method of fixation of Foreign Allowance should be reviewed in order to rationalise the basis of its computation avoiding the need for resorting to slab deductions from time to time.

Ministry of Finance

The posts of Assistant Master and Deputy Works Manager in the Mints should be made interchangeable and the post of Works Manager should be made a promotional post for them.

The post of Deputy Master in the Mints should be filled by promotion of Works Manager only.

Government should consider whether having regard

to the nature of work, duties etc., of the Assistant Engineers in the Mints, the recruitment to these posts could be made from amongst Diploma holders.

Government should consider whether it would be desirable to have a uniform cadre structure for the Engravers in all the Mints.

The posts of Engineer (Mechanical/Electrical) in the Junior Class I scale of pay in the Security Paper Mill, Hoshangabad, should be filled by direct recruitment.

Government should consider whether having regard to the work load etc., there could be an intermediary level between the Assistant Master and the Deputy Master in the Indian Security Press, Nasik.

The pay structure of the tradesman and non-tradesman categories in the Mints and artisan staff in other industrial establishments under the Department of Economic Affairs should be brought in line with the general pay structure for workshop staff recommended in Chapter 19.

Government should consider rationalising the designations of the various supervisory posts in the industrial establishments under the Department of Economic Affairs.

The designations of the posts responsible for the security arrangements in the Mints and Presses should be rationalised.

The minimum educational qualification for recruitment to the posts of District Organiser in the National Savings Organisation should be a University Degree.

Adequate cash awards linked to performances should be given over a fairly wide field to the field staff in the National Savings Organisation so as to induce a feeling of healthy competition among them for mobilisation of small savings.

The cadres of Technical Assistants (Irrigation & Works) and Accountants in the Department of Expenditure should be merged.

S.A.S. Accountants, Accounts Officers and other staff possessing the requisite cost accountancy qualifications and experience should be made eligible for appointment to the posts of Cost Accountant, Assistant Cost Accounts Officer and Cost Accounts Officer in the Central Cost Accounts Pool and for this purpose necessary age relaxation should be allowed.

The posts of Income Tax Officer Class II should continue as a separate cadre. There should, however, be a clear demarcation between the charges normally to be held by Income Tax Officers in the Class I Senior Scale and those to be held by Class II officers and barring unforeseen contingencies there should normally be little or no interchangeability.

Government should consider whether the Class II Executive Officers in the Narcotics Department could also be made eligible for promotion to the Class I post in the Central Excise and Customs Departments.

The qualifications for direct recruitment to the posts of Inspector of Central Excise (Ordinary Grade), Examiner (Ordinary Grade) and Preventive Officer Grade I (Ordinary Grade) should be raised to a University Degree and the recruitment to the posts of Inspector of Income Tax should either be made through the U.P.S.C. or the Subordinate Services Board likely to be constituted.

Sepoys in the Central Excise and Customs Department who are trained in the use of fire arms should be given a special pay of Rs. 10 per mensem during the period they are employed on preventive, guard or other similar duties, which may require the use of fire arms.

There should be no direct recruitment to the post of Chemical Examiner Grade I in the Central Revenue Chemical Service.

The number of posts in the selection grade for the Divisional Accountants should be increased from 10 per cent to 15 per cent of the permanent strength.

The posts of Sorter in the P & T Audit and Accounts Offices should be made promotional posts for the Class IV staff in these offices.

Government should suitably revise the quantum of charge-allowance/special pay admissible to selection grade clerks who are in independent charge of local audit offices etc. in Defence Accounts Department.

The special pay of the Chief Machine Operator in the Hollerith Section under the Defence Accounts Department should be made promotional posts for the Class IV staff.

Government should review the need for special pay to the staff working in the Defence Audit wing of the Audit Department having regard to the liberalisation recommended in the rates of daily allowance.

There should be uniformity of treatment in the matter of grant of incentives to S.A.S. passed clerks in all the Audit & Accounts Departments.

There should be uniformity in regard to the quantum and the system of grant of special pay on appointment to posts in the Headquarters offices of the Indian Audit and Accounts and Defence Accounts Department.

Ministry of Health and Family Planning

As far as possible the isolated Class I and Class II posts in the Ministry of Health and Family Planning should be filled by deputation instead of direct recruitment.

A Post-graduate qualification in public health engineering may be prescribed as essential in future for the posts of Assistant Public Health Engineers in the Rural Health Training Centre and the Jawaharlal Institute of Post-graduate Medical Education and Research.

The Vice-Principal, College of Nursing should be given a special pay of Rs. 150 per month.

The post of Director, National Tuberculosis Institute should be included in Supertime Grade I of the Central Health Service.

The special pay of Rs. 150 per month admissible to one of the posts of Deputy Assistant Directors General in the Medical Stores Organisation should be withdrawn.

The qualifications for the posts of Assistant Professors of Public Health Nursing and Midwifery Nursing in the All India Institute of Hygiene and Public Health should be reviewed.

The scheme of flexible complementing and merit promotions recommended for the Scientific Services should apply mutatis mutandis to the scientific posts under the Department of Health.

Ministry of Home Affairs

Government should review the grant of compensatory allowance admissible to holders of certain posts of Commandant, Deputy Commandant and Assistant Commandant etc.

Unless in future there is any alteration in the role assigned to any police force or in the recruitment qualifications, the infantry soldier should have a slight edge over the Constables in the armed police force.

The scale approved for the matriculate Constable of the civilian Police Forces should not be admissible to Constables assigned purely orderly duties.

The Selection Grade of Rs. 85-110 for matriculate Constables of Delhi Police should be abolished.

Sub-Inspectors in the Delhi Police should be given only one Selection Grade, in the scale of Rs. 455-700, instead of the existing 4 Selection Grades. The strength of the Selection Grade should be fixed at 10 per cent of the number of sub-Inspectors.

Direct recruits in the IB and CBI from the rank of Constable to that of Inspector and equivalent should be allowed the corresponding scales recommended for the Delhi Civil Police. In view of the specialised and complex nature of their work, they should, in addition, be granted special pay on the rates applicable to the deputationists. The same rates of special pay should apply to personnel in the ITBP.

Special pay allowed to Police personnel trained in the use of team-smoke, 3" mortar and medium Machine Gun etc. and armed efficiency pay of Rs. 2 p.m. granted to Constables and Naiks in the CRP and BSF should be discontinued.

Special pay given to Head Constable and ASIs employed as "proficients" and to Inspectors of District Police and those employed on traffic duties in the Delhi Police should be discontinued.

Constables and Head Constables of the Delhi Police should continue to be paid the Metropolitan Allowance which should be redesignated as "Rajdhani Allowance".

No change need be made in regard to the system of ration allowance in the Central Reserve Police or in the rates of this allowance. The present 'belt system' in the Border Security Force should be replaced by two classes of areas, viz. "qualifying areas" and "non-qualifying areas". In qualifying areas ration allowance should be allowed at full rates, in non-qualifying areas at half the rates.

The amount of ration allowance to BSF personnel should be 80 per cent of the monetary value of the rations at the BSF scale in the "qualifying areas" and 40 per cent of the value in "non-qualifying areas".

A reasonable limit, say six months, should be prescribed as the period for which the detachment allowance can he drawn by the CRP personnel after a move. The authorities should determine after a month or two of the move, the approximate period for which the CRP force would have to be retained at that station and, where deemed necessary, to shift arrangements as regards accommodation etc. thus obviating the need for paying detachment allowance indefinitely.

The grant of detachment allowance to BSF personnel is hardly justified and its continuance should be reviewed.

The grades of Assistant Supervisor and Supervisor in the Hindi Teaching Scheme and of Hindi Supervisor and Assistant Supervisor in the Posts and Telegraph Department should be merged.

Ministry of Industrial Development

It is not considered necessary to provide a Selection Grade in the scale of Rs. 2000-2250 for Development Officers in the Directorate General of Technical Development as recommended for other Engineering Officers in view of the availability of a sufficient number of posts in a higher scale.

The proposal for splitting up the scale of Development Officers into two grades is not recommended.

A reorganisation of the grade structure of officers in the Patents and Trade Marks Organisation has been suggested.

The existing system of two grades for Directors and two grades for Assistant Directors in the Office of Development Commissioner, Small Scale Industries should continue.

A restructuring of the grades in the Indian Salt Service has been suggested.

There is no justification for parity of pay scales between the posts in the Office of Chief Inspector of Explosives and Director General, Mines Safety is not justified.

Ministry of Information and Broadcasting

Direct recruitment to Grade I of the Central Information Service should be discontinued and the percentage of direct recruitment to Junior Administrative Grade increased from 12-1/2 per cent to 25 per cent.

Junior and senior scales of Junior Administrative Grade in Central Information Service should be merged.

The posts of Field Publicity Officer in Grade IV of Central Information Service should be upgraded to Grade III of the Service.

The posts of Field Publicity Officers (Border) in the Directorate of Field Publicity should be placed in the same scale of pay as recommended for the other posts of Field Publicity Officer encadred in the Central Information Service.

The cadres of Assistant Director and Photographic Officer in the Photo Division should be merged.

The cadres of Junior Booker and Senior Booker in the Films Division should be amalgamated.

The ordinary grade and the selection grade of Programme Executives should be merged.

Some of the posts of Programme Executive should be placed in the junior Class I scale of pay and direct recruitment to this scale should not be less than 25 per cent.

The direct recruitment to the posts of Assistant Station Director should be discontinued and these posts should be filled by promotion of Programme Executives in the Junior Class I scale of pay.

25 per cent of the posts of Transmission Executive should be placed in a selection grade.

Government should consider making appointments on short term contract basis to the posts of Monitors in the Monitoring Division of All India Radio.

The Stenographers of All India Radio should be given a special pay of Rs. 50 per month during the period they work on the Monitoring Unit.

Ministry of Irrigation and Power

(i) The Member (Commercial) is at present on a scale, the maximum of which is equal to the fixed pay of the other Members. It does not appear that there is any particular justification for such a small differentiation at the Member level and the Member (Commercial) should also have the same remuneration as the other Members.

(ii) There are certain posts in the Farakka Barrage Project which are on the West Bengal Government scales of pay. No recommendations in respect of these scales have been proposed as the project is nearing completion. The nearest revised scales should be given in accordance with our recommendation in respect of corresponding grades.

Ministry of Labour and Rehabilitation

As labour economics is today an integral part of the equipment of the members of the Indian Economic Service, the Government should consider the question of encadering a certain percentage of posts of Assistant Labour Commissioners, Regional Labour Commissioners and Deputy Chief Labour Commissioners in the Indian Economic Service.

Response to recruitment would improve if the Assistant Directors of Mines Safety are placed in the Junior Class I scale, with a simultaneous provision that all the posts in the grade of Deputy Directors Mines Safety should be filled by promotion from among Assistant Directors. There should be a suitable training programme, including a period of attachment to mining corporations in the public sector so as to enable the young recruits to acquire the experience necessary to obtain a First Class Mine Manager's Certificate of competency. There should be a provision as at present for a higher initial start for the mining graduates and diploma holders who join the grade of Assistant Directors on the proposed Junior Class I scale after obtaining a second class Mine Manager's certificate. Direct recruitment would, however, have to continue as at present, to the grades of Assistant Director Mines Safety (Electrical) and Deputy Director Mines Safety (Electrical/Mechanical), since their number is small.

Ministry of Law and Justice

Members of the Central Legal Service mostly work in the Central Secretariat and it is more rational to compare their posts with those in the Secretariat hierarchy rather than with the executive field posts. In order to attract experienced persons from the legal profession and from the State Judicial Services the identity in scales existing at Under Secretary and Joint Secretary's level should be extended to include Deputy Secretary and Director levels also.

The special pay of Rs. 200 allowed to the Government Advocate should be merged with the grade pay and the post should be placed in the scale of Rs. 2500-2750.

Research Officers in the Official Languages (Legislative) Commission should be brought on par with the Research Officers in the Election Commission.

There is no ground for differentiation between the Assistant of the Central Secretariat Service and the Assistant (Legal) in the Ministry of Law. Both should be allowed the same scale of pay.

Department of Company Affairs

The posts of Regional Director may be included in the Central Company Law Service.

The demand for parity in pay scales for legal posts in the Company Law Service with corresponding posts in the Central Service is not justified.

Ministry of Planning

The posts of Adviser, including that of Economic Adviser, should be allowed an appropriate scale of pay within the range of Rs. 2250 to Rs. 3500 p.m. depending upon the job requirements and the qualifications, experience and standing of the person inducted as an Adviser in the Planning Commission.

Ministry of Railways

All the posts of Directors in the Railway Board should be given Joint Secretaries' grade.

The principle of filling up of vacancies in the Railway Board Clerical, Secretariat and Stenographers Service from amongst zonal railway staff is an intrinsically sound arrangement which should be retained.

While not accepting the suggestion regarding exclusive reservation of certain broad categories of posts for Railway Board Secretariat Service officers, these Officers may be given opportunities to hold such posts where field experience is not an essential pre-requisite.

The grade and pay structure of the Railway Board Secretariat Service may be brought in line with that of the Central Secretariat Service.

The pay scales of Directors, Joint Directors, Deputy Directors and Assistant Directors in the Research Designs and Standard's Organisation will be in accordance with the pay structure recommended for similar posts in the Railway Board.

The Divisional Superintendents should be in a single grade instead of two grades as at present.

If an engineering degree is considered essential for the posts of Assistant Directors in the RDSO, there should be no exception, whether the Class II officer under consideration comes from the RDSO or the zonal railway.

The professors in the Railway Staff College, Baroda, who are in the junior administrative grade, may be given a special pay of Rs. 200 per month.

As regards the question of 'major' and 'minor' departments, the idea of having more than one scale of pay for heads of departments is sound. The line of demarcation should not be based on whether a particular post belongs to a 'major' or 'minor' department but whether a post deserves a higher grade or a lower grade on the basis of importance and difficulty of the charge.

The level of Works Managers should be decided with reference to the capital out-lay, annual output, staff strength, product-mix, expansion programme and other related factors. Judged by these criteria, there is justification for the introduction of a higher grade of Rs. 2000-2250 for some of the Works Managers in the Railways.

The problem of temporary officers cannot be satisfactorily solved by the Railway Board alone. The combined resources of the Government and the public sector undertakings would have to be tapped in order to absorb temporary officers with satisfactory records of service in future vacancies in other Government departments and public sector organisations.

The relatively poor career prospects of Class I Railways Services vis-a-vis other Central Services and Engineering Services call for remedial action by Government.

The demand for abolition of direct recruitment of Commercial Apprentices is not justified.

The demand that medically de-categorised staff should not be absorbed in the Commercial Clerks cadre is also not justified.

While the merger of the ticket checking cadre with that of the Commercial Clerks is not favoured, the merger of enquiry-cum-reservation staff cadre may be considered.

Government may consider the feasibility of the merger of the cadre of Weighbridge Clerks with that of the Commercial Clerks.

Government may examine the practicability of merging the cadre of Coal Tracers with the main stream of Claims Tracers and Inspectors, as it would make for uniformity in prospects of promotion and remove a justifiable cause of grievance.

The demand for grant of running allowance to the Travelling Ticket Examiners and Conductor Guards is not reasonable.

The guidelines laid down by the Railway Board regarding filling up of the posts of ASMs which at present, vary widely on different zonal railways.

Government might consider the feasibility of prescribing broad guidelines for the upgradation of posts of Station Superintendents to Class II. With the steadily increasing pace of industrialisation, more stations might qualify for such upgradation.

The demand for abolition of direct recruitment of Transportation Apprentices and lateral induction of allied categories in the Station Master's cadre is not justified.

There is no case for parity of Railway Signallers with the P & T Telegraphists.

The feasibility of establishing uniform incentive rates in the Railways and P & T for Railway Signallers and P & T Telegraphists for performance beyond the prescribed norms may be considered by the Government.

In view of the relatively small cadre of Wagon Movement Inspectors, Government should examine the question of merger of this cadre with that of Transportation Inspectors or, in the alternative, treating these posts as ex-cadre posts.

There should be uniformity in respect of pay scales, grade structure and percentage distribution of posts between the cadre of Assistant Yard Masters and Yard Masters and those of ASMs and SMs to the maximum extent feasible.

On the analogy of upgradation of certain posts of Station Superintendents to gazetted grade, Yard Masters in charge of certain important marshalling yards, who have exceptionally heavy responsibilities, should be given the same scale, which has been suggested for the gazetted Station Superintendents.

There is a case for raising the age limit as well as the quota of Switchmen for promotion as Assistant Station Masters.

The demand for equal scales of pay for Second Firemen and First Firemen on the ground of identical nature of duties and responsibilities is rejected.

The existing classification of Drivers and Guards with reference to the type of trains worked may continue.

The demand for Motormen for parity with the Drivers Grade 'A' on the basis of responsibilities is rejected.

Status quo in regard to rates of running allowance should be maintained, especially as no increase has been recommended in the existing rates of daily allowance. On the other hand, some reduction has been suggested in the rates of daily allowance where free accommodation is provided.

It is not administratively expedient to recommend different rates of remuneration for running staff working on electrical, diesel and steam locomotives.

For the supervisory categories such as Loco Foremen, some posts should be allotted the grade of Rs. 840-1040 on the basis of their worth.

Wherever Mistries are required to supervise highly skilled Grade I workmen as a general rule or wherever the promotion to the grade of Mistries is made from highly skilled Grade II workers, their scale of pay should be Rs. 380-560.

Maintainers should, at present, continue on the same scale of pay as applicable to Workshop staff recommended vide Chapter 19.

The recruitment practice in the P & T Department may be reviewed with a view to elimination of direct recruitment at successive levels, if necessary, by initiating training courses.

A separate 'call duty allowance' for S & T maintainers is not justified.

The demand for increase in the existing rates of out-turn allowance for Wireless Operators is not accepted.

The demand of the Wireless Operators regarding special pay on the lines of Signallers working on the teleprinter service is rejected.

There is no case for grant of high tension allowance for employees working on over-head lines.

There is also no case for grant of breakdown allowance for the traction distribution staff who are required to attend to break-down on overhead electrical equipment.

Regarding different scales of pay of Stores Issuers, Stores Distributors and Material Checkers on different zonal railways, there is need for removing disparities in pay scales as between Railways for performance of identical duties.

The feasibility of filling up of posts of Chief Cashiers by officers of the Indian Railway Accounts Service may be considered by the Government. The Accounts Officer in the senior scale should be given a special pay of Rs. 150 per month when holding the post of a Chief Cashier.

The demand of the Cash Clerks, Cashiers and Shroffs for eligibility to appear in Appendix II-A and Appendix III-A examinations deserves to be considered.

The demand of Appendix III-A qualified staff for reservation of certain percentage of vacancies of Sub-Heads for their promotion is not reasonable.

The demand of the Sub Heads that a certain percentage of vacancies of Accountants should be reserved for unqualified Sub Heads is not tenable.

In view of the large number of Appendix III-A qualified staff awaiting promotion as Accountants for long periods, Government may consider the desirability of holding the Appendix III-A examination at greater intervals, modifying the incentive system, raising the standards of the examination and reviewing the standards for creation of posts.

The principle of a special pay to the staff deployed in the Special Intelligence branch of the RPF is approved. No increase is, however, recommended in the rates of out-fit allowance for these staff in view of the special pay recommended.

Existing rates of special pay for the Armourers in the Armed Wing of the RPF may continue, as at present. Government may also examine the need for granting special pay to specialised trades in the Armed Wing of the RPF.

Pay and grade structure of Operational branch of the Fire Service Wing should conform to the general pattern recommended for the other Wings of the RPF.

Government should ensure a certain degree of continuity and stability in postings of Personnel Officers. Personnel Officers should be given adequate training in personnel and labour welfare matters.

It would be desirable to earmark a substantial percentage of vacancies of Assistant Personnel Officers (Class II) for the Personnel Department staff, the balance being shared by other departments/categories who do not have a regular avenue of promotion to Class II posts.

The question of forming a unified cadre of Welfare, Personnel and Hours of Employment Inspectors may be examined.

Government should consider the question of granting advance increments to employees having specialist qualifications in industrial relations and labour welfare, if such qualifications are considered desirable.

Government should also examine the desirability and feasibility of having intermediate recruitment of persons with Degree/Diploma in Industrial Relations and Labour Welfare, with suitable age relaxation for serving employees having these qualifications.

We suggest that Government may consider the desirability of introducing intermediate recruitment as a regular measure for filling up a proportion of posts of Statistical Inspectors in the proposed grade of Rs. 550-750.

Appointment of an expert departmental committee to rationalise the existing number of designations in the Railways is suggested, so that remuneration is fixed with reference to the duties and responsibilities of a post and its designation correctly reflects the attendant functions and duties.

A comprehensive review of the existing system of grade-wise percentage distribution of posts is suggested with a view to rectifying anamolies.

In connection with the problem of medically de-categorised employees, it is suggested that :—

(i) the occupations or grades in which medically de-categorised personnel are absorbed, should be further widened, if necessary, by arranging re-orientation courses or further training;

(ii) the medically de-categorised persons who cannot be offered alternative employment should be given invalid pension and, if necessary, liberal ex-gratia terminal payments, in addition;

(iii) no medically de-categorised personnel should as far as possible, be forced to remain on extraordinary leave due to administrative delays.

The recommendations made by the Railways Labour Tribunal, 1969, regarding Hours of Employment Regulations need to be reviewed in the light of the following :

(a) Existing principle of 'averaging' for working out the over-time hours is considered salutary.

(b) Over-time allowance may be paid at time rate for the intervening period between the rostered hours and the statutory limits and at 1-1/2 times the normal rate for the period worked beyond the statutory limit as laid down in the Indian Railways Act.

(c) The categorisation of 'essentially intermitent' workers for purposes of rostered hours of work with reference to availability of official accommodation within a stipulated distance of 0.5 km from the place of work is likely to create many practical difficulties.

(d) The existing rules regarding 'travelling spare on duty' appear to be reasonable.

(e) The shifting of the onus for giving notice for relief from the Running Staff to the Railway administration may create practical difficulties.

Ministry of Shipping and Transport

The designation of the post of Chartering Officer in the pay scale of Rs. 1300-1600 should be suitably changed to distinguish it from other posts of Chartering Officer in the pay scale of Rs. 1100-50-1400.

The cadre of Engineering Supervisor should be merged with that of Assistant Engineer.

The cadres of Engineering Assistant and Overseer in the Department of Lighthouses and Lightships should be merged and redesignated as Junior Engineer.

The posts of 'B' grade Light Keeper should be

filled by promotion of Class IV staff. The cadres of Head Light Keeper (Junior Scale) and Assistant Light Keeper (Senior Scale) should be amalgamated and suitably designated. 25 per cent of the permanent posts of Head Light Keeper (senior scale) should be placed in a Selection Grade.

Class IV staff in the scale of Rs. 185-220 should be paid a hardship allowance of Rs. 10 per mensem while working in the Light Houses situated away from mainland. For other staff working in such Light Houses, Government should consider grant of suitable allowance.

The posts of Principal Officer, Mercantile Marine Department, Madras should be placed in the same scale as Principal Officer, Calcutta and Bombay.

In Andaman and Laccadive Harbour Works the cadres of Engineering Assistants and Supervisor should be merged.

Ten per cent of the posts of Civilian Officer Grade I in Border Roads Organisation should be placed in a Selection Grade.

GREF Pioneers should be paid dearness allowance at full rates in future.

For purposes of grant of Project Allowance the qualifying areas should be classified into two categories, 'Construction Project' and 'Maintenance Project'. While in the former both special compensatory allowance and free rations should be admissible, in the latter only special compensatory allowance should be admissible.

Ministry of Steel and Mines

A distinction has been drawn between Senior Technical Assistant of the Scientific stream (geophysics and geophysics instrumentation) for whom an M.Sc. degree has been prescribed and the Senior Technical Assistant (Geophysical Workshop) who is in the Workshop Stream and is promoted from Foreman and Technical Assistant (Geophysical Workshop). The former has been placed on par with other Senior Scientific Assistants and recommended the same scale as proposed for this category in the Chapter on Scientific Services. As for the latter, they should seek their relativity or parity with the workshop category and have recommended likewise. To avoid any confusion the Senior Technical Assistant (Geophysical Workshop) may be designated as Senior Foreman. To maintain this existing internal parity 20 per cent of the posts of Senior Technical Assistants (Geophysical Workshop) should be on the higher scale of Rs. 700-900.

The Senior Technical Assistants in the scientific branches of the GSI should be brought to the level of Senior Scientific Assistants elsewhere and their pay scale should be Rs. 550-900. The pay of Senior Technical Assistants in the mining branch should, on the other hand, conform to what has been generally recommended for the comparable level in engineering categories i.e. the scale of Rs. 550-750. However, in order to maintain the existing internal parity with Senior Technical Assistants in the scientific branch, 20 per cent of these posts should be in the scale of Rs. 700-900.

Ministry of Tourism and Civil Aviation

A substantial percentage of posts of Assistant Aerodrome Officer should be upgraded as Aerodrome Officer and some of the posts of Aerodrome Officer should be upgraded as Senior Aerodrome Officer.

There should not be any direct recruitment to the posts of Assistant Aerodrome Officer. Government should consider whether there should be direct recruitment up to 50 per cent to the posts of Aerodrome Officer.

There should be direct recruitment at the level of Aircraft Inspector only. Direct recruitment at the level of Senior Aircraft Inspector should be resorted to, only if suitable Aircraft Inspectors are not available for promotion.

A flying allowance, to be known as flying bounty, should be paid to both Pilot and Co-Pilot.

Government should consider making licensed Engineers eligible for promotion to the posts of Senior Aircraft Inspectors.

Directly recruited Assistant Aerodrome Officers should be paid full pay scale of the post during the period of training.

A certain number of posts of Assistant Director in the Department of Tourism should be upgraded to junior Class I scale of pay which should be filled up to 50 per cent by direct recruitment. Further direct recruitment to the grade of Director should be reduced from 66-2/3 per cent to 50 per cent of the posts. The posts of Assistant Director in the Class II scale should be filled entirely by promotion of Information Assistants. The Assistant Director in the Class II scale should be promoted to the post of Assistant Director in the junior Class I scale and not to the post of Director.

The posts of Assistant Meteorologist should be filled by promotion only from Professional Assistants.

The employment of scientific staff on purely administrative duties and the promotion of non-scientific staff to the scientific posts in the India

Meteorological Department is not a satisfactory arrangement and should be looked into.

Ministry of Works and Housing, Central Public Works Department

Workcharged staff : The 10 scales of pay applying to the unskilled, semi-skilled and highly skilled categories of the work charged staff should be broad-banded and revised on the lines prescribed in the Chapter on Workshop staff.

The Lift Operators cannot be reasonably equated with either the Assistant Pump Operators or the Pump Operators in the CPWD. However, in view of the fact that Lift Operators come constantly into contact with the public, and further, since they do not have much of a promotion avenue, they should have a better scale than at present.

Town and Country Planning Organisation : Considering the importance in Town Planning, the scale of Chief Planner which is today lower than the pay of a Chief Engineer in the CPWD, has been improved.

Department of Science and Technology : For purposes of promotion within the Class I cadre of the Survey of India the civilian and the army components should be treated as separate cadres.

Direct recruitment to Class I junior grade of Deputy Superintending Surveyors should be resumed without delay from among civilians.

The number of grades in the Division II establishment should be reduced and instead of four there should be only two grades.

In the Division I establishment the grades of Surveyor Grade I and Surveyor Grade II should be merged into a single grade.

Department of Supply : The ordinary and selection grades of Directors in Indian Supply Service and Indian Inspection Service should be merged.

The cadre of Technical Assistant should be merged with that of Examiner of Stores.

Head Clerks in the Inspection Wing of Directorate General of Supplies and Disposals should be placed in the same scale of pay as Superintendents in the Supply Wing.

Cabinet Secretariat : The work done in the Directorate of Revenue Intelligence is comparable with the work of the Central Bureau of Investigation. This should determine the approach to special pays. The special pay of Income Tax, and Customs and Central Excise Officers on deputation to the Revenue Intelligence Organisation should be at the rate of Rs. 200 per month.

Ministry of Petroleum and Chemicals

The difficulties now experienced by the Ministry in recruiting and also retaining suitable men for the posts of Chief Project Officer and Chief of Explorations are not likely to be solved by marginal adjustments of the pay scales. The best solution would be to offer contract appointments on terms to be determined on the merit and availability of the individuals concerned. The recommended scales of pay for these posts are subject to this qualification.

Union Territories : The Union Territories of Delhi, Goa, Pondicherry, Andaman & Nicobar Islands and Dadra & Nagar Haveli, Laccadive, Minicoy and Amindive Island are already following the Central pattern of pay and allowances. This arrangement should continue.

The present linkage of Chandigarh employees with Punjab scales of pay and allowances be continued.

It is not considered worth while to make recommendations regarding the pay and allowances of the employees of Arunachal Pradesh and Mizoram Administration. If the employees and the administrations of these Union Territories express a preference for Central pay scales after the pay scales have been revised, a departmental committee could review the whole position and suggest for posts in Mizoram and Arunachal Pradesh the adoption of one or other of the standard scales introduced on our recommendations.

Where the scheme of revised scales has been recommended in broad terms, the detailed application should be done after some further examination.

The position should be reviewed to identify posts in the headquarters of the Island UT Administrations which could be placed in the scale of Rs. 425-700.

A review may be undertaken in Dadra & Nagar Haveli and if any post carries definite supervisory responsibility over clerical staff, it should be allowed the scale of Rs. 425-600.

In the Andaman & Nicobar Islands, some posts of stenographer attached to senior officers like Chief Secretary, Secretaries and Heads of Departments should be allowed the scale of Rs. 425-700.

Telephone Operators should preferably belong to the clerical cadres.

In Andaman and Nicobar Administration, either 10 per cent of the posts of driver on the scale of Rs. 110-155 and Rs. 110-139 may be placed in the Selection Grade of Rs. 320-400 or if it is possible the posts of drivers of heavy vehicles should be segregated and placed on the scale of Rs. 260-400.

The recommendations made in respect of teaching

posts under the Delhi Administration should be applied to the corresponding posts in the other Union Territories also.

Non-practising allowance should be admissible to doctors on the same rates and subject to the same conditions as recommended for non-C.H.S. posts in the Government of India.

Qualification allowance of Rs. 100 p.m. for possessing a post-graduate degree and Rs. 50 p.m. for post-graduate diploma should be admissible to all the medical posts.

Twenty per cent of the posts of Health Visitor in the various Union Territories be placed in a Selection Grade of Rs. 425-640.

There should be a Selection Grade for the Constables, in the grade of Rs. 225-308.

The number of Selection Grade posts in the Delhi Judicial Service should be raised from 10 per cent to 20 per cent of the permanent strength.

Government should review the provisions regarding the grant of travelling allowance to Patwaris and others working in the Revenue Department. Provisions like the payment of fixed allowance to Patwaris for purchasing articles of stationery and undergoing training at their own expense at the time of promotion as Kanugo should also be reviewed.

Provision of Selection Grade on the scale of Rs. 330-560 should be considered for the Village Level Workers in such of the Union Territories where promotion prospects are not adequate.

Ten per cent of the posts of Mahout in Andaman & Nicobar Islands Administration should be placed in the Selection Grade of Rs. 260-350.

The proposal for a compensatory allowance in Goa has to be considered within the frame-work of the scheme of C.C.A. and not on any special footing.

Increments admissible under normal rules at the time of promotion should not be absorbed in personal pay of the ex-Portuguese employees so that promotion results in an increase in emoluments.

Another option should be allowed to the ex-Portuguese employees who have opted for the Old Portuguese rules regarding pensionary benefits, if Government are satisfied that these employees exercised their option without full knowledge of its implications.

In Pondicherry, the cases of any incorrect equation may be reviewed so that full benefit of the corresponding revised scales becomes available to such employees.

Pensionary contributions at the rate of 8 per cent of pay made by ex-French permanent employees in Pondicherry may either be refunded to them or credited to their Provident Fund on their coming over to the Central Pension Rules.

In Andaman & Nicobar Islands the rate of compensatory allowance should be increased from 7½ per cent to 12½ cent subject to the maximum of Rs. 150 per month. The rates of special allowance would, however, be reduced by 5 per cent in the different areas. The revised rates of compensatory and special allowances should also apply to the officers of the DANI Civil and Police Services and the UT Cadre of All-India Services.

Dependent parents should be included within the definition of 'family' for purposes of free sea passage.

While the temporary character of allowances like compensatory allowance and special allowance and concessions regarding accommodation etc. may be brought out in the Government orders issued on the subject, no specific date need be mentioned after which the matter has to be necessarily reviewed.

The cases of industrial workers serving in the departments of the Andaman & Nicobar Islands Administration on regular operational jobs should be reviewed and these posts brought on to regular establishment where justified.

Our Approach to Armed Forces' Pay

The job evaluation technique can be used with advantage for ensuring a more rational allocation of trades within the different pay groups derived for the personnel below officer rank.

The present structure of pay with the allowances and benefits in kind should continue for personnel of the Armed Forces. The concept of 'all-in' military salary with provision for deduction for ration and quartering charges as now prevalent in the U.K. is not considered suitable.

The most practicable and equitable method for determining the Service pays should be on the basis of fair comparison with the rates of pay fixed for the civilian employees of the Central Government.

Service Officer's Pay

The existing relativity between Service officers and officers of the Class I and the Indian Police Service should be continued as provided a better framework for a broad comparison than any single Service like the Indian Administrative Service.

Factors affecting Service officers generally should be compensated for in the pay itself, unless there is considerable variation as between one group of officers and another. The Special Distribution Allowance which is being granted to all Service Officers up to and including the rank of Brigadier should, therefore, be abolished, the existing rates of this allowance being taken into account while framing the new scales of pay.

Taking into account the Special Disturbance Allowance admissible hitherto, the starting salary of commissioned officers should be higher than in the Civilian Class I Services.

The existing salaries prescribed for officers of the rank of Major General and above in the three Services should be continued.

Although a differential in pay in favour of the officers of the Flying Branch should be continued, the existing lead should be somewhat reduced, with the substantial improvement in the starting salaries of all Service Officers and the increase in the rates of Flying Bounty.

It would be advantageous to consider ways and means for providing opportunities to Service doctors to improve their professional skill so that they do not get the feeling of being isolated from the mainstream of developments occurring in the profession.

The pay scales of AMC officers should be determined with due regard to the existing favourable differentials vis-a-vis the officers of the general cadre as also the pay scales for the medical services on the civil side.

The existing relativities between officers of the AMC and the ADC should be continued.

The rates of Non-Practising Allowance should be related to the rank in the case of medical and dental officers as under :—

Army Medical Corps		Army Dental Corps	
	Rs. p.m.	Rs. p.m.	
Lieutenant	200	175	
Captain	250	250	upto 7 years' Commissioned Service
		400	Captain with more than 7 years and higher ranks.
Major	400		
Lieutenant Colonel and above	600		

The existing parity between pay scales for Army Veterinary Officers and scales of pay of officers of the Army Dental Corps should continue.

Officers of the Military Nursing Service should be provided with comprehensive rates of pay, dispensing with the provision of free services as regards accommodation, allied services, mess servants, etc.

Pay Structure of Personnel below Officer Rank

Inter-Service uniformity in pay scales based on different levels of skills can be considered only after a systematic evaluation of the Service jobs is completed on the basis of a common job evaluation plan acceptable to each of the three Services.

The present practice of establishing equation between the infantry soldier and an industrial workman is the most reasonable.

The relativity in favour of the fully trained infantry soldier should be improved and he should appropriately be placed somewhere between the semi-skilled workmen and those categorised as skilled.

The deduction of a notional ammount representing the anticipated amount of saving to the soldier on account of the provision of free services like food, clothing and accommodation should continue to be made. A deduction of the order of 20 per cent on this account would be fair and reasonable.

The dearness allowance and city compensatory allowance should be allowed to the Servicemen at full rates.

Compensation for 'X' factor, to represent the average degree of hardship, turbulence, hazards etc. inherent in Service life should be taken into consideration while fixing the soldier's pay. An element equal to 5 per cent of the pay would be reasonable for this purpose.

The fully trained infantry soldier should now be viewed as equivalent to the Leading Aircraftsman of Group V with a small differential in favour of the Able Seaman of Group C considering the relatively greater hardship inherent in sea life.

The Army should have 5 pay groups. The existing groups A, B and C should continue without any change, while the existing D, E and F should be amalgamated into one group and G and H into another group. The Air Force should have 4 pay groups, the existing III and IV being combined into one. No change need be made in the case of Navy.

The Army personnel below Junior Commissioned Officers should now be brought over to regular pay scales for each rank as in the Navy and the Air Force, with an appointment pay at the rates specified for the various appointments interspersed between the various ranks in the Army.

The existing system of classes within each pay group for the sepoys and Non-Commissioned Officers in the Army should be continued even after the provision of regular scales of pay for them.

The existing allocation of trades into the various pay groups should not be disturbed except for reallocation consequential to the rationalisation of pay groups in the Army and the Air Force. Reallocation of Service trades to various pay groups should follow the comprehensive and scientific enquiry into the content of Service jobs by a composite team of experts in this line.

Allowances and Benefits of Service Officers

The existing concession of recovery of rent for unfurnished accommodation and concessional rates of recovery of water and electricity charges need not be withdrawn. So long as these concessions are continued, they should be extended to officers of the rank of Major General and above also.

The initial outfit allowance should be raised to Rs. 1400 for the Army and Air Force Officers and to Rs. 100 for Naval Officers. No change need be made in the rates of renewal outfit allowance.

The rate of outfit allowance to MNS officers should be raised from Rs. 600 to Rs. 700 and a renewal outfit allowance of Rs. 500 after every 7 years of service should also be provided to them.

The rates of uniform allowance for MNS (local) officers should be enhanced to Rs. 250 on appointment and to Rs. 375 at specified cold stations.

The need for continuing the Kit Maintenance Allowance should be reconsidered by exploring the possibility of providing an alternative allowing the deduction of a reasonable amount from the annual income, assessable to income-tax. Pending this, the existing rate of Kit Maintenance Allowance of Rs. 50 for officers up to the rank of Brigadier should be continued. This allowance should also be extended to officers of the rank of Major General and above.

The existing provisions relating to free ration and accommodation on posting to field service areas should continue. These concessions should not be extended to Naval Officers serving afloat when the ship is in the home port.

While the Separation Allowance should continue there is no case for increasing the existing rate of this allowance.

There is no need for the grant of a new field service allowance.

The High Altitude and Uncongenial Climate Allowance should be enhanced to Rs. 175 per mensem for Major, Rs. 125 per mensem for Captain and Rs. 100 per mensem for Subaltern, respectively. Officers of the Military Nursing Service should also be allowed this allowance at the same rates.

There is not much justification for providing an addition to pay for acquiring higher qualifications while an other remains on duty and draws his full pay and allowances. The existing system of Qualification Pay should be abolished as soon as possible and replaced by a system of Qualification Grants.

No Qualification Grant should be admissible to officers merely for obtaining the membership of a professional institute without having to pass any examination or obtaining any additional qualification for that purpose alone.

While Flying Bounty should continue as annual allowance, the condition of flying the prescribed number of hours during a year for entitlement to flying bounty should be removed and flying bounty admitted only on the basis of the certificate of the Commanding Officer. The rate of flying bounty should be Rs. 4500 per annum for officers up to the rank of Wing Commander, Rs. 4,000 per annum for officers in the rank of Group Captain and Air Commodore, and Rs. 3600 for Air Vice Marshal and Air Marshal.

The Air Observation Post Pay should be redesignated as Flying Allowance in all the three Services. The rate should be revised from Rs. 50 to Rs. 75 per mensem.

Submarine Allowance should be continued at the existing rates.

The rate of Submarine Pay should be enhanced to Rs. 275 per month for all officers of the Submarine cadre including the Sub. Lieutenant.

The Diving Allowance should be revised to Rs. 100 per month for Clearance Diving Officers and Deep Diving Officers and Rs. 50 per month for Ship's Diving Officers. The normal rate of Dip money should be revised to rates varying, depending upon depth from 10 paise per minute to 70 paise per minute. The Clearance Diving Officers should be paid Dip money at twice the normal rate and Deep Diving Officers at normal rates.

Hardlying Money should not be paid on all classes of ships. The rate of Hardlying Money should be increased to Rs. 45 per month for officers in the rank of Lieutenant and above and Rs. 35 per month for officers below Lieutenant's rank.

Survey Allowance at the present admissible to officers of the Executive Branch employed on survey duties for short spells should be discontinued. Survey bounty should be enhanced to amounts varying between Rs. 1000 and Rs. 2000 per annum.

Allowances—Personnel below Officer rank

Compensation in lieu of quarters should be

enhanced to amounts varying from Rs. 35 to Rs. 80 for Class I cities, Rs. 25 to Rs. 65 for Class II cities and Rs. 20 to Rs. 60 for Class III cities, reclassification of cities being made as under :—

Class I to include existing A, B1 and B2 cities
Class II to include 'C' class cities or towns
Class III to include all other cities or towns

There is no need for providing Special Disturbance allowance for the personnel below officer rank specially after an element is included in their pay on account of the 'X' factor.

Special Compensatory Allowance should be revised to amounts varying from Rs. 15 to Rs. 35 for personnel below officer rank of the Army and Air Force. This allowance should not be extended to cover any station in a peace area.

The rates of High Altitude and Uncongenial Climate Allowance should be revised as under :

Honorary Commissioned Officers, JCOs including Flight Sergeants	Rs. 90 per mensem
NCOs	Rs. 70 per mensem
Sepoys and Aircraftsmen, and Non-Combatants enrolled	Rs. 50 per mensem

The rate of Flying Bounty for personnel below officer rank serving as aircrew in the Navy and Air Force should be revised to Rs. 2250 per annum.

The system of Qualification Pay or Grant for the personnel below officer rank should not be introduced.

The rate of Subsistence Allowance in respect of families of other ranks should be enhanced to Rs. 60 per mensem.

The rates of Outfit Allowance for Junior Commissioned Officers granted Honorary Commission should be increased from Rs. 600 to Rs. 800.

Additional prescribed items of Kit should be provided at Government expense to Non-Commissioned Officers who are promoted as Junior Commissioned Officers.

The initial grant for purchasing items of civilian clothing should be enhanced from Rs. 20 to Rs. 25.

Conveyance Allowance for Servicemen using cycles should be paid at flat rate of Rs. 5 per month.

It does not appear necessary to make changes in regard to Good Service Pay in the Services.

The Master Chief Petty Officers should be entitled to Submarine Allowance at the daily rate of Rs. 2.

The rates of Submarine Pay should be revised to amounts varying between Rs. 100 to Rs. 175 per month for personnel below officer rank of the Submarine branch.

The rates of Survey Bounty should be enhanced to amounts varying between Rs. 300 and Rs. 700 per annum.

The rates of Diving Allowance for Clearance Divers Classes 1, 2 and 3 should be enhanced to Rs. 75, Rs. 65 and Rs. 55 per month respectively. Deep Sea Divers should also be paid Diving Allowance at the rate recommended for Clearance Divers. For Ship's Divers, the rate of Diving Allowance should be increased to Rs. 50 per month.

Dip Money to the Sailors should be paid at the rates as recommended for the Naval Officers.

The rates of Hardlying Money should be revised to accord with the revised rates of the Special Compensatory Allowance admissible to Army and Air Force personnel.

Non-effective Benefits for Service Officers and Personnel below Officer Rank

The grant of pension should be so regulated as to enable Servicemen to earn full pension at a relatively younger age compared to the civilians.

The length of service beyond a point should not be allowed to influence pension rates in the Service as that would induce personnel to stay on in service to earn higher pensions even after they have ceased to be useful.

An element of compensation in the pension rates should be provided explicitly to cover early retirement in Service interest.

The existing system of standard rates of retiring pensions related to rank and prescribed length of qualifying service should continue.

The rate of earning pension should be the same as for civilians, viz. 1/80. Compensatory element for truncated career should be provided (i) by adding to the period prescribed for earning pension of the rank, a period of 5 years for officers retiring in the ranks of Brigadiers and below, with an extra year for officers retiring in the rank of Major and 2 years in the rank of Captain and below and (ii) by assessing pension on the basis of maximum pay of rank.

For senior officers, the pension should be determined on the basis of reasonable differentials.

Recommendations on the DCR Gratuity Scheme on the civil side should apply to the Service Officers also.

The amount of retiring gratuity prior to reduction for DCR Gratuity should be enhanced to Rs. 12,000 for 10 years' service and Rs. 1200 for each additional year of service. In the case of MNS officers, the rate should be enhanced to Rs. 600 for each completed year of service. Deduction for DCR Gratuity should continue to be made at existing rates.

Deduction for shortfall in qualifying service should continue to be made at existing rates from the amount of Disability Pension.

The amount of disability element should be increased to Rs. 200 for 100 per cent disablement with a minimum of Rs. 40 for 20 per cent disablement. For officers of MNS, the amount of disability element should be Rs. 170 for 100 per cent disablement and Rs. 34 for 20 per cent disablement.

Officers invalided out of service for less than 20 per cent disability attributable to service should be given the Service element of disability pension, without addition of any amount as a disability element.

The rate of Constant Attendance Allowance should be enhanced to Rs. 60 per month.

Invalid pension should be determined at the flat rate of 75 per cent of the service element of disability pension.

The Ordinary Family Pension Scheme for Service officers should continue to be based on the corresponding scheme on the civil side. For special Family Pension also the Extraordinary Family Pension Scheme on the civil side should be adopted for the Service Officers.

The existing percentages should be applied to the Extraordinary Pension admissible to the widows in working out pensions admissible to parents. The rate of pension for each brother or sister in the absence of parents, should be raised to Rs. 50 per month, the ceiling being 50 per cent of the Extraordinary Family Pension admissible to the widow.

The existing provisions relating to the 'means limit' and the 'support limit' in the case of Dependent's pension should be reviewed.

The rate of Children's Allowance should be increased to Rs. 600 per annum per child if the mother is alive and Rs. 900 per annum per child in the case of motherless children.

The limit for reimbursement of the actual expenses incurred on the education of children of a deceased officer should be raised to Rs. 50 per month per child.

Entitlement to pension should continue to be for the minimum qualifying service of 15 years. Pension of personnel below officer rank should be calculated by applying the formula of 1/80th of emoluments but weightage of 5 years should be added to the prescribed length of qualifying service subject to the total length of service reckonable for pension not exceeding 33 years.

For calculating the emoluments for pension the maximum pay of the scale, good service pay (and class pay in the Army) and the notional home saving element should be taken into account. For this purpose the following amounts will be taken as the notional home saving elements for the various ranks:

	Rs.
Sepoy	47.25
Naik	50
Havildar	55
Naib Subedar	70
Subedar	80
Subedar Major	85

DCR Gratuity should be provided as per the provisions applicable to the civilian employees.

Reservists who do not earn a pension should be paid an enhanced reservist fee of Rs. 30 per mensem.

The rates of diability element of the Dibability Pension for 100 per cent disablement should be enhanced for the various ranks, ranging from Rs. 45 for the Sepoy, Rs. 60 for the Non-Commissioned Officers, Rs. 110 for Junior Commissioned Officers and Rs. 170 for officers granted Honorary Commission.

In the case of personnel who are invalided out of service with a disability of less than 20 per cent attributable to service, the service element of disability pension should be allowed.

The rate of Constant Attendance Allowance should be enhanced to Rs. 45 per month.

The provisions relating to Ordinary Family Pension and Special Pension prescribed for civilians should continue to apply to the ordinary and special family pensionary awards of personnel below officer rank.

Dearness Allowance

The supply of essential commodities to Central Government employees at subsidised rates is not a feasible proposition. A periodical revision of pay as compensation for rise in prices would also be a highly cumbersome process. The employee should, therefore, continue to be compensated for the increase in prices by the grant of dearness allowance.

Dearness Allowance should be treated as a compensation to the wage earners and salaried employees against a possible rise in prices over the index level to which the pay structure is related.

The All India Average Consumer Price Index Number for Industrial Workers (General) with 1960 base published by the Labour Bureau should be adopted for the purpose of granting dearness allowance to Central Government employees in future.

The existing formula whereunder the changes in the cost of living are measured in term of changes in a fixed number of points over a period of 12 months should continue. However, adjustments in dearness allowance should be made when the 12 monthly average of the index (1960—100) changes by 8 points.

Government should not be bound to automatically sanction an increase in dearness allowance according to any given formula even when the circumstances require that restraint should be exercised on wages and wages and incomes is adopted, it should not be, confined to Government employees alone but should cover the entire organised sector.

The various categories of employees should be brought within the purview of the scheme of dearness allowance in the following manner :—

Rise in prices over the base period (12 monthly average of 200 points of the index with 1960 base) adopted for devising the pay structure	Employees to be covered
(1) For the price rise of first 8 points in the 12-monthly average of the 1960 base index.	(1) All employees drawing revised pay upto Rs. 900 per mensem with suitable marginal adjustments.
(2) On the index average rising by 16 points.	(2) Employees at (1) above plus all employees drawing revised pay upto Rs. 1600 per mensem with suitable marginal adjustments.
(3) On the index average rising by 24 points.	(3) Employees at (1) and (2) above plus all employees drawing revised pay above Rs. 1600 and upto Rs. 2250 per mensem with suitable marginal adjustments.

When employees in any of the higher pay ranges are initially brought within the purview of the dearness allowance scheme, the total amount of dearness allowance to be given to employees in that range should not be less than the amount admissible at the highest pay range for the category already covered by the dearness allowance scheme. When the index average rises above 24 points the various categories of employees should be covered by the dearness allowance scheme in the same manner as for the first rise of 8 points and the cycle should be repeated. The pay plus dearness allowance should in no case, exceed Rs. 2400 per mensem.

The dearness allowance should be granted as per the following formula in future :—

Pay range	Amounts of dearness allowance admissible for an increase of 8 points in the index average (1960—100)
Rs. p.m.	
Upto 300	3½ per cent of pay subject to a minimum of Rs. 7 and a maximum of Rs. 10 per mensem.
Above 300	2½ per cent of pay subject to a minimum of Rs. 10/- per mensem and a maximum of Rs. 20/- per mensem.

Should the price level rise above the 12 monthly average of 272 (1960—100), Government should review the position and decide whether the dearness allowance scheme should be extended further or the pay scales themselves should be revised.

The question whether a portion of dearness allowance should be treated as pay for specified purpose should continue to be decided by the Government having regard to various considerations.

The payments on account of dearness allowance should be rounded off to the nearest 10 paise. Government may also consider whether a similar rounding off could be resorted to in respect of all the other cash payments made to Government employees.

Compensatory Allowances

I. Compensatory (City) Allowance : (i) The existing restriction that the place of duty of a Government employee should be within a distance of 8 kilometres of the municipal limits of a city for the purpose of determining his eligibility for C.C.A. should be relaxed. The allowance should be made admissible to all employees whose place of work falls anywhere within the 'Urban Agglomeration' of a city or town as adopted for the population Census of 1971. An 'urban agglomeration' should be treated as one unit of population for the purpose of determining the class to which the city belongs and C.C.A. at the rate recommended for that class be granted to all employees whose place of duty falls within the agglomeration.

(ii) The proposed rates of Compensatory (City) Allowance are as follows:

Class of city/town	Rate of C.C.A.
'A' Class	
Below Rs. 250	6-1/2 per cent of pay subject to a minimum of Rs. 12.
Rs. 250 and above	6 per cent of pay subject to a maximum of Rs. 75.
'B'-1 Class	
Below Rs. 330	5 per cent of pay.
Rs. 330 and above	4.5 per cent of pay subject to a maximum of Rs. 50.
'B'-2 Class	
Below Rs. 750	3.5 per cent of pay subject to a maximum of Rs. 50.
Rs. 750 and above	Amount by which pay falls short of Rs. 759.
'C' Class	No allowance.

(iii) A city or town which for any special reasons may be abnormally expensive but does not qualify for grant of Compensatory (City) Allowance on the basis of population, should be given special consideration on merits.

II. House Rent Allowance : (i) The Government should take houses on long lease and make residential accommodation available to its employees on payment of 10 per cent of their pay.

(ii) Government should lay down appropriate rates of house rent allowance for different cities and towns not on the criterion of population but on the basis of the prevailing levels of rent. Alternatively, notional rents for different types of accommodation meant for employees in specified pay groups should be laid down for different cities and towns. The difference between the actual rent paid and 10 per cent of the pay should be reimbursed provided the actual does not exceed the notional rent; where it does, the extent of reimbursement will be limited to the difference between the notional rent and 10 per cent of the pay.

(iii) Till the Government is able to make the above mentioned arrangements the rates of House Rent Allowance should be as follows:

Class of City/Town	Rate of House Rent Allowance (H.R.A.)
A, B-1 and B-2	15 per cent of pay subject to a maximum amount of Rs. 400 as house rent allowance.
C Class	7½ per cent of pay subject to maximum amount of Rs. 200 as house rent allowance.

(iv) Production and verification of rent receipts should be made compulsory in all cases. However, the employees who are at present drawing House Rent Allowance without production of rent receipts should be allowed this facility so long as they claim the same amount as House Rent Allowance as they are receiving at present. This concession should apply to fresh entrants also.

(v) In hill stations and unhealthy and remote localities where a house rent allowance is now admissible under special orders, it should continue to be paid.

(vi) Unlike Compensatory (City) Allowance, House Rent Allowance will not be admissible at the same rate as in the main city in areas covered by the Urban Agglomeration around it.

III. Housing Facilities

(i) The Government should redouble its efforts to build more houses. The houses meant for lower classes of employees should receive preference in the construction programmes. Further, the unit cost of construction should be brought down so that the available funds could be utilized for the construction of a relatively larger number of houses.

(ii) There is at present a very wide variation in the ratio between demand and provision in respect of Government quarters in different places and among the metropolitan cities. It would be desirable to allot quarters in Calcutta, Bombay, Madras and other big cities with a concentration of Central Government Employees.

(iii) The Posts and Telegraphs Department lags very much behind the others in the matter of the extent of provision of residential accommodation of its employees. Special efforts are necessary to make up the leeway.

(iv) The percentage of pay charged on account of house rent for Government accommodation will remain unchanged. The pay limit up to which rent is recoverable at 7-1/2 per cent should be raised from Rs. 200 to Rs. 300 in the revised pay structure.

(v) In the case of employees who are regularly or frequently transferred, separate pools of accommodation should be established by setting apart an adequate number of quarters for allotment.

(vi) The Ministry of Defence should increase the housing facility for their civilian employees; further, the feasibility of sparing from the general pool some quarters near the cantonment area for such employees may be examined.

IV. Rent Free Quarters

(i) The existing practice of providing rent-free accommodation to certain categories according to the criteria presented by the Second Pay Commission should continue.

(ii) In regard to the extent of compensation allowed when free Government residence is not actually provided to an employee who is entitled to it, there should be uniformity in different departments. The quantum of such compensation should be equal to the amount charged as rent for Government accommodation from quarters. In the classified cities, this should be in addition to the house rent allowance but the two together should not exceed the actual rent paid. The revised rules should apply only to those who are able to produce house rent receipts; for others the existing rates will continue.

(iii) For linemen in the Posts and Telegraphs Department, compensation should be raised to Rs. 10 in the unclassified towns; in classified cities the same amount should be paid in addition to the admissible House Rent Allowance. In the case of these employees also, the stipulation regarding production of house rent receipts will be the same as in (ii) above.

V. Other Compensatory Allowances

For grant of differential rates of hill compensatory allowance height of the hill stations alone should be the criterion, and hill stations should be classified into the following categories :-

(i) Hill stations situated at a height of 1000 metres of more but below 1500 metres, and

(ii) Hill stations situated at a height of 1500 metres or above.

The Hill Compensatory Allowance should be paid to all employees, irrespective of pay drawn, at the following rates :-

(i) At hill stations situated at a height of 1500 metres or more as per the rates of compensatory (city) allowance applicable in 'A' class cities.

(ii) At hill stations situated at a height of 1000 metres or more but below 1500 metres as per the rates of compensatory (city) allowance applicable in B-1 class cities.

Winter Allowance should be paid at the following rates to all employees getting a pay up to Rs. 1250 per mensem :-

Station	Rate of Allowance
(i) Hill stations situated at a height of 1000 metres or more but below 1500 metres.	Same rate as for compensatory (city) allowance in B-I Class cities subject to a minimum of Rs. 10 and a maximum of Rs. 25 per mensem.
(ii) Hill stations situated at a height of 1500 metres or above.	Same rate as for compensatory (city) allowance in 'A' class cities subject to a minimum of Rs. 15 and a maximum of Rs. 40 per mensem.

The present practice of paying bad climate allowance to Central Government employees at those places where the State Governments allow a similar allowance to their own employees should continue. Bad areas should be granted to Central Government employees getting pay upto Rs. 900 per mensem as per rates applicable for compensatory (city) allowance in B-1 Class cities.

Project Allowance to the Government employees belonging to various departments but working at the same project sites should be sanctioned as follows :-

(i) In respect of Central Government projects, orders should be issued centrally by the Government so that there is no time lag in the grant of the project allowance to the affected employees of the various Ministries/Departments.

(ii) In respect of State projects, Central Government employees should be given the project allowance from the date they join their duties at the project site if State Government employees are already getting the project allowance.

Government should determine the revised rates of the Project Allowance taking into account the revised rates of pay, rates for other compensatory allowances, etc.

The phased reduction or the final withdrawal of the project allowance should be linked with the progress made in the provision of schools, markets, medical facilities and reasonable housing facilities within the project area or in its proximity.

The question whether the existing rates of border allowance/difficult terrain allowance etc. need revision should be decided by the Government in the light of the revised scales of pay and the new rates of other compensatory allowances.

VI. All India Transfer Liability Allowance

With the coming into force of the proposed scales of pay, the rate for purposes of calculating the amount of the all-India transfer liability allowance, where admissible, should be reduced from 10 per cent to 7½ per cent till such time as the orders of October 1970 continue to remain in force. The allowance should not be extended to other categories.

VII. Risk Allowance

(i) The Government should appoint a Committee which should examine cases where the staff are already in receipt of risk allowance with a view to putting it on a rational basis.

(ii) A comprehensive review of the provisions of the Workmen's Compensation Act should be undertaken with regard to possible changes in the rates of compensation, the list of specified hazardous occupations and the coverage of the Act.

(iii) Priority should be given to finding alternative employment for employees of the BCG Vaccine Laboratory who are not allowed, in the public interest to continue in the laboratory even after they have been cured of T.B. infection.

VIII. Transport between Place of Work and Residence

There need not be a general extension of either the free transport facility or the grant of subsidy for expenditure on transport. In cities where CCA is admissible, a part of it is expected to cover the extra cost on transport. However, in the case of employees especially those of Defence, Meteorological installations, Posts and Telegraphs, Civil Aviation etc., who have to come on or come off duty at odd hours of the night or to travel long distances from rest houses in between two spells of duty, some assistance is necessary in the form of free transport, subsidy or a conveyance allowance. The exact nature and scale of assistance will be decided by the Government depending on local conditions.

Travelling Allowance

The revised gradation of Central Government employees for the purpose of travelling allowances, daily allowance etc. should be as follows :-

Grade I	Rs. 1000 and above
Grade II	Rs. 650 and above but less than Rs. 1000
Grade III	Rs. 330 and above but less than Rs. 650
Grade IV	Less than Rs. 330

Reservation charges for a seat (for day journeys) and sleeper berth (for night journeys) should be paid to Grade III and IV employees.

The system of separately paying incidentals and a halting allowance (daily allowance) for journeys on tour should be replaced by a system of daily allowance for the entire period of absence from the headquarters including the journey time, on the pattern of the existing practice followed on the Railways. Full daily allowance should be granted for each completed day of absence from the headquarters reckoned from midnight to midnight. Daily allowance may be paid at the following scale for absence of less than 24 hours :

Absence exceeding 12 hours and upto 24 hours	Full Daily Allowance
Absence exceeding 6 hours but not exceeding 12 hours	50 per cent of the Daily Allowance
Absence of less than 6 hours	30 per cent of the Daily Allowance

Officers drawing the revised pay of Rs. 2250 and above should only be entitled to travel by ACC first class. The levy of surcharge of one paisa per kilometre should be dispensed with. The same limit should apply to railway employees also.

The revised pay limit for air journeys may be Rs. 2250 except that employees drawing pay between Rs. 1800-2250 in the revised scales may also travel by air at their discretion if the distance involved is more than 500 kilometres and the journey cannot be performed overnight by rail.

The rate of road mileage for a journey by car/full taxi should be 40 paise per kilometre and by motor cycle/scooter 15 paise per kilometre. Employees belonging to Grade I and II only should be entitled to travel by car/taxi.

Daily allowance should also be admissible for journeys on tour by road to meet incidental expenses.

The rates of conveyance allowance should be as follows :-

Average monthly traval on official duty	Rates of conveyance allowance for journeys by	
	Owned Motor Car	Other modes of conveyance
	Rs.	Rs.
210-300 kms.	100 p.m.	35 p.m.
301-450 kms.	150 p.m.	50 p.m.
451-600 kms.	175 p.m.	60 p.m.
601-800 kms.	200 p.m.	70 p.m.
above 800 kms.	225 p.m.	75 p.m.

The revised pay limit for admissibility to the conveyance (car) allowance should be Rs. 1000. This limit may be relaxed in the case of doctors and any other special categories.

Conveyance allowance should be attached to a post and not sanctioned separately for each employee holding the post.

The rates of daily allowance, where employees have to stay in hotels or other establishments providing board and/or lodging at scheduled tariffs may be as follows :-

Grade (pay in the revised pay scales)	Ordinary places	Delhi/ Madras, Simla, Jammu and Kashmir etc.	Bombay/ Calcutta and Central Hill Areas
	Rs.	Rs.	Rs.
I. Rs. 1000 and above.	35.00	40.00	50.00
II. Rs. 650 and above but below Rs. 1000	25.00	30.00	35.00
III. Rs. 330 and above but below Rs. 650	15.00	20.00	25.00
IV. (a) below Rs. 330 (Class III employees)	12.00	16.00	20.00
(b) Class IV employees	6.00	8.00	10.00

In other cases, the existing rates of daily allowance should continue. Government should prescribe flat rates of daily allowance based on the existing rates for each grade of employees.

Full daily allowance may be granted to government employees for the first 30 days of halt on tour.

If only free lodging is provided to an employee on tour, he may draw 3/4th of the daily allowance instead of half and in case only free board is provided he may draw ½ of daily allowance as at present. Railways should consider either levying charges for the accommodation provided to the railway employees on tour in the railway rest houses, or reducing the daily allowance of such employees by 1/4.

The definition of family adopted by the Railways for the purpose of transfer travelling allowance may be extended to other Government employees also.

The revised rates of transfer grant may be as follows :-

Grade	Pay Range	Transfer Grants
	Rs.	Rs.
Grade I	2000 and above	500
Grade I	1000-1999	400
Grade II	650-999	300
Grade III	330-649	200
Grade IV	Class III employees other than those covered by Grade II and III	150
Grade IV	Class IV Employees	100

Transfer incidentals may be replaced by daily allowance for the employee as well as for the members of his family, children below 12 years being given half the daily allowance.

The revised scale of baggage allowance may be as follows :-

Grade	With family	Without family
Grade I	Full Wagon	2000 kilograms
Grade II	3000 kilograms	1000 ,,
Grade III	1500 ,,	750 ,,
Grade IV	600 ,,	250 ,,

Employees on transfer may transport their personal effects by road between points connected by rail subject to the cost not exceeding the cost of transportation of the maximum permissible quantity of personal effects by goods train.

A retiring employee should be granted transfer travelling allowance on the same scale and subject to the same terms as admissible to a serving employee on transfer including transfer grant, daily allowance (in lieu of incidentals) and cost of transportation of the conveyance where entitled. Leave travel concession should not be granted in the year of retirement.

A retiring employee should be granted transfer travelling allowance to a station of his choice in India subject to the amount being limited to what would have been admissible to him had he proceeded to his declared home town.

The concessions mentioned in items 19 and 20 above should also be admissible mutatis mutandis to the family of an employee who dies while in service.

There should be uniformity in regard to the rates of daily allowance, road mileage and conveyance allowance between railway and other employees. The Railways should also fall in line with the civil departments in regard to the baggage allowance and transfer grant.

Children of employees staying away from them for the prosecution of their studies may be allowed free travel by third class for a distance beyond 150 kms once a year to and from a school or college during an approved vacation to join their parents at the station of posting of the Government employee.

Leave Travel Concession

A. Railway Employees : The present rail travel privileges of railway employees should, as a first step, be reduced to the level recommended by the Estimates Committee (Fourth Lok Sabha). The number of passes of the gazetted officers should be reduced to the level admissible to the non-gazetted officer at present. The number of PTOs should be reduced from 6 to 3 per year for both gazetted and non-gazetted officers. The facility for taking attendants on First Class 'A' and First Class Passes should be abolished but lady officers including Lady Health Visitors and Nurses may be allowed to take one attendant provided they are not accompanied by their husband or other male relative. Only those members of the family should be eligible to travel on free passes and PTOs as are covered under the Travelling Allowance Rules for journeys performed on transfers.

All railway employees of Class I, Class II and Class III who retire after having rendered more than 20 years' service should be allowed one set of free passes every year. No change need to be made in the provisions concerning the travel concession available to retired railway servants of Class IV.

The present limits for entitlement to different classes of persons should be reviewed to avoid a situation where a very large number of railway employees become entitled to a First Class Pass on the introduction of the revised scales of pay recommended by us. Those who are today entitled to a Second Class Pass should not become entitled to travel in the first class on the abolition of the second class passenger compartment considering the liberal standard already adopted in the grant of First Class passes.

B. Central Government Employees excluding Railway Employees and Armed Forces Personnel

The existing provisions as regards journeys to home-towns once in a block of two years should be continued with the modification that once a block of four years, every Government employee should be allowed to avail of the LTC for journeys to any place in India subject to other prescribed conditions.

The definition of family for purposes of the LTC should be the same as under the Travelling Allowance Rules.

The employees should be permitted to avail of the LTC for journey performed during casual leave also without specifying any minimum period of absence.

C. Armed Forces Personnel

(i) Service Officers : The existing concession should continue and the limit of 965 kms should not apply in the case of journeys undertaken to home-town. Dependent children should be allowed the same travel concession as the officer's wife once in a block of two years. For travel concessions, the definition of family should be the same as for the civilian employees of the Central Government. The extra leave travel privileges enjoyed by officers engaged on flying and submarine duties should be continued.

The use of Form D concessions should be limited to 3 sets in a year, a set covering both the outward and the return journey. This facility should however, be available in excess of this number for certain specific purposes like children going to a boarding school and returning to parents, journeys in connection with medical treatment in military hospitals, etc.

(ii) Personnel below Officer rank : For journey to home station once every year, the free concession voucher should cover the Serviceman's wife and children also and in every alternate year, he along with wife and children should have the option to travel in a leave station with Government bearing the cost of the outward and return journey upto a distance of 965 kms every way. For travel concessions, the definition of family should be the same as in the case of Service officers. The expenditure on account of half the rail fare in respect of family members that is being borne today by the Servicemen should be reimbursed to them.

Educational Facilities and Allowances

All the existing schemes of educational facilities and allowances should continue with the modifications recommended in respect of each.

As in the Railways, the children's educational allowance should be admissible to employees in other departments also only if a school of the requisite standard does not exist at the station where an employee is posted or on account of non-availability of accommodation in such a school. The certificate regarding non-availability of accommodation in a school of the requisite standard should be obtained from the district educational authorities or similar authority.

Children's educational allowance should be admissible to the Central Government employees drawing pay upto Rs. 1200 per mensem at the following rates :

Primary classes	Rs. 15 per child
Secondary and Higher Secondary classes	Rs. 20 per child

The total amount of the allowance should be restricted to Rs. 60 per mensem per employee.

The upper pay limit for admissibility of reimbursement of tuition fee should be raised to Rs. 1200 per mensem.

With a view to reducing the administrative and accounting work, the tuition fee should be reimbursed on production of certificates twice a year from the head of the school giving particulars of the children studying in the school, the classes in which they are studying, the amount of the fee charged, etc. A similar certificate should be obtained when children are transferred from one school to another.

Government should consider opening more subsidised hostels for the children of the Railway employees.

There should be no upper pay limit for payment of hostel subsidy and the hostel subsidy at a uniform rate of Rs. 60 per mensem per child should be admissible to all Central Government employees who because of their transfer are required to keep their children in a hostel. The subsidy should continue to be limited to not more than three children, and the total number of children who may avail of the hostel subsidy and children's educational allowance should not exceed four. The hostel subsidy should be extended to the children residing in the hostels of all recognised schools.

The benefit of the scheme of children's educational allowance, reimbursement of tuition fee and payment of hostel subsidy should, subject to the other conditions being fulfilled, be admissible (i) to all permanent and quasi-permanent Central Government employees, and (ii) to all temporary employees who have completed not less than one year's service.

In order to satisfy the assessed needs of employees Government should take steps to open as many more Central Schools as possible.

Where an employee is transferred from one station to another in the middle of an academic session and shifts his children to a school requiring purchase of a new set of books, he should be granted a subsidy at the following rates :—

Primary classes	Rs. 20 per child
Secondary classes	Rs. 40 per child
Higher Secondary classes	Rs. 60 per child

The subsidy should be available to employees drawing pay upto Rs. 1600 per mensem and be admissible up to a maximum of four children.

Death-cum-Retirement Benefits

The age of superannuation of Central Government employees should continue to be 58 years.

Government should look into the lack of uniformity in regard to the age of superannuation of Class IV employees in the railways and in other Government departments and remedy the position as circumstances permit.

There should be no change in the existing age of superannuation of police personnel in the Border Security Force and the Central Reserve Police under the relevant Acts.

The retirement of Government servants should take effect from the afternoon of the last date of the month in which they attain the age of compulsory retirement instead of the afternoon of the actual date of their superannuation.

The existing provisions for the compulsory retirement of Government employees before they have reached the normal age of superannuation which are directed towards maintaining the efficiency and integrity of the public services are salutary and should continue.

No change should be made in the existing provisions relating to voluntary retirement of Central Government employees.

The benefit of pro-rata pension and gratuity at present admissible to scientific employees on absorption in autonomous organisations like C.S.I.R., I.C.A.R., Central Universities, etc. should be extended to the various categories of technical personnel also on similar absorption in these organisations.

The existing arrangements under which Class I and some of the Class II officers are required to take permission from Government before taking up commercial employment within two years of their retirement should continue. These restrictions should also be made applicable to the employees governed by the Contributory Provident Fund Rules and to those who are allowed to retire voluntarily under the existing rules.

The existing provisions, under which pension can be sanctioned and continued only if certain conditions, mainly related to safeguarding the efficiency and integrity of the Government service, are satisfied, should continue.

Emoluments for purposes of pension should continue to be calculated over a period 36 months as at present.

No change is considered necessary in the existing formula for computing pension. However, the maximum qualifying service for pension should be increased from 30 years to 33 years.

The upper pay limit for the grant of pension should be raised from Rs. 1800 to Rs. 2500 per mensem. The existing ceiling on maximum pension should also be raised from Rs. 675 per mensem to Rs. 1000 per mensem.

Death-cum-retirement Gratuity should continue to be calculated on the existing basis. The qualifying years for earning gratuity should, however, be increased from 30 years to 33 years, and the upper pay limit for earning gratuity should be raised from Rs. 1800 to Rs. 2500 per mensem. The maximum amount of gratuity should also be raised from Rs. 24,000 to Rs. 30,000. The exemption limit on gratuity for purposes of tax liability should be increased from Rs. 24,000 to Rs. 30,000.

The existing provisions regarding service gratuity do not need any change.

Government should fix the special contribution admissible to the railway employees governed by the State Railway Provident Fund Scheme as they deem fit keeping in view the improvements recommended in pension and gratuity in the case of other Government employees.

The existing arrangements under which the Government employees are required to contribute partly toward the financing of the family pension scheme should continue. While the contribution of the employees should continue to be equal to two months' emoluments, the maximum amount of contribution should be raised from Rs. 3,600 to Rs. 5,000.

The rates of family pension as also the ceilings should be revised as follows :—

Pay of the Govt. Servant	Amount of family pension per mensem
Below Rs. 400	30 per cent of pay, subject to a minimum of Rs. 60 and a maximum of Rs. 100.
Rs. 400 and above but below Rs. 1200	15 per cent of pay, subject to a minimum of Rs. 100 and a maximum of Rs. 160.
Rs. 1200 and above.	12 per cent of pay, subject to a minimum of Rs. 160 and maximum of Rs. 250.

In case an employee dies after having rendered a minimum service of 7 years, the family pension should be paid at an enhanced rate equal to 50 per cent of the last pay drawn or twice the family pension at the above rates, whichever is less, for a maximum period of 7 years or till he would have attained the age of 65 years, whichever is earlier. In case of death after retirement the amount of family pension at the enhanced rate should exceed the normal superannuation pension (uncommuted value) to which the Government employee would be entitled to on superannuation. Further, in such a case, the family pension should be given only to those who were members of the family of the Government employee as declared at the time of the retirement.

Government should consider introducing a contributory family pension scheme for the railway employees governed by the State Railway Provident Fund Scheme.

While there should be no change in the existing conditions for grant of invalid pension, the amount of invalid pension should not be less than the amount of family pension at the ordinary rates.

Temporary and quasi-permanent employees should continue to be paid a terminal gratuity only as heretofore.

Temporary employees with a continuous service of 5 years or more and all quasi-permanent employees should be paid a terminal gratuity at the rate of half a month's pay for each completed year of service below 10 years, and for continuous service of 10 years or more at the rate of one month's pay for each completed year of service subject to a ceiling of Rs. 15,000, or 15 months' pay whichever is less.

The amount of terminal gratuity to a temporary or quasi-permanent employee should not be less than the amount which he would have got as a matching

Government contribution to the provident fund if he were on the Contributory Provident Fund Scheme from the very inception of his continuous temporary service. The matching contribution of the Government in such cases should be worked out so as to be equal to the amount actually contributed by the temporary employee himself to the provident fund subject to the matching contribution not exceeding 8-1/3 per cent of his pay. The benefit of a contributory provident fund should not be extended to temporary and quasi-permanent employees who are made permanent, and who should on confirmation be automatically brought over on the pension scheme applicable to the other permanent Government employees.

The benefit of added years of service to specially qualified or experienced personnel appointed to posts where these qualifications are necessary in the public interest should continue. The posts where the grant of this benefit is considered essential should be identified in consultation with the Union Public Service Commission and the Ministry of Finance and a suitable provision incorporated in the relevant recruitment rules so that the benefit is automatically available to all the candidates who are recruited in accordance with the provisions of those rules. Further, in the advertisements issued by the Union Public Service Commission for recruitment to such services and posts, it should be mentioned that this benefit would also be available.

The basic criterion for an award under Extraordinary Pension Rules should be whether the death or injury is attributable to service or aggravated by service rather than the existing distinctions with reference to the 'risk of office' and 'special risk of office'.

The existing classification of injuries into A, B and C classes for the grant of benefits under these rules should be replaced by a list similar to that under the Workmen's Compensation Act, which should form a part of the rules.

The family pensionary benefits to widows and motherless children under the Extraordinary Pension Rules should be rationalised after their rate structure brought in line with the benefits admissible under the family pension scheme. The family pension under the Extraordinary Pension Rules should, however, be paid at the higher rates for the entire period and not limited to 7 years as in the case of family pension scheme. In addition to the widow's pension, gratuity, children allowance and children's education allowance should continue to be admissible as at present.

Pension under Extraordinary Pension Rules should not be granted to an employee if he continues to be in service and earns his monthly salary. In such cases, he should be paid a compensation in lump sum only. However, if the disability results in invalidment out of service, the existing arrangement of paying a monthly pension should continue.

The amount of invalid pension under the Extraordinary Pension Rules should not be less than the amount of family pension that would be admissible to the widow under these rules.

A scheme, under which all Government employees will be required to pay a single rate of contribution of Rs. 5/- per mensem (returnable without interest in cases of superannuation, etc.) for an insurance cover of Rs. 5,000/- should be introduced. The scheme should be optional in the case of existing permanent employees and temporary employees with one year's service on regular establishment but should be made compulsory for all such categories of employees who enter Government service in future. No advance for any purpose should be allowed to the employees out of the amounts contributed by them under this scheme.

The rate of interest on the Provident Fund balances of the Central Government employees should be broadly comparable with the interest allowed by the nationalised banks on long term deposits.

Government should introduce an arrangement of issuing pass books to the employees showing the upto date position of their provident fund balances.

All future pensioners, irrespective of the amount of pension drawn up by them, should be given a relief at the rate of 5 per cent of their pension subject to a minimum of Rs. 5/- per mensem and a maximum of Rs. 25/- per mensem on the 12-monthly average of the All India Working Class Consumer Price Index (1960—100) rising by 16 points. The relief for the first time at these rates should be paid when the 12 monthly average of this index reaches 216.

The recommendations with regard to death-cum-retirement benefits of Central Government employees would also apply to the personnel belonging to the All India Services and with a few exceptions, to the employees of Union Territories.

Hours of Works, Holidays and Overtime Allowance

The gross working hours prescribed in the industrial establishments under the Government should be 48 hours in a week and 8 hours in a day. Within this period of 8 hours the workers should be allowed a break for half-an-hour to take their meals, thus yielding a net of 45 hours per week. As regards the industrial establishments where the net weekly hours of work are less than 45, the position should be reviewed.

The disparities existing in different railway zones due to shorter hours of work in some for purely historical reasons should be removed by increasing the net working hours, where necessary, to 45 per week.

The hours prescribed for the administrative offices should be 7 effective hours a day, exclusive of lunch break.

No change need be made in the existing arrangement of giving only the Second Saturday of the month as a holiday, to employees in the administrative offices.

Some arrangement should be devised for giving the categories of staff, who are not assured a regular weekly off e.g. chowkidars, watchmen, cooks, waiters, sweepers, etc., a rest day at least once in a fortnight.

An employee should be given a compensatory off when he is called to work on his normal off-day, and where it is not practicable to do so in the interest of Government work he should be monetarily compensated.

No section of employees should be allowed more than 16 holidays in a year.

The practice of declaring one of the restricted holidays as a public holiday whenever any of the approved 16 closed holidays falls on a Sunday or a Second Saturday, should be discarded as soon as possible.

No change need be made in the system of restricted holidays except that an attempt should be made to control the number of Festivals declared as restricted holidays.

No change in regard to the number of public holidays need be made in respect of those employees who are entitled only to 3 national holidays or 9 effective holidays.

The existing quantum of casual leave is quite adequate; all operating and maintenance staffs who are entitled to less number of public holidays in a year than the number allowed to the office staff in administrative offices should be allowed 15 days casual leave. No class of employees should be allowed more than 15 days' casual leave in a year but in case a higher amount of casual leave has been allowed in certain cases due to remoteness of the region, one or two days' journey time should be allowed whenever a person goes to his home-town on casual leave.

For workshop staffs outside the railways, the system of special non-cumulative leave should be abolished and the quantum of casual leave in their case should be increased from 7 days to 12 days in a calendar year.

The system of overtime allowance should be withdrawn in respect of categories and establishments to which the practice was extended subsequent to the recommendations of the Second Pay Commission, while it may continue in other cases, including categories which are governed by the provisions of enactments such as the Factories Act, and the Hours of Employment Regulations, but where some of the overtime expenditure now being incurred is due to the shortage of staff, such shortages should be made up expeditiously. Where overtime working, as a regular measure, is unavoidable as happens in certain operative offices, the compensation should be in the form of off-days rather than through cash benefits.

For the categories which would become ineligible for overtime, a system of compensatory offs and payment of honoraria should be introduced. Honoraria should, however, be considered only for compensating the over-stayal during the periods of unusual activity or due to unforeseen circumstances such as the compilation of the Budget, Parliamentary work during sessions, organisation of large conferences, fairs, etc. and work connected with emergencies.

Where the system of overtime work continues the period of overtime should be calculated on a weekly basis and should be admissible only if the work put in during the working week of six days exceeds 48 hours; in reckoning these 48 hours the period allowed for meal break should be included.

In organisations like the Government Presses where the prescribed weekly hours are less than 48, and the work done between the prescribed hours and the weekly norm of 48 hours is compensated in the form of overtime at double the time rate, compensation for such work should be only at the time rate in future.

The definition of 'night' as the period between 2200 hours and 600 hours is reasonable. The present weightage of 10 minutes for every hour worked is also adequate. Government may examine the question of bringing about uniformity among the various departments in regard to the definition of night duty and the weightage.

So far as P & T department is concerned, the employees may be given an option either for cash compensation on the same terms and conditions as recommended for other Central Government employees or for continuance of the existing system of restricted duty hours.

For the calculation of cash compensation, only pay and dearness allowance should be taken into account and other compensatory allowances excluded.

Weightage for night duty or financial compensation

in lieu should be granted only when night duty calls for continuous performance of related tasks without considerable interludes of inaction or rest.

No night duty allowance should be granted in those cases where the weekly working hours have been fixed at a reduced level taking the occurrence of night duty into account.

No weightage for night duty should be allowed to those categories of employees who may be called upon to perform night duties only occasionally.

There should also be no justification for such duty in an inseparable characteristic of the job itself, i.e. nurses, sister-in-charge in hospitals, etc.

Leave Entitlements

No change need be made in the case of workshop staffs whose earned leave is governed by the provisions of the Factories Act, 1948 supplemented by Departmental instructions. The Civilian in Defence Services (Industrial Employees) Leave Rules 1954 should be repeated. The amount of annual leave earned by the railway workshop staff should be reduced by 12 days.

In the case of non-industrial staffs, no change need be made in the rate of earning leave, the limit on accumulation of earned leave and the limit on the period of leave that can be availed at any one time. The existing differentiation between permanent and temporary employees in regard to earning leave in the first year of service should be abolished.

At present employees proceeding on earned leave from a post the maximum of which does not exceed Rs. 300 are entitled to draw leave salary equal to the last pay drawn. The limit of Rs. 300 should be raised to Rs. 600.

The present limit of Rs. 750 on leave salary during half pay leave should be dispensed with.

The present limit of 240 days on commuted leave during the entire service should be removed. Half pay leave up to a maximum of 180 days of such leave should be allowed to be commuted during entire service where such leave is utilised for an approved course of study.

The special provisions made in the Study Leave Rules for officers of the Indian Economic Service, the Indian Statistical Service and medical officers should be extended to many more categories of specialists and technical personnel on merits of each case. For courses of study pursued in India, the emoluments during study leave should be regulated in the same way as during earned leave subject to the emoluments not exceeding the pay that the officer would have otherwise drawn had he remained on duty. No study allowance should be paid during this period. The existing provisions relating to study leave availed outside India should continue. The rates of study allowance admissible in foreign countries should be reviewed by the Government from time to time.

In the case of Departmental Leave, the Department concerned should review the position and allow as leave salary from 10 per cent to 25 per cent of pay. In such cases, leave salary should be paid on a monthly basis for the first three months and threafter it should be payable when the Government servant returns to duty. Departmental Leave should not be debited to half pay leave, and for purposes of calculating the amount of half pay leave due 'year' should be construed, not as meaning a calendar year in which duty is performed but as twelve months of actual duty.

Leave Rules should be amended to specify that a female Government servant should be granted maternity leave only if she has less than three living children at the time of application for such leave.

In case of death in harness, the cash equivalent of the leave salary that the deceased employee would have got had he gone on earned leave on the date of death, should be given to his family subject to a maximum of leave salary for 120 days.

Medical Facilities

The Central Government Health Service Scheme (CGHS) should be extended to other cities and towns on a priority basis.

The facilities provided under the C.G.H.S. should be improved.

Government should review the procedure for local purchase of medicines by the C.G.H.S. dispensaries to make it more expeditious and delegate more powers, if necessary, for the purpose to the medical officers incharge of the dispensaries.

The contributory basis of the C.G.H.S. as also the existing rate of contribution should be maintained.

In rural and other areas not adequately served by the existing authorised medical attendants, selected registered medical practitioners may be declared as authorised medical attendants.

The practitioners of indigenous system of medicine should also be declared as authorised medical attendants provided they are in Central or State Government employment. Employees should have the option to consult them and claim reimbursement.

Industrial and work charged staff should be entitled to the same medical facilities as are available to non-industrial employees and on the same terms and conditions.

Government should review the existing rates of consultation/visiting fees charged by the authorised medical attendants keeping in view the present day conditions.

The revised pay limits in the new scales of pay for reimbursement of diet charges should be Rs. 640 in the case of patients suffering from Tuberculosis and Mental Diseases and Rs. 400 in the case of patients suffering from other diseases.

Prescription of a monetary ceiling on reimbursement of medical claims is not considered desirable. A system of selected review of medical reimbursement claims should, however, be introduced.

Railways employees at way-side stations and on branch lines should be allowed to avail of the medical facilities available at the nearest recognised hospital without the prior approval of their authorised medical attendant and get reimbursement of expenses. A scheme of empanelment of registered medical practitioners for this purpose may also be introduced.

All Central Government employees may be subjected to a compulsory medical examination at the ages of 40, 45 and 50 and thereafter at intervals as recommended by the Ministry of Health and Family Planning. A beginning may be made by extending the scheme to the employees covered by the Central Government Health Scheme, Railways and Ordnance Factories may also cover such of their employees as are posted at places having hospitals run by the Central Government.

Staff Amenities

Uniforms : The Government may take note of the views expressed by a large section of the employees against the use of Khadi for the fabrication of uniforms.

The changes in the existing scales and standards of supply of uniforms as also in the amount of washing allowance, are matters which can be more appropriately settled by the Government in consultation with the staff.

The attention of the Government is drawn to the need for ensuring the timely supply of uniforms of the proper fit.

The demand for the grant of a kit allowance in lieu of the supply of ready made uniforms is not accepted. For the nursing staff, etc., instead of giving a uniform allowance the Government may examine the feasibility of supplying special grades of cloth (cotton, woollen or synthetic) and sanctioning an amount towards tailoring charges, leaving it to the officials to have their uniforms stitched in conformity with the regulations.

Canteens : It would not be possible to bring about uniformity in the standards applicable to canteen provided under the Factories Act and other canteens since the provisions made for the purpose under the Factories Act differ from State to State. However where the provisions made under the departmental rules are more favourable these should be adopted even in respect of the canteens provided under the Factories Act.

Canteens in certain Ministries are often used as meeting places at all hours of the day; these should be kept open only during the specified hours.

Advances to Government Servants : The maximum amount of advance for the purchase of motor cars should be raised to Rs. 18,000, for motor cycles/scooters to Rs. 3,500 and for cycles to Rs. 250/-.

Government should consider whether having regard to all relevant factors, a lower rate of interest could be prescribed in respect of advances for house building purpose at least in respect of loans advanced to employees drawing less than Rs. 900 per mensem.

Government should consider whether the existing amount of Rs. 200 as an advance for purchase of warm clothings could be enhanced in view of the increased prices of woollens. An appropriate advance for the purchase of warm clothings should be paid to Class II and Class I employees also on their first posting to a hill station.

Other Welfare Measures : There is considerable scope for providing more space and for improving the office accommodation in use by better lighting, improved ventilation, use of exhaustive fans, greater cleanliness, and more liberal use of paint. There is scope also for rearranging furniture, record rooms, etc. to make the atmosphere more liveable.

While construction of the new building should take time, improvement to existing buildings can be undertaken quickly and at a comparatively low cost. The other essential facilities like rest houses, rest rooms and dormitories should receive the close attention of the Government. The provision of rest houses etc., is also a comparatively less expensive proposition. The Government should attend to these matters with expedition.

Even though the provision of some of the welfare amenities would have to depend to a large extent on the concentration of staff at particular places, in certain other matters e.g. establishment of and the contribution by the Government to the employees' welfare funds, there should be some degree of uniformity in the different departments.

The idea behind a Holiday Home which provide lodging and other facilities at cheap rates for the benefit of the employees is sound and this facility should be extended further. In locating these holiday homes the Government should pay attention to the usual social habits of the generality of its employees.

A systematic study should be made of the trend of indebtedness among the employees and if its proportions show undue increase, the Government should consider steps to remedy the situation, including a scheme of financial assistance in hard and deserving cases.

Miscellaneous

I. Classification of Services : (i) We are inclined to the view that some kind of a classification based on an assumed equivalence of the work content in the different levels of the various occupational groups and, hence of the pay ranges, is necessary for purposes of personnel administration.

(ii) We have, however, formed the impression that the term 'Class' presently in vogue has acquired overtones that could, with advantage be avoided, so as to create a healthy psychological climate. It should be possible to describe the existing classes and 'Groups' as the Government itself seems to have contemplated at one time. In other words, it may be feasible to redesignate the existing Classes I, II, III and IV as Groups 'A', 'B', 'C' and 'D'. We recommend accordingly.

II. Temporary and Quasi-Permanent Status : (iii) We feel that the existing proportion of one fourth of the staff being temporary is too large and recommend that in permanent departments it should, in course of time be brought down to about one-tenth.

(iv) In departments which are themselves considered temporary, or which, by the very nature of their work (as in Ordnance Factories) must carry a somewhat larger component of temporary staff, the position should be periodically reviewed, so that as large a number of temporary staff as possible are made permanent. Temporary employees should be allowed relaxation in age to compete for appointment to permanent posts that fall in the same category.

(v) The quasi-permanent status is a valuable right specially to those serving in temporary posts in the temporary departments, in as much as efforts are more likely to be made to fit them elsewhere, if the necessity should arise. We, therefore, recommend that quasi-permanent status may continue to be conferred on the eligible temporary staff employed in temporary organisation. Elsewhere, there seems to be no specific need for this practice and the Government should consider dispensing with it.

III. Industrial and Non-Industrial Employees : It appears to us that there are broadly two possible approaches, viz :

(a) to exclude all Government industrial workers from the purview of the labour laws, and treat them as an excludive category to be governed solely by the statutory rules and orders issued from time to time by the Government in exercise of its powers under Article 309 of the Constitution, or

(b) to segregate the industrial workers of the Government from its non-industrial workers, and to give them all the facilities and safeguards to which industrial workers in general are entitled under the labour laws. Simultaneously, it should be ensured that the various rules and orders normally applicable to Government servants generally are not extended to the industrial workers of the Government. Even so, however, without an amendment to Article 311 of the constitution, an industrial Government worker still be entitled to certain safeguards denied to non-government industrial workers.

Staffing and Efficiency in Government Service

The additional expenditure arising out of the implementation of our recommendation can be justified only if there is no wasteful expenditure due to overstaffing and inefficiency; and productivity in the public service is maintained at fairly high level.

The pooled messenger system should be adopted in Government offices in preference to the peon system. The system of appointing helpers to assist the skilled workers in workshops as well as outside should be discontinued to the extent feasible.

The desk officer system should be adopted in the Secretariat with necessary changes in recruitment procedures and personnel deployment.

There is need for a regular and systematic review of the prescribed staffing norms with reference to changing patterns and conditions of work and also for periodical overhaul of the procedures and system of work with a view to improving efficiency in the offices.

The three organisations, namely, Department of Administrative Reforms, Staff Inspection Unit and Organisation and Methods and Internal Finance Branches in each Ministry should be strengthened and their range of activity diversified with a view to achieving the objective of improving efficiency at minimum cost. Outside management consultants should also be used wherever necessary.

The scope for economy and improvement of efficiency appears to be greater in departments like Posts and Telegraphs which employ very large complements of staff. The Railways should explore the possibility of curtailing staff by introduction of mechanised track maintenance, automated marshalling yards, improved signalling and telecommunication facilities for better traffic control, etc. The justification for automation should be based not merely on staff savings but also on the overall cost of the scheme taking into account capital investment, interest, depreciation, etc.

The system of providing peons at residences of certain categories of officers is an anachronism and should be done away with.

(i) Fragmentation of inter-related functions resulting in a proliferation of categories should be avoided by combining such duties in a single person.

(ii) It should be ensured that existing promotion prospects of staff are not affected due to reduction in the number of posts in the base cadre.

There is an urgent need to look into the working of the Armed Forces. In view of the considerable scope for economy, without in any way affecting the fighting potential or the efficiency of the Armed Forces.

The existing pervasive system of checks and cross-checks needs to be replaced by a system where the points of control are few but effective.

It should be possible to curb excessive proliferation of staff by curtailing fresh recruitment and confronting it only to meet the essential needs. Essential manpower requirements for the implementation of different plan schemes should be met by internal recruitment of existing staff rather than by fresh recruitment. Government should exercise maximum stringency in sanctioning additional posts.

Any saving in the total wage bill can be fruitfully utilised for more productive employment elsewhere. The solution of the unemployment problem is not to absorb labour in the Government sector but create conditions under which more labour can be employed for productive purposes within or outside the Government. A shift in investment towards economically sound labour-intensive industries is indicated.

A Pay Body should not be burdened with the task of collection and collation of data concerning the functions, recruitment qualifications, promotion avenues, pay scales and number of various posts under the Government. Such information should be made available to it in a processed form from its very inception.

A permanent machinery for systematic collection of reliable and comprehensive data regarding pay scales, fringe benefits, service conditions, etc. of employees not only in the Government but also in the Public and Private Sectors should be set up. If there are difficulties in voluntarily collecting the relevant data, Government may consider the desirability of enacting suitable legislation for the purpose.

Cadre management should receive urgent attention.

A cautious beginning should be made with the use of job evaluation techniques.

Determination of pay scales of employees not specifically covered in the report should be examined by a Central Agency.

The creation of a 'Standing Body on Pay and Cadre Management' has been suggested to advise Government on the following matters :-

(i) Cadre reviews;

(ii) Regrading of any class of employees based on the results of job evaluation studies;

(iii) Pay revision of any class of employees either on its own motion or on a reference from the Government;

(iv) Creation of new scales not provided in the pay structure;

(v) Determination of pay scales of employees who might not have been covered in our Report.

The proposed scales of pay should be made applicable from the Ist March, 1973.

The recommendations on pensionary benefits should be made applicable to those Government employees who retired on or after Ist March, 1973. In respect of these employees the emoluments for computing the pensionary benefits should include, in addition to pay and dearness pay (wherever applicable), the dearness allowance and interim reliefs drawn by them.

Employees drawing pay up to and including Rs. 1800 per mensem in the existing scales should have their pay fixed in the proposed scales after adding to their existing emoluments an amount representing 5 per cent of the existing pay (whether substantive, officiating or acting) subject to a minimum of Rs. 10 and a maximum of Rs. 50 and subject to the various other conditions stipulated for the fixation of pay in the proposed scales.

Employees drawing pay above Rs. 1,800 per mensem in the existing scales should have their pay fixed in the proposed scales under the Fundamental Rules 22, 23 and the relevant Audit Instructions.

The concordance tables should be regarded as being held in abeyance so far as the fixation of pay in the proposed scales of the existing employees is concerned.

STUDY GROUP ON THE DEVELOPMENT OF THE PRESCHOOL CHILD, 1970—REPORT

New Delhi, Ministry of Education and Social Welfare, 1972; 100p.

Convener : Smt. Mina Swaminathan.
Members : Shri M.C. Nanavatty; Smt. Kitty Shiva Rao; Dr. (Smt.) Margaret Khalakdina; Dr. (Kum) C. Nayar; K.J. Majuna Bai; Dr. (Smt.) R. Muralidharan; Dr. O.P. Ghai; Shri Anil Bordia; Smt. Champalakshmi Ventakachalam.
Member-Secretary : Shri J.P. Naik.

APPOINTMENT

At its 35th meeting held at New Delhi in May, 1970, the Central Advisory Board of Education considered the services provided at present and those needed for the preschool child and made the following recommendations in Resolution No. XVIII :

"The Board recognises the significance of primary education and commends the proposal to try out pilot projects by mobilizing local community resources especially in rural areas".

Accordingly, the Ministry of Education and the Department of Social Welfare (which was then a part of the Ministry of Law and Social Welfare) jointly set up a Study Group to examine the question and to prepare a programme of action for the development of the preschool child through the mobilisation of local resources, especially in rural areas.

TERMS OF REFERENCE

The terms of reference of the Study Group are as follows :

"to examine the question and development of the pre-school child through the mobilization of local resources, especially in rural areas."

CONTENTS

Introduction; Need, Significance and Objectives; Existing Services; A Plan of Action; Operational Moderls; Training of Personnel; Equipment and Literature; Research and Evaluation; Administration; Local Community Participation; An Appeal; Summary of Main Findings and Recommendations; Appendices from I to IX.

RECOMMENDATIONS

Need and Significance

Integrated services combining education, health, nutrition and welfare are essential for the total development of the preschool child and should receive high priority and adequate resources.

Objective

The objective of such services should be to promote the optimum physical, mental, emotional and social development of the preschool child.

The different agencies concerned should make concerted and coordinated efforts to provide these services.

Collection of Data

Basic data collected at regular intervals are essential for a proper planning, implementation and evaluation of programmes for the preschool child. The Department of Social Welfare may be designated and adequately equipped to collect and publish this data annually.

Special Features that need Emphasis

In drawing up a programme of service for the preschool population, special attention needs to be given to the vulnerable groups of children, remedying inbalances in the distribution of services, coordination among the agencies involved in the programme, expansion and reorientation of the training programmes and provision of guidance and supervision.

The New Approach

Strategies that would help in undertaking a sizable programme within the limited resources available include mobilising community support and involvement, employing local women in rural areas, part-time employment of educated women and students, maximum utilisation of existing institutions and facilities, and adoption of a variety of models.

Targets

About one million children in the age-group 3-5 are covered at present by existing services. A reasonable and feasible target of enrolment would be to cover 10 per cent or 5 million children by 1981 i.e. one million more children by 1973-74 and a further 3 milion by 1981, priority being given to children from the urban slums, tribal areas and under-privileged groups in rural areas.

Need for Variety and Experimentation

(a) Flexibility and response to the needs of each situation are essential to maximise the benefits of the programme. A variety of operational models has been suggested which may be adapted to each situation in the most advantageous manner possible. These include the comprehensive Day-Care Centre mainly for urban slums, half-day Balwadis, first stage centres, Anganwadis mainly for rural areas, and Primary school-based centres.

(b) The special needs, difficulties and circumstances of the tribal areas call for an unorthodox approach and increase accent on community participation.

During the initial period (1972-74) greater emphasis will have to be placed on the low cost models. In the subsequent seven-year period, the improvement in the position expected regarding resources and trained personnel will facilitate the adoption of a larger proportion of the more comprehensive and hence costlier models.

Training of Personnel

The training and orientation of various categories of workers is essential for the success of the programme and should be accorded high priority. An adequate training programme of good quality should be designed for all categories of workers. It will also be necessary to create three new categories of workers : the local woman worker and the supervisor.

The special features of the training programme recommended include :

(1) Alterations of the primary teacher training curriculum so as to bring primary and preschool education closer together;

(2) Modification of the pre-primary training course so as to bring it in line with the course for the Balsevikas;

(3) Provision of new training courses for all categories of workers, including sandwich type courses and vaccation and orientation courses;

(4) Orientation towards urban, rural and tribal environments; and

(5) Integration of extension, training and research in all training units.

Equipment

Provision of suitable and adequate play and education equipment is essential for the success of the scheme. Scales of equipment have been suggested for the different models striking a mean between the optimum desirable and maximum possible. The State and local community should both contribute to provide these.

A variety of methods should be adopted to provide the necessary equipment, including mass production, local fabrication, class room improvisation, collection of folk toys, etc. and contribution of simple furnishing by the local community. Assistance should be given to institutions to establish prototype design units and display centres.

Literature

The existing literature on the subject being meagre, immediate steps should be taken to produce the needed literature for teachers, teacher trainees, teacher-educators, supervisors, administrators and planners, the community and the children themselves.

Research and Evaluation

Special emphasis should be laid on the development of appropriate programmes of research.

A programme of evaluation should be built into the different programmes recommended in the report, and should be the continuous responsibility of the supervisory staff and of the agencies at the district, State and national levels.

Administration

Implementation of a comprehensive programme of the kind detailed in this report requires a strong administrative machinery at all levels—National, State, District and Local (Rural and Urban).

National Level

In order to ensure a strong and effective central machinery for the coordination of the programmes at the national level, a National Committee for the Preschool Child should be set up under the Chairmanship of the Union Minister for Education and Social Welfare. A Directorate for Preschool Programmes will look after the effective implementation of the decisions of the Committee.

State Level

The Department which would be responsible for administration of this scheme at the State level will differ from State to State. Where more than one department is involved, a suitable coordinating machinery will need to be created. A full-time officer should be made responsible for the programme.

District Level

The District being the most appropriate administrative unit for effective coordination in the field, a suitable coordinating committee should be set up with representatives from various agencies engaged in schemes of child welfare. A full-time officer of the status of a district officer and working directly under the Collector should look after the implementation of the programme.

Local Bodies—Rural

Supervisors placed under the control of Zila Parishad or Panchayat Samiti should be provided facilities of transport to enable them to function effectively.

Local Bodies—Urban

A Standing Committee of the municipal authority concerned should supervise the programme in Urban areas. A special officer should be entrusted with the execution of the programme.

Estimated Costs

The total cost on the programme during 1972-74 will be Rs. 23.2 crores (Rs. 19 crores recurring and Rs. 4.2 crores non-recurring). This will involve an additional expenditure of Rs. 17.6 crores over and above what is already budgetted for nutrition programmes under the Department of Social Welfare.

Local Community Participation

The maximum amount of community participation should be mobilised for the development of the preschool child. Such participation would include contribution in terms of voluntary services and contribution towards buildings, equipment and feeding programmes. Well-to-do communities should also extend support to those less advantageously placed. In addition, local bodies should explore all avenues to raise resources for preschool child services.

At the field level all the programmes for the preschool child should be coordinated and implemented by a single field worker so as to convey the idea of integrated services to the community.

CENTRAL ADVISORY BOARD OF EDUCATION, COMMITTEE ON SCHOOL BUILDINGS, 1970—REPORT

New Delhi, Ministry of Education and Social Welfare, 1970; 65p.

Chairman : Union Education Minister
Vice-Chairman : Prof. A.K. Kisku.
Members : Shri C.H. Mohammed Koya; Shri Surjit Singh; Shri B. Patnaik; Minister for Education, Government of Goa, Daman and Diu; Shri S.D. Patil; Shri A.C. Deva Gowda.
Member-Secretary : Shri T.K. Jayaraman

APPOINTMENT

The Central Advisory Board of Education in its 35th meeting held on May 2-3, 1970 passed the following Resolution :—

"The Board emphasises the urgent need to provide building to educational institutions, especially at the primary stage. In its opinion, this massive problem can be tackled only if local resources are harnessed and a scheme is devised under which it would be possible to make loans available to State and local Governments and voluntary organisations at minimum rate of interest. The possibility of the nationalised banks making some funds available for this programme should be explored and, as a long-term measure a Central Financing Corporation for educational buildings may be set up. Full use should be made of the work done at the Central Building Research Institute, Roorkee, to reduce constructional costs". The Union Education Minister appointed a Committee in 1970.

TERMS OF REFERENCE

Following were the terms of reference of the Committee :—

(i) to examine the problem; and
(ii) to prepare concrete proposals for action.

CONTENTS

Background; Meetings; School Buildings Requirement; Funds for Loans for Construction of School Buildings; Setting up a Central Financing Corporation; Local Resources; Reduction in the Cost of Construction; Annexures from I to VIII; Charts.

RECOMMENDATIONS

The Committee has estimated that Rs. 90 crores will be required for the additional buildings for the primary and secondary schools started before the commencement of the Fourth Plan. The Committee has assumed that 50 per cent of the amount required for the construction of school buildings will be available through popular contribution. The Committee urge the Government of India to set apart Rs. 10 crores per annum for the next ten years as grants to the State Governments specifically for construction of school buildings. If necessary, half of this amount may be given as loan and the rest as grant.

Since the construction of school buildings would create additional employment opportunities for educated unemployed, teachers as well as engineers, overseers, caprenters etc. a revolving fund of at least Rs. 10 crores may be set up from which loans could be given to the States for the construction of school buildings.

It is considered desirable to set up a Central Financing Corporation for educational buildings. An outlay of Rs. 14 crores spread over a period of 7 years at the rate of Rs. 2 crores per year would allow a revolving fund to be set up to be administered by the proposed Corporation.

In order to mobilise local resources for school buildings following steps are recommended :—

(a) Funds may be collected through lotteries.

(b) Local people may be asked to donate one or two rooms at the time of birthdays, marriages etc.

(c) Religious institutions may be encouraged to donate buildings as part of their programme.

(d) Other avenues like staging plays, organising exhibitions should be explored for raising funds for school buildings.

(e) Contribution in kind such as cement, food for paying for labour etc. may be collected.

The cost of school buildings may be reduced by adopting the designs and suggestions of the Central Building Research Institute.

Priorities may be assigned for construction of new buildings, highest priority being given for schools now being held in open and for completing incomplete buildings followed by schools conducted in tents, and those having rented accommodation.

INDIA, BANKING COMMISSION, STUDY GROUP ON NON-BANKING FINANCIAL INTERMEDIARIES, 1970—REPORT

Delhi, Manager of Publications, 1972; 285p.

Chairman : Dr. Bhabatosh Datta

Members : Shri D.A. Ambekar (replaced by Shri Jawaharlal A. Darda); Shri R.S. Bhatt; Shri A.B. Billimoria; Shri D.N. Kaveeshwar; Shri M. Narasimham; Shri S.D. Pardiwalla; Shri T.S. Santhanam.

Convener : Shri A Hasib.

APPOINTMENT

The Banking Commission which started functioning in March 1969, was appointed by the Government of India to examine the banking system of the country and make recommendations for improving its structure and extending its geographical and functional coverage. According to one of its terms of reference, the Commission was also asked to "review the role of various classes of non-banking financial intermediaries, to enquire into their structure and methods of operations and recommend measures for their orderly growth". In order to make a detailed study of the existing non-banking financial intermediaries and to examine the question whether specialised financial institutions were required by the economy, the Banking Commission constituted the Study Group on Non-Banking Financial Intermediaries vide Office Order No. BC/S/NBFI-1 dated June 4, 1970.

TERMS OF REFERENCE

1. To review the role of the various classes of non-banking financial intermediaries at present existing in the country such as Unit and Investment Trusts, Chit Funds, Nidhis, and Loan Companies, the other finance companies;

2. To enquire into the structure and methods of operations of these non-banking financial intermediaries and to recommend measures for their orderly growth (Insurance Companies and Development Banks such as the I.D.B.I., I.C.I.C.I., S.F.Cs, would be excluded from the purview of the Group);

3. To consider what other types of non-banking financial intermediaries such as specialised savings banks, building societies, consumer finance companies, Export-Import Bank, Small Scale Industries Bank, etc. are needed for the proper development of the economy;

4. To recommend appropriate measures therefor; and

5. To make any recommendations on any other related subject matter as the Study Group may consider germane to subject of enquiry or any related matter which may specifically be referred to the Group by the Commission.

CONTENTS

Part I : Preamble; Scope and Method of Study; Approach of the Study Group;

Part II : Study of Existing Non-Banking Financial Intermediaries, Hire-Purchase Finance Institutions; Investment Trust Companies and Unit Trusts; Chit Funds; Nidhis; Finance Corporations;

Part III : Need for Specialised Institutions; Examination of the General Case for establishing Specialised Institutions; Merchant Banking Institutions and acceptance and Discount Houses; Need for an Export-Import Bank in India; The Need for a Small Scale Industries Bank; The Need for Specialised Savings Banks in India; Need for Specialised Institutions for Housing Finance; Need for Specialised Institutions for Consumer Credit; Summary of Major Conclusions and Recommendations; Appendices from I to VI.

RECOMMENDATIONS

The analysis and the arguments on which our conclusions and recommendations are based, and it is felt that any attempt to smmarise all this may mean some distortion of emphasis. The following paragraphs only bring together our major conclusions and recommendations.

Scope and Method of Study

The current definition of 'banking' (accepting, for

the purpose of lending or investment, of deposits of money from the public, repayable on demand or otherwise, and withdrawable by cheque, draft, order or otherwise) does not help in making an unambiguous distinction between banks and NBFIs. The Study Group to Review Legislation Affecting Banking is examining various definitions relating to banking. Hence, the Group selected for its study, NBFIs which are recognised to be important, viz., (i) Hire-Purchase Finance Institutions, (ii) Investment Trust Companies, (iii) Chit Funds, (iv) Nidhis, and (v) Finance Corporations.

In accordance with its terms of reference, the Gorup also enquired into the need for the following types of specialised financial institutions ; (1) Merchant Banking Institutions and Acceptance and Discount Houses, (2) Export-Import Bank, (3) Small Scale Industries Bank, (4) Specialised Savings Banks, (5) Specialised Institutions for Housing Finance and (6) Specialised Institutions for Consumer Credit.

The major constraints on the work of the Study Group were the non-availability of adequate data on the subjects relevant to its study and limited time within which the Report had to be prepared.

Approach of the Study Group

NBFIs supplement the activities of banks. Their functioning in deposit mobilisation is somewhat akin to the role of the small local non-scheduled or urban banks. In many cases, they perform a gap-filling function insofar as they cater for purposes and to customers who may not be getting required amounts of finance at the required time from the organised banking system.

The operations of the NBFIs have not yet assumed such dimensions as to modify the effectiveness of monetary policy. It is, however, possible that in the absence of regulation, their impact may grow to substantial proportions.

NBFIs should be regulated not only to safeguard the depositors' interests but also to ensure the implementation of credit policy objectives of providing credit to neglected sectors at reasonable rates and restricting its availability for less essential purposes. The present system and methods of regulation do not serve these purposes. There is also need for encouraging the growth of NBFIs which are capable of playing a dynamic role in the economy.

The administrative difficulty of regulating a large number of NBFIs can partly be solved by enacting legislation so that only corporate bodies can accept deposits from the public for the purpose of lending. For purposes of regulation, NBFIs in general may be classified into two categories : 'approved' and 'non-approved'. While a specified minimum degree of control may be exercised on all NBFIs, those units—to be designated as 'approved' NBFIs—which satisfy certain additional requirements to be laid down by the regulating authority, may be accorded a special and favourable treatment. 'Approved' institutions which will be only corporate bodies would be eligible for refinance facilities from the banking system and their own lending operations could also be covered under the Credit Guarantee Scheme, Eventually, the Deposit Insurance Scheme can also be extended to those of the approved NBFIs whose manner of conducting business meets the requirements of the Deposit Insurance Corporation. The basic factor to identify 'approved' institutions will have to be the judgment of the regulating authority regarding the quality of their operations.

The Reserve Bank of India or any other regulating authority which may be set up in this behalf will have to strengthen or build up its inspecting machinery so that these institutions can be inspected at least on a sample basis.

In dealing with the question of regulation, the approach may have to be tailored to the special characteristics of the different types of NBFIs. Some types of NBFIs would obviously need a greater degree of surveillance than others.

Each of the NBFIs falling within the scope of our study as identified earlier is studied with the following objectives in mind : (a) reviewing its operations, (b) examining its role in the economy by reference, wherever necessary and feasible to foreign experience; (c) studying the weaknesses, if any, emerging from the above review; and (d) making suitable recommendations about the action to be taken.

Hire Purchase Finance Institutions

In order to bring down the level of finance charges, strengthen the financial position of financing agencies and facilitate regulation, the policy objective should be to institutionalise hire-purchase credit.

In view of the fact that the amount of borrowing is of crucial importance for a hire-purchase financing unit for its profitability, the permissible debt-equity ratio may increase directly with the size of the capital of the unit.

The liquidity ratio as at present applicable against deposits of hire-purchase finance companies, mobilised from the public, may be made higher for the smaller companies and lower for the bigger companies, with a minimum of 10 per cent in each case.

Wherever necessary, commercial banks may start subsidiaries for hire-purchase finance. The authorities may consider whether Section 19 of the Banking Regulation Act, 1949, can appropriately be amended so as to enable banks to promote subsidiary hire-purchase finance companies in which any single banking company may own shares to the extent of 51 per cent.

Small non-nationalised Indian banks may enter more vigorously into hire-purchase finance business.

The benefit of Credit Guarantee Scheme recently introduced for small borrowers, including transport operators, and SFCs, may be extended to other financial institutions (like non-scheduled commercial banks and approved hire-purchase finance companies) in appropriate cases.

All hire-purchase finance companies may be regulated by the Reserve Bank of India or such other agency as may be set up in this behalf in the following way. They may be classified into 'approved' and 'non-approved' institutions. While regulation may extend to all hire-purchase financing units, the approved ones which will be only corporate bodies, may have special advantages of the following types: (a) commercial banks may extend them credit on more favourable terms; (b) they may be allowed to get more credit in relation to their capital; (c) liquidity ratio may be lower in their case than in the case of non-approved institutions; (d) the Credit Guarantee Corporation may consider extending the benefit of guaranteeing small loans made by them; and (e) ultimately insurance cover of Deposit Insurance Corporation may also be made available to their depositors. The criterion for approval would generally be the working of a hire-purchase finance company determined on the basis of inspections.

All hire-purchase finance units may compulsorily be licensed and the licensing authority may be given powers to revoke the licence in case it is satisfied that the operations of a particular unit are unsatisfactory.

In advertisements as well as in agreements, hire-purchase financiers should clearly indicate the true rate of interest along with flat rate. With the present structure of hire-purchase finance companies and the existing structure of interest rates ceilings on hire-purchase charges at flat rate of 10 per cent per annum for new vehicles and of 12 per cent for old vehicles are considered to be reasonable.

Investment Trust Companies and Unit Trusts

There is no need for more unit trusts and investment trusts in the economy because (a) UTI has introduced a new financial asset which combines the advantages of liquidity, yield and growth; it is also considering the introduction of new schemes with different mix and (b) the capital market in India is not broad enough to be able to serve the requirements of the existing institutions as well as new unit trusts or investment trusts. The new industrial securities which may come into the market as a result of growth of industrial development can be absorbed by the existing institutions and private investors.

Existing genuine investment companies may be encouraged and the Government may consider offering them relief from inter-corporate tax provided that they are prepared to have the same obligations (i.e., diversification of investments, distribution of a specified minimum portion of income and regulation by authorities) as the UTI.

The following criteria may be adopted for identifying a genuine investment company: (a) it should have an independent management and investment policy; (b) it should have a diversified investment portfolio both in terms of companies and groups of companies; (c) it should have adequate public participation in its share capital and it should ensure listing of its shares on stock exchange; (d) a major portion of its funds should be invested in shares, stocks, bonds and other securities; and (e) it should regularly distribute not less than a specified proportion of its income to its members.

Although the number of genuine investment companies at present is small and hence no separate machinery is required to regulate them, it would be useful to enact a separate legislation with the object of protecting the interests of the members of these companies. The legislation may be applied as and when number of investment holding companies convert themselves into genuine investment companies.

The proposed legislation may be framed on the lines of Investment Companies Act of the U.S.A. and also should incorporate provisions forbidding investment companies from entering certain fields. No industrial or trading company should be permitted in any event to hold any shares in investment companies. In order to ensure an independent management and policy, a Government nominee should be appointed on the Board of Directors of each genuine investment company.

One of the members does not agree with the main conclusions and recommendations of the Group on the subject of Investment Companies and Unit Trusts.

Chit Funds

Chit Fund is an indigenous institution which

combines saving (through subscription of members) and lending (thorugh distribution of 'prizes'). There is discrimination in the distribution of profits and losses to the members of chit funds. The more needy a person the higher the rate of interest which he has to pay. Also, the unscrupulous among the foremen resort to unfair methods which are not in the interests of members. At the same time it is popular as an indigenous institution. Ultimately the solution to the problem is that commercial banks should introduce schemes similar to chit funds but without the disadvantages associated with them.

Meanwhile, elimination of chit funds will leave a credit gap. Hence they should be regulated. There are three lines of action. (a) State Governments may, wherever they think it appropriate, consider starting chit funds at strategic places as model foremen. (b) Commercial banks may run chit funds subject to proper safeguards as formulated by the Reserve Bank of India. (c) Depending upon the constitutional position, whether chit funds come under the Union List, Concurrent List or State List, either an all-India chit fund law may be enacted by the Central Government or a model law may be framed which may be adopted by State Governments. The Tamil Nadu Chit Funds Act contains the essential features of legislation regulating chit funds. This may be strengthened with a view to safeguarding the interests of members and ensuring that the foreman works only as a manager and ceases to enjoy the wide powers that he has at present. Since a large number of chit funds working in States having no chit fund legislation are branches of chit funds registered in States which have such legislation, it will be useful to apply the provisions of chit fund laws in these latter States to their branches operating in the former States. Regulation will be easy if only public limited companies are allowed to run chit funds. Also, the offence under Section 294-A of the Indian Penal Code relating to lotteries may be made a cognisable one so that 'prize chits' could be prohibited.

Nidhis

Nidhis are performing useful functions through their operations in the localities where they are operating. It would be useful to encourage the growth of these institutions. Although they deal with their members, it is very easy for any person to become a member of a nidhi. Hence, they are working like commercial banks and should, therefore, be subject to regulation. In the case of nidhis which accept demand deposits the regulation may be similar to that applicable in the case of commercial banks. All other nidhis may be subject to the following regulations :

(a) They may be licensed by the Reserve Bank of India.

(b) A minimum level of liquidity ratio may be fixed which may, however, be lower than that of commercial banks.

(c) Periodical inspections may be conducted.

(d) A minimum amount of paid-up capital and reserves may be prescribed.

While these regulations may be applicable to all the nidhis, incentives may be offered to those among them which satisfy certain requirements. For this purpose, nidhis may be classified into two categories, i.e., 'approved' and 'non-approved'. Approved nidhis will be those companies which are run on sound lines and whose affairs are conducted in a manner not detrimental to the interests of their depositors.

The benefit of availability of refinance, guarantee of loans as well as, ultimately, insurance of their deposits may be extended to approved nidhis. Government may also consider extending to the depositors of approved nidhis the same tax concessions which are available to the depositors of commercial banks.

Finance Corporations

Since the Bangalore type finance corporations are para banking institutions, it is necessary to regulate their activities on the following lines in the interests of their depositors : (a) No finance corporation may be allowed to work without a licence from monetary authorities; (b) A ratio may be prescribed between the owned funds of corporations and their deposit liabilities; (c) Liquidity ratios may be prescribed for them; (d) Periodical inspection of the corporations on a sample basis may be undertaken; (e) Maximum interest rates on deposits may be prescribed which may, however, be higher than those prescribed for commercial banks.

Finance corporations may be classified into two categories—'approved' and 'non-approved'. Approved corporations should be only corporate bodies and be eligible to get the benefit of refinance facilities from commercial banks or the Reserve Bank of India. The benefits of guarantee for their loans and ultimately of deposit insurance may also be extended to them. The criteria for according the status of 'approved' to a corporation will have to be based on the judgment of the regulating authority as to whether its affairs are being conducted in a manner not detrimental to the interests of its depositors.

Ultimately the solution to the problems created by the emergence of a large number of Bangalore type finance corporations lies in the commercial banks competing with them effectively in the localities where such corporations are operating.

Examination of the Case for Establishing Specialised Institutions

New specialised institutions should not be set up merely on general grounds. Each case should be studied on merits and a new institution may be created only if there is a clearly identified credit gap which, for some reason or the other, cannot be filled by the existing financial institutions.

Merchant Banking Institutions and Acceptance and Discount Houses

Institutions of the merchant banking type are required in India to perform the following services : (a) syndication, financing and promotion of Indian projects; (b) investment advisory service; and (c) investment management.

Under present circumstances, they may not take up acceptance and discounting functions because these services can well be performed by commercial banks which have a wide network of branches and an intimate knowledge of the creditworthiness of their borrowers. In due course, however, after the bill market is well developed and the merchant banking institutions get the necessary expertise they could enter the acceptance and discount business. Although, at present there is no need to set up specialised discount houses, in course of time, such institutions could be set up to offer discounting facility as well as a money market intermediary to even out the demand for and supply of short-term funds in the money market.

Initially, there could be four merchant banking institutions located in Bombay, Calcutta, Madras and New Delhi set up by the specialised financial institutions and commercial banks. Later branches can be set up in important centres also by each of the regional institutions.

In the light of experience gained and depending on the integrity, investment expertise and management standards, the erstwhile managing agencies may be allowed to set up merchant banking institutions in the private sector.

It will be necessary for the successful working of the proposed merchant banking institutions to organise a training programme for their staff.

Need for an Export-Import Bank in India

There is no need for a specialised Export-Import Bank in India because the existing institutions, viz., commercial banks, Industrial Development Bank of Indian and the Reserve Bank of India are providing adequate credit on reasonable terms.

The functions of insurance of risks and guaranteeing of loans are performed by the Export Credit and Guarantee Corporation which has progressively liberalised and extended the coverage of its schemes. There are, however, no facilities available for covering risks of exchange rate variation involved in long-term deferred payment exports. The authorities should devise a machinery for providing such exchange cover. The creation of a new institution will not, however, be necessary for performing this function.

There is at present no systematic collection of information regarding exports. A number of institutions like the Trade Development Authority, State Trading Corporation, Export Promotion Councils, Commodity Boards, ECGC and IDBI collect useful information and it will be beneficial from the point of view of promoting exports if such information is pooled.

The IDBI has constituted informal and consultative working groups to utilise the information available within the country. Such groups should co-ordinate the functions of all the export financing institutions so that an exporter is prevented from the necessity of going from one institution to another for meeting his needs.

In course of time buyers' credit will be required. It is understood that the IDBI is examining this problem. A separate institution will not be necessary for the purpose. In fact, the IDBI is already performing many functions expected from Export-Import Bank.

If a new institution is created, its operations would be more costly because it will have to establish branches all over the country and perhaps abroad It is less costly for commercial banks to take up this work because they can combine it with their other activities.

The need for an Export-Import Bank is sometimes advocated on the grounds that it will be able to borrow more economically in the foreign markets for financing the imports of goods like ships and aeroplanes. In the view of the Group, commercial banks with their branches and contacts abroad are in a position to perform the same function efficiently.

Banks should play a more active role in locating, assisting and developing export potential. More emphasis should be given on the training of personnel of commercial banks in the field of export credit.

Need for Small Scale Industries Bank

There is no need to create a separate financing institution for small scale industrial units and/or small business units because (a) the existing financial institutions are adequate for the purpose and (b) the creation of a centralised agency has no special advantages to offer.

Commercial banks, through a wide network of branches, are meeting the working capital needs of widely scattered units to a considerable extent. Their professional expertise and trained personnel are helpful in making technical appraisal of loan applications. Other institutions, such as the SFCs, are also playing a useful role in giving term loans to small units.

If a specialised Small Industries Bank is set up, it would have to find sufficient resources to operate without depending on funds drawn from the budget or Reserve Bank or other existing institutions. It would only duplicate the functions presently being performed by the Industrial Finance Department of the Reserve Bank of India, of co-ordinating the activities of different financial institutions in the field. Since its costs of borrowing are likely to be as high as for other institutions, it may not be able to provide credit to small units more cheaply than the existing institutions.

Need for Specialised Savings Banks

There exists enough scope for mobilising and institutionalising savings, especially in rural areas.

On the basis of a review of the growth and structural changes of financial institutions over the past few decades, and having in view the various measures which are being taken to strengthen and gear the existing financial institutions to the task of mobilising savings, and the general problems associated with the establishment of new savings institutions, there is little support in favour of establishing an entirely new organisation of specialised savings banks.

Need for Specialised Institutions for Housing Finance

Existing financial institutions are not in a position to solve the problem of housing finance because of its large magnitude, the peculiarities of the housing market and (as in the case of commercial banks) the burden of wide and expanding range of functions. Also, as the experience in foreign countries shows, savings can increase substantially if they are linked up directly with the acquisition of houses.

Specialised housing finance institutions are required in India in order to mobilise additional savings for the purpose of giving loans for house construction or ownership. The proposed organisation will have two tiers. The Housing and Urban Development Corporation may work as an apex institution and local and regional institutions may be set up with the active support of the Government.

The local and regional institutions will have the primary function of attracting savings linked to the provision of credit for construction or purchase of houses. The functions of the apex body will be to encourage, supervise and provide temporary finance to the local or regional institutions. This body will also be vested with the responsibility of serving the housing needs in the country in its different aspects. The source of funds for the central housing finance institution will initially have to come from the Government but ultimately the institution should rely on market borrowings. The LIC and the Reserve Bank of India may also give loans to this body.

There should be a machinery to offer suitable guarantee and insurance facilities to cover the risks involved in providing housing finance.

Steps should be taken to create and develop a secondary mortgage market to impart liquidity to housing loans.

Co-ordination may be ensured between the proposed institutions and the existing financial agencies in the following ways: Wherever feasible, Housing Boards and nidhis may be vested with the functions of the proposed housing finance institutions. Social housing schemes which involve an element of subsidy, may be continued. Co-operative housing societies should be strengthened particularly with a view to mobilising resources from members and eliminating malpractices. An apex co-operative society should be set up in each State with primary affiliated societies all over the State. However, as individuals cannot borrow from the co-operative housing finance societies, they would not be a substitute for specialised housing finance institutions. Commercial banks may give short and medium term credit to the builders in order to enable them to undertake mass housing construction programmes. Prospective purchasers of houses may borrow from the specialised institutions to purchase houses from the builders who, in turn, can repay their loans to commercial banks. To the extent their administrative and personnel resources permit them, commercial banks may also give credit to individuals desiring to own or construct houses.

One of the members is of the view that commercial banks with their wide network of branches will be able to provide housing finance and there is no need for setting up specialised housing finance institutions.

Commercial banks may set up specialised departments for receiving housing deposits and making housing loans. The Housing and Urban Development Corporation may guarantee such loans and impart liquidity by taking over the loans when banks are in need of funds.

Need for Specialised Institutions for Consumer Credit

Consumer credit for durable goods on a large scale in the present circumstances is likely to raise aggregate expenditures and thus raise prices of essential commodities.

Loans for the purposes of meeting medical, education and other contingent expenses would have to be provided, preferably, by health and educational insurance schemes and other welfare schemes of the Government.

With the likely increase in incomes in the next decade, there is likely to emerge in the long run an increase in the demand for low income or middle income consumer durables and consequently there will be need for an organisational innovation to satisfy the consequent credit needs of consumers. In this connection, it is suggested that there should be a uniform legislation in the country as a whole, with allowances for regional characteristics insofar as the terms and conditions of consumer business are concerned. Again, in the interest of orderly development of financial institutions it will be desirable to encourage the formation of public limited companies for extending consumer credit. Moreover, from the point of regulation, it will be useful to bring the specialised institutions for consumer credit under the control of the Reserve Bank of India, or any other agency set up in this behalf.

ONE-MAN COMMISSION OF INQUIRY INTO THE DISAPPEARANCE OF NETAJI SUBHAS CHANDRA BOSE, 1970—REPORT

New Delhi, Ministry of Home Affairs, 1974; 137p.

Sole Member : Justice G.D. Khosla

APPOINTMENT

The One-Man Commission of Inquiry into the Disappearance of Netaji Subhas Chandra Bose was appointed by the Government of India, Ministry of Home Affairs vide Notification No. 25/14/70 Poll-II dated 11 July 1970 as cited below :—

S.O. 2375—WHEREAS the Shah Nawaz Khan Committee appointed by the Government of India in April, 1956, to enquire into and to report to the Government of India on the circumstances concerning the departure of Netaji Subhas Chandra Bose from Bangkok about the 16th August, 1945, his reported death as a result of an aircraft accident, and subsequent developments connected therewith, had come to the conclusion that Netaji Subhas Chandra Bose met his death in an air-crash;

AND WHEREAS there is a widespread feeling amongst the public that the problem of finding the truth about Netaji's death still remains;

AND WHEREAS the Central Government is of opinion that it is necessary to appoint a Commission of Inquiry for the purpose of making an inquiry into a definite matter of public importance, namely, the disappearance of Netaji Subhas Chandra Bose in 1945;

Now, THEREFORE, in exercise of the powers conferred by Section 3 of the Commissions of Inquiry Act, 1952 (60 of 1952), the Central Government hereby appoints a Commission of Inquiry consisting of Shri G.D. Khosla, Retired Chief Justice of the Punjab High Court, as Sole Member.

The Central Government is of opinion that, having regard to the nature of the inquiry to be made and other circumstances of the case, all the provisions of Sub-section (2), Sub-section (3), Sub-section (4) and Sub-section (5) of the Commissions of Inquiry Act, 1952 (60 of 1952) should be made applicable to the said Commission and the Central Government hereby directs under Sub-Section (1) of the said section 5 that all the provisions aforesaid shall apply to the said Commission.

To the above Notification may be added the following note prepared in the Ministry of Home Affairs, briefly stating the circumstances which led to the appointment of the present Commission :

"In April, 1956, in response to the public demand, Government of India appointed an Inquiry Committee to ascertain the circumstances concerning Netaji's departure from Bangkok on August 15, 1945 and his alleged death in an air-crash.

The Committee consisted of the following :

(1) Shri Shah Nawaz Khan, M.P., Parliamentary Secretary to the Minister of Railway and Transport;

(2) Shri Suresh Chandra Bose, elder brother of Netaji Subhas Chandra Bose; and

(3) Shri S.N. Maitra, ICS, formerly Chief Commissioner, Andaman and Nicobar Islands.

(1) The Committee examined a number of witnesses in Delhi, Calcutta, Bangkok, Saigon, Tourane and Tokyo. They also examined books and articles about Netaji Subhas Chandra Bose and studied relevant classified records pertaining to the matter.

(2) After fully considering the evidence available two of the Members (S/s Shah Nawaz Khan and S.N. Maitra) came to the conclusion that while taking off from Taihoku (Formosa) in the afternoon of 18th August, 1945, the Japanese military plane carrying Netaji and his companion (One Col. Habibur Rahman) developed some trouble and burst into flames. Suffering from severe burns, Netaji was carried into the Taihoku Hospital, where, after some hours, he passed away. The third member of the Committee, Shri Suresh Chandra Bose, submitted a dissentient report, stating that there had been no plane crash involving Netaji's death. The majority report was accepted by the Government.

(3) Since then there have been repeated demands for undertaking another inquiry into the matter. Rumours about Netaji's survival and whereabouts etc. have cropped up repeatedly. Several Members of Parliament also strongly pressed the demand for a fresh inquiry. The matter was considered by Government and it has been decided to appoint One-Man Commission of Inquiry consisting of Judge of the Supreme Court or the High Court, to make a further inquiry into the circumstances relating to the alleged death of Netaji Subhas Chandra Bose.

TERMS OF REFERENCE

The Commission shall inquire into all the facts and circumstances relating to the disappearance of Netaji Subhas Chandra Bose in 1945 and the subsequent developments connected therewith and to make its report to the Central Government.

CONTENTS

Notification; Introductory; Evidence and Proof; Air Crash Story; Examination of Certain Witnesses; Some Theories and Hypotheses; Some Miscellaneous Matters; Findings; Appendices I to IV.

Findings

(i) Bose was informed on August 12, 1945 that the war was about to conclude and the Japanese had decided to surrender to the Allied Forces. He was at that time at Saranban. The message was brought to him there by Negishi (Witness No. 50).

(ii) Bose at once left for Singapore where he discussed his future plans with his colleagues and the Ministers of his Cabinet, almost all day and night. The decision was taken on the 14th when Sakai arrived and conferred with Bose. It was decided that Bose himself should leave Singapore and try to escape to Russia where he hoped to find asylum.

(iii) On the morning of 16.8.1945, Bose left Singapore accompanied by Col. Habibur Rahman, S.A. Iyer (Witness No. 29), a Japanese Liaison Officer Negishi (Witness No. 50), Col. Pritam Singh (Witness No. 155) and others. The party arrived at Bangkok at 3.30 P.M. and spent the night there.

(iv) At about 8 A.M. on 17.8.1945, Bose and party left by two planes for Saigon, Bose's party included Col. Habibur Rahman, Deb Nath Das (Witness No. 3), S.A. Iyer (Witness No. 29), Hachia (Witness No. 51), Ishoda (Witness No. 68), Gulzara Singh (Witness No. 153), Abid Hassan (Witness No. 157), and others. The party arrived at Saigon at 11 A.M.

(v) The planes in which Bose and his party had travelled to Saigon had to go back, and fresh arrangements had to be made for the next stage of the journey. Bose was informed that one seat could be given to him in a Japanese bomber which had come from Manila and was going to Dairen in Manchuria. The plane, Bose was informed, had, on board, a number of Japanese army officers who had been posted to Manchuria and who could not be left behind.

(vi) Bose was very upset on hearing this, because he wanted to carry all the members of his party with him. Ishoda and Hachia were sent to Dalat where Field Marshall Tarauchi was camping. These two emissaries could not see Tarauchi personally, but his

Adjutant told them that it might be possible to make available two or three seats in all for Bose.

(vii) Ishoda and Hachia returned to Saigon and conferred with the pilot of the plane and the Japanese military authorities there. The conclusion was that two seats were placed at the disposal of Bose.

(viii) After some discussion, Bose decided to avail himself of the two seats, and asked Habibur Rahman to accompany him.

(ix) The Japanese bomber left Saigon at approximately 5 P.M. carrying Bose, Habibur Rahman, Lt. Col. Sakai (Witness No. 47), S. Nonongaki (Witness No. 53), Tarokono, Navigator (Witness No. 63), Takahashi (Witness No. 65), the pilot-in-charge Takizawa, Genl. Shidei, second pilot Ayoagi, all three of whom were killed and some others, whose names need not be mentioned. They were the crew and other officers posted to Manchuria, or to Tokyo.

(x) The plane arrived at Touraine at 7.45 P.M. and the party spent the night there.

(xi) On the morning of 18.8.1945 the bomber left Touraine carrying the previous complement of crew and passengers and arrived at Taipei in Formosa at 2 P.M.

(xii) The party had a snack lunch at Taipei while the pilot attended to a snag, which he declared, had been corrected, after a short while.

(xiii) The plane took off at 2.35 P.M. but within a few seconds one of the engines flew out and the plane crashed near the fringe of the Taihoku airfield. The body of the plane broke into two parts and caught fire.

(xiv) The pilot Takizawa and Genl. Shidei were killed inside the plane. The rest of the crew and passengers came out, but all of them had sustained burn injuries, two of them viz. Ayoagi and Bose had received very severe burns.

(xv) The injured persons were carried to the army hospital a few kilometres from the airfield and given medical treatment.

(xvi) Bose had sustained burn injuries of the third degree and despite the efforts of the doctors to revive him, he succumbed to his injuries the same night.

(xvii) Of the other injured persons Ayoagi, the second pilot also died.

(xviii) Two days later Bose's body was cremated and his ashes were carried to Tokyo in the beginning of September 1945 where they were deposited in the Renkoji Temple.

(xix) There is no reason for believing that the relations between Nehru and Bose were anything but friendly on a personal basis. Political differences between them did not lessen Bose's great respect for Nehru and Nehru's affection for the younger politician whose patriotism no one questioned.

(xx) There is not the slightest evidence of any attempt by Nehru to suppress the truth about Bose at any stage or to make false statements about his death at Taihoku on August 18, 1945. His concession to a public demand for enquiry was an instance of his compliance with democratic procedures and not an admission of his disbelief in the truth of the crash story.

(xxi) The personnel of the Committee appointed by Nehru's government to enquire into Bose's disappearance is ample evidence of his *bona fides*. He appointed Bose's brother, who could be presumed to make an earnest search for truth about his brother and whose appointment would win public confidence. The Chairman was Shah Nawaz Khan, who was a close associate and confidant of Bose and who had taken a very prominent part in I.N.A.'s campaign against the British. Shah Nawaz Khan could, therefore, be depended upon to conduct the enquiry honestly and conscientiously. The third member was Shri S.N. Maitra, a member of I.C.S. and a Bengali. He was chosen because of his administrative experience, his proved integrity and his attachment to Bose who belonged to his own State.

(xxii) There is no evidence of any attempt by the present government to withhold evidence or place impediments in the way of this Commission. All documents called for have been supplied and the delay occasioned in making some files and documents available cannot be construed as placing obstacles in the progress of the enquiry. Such delays are a nominal feature of government red-tape and preoccupation with more urgent matters.

(xxiii) Bose had impressed the Japanese as a great patriot and a competent administrator who could win the confidence of Indians in South-East Asia. The Japanese, however, looked upon him not as an equalally, but as a person whom they could use for their own ends. It was with great reluctance that they allowed Bose to organise the Burma Campaign against the British forces. The Japanese, however, did not give adequate assistance to the I.N.A., and despite promises, they did not hand over the occupied territory to the Provisional Government of Azad Hind. An instance in point was the Nicobar and Andaman Islands, the administration of which was not completely entrusted to Maj. General Loganathan, who was sent as High Commissioner by Bose to take charge of the Islands. All the evidence points to the fact that the Japanese neither had complete confidence in Bose's ability to lead a large army and secure victories over the Allied Forces, nor did they fully trust him. They, nevertheless, had considerable respect for him because they saw that he was a man of remarkable courage and unquestioned patriotism.

(xxiv) The Japanese attitude towards Bose underwent a change when the war concluded. The Japanese were more concerned with trying to retrieve whatever they could of their own resources than with giving large scale help to Bose which would have proved detrimental to their own interests. Also the blow to their self-esteem was so violent that they became indifferent to Bose and his future plans.

(xxv) The numerous stories about encounters with Bose at various times and various places after 1945, are completely false and unacceptable. They are the result either of hallucination helped by wishful thinking or have been invented by persons who wanted to draw attention to themselves and advertise themselves as public-spirited men.

Appendix III

Principal points agreed to-dated 30.6.1956 for draft Report.

(1) It was Netaji's idea to continue to struggle for the liberation of India. This was thought of by Netaji some time before Germany and Japan surrendered and which Netaji had at that time said to a selected few that they would sooner or later lose the war. Netaji also discussed with his Cabinet members about this point.

Since October 1944, when Netaji visited Tokyo, he carried out these intentions of his attempt to contact the Russian Ambassador, and finally decided to go to Manchuria with the purpose in view.

(2) whether the plane crash did take place? The plane carrying Netaji did crash. There is no other evidence to the contrary; the evidence should be considered carefully and in details.

(3) whether Netaji met his death as a result of this accident? The witnesses support this story. There is no reason why they should be disbelieved. After a lapse of about 10 years, these witnesses, who belong to different walks of life and of different nationalities, Habib an Indian and subsequently a Pakistani and the others, who are Japanese who mostly are unconnected with one another and no longer subordinates of their Government and Japan not being a totalitarian State would not be expected to state what was not true.

Enquiries made subsequently (1) by British Intelligence teams operating from Delhi and (2) British and American Intelligence teams operating from Tokyo (3) non-official enquiry appear to corroborate the statements of these eye-witnesses and a few others, who appeared on the scene immediately after.

A person of the status of Netaji as Head of a State, that was not only recognized by Japan, but was helped materially in every way by Japan and vice versa was not given the requisite facility and honours due to him, from the very start, viz., by providing a separate plane or seats for him and for all of his associates; treatment in a small hospital with a junior medical officer—Captain; manner of cremation; disposal of ashes etc. all without due honour and respect, viz., full military funeral; body placed on a gun carriage with full military honours etc.

(4) **Cremation :** Preliminaries—by the 2 doctors and some of the subordinate Hospital Staff.

Main Evidence—by (1) Habib (2) Nakamura and (3) Nagatomo—More or less corroborative.

Re : Habib—Oath of secrecy may be argued only.

Re : other two—no interestedness, so their stories supporting Habib takes away most of charge against Habib for oath of secrecy; in what way could they be obliged to Habib?

No other suggestion that the body was disposed of in any other manner—so body cremeted.

The evidence of the doctors will have to be discussed very carefully, as it will surely be a matter of detailed criticism by eminent doctors throughout the world.

(5) **Ashes :** Ashes from the crematorium to Renkoji temple is a long way—first to Nishi Honganji temple; then to Tokyo etc.

There is nothing to show that there was tampering, but to prove that it was definitely those of Netaji, much more stringent measures required by law should have been taken and a different and very strict procedure by way of seals, guards, etc. should have been taken.

In all probability, the ashes could be said to be those of Netaji.

(6) **Treasure :** Comments should be minimum.

Evidence recorded by us should be placed in a guarded manner.

We may state that out of the quantity carried by Netaji, a portion eventually was deposited in the National Archives.

The dropping of the treasure from the plane, its charred and molten condition and identification of some items, would help the report.

We should state that this may be the subject-matter of a separate Enquiry and this Enquiry should start from the complete assets, in cash and kind and liabilities of the Azad Hind Government.

(7) **Shri Thevar's statements and Statements of Shri Goswami : Their statements should be discussed while dealing with Netaji's death or otherwise and a little more in details separately later on.**

Draft by Shri S.N. Maitra
Draft—10-7-1956
Discussion, correction and finalisation. 13-7-1956
Submission to Government of India 16-7-1956

S.C. Bose
2-7-1956
Sd/-Illegible
2-7-1956
Shah Nawaz Khan
2-7-1956.

NATIONAL HIGH LEVEL SCIENTIFIC COMMITTEE FOR PLANT AND ANIMAL INTRODUCTION AND QUARANTINE, 1970—REPORT

New Delhi, M/o Food, Agriculture, Community Development and Cooperation (Department of Agriculture) (ICAR), 1971; 126pp., 3 maps

Chairman : Dr. J.S. Patel.

Members : Dr. Guy B. Baird; Dr. L.S. Negi; Dr. L.B. Singh; Plant Protection Adviser to the Government of India, New Delhi; Deputy Director General (CS) I.C.A.R., New Delhi; Dr. C.M. Singh; Dr. H.R. Arakheri; Chief Controller of Imports & Exports or his representative; Chairman, Board of Excise and Customs or his representative.

Member-Conveaer : Shri H.B. Singh

APPOINTMENT

The Government of India, Ministry of Food, Agriculture and Community Development vide Resolution No. 3 (2)/69-AS-III/S.C. II dated 11th August, 1970 set up a High Level National Scientific Committee to consider the suggestions for amending the existing rules and regulations relating to plant and animal introduction and quarantine and also to suggest the action to be taken on some important recommendations made at the workshop held in September, 1969, on Plant Introduction and Quarantine.

TERMS OF REFERENCE

(i) To review and examine in a comprehensive manner the organisational and operational aspects of the existing arrangements for plant and animal introduction and quarantine including customs procedures in India, staffing pattern, physical facilities and financial allocation; and

(ii) To suggest measures for rectifying the existing deficiencies for streamlining and strengthening the arrangements in commensurate with the needs and importance of the work.

CONTENTS

Part I : Plant Introduction and Quarantine : Role of plant introduction in agriculture, Phytosanitary considerations; Existing plant introduction procedures; Existing plant quarantine, Post-entry quarantine and other phytosanitary procedures; Recommendations regarding plant introduction, quarantine and post-entry quarantine work; Recommendations regarding domestic quarantine work; Staff and physical facilities; Role of various agencies and departments in plant introduction and quarantine; Export of Plant propagating material to foreign countries; Role of Indian Missions abroad; Revision of rules under the DIP Act 1914 and timely updating of provisions relating to plant material published in Customs Act, Customs Manual, Post Office Guide; Import Trade Control Policy; and Export Trade Control Policy; Standing Advisory Committee on Plant introduction and quarantine.

Part II : Animal Introduction and Quarantine : Necessity of animal introduction in livestock industry and existing animal introduction procedures; Role of animal quarantine in livestock industry (a) Recommendations of an international organization; (b)

Some national organizations; Existing animal quarantine and post-entry quarantine procedures; (a) Present set up, (b) Animal health certificates, (c) Detention in quarantine, (d) Payment of charges, (e) Livestock products, (f) Proposals under the Fourth-Five Year Plan; Certification service in India; Recommendations regarding animal introduction, certification, quarantine, and post-entry quarantine; Staff and physical facilities, (a) Animal quarantine, (b) Animal Certification Centres; Revision of Livestock Importation Act and the Livestock (Import) Quarantine Rules; Necessity for having statutory regulations for the export of livestock and livestock products; Standing Advisory Committee on Animal Introduction and Quarantine; Summary and recommendations; Maps; Appendixes from I to XI.

RECOMMENDATIONS

Plant introduction has played and shall continue to play a pivotal role in development of agricultural, horticultural and sylvi-cultural plant resources of any country. Phytosanitary considerations should be a precondition to the dispersal of any plant material involved in plant introduction activity. In India today, such dispersal of plant material is being carried out by many private, Governmental and foreign technical aid agencies including three plant introduction agencies accredited by the Government of India to carry out this work scientifically. Only two of the officially authorised agencies have some facilities to carry out their functions under relatively high standard of phytosanitary conditions.

Tha present Plant Quarantine Organization of the Government of India is under administration and technical control separate from that of the official plant introduction agencies. This plant quarantine Directorate ensures that imports of plant material by any agency are regulated according to updated regulations made under the Destructive Insect Pest (DIP) Act of 1914. This involves issue of permits to perspective importers (often excluding the three official plant introduction agencies); inspection and treatment of certain categories of plant material imported through authorised air, sea, land ports of entry; and follow-up post-entry quarantine check by arrangement with plant protection experts available in the interior for some types of plant introductions.

Plant introduction and Plant Quarantine Organizations and their operations in India should be based on realistic appreciation of (1) the current magnitude of traffic in agricultural, ornamental and other plant materials, including that of no economic value; and (2) the diseases and pests involved in import of all such plant materials.

Both types of organisations should be equipped with adequate cataloguing facilities for pests and pathogens likely to find entry with imported plant materials from other countries. They should mutually exchange complementary information compiled by them.

It is also necessary to channel all imports of plant propagating materials (at least of those involving quarantine risks of national significance) only through sea and airports of Bombay, Madras and Calcutta and airport of Delhi. This work should be entrusted to competent plant introduction agencies such as: Division of Plant Introduction, IARI, ICAR, (for agri-horticultural plants); Forest Research Institute (for plants of forestry importance); and Botanical Survey of India (for plant of general Botanical interest). These agencies should serve as service agencies for international exchange of plant material for the benefit of all States, institutions and parties. The FRI Agency is located at Dehradun which is not directly connected with outside world. It should have some collaborative arrangement with the ICAR Agency. Since ICAR Agency caters to the needs of all Indian crop scientists, it should be placed under direct administrative control of the ICAR and yet head-quartered at IARI campus-

Licence to import plant materials may be granted to parties other then the official plant introduction agencies in exceptional cases, only after consulting the agency concerned and the Plant Quarantine Directorate. Foreign technical missions would need no such licence, but they should not import plant material through channels having diplomatic immunity. All plant introductions obtained in every manner, including the confiscated irregular ones, should be routed through the Plant Quarantine Directorate and the concerned plant introduction agency.

A national register of plant introductions being maintained at various locations in the country should be maintained at a central place like that of the ICAR agency and sub-registers should be maintained at the other two agencies.

Research and refresher training courses on plant quarantine science should be conducted at IARI by the ICAR plant introduction agency having a strong post entry quarantine base.

The existing post-entry plant quarantine base of the FRI Agency will have to be considerably strengthened. Since the BSI Agency will have relatively limited plant introduction activity, it may forge some working arrangements with the station of the Plant Quarantine Directorate at Calcutta.

The staff and facilities of the Plant Quarantine

Stations at the main points of entry (Bombay, Madras, Calcutta, Delhi) for plant introductions should be considerably strengthened.

The staff and facilities of the three plant introduction agencies need to be strengthened to varying degrees, commensurate with their work load. For example, the ICAR Agency should have additional stations at Jorhat, Kodaikanal, Bangalore and Trombay. Phytosanitary Propagation House facilities, duly equipped and staffed, should be expeditiously arranged at Delhi, Simla, Coimbatore, Trombay, Rajahmundry, Dehradun and Calcutta. The various schemes for establishment of National Seed Storage Laboratory and expansion and consolidation of the ICAR Agency for plant introduction and its Phytosanitation Laboratory Units at IARI should be expeditiously implemented.

With a view to stemming genetic erosion, the ICAR plant introduction agency should be made responsible for plant exploration and collection work within and outside the country. To facilitate former it should be adequately equipped with exploration vans, among other things and to facilitate latter, roving Plant Introduction Attaches should be posted in some important cultivated and related wild plant regions. Plant Introduction and Plant Quarantine scientists should have increasing opportunities to visit countries having efficient services of professional interests to them. The Indian Missions should extend all facilities to explorers of plant introduction agencies and scientific personnel visiting abroad.

The authorised plant introduction agencies should enjoy certain special standing concession such as : blanket licence to exchange plant materials with any country, foreign exchange sanctions, facility to pay for cost and incidentals in foreign currency with the help of Indian Missions abroad, permission to pay freight charges in Indian currency, working arrangements with Indian air or surface shipping lines to pay dues on production of bill, customs duty-free clearance of all introductions, etc. The concerned Government authorities should arrange for these.

The Plant Quarantine Directorate should post its whole-time representatives at the Foreign Post Offices at Delhi, Bombay, Calcutta and Madras to facilitate quick clearance of plant introductions arriving in distinctively marked packages through postal service. The Customs officials should inspect such parcels by opening them only in a laboratory of the Plant Quarantine Station concerned.

All existing and forthcoming provisions and facilities should be made use of for enforcing Domestic Plant Quarantine and no parochial interest should dominate national interests.

Export of plant propagating material belonging to plants of key importance to Indian economy may be banned and that of plants likely to get extinct should be restricted. To ensure that this is done and to keep centralised records of supplies abroad, all exports of plant propagating material should be supported by a 'No Objection Certificate' from the concerned plant introduction agency, in addition to phytosanitary certificate and identity verification plant inspection certificate issued by the same agency or any alternative competent Government of India accredited agencies. Plant introduction agencies and Directorate of Plant Quarantine should jointly prepare publicity material on rules relating to plant collection, and national and international movement of plant materials with reference to India. Copies of such publicity material should also be available from Indian Missions abroad to all persons coming to India.

A standing National Advisory Committee for Plant Introduction and Quarantine should be constituted to : (1) uptodate the rules made under DIP Act of 1914, including those for domestic quarantine by revising them in the light of the latest scientific information available and recommendations made in this Report, (2) arrange simultaneous incorporation of all such changes in the publications, Customs Act, Customs Annual, Import Trade Control Policy, Export Trade Control Policy, Post Office Guide etc., and (3) prescribe norms of facilities and staff the Government authorised plant introduction agencies must have in order that they may continue to retain their delegated authority.

Movement of animals used in lac, silk and honey producing industries may be controlled by the appropriate agencies that control the movement of plant materials.

Import of livestock, including poultry, as individual animals or their eggs or semen, would be essential for a long time to come since performance of indigenous livestock is comparatively poor.

Import of foreign biological materials essential for tackling effectively disease control problems of livestock in India would also be similarly essential.

Import of livestock and related biological materials is presently regulated through issue of Import Permit or Customs Clearance Permit by the Animal Husbandry Commissioner to the Government of India. This Government permits duty free clearance of livestock imported solely for breeding purposes.

The rules relating to animal quarantine and post-entry quarantine procedures are framed by the various State Governments under the provisions of the Livestock Importation Act, 1898 of the Government of India. Customs officials, assisted by Animal

Husbandry officials of the concerned State Government, deal with incoming livestock and allied material of animal quarantine significance at the specified posts of entry viz. seaports of Bombay, Madras, Calcutta and Cochin; air ports of Delhi, Madras, Calcutta, Cochin and Tiruchirapalli; and Attari on Indo-West Pakistan border. The State Animal Husbandry official is empowered to order the detention of any livestock on animal quarantine grounds, at cost payable by the importer.

Imported livestock are being required to be accompanied by specified animal health certificates.

Import of some livestock products is regulated under the provisions of the Prevention of Food Adulteration Act, 1954, the Imports & Exports (Control) Act, 1947, and the Sea Customs Act, 1878. No rules have been framed for import of some products of anima origin, such as wool, hair and skins.

Taking into considerations, among other things the recommended International Zoo-Sanitary Regulations and efficiently organised Animal Quarantine Services of some countries such as USA and Japan, the Government of India sanctioned the setting up of a Central Organization for Animal Quarantine and Certification Service in the Fourth Five Year Plan.

Export of some products of animal origin is regulated by policies backed by Imports and Exports (Control) Act, 1947. There is no statutory regulation to control export of livestock. Health certification of some livestock or its products being exported is being done presently by multifarious agencies in an unsatisfactory manner. The Service Organization mentioned in the preceding para is to be set up for arranging such certification also, with a view to giving a fillip to the export trade in livestock and livestock products.

In view of the foregoing account relating to livestock materials, it is recommeded that the scheme for establishment of Animal Quarantine and Certification Service by the Government of India should be speedily implemented. A comprehensive act for regulating importation of animal products and biological materials such as virulent strains of pathogens, sera and vaccines, should be formulated. Authority to implement the Livestock Importation Act should vest with the Government of India instead of with the various State Governments. All imports of livestock should be centralized through the Animal Husbandry Commissioner to the Government of India and yet the Central Government should authorise competent institutions to certify health conditions of animals held in quarantine at different locations. Adequately staffed and equipped Animal Quarantine Stations and Certification Centres should be set up at each specified port of entry.

A special laboratory in isolation (say on some off-shore island) should be established for developing diagnostic investigation and treatment facilities for curing valuable animals of exotic diseases.

Indian scientists connected with livestock introduction work should be encouraged to go abroad to study quality and quantity of animal wealth available as well as their health and management conditions.

Comprehensive legislation for regulating exports of livestock and its products and for Domestic Animal Quarantine should be framed.

Standing National Advisory Committee on Animal Introduction and Quarantine may be constituted to keep health and other regulations for international and national movement of livestock and its products abreast of the times.

PIPELINE INQUIRY COMMISSION, 1970—REPORT

Delhi, Controller of Publications, 1975; 463p.

Chairman : Shri J. N. Takru one man Commission.

APPOINTMENT

The Committee on Public Undertakings, in their 66th report (4th Lok Sabha), while dealing with the working of the Indian Oil Corporation (Pipeline Division) upto the year 1969, made a number of observations and recommendations for appropriate follow-up action on the part of the Government. Those observations—called 'Conclusions' in the report--and recommendations. Purporting to the act on those recommendations the Government of India, in the Ministry of Petroleum and Chemicals by their Resolution No. 28 (11)/70-OR dated August 22, 1970 appointed a one man Commission.

TERM OF REFERENCE

(a) (i) to determine whether any payment to Bechtels (as design engineers and overall supervisors in Gauhati-Siliguri pipeline and as Design Monitors and Project Managers in Haldia-Barauni-Kanpur pipeline) was made in excess of the amount sanctioned by Government and, if so, was such payment justified ?

(a) (ii) was the induction of Bechtels into the aforesaid projects mala fide, and were they shown any undue favour by officials of the IRL/Government;

(b) to determine whether there have been ommissions in regard to scrutinising, editing, compiling and maintaining contractual documents relating to the investigations, designs, construction and supervision of the Haldia-Barauni-Kanpur pipeline and whether the negotiations leading to the contracts were carried out diligently and whether adequate records of the negotiations were kept;

(c) whether the then Managing Director, IRL, acted on his own by-passing the Board of Directors in his dealing with Snamand Bechtels in vital matters concerning the capacity of the Haldia-Barauni-Kanpur pipeline, and whether the amendment of the contract adversely affected the capacity of the pipeline, and whether negligence or improper motive is substantiated against the MD, IRL, for not bringing these to the notice of the board/Government and, in particular, whether the General Manager and MD were perfunctory and casual in dealing with an important communication of the 26th September 1963 from Bechtels to IRL mentioning the design capacity of Haldia-Barauni pipeline as 1.9 million tonnes per year;

(d) to investigate the circumstances in which the sanction for the total project cost of HBK pipeline was not issued by Government and whether there was any loss to the public interest as a result;

(e) in view of the objections raised by the West Bengal Government and Indian Mining experts over the laying of the pipeline over coal bearing area, to advise whether there was any carelessness and negligence in discharge of responsibilities by Government/IRL/IOC officials;

(f) to determine the circumstances in which the IRL/IOC spent money in excess of the sanctioned estimates in the case of the GSPL project;

(g) to investigate the circumstances under which IRL/Government awarded the construction contracts for Gauhati-Siliguri and Haldia-Barauni-Kanpur pipelines to Snam Saipem on negotiated basis without calling for global tenders;

(h) to advise on whether there has been any negligence or carelessness or malafide motive on the part of any of the officers of Government /IRL/IOC and their staff in the discharge of their duties on any of the foregoing or other related issues, which, in the opinion of the Commission, are relevant;

(i) arising out of (h); to recommend further action, if any, that must be taken against particular officials;

(j) general, to report on any other matter that is relevant, in the opinion of the Commission".

Subsequently, for reasons which need not be gone into here, the Government of India, in the Ministry of Petroleum and Chemicals, by Notification dated 25-10-1971 added the following three terms in place of the original terms (h), (i) and (j) :—

"(h) Whether the Snam-Saipem was shown undue favour by officials of Indian Refineries Ltd., of Indian Oil Corporation or the Government, in connection with the award of the aforesaid contracts and in connection with the execution of the Gauhati-Siliguri and Haldia-Barauni-Kanpur pipeline projects under the aforesaid contracts;

"(i) to investigate the circumstances that caused considerable delay in the completion of Haldia-Barauni-Kanpur pipeline project;

"(j) to investigate the circumstances which led to the continuance of Shri Nittoor Sreenivas an Rau after his retirement as Central Vigilence Commissioner to enquire into the laying of a section of the Haldia-Barauni pipeline over the coal-bearing areas".

Thereupon the original term (h), (i) and (j) were relettered (k), (l) and (m) respectively. Term (l) was later struck down by the Delhi High Court in Civil Writ No. 464 of 1972 filed by Shri P.R. Nayak against the Union of India and another, whereupon the Government of India, in the Ministry of Petroleum and Chemicals by their Notification dated May 3, 1973 deleted term (l) and relettered term (m) as term (l).

CONTENTS

Vol I : Introduction; Historical background; Findings : Term (a) (i); Term a (ii); Term (b); Term (c); Term (d); Vol : II Term (c); Chairman's Inspection report of the Raniganj Coalfield area; **Vol. III :** Term (f); Term (g); Term (h); Term (i); Term (j);

Term (k); Term (l); Vol IV : Appendix I Calendar of event; procedure; Appendix II Extract of the relevant orders of the Commission.

RECOMMENDATIONS

Findings

The 'sanctioned amount' in the case of the Gauhati-Siliguri pipeline was exceeded by Rs. 23.69 lakhs—Rs. 1.21 lakhs under the head of reimbursable costs, and Rs. 22.48 lakhs under the head of income-tax.

The 'sanctioned amount' under both the heads was exceeded without the prior sanction of the Government.

Both Shri P.R. Nayak and Shri M.V. Rao were responsible for permitting these un-sanctioned amounts to be paid, and

There has been no payment in excess of the 'sanctioned amount' so far as the Haldia-Barauni-Kanpur pipeline is concerned,

That all the three reasons which Shri P.R. Nayak advanced before the Board at its meeting dated 3-7-1961, viz.

(i) that Italian credit for the preparation of the Project report was not available,

(ii) that Messrs Bechtel Corporation would prepare a Project report within 4-6 weeks, and

(iii) that they could, if entrusted with the preparation of the Project study, persuade the lending agencies in U.S. and the World Bank to finance the foreign exchange component of the project cost, were mis-statements; and on their bases he succeeded in getting Messrs. John Brown of U.K. eliminated from consideration and Messrs Bechtel Corporation of U.S.A. being given the second preference.

That at the meeting of the Board dated 10-10-1961, Shri P.R. Nayak again made a mis-statement regarding the non-availability of E.N.I. credit, and on the basis thereof, succeeded in getting Messrs E.N.I. eliminated from consideration, for the task of preparing the Project report, and Messrs Bechtel Corporation recommended for it instead.

That at the Board's meeting dated 11-11-1961, he withheld from the Board vital information about the conditions which Messrs Bechtel Corporation had laid down as a pre-requisite to their supplying the Project study by 15-2-1962, and, on the strength thereof, succeeded in securing their appointment for the preparation of the Project report.

That the various actions of commission and omission on the part of Shri P.R. Nayak were motivated by an improper, i.e. mala fide, desire to induct Messrs Bechtel Corporation into the Gauhati-Siliguri pipeline Project for the preparation of the Preliminary Project Study. To this extent he also showed undue favour to Messrs Bechtel Corporation.

The next series of events connected with the induction of Messrs. Bechtel Corporation into the Gauhati-Siliguri Pipeline Project for design and engineering management work, and to which reference has now to be made, start from 12-6-1962. On that date, according to Shri P.R. Nayak, the Minister of Mines and Fuel Shri K.D. Malaviya, gave him permission to "at least go ahead with the design work of the Project". Shri J.K. Srivastava, the learned Counsel for the Commission, challenged the correctness of the said statement, and argued that the permission referred to above was cooked up by Shri P.R. Nayak to expedite the induction of Messrs Bechtel Corporation into the Gauhati-Siliguri Pipeline project for the design and engineering work. The Commission is, however, unable to accept this contention;

Because there are far too many contemporaneous documents in existence in which reference is made to Shri P.R. Nayak's meeting with the Minister on 12-6-1962, and to the direction allegedly given by him to Shri P.R. Nayak at the meeting;

Because Shri K.D. Malaviya in his deposition before the Commission, far from denying the meeting with Shri P.R. Nayak on 12-6-1962, and the permission allegedly given by him to Shri P.R. Nayak on that day, stated that it was "quite possible he might have referred the matter in its generality".

Because Shri P.R. Nayak testified to that fact before the Commission, and his evidence in its generality has remained unshaken, the Commission sums up its findings as below.

That Shri P.R. Nayak deliberately did not bring the income-tax clause in the proposals of Messrs Bechtel Corporation dated 29-3-1962. Ex. A-598, to the notice of the other two members of the Sub-Committee he himself being the third Member—so as to ensure a smooth passage for his recommendation, that Messrs Bechtel Cooporation be entrusted with the design and engineering management of the Gauhati-Siliguri pipeline;

That Shri P.R. Nayak deliberately did not make any inquiries from the firms which had shown interest in the pipeline projects, although he had all the time in the world to do so. Instead, he did everything possible to expedite the induction of Messrs Bechtel Corporation into Gauhati-Siliguri pipeline project for the task of design and engineering work, at the Sub-Committee meeting dated 8/15-4-1962, although he was aware that the objections of the Railways to the laying of the pipeline along the railway-tract and on the railway-bridges, were still pending, and that without a decision on them, no realistic and final design work could be done;

That he settled the terms and conditions on which Messrs Bechtel Corporation were to do the design and engineering management work without the prior knowledge and approval of the Board or the Minister/ Ministry, and, in order to ensure that no inconvenient questions in regard to them were put by any of the Directors at the Board's meeting dated 20-7-1962 (Ex. A-379), he made a patently incorrect statement at that meeting, that the Minister and the Ministry had agreed to the payment terms of the contract;

That after the meeting of the Planning Commission on 28-7-1962, Ex. A-577, he deliberately did not ask Messrs Bechtel Corporation to suspend their work on the design and engineering management, although he knew that the limitation for the exercise of that right by the Government would run out in the next day or two, and the Planning Commission had neither cleared nor were likely to clear, the Gauhati-Siliguri pipeline project within the said period of limitation. He did this with a view to strengthen Messrs Bechtel Corporation's claim for the award of the design and engineering contract to them after the expiry of the period of limitation.

The Commission sum up its findings on the question of Messrs Bechtel Corporation's induction into the Haldia-Barauni-Kanpur pipeline which is as follows :

That, to begin with, Shri P.R. Nayak did the right thing in suggesting at the Board's meeting dated 20-12-1962, Ex. A-318, that "it would be advantageous if the management of the construction of the Calcutta-Barauni-Kanpur pipeline was carried out" by a third party, as not only was such a suggestion in accord with well-recognised international commercial practice, specially in a case in which both the designer and the contractor belonged to the same organisation, but it was, otherwise, also desirable and necessary as at that time, Messrs Indian Refineries Limited had next to no expertise and know-how for monitoring Messrs E.N.I.'s design, and supervising their construction work;

That Shri P.R. Nayak's further suggestion that "it would be advantageous if the management of construction of the Calcutta-Barauni-Kanpur pipeline was carried out by Messrs Bechtel Corporation" because they had been entrusted with similar work in the Gauhati-Siliguri Line, would also have been unobjectionable, provided he had made it in the interests of Messrs Indian Refineries Limited, and not with any ulterior motive or intention. However, his subsequent conduct shows that he made that suggestion, more out of his concern for Messrs Bechtel Corporation, than his solicitude for the interests of Messrs Indian Refineries Limited. This conclusion stands established from the following facts :

(a) that he did not make any inquiry from any other firm, as to whether it would be interested in the monitoring of Messrs E.N.I.'s design in the management and supervision of the construction of the Haldia-Barauni-Kanpur pipeline; and, if so, what its fee for those services would be;

(b) that as soon as he came to learn about the lines of which the Government's thinking in regard to the oil position, arising out of the emergency created by the Chinese invasion, was taking place, he wrote to Shri R.M. Dorman on 11-12-1963, Ex. A-605, inquiring of him whether Messrs Bechtel Corporation "would be in a position to come in, and build a crude oil pipeline 12 "dia. for a through put of 3 million tonnes per annum from Calcutta to Barauni Refinery which was to be ready in 10 to 12 months". Shri P R. Nayak was not justified in making such an inquiry of any firm, before the Cabinet had taken a decision, and that decision had been conveyed to Messrs Indian Refineries Limited. The fact that Shri P.R. Nayak, without waiting for the Cabinet's decision to be conveyed to Messrs Indian Refineries Limited, made the aforesaid enquiry only from Messrs Bechtel Corporation, contrary to his own suggestion that "we should consider inviting certain other well-known firms from the U.S.A. and West Europe to quote for doing the work (vide his letter dated 10-12-1962, Ex. A-357, to Shri K.R. Damle) also, shows the extent of his undue interest in that corporation;

(c) that in all the notes, which he prepared for consideration at inter-Ministerial meetings, as well as in the meetings themselves, he made statements, which were not only incorrect or incomplete to his knowledge, but also, invariably, tended to favour Messrs Bechtel Corporation at the expense of their rivals.

That the tactics, which Shri P.R. Nayak employed in the meetings of the Board of Directors of Messrs Indian Refineries Limited, and with the Ministry of Mines & Fuel, for getting his suggestions or proposals accepted by them, also reveal his undue anxiety to secure Messrs Bechtel Corporation's induction into whatever happened to be going at the time. For instance, in the case of Gauhati-Siliguri pipeline, he succeeded, on more than one occasion, in getting his proposals or suggestions accepted by the Board of Directors of Messrs Indian Refineries Limited, on the strength of some supposed discussion with, or approval of, some unnamed Government representative; and on the basis of the Board's recommendations he succeeded in getting the sanction or approval of the Government to his proposals and suggestions.

Thus on the findings recorded above, the Commission is satisfied that the induction of Messrs Bechtel Corporation into the Gauhati-Siliguri and the Haldia-Barauni-Kanpur pipeline projects by Shri P.R. Nayak was malafide.

Term (b)

That there has been no omission on the part of the officers of Messrs Indian Refineries Limited/Ministry of Mines and Fuel/Ministry of Finance in the 'scrutinising', 'editing', 'compiling' and 'maintaining' of the Preliminary Project report, the Executive Project report, the amendment to the Haldia-Barauni-Kanpur Construction Contract, and the three Supervision Contracts with the Bechtel firms. There has, however, been omission in the 'scrutinising' and 'editing' of the Haldia-Barauni-Kanpur Construction Contract, Ex. B-210.

That the three officers of Messrs Indian Refineries Limited who are responsible for the omission in the 'scrutinising and editing' of the Haldia-Barauni-Kanpur Construction Contract, Ex. B-210 are (1) Shri P.R. Nayak, (2) Shri M. Gopal Menon, and (3) Shri M.V. Rao;

That there was omission on the part of shri P.R. Nayak to 'maintain' records of negotiations, with which he was concerned;

That Shri Daulat Singh, and Shri N. Aravindakshan of Messrs Indian Refineries Limited are not liable for any omission in the 'maintaining' of the contractual documents referred to above;

That none of the officers of the Ministry of Mines and Fuel, and the Ministry of Finance, who dealt with the aforementioned contractual documents are liable for any omission, in regard to the 'scrutinising' of those documents.

Term (c)

That by their letter dated 7-1-1963 Ex. A-309/1, the Ministry of Mines and Fuel, directed Messrs Indian Refineries Limited to construct by 1965/66, a pipeline from Haldia to Barauni, having a capacity of 3 million tonnes per annum;

That Shri P.R. Nayak did not inform the Board of Directors of Messrs Indian Refineries Limited or the Ministry of Mines and Fuel, that the construction of the Haldia-Barauni pipeline was to be done on the basis of a 2 million tonnes per annum capacity initially; and of a 3 million tonnes per annum capacity by 1965-66, or when required;

That the amendment of July 1964 adversely affected the capacity of the Haldia-Barauni pipeline, since it provided for only 2 million tonnes per annum capacity in praesenti but capable of transporting 3 million tonnes per annum in future as against the Government's directive of 3 million tonnes per annum capacity.

That the consent of the Board of Messrs Indian Refineries Limited and the Ministry of Mines and Fuel, was a must, before any amendment to the directive contained in the Ministry of Mines and Fuel's letter, dated 7-1-1963, Ex. A-309/1, could be effected.

That Shri P.R. Nayak by-passed both the Board of Directors of Messrs Indian Refineries Limited, and the Ministry of Mines and Fuel, "in vital matters concerning the capacity of the H-B-K pipeline;

That the communication dated 26-9-1963, Ex. A-243 was an important communication and both the Managing Director, Shri P.R. Nayak and the General Manager, Shri M. Gopal Menon, were perfunctory and casual in their dealings with it, particularly, in not seeking further information from Messrs Bechtel Corporation or/and Messrs Snam Saipem, as to whether 1.9 million tonnes of Kerosene equivalent was equal to 2 million tonnes of crude and, if so, how;

That while no negligence or improper motive is substantiated against Shri P.R. Nayak, the Managing Director, Messrs Indian Refineries Limited, for not bringing vital matters concerning the capacity of the Haldia-Barauni-Kanpur pipeline to the notice of the Board of Directors of Messrs Indian Refineries Limited and the Ministry of Mines and Fuel, he cannot escape responsibility for arrogating to himself authority and power in the matter of implementing his capacity-concept of the Haldia-Barauni pipeline, which did not vest in him as the Managing Director of Messrs Indian Refineries Limited under their Memorandum, or Articles of Association, or Regulations.

Term (d)

That there was no sanction to the total project cost estimates of the Haldia-Barauni-Kanpur pipeline, though a number of individual items of the same were sanctioned;

That there has been no loss to the public-interest

as a result of non-sanction of the total project cost estimates, or of all the items forming part thereof;

That none of the officials of Messrs Indian Refineries Limited/Messrs Indian Oil Coporation—including their Directors—Ministry of Mines and Fuel/Petroleum and Chemicals and the Ministry of Finance acted carelessly or negligently or malafide in the discharge of their duties connected with the implementation of the Haldia-Barauni-Kanpur pipeline project.

Term (e)

That Shri M. Gopal Menon, Shri P.R. Nayak and Shri N.N. Kashyap acted carelessly and negligently in their dealings with the objections of the West Bengal Government and the Indian Mining Experts. In addition Shri M. Gopal Menon and Shri P.R. Nayak, by their obstinacy to preserve the original alignment, come what may, failed to deal with those objections objectively as befitted officers of their status and calibre;

That Shri B. Subba Rao was not responsible for any carelessness or negligence in the discharge of his duties in connection with the objections of the West Bengal Government and the Indian Mining Experts;

That the advice, Ex. F.22, which Messrs Snam Progetti, gave to their clients, Messrs Indian Refineries Limited was improper and incomplete, and consequently of no practical value;

That the advice which Messrs Bechtel Asian Corporation Limited gave to their clients, Messrs Indian Refineries Limited, besides being improper and incomplete, was also incorrect and misleading;

Thus on the findings recorded above, the notices to Shri M. Gopal Menon, Shri P.R. Nayak, Shri N.N. Kashyap, Messrs Snam Progetti and Messrs Bechtel Asian Corporation Limited, are made absolute, while the notice issued to Shri B. Subba Rao is vacated.

Term (f)

That the 'sanctioned estimates' in the case of Gauhati-Siliguri Pipeline were Rs. 591.20 lakhs or say Rs. 6 crores;

That the final revised project estimate as of 15-2-1966 was of the order of Rs. 775.38 lakhs which rose to Rs. 847.38 lakhs as a result of the devaluation of the rupee on 6-6-1966.

That the expenditure in excess of the 'sanctioned estimate' of Rs. 591.20 lakhs or 'say Rs 6 crores' was incurred without the prior formal sanction of the Government.

That the officers responsible for this lapse were Shri P.R. Nayak, Shri M. Gopal Menon and Shri M.V. Rao. However, the lapse on their parts was not due to any malafide motive;

That having regard to the practices and procedures followed by the Government at the relevant period, in providing funds for a continuing project, none of the officers of the Ministry of Finance, and none of the Directors of Messrs Indian Refineries Limited, during whose tenures and unsanctioned excess expenditure was incurred, can be held to have acted negligently or carelessly or malafide in the discharge of their duties in that regard.

Term (g)

That the awarding of the construction contracts for the Gauhati-Siliguri and the Haldia-Barauni-Kanpur pipelines on negotiated basis, without calling for global tenders, was a policy decision, of the Government with which the officers of Messrs Indian Refineries Limited/Government of India had nothing to do;

That under the Government of India—ENI Agreement the Government of India had the option to test the competitiveness of Messrs Snam Saipem's offer for both those pipelines, either on negotiated basis or by inviting global tenders, and hence they did not do anything contrary to the terms of the said agreement if, having regard to all the facts and circumstances of the case, they decided to avail themselves of the first alternative. However, so far as Messrs Snam Saipem were concerned, they were, always ready to have their offer tested by global tenders;

That the offer of Messrs Snam Saipem for the Haldia-Barauni-Kanpur pipeline was subjected to a detailed examination, first by the staff of Messrs Indian Refineries Limited and then by their Manager, Messrs Bechtel Corporation, and found to be competitive;

That Messrs Snam Saipem's offers for both the Gauhati-Siliguri and the Haldia-Barauni-Kanpur pipelines were compared with the quotation, which was accepted by Messrs Oil India Limited for their crude oil pipeline on the basis of global tenders only three years back, and were found to compare very favourably with the quotation, which was accepted by Messrs Oil India Ltd., the putting of Messrs Snam Saipem's offers to global tenders in the case of Gauhati-Siliguri pipeline and also the Haldia-Barauni-Kanpur pipeline, would have been, at best, a futile and time-consuming exercise;

That there has been no negligence or carelessness or malafide motive on the part of any of the officers of Government/Messrs Indian Refineries Limited in awarding the construction contracts for those two pipelines to Messrs Snam Saipen on negotiated basis without calling for global tenders.

Term (h)

That apart from the 'undue favour' which Messrs Indian Refineries Limited/Messrs Indian Oil Corporation showed to Messrs Snam Progetti under Item No. 11, supra they did not show any other favour to Messrs Snam Saipem/Messrs Snam Progetti in the award, or in connection with the execution, of the Gauhati-Siliguri and the Haldia-Barauni-Kanpur pipeline contracts;

That the said 'undue favour' took place unwittingly on account of the failure on the part of Shri P.R. Nayak and Shri M. Gopal Menon to study the offer for the preparation of the Project Report with the care and attention that they deserved, as also their obstinacy to stick to the original alignment of the pipeline through the Raniganj Coalfield area come what may.

Term (i)

It would have been noticed that the Commission has not given any findings on point 3 and 4 delineated under this term. This is because those points have already been dealt with by the Commission under terms (b) and (c), and as the Commission has nothing further to add to them, it will refrain from repeating itself unnecessarily.

Before parting with this term, the Commission would like to mention that it has had the advantage of perusing the conclusions recorded by the Committee on Public Undertakings in paragraphs 6.9 to 6.12 of its 66th report dated 29-4-1970. The Commission respectfully adopts those conclusions and recommends them for the acceptance of the Government. However, in the present case, there is one extenuating circumstance in favour of Messrs Indian Refineries Limited/Indian Oil Corporation for the delay in the completion of the Haldia-Barauni-Kanpur pipeline project, and that is that, except for the delay in the acquisition of the right of user in land, all the other delays were beyond their control. Indeed the moral which can be drawn from the Haldia-Barauni-Kanpur pipeline project is that before the Government decide to undertake any project they should insist upon a realistic appraisement of the time and money which is would entail. In the present case both those vital aspects were given the short shrift in the name of 'emergency' and 'speed' with the result that the cost of both the Gauhati Siliguri and the Haldia-Barauni-Kanpur pipeline projects, escalated by several crores of rupees, and the time taken in the completion of the Haldia-Barauni-Kanpur pipeline project was several times more than what it was expected to take. This is, however, not to say that the increase in the cost, and the delay in the completion, of the Haldia-Barauni-Kanpur pipeline project were not justified, but only to emphasise that if Messrs Indian Refineries Limited and the Ministries of Mines and Fuel and Finance, while processing the said project, had made a realistic allowance for the delays which are inevitable where the implementation of a project depend upon the concurrence of such a large number of departments and organisations as in the present case, and for the increase in costs due to the same, then they would have been in a better position to judge the economics of that project, than otherwise. The Commission would, therefore, recommend to the Government that before they make up their mind to undertake a project, they should satisfy themselves on both those matters, as closely and thoroughly as possible, so that there is no disproportionate fluctuation in that regard between the original estimates and the final results.

Thus as a result of the investigation attempted above, the following facts stand proved beyond the shadow of any doubt:—

That there was considerable delay in the completion of the Haldia-Barauni pipeline project;

That except for the delay involved in the acquisition of the right-of-user-in-land Messrs Indian Refineries Limited/Messrs Indian Oil Corporation were not responsible for any of the delays under the remaining heads. The officers and staff of Messrs Indian Refineries Limited must, therefore, be held to have acted carelessly and negligently in the discharge of their duties in connection with the acquisition of the right-of-user-in-land. However, it is not possible to identify those officers or the members of the staff, firstly because of their large numbers, and secondly because of the non-availability of all the necessary and relevant papers;

That Messrs Snam Progetti/Snam Saipem were not responsible for any delay in the completion of the Haldia-Barauni pipeline project.

Term (j)

That both the Minister, Shri Asoka Mehta and Shri P.R. Nayak acted improperly and unwisely in their handling of the matters connected with the initial appointment of Shri N.S. Rau to conduct the enquiry in question—the former in asking Shri P.R. Nayak to suggest some name for conducting that enquiry, and the latter in giving his suggestion in that behalf—as it was known to both of them that the conduct of Shri P.R. Nayak might also be involved in that enquiry;

That when the impending retirement of Shri N S. Rau from the office of the Central Vigilence Commission, in August 1968, necessitated a consideration of the question as to who was to conduct the inquiry thereafter, both Shri Asoka Mehta and Shri P.R. Nayak again acted improperly and unwisely in their dealings with that matter—the former in leaving the negotiations in that regard to be carried out by the latter, and the latter in undertaking them—for the same reason as the one mentioned as above; and

That Shri P.R. Nayak gave incorrect and misleading information to Shri Asoka Mehta as regards the probable time that Shri N.S. Rau's report was likely to take, and on the strength of it he succeeded in obtaining Shri Asoka Mehta's concurrence to the continuance of Shri N.S. Rau with the inquiry after his retirement as Central Vigilance Commissioner, instead of entrusting in to his successor in that office or to some other person. Shri P.R. Nayak, therefore, acted malafide and in contravention of Rule 3 of All India Services Conduct Rules 1968, which inter alia requires that "Every member of the Service shall... do nothing which is unbecoming of a member of the service". The notice issued to him under section 8B of the Commission of Enquiry Act 1952, as amended by Act 79 of 1971 is, therefore, made absolute.

Term (l)

This term also fell for the consideration of the Commission on an earlier occasion, when it was argued, as indeed it was argued on the present occasion also, that it was a residuary term intended to embrace all matters involved in alleged pipeline muddle which were not covered by any of the preceding terms of reference. Developing his arguments, Shri Chatterjee contended that this term was not to be interpreted ejusdem generis with the preceding terms but was to be considered as a separate term of inquiry covering all matters not specified before, but connected with the construction of the two pipelines in question, and the manner in which some of the matters connected therewith were suppressed. Without a finding on all those points Shri Chatterjee contended, the object of the inquiry would be frustrated and the government would not be able to take steps to 'plug the loop-holes' in the working of the public-sector undertakings in the future. As stated above, this point was considered on an earlier occasion also and the view taken by the Commission then was (vide its order dated 19-8-71 on the application of Shri Arun Roy Chaudhury dated 8/9-7-71) that 'such a provision is included in all such cases to enable the inquiring authority to make recommendations to Government about desired future practice or procedure in matters similar to those covered by the scope of the inquiry' and that it cannot be used to extend the scope of the Commission's terms of reference to a determination on issues not specifically or impliedly referred to the Commission.

It would have been noticed that the aforesaid view does not proceed on the basis that term (m) was to be interpreted ejusdem generis with the terms preceding it, but is based on the ground that it was included in the Commission's term of reference for a different purpose altogether, viz., for enabling the Commission to make recommendations to the Government about the 'desired future practice and procedure in matters similar to those covered by the scope of the inquiry'. Indeed the opening word 'generally' and the expression 'that is relevant in the opinion of the Commission' in the said term, clearly go to show that the matters envisaged therein have nothing to do with the matters connected with the alleged pipelines' muddle, for had that been the intention of the framers of the Commission's term of reference, the Commission sees no reason why they should have left the submission of a report on them to the discretion of the Commission, instead of requiring it to investigate/determine them or give its report/advice thereon in the same way as was laid down by them in the case of the other terms. Futher the tetm 'generally' would not have been used to preface that term. The dictionary meaning of the word 'generally' is 'in a general sense' without regard to particulars', not specifically. Hence if any meaning is to be attached to that word the report on matters under term (m) is to be in general and not any specific sense as in the case of the other terms. Thus both the word 'generally' and the expression 'in the opinion of the Commission' go to show that term (m) is not meant to embrace all residuary matters connected with the alleged pipelines' muddle. On the contrary, the Commission is firmly of the opinion that this term could not have been framed in its existing form, unless it was intended to apply only to matters which the framers of the Commission's terms of reference could neither visualise nor forsee. As all the aspects of the alleged pipeline muddle were within the knowledge of the framers of the terms of reference—particularly in view of the Report of the Public Undertakings Committee—the specific inclusion of some of those matters in the Commission's terms of reference, and the exclusion of some others therefrom, can only be explained on the hypothesis that the matters not specifically included in its terms were not to be investigated by the Commission. This view receives some support from term (k) in which also, the expression 'in the opinion of the Commission are relevant' has been used. That term requires the Commission 'to advise whether there has been any negligence or carelessness or malafide motive on the part of any of the officers of Government/IRL/IOC and their staff in the discharge of their duties on any one of the foregoing or other related issues which 'in the opinion of the Commision are relevant'. It will be noticed that in this term the expression 'in the opinion of the Commission are relevant' has been used in connection with 'other related issues'. The Commission has already held in its order dated 19-8-1971 that the expression 'other related issues' in term (k) means issues which bear some relation or kinship with the terms which precede it. It seems to the Commission that the only reason why the framers of the Commission's terms of reference used the words 'related issues', instead of specifying the same themselves, was their inability to foresee them, and hence they left them to be sorted out by the Commission during the course of the inquiry. Further more the fact that the advice on those issues was left to the discretion of the Commission, and was not made mandatory as in the case of the other terms also lends support to this view. Finally, it is noteworthy that though the Commission's views on the scope and ambit of old term (j) i.e. present term (m) have been known to the Government for almost a year now, and though they added three more terms after the Commission's Order dated 19-8-1971, they did not deem fit to amend or clarify that term so as to bear the construction sought to be placed upon it by Shri Chatterjee. Thus both the preliminary objections have no force and are rejected.

Thus according to the Commission this term was included in its terms of reference with a view to enabling it 'to make recommendations to Government about the desired future practice or procedure in matters similar to those covered by the scope of enquiry'. Pursuant to that construction, the Commission has in the course of its inquiry made suggestions/recommendations at several places 'about the desired future practices or procedure' to be followed in 'matters similar to those covered by the scope of the inquiry'. It is, unnecessary therefore to repeat them here.

There is, however, one matter which the Commission has had no occasion to deal with earlier, and that is the manner in which proceedings used to be conducted at the meetings of the Board of Directors of Messrs Indian Refineries Limited. The recorded minutes of the Board of Messrs Indian Refineries Limited/Messrs Indian Oil Corporation relative to the period of the present enquiry show, that on a number of occasion, items used to be taken up, without prior notice thereof to the Directors, and decisions were taken on them, on the faith of the bare statement of Managing Director, Shri P.R. Nayak, with the result that he was able to get the Board and the Government to agree to whatever he desired. The Commission has pointed out several instances under term (a) (ii), where Shri P.R. Nayak succeeded in getting the Board's approval to his proposals, on the strength of some supposed talk between him and the officials of the Ministry. and the Government's sanction on the basis of the Board's approval. While the Directors cannot be held responsible for this state of affairs (Vide the Order of the Commission dated 20-7-1972, passed on the joint application of Shri L.N. Mishra and Shri K.G.R. Iyer and the order dated 25-9-1972 passed on the applications of Sardar Joginder Singh dated 15-7-1972, Shri B.S. Sarao, dated 10-6-72 and Rana K.D.N. Singh, dated 10-8-1972). The Commission feels that this is not a desirable state of affairs, and that some procedure should be devised to obviate the repetition of such a situation. The Commission would accordingly recommend to the Government (1) that they should require public sector undertakings to send to the concerned administrative Ministries verbatim copies of the recorded minutes of the relevant Agenda Item—and not merely extracts thereof—so that if they contain any inaccuracy, the concerned administrative Ministry may be able to set the record straight before any mischief is done and (2) that, except in cases of extreme urgency and necessity, they should inhibit the Board of Directors from considering any matter unless a self-contained agenda note accompanied by copies of documents, if any, on which it purports to be based, has been circulated to the Directors in good time, to enable them to give due thought to it. In this connection, the Commission cannot help observing that while it is no doubt true that in law, the Directors of Messrs India Refineries Limited were justified in relying upon the statements made at their Board's meeting by the Managing Director, Shri P.R. Nayak, whose integrity they had no reason to doubt, but as those statements were made on the basis of some alleged talk with the officers of the Ministry of Mines and Fuel or/and the Ministry of Finance, one would have expected that at least the representatives of those Ministries on the

Board of Directors of Messrs Indian Refineries Limited, would, as watchdogs of their Ministries, have asked for some independent corroboration of those statements, even if they had no reason to doubt the integrity of Shri P.R. Nayak. Had these precautions been taken in the present case many of the complications, which have been brought to light in the present inquiry, would not have arisen.

The Committee on Public Undertakings in its Report, dated 29-4-1970 has made a number of suggestions/recommendations for consideration of, and implementation by, the Government. The Commission cannot do better than impress upon the Government the absolute necessity of giving effect to them as soon as possible. However, before concluding, the Commission would like to observe that, in its opinion, no amount of rules and regulations, checks and counter-checks, which human ingenuity can devise to ensure that officers and staff in public life perform their duties conscientiously and with scrupulous honesty, can succeed, or even hope to succeed unless high ethical standards are meticulously observed at all levels. The Commission would, therefore, advise the Government not to spend their time and energy in framing rules and regulations to plug all conceivable loop-holes in the working of public sector undertakings and Government Departments—since we have too many of them already—but to concentrate on ensuring that the officers and staff, whom they select for public service, possess not only the requisite ability, but also the necessary character and integrity. As for the officers and staff who are already in service, the Government would be well-advised to take steps to improve their ethical standards, if, and where necessary. The Commission has no doubt that with the qualitative change that has come in the situation with the declaration of emergency, that consummation should not be difficult to achieve.

NATIONAL COMMISSION ON AGRICULTURE, 1970—REPORT

New Delhi, Ministry of Agriculture and Irrigation, 1976; 15 parts

Chairman : Shri Nathu Ram Mirdha (replaced Shri C. Subramaniam who resigned on January 28, 1971).

Vice-Chairman : Shri B. Sivaraman.

Members : Dr. S.K. Mukherjee; Dr. H.R. Arakeri; Dr. P. Bhattacharya; Chaudhuri Randhir Singh; Shri M.V. Krishnappa; Dr. Z.A. Ahmed; Dr. M.S. Swaminathan; Shri T.A. Pai; Shri Balwant Singh Nag; Dr. A.M. Khusro; Shri Hari Singh; Dr. N.K. Panikkar; Shri Triloki Singh.

Member-Secretary : Shri J.S. Sarma.

APPOINTMENT

Agriculture has a dominant role in the Indian economy contributing nearly half of the national income, providing employment to about 70 per cent of the working population and accounting for a sizable share of the country's foreign exchange earnings.

Population has been increasing at a rapid rate, leading to increase in demand for food and other consumer goods, many of which have an agricultural base. There is a legitimate aspiration of the people in rural areas to improve their standards of living and to share the fruits of development.

Rapid improvement in agriculture is possible through advances in research and technological innovations, larger utilisation of inputs and reduction in dependence on the vagaries of weather through irrigation and other improved practices. Recent trends have thrown up vast possibilities of an accelerated growth in Indian agriculture. The experience of the Intensive Agricultural Development Programme (Package Programme), Intensive Agricultural Area Programme and the introduction of the new strategy have shown that the farmers are responsive to the adoption of scientific and improved agricultural practices and to the incentive of prices. Notable break-through has been achieved in respect of one or two crops and there is the promise of a similar break-through in respect of other cereal crops and some non-food crops. There has been increasing evidence of investment in irrigation and other facilities both from private and institutional resources with a view to reducing the dependence on vagaries of weather. The utilisation of technological and non-farm inputs has also been growing at a rapid rate. The development of transport and other facilities is opening up the rural areas and is providing outlet for the farm produce.

During the very process of this development, the need for taking measures to ensure that the benefits of the new technology are shared by the bulk of the farming population and are not limited to the better-off class of farmers has become obvious. It has become clear that besides the irrigated areas which permit of intensive development through multiple-cropping and application of inputs in intensive doses, there are large tracts under rain-fed agriculture requiring special attention both in the matter of evolution of the appropriate technology suited to those areas and of making available the necessary resources to the farmers. Moreover, currently, while there have been impressive increases in foodgrains, critical shortages are developing in respect of fat and protein production. It is, therefore, necessary to diversify agriculture between crops and to extend the new technology to horticultural crops also. The overall objective should be to secure integrated development of agriculture, animal husbandry, poultry, inland fisheries and forestry for ensuring a balanced diet and development.

The possibilities of progress in different directions have made it incumbent to take a coordinated and forward view of the different aspects of development. In spheres such as those dealing with the problems of unemployment and reduction in the disparities between the low and high income farmers as well as irrigated and rain-fed areas, urgent action is necessary. The existing arrangements for research and extension which are basic for sustaining the tempo of development have also to be reviewed for coping with the challenges posed by the adoption of new techonology and providing a two-day channel of communication between the farmer and the scientist.

All in all, it has to be ensured that the development of agriculture caters to the welfare of the vast multitudes of population living the rural areas.

It is in this background that the Government of India have taken the decision to set up a National Commission to enquire into the progress, problems and potential of Indian agriculture. In status as well as in the assignment given to it, the Commission will be of the highest level and Government are confident that its report and recommedations would have a far-reaching and historic impact on the further development of Indian Agriculture in all its aspects.

The National Commission on Agriculture was constituted by the Government of India, Ministry of Food, Agriculture, Community Development and Co-operation (Department of Agriculture) Vide its Resolution No. 25-13/68-Genl Coord. dated August 29, 1970.

In the context of the agricultural situation described in the foregoing paragraphs, the terms of reference of the Commission will be as follows :-

1. To examine comprehensively the current progress of agriculture in India and to make recommendations for its improvement and modernisation with a view to promoting the welfare and prosperity of the people;

2. In particular, investigate and report the following aspects of agriculture:

Crop Production and Land and Water Development

(i) Economics of land and water utilisation and the patterns, and scope for expansion of crops for balanced and nutritious food, industrial uses and exports with special reference to the need and scope for development of horticulture;

(ii) Problems of soil and moisture conservation, particularly those related to the catchment areas of the major irrigation projects on the one hand and the composite implementation of soil conservation measures and improved agricultural practices on the other;

(iii) Problems of water management and ground water exploitation in relation to other surface irrigated projects, major and minor;

(iv) Programmes for land reclamation and development with special consideration of the needs of areas affected by soil salinity;

(v) Requirements of the new strategy of scientific agriculture in the shape of requisite supplies of inputs and production requisites with special consideration of sources of supply and problems and in particular :-

(a) multiplication, distribution of high-yielding varieties of seed and other improved seeds;

(b) propagation of soil nutrients including chemicals, fertilisers and other organic manures;

(c) measures for plant protection keeping in view the risk of pollution, and

(d) agricultural creait from Government, co-operative and other institutional agencies;

(vi) The scope and long and short-term potentiality

for mechanisation of agriculture in the context of the use of advanced technology involving the use of high yielding varieties and adoption of multiple cropping without having adverse effect on rural employment situation.

Animal Products, Fisheries and Forestry

(i) Development of animal husbandry both for providing nutritious diet to the population, draft power for agricultural operations and income and employment opportunities to the rural population;

(ii) Development of poultry, piggery, sheep and goats for increasing income and employment opportunities in the rural areas, besides contribution to balanced diet;

(iii) Measures necessary for disease control in animal population to increase their efficiency;

(iv) Development of fisheries, marine, inland and estuarine for increasing income and employment opportunities for the weaker section of population dependent for their livelihood on this occupation, besides their contribution to balanced diet and export earnings;

(v) Development of forestry, including farm forestry as a factor in agricultural progress and as a source of raw material for industry, exports as well as for sustaining the ecological balance in nature, and for providing employment opportunities to large sections of tribal and other population living in these areas.

Research, Education and Training

(i) Achievements, deficiencies and potential of the development of agricultural research and steps needed for promotion of agricultural research and its application to field conditions in the context of fast developing technology; and the need for scientific demonstrations on farmers' fields, for gearing up extension machinery and for the establishment of a two-way channel between farmers and scientists;

(ii) Education and training of personnel, (a) at the level of Universities and higher agricultural education; (b) middle level training of personnel engaged in occupations ancillary to agriculture, and (c) training of government and other personnel connected with agricultural development;

(iii) Role of farmers' training and education, and methods of mobilisation of human resources and ensuring people's participation in agricultural development programmes.

Organisation and Supporting Measures

(i) Examination of the structure and organisation of existing agencies and personnel both government and non-government engaged in the operation of agricultural research and development programmes and improvements and adjustments necessary to suit the changed requirements for the formulation of policies, preparation of programmes and implementation of action in the field, and the relative role and responsibilities of Central and State Governments.

(ii) Development of transport, marketing and storage and processing industries with particular reference to food processing to support the programmes for growth in agricultural production, including horticulture and animal husbandry.

Employment and Manpower

(i) Employment potential of agricultural sector and the implications of the goal of full employment in agriculture for policies and programmes;

(ii) Scope for pilot projects to demonstrate the types of schemes necessary for creating employment opportunities in the rural areas;

(iii) Manpower requirements for agricultural programmes and methods of recruitment and training;

(iv) Problems of small farmers and agricultural labour viewed in the context of social justice and equality of opportunity and as a factor in securing effective participation of the bulk of the Indian peasantry in stepping up agricultural production.

Other Aspects

(i) Concept, potential and measures necessary for integrating area development with special reference to dry and rain-fed areas, command area of irrigation projects and remote, economical backward, hilly and tribal areas;

(ii) Land reforms, consolidation of holdings and the link between land reforms and agricultural production;

(iii) Study of agricultural price problems as a policy of incentives for agricultural production;

(iv) Crop insurance;

(v) Availability of reliable and timely agricultural statistics for formulation and implementation of agricultural policies and programmes.

CONTENTS

Part I—Review and Progress: Introduction; Historical Review; Progress of Agricultural Development; Some Economic Aspects; Appendices. **Part II—Policy and Strategy:** Agriculture in Economic Development; Growth with Social Justice; Policy and Strategy;

Centre-State Relations in Agricultural Development; Summary of Recommendations; Appendix; Nutrition; Summary of Recommendations; Appendix. **Part III—Demand and Supply:** Demand Projections; Summary and Conclusions; Appendix; Supply Possibilities; Export Possibilities and Import Substitution; Summary of Recommendations; Appendix. **Part IV—Climate and Agriculture:** Climate; Agrometeorology; Droughts; Weather Bulletins for Farmers; External range Forecasting; Crop Weather Relationship; Weather Modification; Artificial Rain Making Experiments; Research; Education and Training and International Cooperation; Organisation of Metereological Observatories and Raingauges for Agriculture; Summary of Recommendations; Appendix; Maps; Rainfall and Cropping Patterns; Methodology; General Information; Rainfall Patterns—Zones; Rainfall Regions; Cropping Patterns; Suggestions for Future Cropping Patterns; Summary of Recommendations; Appendix; Maps. **Part V: Resource Development:** Irrigation, Water Resources; Land Resources for Irrigation; Past Development of Irrigation; Ground Water; Development of Water Resources; Perspective of Irrigation Development; Cropping in Irrigated Areas; Modernisation of Existing Irrigation Systems; Economic and Financing of Irrigation Works; Irrigation Administration; Irrigation Research and Training; Summary of Recommendations; Appendix; Command Area Development; Soil and Soil Surveys; Land Preparation for Irrigation; Preparation of Command Area Development Report; Summary of Recommendations; Appendix; Land Reclamation and Development; Summary of Recommendations; Appendix; Soil and Moisture Conservation; Summary of Recommendations; Appendix; Electricity in Rural Development; Summary of Recommendations; Appendix. **Part VI—Crop Production, Sericulture and Apiculture:** Preamble; Reorientation of Cropping System; Introduction; Rainfed Farming; Irrigated Farming; Cropping System; Summary of Recommendations; Appendix; Foodgrain Crops; Rabi Cereals; Rice; Kharif Cereals Other than Rice, Pulses: General; Summary of Conclusions and Recommendations; Appendices; Commercial Crops, Sugar Crops, Tobacco, Cotton, Best Fibre Crops; Summary of Recommendations; Appendices; Horticulture Crops—Fruit Crops, Tuber Crops, Bulb Crops, Vegetables, Condiments and Spices, Mushrooms, Floriculture, Aromatic and Medicinal Plants; Summary of Recommendations; Appendices; Plantation Crops; Summary of Conclusions and Recommendations; Appendix; Fodder Crops, Cultivated Fodders, Grasslands, Tree and Shrub Leaves as Fodder; Seeds of Fodder Crops; Organisational Aspects; Summary of Recommendations; Appendix; Sericulture; Central Silk Board, Extending Sericulture to New Areas; Multiplication and Distribution of Silkworm Seed; Organisational Structure; Summary of Recommendations; Agriculture, Scope for Increasing Honey Yields Through Organised Agriculture; Induction of Agriculture as an Organised Activity to the Benefit of Crop Production; Summary of Recommendations; Appendix. **Part VII—Animal Husbandry:** Cattle and Buffaloes; Trend in Cattle Population; Estimates of Milk Production and the Demand; Cattle Development; Cattle Breeding Policies; Cattle Breeding Farms; Military Dairy Farms; Gaushalas; Role of Indigenous Breeds of Cattle; Artificial Insemination; Crossbreeding with Exotic Dairy Breeds; The Buffalo; Milk Recording and Herd Books; Problems of City Milch Cattle; Cattle Insurance; Export Trade in Cattle and Buffalloes; Policies and Programmes for Achieving Milk Production Targets; Summary of Recommendations; Appendix; Dairy Development—Introduction; Review of Progress; Marketing; Dairy Plant Management; Manufacture of Dairy Equipment; Projections for Milk Demand, Processing and Marketing; Administrative and Institutional Structure; Summary of Recommendations; Appendix; Sheep and Goats—Sheep; Goats; Summary of Recommendations; Poultry—Introduction; Poultry Statistics; Development of Poultry Farming; Breeding; Poultry Feeds; Poultry Epuipment; Health Cover; Credit, Cooperative and Marketing; Duck Rearing; Research and Education; Summary of Recommendations; Appendix; Other Livestock—Pig; Equines, Camel, Yak; Recommendations; Appendix; Mixed Farming—Introduction; Regional Practices; Scope for Livestock Production in Mixed Farming; Apiculture, Sericulture and Pisciculture in Mixed Farming; Results of Studies on Mixed Farming; Benefits of Mixed Farming; Summary of Recommendations; Live-Stock Feeding—Introduction; Feed Requirements for Livestock; Availability of Feeds; Requirements vis-a-vis Availability of Livestock Feeds; Ways and Means to Increase Availability of Fodders; Ways and Means to Improve Availability of Concentrate Feed; Compound Feed Manufacturing Industry; Further Suggestions; Summary of Recommendations; Appendix; Animal Health—Introduction; Clinical and Preventive Veterinary Medicine; Registration of Veterinarians; Veterinary Biological Products; Control of Animal Diseases; Legislation for Control of Animal Diseases; Animal Quarantine and Certification; Animal Disease Intelligence Service; Veterinary Public Health; Summary of Recommendations; Meat Production and Animal Byproducts—Meat Production; Animal Byproducts and Animal Wastes; Utilisation of Fallen Animals;

Summary of Recommendations; Appendix. **Part VIII—Fisheries :** Inland Fisheries and Aquaculture; Introduction; Riverine Fisheries; Reservoir Fisheries; Derelict Freshwater Fishery Resources and Their Reclamation; Estuarine Fisheries; Aquaculture; Culture in Freshwaters; Culture in Brackish Waters; Mariculture; Leasing of Fishery Rights in Public Waters; Organisational Aspects; Summary of Recommendations; Appendix; Marine Fisheries—Introductions, Production Trends; Resource Potential, Survey and Assessment; Production Means; Tuna Fishing in the High Seas; Fishery Harbours; Training of Operatives; Economic Aspects; Marine Fisheries Policy; Summary of Recommendations; Appendix; Crustacean Fisheries and Their Utilisation—Introduction; Prawn Fisheries; Lobsters; Crabs; Squilla; Utilisation; Research; General Suggestions; Summary of Recommendations; Appendix; Marketing of Fish and Fishery Products—Fish Marketing Within India; Export of Marine Products; Industrial Fishery Products; Summary of Recommendations; Appendix. **Part IX—Forest Policy :** Introduction; Forestry Before Independence; Role of Forestry in Economic Development; Forest Development Under the Five Year Plans; National Forest Policy; Land Requirement for Forestry; Strategy for Forest Development; Summary of Recommendations; Appendix; Production and Social Forestry—Introduction; Demand and Supply Projections; The Interim Report on Production Forestry; Export Potential of Indian Timbers and Processed Products; Expanding Industrial use of Forest Products; Logging and Mechanisation; Infrastructure and Inputs; Control of Forest Diseases and Insects; Social Forestry; Role of Forest in Soil and Water Conservation; Grazing in the Forests; Forest Based Tribal Development; Special Problem Areas; Organisation and Manpower; Summary of Recommendations; Appendix; Minor Forest Produce—Introduction; Production—Actual and Potential, Demand, Collection and Processing; Export; Organisation, Employment; Summary of Recommendations; Appendix; Forest Ecology and Wild Life Management—Introduction; Forest and Environment; Ecological Considerations In Forestry, Wildlife Development; Diseases of Wildlife; Wildlife and Tourism; Summary of Recommendations; Appendix; Forest Protection and Law—Introduction; Forest Fire; Protection from Destruction and Encroachment; Present Status of Forest Laws; The Approach to Forest Legislation; Summary of Recommendations; Appendix; Forest Planning, Research and Education—Introduction; Forest Inventory; Forestry Statistics; Forest Planning; Industry Oriented Management Plans; Organisation; Forest Research and Education; Summary of Recommendations; Appendix. **Part X**—Inputs—Seeds; Introduction; Review; Measures to make Seed Business Attractive; Measures for Quality Improvement; Seed Research, Education, Training and Organisation; Summary of Recommendations; Appendix; Fertilisers and Manures—Role of Fertilisers in Crop Production, Plant Nutrients; Assessment of Fertiliser Requirement; Factors Affecting Efficient use of Fertilisers; Soil Organic Matter and Organic Manures; Chemical Fertilisers and Soil Amendments; Fertiliser Dose; Soil Testing as a Guide to Efficient use of Fertilisers; Chemical Fertilisers and Soil Amendments; Fertiliser Dose; Soil Testing as a Guide to Efficient use of Fertilisers; Summary of Recommendations; Appendix; Plant Protection Chemicals—Introduction; Role of Chemicals in Pest Control for Enhanced Crop Production; Extent of Crop Loss due to Insect, Pests and Diseases; Efficiency of Chemicals in Pest Control and Increasing Crop Production; Chemicals in Farming System: Surveillance and Warning; Economics of the Use of Agricultural Chemicals; Basic Raw Materials, Knowhow and Indigenous Availability; Fertiliser Pesticide Mixture; Residual Toxicity and Hazards of Pesticides; Quality Control of Pesticides; Plant Protection Services; Summary of Recommendations; Appendix; Farm Power—Introduction; Farm Power and Productivity; Requirements of Farm Power; Manufacturer; Quality Control; Supply and Services; Organisation; Education and Research; Summary of Recommendations; Appendix; Farm Implements and Machinery—Introduction; Hand Operated and Animal Drawn Implements and Machinery; Inanimate Power Operated Implements and Machinery; Manufacture; Quality Control, Supply and Services; Summary of Recommendations; Appendix. **Part XI—Research, Education and Extention : Research**—Introduction; Categories of Research; Historical Background; The Indian Council of Agricultural Research; Agricultural Universities and State Departments *vis a vis* Research Institutes; Research Organisations Other Than Agricultural Universities and ICAR Institutes; Research Administration; Some Topics For Research; Summary of Recommendations; Appendix. **Education**—Introduction; Brief Historical Development; Primary and Secondary Level Education; Nondegree Education Programme; University Level Education; Preservice and Inservice Training; Education and Training in Animal Science; Education and Training in Fisheries; Summary of Recommendations; Appendix. **Extention**—Introduction; Scope and Objectives; Demonstration; Farm Information and Communication Support; Farmers Education and Training; Extension

Personnel and Professional Development; Role of Various Agencies; Summary of Recommendations. **Part XII—Supporting Services and Incentives** : Credit and Incentives—Introduction; Evolution of Institutional Finance System; Achievements and Limitations; Major Components of New Credit Policy for Financing Agriculture; Organisation of Credit and Farmers' Service Societies; National Programme for Organisation of Farmers Service Societies; Mobilisation of Institutional Financial Resources; Measures for Implementation of National Policy; Other Incentives Including Subsidies; Summary of Recommendation; Appendix; Marketing; Transport and Storage : Preamble; Markets and Marketing Institutions; Input Marketing; Output Marketing; Transport; Storage; Marketing Education, Research, Extension and Administration; Summary of Recommendations; Appendix; Processing and Agro-Industries—Preamble; Processing; Expanding Uses of Agricultural Commodities; Utilisation of By-products and Wastes Commercial Exploitation of Agricultural Products; Role of Agro-Industries Corporations; Summary of Recommendations; Appendix. **Part XIII—Rural Employment and Special Area Programmes** : Rural Employment—Introduction; Growth of Rural Labour Force; The Unemployment Situation; Programmes and Planning; The Strategy and Policies; Summary of Recommendations; Appendix. Special Area Development Programmes—Introduction; Hill Areas; Tribal Areas; Arid and Semi-arid Areas; Kutch and Sundar Ban; Small and Marginal Farmers and Agricultural Labourers; Summary of Recommendations; Appendix. **Part XIV—Planning, Statistics and Administration** : Planning —Introduction; Historical Background; Approach to Agricultural Planning; Planning Process; Plan Implementation; Planning Machinery; Methodological Problems; Regional Planning for Balanced Development; Lessons of Planning; Summary of Recommendations. **Statistics**—Introduction; Land Utilisation and Area Under Crops; Statistics of Crop Production; Reliability of Estimates of Foodgrains Production; Improvement of Crop Statistics; Fruits and Vegetables Statistics; Irrigation Statistics; Livestock Statistics; Fisheries Statistics; Forestry Statistics; Input Statistics; Market Intelligence; Agricultural Census; Integrated System of Agricultural Surveys; Research Statistics; Derived Statistics and Indicators of Agricultural Economy; Tabulation, Publication and Dissemination; Organisational Set-up for Statistics; Agro-Economic Research; Summary of Recommendations; Appendices. **Administration**—Introduction; Role of State; Field level Administration; State level Organisation; Central Agricultural Set-up; Training in Agricultural Administration and Management; Summary of Recommendations; Farmers' Organisations; Need for Setting up an All India Farmers' Organisation; Existing Farmers' Organisations in India; Farmers' Organisations in other Countries; Farmers' Organisation A Suggested Pattern For India; Representation; Summary of Recommendations. **International Cooperation**—Introduction; Review; Scope and Progress of Further Assistance in Agriculture; Summary of Recommendations; Appendix. **Part XV—Agrarian Reforms** : Land Reforms Policy—Pre-Independence Land Tenure System; Evolution of Policy; Land Reforms Legislation and Implementation—Introduction; Legislation for Abolition of Intermediaries; Tenancy Legislation; Ceiling Legislation; Implementation; Appendix. **Agrarian Structure and Perspective**—Introduction; Pre-Independence Agrarian Structure; Emerging Agrarian Structure; Future Course of Development; Recommended Structure; Summary of Recommendations; Appendix. **Consolidation of Holdings**—Introduction; Experience in India and abroad; Review of Progress; Land Consolidation in Socio-Economic Background; Principles and Techniques of Consolidation; Procedures; Survey and Record of Rights; Organisational and Administrative Set-up; Integrated Approach to Consolidation of Holdings; Special Problem Areas; Priorities and Financing; Summary of Recommendations; Appendix. **Agricultural Labour**—Introduction; Policy for Minimum Wages in Agriculture; Housing Amenities and Subsidiary Occupations; Phasing and Integration of Programmes; Summary of Recommendations; Appendix.

RECOMMENDATIONS

Policy and Strategy

The future policy of agricultural development should consciously attempt to combine social justice with growth. The main thrust should be on the creation of large scale opportunities for productive employment with a view to raising the level of incomes of the less privileged among the rural population through increased production. The accent should also be on the development of secondary and tertiary sectors not only to meet the increasing demand for rural services such as credit, transport, marketing and trade, etc., but also to increase the prospects of employment and income in the rural areas through greater diversification.

Decentralisation of industries and services would be the means through which such a diversification could be achieved. Necessary support to rural crafts will be required for fuller utilisation of the local skills. Only such measures can tackle the problem of unemployment and under-employment in the rural areas as well as the problem of rural-urban disparity. Both the agrarian structure and the institutional arrangements will require fundamental changes to enable the small farmers, tenants, share croppers and the landless agricultural labourers to participate in the process of development and share its benefits. Land reforms must be considered as basic to ensuring growth with social justice. In the context of the predominance of small sized farms and low level of output, layers of intermediary interests sharing the small produce will only perpetuate poverty. Tenancy in such a situation is clearly untenable except perhaps in very special cases. State policy should be to encourage peasant proprietorship with necessary backing of supplies and services to derive the maximum benfit out of the small piece of land. Measures will have to be taken for fuller utilisation of the limited land area and for diversification of agricultural activities for sustained growth. The concept of social justice has many facets. The policy instruments to achieve growth with social justice have to be varied and their choice will have to depend upon the peculiar needs of each situation. The policy should be to not only reduce inequality among the various strata in the rural society, but also among different regions by utilising the endowments of each region to the maximum. Necessary backing of research, extension and services will have to be provided for the purpose. Sufficient funds should be earmarked for research which should be directed towards evolving suitable crop varieties and practices for areas with different rainfall conditions so as to extend the benefits of scientific agriculture to more crops and areas. Special attention has to be paid to the vulnerable and backward regions which, because of their social, economic and political limitations and peculiarities, have so far been outside the mainstream of development in the country. In fixing priorities for development and deciding upon the pace of such development, due consideration should be given to specially backward areas. Development of infrastruture in such areas will need priority attention. Larger state assistance will be called for to activise these areas.

The amelioration of poverty in the rural areas cannot, however, be accomplished quickly. Complete eradication of poverty may yet be a distant goal. The availability of overall resources in the country sets a limit to the pace at which the disparities can be mitigated and ultimately removed. While every effort has to be made to continuously move in the direction of removal of poverty and inequality and reduction of regional imbalances, what may be feasible is to reduce the order of disparities between class and class and area and area. The agricultural policy must be designed accordingly.

These considerations provide an important basis for the future agricultural development policy in the country. We have, therefore, kept these in view while formulating our approach to and making our recommendations later in this Report on the development of agricultural and the rural economy in India.

States also should be closely associated with the formulation of the central and centrally sponsored sector of the agricultural plan which can be done through joint Working Groups consisting of the central and the state representatives.

There has to be a close integration between Plan and the budget at both the state and the central levels through the planning units at these levels.

Centre has a genuine role in laying down the broad framework of developmental policies and providing guidelines on some of the basic issues connected with the administrations of programmes. Alternative approaches to a problem with their implications should be fully spelt out so that the states are able to take their own decisions adopting the general guidelines to local conditions.

The decision-making process should be improved through suitable organisational and other measures. Results of evaluation should be fed into the policy-making process. The process of feed-back can be facilitated through close contacts between research and development organisations under the control of the central and the state Governments. Other important measures are constitution of Agricultural Development Council at the state and Consultative Council at the central level, activisation of the advisory bodies and panels, decentralisation of decision-making and training in agricultural administration and management and economic decision-making.

Reaction of the state governments to the national policies in non-agricultural sectors should also be sought for taking decisions. The consultative council under the central agricultural set-up could be the appropriate forum for this purpose.

A long-term perspective has to be developed in respect of central and centrally sponsored schemes being implemented through the state agency and a strategy has to be followed under which these schemes ultimately form part of the state sector. The number of such central or centrally sponsored schemes should be kept to the minimum.

Earmarking of resources for key sectors of development can be secured even while such programmes form part of the state sector. States can issue sanction for these schemes after their details have been worked out in cosultation with the centre and the central assistance can be released on the basis of expenditure reported by the states, on the earmarked basis.

The system of ad-hoc central assistance for emergency production programmes and such other purposes should normally be avoided. Where emergency assistance becomes unavoidable, it is necessary that the assistance should be accompanied with an assurance of follow-up and complementary measures by the states.

There should be a definite assurance about the flow of supplies through forward planning so that crop production can be planned effectively. At the central as well as the state level, there should be a co-ordinating cell in the Inputs Division under the agricultural set up for securing co-ordination in the organisation of individual supplies and services.

Growth of state level seeds corporations will be necessary in order the states assume full responsibilities in the development of seed industry. The state level corporations can be set-up with joint participation of the Agricultural Universities, State Department of Agriculture and the National Seeds Corporation.

The basic objective of the National Co-operative Development Corporation (NCDC) should be to help the state Governments in the process of co-operative development in the states. The model of NCDC can be followed by other promotional co-operations at the national level for allowing state participation in their management.

The co-ordination committees at the central and the state levels responsible for drawing up and supervising the implementation of a unified storage development programme should be made effective.

Centre must be a source of effective guidance in various technical, economic and administrative matters affecting the total agricultural sector and not only the central and centrally sponsored sectors. States should be encouraged to utilise the experts under the central agricultural departments and the ICAR.

The All-India Agriculture Service can be utilised as a channel for exchange of experience and expertise between the centre and the states. The technical posts at the centre including those at intermediate levels should be tenure posts.

A close working relationship should be established between the field units under the central agricultural set-up and the counterpart organisations at the state level, so that complementary action in the state sector in regard to the utilisation of facilities created in the central sector is ensured.

Development corporations at the national level should act as a national grid of development giving full freedom to the state units where in existence, and proper representation to the state interests in the management of the national body. The autonomous corporations and agencies should not work in isolation from the central development and extension set-up under the state governments. These bodies can be instrumental in depoliticising decision-making and securing a better accord between the centre and the states.

In the case of key sectors needing large investments such as Command Area Development, a central representative could be associated with the management of the development authority at the state level with the object of evolving a commonly agreed programme on points of mutual interest.

The shortcomings in land management legislation, other agrarian legislation and regulatory acts under their administration can be avoided to a great extent through on setting definite norms at the national level in a number of important areas. A comprehensive code or manual dealing with agrarian legislation in the state should be prepared by the centre which could be adopted by the states with suitable modifications to suit their local requirements. There should be a well-organised Division in the central Department of Agriculture and a small Cell in the Department of Agriculture at the state level for making continuous study of agrarian legislation and preparing a code.

Central teams could be more effective if these are posted in advance with the details of bottlenecks faced by a particular state so that the discussions with the state are more specific.

There could be written Memoranda of understanding on the working programmes between the centre and the states in suitable cases specifying respective roles responsibilities of the central and the state Governments or agencies under them, in the formulation and implementation of the concerned programmes. Streamlining of the administrative machinery from the field to the central level is necessary in order to build joint commitment between the centre and the states covering the total plan of agricultural development.

Nutrition

There is urgent need for the processing of foodgrains and improving storage structure to prevent appreciable loss both in quality and quantity caused by rodents and insects, by providing ratproof godowns. Such facilities should, as far as possible, be cheap and developed indigenously. Measures to control storage pests by using chemicals should take precaution against pollution.

Production patterns should preferably be oriented

to meet nutritional needs of each region. For this purpose, priority should be given to meeting the quantitative deficit in calorie requirement. Nutrition oriented food production planning should be initiated at the district level. For better nutrition the high yielding and improved varieties of cereals, pulses and oilseeds should have preference.

A diversification of foods is desirable even for a single nutrient, not because of taste but for the sake of complementarity, as is especially true in the case of proteins.

Possibility of microbial production of oil for non-edible purposes should be explored.

Edible oilseeds and oilcakes being supplementary sources of oil and protein, their antinutritional and toxic constituents, if any, should be removed before they are used. Promotional measures should be taken to increase internal consumption rather than exporting them as cheap raw materials. It would be more appropriate to process oil meals for export purposes.

In order to meet the shortage of edible oils, besides stepping up production of traditional oilseeds, new sources of edible oils should be fully explored. Oil yields from available sources should be extended by solvent extraction by the use of food-grade solvents.

The nutritional significance of vegetable and fruits in general and more particularly leafy vegetables has not been fully recognised by consumers. Their current production and consumption should, therefore, be augmented through research and extension efforts. Appropriate incentives and adequate facilities for their storage, transport and marketing should go hand in hand with production.

Measures to increase the production of foods of animal origin, such as milk, fish, meat and eggs have to be intensified in a phased manner. There should be adequate infrastructure for cold storage, quick means of transport and marketing facilities for efficient delivery at the consumer level. On conventional foods such as algae, yeasts, mushrooms, petroproteins, leaf proteins are expensive from the point of view of initial cost of outlay and energy imputs. However, since technical know-how for commercial production of such foods is available whithin the country, efforts should be made to explore the scope of utilisation of these sources as animal feeds. Until research provides clearance on the basis of toxicological evaluation, these sources should not be utilised for human consumption.

Food quality, food safety and food sanitation have been the weak areas leading to health hazards and improper utilisation of good foods and nutrients derived from them. The quality control in regard to raw foods looked after by the Food Corporation of India does not adequately cover all items and, wherever covered, is not properly enforced, as seen by the results at the consumer's level. The defects have to be eliminated, for which stringent measures are called for.

The danger of food contaminants such as naturally occurring toxins, chemicals such as pesticides and food additives needs to be elaborately studied. Methods of detoxification as in the case of Lathyrus sativus and control of fungal contamination by quick drying and better storage should be popularised through education and extension work. The increased use of pesticides in preharvest and postharvest conditions is apt to result in appreciable pesticide residues which are likely to be harmful to consumers. There should be a permanent machinery to conduct a continuous surveillance of the effects of pesticide residues in foods.

The use of irradiation as a means of extending storage life and prevention of deterioration and insect infestation should be examined from the point of view of economic feasibility as well as possible harmful effects of irradiation on the consumer and the nutritional quality of foods. For the purpose of eliminating possible harmful effects, wherever necessary, a minimum period of storage after irradiation should be made mandatory before such irradiated foods are distributed to consumers. For both radioactive fallout and possible harmful effects of irradiated foods, appropriate monitoring agencies should be set up.

Food adulteration has become a great menace to health and its effects may be aggravating to the undernourished population. The existing loopholes in the Prevention of Food Adulteration Act should be plugged and punishment for food adulteration made severe and deterrent. Facilities for checking adulteration by on-the-spot tests must be provided and consumer awareness should be aroused through education and consumer guidance societies. There is need for an exhaustive National Food Sanitation and Safety Act to ensure consumer safety in regard to raw foods, processed foods and food preparations served in catering establishments.

Many industries dealing with processed foods have come into being as a result of industrialisation and urbanisation. Depending as they do on surplus agricultural produce spread over wide areas in the rural sector, industries have to think of smaller viable units of processing located in rural and semi-urban areas. Many of the products currently marketed are not covered by the ISI marking. They and the new ones should be brought under the purview of the ISI as quickly as possible.

Nutritional upgrading of foods through food fortification must be carefully examined in the context of food habits. Fortification of cereals in a big country like India involves enormous cost apart from problems of logistics. Unless backed by proper monitoring and follow-up studies fortification of foods would illserve its purpose.

Public eating places in towns and cities are an outcome of urbanisation and industrialisation. But the hygienic condition and quality of food served there leave considerable room for improvement. There should be one eating houses sanitation committee attached to the municipality or the corporation, to supervise periodically all public eating places and enforce minimum sanitary conditions. The assistance available with the regional institutes of catering technology and applied nutrition should be taken advantage of by industrial managements in organising model canteens and restaurants in industrial locations for the benefit of their workers.

In the implementation of nutrition propgrammes, organisational lapses stand out prominently. The Government should, therefore, examine their achievements and bottlenecks and lay greater emphasis on cost, efficiency, management, exploitation of locally available foods, motivating greater participation of the people, effective reach out to the beneficiaries, and efficient delivery systems.

The co-ordination committee set up at the district level for the integration of nutrition programmes involving several organisations should be made to function effectively by bringing into its fold other interrelated aspects of community development, such as environmental sanitation, control of infection, early immunisation, family care, family planning, etc. The Integrated Child Development Services Scheme of the Ministry of Education and Social Welfare, which embodies a package of services in a spirit of co-operation and co-ordination amongst various departments, merits support.

Supplementary programmes can be made more effective through education and choice of cheap and locally available foods. In this task governmental departments such as those of Health, Agriculture, Social Welfare, Rural Development and the home science faculties of agricultural universities should work together.

A review of researches carried out so far by various organisations in the country on food science and allied disciplines suggests thal there is urgent need for creating a national grid of operational research for streamlining and co-ordinating results of research with the definite objective of applying them to solve actual problems in the field. In the light of experiences in the fields of research on food science and allied disciplines, it is possible to pinpoint a number of important areas in which research programmes should be either initiated or intensified on a priority basis.

To realise fully the impact of nutrition education programmes and to have an extensive coverage, the existing infrastructure needs to be strengthened.

A vast scope exists and sufficient manpower available for the extensive use of mass media for nutrition education in the rural and urban areas. All such possible means should be vigorously exploited.

Nutrition education should be made compulsory in agricultural, animal science and medical faculties right from the under-graduate level. Nutrition should also be included in school curriculum and teachers training curriculum.

On a national level nutrition is liked with economy of the country. The aim should be to provide proper nutrition to the people and to fight malnutrition and associated maladies. The formulation of a sound nutrition policy becomes in this context obligatory.

The nutritional status should be assessed by means of carefully planned surveys. They should elicit information about the nutritional status of the vulnerable groups of the population. The major nutritional problems to be identified are : Calorie-protein deficiency, vitamin A deficiency, nutritional anaemia, goitre, fluorosis, pellagra and lathyrism.

Depending on the pattern of food production as determined by exigencies of the prevailing situation, broad formulation should be made of the best possible balance sheet, commensurate with minimum nutrition and socio-economic status of the population groups.

The diversion of primary foods for conversion into processed and sophisticated foods to meet consumer demands of urban area should be restricted to surplus foods only.

Demand and Supply

Demand Projections

An important aspect of agricultural planning is the estimation of requirements of various agricultural commodities to cater to the growing population at rising levels of incomes.

The projections of economic demand presented in this chapter are based on our best judgement on the key factors which have a bearing on it. It is possible that some of the assumptions underlying these projections may not turn out to be valid and may thereby vitiate the estimates of demand. For instance, a progressive reduction in income disparities might also change the pattern of demand for the various agricultural commodities. Besides, trends in the age-structure of population and the pace of urbanisation could also have a significant bearing on the pattern of demand. These are some of the postulations and imponderables which will have a bearing on the pattern of demand in the long run. These factors have not been taken into consideration in this chapter since it is difficult to quantify their effect.

The demand for certain commodities viz., cotton, Sugarcane, etc. also depends on the development of alternative products. For instance, the demand for raw cotton would be greatly influenced by the extent of production of synthetic cloth. Similarly, the potentialities of development of sugarbeet as a raw material for the production of sugar would determine the demand for sugarcane. It will be necessary to carefully watch these factors and adjust the demand projections suitably.

The following table indicates the expected increases in the demand for selected agricultural commodities during the period 1971-1985 and 1971-2000 A.D.

Table 10.11
Percentage Increase in Demand for selected Agricultural Commodities

Items	Increase in 1985 over 1971		Increase in 2000 AD over 1971	
	Low	High	Low	High
Foodgrains	39.3	51.0	90.3	108.6
Sugar & gur	47.1	84.7	109.0	160.5
Oils	67.8	107.6	160.3	220.5
Tea	54.6	109.0	136.6	226.4
Coffee	64.9	143.9	173.1	319.0
Tobacco	39.1	68.7	87.7	131.5
Cotton	37.3	118.6	76.3	191.5
Jute	102.1	145.8	257.9	389.6
Milk	53.9	103.7	127.4	196.8
Eggs	69.2	164.4	188.4	372.0
Meat	52.2	102.9	127.5	205.8
Fish	59.7	92.6	160.8	205.6
Industrial wood	84.3	115.9	189.6	295.6
Fuelwood	34.7	34.7	50.0	50.0

It would be seen that in the years ahead, though the demand for foodgrains would increase, the order of increase would be considerably less than the step-up in non-food grain agricultural products. More particularly, the expected demand for oils and animal and dairy products is likely to grow at a phenomenal pace. As already stated, the increase in demand for agricultural commodities presented in Table 10.11 are derived without taking into account the price effect. The question of providing an appropriate price incentive to stimulate agricultural production has often been raised. This would involve adoption of policy measures, fiscal and economic, to turn the terms of trade in favour of agriculture. In that event, while increase in the price of agricultural commodities without affecting the overall price level will lower the demand for agricultural commodities, it will tend to push up rural demand resulting from net increase in rural income.

Apart from the crops studied in this chapter, tuber crops and fruits and vegetables are also important items in the food basket. Particularly the tuber crops viz. potatoes, sweet potatoes and tapioca have a high carbohydrate content and to that extent, would supplement cereal diet. If the levels of production anticipated by the Commission in chapter 23 on Horticultural Crops are achieved by 2000 AD, the tuber crops would provide a per capita availability of about 15 kg per annum in terms of cereal content or 50 kg per annum in terms of fresh weight of tubers. Since firm estimates of availability of all starchy roots and fruits and vegetable for human consumption in the base year as also the expenditure elasticities of demand are not available, it is not possible to forecast their demand. However, considering the importance of these crops in the food basket, we feel that efforts should be made to collect these data so that reliable long term demand projections could be worked out.

The implications of the alternative sets of demand projections on the average per capita availability of calories and proteins in 1985 and 2000 A.D. are as under :

Table 10.12
Availability of Calories and Proteins per day in 1971, 1985 and 2000 A.D.

	Base level	Projected level			
	1971	1985		2000 AD	
		Low	High	Low	High
Total calories	2,080	2,200	2,480	2,300	2,600
Proteins (gm)					
(i) vegetable	44.1	45.8	50.4	47.1	51.8
(ii) animal	6.1	7.1	9.3	8.2	10.9
Total	50.2	52.9	59.7	55.3	62.7
Percentage of animal to total Protein	12.2	13.4	15.6	14.8	17.4

The above estimates of availability of calories and proteins have been derived on the basis of apparent level of consumption of food items and include table losses. The per capita availability of calories (net of table losses, etc.) would range between 1,980 and 2,230 units in 1985 and between 2,070 and 2,340 units in 2000 A.D. against 1,870 units in 1971.

Besides, fruits and vegetables, starchy roots and tuber will further supplement the availability of calories with tubers alone contributing an estimated 125 gm in 2000 A.D. The per capita availability of proteins will range from 47.6 gm to 53.7 gm in 1985 and 49.8 gm to 56.4 gm in 2000 AD against 45.2 gm in 1971. Proteins of animal origin are expected to comprise 13 to 16 per cent of the total protein in 1985 and 15 to 17 per cent in 2000 A.D. against 12 per cent in 1971.

Export Possibilities and Import Substitution

A summary of the main recommendations is given below :

A well thought out and effective programme of import substitution is essential. In such a programme there should be a clear demarcation of areas where :

(i) total import substitution is immediately possible;

(ii) total substitution could be envisaged within a short-term period; and

(iii) the present resources will not permit import substitution in the near future because of which imports must continue for meeting the essential requirements.

Import substitution efforts in the first two areas should receive high priority. In particular production of milk powder, animal fats, raw cashewnuts, raw wool, wool tops, wood pulp and vegetable oilseeds should be stepped up as quickly as possible.

Research in developing new uses of jute should be intensified in the context of the competitive situation between jute and its synthetic substitutes in the various consumer markets. The competitive situation should be kept under continuing review. Exports of fine raw wool should be progressively restricted and those of manufactured woollen goods should be encouraged instead. Programmes for developing fine quality fleeces should be given high priority.

Efforts have to be made to maintain the export levels of lemongrass oil already achieved in the early sixties and increase the volume of exports of other essential oils, like sandalwood oil, so that the country could have a share of the rising world demand for essential oils.

Modernisation and improvement of slaughter houses and facilities for processing hides, skins and animal byproducts will help in stepping up the production of quality hides, skins and other animal products like casings for export.

There is need for setting up a suitable agency charged with the responsibility for co-ordinating the activities of the various organisations handling export of lac. The capacity of the lac bleaching industry in India needs to be developed to meet the rising export demand of this item. Efforts should be made to develop a consortium approach towards export of lac.

The possibility of re-capturing the markets of USSR and East European countries in banana with the re-opening of the Suez Canal has to be carefully examined.

There is scope for exporting disease-free seed potato particularly to European countries during off-season months around January. The export possibilities in dehydrated potatoes and onions need a careful study.

Production of vegetable for export purposes should be organised in compact areas on scientific lines. This could preferably be done by a public sector or a co-operative agency. Marketing infrastructure for export needs to be developed so that quick transit is possible from the producing areas to the export points.

The cost of indigenous production of cashewnut shell oil has to be reduced in order to compete with the world markets. Research on conditioning of nuts, heat control, oil bath machinery, etc. needs to be intensified.

Selective modernisation of exporting or export oriented cotton textile units is essential to streamline the production for export. The production base needs to be improved for the manufacture of high density fabrics apart from a wide range of sophisticated fabrics.

Fifty export-oriented pilot production units should be set up in important handloom centres in the country. Sericulture should be extended to new areas to make the industry self sustaining. Silk production techniques should be modernised and greater care exercised as regards quality control.

A continuing countrywise assessment of export possibilities of tea to traditional buyers and to the new markets should be made. There are good prospects of expansion of exports of tea in the long run provided a bold export promotion programme, backed by a high level of production, is taken up.

An assessment of the export possibilities of Indian

coffee should be made on the basis of an estimation of the likely increase in the demand on a country-wise basis according to different types of coffee and of the share which India can meet of such demand. Given the proper export promotion measures, it should be possible for India to improve its exports of coffee to major importing countries like U.S.A., Germany (FR) and France. The possibilities for stepping up export to 'non-quota' countries should receive special attention. The scope for increasing exports to Japan should be particularly investigated. Work on evolving and testing high-yielding varieties of pepper other than Panniyur-I has to be undertaken. In selecting the varieties, the yield rate cost of cultivation and the quality acceptability in export markets should be kept in view.

USA and USSR offer good scope for Indian cardamom and the STC should be entrusted with the task of exploring these markets. Possibly Australia will provide a good market for Indian cardamom.

Efforts should be made to evolve fibreless and high yielding varieties of ginger to recapture India's export-markets of the West. Stability in prices is essential for ensuring steady exports. A study of the reasons of fluctuations in exports of spices like coriander (in fruit form) and turmeric may be made.

Measures needed to improve the long term export prospects of minor spices, viz., maintaining production at levels higher than domestic consumption, controlling speculative trading, subjecting minor spices meant for export to compulsory grading and pre-shipment inspection under Agmark and improving packaging, should be undertaken.

Particular emphasis should be laid on increasing export availability of processed fruits and vegetables as there is considerable scope for expansion of exports of citrus and mango products and orange segments.

Adequate capacity should be created in the country for producing banana powder for export to European countries. Efforts should be made to produce larger quantities of dehydrated vegetables. The possibilities of exporting new items of fruit and vegetable products should be explored.

Production of garlic powder for export should be encouraged as there is an increasing demand for this item for food preparations in several Middle East, South East and African countries.

In the case of marine products, there is scope for exploring diversification of products as well as markets. For rapid growth of exports, there is, however, need to maintain strict quality standards and develop facilities for proper grading and packing.

A significant proportion of increase in sugar production should be diverted for export. Improvements in refining and packing sugar are also needed.

Exports of meat may be canalised through a public sector agency like the STC. There is considerable scope for producing certain types of meat for export for which there is little pull from the domestic market. Special steps should be taken to improve the meat characteristic of buffaloes and utilize unwanted male buffaloes for the export market.

Pig rearers and bristle merchants should be educated in regard to export possibilities of bristles. The Indian brush industry should also be encouraged to utilise bristles of higher lengths and turnout brushes of the standard and finish required by developed countries.

Finished leather garments and other leather manufactures have to be developed as export items and adequate infrastructure development for finished leather and footwear branches of indigenous industry should be ensured.

The possibilities for expanding India's exports of oilcakes to countries like Belgium, Luxembourg, Canada etc. should be explored. Compulsory preshipment inspection may be introduced to ensure that quality specifications, as prescribed in the export contracts, are rigidly adhered to. The existing small and uneconomic expeller units should be replaced by large composite crushing-cum-solvent extraction units.

Assessment should be made of the export possibilities of items (like rice, coconut, silk, meat etc.) where India's exports constitute a very nominal share in the total world trade. In the case of oilcakes derived from minor oilseeds the possibility of exporting after subjecting them to the extraction process has to be explored.

Efforts should be made to export sophisticated in these countries will be comparatively easy as milk products are already greatly valued. There is also a good market for ghee in the neighbouring countries which have a sizable population of Indian origin.

Animal feed resources of the country should be utilised optimally within the country to provide better feed to milch animals, so as to augment their milk production. The economies of exporting animal feed items vis-a-vis importing dairy products should be carefully studied and to the extent that imports of dairy products could be reduced, there could be corresponding reduction in the export of cattle feed. A balanced view has to be taken keeping in mind the various aspects of the animal feed situation in the country.

The type of repackaging/processing done by certain countries (like Singapore, Hongkong and Kuwait) which have specialised in importing agricultural raw materials for re-export, should be studied so that these techniques could be indigenously developed or duplicated.

Export promotion effort should encompass measures for (a) pin-pointing areas of demand for various agricultural commodities in raw, semi-finished or finished form, the production of which can be developed indigenously; (b) undertaking development programme for producing these items at competitive prices; and (c) developing the infrastructure for processing agricultural commodities into exportable form and moving them to ports of exit. The necessary investment should be made for building up export production infrastructure.

Funds should be earmarked for development schemes which have a bias in favour of export promotion or import substitution. Such investment should be made on integrated projects for production, processing and export of suitably identified varieties of agricultural products in actual demand in different importing countries.

Some areas which require serious attention in research and development effort, from the point of view of stepping up exports are : (a) Preparation of instant tea in ready-to-drink form; (b) processing of spices and derived spice products in forms acceptable to foreign buyers (care would have to be taken to prevent adulteration in export consignments of these items); (c) distillation of cardamom oil to specifications required in foreign markets; (d) preparation of ginger oil and oleoresin from ginger, ginger pickle and sugar preserves etc.; (e) developing new uses of cashewnut shell oil; (f) exploring possibilities of producing cattle feed, rum and gin from molasses; (g) developing non-traditional uses of press-mud and commercial exploitation of pulp obtained as a by-product from sugar-cane/beet industry; and (h) identifying new uses of coir.

The fruit and vegetable processing industry has to be developed keeping in view the seasonal flow of fruits and vegetables. There has to be a parallel coordinated development of cold storage facilities so that the load on the processing industry could be staggered by regulating supplies of raw material.

Export strategy should take into consideration the advantage which India has in producing labour intensive crops. The strategy should also include provision for producing for export superior varieties of agricultural commodities and importing instead cheaper varieties for internal consumption.

The need for exploring the possibility of increasing trade with other developing countries is important. An integrated approach to the problems facing intra-regional trade in rice has been adopted by the ESCAP. Similar approach to the problems facing other commodities needs to be adopted and formation of commodity communities or producers' association encouraged.

Increase in productivity is essential to generate exportable surpluses in case of items like cashewkernels, oilseeds, raw cotton, raw jute, spices, tobacco and sugarcane which have hitherto remained practically untouched by the recent advances in agricultural technology.

Scientific processing of forest produce should be taken up on a more systematic basis to augment exports of processed timber/wood, shellac, gums and resins. Problems of insufficient catch, inadequate deep sea fishing fleet and lack of processing facilities should be attended to for augmenting exports of sea foods.

The types of consumer controls to be exercised on the internal market for exportable goods where the overall production has to be apportioned between domestic consumption and exports should be examined. A suitable link between production export and domestic consumption of such commodities has to be established in the long run.

Measures should be taken to correct the disequilibrium between the export prices in India and the competing countries in respect of major agricultural commodities, which are inhibiting the expansion of the export capacity.

Quality packing and packaging are important considerations in export trade. The establishment of an organisation on the lines of the International Cargo Handling Coordination Association in U.S.A. might be of help.

Work has to be initiated on some important aspects of export marketing e.g. identification of markets, collection of information, intelligence and statistics on foreign markets, publicity, etc.

With improvements in the present reporting system through trade representatives of India in a limited number of countries, Indian exporters might be better informed of possibilities of actual sales. The expert services available in International Trade Centre and ESCAP Trade Promotion Centre could be availed of.

Export Promotion Councils need more autonomy and facilities in the matter of undertaking marketing surveys and research. These councils may be suitably strengthened for playing their due role in the export effort.

An export corporation to handle certain export oriented agricultural commodities like rice bran, compound animal feeds, caster, pepper, some types of pulses, starch, meat and meat products, forestry and horticultural items may be set up. The corporation should be the sole import-export agency for agricultural commodities charged with the responsibility for planning and developing their production, processing and marketing in an integrated manner.

As a subsidiary of the Reserve Bank, to provide medium and long-term export credit and also meet the short term credit requirements of exporters both at the preshipment and post-shipment stages, the establishment of an Export-Import Bank may be considered.

An element of flexibility should be introduced in export financing producers by developing institutions like factor houses.

The freight structure needs rationalisation for eliminating uncertainties regarding rates. Unilateral changes in rates should be eliminated through voluntary arrangements under the aegis of an international body like the UNCTAD. A cooperative endeavour between trade and shipping interests in assessing the supply position of reefer space in relation to the requirements, periodically, through a joint machinery of shipping agents, freight brokers and trade representatives, is necessary.

The development of export business in perishables, specially fruits and vegetables, would be facilitated by the provision of package-rates by Indian Airlines.

Following measures to streamline the transport arrangements for perishables with a view to realising the export potential in them should be taken :

(i) liberalisation of permits for road operators and opening of new roads;

(ii) removal of restrictions on movement of perishables and cutting down time of detention at transhipment points, road barriers and inter-state check-posts and provision of large covered sheds at these points;

(iii) laying down standards for packaging and crating to reduce spoilage in handling by different modes of transport;

(iv) evolution of special type of road vehicles for quick transit for export;

(v) strengthening and streamlining of arrangements for rail transport for long journeys and provision of special type of wagons;

(vi) ensuring adequate supply of wagons at important export points for specific destinations during peak seasons;

(vii) reducing transit time by accelerating the speed of services and eliminating en-route detentions; and

(viii) rationalisation of freight structure for fresh fruits and vegetables.

Cultivation of varieties of cashewnuts which are being imported at present should be encouraged since the competing producing countries are developing their own processing industry and the import availabilities are likely to go down rapidly in the coming years.

The indigenous availability of vegetable oils should be augmented by tapping sources like minor oilseeds, cotton seeds, rice bran etc. to reduce imports of animal and vegetable oils and fats. Full and rational utilisation of animal fats which are available in large quantities from fallen and slaughtered animals is also important.

For some years to come, imports of SMP might have to be permitted for meeting essential shortages in milk supply schemes or for manufacture, for export of dairy items. Import quotas in respect of sophisticated dairy equipment should be made freely available for meeting requirements of new dairy plants and for replacemants.

The use of sulphur in the manufacture of phosphatic fertilisers should be avoided as far as possible. Geological explorations should also be intesified in search of new sources of raw materials for manufacture of fertilisers.

The annual maintenance, imports of leathar and tanning industries should be treated as essential imports, since their development is important both from the point of view of export promotion and import substitution.

In view of the development programmes in respect of forestry products, the dependence on imports in respect of items like pulp, paper, and paperboard should get reduced.

The recommendations given below are not comprehensive, only the more important ones are stated here for special notice. On an average, precipitation in the country contributes about 400 million hectare metres of water anually. Of this only about 105 million hectare metres can be utilised in the long run. That would suffice for irrigating about 52 per cent of the sown area of 210 million hectares expected in the early part of the next century. In view of the insufficiency of water resources to meet the requirements, there is need for a great deal of efficiency and economy in their use.

Wherever feasible surplus water in a river, such as in the Brahmaputra, the Ganga and the west-flowing rivers south of the Tapti, should be utilised in other basins where there is paucity of water. All such possibilities should be examined and considered.

While planning for a storage scheme a study should be made to find out the effect of constructing the dam on the existing wells down stream. The study should be repeated on the basis of actual observations a few years after the construction to check on the assumption made.

In the Act that the State Governments may enact for the development of ground water, there should be a provision that the drilling agency which drills to depths of more than 30 metres must furnish a copy of the drilling log to the State Ground Water Board for record and use in subsurface geological mapping. Further, the State Ground Water Boards should make a systematic attempt to secure copies of logs of existing private deep tubewells for the same purpose.

The deep tubewells, because of the high cost involved in their construction and the skill and equipment required for them, are best undertaken by public sector, all other ground water developments should preferably be in private sector. Jointly owned private tubewells would run for more hours than individually owned ones making them more economical and should, therefore, be encouraged.

Electric pumps are much more economical to run than diesel pumps. To encourage the former, the power requirements for irrigation pumps should be met on a priority basis and an unfluctuating and uninterrupted supply ensured.

In areas where ground water is getting over exploited, the state must intervene and rationalise the extraction and distribution of water. The legislation for regulating and controlling the use of gound water is urgent specially in states where over-exploitation is already in evidence.

If a farmer constructs a private tubewell which yields more water than what the size of his holding justifies, then it should be permissible for the farmers having contiguous holdings to avail of their share of tubewell water on payment of share cost.

Comprehensive river basin plans should be drawn up giving an outline of the development possibilities of the land and water resources of the basin establishing priorities in respect of water use for various purposes, earmarking water for a specific purpose where necessary and indicating *inter se* priority of projects.

Irrigation policies should envisage :-

(i) maximum production per unit of area through multicropping in areas with ample water resources;

(ii) maximum production per unit of water in regions of medium and low rainfall in which a large part of the country lies;

(iii) provision of maximum protection in drought areas;

(iv) irrigation of maximum area during the rainy season by supplementing rain;

(v) maximum utilisation of irrigation supplies from storage during eight months of the year excluding summer when evaporation losses are highest; and

(vi) conjunctive use of surface water and ground-water.

River diversion schemes should be investigated even on nonperennial streams for *Kharif* irrigation.

In formulating new irrigation projects, particularly in low rainfall areas, an attempt should be made to create irrigated plantations in compact blocks to provide fuelwood, small timber and tree fodder in the area. Investigations of irrigation projects take a fairly long time. It is important that a number of fully investigated projects should be kept ready to choose from to suit the availability of resources and fulfilment of other considerations.

An irrigation project report should be formulated in three parts as under :

Part I : All engineering works from source of supply to outlets and drains.

Part II : All engineering works in the command area comprising land levelling and shaping, construction of water courses, lined or unlined, field channels, field drains and farm roads.

Part III : All other items pertaining to agriculture, animal husbandry, forestry, fisheries and cooperation.

Investigations of all the above items should be done simultaneously, and the report considered for sanction in its entirety.

The priority with regard to the lining of channels is recommended as below :

(i) On new projects and projects being remodelled, channels which are designed to run constantly or most of the time, should be preferred because of the difficulty and in some cases unfeasibility of lining them later once they are opened for irrigation.

(ii) On existing projects the smaller channels including water-courses should be preferred because lining these would bestow greater benefit and is easier to carry out.

Research on evaporation retarders with newer materials and techniques should be intensified.

The circle system of inspection and repairs of tanks, as in vogue in erstwhile Madras state should be introduced in all states which have fairly large tank irrigation.

Where panchayats are responsible for maintenance of tanks, they should raise sufficient financial resources through water charges for satisfactorily maintaining the tanks and should employ sufficient staff for the purpose.

There should be a suitable legislation for recovering water charges from beneficiaries of tank irrigation, at present exempt under 'Fard-abpashi' or 'Wajib-ul-arz', in order to cover maintenance cost of the tanks.

State Governments should assume necessary powers to enforce suitable cropping patterns.

The irrigation requirement in an area depends upon the type of soil, climate, contribution from effective rainfall, crop types and their duration, etc. As these vary from project to project, channels should be designed individually taking these varying factors into consideration instead of applying a uniform yardstick to them.

The schedule of channel operation should be made known to irrigators as much in advance of each cropping season as practicable to enable them to plan their cropping suitably.

Rice should be preferably grown where there is a good support from rainfall and where the soil has low permeability, say, 5 mm per day or less.

In preparing schemes for drinking chaurs for reclaiming land for crops, the alternative use of chaurs for pisciculture should be considered.

A comprehensive review of pre-plan and earlier plan projects should be undertaken by the states to farmulate a programme for their improvement. It would be desirable to complete these reviews within the next five years, so that these improvements are taken into account in the preparation of river basin plans.

In evaluating irrigation projects, the use of internal rate of return criterion is recommended. In making the economic appraisal, the cost of works and that of land shaping and construction of field channels and field drains should all be taken into consideration. The cost of soil conservation measures in the catchment, however, need not be taken into account from practical considerations.

Irrigation works, remunerative before Independence, started showing a loss soon thereafter. The annual loss had risen to about Rs. 141 crores in 1971-72. The water rates should be revised upwards to meet the loss. In fixing these rates, the overall consideration should be that, taken as a whole, the irrigation works in a state should not impose any burden on the general revenues. On canal systems where farmers are prone to speculate on rainfall to avoid paying irrigation charges, a two part tariff should be adopted.

In order to carry out construction of large projects at the optimum pace, centre should provide additional outlays for them after ascertaining the outlay which can be reasonably met from the state plan.

Instead of setting up a separate Directorate of Hydrology under a Director General the Central Water Commission should be allowed to continue to perform its important function of collecting, collating and publishing hydrological data. Its Hydrology Directorate should be adequately staffed and equipped with necessary aids. Also the Government of India should take steps to make it obligatory on the part of the states to furnish to the central organisations the hydrological data which they observed.

The preparation of river basin plans is of great importance in the proper utilisation of the limited water resources of the country. We, therefore, support the recommendation of the Irrigation Commission to set up the river basin commissions.

There should be in every state an organisation for water budgeting. This is best located in the Irrigation Department that being the major user of water. There should be adequate arrangement for flow of information to this organisation from other water using departments.

A national water reasources council should be set up to lay down broad technical, economic and financial policies in irrigation for the country as a whole, keep a watch on the problems of interstate rivers and ensure that irrigation projects are formulated to conform to the highest national interest.

There should be a legal provision for the interbasin transfer of water by making the necessary constitutional amendment.

As purveyors of irrigation supplies, the Irrigation Department should be responsible for the efficient conveyance of water from its source to the field and for its fair distribution.

More attention should be paid to the following items of research than hitherto :

(i) Snow gauging and contribution from glaciers;

(ii) effect of soil conservation measures and change in land use on run off and infiltration;

(iii) Hydrogeological investigations and assessment techniques of ground water in hardrock areas;

(iv) reduction in evaporation from reservoirs;

(v) lining materials and techniques; and

(vi) optimum size and spacing of field drains;

(vii) reduction in yield due to root submerge for different length of time during different periods of growth for various crops;

(viii) effect on yield of the number and timing of irrigation for other crops besides wheat; and

(ix) water pollution due to the use of fertilizers and pesticides and discharge of industrial affluents into streams.

Essential elements of agriculture should be included in the syllabus for engineers. On joining service, irrigation engineers should be given training in agriculture for some time at an agricultural university as also in revenue matters in Revenue Department. Also in-service training courses should be held at suitable intervals.

The recommendations given below are not comprehensive. Only the more important ones are stated here for special notice.

All the steps necessary for development of land

in a command area have to be taken together in an integrated manner. These comprise :

(i) Layout of plots and of common facilities like water courses, field channels, drains and farm roads;

(ii) Consolidation of farmers' scattered plots into one or two operational holdings;

(iii) Construction of water courses and field channels;

(iv) Construction of field drains where necessary and linking them with connecting drains;

(v) Provision of farm roads; and

(vi) Land formation to suitable slopes.

For the layout of fields and other facilities the contour method of layout is recommended.

The maps of the land development in the command area should be on a scale of 1 : 2,500 or 1 : 4,000 with 10 cm contour.

Land preparation for irrigation on steeper slopes becomes expensive and in areas with natural slopes exceeding 10 per cent it may cost so much as to make introduction of irrigation uneconomical.

It is desirable that small holdings should be grouped in a contiguous area near the periphery of the village within the command of an outlet, the smaller holdings should be located at the beginning of the water course and the larger ones farther away. This will facilitate equitable distribution of water to the small holdings.

Once approval of government is accorded to the preparation of a project report, the Irrigation Department should immediately notify other concerned departments of this approval, and giving an outline of the project, advise them to take up investigation of the items which pertain to them. These concerned departments should prepare their own estimates for any field investigation which they may need to carry out and obtain the necessary sanction and funds through their own departmental channels.

An irrigation project report should be prepared in three parts, besides the general report as under :—

Part I : All engineering works from source of supply up to outlets, including drains.

Part II : All engineering works in the command area comprising land levelling and shaping, construction of water courses, lined or unlined, field channels, field drains and farm roads.

Part III : All other items pertaining to agriculture, animal husbandry, forestry, fishery, communications and cooperation.

The general report and part I and II of the project report should be prepared by the Irrigation Department. As the work involved in part II of the report is not being handled by the Irrigation Department at present, that department should organise a special set up for the purpose for which agricultural engineers should also be inducted into the department. The personnel should be given the necessary training. The part III of the report should be prepared by the concerned departments and sent to the irrigation department for compilation. The Irrigation Department should then submit the complete report comprising all the parts for sanction to the appropriate authority.

In part III of the report the Agriculture Department should deal with tillage practices, cropping pattern, production of seeds and their distribution requirement and distribution of fertilisers and manures, soil testing, plant diseases and distribution of pesticides, role of agro-industries, extention services, horticulture, transformation, storage and marketing and credit facilities.

The animal husbandry department should deal with the requirement of livestock, fodder and feed, the dairy development, arrangements for processing and marketing and extention services.

The Forest Department should indicate the proposals for farm forestry, raising of grasses, arrangement for nurseries and extension organisation. The scheme for irrigated forest plantation may also be included.

The Fisheries Department should be consulted in respect of extent to which reservoir area should be cleared of trees and scrub, the structures to be provided in the interest of fishery and the minimum flows that may be required from the reservoir for riverine fishery. These matters should be included in part I of the report. In part III they should deal with the arrangements for fishery in the reservoir, setting up of seed fish, farms, the scope and proposals for pond and tank fisheries in the command areas, leasing policy, credit facilities, and marketing and processing arrangements.

Land formation work should be taken in hand concurrently with the construction of irrigation channels.

At present, command area awaiting land formation work is of the order of 10 Mha, including that where irrigation supplies would become available in the next two to three years. Land formation work would need to be completed in about 30 Mha by the year 2000.

The problems pertaining to organisation and finance in command area development should be given immediate and serious attention.

Proper land formulation is equally important in the commands of minor irrigation projects. By the turn of the century there would be about 9 Mha that would have required action. In the case of ground-water, the sinking of tubewell and the land development in its command should be a single composite work to be carried out simultaneously.

It would be desirable that the work of land development should be placed under the purview of the same department as is responsible for the construction of irrigation works, namely, the Irrigation Department.

The land development works should be entrusted to Land Development Corporation. The corporation should be invested with the necessary authority to enable it to adequately discharge its functions. To begin with it should borrow technical and skilled personnel particularly for its top echelon from the irrigation, agriculture and other departments making also direct recruitment. Gradually it should have mostly its own staff. Agricultural and other engineers which it may recruit should be put through a course of training to specialise for the work. At the secretariat level the corporation should be the responsibility of the Irrigation Department.

In some States the agro-industries corporations have taken up the land levelling work. Since the work has to be done along with the construction of water cources, field drains and farm roads as a single operation, the agro-industries corporation is not the best agency for this work.

There should be a legal provision that once it is declared that in a command area land formation operations are to be taken up consolidation of holdings would be obligatory. It would be desirable to deploy special revenue staff well in advance of the land development activities to bring land records up-to-date before actual start of work.

During the period of Land Development Corporation is engaged in land formation in a command area, there should be a project development officer in overall charge so that the requirements of farmers during the transition period receive concentrated attention and the various activities in the command area get properly coordinated.

Considering the magnitude of the land formation work to be undertaken the most sophisticated techniques of mapping will need to be adopted from consideration of speed of work, accuracy and cost. It would be advisable to have a separate Land Survey and Mapping Corporation or a separate Command Area Mapping Wing under the same ministry as administers the Survey of India, for the purpose. This organisation would also arrange for ground control work and detailed levelling necessary for preparing accurate contour maps from photographs. This corporation or the wing can initially draw some of the required personnel from the Survey of India and Indian Photo-Interpretation Institute, Dehradun.

Aerial photographs and most of the maps are at present treated as restricted material for security reasons and as such are not available freely even to government departments for planning developmental work. If the developmental work is not to be unduly hampered, then it is necessary that these restrictions should be relaxed to the maximum extent feasible.

In order that the preparations of the irrigation project report is not delayed it would be necessary to have a planning cell at state headquarters in each of the concerned departments dealing with other fields of development such as agriculture, animal husbandry, fisheries, forests, co-operative etc. which would devote sustained attention to formulation of proposals in respect of command areas.

The Land Development Corporation would carry out land formation work on behalf and at the cost of the farmers, allowing for any subsidy which the centre or the state may give for the purpose. The corporation would require some funds of its own for equipping itself with the necessary equipment and machinery and for meeting the organisational expenses. The funds required for actual work have to come from institutional sources as long term loan to individual farmer passed on to the corporation for the purpose.

The farmer should be enabled to obtain all his loan requirements, short, medium and long terms, from one and the same institution. This is particularly important where small and marginal farmers are concerned. As such the setting up of farmers service societies should be given priority in the command areas.

The Land Development Corporation should be given an accommodation to the extent of 50 per cent of the total requirement to enable it to get on with the actual work in the field after the plans for a particular area have been drawn up, while the full credit requirement is being examined by the bank. On completion of the work necessary adjustments in the credit account of each farmer should be made. The amount advanced to the corporation would thus get finally debited to the farmers' account and the corporation cleared of its loan liability to the bank.

Every attempt should be made to carry out the work in the field for the maximum number of days in a year even by giving sustenance loans to farmers on their having to miss a crop in the process. During land formation operation the idle time of farmers can be used for non-skilled work to the extent they be willing to do the work. This would provide employment and relief to them.

Even before the consolidation of holdings is undertaken, it would be necessary to enforce the land ceiling law so that the allottees of surplus land become entitled to credit. But where land ceiling cannot be enforced immediately the loan can be given to the present owner with the proviso that liability for the loan would be transferred to the new allottee to the extent it pertains to the allotted land.

In the case of share cropper the entire loan should be in the name of the land owner. But in the arrangement for crop sharing, he should be entitled to recover annually a stipulated amount from the recorded share-cropper towards payment of his share of loan. This arrangement should be legalised.

Since no part of the irrigable land in the command area can be left out of the development operation, Government should provide the necessary funds for completing this work, and recover the amount as arrears of land revenue in reasonable instalments in the case of those farmers who are unwilling to take a loan. In the case of farmers whose title is not clear but who are willing to take a loan and have the capacity to repay, the credit should be allowed by the financial institution under a Government guarantee.

Since it is the ARC which has ultimately to provide finance to the bank or the cooperative societies for land development work, it would be desirable to appoint a representative of the ARC on the Board of Directors of the State Land Development Corporation. The land development proposal which the corporation may sponsor should be technically and economically examined, to the extent really necessary, only by the ARC. The bank can then advance the credit on ARC's certification.

By 1980 the pace of land development should reach one million hectares per annum requiring term credit of the order of Rs. 120-150 crores per annum from institutional sources. This would further rise to Rs. 170-210 crores per annum by 1985.

The full requirements of finance for command area development from institutional sources along with the contribution from governmental sources to the extent it is required to be provided, must be made available to maintain the stipulated pace of development.

Experimental farms should be established in the command area well before irrigation supplies become available. A fairly large number of demonstration farms would need to be established as irrigation water becomes available. The farmers should be given training in water management, appropriate tillage practices, raising of irrigated crops and the use of fertilisers and pesticides, likewise, training of women-folk in the more efficient way of carrying out farming duties should be arranged.

In any new irrigation system night irrigation should also be enforced through the system of 'warabandi'. This system of 'warabandi' would also protect the interests of the weaker farmers who may be otherwise deprived of their due shares of supply during a period of keen demand.

The important recommendations made in the chapter are as follows :-

In the command areas of major irrigation projects, where problems of waterlogging and salinity exist, apart from the provision of drainage, water courses and field channels, an economy in the use of water and exploitation of ground water to lower the water table should be insisted.

The areas liable to flooding and waterlogging in the country should be identified. They should be brought under suitable crops avoiding flood periods.

In areas where reclamation projects are being launched, detailed mapping indicating classification of the self-affected soils together with their characteristics should be initiated.

Reclamation of saline and saline-alkali lands should be attempted in a large scale in order to prevent infestation of soils from neighbouring areas, physico-chemical characteristics of the soils should be periodically observed to enable modifications if any of reclamation methods.

A suitable subsidy may be given to small and marginal farmers owning alkali affected lands for purchase of gypsum for reclamation.

Pilot operational research projects on watershed basis covering 2,000-3,000 hectares of land should be taken up to assess the economic feasibility of developing rangelands. Standard soil survey should be carried out to selineate different land capability classes suitable either for cultivated crops or grasses or forest plantations.

There is an urgent need to carry out soil surveys in the ravine lands for the purpose of differentiation of the soils. For whatever areas aerial photographs are available they should be interpreted to find out the physical features of the land, characterising ravine systems. For those areas for which aerial photographs do not exist, urgent steps should be taken to have them.

Property boundaries and field boundaries should not be allowed to interfere in the way of scientific planning of ravine land reclamation. The land consolidation and settlement operations should be simultaneously undertaken. Areas considered suitable for horticultural crops should similarly be planned on contours and redistributed to facilitate speedy development. Areas recommended for forestry should also be subjected to run-off management.

The economic benefits should not form the sole basis in the reclamation of ravine lands, poverty and the objective of curbing of activities of antisocial elements should receive due consideration. Ravine reclamation as such should receive national priority and investment should not be denied on account of unfavourable benefit-cost ratio.

In multiple channel rivers occupying vast areas under their beds, the subsidiary channels should be diverted, wherever feasible, into the main river and the land under the bed reclaimed. The canalisation of such rivers on which dams have been constructed may be effected downstream of the dam so as to bring large areas of riverine waterlands for profitable land use.

Wherever feasible, the technique and experience already available in grouping 'Chos' for their canalisation and the reclamation of 'Cho' devasted land for better land use should be adopted extensively.

About half the coastal areas, which are partly saline, would be amenable to reclamation through plantations. Using the available technology, coastal plantations of '*casuarina*', eucalyptus, coconut, cashew, *chikku* etc. should be taken up extensively for profitable land use.

Stony and gravelly lands lying extensively as waste land should be closed to grazing for a few years to establish good vegetable cover before controlled grazing is permitted.

Intensive research and development programmes should be taken up for evolving rational land utilisation and obtaining economic production from shallow laterite soils through establishment of orchards of certain fruit trees, plantations of quick growing fuel species or pastures and grassland.

Urgent measures should be taken to put steep slopes in the Himalayas watershed under permanent vegetation and grasses to prevent soil erosion and heavy silt discharges from endangering life of reservoirs.

The causes of land lying waste should be examined by the concerned state departments in order to chalk out a strategy for its reclamation. The schemes for development and utilisation of the wastelands should be formulated in coordination with the Forest and Revenue Departments and democratic institutions like the Zila Parishad.

The categorisation of all wasteland in the country in blocks less than 100 hectares should be completed on priority basis as a centrally sponsored scheme. Aerial photogaphs and remote sensing techniques for survey of location and planning the use of wastelands should be adopted. The interpretation of the aerial photographs and that of soil survey reports of wastelands should be done on uniform basis so as to have uniform results. During the soil survey of wastelands, data on water table should be collected and compiled since these data would help in better and more economic utilisation of land.

Extensive areas are lying unutilised or underutilised along the railway lines, national highways, rivers, canals, etc.

Such land needs to be reclaimed and utilised according to the land use capability. For effective implementation of the programme, it would be necessary to have a co-ordination committee consisting of representatives of the concerned ministries/departments at the central level.

While distributing wastelands to the landless agricultural labour, ex-servicemen, etc., provision for necessary inputs to undertake cultivation and scientific reclamation, viz., agricultural implements, improved seeds, pesticides, irrigation and credit facilities should be made by the government.

Afforestation of wastelands with fast growing species could be helpful in converting large areas of such lands for other useful purposes. In the earlier stages of development afforestation of such wastelands should, therefore, be considered from the larger perspective of utilisation for protective purposes rather than for purely financial returns. There is an urgent need for attaining self sufficiency in fodder, fuel, small timber and soft wood for pulp. In this cantext, country's wasteland or unutilised land offers great scope. Reclamation of wasteland should be planned to meet the above demands of national importance.

To enable the local livestock industry to develop faster than hitherto in hilly and desert areas, development of pastures should be an important programme. In no case should such lands be distributed among local landless and agricultural labourers.

Necessary legislation should be enacted to enable consolidation of wastelands inclusive of the scattered patches of sown area and allot the displaced land owners alternative lands of equivalent value elsewhere in the vicinity of affected villages.

Efforts should be intensified to bring substantial portions of wastelands under fuel and small timber plantations for meeting the needs of expanding rural and semiurban population.

A continuous up-dating of knowledge regarding the most remunerative and fast growing species is required in order to suit different ecogeophysical situations.

The available wastelands should be reclaimed and converted into suitable fodder reserves to support the intensive programmes of cattle and sheep development.

On the basis of available technology and past

experience in the fields, there is a great need for rapid reclamation of the ravine areas of Gujarat, Rajasthan, Madhya Pradesh and Uttar Pradesh in order to provide timber, fodder and cultivable land.

The recommendations made on sand dunes reclamation and stabilisation in our interim Report on Desert Development are reiterated.

Researches on alternative and less expensive land utilisation methods by raising suitable grasses and economic forest species may have to be explored for reclamation and better utilisation of saline and sodic soils. In view of this, there is a need for intensification of research at the Central Soil Salinity Research Institute, Karnal. Operational pilot research projects should be taken up on contiguous problem areas of about 1,000-2,000 hectares with a view to evaluating the economic feasibility of the practices under alternative land use like agriculture. Studies should be made for exploring the possibility of composite fish culture in dug out ponds in the salt affected land which generally has low permeability.

The problems of riverine wasteland known as 'Diara' lands need to be investigated and suitable practices evolved for the management of sandy areas, flooded and water-logged land and salty land, apart from evolving a suitable crop and forage production technology.

In view of the extensive nature of wastelands, it is necessary to intensify research for developing technology for successful establishment of permanent cover of economic species of fuel, fodder, inferior fruit trees and fast growing industrial species. Pilot research studies in large contiguous blocks should be undertaken to standardise the management methods and to evolve working plans for maximising production and econonmic returns. There is also a felt need to improve further the design and specifications of costly structures in canalising the 'Chos'. Irrigation research institutes and river research institutes located in the 'Cho' affected areas and concerned agricultural universities may initiate co-ordinated programme of field investigations in this direction.

Rocky, stony and hilly areas with skeletal soil are not considered suitable for agriculture and forestry but can be developed for recreation purposes and nature reserves. The Forest Research Institute and State Forest Departments should initiate research in this direction.

Research work should be taken up to identify proper grass species suitable for wastelands occupied by shallow laterite soils and develop technology for increased production from such lands. The Indian Grassland and Fodder Research Institute, Jhansi should undertake suitable investigations for development of grassland on these soils. In collaboration with the State Governments pilot research projects for grassland development should be undertaken to transfer the available technology to the field.

Research work leading to increased agricultural production and for development of alpine pastures and meadows at high altitude location should be intensified at the Indian Grassland and Fodder Research Institute, Jhansi.

The Indian Council of Agricultural Research should initiate watershed research for soil conservation and proper land utilisation with a view to rationalising land use practices for watershed protection and reduction of silt discharges thereby saving the life of costly reservoirs.

The rehabilitation of tribal people who practice *jhum* cultivation in one form or the other may be attempted in one or more of the following ways.

(i) Reclaiming land and providing irrigation, where necessary, and other inputs and facilities so as to encourage settled cultivation;

(ii) identifying areas suitable for plantation crops which would give subsidiary occupation;

(iii) developing grass reserves to support a subsidiary programme of animal husbandry; and

(iv) developing areas for agri-silvicultural operations and commercial forest plantation which would give full occupation.

Land reclamation should substantially be done through institutional investments availed of by the allottees. Alternatively, it may also be possible for a land reclamation organisation in a state taking up advance reclamation of an annual area then selling the land at a fair price to the settlers. The land reclamation programme should be attempted on either of these bases so that direct investment by the state is limited and substantial investment comes from the farmers themselves through borrowings from institutions for long term agricultural credit.

The land reclamation should form part of area development and would not require any separate organisation. The central planning division will have to formulate the overall national programme, with the help of state planning units, keeping in view the relative needs in the states for land, of growth with social justice and depending on funds available from the state investment and institutional borrowing.

The following is a summary of the important recommendations made in this chapter.

In view of hazards of rapid siltation of rivers and streams, a firm strategy for taking the conservation works in the water-sheds of river valley projects should be planned quickly, preferably within five years.

In conformity with the international standard, a soil map of India in the scale of 1 : 1 million is considered necessary and adequate. The comprehensive system of soil classification developed by the United States Department of Agriculture (USDA) should be suitably modified, where necessary and adopted and brought in line with the International system of soil classification as adopted by Food and Agricultural Organisation. Expeditious measures should be taken to prepare the soil map of India in 1 : 1 million scale and to organise additional 170 soil survey parties in accordance with the specific requirements of the states and the centre. Aerial photographs, at least for the nonsensitive areas, should be made available for accelerating soil survey work. The Directorate of All India Soil and Land Use Survey which is charged with the training of soil survey personnel and soil correction and classification at the national level, should be appropriately strengthened. An integrated training course in collaboration with the Indian Photo Interpretation Institute of the Survey of India should be organised. The State Soil Survey Organisations should be strengthened with properly trained personnel in order to carry out all new surveys as well as resurveys on the standard pattern. A close liaison between the central and state soil survey organisations is imperative. For this purpose, the state coordination committees, wherever formed, should be activised and wherever not yet formed, should be constituted as early as possible. State coordination committees should utilise the existing data on soil survey for land use and crop planning after due interpretation.

The programme of soil survey should include hydrological and erodibility groupings of recognised soils in order that soils producing sediment get quickly identified. Soil and land use survey should precede soil conservation measures, so that the latter can be based on the recommendations of the former. Gaps noticed in the progress of either should be expeditiously bridged.

In view of the irreparable damage done to reservoirs by siltation, high priority should be attached to the treatment of those lands in the watershed which deliver the largest amount of sediment to the reservoirs.

A time-bound programme needs to be drawn up for the aerial survey of the remaining catchment area and for correlation with sediment inflow and its transport via rivers and streams and delivery into reservoirs. This would help better identification of priorities for treatment.

The inadequacy of rainfall data in the watersheds of the various river valley projects calls for the following urgent measures.

(i) the location of all rain-gauges should be fixed if necessary by a special scheme within two years;

(ii) all non-standard rain gauges should be replaced by standard ones;

(iii) IMD's plan for installation of 1200 additional raingauges on the basis of WMO's recommendations should be re-examined;

(iv) a special unit should be established in the IMD with powers and responsibilities and suitable financial assistance to instal additional network of raingauges, and collect and publish all available data within a period of 3 years;

(v) correction factors applicable to all the defective raingauges should be determined as early as possible; and

(vi) a minimum network of self-recording raingauges as would enable publication of maps of short duration rainfall and frequencies within a period of 10 years be established.

Conservation measures in catchment areas should have the same priority as the development of command areas.

Due consideration should be given to the physical and morphological characteristics of soils in the development of precise techniques for soil and moisture conservation.

Alternating grass and crop varieties is an important measure of soil conservation and moisture preservation. In the multiple cropping programmes grasses should find a place.

Private degenerated lands which may be the foci of erosion should be treated for purposes of conservation, e.g., for farm forestry with technical help from the forest department; or else the State Government should notify the owners of such lands for including them in land development schemes.

Instead of treating soil conservation in catchment areas as one of saving life of reservoir, it should be looked at as part of programmes for maximising land use. To attain this end, all related programme should be drawn up in a coordinated manner.

Considering the limited forest area available in the catchment areas, every bit of degraded forest land should be replanted with intensified efforts. According to suitability and feasibility, a programme of either farm forestry or commercial forestry should cover a substantial portion of the catchment areas.

Grass reserves should be created in forest areas and community lands. This would link up soil and moisture conservation of degraded areas in the catchment with programme of milk production and make both of them economical ventures.

Areas showing reasonable rise in productivity as a result of conservation measures should be identified in catchment areas and an institutional programme of credit should be developed, so that farmers would find it profitable to take up soil conservation work. This step would substantially minimise direct investment by State Governments for the overall soil conservation work.

In soil and moisture conservation works covering wide areas in the watersheds and involving a large number of people, extensive participation of the people at the district, block and village levels would ensure superior performance and higher achievements, particularly in respect of the maintenance programme.

All storages with a hypothetical limit of 12.5 thousand harm and above should be treated as having interstate implications. In such a situation the centre should provide financial and supervisory assistance for the watershed management. Since the benefit accrues directly to the states in various ways, such projects should be financed by the centre and the state concerned.

The work of gauging silt and discharge of various rivers and their tributaries should be a central responsibility. Adequate funds should be provided for the purpose.

Particulars of watersheds should be continually collected and systematically studied in order to take corrective measures. For river valley projects, the catchments of which are situated in more than one state, the data should be collected by the Ministry of Agriculture and Irrigation with the assistance of the concerned states, analysed, and stored in one place for the benefit of users.

The location of gauging stations should be planned carefully to cover all major situations. In view of the urgency and importance of sediment data, it should be made obligatory on the part of all the discharge observation sites to obtain sediment data as well. At least 10 per cent of the observation units should be run by the central agency and classed as 'A' class stations after having been provided with sophisticated equipment and standard arrangements for observations and checks.

Watershed management should be initiated well in advance preferably before the execution of the project itself. Advance action results in stabilisation of the watershed thereby putting the water resource development project on a firm basis. Priority determination should be based on sediment yield and experience in similar catchment areas.

At present the water resources projects are handled by one organisation whereas watershed management projects are handled by another. The two are so intimately related that whenever a water resource development project is planned, the authority responsible for watershed management should be simultaneously associated with it, so that both works run complementarily and parallely.

For comprehensive planning and effective execution of soil conservation programmes, the organisation should be adequately strengthened so as to meet the requirements of a coordinated programme of conservation, use and management of soil and water.

The jurisdiction of an Assistant Soil Conservation Officer should be fixed and he should be required not only to tackle fresh problem areas but also to maintain the areas already treated. And treated once can be taken up for fresh treatment after 5-7 years depending on the condition of deterioration.

An inter-directorate committee presided over by the Agriculture Production Commissioner may take up soil conservation on a coordinated basis and as a special action programme.

The amount due from each landholder as cost of soil conservation works in a cultivated land should be recovered in suitable instalments depending on the nature of operations and cost involved. The number of instalments may be made conveniently larger in case of small and marginal farmers. In course of time this concession should apply to marginal farmers only.

For lands suitable for afforestation and grass production the Forest Department should suitably include them in their programmes of afforestation and conservation and realise part of the expenditure from the sale of either forest produce or grasses.

Indigenous research set up is essential for investigating the quantitative aspects of watershed management under conditions prevailing in the catchments of the river valley projects in India.

A scientific appraisal of the land and soil resources should be made by the Directorate of All India Soil and Land Use Survey to enable preparation of an inventory of the above resources, assess the nature and extent of soil and moisture conservation problems in the country, classify the country into different land resource regions and subregions and map them on a suitable scale.

Studies on conservation hydrology already being conducted at various research centres should be intensified so as to include the following aspects: (a) watershed hydrology with special reference to precipitation frequency distribution etc; (b) rainfall erosion indices; and (c) infiltration rates and cumulative intake for different hydrological soil units.

Research work on conservation agronomy should be strengthened to include the following aspects: (a) Selection of crops, cropping systems, geometry of cropping, crop rotations, mixed cropping, inter-cropping and strip cropping with reference to rooting habits of crops; (b) tillage practices to optimise soil moisture regime in the root zone; (c) crop response at different stages of growth under various moisture levels; and (d) development of proper, water harvesting and water recycling techniques for rainfed agriculture.

Studies on mechanical measures with reference to conservation structures, such as contour and graded terracing, bench terracing, grassed waterways and diversions should be augmented. Criteria for design of bunds, earthen dams and other soil conservation structures should be developed. Studies should be initiated on parallel terracing and zigzag terracing with a view to avoiding point rows and sharp turns for various agricultural operations using tractors.

The gap in available knowledge for improving extensive grazing land and maintaining grass reserves should be filled up.

Studies on torrent control, landslides and ravine control, specially in hilly regions, should be initiated with the ultimate objective of (a) classifying, controlling and reclaiming gullies; and (b) evolving package of practices to control roadside and railside erosion and techniques of stabilisation of problem areas, such as those frequently affected by landslides and hill torrents. Extensive studies on the problems of shifting cultivation and consequent hazards and steps to prevent them should be undertaken.

Priority should be given to studies aimed at evaluating the various factors in the universal soil loss equation particularly for the adopted crop rotations.

In view of the large gap in the requirement and availability of trained personnel the training facilities at the various soil conservation research and training centres should be strengthened. The training of officers and of graduate assistants may be imparted at the Soil and Water Conservation Research and Training Institute and its substations. The in-service training of the field assistants and sub-assistants may be imparted by the soil conservation organisations existing in different states. This programme should receive a high priority.

Agricultural universities should gradually build up expertise in the field of research and education on soil and moisture conservation. The Krishi Vigyan Kendra would be eminently suitable to educate the farmers on the principles and benefits of soil and moisture conservation.

Suitable action should be taken to bring out manuals and handbooks incorporating research data and recommendations emanating therefrom for adoption in the field. The ICAR should be entrusted with the task of preparation and publication of such manuals for the benefit of the State Governments. Afforestation being an important aspect of soil conservation, the collaboration of the Forest Research Institute may be sought in the preparation of the manual. The task of preparing field manuals necessary for the execution of soil conservation programmes in the states should be entrusted to the respective State Governments. The regional centres which are to help the State Governments in planning and designing soil conservation measures should periodically review these manuals and make them uptodate.

Certain priorities should be assigned in the implementation of the recommendations regarding training and research in soil and water conservation. The following priorities (not yearwise) are suggested:

Priority I—affording training facilities after ascertaining requirement of personnel from the State Governments.

Priority II—Strengthening research (both basic and applied) at the existing research stations to fill up the gaps in knowledge pointed out above.

Priority III—opening additional research stations.

Priority IV—starting comprehensive pilot watershed studies.

The more important recommendations are given below:

The tempo of rural electrification should be stepped up so as to make electricity available for pump sets and rural industries in practically all the villages by 1990.

The state electricity boards should prepare a well-considered and coordinated programme of rural electrification in consultation with the other development at the state, district and block levels.

Advance planning for the future programme of electrification is essential and the state electricity boards should take early action on the following aspects:

(i) assessment of requirement of power and making arrangements to meet the same;

(ii) assessment of requirement of Extra High Tension (EHT) and High Tension (HT) net works and initiation of appropriate action to meet the same;

(iii) assessment of requirement of materials and

arrangements for their indigenous procurement;

(iv) assessment of requirement of Personnel and arrangements for their training; and

(v) carrying out of connected research and development work.

The present difficult power position should not be permitted to hamper agricultural development and the requirements of rural electrification should continue to be accorded a high priority. The State Government should take steps to encourage rural loads by promoting dispersal of industries to rural areas.

The state electricity boards should take advantage of the funds, placed at the disposal of the REC for granting loans, to provide street lights in *harijan basties* as were left out while electrifying the village within the next two years. The charges of electricity consumed by these *basties* should be borne by the State government concerned.

The State governments should take suitable action to extend electricity to primary heatlh centres for which 50 per cent subsidy is allowed by the centre, within about two years.

The electricity boards should give special consideration to extending electricity to fisher men colonies along the sea coast.

Wherever famine relief funds are used for deepening of existing wells or digging of new wells, funds should also be provided for electrifying them.

In order to minimise the financial loss on rural electrification schemes, it is important to bring about maximum economy in capital costs through standardisation without sacrificing safety considerations and also to take steps to improve the load factor and thus the revenue through larger use of power.

The electricity boards should take urgent steps to bring down the losses in the existing systems and ensure that the future distribution systems are designed to give only tolerable line losses.

The state electricity boards should have the authority to disconnect the power supply to a consumer who is adopting various malpractices. This authority should be exercised only by a responsible officer of the electricity board.

The centre/state governments should subsidise part of the capital cost of the schemes for transmission and subtransmission lines to be installed by state electricity boards in backward areas so as to satisfy the norms prescribed by the REC. Similarly, where villages are far away from each other and the inclusion of the cost of 11-KV lines makes the schemes for electrifying them unremunerative; the REC may consider giving special loans for the 11-KV lines by treating them as transmission lines.

Credit facilities should be extended to farmers and small scale industrialists, including for the electrification of their homes, for meeting the initial cost and connection charges etc.

The state agro-industries corporations should be charged with the responsibility for the supply of quality equipment at reasonable prices.

Agro-service centres should be set up to provide the services of licensed electrical wiremen/electricians for attending to repair work including rewinding of motors at reasonable rates.

Pending investigation of a contested bill, the consumer should be charged on the basis of average consumption for the past two months. Ficticious reading of meters which is generally the cause of wrong billing should be considered a serious offence and persons found responsible for it should be suitably punished.

The system of sending bill collectors to specified places in the villages on specified days should be introduced by the electricity boards, who have not done so, so far.

The theft of transformers, conductors and other materials and the possession of such stolen articles should be made a cognizable offence under the Electricity Supply Act, as in the case in the Indian Telegraph Act.

The state electricity boards should make stamp paper available at the time of signing the agreement.

The imposition of minimum consumption guarantee charges should be waived if the circumstances are beyond the control of the consumer. When a farmer has secured electric connection on his tubewell or pump set, he should not be restrained from sharing with or selling water to other farmers.

For expediting the electrification programme in an area, voluntary labour offered by the people should be fully utilised and encouraged which would also bring down the cost.

Climate and Agriculture

The main recommendations are summarised below :

Climate : Present rainfall normals (1901—50) which are more than two decades old should be revised and published early. Normals of stations computed with records for shorter periods should be reduced to the same period as those with complete records.

The method of working of district normals should be reviewed. Percentage departures from normal of rainfall for the various meteorological subdivisions should be worked out for all the years from the beginning on a uniform basis and using the latest normals.

Frequency distributions of daily rainfall should be prepared for all taluk stations and published. Weekly totals of rainfall of all stations with data of at least 20 years should be published.

A good network of snowfall recording stations should be extended. Studies on the contribution of snow to river flow should be undertaken.

Glaciology : IMD, Geological Survey and other concerned departments should draw up co-ordinated programme of work in this field with a view to understanding their role in Indian weather.

Rainfall Variability : Whenever normals of rainfall of a station, or area computed, they should always be accompanied by their respective standard deviations and values of coefficient of variation.

'Breaks' in rainfall should be analysed for taluk areas and published for general use.

Temperatures : Frequencies of daily maximum and minimum temperatures, heat and cold wave spells and duration in hours of temperatures in different ranges should be prepared and published.

Reference publications (i) Climatological Tables of observatories in India (1931—60) and (ii) Climatological Atlas of India (abridged) should be reprinted early as copies of these are not readily available.

Wind : Averages of hourly wind data and frequencies of speeds in different intervals and durations should be published for all the stations for which data are available.

Complete series of rainfall of all the stations in the country with records of 70 years or more, percentage departures from normal of all the meteorological subdivisions should be published to facilitate detailed studies of trends and periodicity in Indian rainfall.

Climatic Change : The problems concerning climate change and prediction should be taken up as a research project by the Indian Institute of Tropical Meteorology, Poona in cooperation with India Meteorological Department and ICAR etc.

Agrometeorology : ICAR should examine the feasibility of inclusion in their future programme of research biochemical studies for a fuller understanding of crop weather relationships.

There is urgent need to go in for phytotrons at all the agricultural universities to have clearer ideas as crop weather relationships under controlled conditions.

Each one of the rainfall zones into which the country has been divided should have at least one fully equipped agromet observatory. Every taluk should have at least one soil moisture measuring station. The total for the country would be about 3000 and this network should be built up by the State Agricultural Departments during the next few decades. They should also arrange for the publication of these data.

Studies of evapotranspiration under varying conditions of soil moisture in different soils and using as many plant species as possible are urgent and this work should be started at all the agricultural universities, the central institute of ICAR and the Forest Research Institute, Dehra Dun. Based on the results of these studies, a suitable network of stations, one at least in each district, for actual observational measurements should be started.

The network of stations recording phenological observations should be expanded so that there is at least one station in each taluk. The selection has to be of nature-grown plants as far as possible.

ICAR should organise a joint meeting of plant pathologists, entomologists and agricultural meteorologists for organising a unified approach to the study of problemf of pests and diseases. These will not only include the relationship under field conditions between weather and pests and diseases but also steps for starting a surveillance service based on meteorological factors which should be helpful in forecasting and controlling the epidemics.

Meteorological observatories in adequate numbers should be set up in orchards, plantations and forests.

India Meteorological Department in consultation with Forest Research Institute, Dehra Dun and State Forest Departments should draw up a long term research programme in forest meteorology.

All institutions and organisations dealing with animal research and dairy, piggery and poultry should arrange for meteorological observations needed for their work and conduct micro-climatic studies with in paddocks and barns.

Research studies should be undertaken with a view to forecasting animal diseases.

Droughts : Comprehensive and systematic studies of all past droughts by dynamic and synoptic climatological methods should be undertaken as a joint project by the India Meteorological Department and the Indian Institute of Tropical Meteorology, Poona, for developing techniques for forecasting them.

Crop Weather Calendars : Existing crop weather calendars should be brought up-to-date. Separate calendars should be prepared for early, normal and late sowing varieties of each crops in different areas of the country. They should also be prepared for crops like soyabean, cow-pea, safflower, sunflower, etc.

Weather Bulletins : Weather bulletins for farmers should include advice on agricultural operations and should be prepared daily after joint discussions between Forecasting Officer and Agricultural Officer deputed by local agricultural departments to make them purposeful. In the light of Karnataka and Tamil Nadu experience this arrangement of joint daily discussions in preparation of operational weather bulletins should be compulsorily extended to all states. The trial SITE programme of weather broadcasts for farmers issued after joint discussions of representatives from ICAR, Agricultural Meteorologist and the Weather Eorecaster should become a regular feature.

IMD should evaluate each year the performance of weather bulletins for farmers and discuss at conferences of agriculturists at state level.

ICAR should consider convening of such periodical conferences for evaluating weather service to farmers and for their improvement.

Every State should issue a weekly crop weather bulletin containing description of week's weather and crops in the state and outlook for a week ahead. The responsibility for the compilation and issue should be that of the Directorate of Economics and Statistics with cooperation from the local Meteorologist, the Director of Agriculture of the State and a representative from local agricultural university.

Extended Range Forecasting : Research into various aspects of "Extended Range Forecasting" should be given priority and work distributed among the IMD, Indian Institute of Tropical Meteorology, Poona and other interested institutions. An advisory working group may be set up with the Director General of Observatories as chairman and membership from IMD, ICAR and State Agricultural Departments to periodically assess and review the speedy implementation of programmes of work.

Crop Weather Relationships : (i) Crop weather studies in progress in the IMD should be intensified and formulae developed on a districtwise basis.

(ii) Detailed data on acreage, yield etc. according to varieties, irrigation, cultural practices etc. are essential for crop weather studies and these should be compiled in standard format by Directorate of Economics and Statistics. Formulae for forecasts of crop agreage should be developed using climatological factors.

Weather Modification : The research and operational aspects of the present organisation for weather modification in the India Meteorological Department and Indian Institute of Tropical Meteorology should be strengthened to conduct further trials and experiments to arrive at dependable conclusions.

Research Education and Training

Work in the field of Mathematical Simulation Modelling should be reviewed and attempts made with data available in India. IMD in consultation with ICAR should work out a joint programme of study using this approach.

Production functions for crop yields should be worked out using techniques of analysis developed in the Indian Statistical Institute and in the paper on irrigation evaluation under monsoon rainfall conditions

The present position regarding agroclimatological atlas should be reviewed and as soon as feasible, a detailed and comprehensive atlas should be prepared.

In service training of staff for manning various types of Agromet observatories should be arranged by the state agricultural organisations in cooperation with IMD.

Agricultural Meteorologists should be deputed to meetings of the Commission of Agricultural Meteorology of World Meteorological Organisation.

Observational Organisation : As a policy, the observational organisation needed by State Departments of Agriculture etc. should be controlled and maintained by them. They should provide all the finances needed for the purpose. Every state should immediately review their observational requirements and the organisation needed by them for necessary action.

Every Block should have at least one raingauge and they should be located in Block Development Office.

Rainfall Organisation in the states which is primarily needed by the state agricultural departments should be placed under their direct control; they will examine the present locations etc. of raingauges and take action to shift them to block offices in consultation with and cooperation of the Director General of Observatories who will continue to be technical adviser on all matters concerning meteorological observations.

Departments of Agriculture will have a planning unit for dealing with planning progress and evaluation of agricultural programmes. Each unit must have a qualified agricultural meteorologist who should look after all matters pertaining to meteorology including the rainfall organisation. He will arrange for the collection, scrutiny, checking, processing and publication of the data and for supply of data to all concerned. At the centre, these items of work should be handled by the Directorate of Economics and Statistics. As those form basic data for analysis they should also be punched in prescribed formats in consultation with India Meteorological Department.

The proposals regarding reorganisation of state

rainfall organisation will involve considerably increased work to the India Meteorological Department and they should be provided with additional staff for the purpose.

Rainfall and Cropping Pattern

The main conclusions and recommendations are summarised in this section. Our observations and suggestions regarding cropping patterns in Rainfall Regions are as under :

Region 1 : This is the area of lowest rainfall distribution in the country. Arable crops will have to be restricted to low lying areas with good retentive soils. It is advisable to divert the areas from arable to forage and economic tree crops either as sole crops or in mixture. More research and extension efforts will have to be put in with this objective.

Region 2 : Reasons for low yields of bajra and rabi jowar in Maharashtra and cotton in Andhra Pradesh and Karnataka should be examined and necessary measures taken urgently to increase the yields of these crops or for substituting them with more suitable crops.

Region 3 : Excepting Gujarat, the yield levels of crops without irrigation are on the low side, some of them being less than 50 per cent of all India average as in the case of bajra. The position has to be remedied by adopting better varieties or agronomic practices or by substitution of more suitable crops.

Region 4 : Although the crops grown appear to be suitable according to rainfall distribution, the yields are low in the case of almost all crops grown in the portion of the Region covering areas in Maharashtra, Madhya Pradesh and Rajasthan. There is, thus great need for detailed analysis, research and developmental efforts. Similar efforts are needed in the case of gram and other crops which have low yields in Andhra Pradesh and Karnataka.

Region 5 : There is need for adopting better water management and agronomic practices for improving the yields of maize and bajra in Rajasthan area; groundnut in Surendra Nagar district (Gujarat) may be substituted by sunflower after carrying out trials.

Region 6 : Though the crops grown are nearly suited to rainfall distribution, yields levels in Rajasthan area are low. These could be improved by adopting better agronomic practices and improved varieties or hybrids.

Region 7 : (a) In spite of fairly good irrigation support wheat yields in Rajasthan and Uttar Pradesh areas of the Region, are low. The reason as to why these should not be at almost the same level as in the Punjab needs to be looked into. Similar remarks apply to maize in Rajasthan and paddy in Uttar Pradesh.

(b) In case it is not possible to provide irrigation support to wheat and if it is difficult to increase yields under rainfed conditions, it may be considered as to why this area should not be diverted to barley, gram, safflower or other such crops.

(c) Paddy yields connot be high without irrigation support and it may be advisable therefore to divert paddy area to maize or other suitable crops after providing for proper drainage facilities.

Region 8 : Growing of paddy and wheat does not appear to be advisable in areas where yields are low for lack of irrigation support. In areas where irrigation development is not possible should be diverted to other appropriate crops after study.

Region 9 : Paddy crop dominates but rainfall is insufficient and required irrigation facilities are not available. Yields of other crops are also low. Careful examination is necessary.

Region 10 : The Region is entirely in Gujarat and with the rainfall distribution with a type in July there could be a temptation to go in for paddy. However, crops other than paddy are being taken with good yields. This could be cited as a good example of an area where cropping patterns have stabilised after taking the minimum likely rainfall into account. In areas with above average rainfall, drainage aspect is fully taken care of. This example of Gujarat is worth emulation by others.

Region 11 : Yield levels of many of the crops are low except in Gujarat areas though rainfall distribution is good for majority of the crops. Paddy yields cannot be high unless crop is irrigated. The cropping structure of the Region should be examined in detail with a view to bringing about improvement in both structure and productivity.

Region 12 : (a) Rainfall distribution seems more suited for millets, maize and cotton but not for paddy without supplemental irrigation.

(b) Reasons for low yield of crops in some states of the Region and good yields in others like Gujarat, need to be looked into.

(c) Cultural and other practices in states where the yields are good should be studied and extended to other areas in the Region, in addition to carrying out the needed research.

Regions 13 & 14 : Yield levels of paddy and wheat, the two major crops of the Regions are on the low side. Rainfall in September is not sufficient to support paddy crop and irrigation facilities are wanting both for paddy and wheat. The crop distribution needs detailed examination for evolving and adopting appropriate measures.

Regions 15 & 16 : Paddy is the main crop of these Regions but yields are low, the chief reason being insufficiency of rainfall in September. These Regions are more suitable for paddy than other crops and hence necessary steps should be taken for providing irrigation facilities. In case this cannot be done, paddy areas may be diverted to other crops.

Region 17 : (a) Rainfall resources are more than adequate for growing paddy in valleys and hill millets in elevated areas. Paddy yield in Bulsar district (Gujarat) could be raised. There is good scope for increasing the yields of ragi by adopting better varieties and agronomic practices.

(b) There is scope for introducing improved varieties of grass and forage legumes; soyabean in rotation with ragi could be tried. Maize also could be tried.

(c) Region is good for production forestry and economic tree crops.

Regions 18 to 22 : Paddy yields are high in general. Millet yields are very good in Tamil Nadu and moderate in Andhra Pradesh. Pulse yields are low. The reason for the same are required to be looked into and improvements brought about.

Regions 23 to 26 : Paddy can be grown only with irrigation and this is what is being done. Conditions are nearly favourable for maize in regions 25 & 26. Introduction of this crop along with soyabean is worth examining. Measures required to be taken to further increase the yield levels of the existing crops also need examination.

Regions 27 to 29 : There are possibilities of diverting areas under crops like paddy with a view to introducing protein yielding crops and fodder crops which may be examined along with the possibilities of increasing yield levels of existing crops.

Regions 30 to 36 : Paddy dominates whether rainfall is sufficient or not. The only good feature is that it is grown mostly under irrigation and yields are high. It may, however, be necessary to consider as to whether available water could be better utilised for raising other crops on larger areas with advantage. This suggestion especially applies to regions 30 and 31, where the rainfall is good for raising crops like jowar, ragi, etc. Maize can be a good crop for these regions and may be tried. Similarly soyabean and cotton can be good crops in regions 31 to 36. Plantation crops should also be considered especially in regions 33 to 36 since there is rainfall in October month in addition to monsoon months, possibilities of raising pulses and fodder crops in paddy fallows with supplementary irrigation is worth considering.

Regions 37, 41, 42, 44, 45, 47, 48 and 55 : Paddy is the major crop of these Regions. Regions 41, 42, 44, 47 and 48 do not have favourable rainfall distribution for paddy. Regions 41 and 48 do not have even one month of a type rainfall. Region 42 has only one and 44 two months of A type. Moisture stress in September and floods affect the yields. There is scope for substitution of paddy with maize and similar crops in Regions 41, 44, 47 and 48. Soyabean too can be a good crop for these Regions.

Regions 38 to 40 : These are scanty rainfall Regions with long intervening breaks. It is therefore necessary to examine possibilities of putting larger areas under grasses and economic tree crops which can stand prolonged drought better than arable crops.

Regions 43, 46 and 50 to 53 : Cropping structure in general appears to be appropriate. With long rainy seasons and with milder temperature, it would be advisable to pay more attention to fruit crops and grassland development in high lying areas.

Region 54 : More attention to grassland and fruit crops may be desirable.

Regions 56 to 62 : Cropping structure appears to be satisfactory. In Regions 56-57 paddy could be replaced in high lying areas with maize and soyabean with advantage. Possibilities of taking short duration pulses, oilseeds, fodder crops and vegetables appear to be feasible before and after paddy.

The high lying areas where raising of plantation crops is difficult could be used for developing grasslands. These regions are good for production forestry and plantation crops. Tendency of opening up slopy lands for arable crops has to be discouraged.

General observations and suggestions regarding cropping patterns etc. are as under :—

(i) Rice crop is prone to suffer in areas under rainfall categories A-2 to B-2 unless due provision is made in the rainy months to collect and store water for irrigation in the lean periods. For other crops there is always danger from water logging to avoid for which suitable agronomic measures should be adopted right from the beginning

(ii) Studies on optimum dates of sowing should be completed for the whole country in close liaison with the scientists of agricultural universities, institutions and departments for adoption of the results after large scale trials in the field.

(iii) In about 25 per cent area precarious conditions prevail, rainfall being 10 to 20 cm pm in not more than two months in the year which are not even consecutive months in some areas. Variability of rainfall in these areas is also high. High priority should be given to these regions in providing irrigation for as much as possible area. All kinds of water harvesting techniques within each holding as well as outside on community basis are necessary for stabilising production.

(iv) There is too much emphasis on arable crops irrespective of the suitability of land or sufficiency of rainfall. Land use planning has to be done on a scientific basis and implemented.

(v) Field crops should be restricted to most favourable areas which have good retentive soils and are situated in valleys so that the rainfall could be preserved in soil profiles and water harvesting techniques adopted. The remaining areas should be put under forage and economic tree crops either as sole crops or in mixture. Research efforts in these directions should be intensified and suitable recommendations developed as applicable to different regions.

(vi) Attempt should be made to introduce crop and varieties which fit best in the environmental rhythm of a place. Cropping patterns should be flexible for adjustment to changing needs taking into consideration advance in technology.

(vii) If rainfall pattern of a Region includes A,B and C classes of rainfall amounts in each of the three consecutive months, it is better to go in for crops that require C or B amounts of rainfall and not A. In such cases, steps should be taken right from the beginning for drainage of excess water.

(viii) All irrigation resources in Andhra Pradesh, Tamil Nadu and Karnataka are used mainly for growing paddy. It is necessary to examine as to whether water resources could be put to better use from socio-economic as well as from human nutrition and other agronomic points of view.

(ix) There is a case for restricting paddy to one season only in the Southern States with rainfall amounts in higher ranges in one or two months and utilising irrigation water for growing other crops. Farmers will switch over only when it is economical to do so. Research attempts should be intensified keeping these various objectives in view.

(x) Rainfall distribution patterns with a knowledge of monthly variability could be used as an important basis in any scheme for changing cropping patterns.

(xi) Urgent steps would have to be initiated on priority basis for determining and adopting more suitable cropping patterns than the existing ones. Detailed studies should be taken upon the lines indicated and keeping in view the proposed targets and suggestions made in the crop chapters, formulate research and extension programmes to achieve the main objective of putting every hectare of land to its best use.

Crop Production, Sericulture and Apiculture

This chapter is more meant to present a synthesized picture of the various issues which have been discussed individually in various other chapters and which have a bearing on crop production. Recommendations made in other chapters are not repeated here ordinarily. Those arising from this chapter are given below:

(1) Appropriate research organisation is required to evolve diversified cropping systems in heavy rainfall areas instead of the mainly monocropping system with paddy that exists at present. Allied socio-economic problems and problems relating to soil conservation and maintenance of soil fertility will also have to be studied.

(2) Attention should be devoted to store water in deep valleys at appropriate places towards the end of the rainy season in heavy rainfall areas, in order to lengthen the cropping season.

(3) In order to ward off the danger of water scarcity for irrigation of paddy during prolonged spells of drought shallow wells may be dug for storing water in every paddy field in heavy rainfall areas.

(4) Seed material for high rainfall areas has to be produced elsewhere because of fast deterioration inherent in these areas.

(5) Implements and machinery particularly suited to high rainfall areas will also have to be developed.

(6) A farming system designed to cultivate crops in flood-free periods has to be developed for Assam and Bihar. The Kharif crops of rice and jute must be either sown early in order to escape/withstand damage or the varieties should be such as to endure flooding (e.g. deep water rice).

(7) Increasing use of forage crops in low rainfall areas in crop rotations or as lays is required to be effected.

(8) In recognition of the importance of detailed crop planning in meeting the challenge of aberrant weather, as illustrated in the case studies mentioned in the text. Similar analysis and contingent cropping plans should be developed for all the 72 drought prone districts in the country and implemented as farmers' programmes for drought proofing of the areas.

(9) In view of the available technology, any strategy for crop planning in drought prone areas in the country should include the basic practices described in the text as essential constituents of the package programme for implementation under a rotational system of land utilisation.

(10) Kharif fallows of Madhya Pradesh which are

at present utilised only for raising wheat or other rabi crops, could be utilised for growing crops in the South West monsoon season too through suitable water management programmes.

(11) Cultivation of pulses/leguminous crops in rotation or as inter-crops is recommended in canal irrigated tracts for purposes of green manuring and maintenace of soil fertility.

(12) Weed and disease-pest control measures are specially needed to be developed for irrigated conditions and heavy rainfall areas.

(13) River bed farming has to be developed as a direct way of cultivation, specially for vegetables and melons. This has been a neglected sphere and, therefore, requires the attention of the scientists and developmental authorities alike.

(14) Sewage farming utilising town effluents for irrigation should be developed to the maximum possible extent. Some of the expenditure incurred on this could be recovered through charges which can be levied on effluent irrigation and the balance, if any, could be treated as developmental expenditure.

(15) Scientific investigations into the subject of multiple cropping and crop rotation in various parts of the country have yielded valuable data on new patterns of cropping suitable to the respective areas. There is now a pressing need to make a reappraisal of the various possibilities to evolve cropping systems for covering all kinds of soil, rainfall and irrigation conditions as obtains in every taluk. The cropping systems so determined should be put into operation through active extension efforts and there should be a machinery to assess the progress and to effect mid-course alterations according to need.

The targets of area and yield for the various grain crops as contemplated for 2000 AD are given in Table 21.7. The present position has also been indicated for comparison. The salient aspects of suggested changes in cropped areas are stated below :

1. Significant increase has been suggested in barley area. About 0.34 Mha are for cultivation on saline and alkaline lands, 0.46 Mha to be transferred from wheat area and the remaining excess over the present acreage is mainly to come from rabi fallows in Uttar Pradesh, Bihar, Punjab and Haryana.

2. Major reduction of paddy area has been suggested in Uttar Pradesh, Madhya Pradesh and Bihar, West Bengal and Andhra Pradesh, Tamil Nadu and Karnataka. Preference should be given to crops like cotton, groundnut and maize in the surplus areas of the south and maize, soyabean and blackgram etc. in the other states. In rice, area should be withdrawn from uplands or other unfavourable situations where irrigation water cannot be provided easily to supplement rain-water. Wherever tank irrigation is prevalent as in the south, rice should be confined to the areas where water can reach through flow irrigation, lift irrigation should be avoided as far as possible.

3. Additional area of 4.7 Mha has to be brought under maize mainly from the surplus rice areas of Uttar Pradesh, Madhya Pradesh, Bihar and West Bengal (3.8 Mha) and Andhra Pradesh, Karnataka and Tamil Nadu (0.9 Mha). A rabi crop of maize should be encouraged in Orissa, Andhra Pradesh, Karnataka and Tamil Nadu.

4. Out of the total existing area of 4.7 Mha under small millets, 2.7 Mha are proposed to be diverted to fodder raising and only 2 Mha are to be retained for grain production.

5. For Pigeonpea, until medium duration varieties become available the main thrust of area expansion will have to be in frost-free areas of the north, because the peninsula does not hold promise in this regard owing to competition from crops like cotton.

6. For increasing area under miscellaneous pulses, due consideration should be given to multiple cropping. Off-season cropping in April to June period in river beds and tank beds should also be given a trial wherever feasible.

21.6.2. Emphasis in researches has usually been on improving yield by quantity rather than quality except for cotton and agronomic aspects have not received due attention. Specific recommendations are indicated below :

1. There is need to make a realistic distinction in crop research relating to irrigated and rainfed conditions proportionate to the area obtainable under each condition. For example, a crop like maize requires emphasis on rainfed conditions, whereas the emphasis has usually been for irrigated conditions. For wheat, the efforts are also required to be directed towards successful rainfed crop raising whereas the attention has been mostly given to irrigated crop so far. Crops like barley, jowar and pulses also require attention in research for rainfed conditions.

Wheat : 2. Whereas the existing tempo has to be maintained in all-round research, a special programme of evolving varieties and agronomic techniques suited to warmer winter conditions of the peninsula should be put into operation.

3. Due attention should be paid in research work to durum and dicoccum species which hold better promise for the south. Special varieties of wheat are required to be bred and cultivated for milling, baking and confectionary industries also.

4. The rust problem and the problem of storage pests should also get the best possible attention. In order to minimise rust menace, it is worth while to

eliminate wheat cultivation in the high hills or to saturate their area with resistant varieties. If wheat is continued to be grown in these areas, only rust-resistant varieties should be permitted. As all varieties may develop susceptibility with the passage of time, a surveillance service for rust detection on cultivated wheats will have to be organised.

5. Extension workers have to see that the capacity of the new dwarf varieties to adjust to late sowings is not stretched too far to the detriment of yield performance.

6. Breeders have to provide ample choice with maximum possible diversification of genotypes in the case of wheat in order to avoid disadvantages of a narrow genetic base throughout the length and breadth of the country and extension workers have to ensure that only a couple of varieties do not catch the fancy of the farmers.

Barley : 7. Research work on cultivation of barley under saline and alkaline conditions should receive attention. Many pests and diseases (e.g. corn leaf aphid and molya disease) and problems like lodging have to be tackled. The nutritional quality and digestibility of grain should be improved. Varieties like Hiproly are worth developing. Attempts to increase total lipids are also necessary. Hulled barleys cause digestive difficulty and hull-less types are at present low yielding. Attempts are necessary to remove this drawback and also to breed varieties with less percentage of crude fibre because crude fibre also impairs digestibility.

Oat : 8. As this crop is only of local importance from cultivation point of view its research aspects need to be looked after only by the central institutes and the agricultural universities, which are situated in the main wheat growing belt. Prevention of lodging, response to fertilisers and improvement in nutritional quality and digestibility of grain are some of the problems which should engage attention.

Rice : 9. The areas and production of rice crops should be reported in official statistics with reference to the dates of sowing. An experimental project is necessary to determine the most feasible arrangement.

10. The non-consumer areas like Punjab, Haryana, Rajasthan and West Uttar Pradesh hills and adjoining parts should be encouraged to grow high quality rice for exports. But due to the heavy pressure on irrigation resources for growing rice with inadequate rainfall, attempt should be made as far as possible to confine paddy cultivation to low lying areas or those lands which suffer from salinity and alkalinity.

11. Excessive rainfall should be suitably stored and used during the spells of drought as well as in the month of September when the rainfall is much less. Attempt should be made to transplant the crop in June with the backing of irrigation water to facilitate completion of its vegetative phase by the end of August. Under this arrangement it would not be subject to want of rainfall in the month of September.

12. The summer sown crop (April $\pm$ 15 days) in Orissa should be given up and whatever little irrigation water is used at present for its raising in the months of April and May could be utilised for raising nurseries for monsoon crop. The monsoon crop receiving astart in June would get the full advantage of the monsoon rainfall of July and August for its vegetative growth.

13. Varieties for the summer sown crop (February-May) have to be of early duration, say within 90 days, so that these could finish their life cycle before the onset of SW monsoon. Those for the monsoon crop could have a duration of 90-120 days and October-January sown crop could be even 150-160 days' long. Breeders should provide the information regarding the correct yield potential of the varieties when they release the varieties.

14. Serious endeavours are required to be made to lay emphasis on the cultivation of rice in Assam and adjoining parts in the flood-free period of October onwards. This poses a connected engineering problem of harnessing rain water of the monsoon season in such a manner that it would be available for irrigation purpose in later months.

15. If irrigation could be assured in the clear season in Assam; West Bengal and Orissa, the area under different rice crops could be readjusted in the following manner giving more weightage to the October-January sown crop than at present :

	area per cent		
	Feb-May	June-Sept	Oct-Jan
North Eastern States	20	60	20
West Bengal	10	80	10
Orissa	5	80	15

16. Considering the peculiarities of this crop, rice research could be regionalised in the following manner: (a) Jammu and Kashmir, Himachal Pradesh and West Uttar Pradesh hills, (b) Punjab, Haryana, Delhi and Rajasthan, (c) Gujarat and Maharashtra, (d) Uttar Pradesh, Madhya Pradesh and Bihar, (e) West Bengal and Orissa, (f) North-Eastern States, (g) Karnataka, Andhra Pradesh and Tamil Nadu and (h) Kerala, Coastal Karnataka and Coastal Maharashtra. Each region should be independent and self-sufficient

by itself in research as well as extension efforts. Each region should have its own research institute of All-India status. The overall all-India problems could be looked after by the CRRI in collaboration with these institutes. On extension side, the Ministry of Agriculture and Irrigation can develop suitable regional machinery with the involvement of the State Department of Agriculture.

17. The main research problems which call for special attention in the case of rice are (a) to fit the varieties as well as agronomic practices to local rainfall rhythm of different parts, (b) water and soil management under excess as well as deficient rainfall conditions, and (c) finding suitable varieties for different situations (hills, valleys and plains etc.) and for different crop seasons.

18. It is desirable to improve drainage of maize fields through cultural practices in order to avoid damage due to water logging.

19. The existing drawback in maize is that the early varieties are low yielders and the high yielding hybrids are too late for the rabi crops to be sown in time. This drawback is to be removed through persistent breeding efforts. Response to high population stress and resistance to borers are the other characteristics which have to be kept in view in breeding work.

Jowar : 20. Breeding efforts should attempt to introduce a proper leucine and isoleucine balance in jowar grains in order to ward off pellagra disease. It is also necessary to breed medium duration fertilizer responsive rabi jowar. Striga the plant parasite also needs attention either through developing resistant hybrid or through proper control measures. Extension efforts are required to ensure that beneficial practices relating to time of sowing, manuring, optimum plant population, weed control and plant protection are adopted by farmers on a large scale.

Bajra : 21. The need is to develop high yielding, disease and bird resistant varieties along side due agronomic methods including dry sowing and transplanting for different circumstances. Digestibility and keeping quality of flour are the other factors which require attention.

Ragi : 22. Breeding for short duration, bold grain with less husk and uniform maturity is desirable. Introduction of dormancy is necessary.

Small Millets : 23. Fodder and grain aspects have to be separated in research work. A contrasting study is also needed for the small millets which are grown in apparently two dissimilar conditions, viz. high and low rainfall areas.

Gram : 24. Improvement of yield in gram can be achieved by breeding significantly better varieties of this crop and provision of at least one irrigation between sowing time and flowering date according to exigencies.

Pigeonpea (arhar or tur) : 25. In the case of pigeonpea, attempts have to be continued to seed for medium duration single-season high yielding varieties suitable for different parts and for frost as well as wilt resistance.

Lathyrus (Khesari) : 26. The main problem in the case of this crop is to educate people in the proper use of the pulse and here the help of extention and revenue authorities could prove quite beneficial.

Other Pulses : 27. Due attention is required to be given to black gram, green gram, horse gram, *moth* and many others like cowpea, french bean, Dolichos lablab in order that different conditions of rainfall and soil could be met successfully in different parts. The agricultural universities and State Departments of Agriculture will have to draw up their own strategies concerning typical problems in regard to the pulses of their regions. Co-ordination could be broadly arranged for the peninsula, northern plains, hills and eastern parts. The extension machinery should be made to give top priority to make available to farmers the existing know-how and associated inputs.

The targets of area and yield for the various commercial crops as contemplated for 2000 AD are presented in Appendix 22.6, Statement I. The present position has also been indicated for the sake of comparison. The salient features pertaining to area changes are stated below :

(i) The major areas under groundnut will have to continue under rainfed conditions only. Because of this reason, the extension of area under groundnut should be effected as far as possible, (a) in such parts which receive rainfall of 10 to 20 cm per month in three or all of the South West monsoon months of June to September or, (b) where it is 20-30 cm per month in two of these four months (i.e B2-C4/C3) or, (c) in the South where the rainfall of September to November ranges between 5 and 20 cm per month (Sept. 20-30 cm, Oct. 20-30 or 10-20 cm, Nov. 5-10 cm).

(ii) The area increase in sesamum crop should preferably take place in such rainfall zones where the South West monsoon months involve rainfall month 10 to 20 cm or 20 to 30 cm for at least one month (i.e., between B1 and C1 types of rainfall patterns).

(iii) The area increase for niger should take care of the possibility of utilising the wheat fallows of Madhya Pradesh.

(iv) 50 per cent of the total proposed area for brassicas should come under irrigation. The crop in Uttar Pradesh should get utmost attention in this respect.

(v) Safflower can suit paddy fallow in majority of the paddy growing areas. It can be a fit substitute for lathyrus in Madhya Pradesh, Bihar and West Bengal.

(vi) Soyabean can be considered as one of the substitute crops in such areas where rainfall, though high, is not adequate for paddy all through, it can be considered with irrigation pulses like horsegram.

(vii) Out of the total area of 2.0 Mha under sunflower, only 0.75 could be put under irrigation, the rest will have to be raised under rainfed conditions as an early *Kharif* crop in general (wherever possible) and late *Kharif* crop with the help of September-October rains in the South.

(viii) Sugarbeet could be specially considered in the north-western parts comprising Jammu & Kashmir, Himachal Pradesh, West Uttar Pradesh, Punjab, Haryana and Rajasthan.

(ix) For sugarcane, about a million ha have to be added in the peninsula and 1.5 Mha in other parts. Uttar Pradesh and Bihar can certainly take in more area but the needs of other promising states like Madhya Pradesh, Orissa and irrigated parts of Rajasthan should also be given due consideration.

(x) The districts of West Uttar Pradesh bear the same promise for cotton growing as is obtained in the States of Punjab and Haryana. An allocation of 0.8 Mha has been made for these districts. Cotton growing may also be encouraged in West Bengal, Bihar and Orissa. In these parts, the crop can be taken during the period December to April and, therefore, can be easily fitted into the paddy fallows.

(xi) Irrigation is at present the most important factor for increasing jute yields and eighty per cent of the proposed jute area is, therefore, recommended to be irrigated. Further, out of the remaining 0.2 Mha 0.1 Mha may be brought within a more assured rainfall distribution, which in practice involves a sowing date not later than the 15th of May. This may be tried on an experimental basis, and for this purpose early maturing varieties may be used.

(xii) Ramie plantations may be established in the Himalayan West Bengal, Assam and other suitable parts of the North Eastern States. It could be tried even along the west coast. The advantage of starting these plantations could be given to small farmers by encouraging them to form cooperatives. Planting material sufficient for the purpose may be produced in time.

(xiii) The Ministry of Agriculture and Irrigation should ensure the fulfilment of the area targets under agave recommended by the expert sub committee appointed by the Indian Central Jute Committee in 1959.

Recommendations on general, research and developmental aspects of oilseed crop are as under :

(i) Due attention should be given to all oilseed field crops in order to increase their production capabilities. Many of the known results of research should be extended to them immediately and in the case of ground nut and brassicas, extension efforts should aim at covering the entire area with useful practices as quickly as possible.

(ii) **Ground nut :** As it may not always be possible to allot the best lands to this crop, agronomic techniques to be developed should be able to give maximum possible returns under different kinds of soil. The crop could be given an early start in the *Kharif* season with the help of irrigation, at least in some project areas as an experiment.

(iii) In order to raise the yield standards of groundnut, it is necessary (a) to develop better drainage fields in high rainfall areas, (b) to take all possible measures for covering soil moisture in low rainfall areas, (c) to adjust growing season to fit into local rainfall rhythm, and (d) to increase plant population per unit area.

(iv) **Sesamum :** In the case of sesamum the main strategy for increasing the yield will be the improvement of drainage conditions in high rainfall areas and the better utilisation of rainfall facilities elsewhere.

(v) **Niger :** High yielding Ethiopian varieties could be introduced directly after testing or used for improvement of Indian varieties through hybridisation.

(vi) **Soyabean :** For popularising soyabean, an alternative to the exotic varieties can be to try the indigenous hilly varieties. The latter have the advantage of being accepted as a pulse, while the former do not have this and, therefore, indigenous varieties can be sold as pulse when the oil industry fails to utilise due quantity. Researches in this direction are desirable. Attempts to introduce disease resistance in new varieties, specially against mosaic should continue.

(vii) In the extension programme of soyabean, the spheres of utility of this commodity should also be expanded. For example popularising a blended mixture of wheat and soyabean flours, putting to use the soyabean flour and meal in confectionary articles and exploiting soyabean for the manufacture of vegetable milk are some new uses. It may be pointed out here that groundnut cake has also the same potentialities.

(viii) **Sunflowers :** Seed-setting, seed viability and oil content of seed require to be improved. Since better pollination through the agency of honey bees could be an effective answer to proper seed-setting this factor should be studied thoroughly. Other responsible factors, if any, for seed-setting and viability should also be studied.

(ix) Utilisation of oilseed cakes, cotton seed and rice bran, which should rightly be given preference for obtaining oil, are at present used for livestock feeding. Extension agencies should see that the farmers get accustomed to feed their animals with the cake or meal of these subsidiary products which are equally nutritive or even better.

(x) The full utilisation of cake or meal of all the oilseeds in general is an imperative necessity, because if the cake is not disposed it will discourage the further offtake of oilseeds for crushing and in turn to the very cultivation of oilseeds themselves. The maximum utilisation of cakes should be for livestock feeding. Utilisation of cakes as manure and for preparation of germicides and pest repellants may be developed and popularised. Internal demand and export may be properly balanced so that annual fluctuations in the quantity exported are avoided as far as possible.

(xi) **Organisation** : For giving proper attention to oilseed crops, there is need for four well coordinated wings, one each to deal with (a) field crops, (b) subsidiary oilbearing products of field crops, (c) oil bearing shrubs and trees, and (d) byproducts of oil industry. These wings may be set up both on the research and production side, i.e., in the ICAR as well as in the State Departments of Agriculture with due participation of the agricultural universities on research side. A Central Technological Laboratory for oilseeds and their byproducts is also necessary and this may function under the ICAR.

(xii) Each State should be fully responsible for research as well as developmental work on the oilseed crops of their region. Regional coordination should in the first instance be organised among the contiguous states having identical crops and identical problems. The central coordination should be confined to problems of all-India nature only and the Oilseeds Development Council at the centre should be a broad based apex body charged with this responsibility. Its composition could include representatives of the States, ICAR, Union Ministries of Agriculture, Industry and Civil Supplies and Commerce, Forest Research Institute, Dehra Dun, Khadi and Village Industries Commison and oil millers. The states may also have similar apex bodies with representation from the agricultural universities, plantation crops (if any), Forests, Industries, Khadi and Village Industries Board, representatives of oil industry and growers. It is this body which could represent a State on the central apex body as well as in the inter-state coordinating councils. Recommendations pertaining to other commercial crops are summarised below :

(i) **Sugarcane** : Ratoon cropping may be encouraged because it reduces cost of cultivation. As the ratoon crop has to be given as much attention as the plant crop separate agronomic and plant production schedules should be drawn up for both of them.

(ii) Varieties have to be bred separately for (a) plant and ratoon crops, and (b) Gur and white sugar. Varieties of the future should have the highest possible sugar recovery, tillering capacity and tolerance to high population stress. Agronomy has to aim at maximum percentage of germination, least morality and the maintenance of an optimum plant stand up to the end. In the field of plant protection, efforts have to be continued for introducing genetic resistance and for finding out effective methods of chemical control, while biological methods of control also require to be developed and put into practice. Biochemical techniques should be developed for stimulating ripening in adverse circumstances.

(iii) Research activities other than breeding should be made the responsibility of the agricultural universities in order to render effective solution of regional problems. Breeding aspects in sugarcane presents, of course, a special problem, viz. that of flowering, because of which Coimbatore has to continue to play a central role in hybridization work. Hebbal (Bangalore) is another station not far away from Coimbatore which has shown promise in this type of work and it may also be fully developed as a companion station to Coimbatore. Hebbal can specifically look to the breeding needs of the Southern States and Coimbatore should have an all India slant, more directed to northern needs. The Sugarcane Research Institute, Lucknow has to develop as a sister station alongwith Coimbatore specialising in selection and development of suitable varieties after the 'fluff' stage for the northern parts of the country.

(iv) Multiplication and distribution of disease-free planting material of sugarcane should be given special attention because the existing stock is highly degenerated and disease-ridden.

(v) The developmental activities pertaining to sugarcane should be the responsibility of the Director of Agriculture on a uniform pattern in all the states including Uttar Pradesh. The Departments of Agriculture should look to all round development of sugarcane—whether it is for sugar or *gur* or *khandsari* manufacture. Even the industrial aspects with regard to the production of sugar or *gur* or *khandsari* may be looked after by the Department of Agriculture by creating a special cell for the purpose.

(vi) Sugar factories should be encouraged to participate directly in promotional and advisory activities on the developmental side as much as in procurement activities in their concerned areas to the maximum possible extent. It should be made mandatory for the factories to have a Cane Development Wing for this role, such a wing in every factory should have a Cane Development Officer in the same way as a Chief Chemist or a Chief Engineer. The functions of such a Wing should relate to the provision of all inputs including credit in the factory area. It should advise growers on all aspects of sugarcane cultivation. It should have its own mechanised units available for operations on the growers' fields at appropriate charges. In short, a very effective and intimate two-way direct contact between the grower and miller should develop. Governmental involvement in these matters should be limited to a supervisory role.

(vii) **Tobacco** : Varietywise and usagewise area and production statistics of tobacco has to be collected. Collaboration between the Directorate of Economics and Statistics, Ministry of Agriculture and Irrigation, Directorate of Statistics and Intelligence in the Department of Central Excise and Customs is desirable for this purpose.

(viii) Future research work should be in the direction of achieving higher yields per plant and per unit area of land under all kinds of tobaccos. Aircured and/or aromatic tobaccos like Burley, *Natu* and *Lanka* which have better appeal from export point of view need encouragement. The agricultural universities of the tobacco growing regions should be increasingly associated in future research work. Some specific aspects which require investigation area: (a) avoidance of harmful effects of irrigation on leaf quality due to the presence of chemicals in irrigation water, (b) biological control of pests and the role of harmless chemicals for use in plant protection work, e.g. fungicides of organic origion, and (c) elimination or reduction of carcinogenic or other harmful properties of tobacco.

(ix) Grading of tobacco leaves should be made compulsory, whether the product is meant for export or internal consumption. The system of grading tobacco leaves according to position on plant should be investigated with due regard to the economic operation of barns.

(x) The Ministry of Agriculture and Irrigation together with the concerned State Governments should make a review of all developmental activities (including extension and training) in order to make the development organisation effective in every important tobacco growing district for increasing production of all kinds of tobacco.

(xi) **Cotton** : There is need to study why the cotton crop in Madhya Pradesh and Maharashtra is not able to perform as well as in Gujarat under the same pattern of rainfall distribution since irrigation does not fully explain the existing difference in performance.

(xii) The districts of poor performance of cotton, where sure support of irrigation is called for are Aurangabad (Maharashtra), Belgaum, Gulbarga, Dharwar (Part), Bijapur, Raichur, Bellary, Chitradurga (Karnataka), Mahaboobnagar, Kurnool and Anantapur (Andhra Pradesh). Judicious use of rainfall and irrigation water, one supplementing the other, is the keynote on which future strategy lies also in general.

(xiii) In order to fix proportion between long, medium and short staple cottons for the sake of a production programme, it is necessary to make a periodical review of the domestic as well as export demands. More of medium and short staple cottons may be required in future and suitable high yielding varieties have to be bred for the purpose.

(xiv) The results of practical utility already available should be fitted into suitable agronomic and plant protection practices in the different regions. The emphasis in future years should be that every State tackles its own research and developmental problems with the involvement of the agricultural university and department of agriculture. For purposes of inter-state consultation and cooperation the important cotton growing states can be formed into groups as follows :

(a) Punjab, Haryana, Rajasthan and Uttar Pradesh.
(b) West Bengal, Bihar and Orissa.
(c) Gujarat, Madhya Pradesh and Maharashtra.
(d) Karnataka, Andhra Pradesh and Tamil Nadu.

It is not sufficient if the Central Cotton Research Institute, Nagpur has few substations. It is more important that it also develops a working partnership for solving regional problems with the concerned agricultural universities.

(xv) Wherever feasible, adjustment of cropping season may be considered from the view point of insect or disease free period also on the same analogy as the "Potato Seed Plot Technique." Methods of biological control may be investigated, developed and popularised. Co-operative pest management practices involving the whole village approach should be encouraged.

(xvi) Breeding work should also take into

consideration some special requirements like (a) varieties which can withstand the effects of high soil moisture in high rainfall areas, (b) varieties for early sowing under such high rainfall conditions, (c) varieties with gossypol free seed, (d) increased oil percentage in seed without detriment to quality or quantity of lint, and (e) varieties with fibre suitable for blending with synthetic fibres. Suitable combination of agronomic and plant protection schedules is also required to be developed for making the varieties yield their best in high rainfall areas. Developing varieties and agronomic and plant protection techniques for cotton cultivation during the months of December to April in West Bengal and the adjoining States of Bihar and Orissa should also engage attention.

(xvii) The Cotton Technological Laboratory should continue to study all facets of fibre quality and treatment which will promote the use of cotton varieties for blending purposes and incorporate easy care properties even in pure cottons.

(xviii) **Best fibre** : The comparatively low price of jute and allied goods is an advantage which has to be maintained by continuous attention to productivity as this is the only way to save this crop from competition from other sources. New uses of jute and allied fibres such as textiles, flooring and construction materials, woollenised goods should receive constant attention. Woollenised goods in particular may have a great attraction in this country as well as other similar developing countries because of their low cost.

(xix) Developmental measures should be intensified in order to bring home to the farmer the full benefits of research work and provide him with all necessary inputs and extension agencies should be specially geared up for this purpose. Extension agencies have to educate farmers that they can use the ideally stored seed up to two years rather than seeking renewal every year. Extension agencies should impress on farmers that well stored seed may be used upto two years and annual renewal is not necessary. This will relieve pressure the demand for fresh seed and enable a larger coverage within the same amount of seed.

(xx) The most important problem that needs attention in the case of sannhemp is to break the barrier of self-sterility and bring forth durable hybrids or synthetics. Another is the breeding of varieties separately for green manuring and for fibre purposes. The third important problem relates to a special seed multiplication programme to overcome deterioration caused by cross pollination.

(xxi) The Jute Agricultural Research Institute (JARI) and the Central Ramie Research Station, Sorbhog (Assam) should continue to be responsible for research work on ramie for the time being. It is necessary that the mesta and sannhemp growing states should themselves be made directly responsible for research work on these crops through the involvement of their agricultural universities. The JARI should play only a coordinating role. Insofar as agave is concerned, the basic work being done by the Barma substation of the JARI can continue as at present. The technological aspects relating to all these crops should be continued to be dealt with by the Jute Technological Laboratories for the country as a whole.

(xxii) The minimum viable unit of agave plantation is 105 hectares. Such plantations should be organised on co-operative lines by small enterprising farmers. Because of the agronomic and decortication techniques involved it will be a fit venture for agricultural graduates and preference should be given to them to establish agave plantations.

(xxiii) The ICAR institutions relating to agave should not directly involve themselves in multiplication programmes except for the supply of nucleus material. The State Governments concerned should have their own nursery stations with facilities to take up research work for an adaptive nature. The ICAR institutions should devote their attention mainly to research problems, wherein due emphasis has to be given to breed varieties, which should give increased outturn, better quality of fibre and be at the same time resistant to pests and diseases. As seed-setting in agave requires a cool climate, the ICAR should choose a suitable station for this purpose at some higher altitude. Because the land which will be available for this crop will be mostly marginal or sub-marginal, improvement in its productivity should also engage attention in research programmes. Arrangements may have to be made for the exchange of knowhow on this crop from other countries advanced in the cultivation of this crop.

(xxiv) The Central Arid Zone Research Institute at Jodhpur and the university which may be established in Rajasthan should undertake the responsibility of research work for the propagation of agave in dry conditions.

The important conclusions and recommendations which emerge are discussed in this section. The targets of area and yield for the various crops as contemplated for 2000 AD are given in Appendix 23.6. The present position has also been indicated therein for the sake of comparison. Important recommendations regarding areas under different crops are given below :

(i) The target of area under fruit crops for 2000 AD

should set at 4 Mha.

(ii) The imposition of land ceilings would necessitate making available data collected through scientifically conducted experiments with regard to the minimum economic size of an orchard and also with regard to the comparative economics of raising a food or commercial crop as against fruit crops in order to help the farmers determine the proportion of area which they would like to put under fruits. It might also be necessary to give special loans for inducing farmers to go in for fruit cultivation.

(iii) Seedling mango trees should be protected and the area under them could also be increased. Their felling has to be regulated so that only useless trees are cut and the correct proportion between removal and replenishment is maintained.

(iv) Orchards of grafted mango can be favoured in all such areas which are easily commanded by the markets, whereas seedling mangoes could predominate in the interior.

(v) Besides many other situations, community lands like those of the Panchayats and the areas released from 'shifting cultivation' in the States of Madhya Pradesh, Bihar (South) and the adjoining areas in Orissa could also be considered for mango planting. Road and canal sides also afford possibilities for this purpose. A study is needed to determine the relative feasibility and proportion of planting road and canal sides with mango and other kinds of trees.

(vi) Efforts should be made to increase area under banana considerably. The strategy should be to make its cultivation widespread with preference to small scale production.

(vii) It is desirable to encourage the cultivation of guava in as many congenial situations as possible. It is a good tree for homesteads. It could be tried on ravines and common lands under panchayats, etc.

(viii) For sour varieties of apples, the area of cultivation specially requires to be extended in order to cope up with the demands of South India. Elevations of less than 1,500 m or more than 2,000 m offer scope for apple cultivation, if and when suitable varieties become available.

(ix) It is necessary to study the comparative economics of cultivation of grapes as against the other field crops, which are usually grown in Punjab, Haryana and adjoining irrigated area of Rajasthan with a view to encourage grape cultivation in the area.

(x) There is a good scope for introduction of pine-apple in the areas reclaimed from 'shifting cultivation' in the North-Eastern region.

(xi) Walnut area in the producing States requires at least to be doubled by 2000 AD, the existing area being 6,000 ha.

(xii) Besides the need for area increase through new plantations, there is urgent need for replacing the non-descript or disease-ridden trees in many of the fruit crops through interplanting with the better material and then removing the old ones at an appropriate stage. This specially applies to mango and citrus.

(xiii) The area under tapioca in the country should be raised to one million hectares by 2000 AD.

(xiv) The agronomic and economic aspects of inter-cropping in bananas should be worked out in detail. Studies should be conducted on the economics of under planting banana in coconut groves.

(xv) Production of vegetables needs to be under-taken in : (a) belts around towns and cities over 2.8 Mha, (b) hills over 0.2 Mha, (c) along tanks, lakes, rivers and canals over 0.8 Mha, and (d) kitchen gardens in the interior villages and towns and cities over 0.2 Mha. Kitchen gardens in cities and towns could be developed simultaneously with the necessary promotional activities pertaining to vegetable production.

Recommendations regarding fruit crops pertaining to aspects other than area are given below :

Mango

(i) Seedling mango should receive due attention in future research and development efforts.

(ii) It will be necessary to train a large number of *malis* in the art of budding, grafting and top working so that they can operate an effective custom service. A vigorous extension programme will also be necessary to educate people to replace their inferior trees and groves.

(iii) Hybridization efforts illustrated by the evolution of *mallika* for incorporating the characteristic of annual bearing has to be pursued tenaciously until it becomes possible to release a good number of hybrids with proven record of annual bearing. Similarly, it is also necessary to intensify research efforts to eliminate or control malformation of vegetative and floral shoots.

(iv) The commercial varieties, which are under cultivation, at present, require to be screened from the view point of genetics and once the cultivars with stable and identical characters relating to plant behaviour, productivity, disease resistance, adapta-bility, quality and flavour have been identified, these only should be propagated vegetatively on standardis-ed root stocks. Use of polyembryonic root stocks would further ensure uniform performance. Breeding efforts have also to go on for evolving better varieties, some of the desirable characters are dwarfness, resistance to pests and diseases and different maturity periods. Some polyembryonic varieties have shown promise as dwarfing root stocks and hence could be tried for this purpose.

Banana

(v) Improvement in the yield and quality standard of banana crop should be aimed at for the entire area. The problems which need attention in future are spacing of plants for the healthy development, introduction of ratooning, beneficial combinations and techniques of mixed cropping, combating pest and disease problems like those of 'hunchy top', leaf spot (sigatoka) and nematodes, means and methods of reducing water requirement, harvest techniques and ways of protection of banana bunches from external injuries, insect bites, sunburn etc.

(vi) Pending the outcome of spacing trials, 92m ×2m distance between plants could be advocated as an interim measure. Pending solution of 'bunchy top' disease, in areas where it has assumed very serious proportions (e.g., Kerala), a complete replanting programme is necessary with healthy disease free suckers. In those areas wherein disease is not serious, a suitable package of practices for eliminating it could be popularised.

Citrus

(vii) It is necessary to find out through experiments compatible stocks for different varieties of citrus for different regions. Future research work should also include evolving of nuclear line plant material; hybridisation work with a view to evolve varieties resistant to root rot and viruses, saline conditions and nematodes.

(viii) Studies are also needed to standardise cultural practices for commercial varieties, suitable schedules of intercrops have also to be developed. The effect of various nutrients in different doses on commercial varieties raised on different root stocks requires to be studied.

(ix) Biochemical changes, which are produced in citrus plants by viruses and die back diseases also require to be studied. The study of virus-vector relationship and sterilisation of vector by irradiation techniques will prove helpful. Another useful direction of research would be to induce resistance against severe strains of known viruses by cross-protection with mild strains.

(x) The programme of certification, inspection and registration of virus-free mother trees requires to be rigidly enforced. For this purpose it is necessary to multiply virus-free material. It is desirable to draw a programme of replantation of citrus orchards with the best possible disease-free material.

Papaya

(xi) Research work in other countries indicates that gynodioceism with complete elimination of males can be introduced in dioceious cultivars. Either this technique could be adopted or other efforts could be made for breeding stable cultivars. The other desirable characters to be introduced are dwarfness; high yield of fruit as well as papin; and uniform shape, size, texture and flavour of fruit. Suitable control measures and breeding efforts are required for combating diseases like 'damping off', collar rot, mosaic, leaf curb and distortion ringspot. Development of frost resistant varieties is also necessary.

Guava

(xii) It is necessary to study which of the guava seasons in a year is better in a particular region with regard to yield and quality. Resistance to wilt disease is required to be introduced in new varieties. It is necessary that unless resistance is proved pathogenitically, no cultivar should be taken as resistant even if it might have been growing unaffected for many years.

Apple

(xiii) It is necessary to broaden the genetic base of sweet varieties of apple and in this connection the possibility of utilising wildgerm plasm has to be explored.

(xiv) Varieties of apples are required to be evolved for elevations lower than 1,500 metres and more than 2,000 metres, the economics of successful apple cultivation at greater heights will also have to be worked out besides the breeding of suitable varieties.

(xv) The relative economics of the new method of cultivation of dwarf apples comprising dense planting with specialised training techniques for branches as against the established methods requires to be tried experimentally.

Pine apple

(xvi) Pine apple research has to be done on a

regional basis. Suitable agronomic and plant protection schedules for different areas are required to be developed and recommended. Methods for activating slip production by using vegetative bud dormancy breakers and reducing the unproductive off-type population require to be worked out. It is desirable to breed a number of good varieties for table purposes as well as for canning.

Walnut

(xvii) Walnut needs special attention because it has good potentiality of earning foreign exchange. The problems, which need attention, are production techniques and care of plantations in general and making available walnut grafts for replacing the seedling trees.

All fruits

(xviii) In order to expand the export trade in fruits, it is necessary to evolve a standard procedure for the Indian embassies for enabling them to maintain a constant survey of the changing tastes and requirements abroad so that production programmes within the country could periodically be given the required orientation.

(xix) It is desirable that ICAR undertakes research work on the maintenance of ecological balance in the context of minimising damage to fruit crops through animals and birds.

(xx) The States should strengthen their horticultural set-up in order to be effective enough to undertake the expansion programmes relating to fruits and vegetables etc.

(xxi) Clonal selections to choose the best cultivars have to be made in all possible fruit crops in order to ensure a consistent standard of yield and quality.

(xxii) More attention is required to be given to tillage aspects of orchards. There should also be provision for irrigation and adoption of plant protection measures. In short, better agronomic practices have to be developed for different fruit crops and also popularised. Foliar Analysis Laboratories are required to be established in the agricultural universities for estimating nutritional requirements of fruit trees and an associated advisory service is also required to be organised in order to help the growers in this regard.

(xxiii) Research is also necessary to determine :

(a) which crops could be grown under rainfed conditions and in which parts,

(b) which crops would require the full irrigation support, and

(c) which crops would have to depend partly on rainfall and partly on irrigation and in their case to define the periods of dependence on rainfall and on irrigation.

(xxiv) The problem of residual toxicity will also need attention when the use of plant protection chemicals becomes popular in orchards and groves.

(xxv) Improving production through top-working should be extended to as many fruits as practicable. The technique of top-working should be standardised for different crops for large scale adoption.

(xxvi) Model orchards are required to be established in every district in order to determine the economics of fruit production. These orchards could also be used as centres of practical demonstration in better methods of cultivation. Research work should be intensified in Agricultural Universities. Establishment of progeny orchards and supply of genetically uniform nursery stock is of utmost importance on the development side.

(xxvii) Two institutes of temperate fruit crops are required to be established, one in the north-western Himalayan belt and the other in the north-eastern hills. Researches pertaining to temperate fruit crops should be the responsibility of these two institutes.

(xxviii) The crops which are of local importance from production point of view, should be dealt with by the concerned State Governments and Agricultural Universities.

Recommendations applicable to many crops in common are given below :

Vegetable Crops

(i) It is necessary that arrangements are made to collect data simultaneously on area and production of vegetable crops, onions, garlic, ginger and coriander in all the states through sample surveys on a periodic basis.

(ii) The varieties, requirements and seasons of various minor crops like onion, garlic, vegetables, ginger, turmeric and chillies vary from place to place. Hence, the research and development work on these crops should be the responsibility of the State Governments. Besides individual states looking after their own problems, continguous states can set up suitable inter-state machinery for mutual benefit.

(iii) Diseases take a heavy toll of the crop in the case of chillies and coriander. Therefore, breeding for disease resistance and developing suitable agronomic and plant protection schedules for combating the menace needs to be given special place in research programmes.

(iv) In order that seed, fertilisers and plant

protection chemicals become available within the financial capacity of small growers, the sale of such inputs in mini kits should be popularised in the case of vegetables and floriculture.

Recommendations regarding tuber crops, bulb crops, vegetables, etc. are summarised below :

Potato : (i) The method of crop cutting surveys for estimation of yield of potato should be extended to all important producing states.

(ii) The programme for increased potato production must be accompanied by effective marketing system whereby it becomes possible to distribute the produce to different consuming centres throughout the country in order to avoid gluts in the producing areas. It is also necessary to have adequate cold storage facilities for accommodating surpluses which might still remain.

(iii) Disease-pest forecasting, surveillance and plant protection measures are specially required to be developed in the case of potato crop. The problem of residual toxicity of pesticides has also to be solved alongside. The use of polyhaploidy and tissue and organoculture techniques should be increasingly made in developing new varieties.

(iv) In the case of sweet potato and tapioca, the Central Tuber Crops Research Institute at Trivandrum should devote attention to basic work including that on breeding. In subsequent stages of breeding work like selection and multiplication, this institute should take full help from the agricultural universities and the farms of different states. Researches of local importance should also be done in the various states where the crops are actually grown.

(v) There should be a clear-cut programme for developing separate varieties and techniques for culinary and industrial purposes in the case of tapioca. Some of the characters which have necessarily to be incorporated in the culinary varieties are : stalked tubers, medium in size and with good drying-ratio. Small size plants, early maturity and mosaic resistance are some other characters which will be equally good for both the purposes. There is need to lay special emphasis on improving the keeping quality of tapioca tubers through breeding.

Onion : (vi) Arrangement should be made whereby uptodate statistics on area and production on onion become available through sample surveys at least once in every five years.

(vii) The existing varieties need to be screened for isolating genetic bases. High yielding, disease-pest resistant varieties suitable for different kinds of uses have to be developed together with proper agronomic and plant protection schedules. Botanical studies will have to be undertaken for finding out optimum conditions of flowering, pollination and seed setting.

(viii) It is desirable that the Home Science Colleges in general and such colleges or divisions of the agricultural universities undertake research work in order to develop various kinds of palatable recipes from the tuber crops. The ICAR should provide guidelines and coordinate research work in this regard. The Departments of Agriculture in the Centre and the States could undertake a coordinated programme of publicity thourgh press, audiovisual means and public contact for popularising the use of tuber crops as a part of cereal substitutions. Practical demonstrations of taste and preparation of recipes could prove helpful in this regard.

(ix) An exhaustive cataloguing could be made of such wild plants, the various parts of which are consumed in the countryside as vegetables. The growth of most useful ones can then be encouraged. This work could be done in cooperation with the forest departments.

(x) In cities and towns, the liquid and solid products of sewerage should be harnessed and their use popularised to maximum possible extent.

(xi) organising the vegetable holdings in a collective manner for making possible large scale mechanised tillage as well as plant protection operations should be the responsibility of the Department of Agriculture/Horticulture. The Government has to assume responsibility for establishing custom services for various kinds of operations either through cooperatives or governmental organisations. Ensuring the individuals the facility of irrigation should also be the responsibility of the government. The individual growers should be encouraged to sink wells on joint ownership basis. All possible guidance and assistance in material or finance should also be provided to them.

(xii) Crop rotations and companion cropping beneficial from the soil point of view could be introduced in vegetable cultivation and in this respect, short statured beans or fodder legumes like berseem and lucerne could prove very useful.

(xiii) Breeding programmes should take into consideration the requirements of processing industry and export and the choice of various countries which have an import potential from India. Hybrid vigour should be increasingly utilised for producing high yielding varieties of quality suited to various purposes and tastes. It will also be good to introduce disease resistance in F1 hybrids, when possible.

(xiv) Leafy vegetables belonging to different species of *Amaranthus*, *Portulaca*, *Trigonella*, *Aerva*, *Alternanthera*, *Basella*, *Celosia* and various other species should be collected and evaluated for their nutritional and other desirable characters.

Ginger : (xv) It is necessary to evolve high yielding fibreless varieties of ginger which have a demand in foreign markets.

(xvi) Variety Rio de Janeiro is suggested for immediate adoption for internal consumption and processing as an interim measure, but it should not be grown in Kerala.

(xvii) Ginger research stations will have to determine the optimum stages of maturity required for the manufacture of various processed articles. Kerala and the North Eastern States of Assam, Meghalaya, Nagaland, Mizoram, Manipur, Tripura, which are important for ginger, should collaborate their research and development programmes. The potential existing in the North Eastern States should be fully exploited both for internal as well as external ginger trade. Other states should also undertake research activities according to their need.

Mushrooms : (xviii) The import of canned *Agaricus* should be replaced by indigenous manufacture. At present *Agaricus sp.* is the only one which is cultivated but other types like paddy straw mushroom also require to be encouraged.

(xix) The artificial cultivation of mushroom should be organised near such cities where it is possible to provide the dehydrating and canning facilities and this work has to be confined only to such persons who possess the requisite knowhow. They should be preferably agricultural graduates.

(xx) In order to provide true to type quality material for production of mushrooms, spawn laboratories have to be started under governmental control. Import of spawns has to be banned, except when required for experimental purposes and that too under rigid quarantine procedure.

(xxi) States undertaking the collection programme of wild mushrooms or production programme of cultivated ones will have to create necessary set up in their Departments of Forest and Agriculture/Horticulture. The Departments of Agriculture/Horticulture should be responsible for inspection and extension activities including training of personnel.

(xxii) Agricultural universities of the concerned states, the Mushrooms Research Institute, Solan (Himachal Pradesh), Hill Fruit Research Station, Chaubattia (Uttar Pradesh), the Indian Agricultural Research Institute (Mycology and Plant Pathology Division), New Delhi, the Indian Horticultural Research Institute, Bangalore (Karnataka) should be responsible for mushroom research.

(xxiii) All possible measures should be taken to popularise truffles throughout the Sub-Himalayan Oak belt and the Hill Fruit Research Station, Chaubattia should take up the necessary research work.

(xxiv) The Mushroom Research Institute, Solan, the Indian Agricultural Research Institute, New Delhi, and the Indian Horticultural Research Institute, Bangalore, should try to provide necessary data and advice to the Agricultural Marketing Adviser to the Government of India and the Indian Standards Institutions of enable them to lay down quality standards for dried mushrooms so that grading is made possible as a compulsory measure in due course.

Floriculture (xxv) An intelligent selective approach is necessary for capturing foreign markets. For example, the best period which can be exploited to India's advantage in winter when temperate and cold countries have the natural handicap of not being in a position to grow plants ordinarily. As far as bulbs are concerned, the country should specialise in exporting such tropical material which is not commonly grown there.

(xxvi) For promotion of exports of various kinds of cut flowers, it is desirable to develop special floriculture blocks in the neighbourhood of airports and this activity could preferably be entrusted to agricultural graduates.

(xxvii) Dry flowers also offer a very good export market and this technique has, therefore, to be increasingly utilized.

(xxviii) Production of new and attractive hybrids of orchids under controlled conditions requires attention. In addition, there is need to protect and proliferate the natural orchid flora of the country. It is necessary to create orchid sanctuaries in the natural habitats of these plants and regulate their exploitation.

(xxix) Landscape planning with the help of attractive flowering and hecter bearing plants on a countrywide scale will also go a long way towards increasing the scope of a floriculture in the country. A central committee for landscape planning should be formed by the central government to prepare various alternative landscape plans to fit into the programmes of development of villages, towns and cities. The State Governments should actively collaborate with the central committee in the preparation and execution of the master plans which should also include in their scope the national highways, canals, railways and riversides.

(xxx) The flowers of Lotus family should engage special attention in research and developmental activities. The ICAR should encourage research on ornamental as well as edible aspects of this flower.

A survey also needs to be undertaken in order to determine the scope for cultivation of the various species of Lotus family which have economic value. The concerned State Governments have to evince due interest for organising production in a systematic manner. The Departments which have a part to play are Agriculture/Horticulture, Fisheries and Revenue.

Aromatic and Medicinal Plants

(xxxi) Production research of all kinds of medicinal plants should be the responsibility of the ICAR. The ICAR should also be responsible for introduction of exotic plants. Processing and utilization research should be the responsibility of the Central Indian Medicinal Plants Organisation (CIMPO) of the Council of Scientific and Industrial Research. The ICAR and CIMPO should develop a proper coordination machinery.

(xxxii) Insofar as *khastha aushadhis* or herbal medicines which are prevalent throughout the country for home medicines, are concerned, the Botanical Survey of India, Calcutta and National Botanic Gardens, Lucknow in consultation with Central Council for Research in Indian Medicine and Homaeopathy should list all the concerned plants and prepare illustrated description in popular languages giving the names, the part of the plants used, medicinal importance and the methods employed for their use in various common ailments. It is necessary to indicate the best time of picking for maximum potency as also the period of expiry. If necessary, legislative measures should be taken for the enforcement of the various standards and for this purpose, even licensing of traders may have to be resorted to.

(xxxiii) The CIMPO should standardise procedures to certify (a) the correct identification of plants, (b) the parts of the plants used and (c) their expiry periods. They may constitute a committee for this purpose with representatives from (a) National Botanic Gardens, Lucknow, (b) Central Council of Research in Indian Medicine and Homoeopathy, (c) Indian Council of Agricultural Research, (d) Botanical Survey of India, (e) Forest Research Institute, (f) Central Drug Research Institute, and (g) Indian Council of Medicinal Research.

Summary of Conclusions and Recommendations

The main recommendations are as under :

1. The targets of area for various plantation crops for 2000 AD are given in Appendix 24.4. Main proposals for area extension are :-

   (i) Out of proposed 175,000 ha additional land to be brought under rubber crop, 100,000 ha be earmarked for the North-eastern Region and the remaining 75,000 ha could be spread over congenial locations along the western ghats. Areas could be sought for even in Andhra Pradesh and Orissa.

   (ii) It is possible to increase the area under cashewnut in the Peninsular States and Orissa. Besides thinking of absolutely new areas for this crop, the plantations from the existing unproductive sites should also be shifted to highly promising ones, both in private as well as in forest lands. Insofar as private lands are concerned, certain incentives like the replanting subsidies, as in the case of Rubber, could be given for this crop too.

   (iii) The ICAR should arrange to conduct feasibility trials on oil palm in the areas which are thought to be congenial. Side by side, it would also be worth while to find out experimentally the manner in which the tree could be grown successfully within the limitations of the agro-climatic conditions prevailing in the country.

   (iv) Congenial conditions for the cultivation of clove and nutmeg exist in the hill regions of Kerala, Tamil Nadu and Karnataka. It is necessary to undertake cultivation of these spices to an extent sufficient to replace their imports. The possibility of their cultivation in the Islands of Andaman and Nicobar should also be explored.

   (v) Besides the Andaman and Nicobar Islands and the States of Karnataka, Tamil Nadu and Kerala, it is worth while to examine whether cacao plantations could be established in other parts also, particularly, Orissa.

2. Special programme for the supply of fertilisers and plant protection chemicals in small pockets should be started for the benefit of small pepper growers.

3. The Rubber Boards schemes for assistance for rubber plantations should be so modified that small growers get due benefit. They should be given all possible facilities by the institutionalised agencies for which it might be necessary to organise them into effective co-operatives. Cooperatives and other kinds of farmers service societies may be created with state support in order to assist small growers in plant protection measures or processing of Latex.

4. Attempts should be made to breed varieties of rubber resistant to abnormal leaf-fall and powdery mildew. It is also necessary to breed special varieties for the proposed new areas in the States of Maharashtra, Andhra Pradesh and Orissa, which represent

comparatively less hum id conditions than Kerala and Assam.

5. In the existing private rubber plantations, the technical competence of management can be gradually improved by encouraging the dependents of growers to go in for agricultural education. It is also worth examining whether agricultural graduates could be given preference in new areas meant for rubber plantations.

6. Increasing the proportion of hermaphrodite flowers and removing other defects should be given priority in research work on cashewnut. It is also very necessary that the existing high yielding varieties are first experimentally tried for their suitability to different agroclimatic conditions before being recommended for adoption.

7. If the technique of *in situ* grafting proves successful, it could be adopted for interplanting in cashew plantations so that the urproductive trees can be removed ultimately.

8. It is necessary to effect proper coordination between the State Departments of Agriculture/Horticulture and Forest for carrying out all activities pertaining to cashew improvement on common lines. The former should pay attention to yield aspect rather than laying emphasis merely on soil conservation, whereas the latter should bestow attention on this crop in the same manner as is given to any plantation crop. Besides other applicable scientific methods the existing trees—whether in forests or elsewhere—should be improved through the technique of topworking.

9. It is necessary that the cashew apple, the shell liquid and the testa tannin should be fully exploited industrially in future. Recommendations, which have been made by the ealier committees and are lying unimplemented, have to be freshly considered and new avenues should also be quickly explored.

10. The development of high yielding varieties and accompanying package of practices deserve attention in the case of arecanut. The Central Plantation Crops Research Institute, Kasaragod together with its regional and substations should try to seek cooperation of the Agricultural Universities of the states concerned. It will be advantageous in research work to get the requisite knowhow from Sri Lanka for improving the standard of production.

11. Sea water should be tried to irrigate coconut plantations in light soils in coastal areas during summer season.

12. The existing low yielding plantations of coconut should be rapidly replaced by resorting to (a) under planting with new hybrids/varieties and (b) by change to new sites according to need. The emphasis has to be on giving attention to individual trees as well as to the plantation as a whole. Extension campaigns have to be conducted in order to educate the growers in the advantages of utilising the new agronomic and plant protection methods coupled with the use of new hybrids/varieties. The State Governments may provide plantation subsidies and input materials. Supply of fertilisers and plant protection chemicals in small packets would prove very helpful to individual household growers.

13. The seed of oil palm for planting has to be multiplied within the country itself in order to avoid reliance on imports. Extraction plants are required to be established in close proximity of the growing areas in order to avoid deterioration of the kernels during transport or storage. Arrangements have also to be made to organise quick collection of fruits from small individual growers too. Proper extraction machinery is also a necessity.

14. Sterility, irregular annual fruiting and the absence of suitable methods of vegetative propagation are some of the difficulties in the case of clove, which have to be solved through research. It is also necessary to evolve methods for increasing germination of clove seed and reducing mortality of seedlings. Techniques in respect of trimming and pruning of clove trees in order to induce formation of low broad bushy crowns have also to engage attention. In addition, manuring and irrigation requirements have also to be determined.

15. The problem of identification of sex of seedling of nutmeg before planting needs attention. The possibilities of conversion of male plants into females by suitable techniques as well as the various methods of vegetative propagation should be studied.

16. Cacao growing could be encouraged as a part of mixed plantations and when this is achieved, a common service for plant protection operations and processing of beans may be organised to assist the small growers.

17. It is advisable to select 150 ha for seed nurseries in the best possible locations out of the existing 1,200 ha of cacao plantations. This seed production programme should be conducted in the concerned States with the cooperation of the Central Plantation Crops Research Institute, Kasaragod and the seed material so produced should be made available to meet the need of Andaman & Nicobar Islands too. Besides propagation through seed, the possibility of clonal propagation should also be experimented with.

18. When the availability of cacao seed has been ensured, seedling nurseries should be established in all

producing areas of the country. Planning for the nurseries and the actual plantation areas should start right from now. The Ministry of Agriculture and Irrigation and the Indian Council of Agricultural Research should render all help to the concerned States in this work.

The following is a summary of the important recommendations made in this Chapter.

1. The available feed resources being extremely limited should be distributed in such a manner that these are put to best use for increasing the production of milk, meat, wool, eggs, etc.

2. There should be a strong research base for undertaking effective programmes for the evolution of high yielding, nutritionally superior and disease resistant varieties and for standardisation of package practices as applicable to different agroclimatic regions. Massive farmer-oriented extension programmes both for fodder production and conservation should be organised.

3. Efficient arrangement for production and supply of high quality fodder seeds should be made.

4. Selection and introduction of high yielding fodder varieties need attention.

5. High yielding fodder varieties are usually shy seeders. Efforts should therefore, be made to incorporate high seed yielding character in them.

6. Efforts should be made to combine high nutritive quality with high yield.

7. Dual purpose and multi-cutlegume fodder varieties which can overlap the fodder scarcity periods May-June and October-November should be evolved for inclusion in crop rotations.

8. Arrangements for seed production of the root crops with high tonnage should be made in the hills of northern India.

9. Suitable high yielding, quick growing and shade tolerant legumes which can combine well with cultivated fodders should be evolved for irrigated as well as rainfed areas.

10. In order to build up the required germ plasm collection, experts should be sent to tropical and subtropical countries to locate promising grasses and legumes.

11. Optimum sowing and harvesting schedules should be determined for each fodder crop for each region.

12. In rainfed areas where pre-monsoon showers occur, possibilities of growing short duration fodder crops should be explored.

13. Studies on the economics of fodder crops grown as a mixed crop with broadly spaced food or cash crops and as a single crop should be carried out.

14. It is necessary to limit the stocking rate of grasslands and to undertake measures for improvement of their productivity by controlled grazing.

15. In grasslands of arid and semi-arid regions, conservation of rain water by fully plugging, putting small dams, removing shrubs etc. should be practised.

16. In degraded grasslands, reseeding of desirable species with proper management should be resorted to.

17. Work on ecological improvement of grasslands should be undertaken by the institutes working on grasslands management.

18. Grass seed production programme should be undertaken by the organisations presently conducting researches on these aspects.

19. In order to improve the herbage quality and the soil fertility, it is necessary to evolve and introduce a suitable legume component in grasslands.

20. Intensive studies should be undertaken to ascertain the optimal mode of utilisation of fertilisers in grasslands.

21. A systematic survey of wastelands and village common lands should be made to prepare a land use plan as part of social forestry incorporating therein programmes of development of fodders and grasses. The wastelands not covered under social forestry programmes should be developed by the Animal Husbandry Department for additional grazing and production of hay.

22. While formulating programmes of soil forestry on lands on the sides of roads, canal banks and railway lines due regard should be given to the growing of grasses and fodder along with trees.

23. Available land in possession of Government, consolidated where necessary, in blocks of over 200 ha should be taken up progressively for development as rangelands by the Animal Husbandry and Sheep Development Departments. There should be a regular consultation between the concerned officers of these departments.

24. Large blocks of Government rangelands located far away from habitation should be developed as grass reserves for hay making and this could be entrusted to the Forest Department if necessary. The village panchayats and individual farmers should also be encouraged to conserve grass on a cooperative basis.

25. Government lands, developed as grazing lands, should also serve as demonstration plots to the village panchayats and farmers. All extension media should be used to educate the farmers on the need for proper protection and regulated utilisation of

grasslands.

26. In order that grassland development becomes economical, the programme should be combined with that of improvement of livestock.

27. Existing pastures, grazing lands, village common lands and other waste lands to be brought under social forestry and other grassland development programmes should not be allotted to landless labourers.

28. Planting of fodder trees on farm boundaries, village surroundings, along road sides, railway tracks, canal banks and in grass lands should be encouraged as part of social forestry.

29. The Indian Veterinary Research Institute, National Dairy Research Institute and the agricultural universities should undertake trials to find out the nutritive value of leaves of fodder trees.

30. The Directorate of Extension of the Union Ministry of Agriculture and Irrigation should bring out suitable farm bulletins on growing, proper lopping/pruning etc. of fodder trees.

31. The Indian Council of Agricultural Research should take immediate steps for streamlining the production of breeder seed of the fodder varieties already evolved so that agencies like National Seeds Corporation, Regional Forage Production-cum-Demonstration Stations etc., could start seed multiplication.

32. The State Seed Corporation should take up production of foundation and certified seeds of fodder crops and should develop their own seed certification agency.

33. The services of the various seed corporations, seed cooperatives, seed growers organisations, agro-industries corporations and private agencies should be utilised for the production and distribution of certified seeds. Registered growers should be encouraged by means of incentives to produce seeds of fodder crops.

34. The State Governments should develop a machinery for proper check and quality control of seeds produced by all the agencies engaged in seed production.

35. The existing fodder crop seed production farms should be provided with necessary inputs like machinery, equipment, staff etc. so that maximum production could be achieved.

36. As the requirement of improved fodder seed is very large, additional fodder seed production farms should be established. A regular and constant demand for quality seed should be created among cultivators through extension and holding demonstrations on the farmer's field.

37. Mini kit demonstration programme on fodder crops should be initiated on the lines of 'Rice Mini Kit Programme'.

38. Proper storage arrangements for seeds specially of grasses should be made at each district headquarters since these quickly lose viability unless properly stored, and they should be supplied to farmers well in advance of sowing-time.

39. Agricultural Universities should have separate departments or units devoted to cultivated fodders and pasture grasses.

40. The present official set-up for fodder development is extremely inadequate, considering the magnitude of the task; a much stronger organisation should function preferably under the Agriculture Department.

41. To achieve the targeted production of green fodder, a strong base for undertaking massive extension programme should be created.

42. For grassland development, the Forest Departments should employ adequate number of agrostologists/agronomists and range management specialists. Area once taken up for grassland development, including grass reserves, should not be converted later into forest plantations.

43. In every state, where there are large areas under grasslands and waste lands outside the programme taken by the Forest Department, the Department of Animal Husbandry should be created a separate wing for their development.

44. Since grassland development is a specialised job adequate numbers of specialists should be trained within the country as well as abroad to man the higher supervisory cadres to whom all development work should be entrusted.

45. Every state should constitute standing committees both at state and district levels for coordination in planning and execution of fodder and grasslands development programme.

46. The fodder and grassland development unit in the Union Ministry of Agriculture and Irrigation should be strengthened.

Summary and Recommendations

The main recommendations made in this chapter are summarised below:

1. Agriculture is proposed to be extended to every village. Six million bee colonies are to be developed in modern apiaries at an average rate of 10 colonies per village. Present annual yield of honey of about 5 kg per colony is to be developed by developing and harnessing bee fauna both for honey and crop production. While this will be achieved through research on all species of honeybee, special emphasis

is to be given to the domestication of rockbee, whose yield potential is very high. There should be no haste to introduce exotic breeds unless it has been fully ascertained and ensured that their popularisation would mean no harm to indigenous species through diseases etc.

2. The impact of man-made apiaries on crop production will be by itself very insufficient unless the natural fauna of honeybees is also fully utilised. For this purpose, all possible efforts have to be made to protect and multiply natural bee fauna.

3. The infrastructure and expertise available with the All India Khadi & Village Industries Commission and similar state boards have to be fully utilised for the production, collection and marketing of honey and honey products. However, the Departments of Agriculture at the Centre and States have to participate with or support fully the Khadi Commission in all the developmental and extension activities relating to apiculture. They should introduce this activity in their set up. The Departments of Horticulture (wherever they exist separately from Agriculture) and those of forests will also have to work in collaboration with the Khadi Commission for planning of orchards and forest trees respectively in the interest of bee fauna. Forest departments have a significant role in the protection of honeybees in the forest areas.

4. The Central Bee Research Institute of the Khadi Commission has to be developed both in the fields of research as well as training and given the status of the central institute of the ICAR. How to administer this Institute can be decided by mutual discussion between the ICAR and Khadi Commission.

5. Besides the Central Bee Research Institute, the agricultural universities will have to strengthen research on the subject. Apiculture education and training needs would also increase in future. For research, education and training it will be desirable to develop a section on apiculture under the entomology division of every university. The divisions of plant breeding and agronomy should take due interest in the concerned aspects.

6. One queenbee multiplication station is required to be established for every 5,000 villages. It is also necessary that such stations associate with their multiplication work, the progressive beekeepers and their recognised co-operative societies whereas these stations could conveniently work under the universities concerned, a working relationship should be established between the central institute and the agricultural universities so that the facilities available at the multiplication stations are also available to the Institute and the Institute is also in a position to exercise control on the methods and quality of queenbee production. Participation of Forest Research Institute, Dehradun is also necessary. It could indicate specifically which type of vegetation should be introduced for the bee fauna in different types of forests including the lands which are going to be under social and production forestry and roadside plantations.

7. A committee for policy and coordination should be formed in every state with members representing the Agricultural University, Departments of Agriculture, Horticulture and Forests, the Khadi & Village Industries Board and private beekeepers or their cooperatives. A similar committee should be set up at the centre consisting of representatives of the ICAR, Union Ministry of Agriculture and Irrigation, Forest Research Institute, Dehradun, Khadi & Village Industries Commission, State Committees and All India Beekeepers Association.

CHAPTER 28

Animal Husbandry

Cattle and Buffaloes

(Summary and Recommendations)

The following is a summary of the important recommendations made in the text of this chapter.

1. Massive programmes for improving the reproductive and productive efficiency of cattle and buffaloes should be undertaken. Low producing stock should be progressively eliminated so that the limited feed and fodder resources are available for proper feeding of high producing animals.

2. All the States should carry out simultaneously integrated surveys for estimation of milk and other livestock products.

3. The working of the key village scheme should be quickly reappraised by a team of experts so that the scheme could function on sound lines. The key Village Blocks should be developed into nucleus cattle breeding centres as originally envisaged under the scheme.

4. Early action should be taken to implement the suggestions made by the Indian Institute of Management. Programme Evaluation Organisation of the Planning Commission and at the Symposium on Statistical Assessment of ICDPs for improving the working of the projects. Particular emphasis should be laid on the involvement of State Agriculture Departments in fodder development programmes. Rural Milk Cooperative Societies should be organised and

periodical surveys and reviews for assessment and evaluation work in areas covered by ICDPs should be made.

5. Emphasis on future cattle and buffalo development should be on increasing milk production and improving the working efficiency of bullocks through planned breeding system.

6. Each State Government should set up a team of animal breeding and farm management specialists to study the working of the existing cattle/buffalo breeding farms and to make comprehensive suggestions for their working on scientific and economical basis. Such of the small farms which do not offer scope fcr breeding programmes should either be closed down or utilised for maintaining other livestock.

7. Setting up of new large farms should be avoided unless facilities and finances for their establishment within a reasonable period of time are assured.

8. The Central Government should identify more farms where planned progeny testing programmes can be undertaken and extend financial assistance to them. The State Governments should be discouraged from spending on smaller farms or on establishment of farms with small herds. Farms for draught breeds should be set up in areas where the draught breeds are of excellent quality.

9. For taking up a proper breeding programme there should be at least 150 cows/mature heifers at each of the exotic cattle breeding farms. Wherever possible small herds should be combined to form large herd at the most convenient farm.

10. The Military Farms Directorate should examine their present cross breeding policy in consultation with the leading animal breeding specialists in the country and lay down a definite large range programme.

11. The Military Farms Directorate should group the crossbred stock in the military farms according to their genetic make-up and take up studies on their comparative performance and adaptability in different agro-climatic regions.

12. The Union Ministry of Agriculture and Irrigation and ICAR should actively collaborate with the crossbreeding programmes in the military dairy farms and extend expert advice and financial support for their breeding experiments.

13. The experience gained in the adoption of improved dairy management practices at the military farms should be made use of in the production of purebred exotic bulls. One of the military farms having facilities for housing and fodder production should be earmarked for developing a purebred exotic cattle breeding farm.

14. Superior female calves born in the military dairy farms should be reared at their young stock farms.

15. The State Governments should convert some of their existing farms located in areas of surplus grass production into young stock rearing farms so that growing heifers can be maintained economically on grass and hay.

16. Facilities available with selected gaushalas should be utilised for developing sizable herds of purebred cattle and for undertaking a cross breebing programme for increased milk production. Government of India should provide financial assistance for creating adequate facilities for meeting operational cost on such programmes.

17. Gaushalas maintaining small herds but otherwise having progressive management should be assisted by the State Government to strengthen their herds for production of milk and quality bulls.

18. Non-official institutions maintaining dairy herds and needing technical advice and financial support for increasing their herd size and milk production should be included in the gaushala development programmes.

19. Breeding for milk production should be concentrated in milkshed areas that can be conveniently linked up with the existing and the proposed dairy projects.

20. Milk production should be on commercial and remunerative basis to attract the farmers and should be attempted through planned cross breeding, selective breeding and grading up of indigenous cattle; selective breeding and grading up of buffaloes.

21. In indigenous cattle with high level of milk production, where cross breeding with exotic breeds is not likely to be introduced intensive selective breeding should be undertaken.

22. Bulls used for breeding should be of superior pedigree and preferably progeny tested.

23. Areas which do not offer scope for marketing of milk and where introduction of cross breeding is difficult, farmers should be helped to replace progressively their low producing nondescript cattle by general utility type animals by grading up local stock.

24. Large size artificial insemination centres should be organised on district/regional basis.

25. Each AI centre should have a well equipped laboratory and arrangements for quick and efficient collection, examination and storage of semen samples.

26. New dilutors should not be used on field scale without proper trials under controlled conditions.

27. Until preparation of semen extenders is taken up on commercial basis, the State Departments of Animal Husbandry should arrange for centralised manufacture of approved dilutors.

28. Desirability of designating one of the centralised

semen laboratories in a region for manufacturing and supplying extenders to different AI centres should be explored.

29. Each State Department of Animal Husbandry should advocate the use of only one type of dilutor and continue the same till a better one is recommended after controlled experiments both under laboratory and field conditions.

30. Uniformity in procedures for semen evaluation both for routine and periodical testing should be laid down, so that it may be possible to evaluate and compare the results achieved in different states/centres.

31. In order to maintain a satisfactory level of conception rate, semen from AI centres should be despatched daily or at the most on alternate days. The AI sub-centres in areas, which are not easily accessible and where semen cannot be supplied even on alternate days, should be provided with small refrigerators.

32. Wherever possible transport facilities of dairy schemes should be availed for semen transport.

33. For increased coverage and providing AI service economically, insemination work should be entrusted to properly trained village educated youths.

34. A reasonable fee for insemination services should be levied.

35. Special fee should be charged for providing the AI services at the door of the farmers.

36. The Animal Husbandry Division of the Union Ministry of Agriculture and Irrigation should investigate the causes for poor response to AI and suggest measures for increasing breeding coverage by the AI centres.

37. Adequate number of bulls of superior quality preferably proven sires should be maintained at each AI centre to ensure regular despatch of high quality semen.

38. Insemination services should be ensured from morning till evening on all the days of the week.

39. Areas where AI is to be introduced should be adequately served by dairy extension work.

40. Laying of minimum targets of work would be advantageous in areas where AI is introduced for the first time and in areas where AI work continues to be poor. Incentives should be provided for those who show evidence of special interest.

41. A uniform method of recording inseminations, estimation of results and calculation of conception rate should be evolved by the Animal Husbandry Division of the Union Ministry of Agriculture and Irrigation in consultation with the states of adoption.

42. The officers-in-charge of AI centres should have thorough practical and theoretical training in AI and physiopathology of reproduction. A minimum training course of three months in these subjects is considered essential.

43. For ensuring sufficient practical knowledge for stock assistants and field inseminators, the training course should be at least for three months.

44. Introduction of frozen semen technique in AI should be planned carefully. Each State Government should depute three or four experienced AI officers for practical training in the organisation and management of a frozen semen station and in the field use of this technique. These officers after training should be entrusted with the responsibility of developing frozen semen stations in their respective states as training centres. As far as possible standard procedures and equipment should be practised in freezing and using the frozen semen.

45. The experience of the Indo-Swiss project should be gainfully utilised for planning cross breeding programmes with clearcut objectives.

46. In all the cattle and dairy development projects a clearcut breeding policy should be laid down in advance about the exotic breeds to be used, level of exotic inheritance to be reached, the type of crossbreed bulls to be used for *inter se mating* etc.

47. Bulk of exotic inheritance should be obtained through Jersey breed. When efficient animal health coverage and adequate supply of feeds and fodder can be ensured Holstein-Friesian breed should also be used along with Jersey.

48. In hilly regions of the North-Eastern States where beef consumption is popular, heavier exotic breeds like Brown Swiss and Red Dome should be used for cross breeding, provided grassland development and fodder production could be augmented in those areas.

49. Cross breeding policy should broadly aim at producing cross bred stock with 50 to 75 per cent exotic inheritance.

50. Under the fifth plan there is a proposal to set up 10 to 12 large exotic cattle breeding farms. These should be established in the states where there are no large exotic herds and where progressively more and more areas are to be brought under cross breeding programme.

51. Each cross breeding project should ensure that the exotic inheritance in the cross breds is stabilised and maintained at the desired level.

52. If policy in a State is to use crossbred bulls having exotic interitance from a particular exotic breed and an indigenous breed, the State should have a planned breeding programme implemented in one of their large farms for producing crossbreed foundation

stock with the required level and type of exotic and indigenous inheritance.

53. A panel of Animal Geneticists should define the mechanics of undertaking a systematic progeny testing of bulls used in the cross breeding areas.

54. Incentives should be given to encourage importation of dairy cattle through individuals of Indian origin who have settled abroad. Government of India may provide foreign exchange to meet the cost of transport of animals from abroad which can be recovered in 'rupee payment' basis from the recipients. Coordination of work relating to collection of animals in foreign countries, their transportation and distribution to their respective recipients in India after inspection, quarantine and prophylactic vaccination may also be undertaken by Government.

55. A fresh review and a study in greater depth should be made for a more satisfactory breed classification of the Indian buffalo stock.

56. The baffalo should be developed not only for enhancement of milk production but also for making it a source of production of quality meat.

57. Major emphasis should be laid for improvement of only the Murrah and Surti breed of buffaloes.

58. Under the prevailing conditions attempts need not be made to develop distinctly separate milk and meat breeds or types of buffaloes.

59. Both official and unofficial organisations interested in dairy development should put in all possible efforts to achieve a high national level of buffalo milk production with time bound programmes.

60. Considerably greater attention than what has been given so far should be directed to the buffalo for milk production enhancement without delay.

61. Wherever possible studies on reproduction of the female buffalo should include study on animal behaviour during oestrum. This should be done with the particular objective of developing husbandry for accurate and early detection of oestrum.

62. Agricultural universities should draw up short term and long term research programmes for studying reproduction and production physiology of the buffalo. Coordinated research programmes should be undertaken when such a procedure is expected to yield the best results.

63. The Central and State Governments should critically re-examine the position of progeny testing programmes in buffaloes with a view to identifying the constraints that are impeding early implementation of the programmes and for taking remedial measures.

64. Seed stock buffalo farms should be created in the states with large buffalo population and in the central sector. Military dairy farms with good buffalo stock offer good prospects for establishment of such farms.

65. A number of seed stock farms with at least 150 breeding she-buffaloes should be established.

66. In buffalo farms and research institutes wide scale investigations and studies should be undertaken on early weaning of buffalo calves and their rearing as low cost calf starters.

67. Research studies on the effect of feeding and husbandry on fattening of buffalo calves should be undertaken. Promotional activity for consumption of buffalo meat in the country and consumer educational programme should be undertaken on a countrywide scale.

68. A deliberate and energetic drive should be made to develop trade in buffalo meat.

69. A committee of experts should study the position and suggest measures to improve the milk recording system.

70. For proper coordination and for avoiding duplication of efforts milk recording scheme should be administrated by a single agency.

71. Institutions and individual farmers owning five animals or more should be organised on the lines of dairy herd improvement associations in the west. The animals should be recorded by the project authorities according to the approved system on payment of a nominal fee by the owners.

72. Farmers should be organised into herd improvement associations for implementation of milk recording programmes. Registration of eligible animals in herd books should be progressively introduced.

73. A procedure for registration of all imported pure bred cattle and their progeny should be evolved and their herd books should be maintained by the central herd book organisation (CHBO).

74. Maintenance of herd books for cattle breds like Sahiwal, Sindhi and Tharparkar and Murrah breed of buffaloes which are used in many states should be the responsibility of the central organisation.

75. Registration and maintenance of herd books in respect of breeds whose breeding tracts are confined to a single state should be the responsibility of the concerned state.

76. To ensure adoption of uniform procedures of inspection, recording and registration, the CHBO may act as the coordinating agency.

77. The CHBO should lay down procedures for milk recording and registration of cross bred cattle.

78. The CHBO in the Animal Husbandry Division of the Union Ministry of Agriculture and Irrigation should be suitably strengthened and headed by a whole time Registrar. Herd book and milk recording cells should be organised under the State Animal

Husbandry Departments.

79. The Indian Dairy Corporation (IDC) in consultation with the Maharashtra and West Bengal Governments should carry out an intensive survey of the present position regarding disposal of cattle and buffaloes, when they go dry in cities of Bombay and Calcutta. Suitable programmes for timely artificial breeding of she-buffaloes and their purchase, when they go dry should be drawn up. As an interim measure, a network of AI centres should be set up within the cities and funds for establishment of centres and financing extension surveys should be provided by the IDC.

80. The insurance agencies and the project authorities should jointly pilot projects on cattle insurance in collaboration with the credit giving institutions on areawise basis.

81. In areas where the General Insurance Corporation would take time in initiating cattle insurance, the Cooperatives handling milk production and, or marketing or the project agencies should take up this activity.

82. Areas covered by projects such as SFDA/MFAL, OFP, where regular cattle insurance has not been undertaken, an alternate system of creating a Cattle Mortality Risk Fund should be adopted. Similar efforts should also be made in districts covered by other cattle development and milk production projects.

83. The insurance scheme should also cover working bullocks in the areas where cattle insurance for milch cattle is taken up.

84. There is an urgent need for taking up promotional measures to build up export trade in cattle and buffaloes.

85. Possibility of exporting frozen semen from superior buffalo bulls should be explored.

86. A separate agency under the Union Ministry of Agriculture and Irrigation should be created for promoting export trade in cattle, buffaloes and other livestock. Alternatively, the Government of India may consider entrusting this function to an organisation like the IOC.

87. Milk production enhancement programmes as recommended for SFDA/MFAL projects should also be started in districts to be covered by the Integrated Cattle Development-cum-Milk Marketing Projects and Special Area Programmes. The proposed cattle and buffalo development programmes should be taken up in about 150 selected districts by 1985 and in 200 selected districts by 2000 AD.

88. The Animal Husbandry Division of the Union Ministry of Agriculture and Irrigation should assess annual requirements of exotic bulls and arrange for foreign exchange for their importation. Possibilities of importing large quantities of frozen semen from bulls of above average quality through foreign assistance and bilateral collaboration programmes should be explored.

89. The task of cattle development, milk collection, processing and marketing in the shape of an integrated project should be entrusted to a single agency, preferably a co-operative of the producers.

CHAPTER 29

Dairy Development

The main recommendations made in this chapter are given below :

1. Cooperative measures should be taken to ensure adequate production of milk to meet the market demand and development of efficient systems of movement of milk from production to demand centres. Adequate facilities should be created for conservation of milk during the flush season for utilisation during the lean season. A rational milk pricing policy should be adopted to encourage milk production.

2. Techno-economic feasibility studies should be made to explore the possibilities of large scale production of traditional milk food delicacies in manufacturing plants. Similar studies should be undertaken to determine the optimal balance that a dairy organisation has to maintain between processing of fluid milk and manufacture of milk products to make it a profitable commercial enterprise.

3. Processes for utilisation of milk by-products should be developed for commercial exploitation. Dairy and Food Research and other Institutes should standardise methods of manufacture of milk food delicacies and undertake research studies for improving the storage life, flavour and taste of various traditional milk food delicacies and their packaging.

4. Energetic steps should be taken in milk producing regions to establish strong cooperative organisations of milk producers.

5. Chilling centres should be installed by the dairy organisation only when unavoidable.

6. A clearcut policy should be laid down by the Government of India for purchase of marketable surplus skim milk powder for creating an adequate buffer stock of this product.

7. Delivery systems with different kinds of milk cans and more particularly with temper proof sanitary cans should be given trials on a wider scale to determine the convenience and economy of

operation of the system and its acceptability to the consumers.

8. Detailed techno-economic feasibility studies should be undertaken by large city milk plants for processing, packaging and delivery of milk. This should be done by the plants in collaboration with the National Dairy Development Board, National Dairy Research Institute and other Institutions with good dairy engineering workshops.

9. While planning is done for a city milk supply project, steps should simultaneously be taken to ensure sale of milk in the connected milkshed areas through cooperative organisations.

10. Dairy development programmes should keep in view the prospective growth centres is non-milkshed areas for organising milk supply to these regions as necessity arises.

11. Consistent with demand-supply situation a dairy organisation should adopt a pricing policy for milk procurement that would ensure an even supply of milk throughout the year.

12. Dairy industry should accept the two-axis pricing policy for milk procurement as this is rationally based on evaluation of both the fat and solids-not-fat content of milk.

13. The sale price of milk and its products should be fixed in a manner that would enable the organised dairy industry to pay remunerative price to the milk producers and meet the cost of collection, processing and distribution of milk and milk products. The sale prices should also cover the cost of services rendered in connection with channelising the inputs for milk production, keep a fair margin of profit and yet make the price of the commodities competitive.

14. The dairy industry should achieve efficiency in organising service to the milk producers for marketing inputs for milk production enhancement.

15. An efficient milk pricing organisation should be set up in each dairy plant and in each state to fix the producer and consumer prices of milk from time to time. An inter-state authority should be established for the same purpose to coordinate the activities of the dairy plants that collect milk from more than one state. These and other recommendations contained in the report of the Milk Pricing Committee 1972 appointed by the Government of India should soon be implemented.

16. So long as the private industries do not come in the way of development of cooperative organisation of milk producers they should be allowed to function subject to their providing inputs for enhancement of milk production in their respective milkshed areas.

17. To encourage the milk producers to become share holders of joint stock companies working in the field of dairying, the companies should keep a stipulated minimum percentage of shares reserved for the milk producers. The companies should also have an effective representation of the milk producers on the board of management so that the interests of the producers are fully safeguarded.

18. As dairy development programmes can best be organised by the co-operatives of the milk producers, the producers should first be organised into primary/village level co-operative societies. Persons not involved in milk production or those associated with private milk business should not be allowed membership of these societies.

19. The primay milk producers' societies should be federated into a district level milk producers union.

20. The responsibility of forming the primary societies and the district unions should be entrusted to a team of specially trained persons with experience in the field of cooperative organisation.

21. In the states where complete cooperative structure of milk producers' unions does not exist but State Dairy Corporations have been formed, the corporations should take up the functions of the unions that have not yet come into existence strictly as an interim measure. State Dairy Corporations should promote the formation of the complete structure of cooperative unions as early as possible and hand over the operations and facilities of the organisation to the unions as soon as those are established.

22. The problems now being encountered by the dairy equipment manufacturing firms should be examined by the Government in collaboration with the concerned interested parties to find out satisfactory solutions.

23. The possibility of indigenous manufacture of the dairy equipment now being imported should be explored.

24. The Government of India should negotiate with the Governments of foriegn countries to explore the possibilities for the supply and installation of complete dairy plants on turn-key basis which should include advisory service and training of personnel.

25. The Indian Dairy Corporation should be encouraged to enter the field of manufacture of dairy and allied equipment.

26. The dairy development wing of the Union Ministry of Agriculture and Irrigation should be adequately strengthened to equip itself properly to meet the needs of increasing dairy development in the country. The Ministry should not undertake commercial operation and should absolve itself of the responsibility for the operation of the Delhi Milk Scheme.

27. The State Governments should set up a unified

department to deal with production, processing and marketing of milk. Operation of dairy plants should not be undertaken by government departments.

28. The State Diary Development Corporations should build up the capacity for project designing and development and for coordinating the functioning of the respective state milk grids.

29. The Indian Diary Corporation should be strengthened so that it can function as a finance house and a promotional institution for speeding up modernisation of the organised dairy sector.

30. The National Dairy Development Board should be merged with the Indian Dairy Corporation to form its research and development wing. This wing should continue to enjoy the operational flexibilities and facilities which are being enjoyed by the Board at present.

31. The reorganised Indian Dairy Corporation should continue to have technically qualified Chairman and Managing Director. The Board of Directors should also be constituted with persons professionally qualified in dairying, animal husbandry, management and finance.

32. Enforcement of Prevention of Food Adulteration Act should be intensified to ensure that consumer confidence in milk and milk products obtained from organised dairy plants is not eroded by adulterated/imitation products.

33. A draft of Milk and Milk Products Control Order is under consideration of the Union Ministry of Agriculture and Irrigation. The draft should be scrutinised expeditiously by the Ministry for early enactment of necessary measures.

SHEEP AND GOATS

Sheep

Summary of Recommendations

The following is a summary of the important recommendations made in the text of this chapter.

1. The State Animal Husbandry/Sheep Husbandry Department should set up service centres on the sheep migration routes.

2. Cheap houses with thatched roofs made of locally available material and thorny fences should be provided to give shelter to sheep flocks, particularly to young lambs, pregnant ewes and breeding rams. In areas normally experiencing extreme cold or hot winds, some protection against the winds should also be provided.

3. The ICAR and agricultural universities should initiate studies on the economics of supplement feeding of sheep during growing stages, breeding seasons, later part of gestation, lactation etc.

4. From the next census onwards break up figures in respect of different categories like ewes, rams and young of the exotic, cross bred and indigenous stock should be collected on a sample basis.

5. The sampling design formulated by the Institute of Agricultural Research Statistics should be used by the States for estimation of wool production.

6. Every effort should be made to fully develop within the shortest possible time the State Sheep Breeding Farms started during the Fourth Plan, as these Farms are to play a very important role in sheep development programmes through the supply of superior germ plasm.

7. Sheep to be imported should come from the regions having more or less the same type of climate that prevail in the areas where they are to be stationed in the country.

8. Sheep for import should be selected from as large a number of flocks as possible to ensure greater genetic variability.

9. The level of exotic fine wool inheritance should be stabilised around 50 per cent in arid and semi-arid areas and the crossing of exotic fine wool breeds with black faced indigenous breeds should be avoided.

10. Since the All-India Coordinated Research Project on sheep breeding is of great importance, necessary steps to remove bottlenecks for its expeditious execution should be taken.

11. The total sheep population in Jammu & Kashmir, Himachal Pradesh, hilly regions of Uttar Pradesh, sheep of Chokla and Nali breeds in Rajasthan, Nali sheep in Haryana, Pattanwadi sheep in Gujarat, Nilgiri sheep of Nilgiri hills in Tamil Nadu and better type of wool sheep in Arunachal Pradesh may be brought under cross breeding for fine wool production using Rambouillet and/or Merinos.

12. Selective breeding among sheep of important carpet wool breeds in Rajasthan such as Marwari, Jaisalmeri, Pugal and Marga and among Marwari and other woolly sheep except Pattanwadi in Gujarat should be undertaken.

13. A few large sheep breeding farms of Marwari, Jaisalmeri, Pugal and Marga breeds should be established in their respective home tracts.

14. Since Indian carpet wool lack lustre, improvement through selection or through crossing with carpet wool breeds from some middle eastern countries which produce lustrous wool may be undertaken by the ICAR on experimental basis.

15. In view of great potentiality for export of mutton, work on evaluation of carcass quality,

laboratory evaluation of meat quality and meat processing should be initiated on priority basis at the CSWRI, IVRI and in agricultural universities.

16. The population of woolly type sheep in Haryana, Punjab, Western Uttar Pradesh, Rajasthan, Maharashra, Andhra Pradesh, Karnataka, Tamil Nadu, and Bihar should be crossed with exotic dual purpose breed like Corriedale to evolve a dual purpose breed for producing better carpet quality wool, better liveweight and higher dressing percentage.

17. The hairy breeds other than Mandya and Nellore should be graded up with Nellore and Mandya. In Mandya and Nellore selective breeding based on six monthly body weight should be practised.

18. It would be advisable to establish four large exotic sheep breeding farms in different regions of the country for undertaking cross breeding with Corriedale.

19. In view of the large scale crossbreeding programmes that are to be undertaken for rapid increase in wool and mutton production, serious attempts should be made to try out the techniques of artificial insemination (AI) in the breeding of sheep.

20. In Rajasthan some flock-owners have been trained in detection of oestrus in ewes and for practising AI in sheep flocks. This practice should be tried on an experimental basis in other important sheep rearing states.

21. For meeting the nutritional requirements of sheep to express their genetic potential for wool/meat production, the greater part of arid region which is suitable only for livestock farming should be utilised more profitably for range land and pasture development.

22. The development of village grazing lands should be entrusted to the village panchayats or Sheep Breeders' Cooperatives.

23. Improvement of natural pastures in States like Himachal Pradesh, Jammu and Kashmir and hilly areas/regions of Uttar Pradesh and southern States should be undertaken. Large blocks of government range lands located far away from villages should be developed mainly as grass reserves for hay making.

24. Fodder crops, especially leguminous fodders, should be included in the cropping pattern in irrigated areas.

25. There is an urgent need to carry out survey on the micro-nutrient (sulphur, cobalt, copper and zinc) status of soils and plants including fodder and their availability to sheep in areas of intensive sheep rearing and investigate the effects of their absence.

26. The feed compounding industry should manufacture cheap supplementary rations for sheep, utilising agricultural and industrial wasters and nonprotein nitrogenous substance.

27. The extension veterinarians should visit the sheep flocks frequenty for undertaking vaccination against the sheep pox, enteroloxaemea etc. and for periodic drenching of sheep with anthelmintics and for arranging sheep dips.

28. The IVRI should undertake large scale manufacture of the irridiated against lung worm infestation for field use.

29. The Animal Husbandry Division of the Union Ministry of Agriculture and Irrigation should lay down a policy for eradication of blue tongue which at present is confined to a small area.

30. The IVRI should initiate research work on blue tongue and should keep itself in readiness to start the manufacture of blue tongue virus vaccine.

31. A systematic survey to determine the incidence of infectious epedidymitis/orchitis at the different sheep farms in the country should be undertaken. The epizootiology, pathology and pathogenesis of the disease should be studied and suitable preventive measures against the disease should be devised for the guidance of breeding farms.

32. The IVRI and agricultural universities should carry out detailed studies on the pathology and pathogenesis of pneumonis in sheep with a view to devising suitable preventive measures.

33. Shearing should be done twice a year, as once a year shearing causes problems of wool shedding and skin disease while thrice a year shearing reduces stable length.

34. The sheep and wool extension agencies of the State Animal Husbandry/Sheep Husbandry Department should educate the sheep farmers regarding improved shearing practices.

35. The present wool grading system is very cumbersome and should be revised to have lesser number of grades.

36. A central wool testing laboratory should be set up in all the important wool producing states to provide wool testing service.

37. The State Governments should enact legislation to ensure that all the wool produced in the state is passed through the grading centres.

38. The grading and marketing of wool should not be the responsibility of the State Animal Husbandry or Sheep Husbandry Department. These departments should primarily concentrate on sheep development activities.

39. It is necessary to have organised wool markets by making provision of Agricultural Produce (Grading and Marking) Act applicable to wool in the

important wool producing states.

40. Wool marketing in important wool producing states should be properly organised either through Sheep Farmers' Cooperatives or through statutory Wool Boards which should take up the responsibility of sheep shearing, wool grading, warehousing and marketing wool.

41. Marketing yards for the sale of live animals preferably with facilities for slaughter, meat packaging and utilisation of slaughter house byproducts should be set up in the major sheep rearing tracts.

42. Progressive restrictions on export of raw wool should be placed and export of manufactured woollen goods should be encouraged.

43. Wool production and manufacture of woollen goods and hand woven carpets should be tied up with the schemes of Handicrafts Boards/Khadi Boards functioning in the area.

44. The procedure of payments of drawback claims of duty on woollen goods for export should be simplified.

45. Shearing, flaying and curing of hides should be undertaken only by trained persons.

46. The sheep population should be raised to about 45 million by 1985 and to about 60 million by 2000 AD.

Goats

47. Approach for raising meat production from goats should be selective breeding among taller and medium sized breeds and outcrossing the non-descript type with selected meat type bucks.

48. Cross breeding with exotic dairy breeds of goats may be undertaken for increasing milk production.

49. Milk capabilities of better indigenous dairy breeds like Jamnapari, Barbari and Beetal should be improved through selective breeding. For production of stud bucks some goat breeding farms should be set up and progeny testing work undertaken.

50. Bucks from high producing dams in flows of progressive goat breeders may be selected and distributed among goat farmers.

51. Progressive goat breeders may be advised to maintain milk records and other relevant information that may be helpful in selecting prospective stud bucks.

52. Work on All-India Coordinated Project for developing a strain of high pashmina producing goats should be pursued vigorously.

53. Field programme to take up production of mohair by crossing hairy breeds of goats with Angora in cold arid areas should be initiated.

54. Slaughter of goats for meat purposes should be increased so that the rate of growth population may come down to a level of 67 million by 1985 and go down to about 40 million by 2000 AD.

Polutry

Summary and Recommendations

The main recommendations made in this chapter are given below :

1. Steps should be taken for obtaining sexwise classification of poultry population and breedwise break down of imported fowls during livestock censuses so that more effective poultry development plans may be drawn up.

2. Research should be continued and expanded for development of methodology to obtain reliable information on all aspects of poultry farm economics.

3. The existing organisations for livestock statistics in the states should be strengthened for conducting regular, periodic intercensus sample surverys. The statistical cell in the Union Ministry of Agriculture and Irrigation needs strengthening to effect necessary coordination and provide guidance to the state organisations.

4. Hybrid chicks should be produced locally in adequate numbers out of breeding stock developed indigenously. The quality of hybrid chicks produced should be of a standard equal to or better than that achieved by the franchise hatcheries.

5. Remedial measures are necessary to remove the constraints standing in the way of proper execution of the Co-ordinated Poultry Breeding Project of the Government of India. The project should be remodelled as a National Coordinated Poultry Breeding Project. Persons in charge of important breeding projects should not be transferred during the tenure of the project. If necessary such persons should be retained in position with proforma promotion.

6. The Central Poultry Breeding Farm at Hessarghatta should serve as the Central Unit of the proposed National Coordinated Poultry Breeding Project and the officer-in-charge of the farm at Hessarghatta should function as the Project Coordinator.

7. The stock developed under the All India Coordinated Research Project (Poultry) of the Indian Council of Agricultural Research should be regularly subjected to the random sample tests conducted at Hessarghatta.

8. The ICAR should initiate a programme to collect and preserve native fowl germ plasm resources.

9. Central Germ Plasm Banks should be created in different agroclimatic regions for maintaining

large populations of distinctly identified strains/lines of poultry as also indigenous fowls under the control of a Standing Committee on Poultry Development (SCPD).

10. Test sample size should be increased to at least 60 Pullets per entry per test centre to attain greater accuracy in Random Sample Tests (RSTs) for egg-laying. RSTs should be conducted under the control of the SCPD to generate confidence among the participants.

11. Work on RSTs in broilers should be extended at Hessarghatta and this facility should de developed at the other regional RSI units when established. Besides testing the commercial broiler chicks the breeder flocks should also be subjected to test.

12. All commercial hatcheries should be licensed to ensure maintenance of high quality of the stock. Extensive field trials should be required to be given to a commercial strain before it is released for general sale by a hatchery. The reliability of the claim of performance of a stock and its suitability for release for sale should be decided by the SCPD.

13. Chick-sexing training courses should be organised on a regular basis. To ensure high quality of training it may be desirable to send a few suitably qualified persons abroad for advanced training. Persons trained in chick-sexing should appear in an examination every three years for recertification of their competence.

14. Steps should be taken to incorporate auto-sexing genes in the stocks being developed under the Central Government and ICAR Poultry Breeding Projects.

15. Broiler Production Programmes should be taken up around all the seventeen poultry dressing plants on a priority basis. Around each of the fifteen 1,000 bird dressing plants located in or near the IPDP centres, a poultry farmers' cooperative with hundred numbers should be formed. The broiler production programme should be so arranged as to enable two members to supply one day's full requirement for the plant. The broiler dressing should be undertaken for 200 days of a year whereas for 100 days, dressing and processing of culled hens from egg producers should be undertaken in these plants.

16. The IVRI and the Central Food Technological Research Institute should attempt at evolving a cheap process of cooking and packing of meat from hens that are sold as table birds after the laying period. The process evolved should be easily operable even under rural conditions.

17. High producing straincross or incross hybrid chicks should be reared in places where high standard of poultry husbandry exists.

18. Where poultry husbandry has not attained a high standard, but is at the intermediate level, exotic crossbred chicks should be raised.

19. Poor backyard poultry keeping in rural areas, cross bred cocks obtained either by crossing White Leghorn males and Rhode Island Red females or White Leghorn males and Australorp females, should be used for grading up the indigenous stock.

20. Poultry estates should be established in selected localities in different States and Union Territories for providing employment to the educated unemployed and for rehabilitation of the physically handicapped.

21. Agricultural Universities in orchard growing states should undertake studies on the economics of poultry keeping in orchards and determine the optimal conditions of poultry raising under this system.

22. Poultry production through SFDA/MFAL projects should be organised following the recommendations made in the Interim Report of the National Commission on Agriculture on Poultry, Sheep and Pig Production through Small and Marginal Farmers and Agricultural Labourers for supplementing their income. Every effort should be made to implement the programme in all the 167 districts identified for this purpose at least by 1985, if not earlier.

23. Till the stage is reached by 2000 AD when there should not be any shortage of grains for poultry feeding, attempts should be made to procure ingredients of poultry feeds at reasonable cost and to use industrial byproducts in greater measure. Extensive studies should be undertaken for greater use of agroindustrial byproducts in poultry feeds.

24. Inedible marine animals or marine animals like mussel, for which there is no local market, should be explored as an alternative source to meet the shortage of supply to the fish meal plants.

25. Sterilised meat and blood meal and silk worm pupae meal can replace fish meal to a considerable extent in compounding poultry feeds and steps should be taken for increased production and use of these materials.

26. A few dehydration plants should be set up in selected places to make pilot studies on the manufacture of lucerne and barseem meals for inclusion in poultry feeds as well as on their economics.

27. Investigations on least cost formulation of balanced poultry feeds should be undertaken on an extensive scale.

28. Raw materials of standard quality should be made available at controlled rates to the poultry equipment manufacturers on recommendations of the Central/State Animal Husbandry Departments.

29. Veterinary Departments should create a cadre of veterinarians specially trained in poultry diseases to

provide effective health cover to the poultry farms.

30. Early action should be taken to introduce licensing of commercial hatcheries under suitable legislation in consideration of disease hazards. The licences should be granted only by the Central Government on recommendation of the SCPD.

31. For imparting special training in poultry diseases to the veterinarians, agricultural universities should introduce special in-service training courses during the summer vacation.

32. Action should be taken to enable landless labourers and small and marginal farmers to obtain loans on personal surety expeditiously, but it should be ensured that the loans are given only to bonafide farmers and landless labourers.

33. Multitiered structure of poultry farmers, cooperatives should be organised on the lines recommended in our Interim Report on Poultry, Sheep and Pig Production through Small and Marginal Farmers and Agricultural Labourers for supplementing their income.

34. Market survey studies should be taken up at regular intervals to collect information on the factors influencing the pricing of eggs and other poultry products. Extensive research on processing and packaging of poultry products should also be taken up early for promotion of poultry industry.

35. All the four proposed Regional Cooperatives Marketing Federations of the National Egg and Poultry Products Marketing Federation should be fully equipped for quick disposal of eggs. This organisation may enter into agreements with milk drying plants to manufacture egg powder.

36. The State Animal Husbandry Department should launch a massive drive to educate poultry farmers in producing clean and infertile eggs.

37. Preliminary work relating to the establishment of the National Egg and Poultry Products Marketing Federation should be completed expeditiously. State Marketing Federations should be set up quickly where these do not exist.

38. As a practical solution to the prevailing problem of marketing of eggs during summer, the egg production programme may be modified both in the rural and urban areas.

39. Research studies should be undertaken to find out if the peculiar odour problem of duck eggs could be eliminated through alterations in the management and dietary of the birds or by chemical treatment of eggs.

40. Systematic research investigations should soon be initiated on various aspects of duck husbandry in the states where ducks constitute an important species of poultry. Initially the ICAR should sponsor such research projects. Subsequently the agricultural universities of concerned states may pursue studies on different problems of duck husbandry.

41. To develop the expertise required for operation of large size duck farms with superior quality exotic ducks, systematic studies should be undertaken on different aspects of duck husbandry in the proposed Central Duck Breeding Farm.

42. Some international agencies should be approached for making expertise available for building up duck farming in the country on modern scientific lines.

43. A National Avian Research Institute dealing will all species of poultry and allied subjects should be established to give research support to the poultry industry.

44. Some of the pre-university level training courses in poultry science now being offered are so poor in standard and quality that they should better be discontinued. Poultry science education should be reorganised as recommended in Section 7 on Education and Training in Animal Science of Chapter 53 on Education.

OTHER LIVESTOCK

Pig, Equines, Camel and Yak

The following is a summary of the important recommendations made in the text of this Chapter :

Pig

1. The Institute of Agricultural Research Statistics (IARS) should develop proper methodology for obtaining dependable population estimate of Pigs through sample surveys during intercensus periods.

2. The IARS should undertake research investigation on economics of pig production on a priority basis.

3. Surveys should be conducted at regular intervals for determining the demand, consumption and supply of pork and pork products.

4. In all cities and big towns where pigs are slaughtered regularly arrangements should be made for licensing of pig slaughtering.

5. The IARS should evolve sampling technique for estimation of the number of pigs slaughtered in rural areas.

6. A cell should be created in the Directorate of Marketing and Inspection of the Central Government for regular periodic surveys on livestock and livestock products.

7. Immediate steps should be taken to remove the

constraints standing in the way of undertaking suitable pig breeding programmes in the Regional Pig Breeding Stations and the Pig Breeding Farms/Units near the bacon factories.

8. Bacon factories should adopt a pricing policy for pork and pork products that would encourage the farmer to take to pig rearing.

9. Producers of pork and pork products in the private sector should be induced to obtain carcasses through licensed pig slaughter houses and a system should be evolved for strict quality control.

10. The bacon factories should take steps to popularise their products. This should include consumer education programmes.

11. The nucleus breeding herd in the Regional Pig Breeding Stations should be strengthened.

12. Considerably more exotic pigs are required to be imported for undertaking selective breeding programme on scientific lines in the Regional Stations.

13. A comprehensive coordinated breeding programme should be drawn up for all the seven regional stations. Simultaneously, a well planned programme of commercial pig production should be undertaken so that genetic improvement of the stock and adequate supply of the bacon factories can be achieved.

14. For some of the orth-eastern States breeds like Berkshire, Hamphire, Saddle back or Poland China should be selected for breeding as the people in those areas prefer black coloured pigs.

15. Artificial insemination (AI) should be tried in the pig to find out how this method of breeding will pan out under Indian conditions. If found satisfactory, it should be adopted in the important pig breeding stations.

16. Attempts should be made to get Indian manufacturers of AI kits interested in fabrication of AI kits for swine.

17. A coordinating cell should be created for proper execution of the coordinated pig breeding programme.

18. The working programme of the All-India Coordinated Research Project of the Indian Council of Agricultural Research (ICAR) on pig breeding should be suitably modified and the herd strength enlarged to obtain useful results.

19. Agricultural universities should undertake studies on pig breeding with indigenous and exotic breeds of pigs.

20. The programme for pig development in the north-eastern states should be implemented soon.

21. So long grain position remains difficult, greater use of agro-industrial by-products should be made in the formulation of pig ration, ensuring satisfactory production performance.

22. Research studies on the nutritional requirements of various classes of pigs should be undertaken without delay.

23. For evolving pigs with better feed conversion efficiency, suitable breeding programmes should be initiated as soon as possible.

24. The Indian Veterinary Research Institute should intensify research to develop an efficacious and inexpensive vaccine for protection of pig from foot and mouth disease.

25. Studies should be undertaken on designing and construction of suitable cheap houses for pigs using locally available material.

26. The Government should permit importation of a few sonoscopes to serve as a model for fabricating the equipment in the country.

27. Necessary steps should be taken to make institutional credit facilities available to pig farmers.

28. Till such time chilled pork products can be supplied at reasonable prices consumption of fresh pork should be encouraged.

29. Meat Food Products Order, 1973 should be implemented and rigidly enforced to prevent the private bacon factories from procuring carcasses through unauthorised sources.

30. The Central Food Technology Research Institute should extend research studies on processing and packaging of pork and pork products so that these products can be manufactured in India matching the standards attained by countries with international reputation for high quality pork and pork products.

31. For imparting scientific knowledge on different aspects of pig production and processing of pork, a three tier training programme should be organised.

Equines

32. The Union Ministry of Agriculture and Irrigation should constitute a committee to advise how and on what points information should be collected and enumeration done during the livestock census.

33. Detailed critical study should be made about the needs and requirements of people engaged in equine based trade for planning equine development. Separate studies are required for trades based on horses, mules and donkeys.

34. Equine development programmes aimed at providing assistance to the weaker section of people should be fully or largely supported by the Central Government as its contribution towards social justice and for removal of regional imbalances.

35. There should be collaborate work between the

civil and military establishment for development of national equine wealth.

36. The Government should take full control of horse racing in the country.

37. A fresh review of the entire field of horse racing and race horse breeding industry is necessary. The Union Ministry of Agriculture and Irrigation should soon convene a meeting of all interests and specialists concerned with import breeding, racing and training of horses for this purpose.

38. Breeding of race horses may for the present be left in private hands but immediate steps should be taken for more effective control as various malpractices alleged to be now prevalent.

39. An Equine Development Bcard (EDB) should be established to exercise control on racing and all organised equine breeding activities.

40. To control race horse breeding steps should be taken to register all private studs with the EDB.

41. The EDB should be responsible for making assessment of fresh blood requirement of exotic stock. The Union Ministry of Agriculture and Irrigation should constitute a purchasing mission from time to time on advice from the EDB for procuring superior quality horses from abroad.

42. Steps should be taken to maximise the utilisation of imported and other high quality horses.

43. As equestrain sports are excellent activities for body building, development of courage and daring, cultivation of sense of discipline, team spirit and love of animals, promotional activities for such games should be undertaken by both government and private organisations.

44. Preservation and development of indigenous breeds of horses is justified on utilitarian considerations and should be undertaken as centrally sponsored programmes.

45. A national equine breeding farm should be established under the direct control and management of the central government.

46. The ICAR should undertake the task of defining the Indian breeds of horses.

47. For proper maintenance of records, the State Departments should open equine stud registers and the Union Ministry of Agriculture and Irrigation should open a National Stud Register.

48. In those states where equines are important animals, the Government should take steps for reopening and increasing the number of horse and jack stallion studs.

49. Only horse/donkey stallions of superior quality should be selected for stud purposes and maintained properly at the stud centres. All stud centres must maintain proper records.

Camel

50. Studies should be undertaken to ascertain if under the changed circumstances there is a necessity of making a special endeavour to retain the distinct types of camels that have been evolved.

51. Animal Husbandry Departments of Rajasthan and Gujarat should take the initiative in organising the camel breeders to create cooperative societies. Financial assistance and technical guidance required for this purpose should be provided by the State Governments.

52. Possibilities of training one or two persons in the USSR in artificial insemination of camels should be explored.

53. For handmating of camels in Rajasthan, Haryana, Gujarat and Punjab stud camels should be stationed in suitable locations.

54. Research studies on nutrition of camels and on formulation of least cost balanced ration should be undertaken without delay.

55. Arrangement should be made for manufacture in the country of drugs specified for treatment of "surrah" in camels.

56. Till such time the drugs become available indigenously, the Union Ministry of Agriculture and Irrigation should arrange for their import after making an assessment of the requirement of the whole country.

57. The Indian Council of Agricultural Research should initiate research studies on camels in the agricultural universities located in the states where the camel is an important livestock.

58. The camel farm at Bikaner should be expanded for research studies and developmental work.

Yak

59. Research studies on yaks should be undertaken at the Agricultural University, Himachal Pradesh as very little is known about the animal.

60. Because of the small size of the herd at the yak farm of the agricultural university, field studies on yaks should also be undertaken in selected locations.

61. Along with research studies on the animal, socio-economic studies should be undertaken to ascertain the economics of utilisation of yaks for different purposes and the social implication of yak rearing.

62. The ICAR should initiate a coordinated research programme for yak development in Jammu & Kashmir and Himachal Pradesh.

Livestock Feeding

Summary of Recommendations

The following is a summary of the important recommendations made in the text of this chapter :

1. Regions having soil conditions leading to deficiency of essential feed nutrients in feeds and fodders and regions having large quantities of toxic minerals should be identified and deficiencies or toxicities should be rectified.

2. Livestock feed resources must be greatly enhanced for increasing production of animal products like milk, meat, eggs, wool etc. and for properly maintaining the animal for efficient draught purposes.

3. The young ones of improved animals and cross breds have higher food requirements. They should be provided with extra feed like creep feed and milk substitutes.

4. Studies should be carried out to determine the optimum nutrient requirements and feeding level under different physiological conditions for production of work meat, milk, eggs and wool. These studies should be up-dated every five years, compiled and published as a guide for scientific and economic feeding of livestock.

5. Area and yield data in respect of different fodder, cereal and cash crop should be collected.

6. Studies should be undertaken by the Institute of Agricultural Research Statistics to develop standard methods of estimation to evaluate total feed availability and requirements of feeds.

7. Efforts should be made to decrease livestock numbers and feeds required by using available stock more efficiently—sharing bullocks, reducing unproductive periods and increasing breeding and productive efficiency. Efficiency of feed utilisation can also be increased by improvement in feed handling and feeding practices particularly by feeding balanced rations.

8. Available feeds should be used for feeding of productive animals and their followers. All the unproductive animals should be progressively eliminated.

9. Restrictions on grazing and/or levying of progressively heavier charges on free grazing should be introduced as a means for the elimination of uneconomic cattle and other livestock and for improvement of pasture yields through systematic grazing and scientific management of grazing lands.

10. In the selection of grasses, trees and bushes for control of soil erosion, their possible feed value should be given due consideration.

11. Pastures and grazing areas owned by individuals or jointly by the community should be improved through controlled grazing and introduction of nutritious grasses and legumes and application of fertilizers.

12. In areas where intensive livestock production programmes are taken up, a study should be made of the cyle of growth, productivity and nutrient yield of the locally available natural grasses. The potential for improvement should be evaluated and action programme drawn up by teams including experts in grassland management, livestock development and agricultural economics.

13. Efforts should be made to rejuvenate and maintain productivity of over grazed pastures and to increase utilization of presently underutilized pastures and grazing areas due to inaccessibility.

14. There should be coordinating bodies in the state headquarters consisting of heads of Departments of Forest, Sheep Development, Animal Husbandry, Dairy Development and Agriculture for planning conservation and utilization of grasslands and hay and for reviewing the progress of plans. Similar committees will be necessary at district level.

15. Cutting of grasses from inaccessible areas (as opposed to grazing by animals) and its storage in fodder banks should be encouraged. Concessions should be given for the transport of baled hay from railheads to rural areas of intensive livestock production. These concessions should not be available for urban areas.

16. Research for evolving high yielding varieties of fodder grasses and legumes and for development of cultivation practices so that higher economic returns can be obtained for land, capital and labour used for fodder in comparison with other uses of land should be intensified.

17. In areas where intensive livestock production is taken up, cultivation of fodder should be encouraged by educative propaganda, advice, supply of seed materials and fertilizers.

18. Silage making from seasonal surplus of fodders, grasses and other plant material may be adopted by large cooperatives of milk producers or producers of other livestock products on a cooperative basis.

19. In hilly areas where surplus grass is available and conditions for hay and silage making are not favourable, artificial drying of forages may be practised. Feasibility studies regarding the economics of such enterprise may be conducted by the IGFRI, and agricultural universities.

20. In each intensive livestock production project a survey of feeding practices should be conducted to

minimize waste and to utilize nutritive fodders more efficiently. An animal nutrition officer should be employed for each major intensive livestock project.

21. While selecting varieties of food grains for extensive cultivation, special varieties with high yield of total nutrients for livestock feeding should be given due importance.

22. Research and extension on high yielding course foodgrains should be intensified.

23. Improved milling of rice should be popularised to make rice barn of suitable quality available for feeding animals.

24. As solvent extracted rice polishings have better keeping quality and can be used for livestock feeding, the extraction of rice polishing for recovery of oil should be encouraged.

25. Proper processing of by-products for feeds should be made a condition for licensing of food industries so that suitable by-products in larger quantities are made available for feeding of livestock. Feasibility studies should be carried out to determine the economics of taking over the raw by-product by the compounded feed industry for further processing and use.

26. Feeding of cotton seed should be discouraged through educative propaganda. It should be replaced with cotton seed cakes and other cheaper substitutes for saving oils for other use. The substitutes or compounded feeds should be provided to the users at reasonable costs and in adequate quantities.

27. Research should be initiated to identify the harmful substances in nonedible oilcakes and other by-products and to devise commercially feasible methods for making these cakes suitable for livestock feeding.

28. Solvent extraction of oilcakes should be encouraged to increase availability of oils and decrease cost of cakes as livestock feeds. Vigilance should, however, be directed to enforce that solvents carrying harmful residues in cakes are not used for extraction.

29. Soyabean cake is of high value for livestock feeding. Soyabean production should be encouraged.

30. Improved methods of processing inedible fish and fish industry wasters into fish meal including the setting up of small sized rotary fish meal plants developed by the Central Institute of Fish Technology at fish landing centres and fish factories should be encouraged, preferably in the cooperative and small scale sectors.

31. The State Animal Husbandry Departments should ascertain the availability of kitchen wasters from large hotels, messes, catering establishments set up by the tourist corporations, airlines, teaching institutions and private concerns. The economics of their use as livestock feed with or without processing should be studied.

32. Molasses should be allotted to the livestock industry in adequate quantities at reasonable rates for enriching feeds and fodders with urea and for pelleting feeds.

33. The use of sugarcane tops as livestock feed should be encouraged. Research on processes like derinding of canes for use as feed should be undertaken.

34. Reasons for the inadequate availability of bone meal and other ingredients for mineral mixtures and additives for balanced livestock feeds should be studied. The livestock feed manufacturers in the Public, Private and Cooperative sector should develop resources of these scarce materials. The State Governments may utilise provisions in the existing laws for making scarce raw materials available to the compounded livestock feed industries at reasonable cost.

35. Import of lysine and methionine should be allowed so that these amino acids can be added to poultry and pig rations. The pharmaceutical industry should be encouraged to manufacture these essential amino acids within the country.

36. Arrangements should be made for the manufacture of feed grade urea in India and popularizing its correct use for feeds and fodders.

37. To minimise the cost of production of compounded feeds for ruminants, one per cent urea should be incorporated according to ISI recommendations.

38. In order to make more milk available for human consumption, use of calf starters should be popularised, compounded feed manufacturers should be encouraged to manufacture calf starters and creep feeds.

39. Even in 2000 AD, the production from conventional sources may not be sufficient to meet the total requirement of feed constituents. As such, other unconventional by-products from slaughter houses, fallen animals, distillary wastes, caning industry, starch industry, forest by-products, sea weeds, algae etc. which are not utilized or inadequately utilised, should be exploited for augmenting feed resources. Research on this aspect both in the laboratory and field and extension programme should be intensified on a continuing basis.

40. Studies should be undertaken to evolve more economical balanced feeds for livestock without any sacrifice of nutritive value for productive purposes and to compare the economics of these rations with

traditional methods of feeding livestock in different parts of the country. Sufficient incentives during the first few years should be provided to livestock owners so as to encourage them to change over to balanced compounded feeds particularly for improved animals and their growing young stock.

41. State Animal Husbandry Departments should have laboratories where feed samples can be got analysed by the producer, seller or purchaser.

42. The livestock feed diverted from export should be fed to high producing livestock. For this purpose an efficient organisation should be built up for transfer of feed from places of production to areas of intensive livestock production.

43. The economics of export of livestock feed vis-a-vis export of livestock products should be studied so that loss of foreign exchange through diminished export of livestock feed ingredients may be made good to our advantage through the export of livestock products.

44. Legislation similar to that of Food Adulteration Act should be enacted and enforced to ensure that only feed materials and compounded feeds which conform to the quality standards are sold.

45. Biochemical pathways in which different nutrients are utilised for production of growth, milk, meat, eggs etc. should be investigated to determine nutrient requirements for economic traits.

46. Every State Animal Husbandry Department should have an officer at a fairly high level to coordinate development and extension of livestock feed production, procurement, compounding and distribution.

47. In order to coordinate the work of the State Animal Husbandry Departments in the field of livestock feeding there should be a specialist of Animal Nutrition in the Animal Husbandry Division of the Union Ministry of Agriculture and Irrigation.

48. A post of Assistant Director General should be created at the headquarters of the Indian Council of Agricultural Research for coordination of research activities in the field of animal nutrition at the various research institutes and veterinary and agricultural colleges.

49. An Institute for Animal Nutrition Research should be established at an early date.

Animal Health

Summary of Recommendations

The following is a summary of the important recommendations made in the text of this chapter.

1. There was one veterinarian for about 26,000 cattle units in the country by the close of the Fourth Plan. This number is considered inadequate to ensure the health and production of livestock. The ratio of veterinarians to the livestock population should therefore be narrowed down. There should be at least one veterinarian for every 20,000 cattle units by 1980, 10,000 cattle units by 1990 and 5,000 units by 2000 AD.

2. All veterinary hospitals/dispensaries should have sufficient stock of medicines and facilities for undertaking surgical operations and routine laboratory examinations. A mobile veterinary clinic should be provided at every veterinary hospital so that veterinary aid can be carried right to the door of the livestock owner, whenever necessary. Polyclinics should be established at district and state level in order to introduce multi-disciplinary approach in combating animal diseases, reproductive disorders and nutritional imbalances.

3. For improving the quality of veterinary service, it is necessary to supplement the funds of the veterinary departments. A phased programme of levying a charge for the treatment of livestock should be introduced immediately.

4. In some hospitals, there is a great demand for the services of veterinarians to attend to cases at the premises of livestock owners. Two veterinany doctors should be posted in such hospitals so that one goes for out-door duty and the other may be available for attending to the cases in the hospital. Fees for such visits should be charged from the livestock owners. Half of the amount of the fees should go to the veterinarian and the remaining half to the government revenue.

5. Prophylactic vaccinations should be charged on a no-profit and no-loss basis from the beginning of 1985. However, the services rendered and the biologicals used under the national programmes of disease control and in the event of natural calamities should continue to be free.

6. The Government should give incentives to veterinarians to set up private practice.

7. The disease investigation centre at the state level should have adequate laboratory facilities including those for tissue culture. This centre should be manned by specialists in disease of different species of animal as well as in different related disciplines.

8. The state disease investigation centre should be under the administrative control of the director of veterinary services.

9. The departments concerned with disease diagnosis and investigation work in the agricultural universities should be suitably strengthened.

10. The disease investigation unit at the IVRI

should have experts of a very high calibre capable of rendering specialized service in their respective fields. The IVRI should also undertake the supply of standard antigens, antisera and diagnostic agents for standardization of biologicals and should serve as a repository of important cultures of micro-organisms.

11. An organisation consisting of veterinarians specialized in exotic disease should be established so that it can be pressed into service as soon as an exotic disease is suspected to have gained entry into the country.

12. High priority should be given to the formation of statutory veterinary councils in the states. The Union Ministry of Agriculture and Irrigation should also constitute an Indian Veterinary Council immediately.

13. All state biological production centres should be suitably strengthened on a priority basis, so that they may be in a position to meet the full requirements of their respective states, at least in respect of the simple types of biologicals. As regards the more sophisticated products, the state biological production centres which have fairly good laboratory facilities and equipment, should be encouraged to take up their production. These centres should meet the demands of the whole country in respect of these sophisticated biologicals till the remaining states are also able to start their manufacture. The IVRI may concentrate on the development of technical know-how and methodology for the production of new and improved biologicals.

14. All the state biological production centres as well as the division of biological products of the IVRI along with the Foot-and-Mouth Disease Vaccine Production Station at Bangalore should be converted into Biological Products Corporations and run on commercial lines.

15. The Biological Production Centre, Gauhati, should be developed into a Regional Biological Products Station to meet the demand of biologicals of the States/Union territories in the north-eastern region.

16. An Expert Committee on Biological Products may be constituted by the Government of India to assess the requirements of the state biological production centres in respect of laboratories, equipment, personnel and training.

17. An Expert Committee on standardization of Biologicals should be constituted to revise the schedule F1 giving the specifications for the standardization of biological products and bring it up-to-date.

18. For enforcing the provisions of the Drugs and Cosmetics Act in respect of veterinary biological products and veterinary drugs, a post of Controller, Veterinary Biological Products and Drugs should be created in each state. At the centre, a post of Chief Controller, Veterinary Biological Products and Drugs should be created in the Department of Agriculture, Union Ministry of Agriculture and Irrigation.

19. A Veterinary Biological Products and Drugs Advisory Board should be set up to advise the Government of India on all matters concerning the veterinary biologicals and drugs.

20. A National Veterinary Biological Products Quality Control Institute for standardization of veterinary biologicals should be set up under the administrative control of the Department of Agriculture, Union Ministry of Agriculture and Irrigation.

21. A final thrust should be made to wipe out rinderpest infection from the few areas in which it is still lingering. For achieving this objective the following strategy should be followed :

(i) Morbid material from each and evey suspected outbreak of rinderpest should be expeditiously subjected to laboratory examination.

(ii) The source of each and every outbreak should be scrupulously traced and definite remedial measures taken to ensure that the lapses responsible for the outbreaks do not recur.

(iii) The number of rinderpest check posts on common cattle routes at the international and inter-state borders and the number of vigilance units at inter-state borders should be increased.

(iv) All cattle and buffaloes going into the forest for grazing should be vaccinated at the forest check posts.

(v) The State Veterinary Departments should intensify the follow-up vaccination programmes.

(vi) Stamping out policy should be gradually introduced.

22. Rinderpest tissue culture vaccine should be used since it has been found to be safe for all types of cattle, buffaloes, sheep and goats.

23. The State Biological Production Centres at Mhow, Lucknow, Hyderabad, Bangalore, Calcutta and Hissar should also take up the manufacture of rinderpest tissue culture vaccine.

24. Epidemiological studies with particular reference to the role of carriers or reservoirs in the dissemination of rinderpest infection should be undertaken.

25. Studies to determine the duration of immunity

conferred by the rinderpest tissue culture vaccine in indigenous, crossbred and exotic cattle as well as in buffaloes, sheep, goats and pigs should be intensified.

26. A systematic programme for control of foot-and-mouth disease should be taken up immediately.

27. Production of foot-and-mouth disease vaccine should be stepped up and efforts should be made to reduce its cost of production. The state biological production centre should also take up its manufacture.

28. Strict quarantine measures should be rigorously enforced to ensure that SAT I, SAT II, SAT III types of foot-and-mouth disease virus or any other new strain do not gain entry into the country.

29. Foot-and-mouth disease typing service should be strengthened by opening more centres particularly to cater to the needs of the areas of intensive livestock development.

30. IVRI should intensify research on foot-and-mouth disease in pigs and take early steps for production of an efficacious and inexpensive vaccine.

31. Research work on foot-and-mouth disease in sheep and goats with particular reference to the study of its epidemiology should be intensified as these a specise may be playing an important role in dissemination of the infection.

32. A National Advisory Committee on Foot-and-Mouth Disease should be constituted to supervise the control programme and to offer expert technical guidance in its implementation.

33. A systematic programme to control tuberculosis and brucellosis among animal with the ultimate objective of their eradication should be taken up immediately on a country wide basis

34. A Tuberculosis and Brucellosis Eradication Officer should be appointed in each state. At the centre, a Chief Tuberculosis and Brucellosis Eradication Officer will be needed for coordinating and guiding the programme on a country wide basis.

35. A National Tuberculosis and Brucellosis Eradication Committee should be set up to chalk out a detailed technical programme, to lay down important guidelines for its implementation and to exercise supervision over the progress of the Tuberculosis and Brucellosis Eradication Campaign.

36. An effective organisation to undertake systematic control of mastitis on a country wide basis should be built up and a well-equipped laboratory for mastitis work should be established in each state.

37. A massive audio-visual programme should be launched to educate livestock owners regarding the economic importance of control of mastitis in dairy animals.

38. Epidemiological maps indicating the endemic areas of haemorrhagic septicaemia, authrax and blackquarter should be prepared by the State Veterinary Departments and a more systematic vaccination programme should be taken up in the endemic areas.

39. Contagious bovine pleuro-pneumonia which is confined only to a few districts in Assam should be eradicated as quickly as possible by stamping out policy.

40. A Committee of Animal Disease Specialists should be constituted immediately to carry out a thorough on-the spot study of the factors responsible for the increase in mortality due to contagious bovine pleuro-pneumonia during recent years.

41. A systematic programme for control of fascioliasis (liver fluke disease) in cattle should be launched. It will be necessary to appoint a liver fluke control officer in each state where the disease is a serious problem.

42. Research work on fascioliasis particularly on ecological behaviour of the intermediate host and the effect of different molluseicides on the snails and the environment should be intensified. The drugs that are being marketed for treating fascioliasis in domestic animals should be subjected to carefully controlled trials to pick up the most effective and safe drug for field application.

43. The State Animal Husbandry Departments should give priority to duck raising programme in the fluke-infested areas as a step towards the biological control of snails.

44. In view of the serious loss suffered by the animal industry due to warble fly infestation, a systematic programme for its control should be taken up at an early date.

45. Research work on theileriasis with particular reference to the study of the antigenie make-up of the local theileria strains and for development of an efficacious prophylactic vaccine should be intensified. Research work should also be undertaken to develop simple serological tests which could easily be applied in the field for detection of early and latent cases. The relative efficiency of various compounds put up recently in the market by some pharmaceutical firms for treatment of theileriasis should be tested under carefully controlled conditions in research institutes and agricultural universities for selection of the most suitable drug.

46. Large scale production of inactivated sheep pox virus vaccine according to the Russian method, should be undertaken immediately at all the biological

production centres. This vaccine should be used for prophylactic immunization of sheep till such time a better vaccine is available. Research work at IVRI and at other suitable centres should be intensified for developing a more efficacious vaccine.

47. Effective measures for control of rabies should be immediately undertaken. The programme should be launched during the fifth five year plan in the capital of each of the States/Union Territories and it should be gradually extended to other cities and towns till the whole country is covered.

48. Should an outbreak of swine fever occur in future in any other state than Meghalaya and Nagaland, stamping-out policy should be followed. In case of Meghalaya and Nagaland, if the disease still persists and if the foci of infection spread, prophylactic mass vaccination programme should be undertaken without any delay.

49. Free movement of pigs from Meghalaya and Nagaland to other parts of the country should not be allowed till these states are absolutely clean of swine fever infection

50. In order to meet any future emergency, it should be ensured that adequate quantities of lapinised swine fever vaccine are stored all the year round at Izatnagar, Hissar, Ranipet, and Calcutta where the vaccine is being manufactured at present. The Biological Products Station at Gauhati should also undertake the production and storage of this vaccine, since extensive pig development work has been taken up in the north eastern region of the country.

51. As swine fever is almost wholly under control. quarantine regulations should be rigidly followed in the case of all pigs imported from abroad.

52. Studies should be undertaken to investigate if wild pigs or some other non-swine reservoirs of this infection exist so that appropriate action may be taken for the elimination of the swine fever virus and for checking its spread to domestic pigs.

53. For bringing down the incidence of Ranikhet disease to an insignificant level, it is necessary to raise the target of vaccination to cover at least 80 per cent of the poultry population within a couple of years and to maintain this level of vaccination target for a period of about 10 years. At that stage, it would be worth while to start a pilot-project in some selected areas, where vaccinations may be stopped and reliance placed on hygienic and sanitary measures for keeping the poultry farms free of the disease. Should an outbreak occur in such an area stamping out policy should be followed. If this approach proves successful, the programme should be gradually extended to bring more and more poultry farms in contiguous areas under its orbit till the whole country is covered.

54. A national programme for control of Marek's disease with the ultimate objective of its eradication should be initiated immediately

55. Since Marek's disease vaccine is not being produced at present anywhere in India it should be imported from abroad till it can be manufactured indigenously. Only tirkey herpes virus vaccine should be imported till a better vaccine is available.

56. Complete records pertaining to mortality and productive performance of the vaccinated birds should be maintained at farms where vaccination is resorted to. These data should be carefully analysed by a committee of experts which should be appointed by the Government of India, for finding out the effectiveness of vaccination as a method for control of Marek's disease.

57. To conserve foreign exchange, manufacture of turkey herpes virus vaccine should be taken up on priority basis by IVRI and other biological production centres.

58. Research work on Marek's disease with particular reference to its epizootiology and factors relating to virus shedding viability of the virus under field conditions and development of a more effective vaccine should be intensified at IVRI and some agricultural universities.

59. A systematic programme for control of chronic respiratory disease (avian respiratory myco plasmosis) should be taken up at a very early date.

60. Production of the antigen for serological diagnosis of chronic respiratory disease should be taken up by some more biological production centres so that the antigen is available in adequate quantity for the national programme for control of the disease.

61. A National Pullorum Eradication Campaign should be launched immediately with a target to complete the work before the close of 1980.

62. A suitable vaccine strain against duck virus hepatitis should be imported from abroad and vaccine as well as hyperimmune serum against this disease should be produced in the country.

63. Vast majority of animals in India manifest subclinical syndromes of deficiency diseases in a complex form resulting from an overall low intake of nutritional substances. In order to save the livestock from further degeneration, production of animal feeds and fodders should be augmented and the number of unproductive and uneconomic stock should be reduced.

64. Systematic control of diseases like Johne's disease, exterotoxaemia, babesiosis, amaplasmosis,

schistosomiasis, amphistomiasis, cocci-diosis, lungworm infestation, contagious caprine pleuro-pneumonia, fowl pox, fowl sprochactosis, fowl typhoid etc. should be undertaken.

65. Programmes for the systematic control and eradication of foot and mouth disease, tuberculosis, brucellosis, contagious bovine pleuro-pneumonia, Pullorum disease and Marek's disease should be financed wholly or partly by the Government of India. As for the remaining diseases discussed in section 5 of this chapter, it should be the responsibility of the State Veterinary Departments to intensify measures for their systematic control.

66. The Joint Commissioner (Livestock Health) in the Animal Husbandry Division, Union Ministry of Agriculture and Irrigation should analyse periodically the trends in the incidence of the diseases and the progress achieved in their control on a country wide basis and keep the states informed.

67. The Livestock Importation Act should be suitably modified, so that the authority to implement this Act vests with the Government of India and not with the State Governments. Regulations should also be added to control import of cultures of micro-organisms, semen and veterinary biologicals and to enforce laboratory examination of imported livestock products like eggs, meat, cheese, butter etc. Animals to be imported for zoological gardens should also be brought under the provisions of this Act.

68. Suitable legislation should be enacted on a priority basis to regulate the inter-state movement of livestock to prevent the spread of diseases from one state to another.

69. Enforcement of the quarantine and certification regulations should also be entrusted to the quarantine organisation in the Animal Husbandry Division of the Union Ministry of Agriculture and Irrigation, which should be suitably strengthened.

70. Quarantine stations should also be established on Indian borders adjoining Bangla Desh, Burma, Bhutan and Nepal.

71. All quarantine stations should have adequate facilities for keeping animals under quarantine and for carrying out laboratory examinations.

72. Official recognition should be accorded to some well-equipped laboratories in India having specialised facilities for undertaking specific tests so that their reports may be legally acceptable.

73. Two pre-export quarantine stations may be built up during the Fifth Plan in well isolated locations, such as on off-shore islands. Should the livestock export demands justify, more such stations may be established subsequently.

74. A Central Bureau of Animal Disease Surveillance and Intelligence should be set up on priority basis in the Animal Husbandry Division of the Union Ministry of Agriculture and Irrigation. Every State and Union Territory should establish under the Directorate of Veterinary Services, an Epidemiological cell.

Meat Production and Animal By-products

The following is a summary of the important recommendations made in the text of this chapter.

1. Urgent steps should be taken to considerably enhance production of wholesome meat as there is a wide gap between the availability and the demand for meat for human consumption. Programmes for development of sheep, goats and pigs particularly to improve their meat qualities should be intensified.

2. Export trade for buffalo meat should be developed by improving the meat characteristics of the buffalo and fattening unwanted male buffalo calves.

3. Modernisation of slaughter houses should be undertaken immediately.

4. An organised marketing service for meat animals should be established in the cooperative sector. The livestock markets should be operated as terminal markets owned by the State Governments or Cooperatives and should provide facilities for yarding, feeding and watering of meat animals. These should also provide veterinary services and banking facilities.

5. Studies should be undertaken immediately by the Directorate of Merketing and Inspection, Government of India and State Marketing Organisations to work out the *modus operandi* by which the farmers or the primary producers receive fair price for their animals and the consumers get good quality meat and meat products at a reasonable price.

6. The export of meat and meat products should be brought under the control of some organised agency like the State Trading Corporation and the quality control should be entrusted to the Directorate of Marketing and Inspection.

7. A Slaughter House Advisory Committee should be constituted under the Union Ministry of Agriculture and Irrigation for formulating a national policy for the betterment of the meat industry and to advise the government on connected problems. The existing Slaughter House Unit in the Division of Animal Husbandry of the Union Ministry of Agriculture and Irrigation should be suitably strengthened.

8. In order to provide incentive to the State Governments for setting up slaughter houses, the Central Government may give about 50 per cent assistance as direct grant for establishing one modern

slaughter house complex in each state during the Fifth Plan.

9. The scope of the Meat Food Products Order, 1973 should be enlarged so as to cover unprocessed meat as well.

10. Training courses should be arranged periodically for imparting in-plant training to technicians required for work in the modern slaughter houses.

11. Research work on problems connected with production, processing and storage of meat and meat products should be intensified.

12. Improved methods of flaying should be introduced in the slaughter houses and better flaying should be encouraged by payment of premia of good flayers. More village flaying centres should be established for skilled flaying of fallen animals.

13. Demonstration-cum-training centres should be established in important places for imparting training in curing, tanning and rational utilisation of hides.

14. A system of compulsory preshipment inspection should be introduced for hides and skins meant for export.

15. Cold storage facilities for preserving raw hides and skins may be provided, wherever possible.

16. For effecting an improvement in the quality of the castings to boost export, sanitary conditions in the slaughter houses must be improved.

17. The byproducts wing of each slaughter house should have a gut processing unit where it should be possible to process the guts under hygienic conditions.

18. For increasing collection of raw bones, cooperatives of bone collectors should be formed and bone purchasing depots established in blocks. Flaying of carcasses should be allowed only at the flaying centres.

19. New bone digestors should be set up only in areas capable of utilising the bone meal and should preferably be located in remote places unconnected by rail or road. Co-operatives of bone collectors should be provided with the digestors on rent.

20. All big slaughter houses should have a byproduct plant within their precincts or in close proximity so that all available fats from slaughtered stock could be processed.

21. The pig rearers and bristle merchants should be educated regarding the economic importance of bristles, particularly as an earner of foreign exchange so that more bristles are collected and dressed for export.

22. Blood from slaughtered animals should be suitably collected and incorporated in the livestock feeds or used as fertiliser.

23. Vigorous propaganda is necessary to educate the goat rearers and the goat hair merchants regarding the economic importance of goat hair and its proper processing for export.

24. Export of horns and hoofs should be increased. Horns and hoofs left in the country should be processed for manufacture of gelatine and the unutilised portion should be converted into meal for use as fertilisers.

25. Meat unfit for human consumption should be converted into meat meal and used as an ingredient of the poultry feed and as fertiliser for tea and coffee plantations.

26. A chain of well equipped carcass utilisation centres should be established by the State Governments.

27. The municipal corporations/committees, gram panchayats and other local bodies while giving contracts for lifting the dead animals should ensure that the contractors have adequate facilities to process the carcasses. Preferences should be given to the Animal Husbandry/Industries Departments and Khadi and Village Industries Commission/Boards in the matter of allotment of contracts.

28. The areas where there is hereditary/proprietory rights for lifting the carcasses of fallen animals, Government should establish service centres with all facilities for the flayers. The flayers who bring dead animals to the centres may be permitted to process the carcasses on nominal charges.

29. Carcass utilisation centres, where more than 4-5 carcasses of large animals are likely to be collected daily, should be suitably equipped for processing the carcasses and for production of end products.

30. In places where new slaughter houses are being established or modernisation of the existing ones is taking place, it is necessary to make simultaneous arrangements for establishing of carcasses utilisation plants so that slaughter house offals could be processed economically.

31. The existing Acts of the Municipal Committees, Corporations and Gram Panchayats should be suitably modified to make it obligatory on the part of the owners of the dead animals to handover the carcasses only to approved carcass utilisation centres.

32. Wide publicity should be given through modern audio-visual methods about the carcass utilisation programmes to arouse awareness among the masses.

FISHERIES

Inland Fisheries and Aquaculture

Summary and Recommendations

The main recommendations are given below.

1. Fisheries from inland waters should be developed as a priority industry because of the high demand and market value for fresh and brackish water fish which could be raised and distributed as low-cost protein food.

2. Improvements in capture fisheries will be possible only through refinements in fishing techniques which should be solved by Craft and Gear Research Section of the CIFT (ICAR).

3. The fisheries organisations in the states should effectively manage fishing operations in rivers through appropriate regulations to conserve stocks.

4. While Indian major carps (*rohu catla*, and mrigal) form the principal yield of the river systems of the Indo-Gangetic plains, greater reliance should be placed on indigenous species in the rivers of peninsular India.

5. To stem the rapid decline of the *Hilsa* fisheries, particularly of the northern rivers, suitable measures of conservation should be formulated and enforced without delay. Research work on establishing *Hilsa* culture should be intensified by ICAR.

6. Improvement in trout hatchery practices should be introduced for higher survival rate of seedfish to enable more intensive stocking in the existing trout streams and for establishing new fishery areas in Jammu-Kashmir, Himachal Pradesh and other high altitude regions. Breeding and hatchery practices should be developed towards the production of seed fish for undertaking commercial culture in suitable cold water areas.

7. Considering the importance of mahseer as a top-class commercial and sport fish there is need for extensive surveys and investigations on different species of mahseer for establishing viable capture and culture fisheries.

8. Pre-impoundment surveys of rivers should help formulate proposals for development reservoir fisheries and for preserving down stream icthyofauna. The proposals should be jointly developed by Fisheries and Irrigation Organisation in the states for inclusion in the river valley projects, and the required works should then be got done prior to impoundment.

9. Reservoirs and tanks built for domestic water supplies should also be utilised for fish rearing but with adequate health safeguards.

10. To keep the continuity of stock of major carps which take long periods of acclimatisation for natural breeding it should be ensured that the adequate level of water is maintained in the dead storages of medium and major reservoirs.

11. Fishing in the reservoirs should be rationalised by systematic removal of trashfish and observing closed seasons to stop indiscriminate killing of brood-fish particularly of major carps.

12. To maintain the productivity of reservoirs, the possibility of cultivating suitable types of legumes in the foreshore areas exposed during summer months, should be explored. The top cuttings of these crops would be useful as green fodder.

13. The State Governments, while formaluting the policy for land and water utilisation, should consider fresh water swamps as naturally advantageous areas for the development of fisheries and other uses, if any, should be treated as subsidiary.

14. To improve production from capture fishery of estuaries, regulations for fishing and 'closed seasons', if necessary, should be adopted for the coastal districts by the maritime states.

15. To restore the fall in production from the capture fishery of brackish waters, particularly in Chilka and Pulicat lakes, as a result of silting of the connection with sea, and to maintain the level of agricultural and fisheries production in the entire area, integrated plans should be developed by coordinated action on the part of Irrigation, Agriculture and Fisheries Departments.

16. The production base by aquaculture from fresh, brackish and sea waters should be enlarged with the application of new technology.

17. The seedfish supplies of major carps have to be increased several fold by all methods of production for undertaking increased stocking densities to obtain optimal yields from all culturable waters.

18. Necessary conservational measures should be undertaken to project breeding grounds of major carps. Riverine stretches which harbour large scale concentrations of seedfish should be kept only for seedfish collection.

19. The State Governments should intensify investigations to locate as many wet bunds as possible for increasing seedfish production. Central fisheries agencies should undertake detailed investigations in collaboration with the states where wet bunds are being exploited to identify the factors responsible for the success of natural breeding of the major carps in the wet bunds, so as to help in bringing about the natural breeding in as many stocked perennial waters as possible by providing the optimal conditions.

20. States should expand the facilities for dry bunds breeding of major carps after surveying suitable

areas where they could be constructed at the minimum cost, with a view to increasing seedfish production, as has been done in Madhya Pradesh.

21. Considering the quality of seedfish produced through induced breeding by giving injections of pituitary hormones or suitable substitutes the state should considerably intensify the programmes for seedfish farms located near reservoirs and other areas where perennial water facilities exist.

22. To meet the mounting demand of injection material in the circumstances of shortage of pituitary glands experienced even at the present level of activity, the ICAR should intensify research on fish gonadotropins in collaboration with the universities and Pharmacological Laboratories in India where allied work is being done, so as to expedite the process of finding out suitable substitutes.

23. The frequency of success in induced breeding method being dependent on favourable environmental factors, not yet clearly defined, the ICAR should intensify studies, on this relationship with a view to establishing the exact environmental factors necessary for success.

24. The state should increase available area for nursery tanks and adopt improved management practices developed by ICAR in fish nurseries. There is need to bring out relevant extension literature and organise training-cum-demonstration in these practices. Floating fish nurseries can be of considerable advantage when adequate space for ground nurseries is not available. The ICAR should study the possibility and economic feasibility of adopting floating nurseries.

25. Whenever stocking of fingerlings is considered necessary, the states should give preferential consideration to grant fallow lands near culturable waters for creating rearing ponds. The possibilities of rearing fry to fingerlings on artificial feeds in net enclosures of synthetic material should be examined by the ICAR.

26. For experimental work on indigenous and exotic carps in areas potentially important in fish culture, the establishment of large fish farms for adoptive research is recommended for each state.

27. As the use of fertilisers in raising productivity of ponds and tanks has to be rational and economic, the ICAR should intensify studies on the uses of different types of fertilisers as applied to fish culture under different conditions. While setting up a service for soil and water analysis the State Fisheries Departments should entrust it with an advisory role on use of fertilisers also.

28. Considering the important role of artificial feeds in increasing production by aquaculture, the ICAR should step up research on utilisation of cheap or waste materials for artificial feeds, which should be available in large quantities and could be easily stored.

29. With the increased stocking density of seedfish of carps in right proportion for optimal utilisation of natural feeds and with the introduction of fertilisers and artificial feeds wherever intensive cultural practices are economically feasible, the states should see that these water resources are put to maximum utilisation thereby increasing the base of carp production several times.

30. Introduction of large scale monoculture of common carp in net enclosures kept afloat in reservoirs, canals etc. to substantially increase inland fish production seems to be a promising line to be developed in the country. This system has also significance in solving to some extent the problem of rehabilitation of people displaced as a result of impounding reservoir basins. The ICAR should find out the most economical types of enclosures to enable the introduction of this system of fish culture.

31. Fresh water swamps, unsuitable for economic reclamation into farming units for carp culture, should be increasingly utilised for culture of air-breathing fishes.

32. The maritime states should undertake detailed surveys of brackish water swamps for mapping out suitable areas for reclamation into farming units, and carry out systematic prospecting of brackish water resources for seedfish. To supplement seedfish production under captivity conditions, ICAR should intensify research on artificial breeding of mullets and other estuarine species.

33. Maritime states should undertake, in coordination with research agencies, pre-investment studies on brackish water culture by establishing experimental and pilot commercial fish farms at selected centres.

34. The maritime states should undertake surveys of coastal regions for locating productive areas for culture of molluscan shellfish, mainly edible oysters, mussels and clams. The most economical methods of cultivation should be evolved for adoption in the states. Alternative use of mussels, constituting the most productive form of mariculture, should also be examined, particularly their reduction into mussel-meal, for livestock and poultry feed.

35. Priority consideration should be given by ICAR to the furtherance of indigenous technology of culture pearl industry with a view to establishing its economic viability and its early development as a commercial undertaking, particularly off Tamil Nadu and Gujarat, where the pearl oyster beds have become

unproductive for the extraction of natural pearls. New developments in spat collection for pearl oysters in Kerala appear promising.

36. ICAR should bring out necessary extension literature on the technique and economics of the culture of marine algae, so that the industry based on these algae as raw material can take advantage of new technology developed by the appropriate institutes of ICAR and CSIR.

37. In granting leases of fishery rights in public waters, State Governments should take a long-range view of enlarging the base for increasing inland fishery production with necessary steps favouring development activities.

38. Fishery rights of inland water resources, now vested in other departments of the State Governments, should be transferred to Fisheries Departments.

39. For fishing in rivers, canals, estuaries and backwater, a licensing system should be adopted in the states after notifying waters under the necessary legal provisions.

40. For fishing in reservoirs, *beels*, *jheels* etc. any system—licensing, royalty, bifurcated leasing, or outright leasing—may be adopted keeping in view the conditions laid down for each system.

41. Rights in culturable fisheries should be granted as outright leases on adequate tenures to enable utilisation of long term credit. There should be a provision for extension of lease periods on satisfactory fulfilment of lease conditions, and on fair amount of annual rentals based on rating waterspreads into suitable categories on the basis of estimated yields and price of produce.

42. In leasing out fishery rights of waters vested in local bodies such as municipalities, gram panchayats, etc., similar procedure as for governmental waters should be adopted. However, local bodies interested in undertaking developmental activities themselves should either engage trained persons or get their personnel trained, and the State Governments should accept such schemes duly approved by the Fisheries Departments.

43. In leasing out portions of reservoirs, canals, lakes and coastal region for intensive aquaculture in new system such as floating net enclosures, cages rafts etc. same procedure should be adopted as for culture fisheries, except that in case of reservoirs first preference should be given to persons affected by impoundments and in case of coastal region consideration should also be given to any private enterprise including the corporate sector.

44. Engineering cells and Extension cells should be developed in the research and developmental agencies at the centre and in the Fisheries Directorates in the states.

45. Training in field adoption of improved technology should be organised at the state level, with the main emphasis on demonstration and practical management.

46. The centre should frame model byelaws for two types of Fisheries co-operatives laying emphasis on capture or culture fisheries separately, but with the common proviso making the marketing of catches by the members through the co-operative an obligatory feature. Necessary credit for marketing should be made available to the co-operatives. The states should identify the minimum scale of economic operation for inland fisheries co-operative and work out the scales of necessary assistance to the new and existing units.

Marine Fisheries

Summary and Recommendations

Amongst the various recommendations given in different sections, only the important ones are given below :

1. Considering the potentials of fisheries resources around India, the production of marine fish should be increased from the present average of 1.0 million tonnes per annum to at least 3.5 million tonnes per annum after 25 years.

2. The strategy for utilising the extended resources of pelagic fisheries, recently discovered beyond the traditional zone of exploitation off Kerala and Karnataka, should be soon developed by the centre and the concerned states but without hindrance to the fishery in the traditional zone.

3. For increasing production from the Wadge Bank fishery, the State Governments of Kerala and Tamil Nadu should formulate specific schemes, particularly developing fishing effort by mechanised boats.

4. The progress in marine fisheries resources survey, carried out in the last 25 years, has been very unsatisfactory. Some of the deeper water resources already surveyed and found productive are not being put to utilisation by the private sector or the state public sector organisations in the industry, indicating a need for public sector organisation supported by the centre to give a lead to the industry. The DSFO and IFP both under the Union Department of Agriculture, should be restructured into a Marine Fisheries Development Organisation or Cooperation, giving it a considerable autonomy in operations. Unserviceable vessels should be scrapped without further loss to the public exchequer. The remaining vessels of the DSFO and IFP should be regrouped into two fleets :

(a) A research fleet for survey and assessment to be directed by the research agencies of the ICAR and (b) a fishing fleet for experimental and commercial fishing to be handled by the proposed Marine Fisheries Department Organisation.

5. The CMFRI in coordination with NIO, should lay greater emphasis in the future programmes of research on the effects of environmental factors on different types of fisheries, particularly correlation of oceanographic and fishing conditions.

6. The resources survey and assessment being a research function, should be the responsibility of ICAR, through the CMFRI, in coordination with CIFT, NIO and other central and state fisheries organisations. The combined leadership of the programmes may be vested in a senior scientist to be nominated by the ICAR from any one of these organisations but with unambiguous delegated authority for the framing and execution of survey and assessment programmes. The ICAR should see that the provision for adequate fleet of research vessels and prevailing rules and procedures for their maintenance do not constitute a constraint in the progress of work.

7. The Ministry of Agriculture and Irrigation should set up a working machinery in coordination with the Chief Civil Hydrographic Office, NIO, CMFRI and other concerned research organisations for the preparation of fishery charts.

8. In the absence of repeat subsidy to the fishermen for replacements of unserviceable mechanised boats, the State Governments should institute a system of preferential loans for boat and/or engine replacement.

9. It should be seen that the withdrawal of subsidies by the State Governments does not constitute a constraint on the progress of mechanisation of fishing boats in those areas still having further scope for expansion of coastal fisheries.

10. Construction of larger fishing vessels with steel hulls should be limited to those yards willing to specialise in this work, execute orders in good time and be responsible for a package deal for assembling the complete vessels, their repair and maintenance. Design improvement and operational efficiency should be included in the working system of these yards.

11. The need for further import of larger trawlers beyond the numbers which are in the pipeline should be reviewed carefully by the Government. But the import of new prototype vessels should be liberally allowed to help the development of indigenous construction of fishing vessels for off shore fisheries. The CIFT should strengthen its craft and gear section with personnel qualified in naval architecture for developing designs to suit Indian conditions.

12. To avoid conflicts amongst the operators of non-mechanical craft, mechanised boats and larger fishing vessels, and between the fishermen of adjoining states the government should undertake necessary measures for delimitation of fishing zones through legislation.

13. The practice of discarding the trash fish overboard by the operators of the larger fishing vessels with refrigerated holes or freezing facility on board, should be curbed, and if need be, the possibility of installation of 'Pocket' size fish meal plants on board should be examined. Reporting the catch, in quantity and quality, by all vessels above 25 GRT to CMFRI should be made obligatory.

14. The CIFT should actively study the use of fibre glass reinforced plastic for mass assembly of smaller Craft in view of the high cost and shortages of timber, particularly for canoes and catamarans. The Institute should evolve a clear categorisation of craft and the material to be used to give the most economic results, short term and long term. Wider trials of ferro concrete craft should also be made.

15. It should be seen that marine diesel engines are marketed with ISI certification after working out standard tests jointly by CIFT and ISI, and should have a reasonable period of guarantee. The manufacturers should develop adequate repair facilities at important fishing centres so that the mechanised boat operators do not lose fishing time due to engine breakdowns.

16. As the prevailing prices of marine diesel engines are prohibitively high, the government should examine the possibility of scaling down the cost through: (a) examination of the price structure to regulate profitability; (b) limiting manufacture to a reduced number of industrial units; and (c) giving relief in the sales tax and the excise duty.

17. The CIFT and the Fisheries research organisations in the maritime states should intensify research in co-ordination, on the traditional gear systems with a view to bringing about improvements in per capita productivity and economic returns to the marine fishermen. Investigations engear technology of mid-water trawling, semi-pelagic trawling and purse-seining should also be intensified, seeking foreign expertise wherever necessary.

18. The CIFT along with fisheries departments of maritimes states should strengthen their extension services and demonstrate the economic advantages of various types of modern fishing devices, particularly fish finders/echo sounders and deck equipment for the operation of different types of gear. The CIFT should liaise with the electronic industry to develop and

market in the country a robust and versatile echo-sounder for the smaller mechanised craft and trawlers. The instruments and deck machinery required and now manufactured in India should be standardised through the cooperation of the CIFT and ISI, keeping in view the need for reducing the number of items and their specifications, and the need for inter-changeability of equipment.

19. With considerable prospects of increasing export earnings from the products of oceanic tuna, India should make an early entry into commercial fishing for high seas tuna in the Indian ocean. This would also enable India to have more effective participation in the international management of the tuna resources in the Indian ocean. Expert foreign assistance may be sought to accelerate the process of developing tuna fishing by Indian private industry and the proposed Marine Fisheries Development Organisation.

20. The exploitation of skip jack fishery resources in the Indian ocean by purse scining, particularly around the Indian Islands should be given special attention in the development of high seas fishing for tuna.

21. Despite the importance of fishery harbour facilities in the development of marine fisheries, the progress in this work has been very slow. For provision of basic facilities at suitable fishing centres in each maritime state, a comprehensive report on planning of minor harbour works should be prepared as expeditiousty as possible for immediate action, priority consideration should then be given to the construction of these smaller works for giving an early relief to the fishing industry.

22. The Ministry of Agriculture and Irrigation, in consultation with the governments of the maritime states, may work out a scheme for the re-organisation of the pre-investment survey of Fisheries Harbours Project so as to make it responsible not only for the formulation of the projects of the Fishery Harbours outside the jurisdiction of the Port Trust Authorities, but also for the execution of the harbour works. The same organisation should estimate the requirement of the dredging work and procure necessary dredgers as a central pool for the construction of fishery harbours.

23. The procedures for sanctioning fishing harbour projects by the Government of India should be streamlined to avoid undue delays which have occurred in the past resulting in several cases in the revision of estimates and need for fresh sanctions.

24. On commissioning the fishery harbours, the State Governments should devise a suitable machinery for management and proper maintenance of fishery harbours as well as for levy and collection of port dues and other charges.

25. To expedite the construction of major fishery harbours by the port trust authorities, the government may accept the procedures suggested.

26. To make fisheries harbours fully functional at the time of their commissioning, planning for provision of facilities such as roads, processing plants, water supply, electricity etc. by the State Governments should be synchronised with the construction of fishery harbours by the Central Government. The centre and the State Governments should formulate specific schemes for expansion of fishing effort involving operations of fishing vessels based from harbours and when they are commissioned.

27. In the absence of specific rules and regulations, under the Indian Merchant Shipping Act (1958) for the navigation, registration and manning of mechanised fishing boats below 25 Gross Registered Tonnage, difficulties are being experienced by the fishing industry. The Ministry of Agriculture and Irrigation should arrange to get the necessary rules framed, as expeditiously as possible, by the Director General of Shipping, giving due consideration to the specific conditions of the industry and recognition of the certificates awarded by the State Directorates of Fisheries and the Central Institute of Fisheries Operatives as the necessary competency certificates for operating the boats outside the harbour limits.

28. There should be a uniform pattern of training at all the fishermen training centres in the states, and rules for proficiency test, syllabus etc. should be framed jointly by the fisheries organisations in the maritime states and the centre in consultation with the Director General of Shipping.

29. The fisheries organisations in the states should take necessary steps to enable the fishermen training centres to assume additional function of developing necessary liaison and building up extension service among the working fishermen in the coastal region with a view to improving their working systems.

30. The grant of remissions in the seatime/workshop time, being given as a matter of discretion by the Mercantile Marine Department to the institutional trainees, should be a general rule applicable to all candidates sponsored for examination by approved institutions.

31. All the rules and regulations pertaining to navigation, registration, manning and examination should constitute a separate chapter in the provisions of the Indian Merchant Shipping Act (1958), and a separate booklet containing this chapter alone should be brought out for the use and guidance of the fishing industry.

32. The candidates appearing for the competency

certificate examinations of fishing secondhand and skipper held by the Mercantile Marine Department only in the disciplines of Navigation and Seamanship, should first qualify for the proficiency certificate in fishing to be awarded under the authority of the Ministry of Agriculture and Irrigation.

33. The present system of institutional training should be modified in such a way that the institutional candidates, appearing for competency certificate examination of fishing secondhand and engine driver, should gain necessary qualifying sea-time/workshop time in between the institutional training.

34. The key post in manning fishing vessels larger than 25 GRT being that of a skipper requiring 60 months of sea-time to qualify as a candidate for the competency certificate, it should be seen that in planning for the development of offshore fisheries the availability of skippers should not constitute a constraint.

35. Economic studies on the cost and return functions in different fishing methods and on the status of the fishermen in different maritime states should be jointly undertaken by the state fisheries organisations and bureaus of economics and statistics for subsequent review at the centre for planning development programmes and determining their economic impact.

36. To involve the small and marginal section of the marine fishermen community in the production process, the feasibility of organising cooperatives of the type of Farmers Service Societies on a pilot basis may be examined by the maritime states.

37. A comprehensive review of the existing marine fisheries cooperatives may be undertaken with a view to assessing the type of assistance needed, both marginal and financial, to make the uneconomic cooperatives viable. The feasibility of reorganising some of the non-viable units on the lines of the Farmers Service Societies should also be examined.

38. The cooperative societies should perform the additional functions of mobilising savings considered necessary for consumption by fishermen during the cessation period of fishing in monsoon, so as to save them from the exploitation by the middlemen.

39. With a view to expanding fishing effort in the exploitation of offshore fisheries, the Government of India should suitably modify the grant of subsidy scheme so as to cover fishing vessels of all types of hull materials and of adequate sizes as to have the minimum endurance capacity of remaining at sea for more than 72 hours.

40. There being a need for giving incentive support of the industry in developing offshore fisheries the grant of preferential loans with grace periods of low interest to be routed through the public sector fisheries corporations in the states in case of fishing vessels upto 25 GRT and through Marine Products Export Development Authority in case of vessels above 25 GRT may be examined.

41. Concession on diesel oil duty should be extended to all sizes of mechanised fishing craft. A high level committee should be set up to periodically review the question of diesel oil to regulate the retail price of diesel oil for marine fishing both in shore and offshore.

42. Instead of charging variable rates of insurance premiums as at present for mechanised boats operating different states, the LIC should examine the adoption of uniform rates tenable throughout the country, with necessary surcharges for boats without monsoon lay-up. The need for insurance coverage of the entire value of mechanised boats should be fostered by the LIC in co-ordination with the state fishing organisations.

43. Marine fishery policy for India should be recast in the light of an exclusive fishery zone adjoining to coast. The accent on distant water fishing fleet should be replaced in favour of more concentrated effort for the exploitation of the seas within 320km of the Indian coast. The requirement of vessels in future should be more for medium-sized vessels rather than large vessels capable of long absence from the base.

44. The economic zone adjoining the coast will, in future, be the area of intense activity in fishing, mineral exploration, defence and navigational installations, oil drilling and coastal aquaculture. Such intense development can lead to conflicting interests and damage to living resources. These activities should be coordinated at the highest level involving the National Environmental Committee and the proposed Ocean, Science and Technology Agency and the maritime states.

45. In the development and utilisation of the exclusive fishery zone adjoining the coast, the concerned states should have a responsible share.

46. On the question of scientific research on fish stocks and related problems, the ICAR should ensure the fullest development of research facilities, expertise and opportunities for cooperation with the neighbouring countries, enabling India to have the most uptodate information on the fish stocks around the country.

Crustacean Fisheries and Their Utilisation

Summary of Recommendations

The following is a summary of the important recommendations made in this chapter.

1. Mechanised fishing vessels around 10 m length and 40 BHP are recommended for prawn fishing in coastal waters. These should be built on mass assembly basis. Boats with outboard motors are recommended for creek fishing. Prototypes of larger vessels for offshore operations should be imported and tried for selection of designs for large scale construction in Indian ship-building yards.

2. Immediate attention should be given by ICAR to the survey and assessment of marine prawn resources on all-India basis for rational exploitation in the areas under heavy fishing pressure and for finding out under-exploited and new areas.

3. The prawn fishery is multi-species in composition and operated by different types and sizes of gear. The CMFRI should work out statistical methods to compare the catch data by different gears, enabling detailed estimates on the landing of important prawn species for the marine prawn fishing centres of the country. Continuing data on catch per unit of fishing effort should be built up so that deleterious effect on fisheries could be diagnosed early. To enable reliable collection of data the CMFRI should bring out illustrated manuals for quick field identification of prawn species of commercial value. The capture fisheries of prawns should be regularly monitored by the CMFRI from different centres of the country to determine the effects of exploitation on stock. The information thus obtained should be quickly disseminated to the industry and governmental agencies for regulatory action, if any.

4. Prawn fishery statistics collected by CMFRI institutes should include detailed catch data on estuarine prawns which are now left out.

5. Model prawn culture farms should be established in suitable brackish water areas as extension centres.

6. In the context of prawn fisheries in particular, and fishing industry in general, the Indian Fisheries Act of 1897 should be replaced by a new legislation with necessary provisions for enforcing management and conservation measures. State fisheries organisations should institute a system of categorising and registering fishery boats undertaking prawn fishing with reference to operational bases and areas of fishing. Suitable regulatory measures should be introduced in appropriate areas to protect the stocks which should be regularly monitored by the CMFRI.

7. The CMFRI should evolve processing techniques for the nompenacid prawns caught in large quantities along with penacids for utilising them for export as well as for internal consumption.

8. The prawn waste obtained in processing plants should be utilised for the preparation of industrial products such as chitosan, peptone etc.

9. Separate financing arrangement for import of trawlers and their indigenous manufacture should be made. Material and machinery for processing and packaging should be made available to the industry on priority basis.

10. Systematic resource survey and assessment of deep water prawns should be urgently carried out for early commercial exploitation of this resource.

11. Investigations should be undertaken by CMFRI in coordination with CIFT for locating lobster grounds and finding out suitable types of gear and baits for expanding fishing effort for them with a view to increasing their production for export purposes.

12. State fisheries organisations, particularly of south-west coast, should undertake necessary measures to control lobster fisheries wherever it is over-exploited.

13. Detailed exploratory work on the resources of deep sea spiny lobsters should be undertaken by the CMFRI and the restructured deep sea fishing organisations.

14. Culture of the crab, *scylla serrata*, on pilot scale should be undertaken by the CMFRI and CIFRI in some select areas.

15. The CMFRI and CIFT should undertake the resource study of *squilla* fishery and its utilisation since they constitute an appreciable quantity of the trawl catch which is now being discarded.

16. There is an urgent need for diversification in the present trend of export of marine products. At present it is almost comprised of frozen prawn export from only a few centres in the country mostly to USA and Japan. This would involve the spread of fishing effort for prawns and development of necessary infrastructure to as many centres as possible and export of a variety of crustacean products to as many countries as possible.

17. Steps should be taken to bring about improvements in the processing sector for better quality products in smaller packs to avoid thawing, refreezing and repacking in the importing countries. This commodity should, as far as possible, be sold in the foreign markets under Indian trade labels. High standards for the products should be kept up by strict quality and inspection control.

18. Owing to the importance of fundamental

research on crustacea of commercial importance, field and laboratory facilities should be established with particular emphasis on endo-crinology, ecology, physiology and fishery biology. Research work on the migratory movements of different species of prawns of commercial importance in estuaries and in the sea should be intensified. ICAR should give priority in fishery research programmes to all aspects of prawn culture to make it economically feasible.

19. With considerable commercial importance of crustacea in both capture and culture fisheries of fresh, brackish and sea waters the ICAR should constitute a separate division for research on crustacea which in course of time could develop into an institute for crustacean research.

20. The government should set up a high level machinery for taking decisions regarding the exploitation, management, research, technology and utilisation of crustacean resources and trade, instead of decision making being fragmented in different ministries and departments of the same Ministry.

21. The fishermen who are primary producers of prawn should be given financial support for boats and gear for inceasing their production. They should be assisted to form cooperative marketing organisation.

22. There is ample scope for both small scale entrepreneurs and large business houses in the marine products trade and export industry. The large business houses should however be allowed to enter only on the basis of at least 50 per cent of the raw material from their own operations for their processing plants.

Marketing of Fish and Fishery Products

Summary of Recommendations

A summary of the main recommendations is as under :

1. Marketing base for marine fish caught in large quantities and comparatively cheap in price, should be extended to the Island areas, particularly in the eastern states where there is considerable demand for fish.

2. With a large variety of fishes composing marine catch and the demand getting concentrated only to a few popular and prime fishes, there is an imperative need of improving the marketability of lesser known fishes. The fish consuming public should be made conscious about the necessity of chilling fish for maintaining the freshness and nutritive value. The preparation of wholesome fish fillets on industrial scale should be encouraged. Fish offal obtained as by-product could be used for fishmeal manufacture. These objectives may be achieved through various media of mass communication.

3. To help data collection for market intelligence and evaluation of production economics, the states should examine the introduction of a system of standards for different types and sizes of marine fish at the primary marketing stage.

4. Hygienic marketing sheds should be provided at suitable fish landing centres.

5. The fish landing sites with adequate marketable surplus should be linked with nearest railway stations or motorable roads by providing feeder roads for quick transport and distribution of fish.

6. The state fishéries organisations and marketing authorities should jointly examine the question of eliminating unnecessary links in the prevailing trade practices and introduce the system of licensed functionaries to the best advantage of the producers and the consumers.

7. Fisheries co-operative should assume an increasing role in developing marketing functions by raising the standards of efficiency in marketing methods and by making marketing as an obligatory function in the bye-laws of the co-operatives. The co-operatives should be provided with necessary credit for working capital from governmental resources and from the financial institutions.

8. For improving quality control and inspection of fish and fishery products, short-term training courses should be organised at suitable central fisheries institutes for public health services personnel. Necessary national standards for analytical methods for quality control and inspection should be formulated jointly by the ISI and central and state fisheries organisations.

9. The CIFT should intensify research on proper procedures for chilling different types of fishes and then formulate necessary specifications on the methods of packing fish and ice in suitable containers with economical insulation materials as early as possible so that these could be adopted by the trade.

10. The CIFT should undertake pilot projects in co-ordination with state fisheries organisations to demonstrate the economic advantages of mechanical air-dryers over the existing traditional methods in some of the suitable areas where sun-drying of fish is being predominantly undertaken.

11. The central fisheries corporation in coordination with state fisheries corporations/organisations should establish freezing plants and storages near the production centres wherefrom bulk quantities of marine fish could be absorbed at comparatively

cheaper price. This would relieve gluts, thereby giving an economic advantage to the producers and also increase supplies of fish in seasons of shortage at reasonable price to the consumers even at distant centres, particularly in the sectors of the country where fish constitutes an important item of food.

12. For improving the transport system for carriage of iced and frozen fish to be sold as thawed fish (iced fish) the question of introducing insulated rail and road vans on a large scale to meet the expanding marketing activity should be examined as a step towards the development of refrigerated transport systems.

13. India's share in the international export trade of marine products being negligible, the MPEDA should intensify promotional measures to expand the export trade.

14. The anomaly regarding to assumption of the functions by the MPEDA with reference to development, conservation and management of off-shore and deep sea fisheries as laid down in the Act 13 of 1972 should be removed by the Government in the interest of this Authority directing its well-concerted efforts towards the promotion of export of marine products.

15. The installed freezing capacity remaining considerably unutilised, the MPEDA should examine the question of its increased utilisation for increasing exports of marine products and for freezing products for domestic consumption.

16. The MPEDA should increase the export of froglegs by popularising this product in affluent countries. The need for increasing production of froglegs both by capture and culture operations would then arise. For increasing production by capture operations the CIFRI should prepare detailed methodology and set guidelines for undertaking population surveys for commercial species of frogs by the state fisheries organisations. As regards culture operations, the ICAR should undertake a pilot project for establishing economic feasibility of frog culture with a view to adopting field practices in utilising fresh water swamps for frog culture.

17. With considerable prospects of increasing exports of diversified canned products by necessary promotional measures by MPEDA, it should not only be possible fully to utilise the installed fish canning industry to compete in the international export trade, empty cans, manufactured from imported tin plate, should be supplied at subsidised rates.

18. With main dependence for cured products only on Sri Lanka, the MPEDA should diversify the export of dried and cured products.

19. To improve the quality of export products, the MPEDA should set necessary guidelines and procedures for the processing sector of the fishing industry oriented for export purposes. Further the State Governments should give priority considerations to the adequate supplies of potable water and uninterrupted electricity supply to the fish processing industry and the Central Government should see that the export consignments are given expeditious clearance.

20. To increase production of fishmeal and incidentally fish oil in the same plants, introduction of a few small scale factory ships with fishmeal plants on board should be encouraged.

21. The CIFT should prepare techno-economic feasibility reports for manufacturing various minor fishery industrial products on small scale industry basis.

Forest Policy

Summary of Recommendations

The more important recommendations made in this chapter are given below :

1. Forests must have an adequate share of land for the productive, protective and aesthetic functions. There should be a minimum diversion of forest land for other purposes, and where some diversion does become inevitable an attempt should be made to make up the loss by bringing some other areas under forests.

2. No disforestation should be permitted without the approval of the State Legislature.

3. Functionally, all forest lands should be classified into :

(a) Protection Forests;
(b) Production Forests; and
(c) Social Forests.

4. A quick reconnaissance should be done in all the states to sub-divide the production forests into :

(a) mixed quality forests,
(b) valuable forests, and
(c) inaccessible forests.

5. Protective influences of the forests, specially on soil and water, should be developed in full by suitably managing the existing forests and providing for their rehabilitation and improvement.

6. The production forests should not be permitted to be diverted to any other forests use. Growing of plantation crops, like rubber, coffee, cashew etc., in suitable localities on forest lands may be undertaken, consistent with the objects of forest management under planting of such crops as turmeric, ginger, cardamom, etc. should also be encouraged, where possible.

7. Instead of supplying agricultural small timber and fuelwood to the rural population free or at concessional rates, a reasonable price should be charged.

8. Forest grazing should be strictly controlled and regulated for feeding of essential livestock. Wherever grasses can be grown in forest lands without detriment to tree growth, and where an effective demand for grasses exists, such lands should be utilised for grazing and for provision of hay for feeding livestock outside the forests. Grazing by goats in forest lands should be prohibited and that by sheep allowed only in specially earmarked grasslands under strict rotational control.

9. Shifting cultivation should be regulated, contained and replaced as expeditiously as possible, by resorting to agri-selvicultural methods apart from other methods. This should be explored, planned and implemented in co-operation with other concerned departments. But regulation of shifting cultivation should form a part of a wider plan for the tribal welfare.

10. Tribal welfare should also be ensured by satisfying their domestic needs of various forest products and by recognising the priority need of their direct employment in forestry operations.

11. Resources for forest raw materials, both for internal consumption and export, should be stepped up through large scale industrial plantations. An adequate investment of capital in forest based industries should be ensured in keeping with the production forestry programme. The forest based industries should be located to the extent possible nearer the source of raw materials, and their establishment should be carefully phased with the development of forest raw material. The price of the forest produce for the industries should be so fixed as to pay for the cost of clearfelling and plantations, and maintenance of production forests, and leave a profit.

12. In inaccessible areas, development of communications should be particularly ensured, so as to utilise the forest potential to the maximum extent possible.

13. Scientific and technologically superior exploitation techniques should be adopted to reduce wastage and improve efficiency of conversion.

14. Adequate protection should be afforded to wild life and plants, particularly of species with dwindling numbers. A core area, about 4 per cent of the forest lands, distributed amongst varied natural conditions and ecological associations, should be dedicated to nature and wildlife conservations. The core area should be surrounded by sizable areas of well managed forests.

15. Forest research should be accepted as basis to efficient forest management, and adequate funds provided for research both in forestry and forest products.

16. Extention and publicity work should be undertaken by the Forest Departments, for making the people tree and conservation conscious and for obtaining their goodwill and cooperation. The state should take steps to include nature conservation and environmental preservation in the curricula of schools and colleges.

17. Existing legislation on forestry should be strengthened for effective implementation of forest policy, and a revised all-India Forest Act enacted.

18. Forest administration should be strengthened at the professional level. The forest policy should recognise the need for :

(a) rational manpower planning by the centre and the states;

(b) adequate training at all levels of forest services; and

(c) coordination of forest and forest industries activities, particularly the planning of industrial investment in forestry.

19. Provision of employment of local people through forestry practices should be recognised as an important element, and all forestry works should be carried out either departmentally or through Forest Labour Cooperative Societies.

20. After obtaining the approval of a draft of the revised National Forest Policy by the Central Board of Forestry, it should be legislated by the states.

21. All forests under management of other departments of the Government should be transferred forth with to the Forest Department. Regulation and control of private forests by the states are imperative.

22. Social forestry, particularly farm forestry and extension forestry, should be adopted for increasing the tree wealth.

23. Steps should be taken to see that the increasing rural employment, created through production and social forestry and through development of minor forest produce, goes mainly to the socially backward, unemployed and underemployed agricultural labour.

Production and Social Forestry

Some important aspects of the production and social forestry have been dealt with by us in our Interim Reports on Production Forestry—Man-made Forests and Social Forestry. The recommendations made in the two Interim Reports may be referred to.

Some of the important recommendations made in this chapter are given below :

1. In order to meet the industrial wood requirement projected for 1980, 1985 and 2000 AD, an extent of about 48 million ha of forest lands should be identified immediately for being dedicated as production forests in use.

2. With regard to sawnwood and roundwood, studies should be taken up on consumption trend for the next 10 years, in order to revise the requirement on more realistic data.

3. A dynamic programme of social forestry should be taken up to supplement fuelwood and small timber production, in order to meet fully the requirement in the rural areas. The transportation of fuelwood to urban areas should be discouraged in the long run.

4. Forest lands should not be leased to the forest based industries for raising plantations to meet their own industrial wood requirement. The produce, however, should be allocated to different industries at an economic price.

5. Trade names for export purposes should be standardised. The Forest Research Institute, Dehra Dun should immediately take up preparation of publicity material, pointing out the characteristics and uses of each species and its equivalence with those already in demand in the export market.

6. Export of well known species that are in demand in the export market should be allowed liberally, and use of other available hardwood species popularised as substitutes in the domestic market. Export of roundwood, however, should be progressively discouraged and that of processed sawnwood and panel products encouraged.

7. The prospect of diversion of sawnwood for export should be studied in depth. Imposition of a severe excise duty on teak sawnwood should be considered so as to restrict domestic consumption.

8. It should be necessary to locate the areas of abundant availability of timber for establishing saw mills and other industries for export purposes, by undertaking an inventory of resources. In such saw mills, precision machinery should be installed and kiln-drying facility introduced. There should be a strict adherence to grading.

9. This country should be associated with the various technical and other studies being carried out by the Economic and Social Commission for Asia and the Pacific (ESCAP) in regard to timber exporting countries of Asia and the Pacific.

10. The installed capacity in the sawmilling industry should be such that over and above meeting the domestic needs completely by 1985 there is enough surplus capacity for export.

11. Over and above meeting the entire domestic requirement by 1985, at least an equal quantity of plywood and veneer should be exported through aggressive export promotion and production of quality materials.

12. For greater export of panel products, the markets in the West Asian and North African countries should be cultivated.

13. Glue of international quality and at international prices should be made available to plywood factories specially oriented towards export.

14. For increasing export of half-wrought and shaped wood products, market intelligence about the kind of wooden toys and articles in demand should be collected, Indian entrepreneurs encouraged to open shops in foreign countries and export promoted through the All-India Handicrafts Board.

15. An Export Promotion Council for forest products should be set up.

16. The forest development corporations should undertake promotion of exports and allocate necessary finance for it.

17. A suitable training programme should be devised for persons to be in charge of export oriented forest industries.

18. The range of species and quality of timber utilised in different forest based industries should continue to be extended in order that this country can enter the export market aggressively after meeting the domestic requirement or substitute imports of products like newsprint. Research is required to be initiated so that the number of simultaneously used wood species of mixed tropical forests is considerably widened for utilisation in the fibre board and pulp industries.

19. Since particle boards and fibre boards make a greater use of secondary raw materials and residues from logging, sawmilling and other industries, the poor record of production of these two categories of industries should be looked into.

20. The growing demand of the match industry should be met both by conserving the existing resource and by creating new plantations. In addition to raising plantation of traditional match wood species, poplar should be raised where feasible in pure plantations in forest areas and encouraged for planting under the programme of farm forestry.

21. All matchwood species should be reserved for the exclusive use of match industry. Expansion of large scale matchwood industry, particularly for making splints and veneers, may be confined in future to the Andaman & Nicobar Islands, in view of the shortage of matchwood in the mainlands.

22. A selective mechanisation in logging should be adopted, so that any impediments in opening up of inaccessible forest areas may be removed and a reduction in logging and transport cost effected. Generally the emphasis should be on mechanical innovations of lower technical sophistication, such as skyline cranes, ropeways, mountain tractors and improved logging tools.

23. For loading and unloading mechanisation should be adopted only where the quality of timber to be handled annually is large.

24. As far as possible no sale of timber standing in the forests should be made. After departmental logging, either through direct employment of local labour or through labour cooperatives, all timber should be brought to a sale depot outside the forests and sale should be made at that point only.

25. It should be necessary to plan for construction of about 2,15,000 km of additional forest roads in the next 25 years for successful implementation of production forestry programme.

26. A review of the fertiliser requirements, current as well as prospective, should be undertaken, and the requirement of the forestry sector arranged without any conflict with the agriculturists' demands.

27. The seed testing rules and seed certification scheme framed by the Forest Research Institute, Dehra Dun should be adopted by the State Forest Departments. The state forest research organisations should carry out selection of *plus* trees of important species and establish seed orchards and clone multiplication plots where necessary.

28. In the case of imported seeds, a list of quarantine procedure and regulations affecting trees, seeds, seedlings and wood products should be compiled, with a view to encouraging standardisation of plant quarantine regulations among countries leading eventually to greater reliance being placed on pre-entry quarantine inspections in the country of origin. There should be regular post-entry quarantine inspections of all nurseries and plantations raised on important seeds.

29. The Forest Department should identify the waste lands and marginal lands within the canal commands, and the estimates of the fund and water requirement where a minimum of 100 ha at one place is available for raising irrigated plantations, should be made for inclusion in the report for the irrigation project.

30. The Council of Forest Research and Education should initiate research on the water consumption of different species in order to minimise the expense on irrigation as well as to avoid over-irrigation.

31. The forest planning cell in the Union Ministry of Agriculture and Irrigation should take up a study of the quantum of institutional credit required by the forest development corporations at least upto the year 1985.

32. Amendment of the tax laws should be considered so that reasonable deductions are allowed to the forest development corporations, from the next income from the sale of the existing crop, for creation and maintenance of man-made forests on the felled areas.

33. The programme of identification of forest diseases and insects should be enlarged and check lists prepared giving their geographical distribution as well.

34. Secondary species and less valuable timber should be used for domestic requirement after seasoning and chemical treatment. The Government departments should give more importance to the use of such timber.

35. Before deciding upon any control measures, the impact of the disease or insect attack should be evaluated, if possible, by techniques of cost-benefit analysis, and the feasibility and the magnitude of control measures worked out. The control measures would broadly be : (a) biological and silvicultural, (b) chemical, (c) integrated management, and (d) quarantine.

36. Genetic control should also be resorted to by breeding strains, immune or less prone to non-injurious organisms. Chemical control should be used after careful consideration of the effect of chemical on non-target organisms, which may include the predators or parasites of the target organisms and many others useful to man.

37. While taking up man-made forests programme, the eventualities of increased danger from disease and insect pests should be considered and protective measures provided for before undertaking the programme.

38. Exemption of the value of trees standing on agricultural land (not being trees in any orchard or plantations) from wealth tax should form a permanent provision in the Wealth Tax Act.

39. The condition, management and improvement of forest lands in the river-valley catchments should, as a matter of rule, be a concern of the watershed management programme. Particular attention should be paid to the degraded forest lands in the catchments, and they should be brought back to proper condition through reforestation wherever necessary.

40. In order to get full benefit from forest management in catchment areas, measures suggested with respect to forest grazing, shifting cultivation and forest protection in sections 11 and 12 of this chapter

and in chapter 43 should be rigorously pursued.

41. The degraded lands in the catchments outside the forest should be brought under social forestry, either for plantation of quick growing fuel species or for development of grasslands and grass reserves by linking it up with the programme of improvement of livestock.

42. The ravines starting from their upper end to their confluence with the main river should be treated as a whole. In general, the heads of the ravines should be treated for developing grassland, while the middle to lower slopes and deep ravines should be tackled by afforestation, supplemented by necessary engineering structures. Grazing should be prohibited in the treated areas and only cutting of grass allowed.

43. The technique already evolved by the Punjab Forest Department for afforestation for the control of *chos* and reclamation of *cho* lands should be extensively adopted.

44. The degree of regulating grazing in forests should be guided by their classification according to the functions they are primarily to fulfil under management. Attempts should be made to prohibit grazing in protected forests. In the production forests, grazing can be treated only as a fringe benefit. The provision of grazing and grass would be one of the primary objectives of social forestry.

45. Research should be taken up immediately for fixing the optimum carrying capacity of all types of forests including those to be created under social forestry programme. A few upper catchments of river valley projects should be selected for investigations on the effect of grazing on soil and water conservation.

46. People owning livestock in the vicinity of wildlife preserves should be persuaded to take to stall feeding, for which permission to cut grass and fodder in a controlled manner may be given.

47. Grazing rules should be promulgated by each State Government, specifying the grazing rates and providing for the manner in which grazing should be permitted, grazing units constituted, carrying capacity fixed, grazing and closure cycle indicated and administration of rules carried out.

48. Grazing rates should be upgraded substantially to curb non-essential cattle in forests, though grazing should not be looked upon as a source of revenue.

49. Grazing should be completely prohibited in the young regeneration areas, grasses should be allowed to be cut from these areas and the hay utilised for feeding the essential livestock outside the forests.

50. Where a large programme of grassland development is taken up by the Forest Departments, they should employ adequate number of agrostologists/ agronomists and range management specialists. In the state forest research organisations, these specialists should conduct research in collaboration with the agricultural universities and experts from Agriculture, Animal Husbandry and Sheep Development Departments.

51. The improvement and maintenance of grasslands and open forests suitable for management as grass reserves should be part of a multidisciplinary approach to the livestock feeds and fodder problem, as elaborated in the text.

52. Plantation of fodder trees should be taken up as a part of social forestry, and the programme should be coupled with those for hay making and ensilage on a wide scale of livestock development. Provisions should be made in the working plans and project plans for allowing lopping of fodder leaves in the felling coupes just ahead of the felling.

53. The approach to the solution of the problem of shifting cultivation should be by permanently settling the shifting cultivators along with a simultaneous programme of afforestation through agri-silvicultural methods, pasture and grassland development, introduction of horticulture crops as well as plantation crops.

54. Suitable areas in the lower reaches and valley, lands and on gentle slopes should be terraced for fixed agriculture by the shifting cultivators. Before taking up the works, the possibility of continued financing of maintenance of terraces and institutional arrangements for irrigation, seed, fertiliser, etc. should be ensured.

55. Fair price shops should be opened for assured supply of essential commodities at reasonable rates to the tribals, including opening of *nistar bhandars* (depots) for supply of domestic requirement of the tribals in respect of forest produce.

56. The tribals should be allotted homestead lands, where programmes of afforestation, pasture and grassland development, introduction of horticulture crops, etc. are taken up.

57. The tribals should be trained for absorption in the forest based industries that may be set up as a part of commercial production forestry programme in the tribal areas, so that dependence on outside labour is reduced.

58. The Forest Departments should coordinate all activities concerning the problem of shifting cultivation. Adequate use of the organisational capacities of the Forest Departments should be made to tackle the problem of tribal development generally. There should be multidisciplinary approach and involvement right from the planning stage.

59. The economic development of the Andaman

and Nicobar Islands should be based on the forest development programmes.

60. The existing working plan organisation should be strengthened for preparing a production oriented management plan for forests of South, Middle and North Andamans. A new working plan organisation should also be set up for taking up immediately the initial working plan works in other islands. A planning and project formulation cell should be established under the chief conservator of forests immediately, so that the planning of chosen existing and new industries can also start simultaneously.

61. A research centre should be established at Port Blair immediately and by 1980 converted into a fullfledged regional research institute in order to strengthen the research base in the Islands and to provide information for preparing production oriented management plan.

62. A Forest Department Corporation in the Islands should be set up very early in line with the recommendations in our Interim Report on Production Forestry—Man-made Forests.

63. The Logging Training Centres Project in Dehra Dun should be associated with preparing logging plans suited to the topography and environmental conditions of the Islands. Importance should be attached for the completion of logging plans before the proposed corporation starts functioning.

64. For the integrated approach to planning for development of forest and forest based industries locations should be carefully selected so that these become the focal points of growth in the economy of the Islands.

65. Arrangements should be made for direct shipping of forest products from the Islands for export to foreign countries for which port and loading facilities should be developed in the focal points of growth.

66. Mechanisation of felling and transport and an efficient system of water transport should be evolved. Knowhow and expertise from other countries should be arranged. A study team of the Government of India should visit Malaysia and Indonesia to get information about the methods and facilities of loading and stowage of forest products for export.

67. While the type and quality of labour to be imported from the mainland should be regulated and tied to different development programmes, the Island Administration should introduce training schemes for generating skills in the prospective employees of the settler population.

68. A mainland posting of forestry personnel in the professional grade may be alternated with a posting on the Islands, if this does not work satisfactorily, the possibility of the distribution of the Island cadre to some of the mainland states for the purpose of an exchange of posting may be considered.

69. For running the public sector industries and logging operations, the employment of retired defence services officers should be considered.

70. Building and other amenities should be constructed in a planned way in the selected growth centres and the headquarters of the forest and other departments should be suitably dispersed in the centres.

71. In the cold desert areas of Ladakh in Jammu and Kashmir and Lahaul-Spiti and Hangrang Valley in Himachal Pradesh, future forest development activities should be taken up with the active involvement of the local population, mainly to meet their requirements of fuel, fodder and small timber.

72. Provision of improved fodder for the local livestock through range management and grassland development should have the utmost priority. It will be necessary to regulate the entry of migratory graziers strictly in accordance with the carrying capacity of the grazing runs.

73. For a large scale afforestation and pasture development programme, a separate canal system with field channels should be constructed. Adequate administrative organisation should be built up, as suggested in the text.

74. Indiscriminate introduction of species should not be made, unless supported by an intensive research effort. Experimentation on conservation and best utilisation of available water should be taken up by the concerned agricultural development department and its findings should be available to the forestry personnel for optimum utilisation of water resource.

75. The Government of India should set up a centre for forest research on cold desert at Leh (Ladakh) with an experimental station under it in the Lahaul-Spiti area. Among other things, research should be taken up on improvement of alpine pastures, introduction of legumes, identification of deep rooted quick growing hardy species suitable for fuel and fodder, etc.

76. The Central Board of Forestry should regularly meet every two years and its standing committee more frequently. The institution of the standing committee should be more effectively used.

77. The Central Forestry Commission must meet once in three months and perform the functions indicated in the text, its strength should be augmented, so that it can function effectively as a permanent coordinating body at the professional and techincal level, in addition to providing the necessary support to the Central Board of Forestry and its standing committee.

78. There should be a fullfledged Department of Forests in the Ministry of Agriculture and Irrigation with the Inspector General of Forests as the Secretary in-charge of the Department. The Department should have three Divisions, namely (a) Division of Forest Inventory, Planning and Evaluation, (b) Division of Wildlife and (c) Division of Forest Research and Education. Each Division should be under the charge of an Additional Inspector General of Forests with the rank of Additional Secretary to the Government of India.

79. The Chief Conservator of Forests should function as Secretary to the Government, and where there are more than one Chief Conservator of Forests in a state, the Principal Chief Conservator of Forests should be accorded.

80. Each state should set up a committee under the Chief Conservator of Forests to fix up norms for delimiting circles, divisions, sub divisions, ranges, etc. both for territorial and non-territorial charges. Special functions of planning, utilisation, wildlife management, research and education, etc. should be taken into account.

81. The augmentation of the education and training facilities for different categories of forestry personnel should be planned somewhat ahead of the period in which the personnel are required to be in position, and should be based on the requirement projected in the text.

Minor Forest Product

Summary of Recommendations

Some of the more important recommendations are summarised below :

1. There should be a uniform legislation on the possession and transit of sandalwood applicable to all the states.

2. Export of sandalwood billete should be gradually reduced, and instead distillation of oil and the products of cottage industries based on sandalwood carving should be developed for export.

3. The tempo of artificial regeneration of sandalwood in afforestation programmes in sandal bearing areas should be increased, and possibilities of growing sandal in other parts of the country explored. The research on sandal spike disease should be intensified.

4. A target of production of 1.2 million tonnes of oil by 2000 AD should be planned through the use of various minor oil seeds of tree and shrub origin. Necessary incentives should be given to industries for using larger quantities of such minor oil seeds.

5. Research and extension efforts should be directed towards popularising the deoiled *sal* meal for cattle and poultry feed.

6. A survey of *harra* tree (*Terminalia chebula* Retz.) should be taken up to determine the total number of trees and the average yield of drupes per tree in order to estimate the production of myrabolan. Experiments regarding the successful raising of myrabolan plantations mixed with other species should be undertaken. Plantations of exotic species, like wattle and *schinopsis lorentzu* ENgl., should be extended.

7. Well equipped factories for the manufacture of tannin extracts from all tannin yielding materials should be set up as early as possible to maximise the earnings from exports. Existing capacities for myrabolan crushing should be fully utilised, and new capacity added, in order that more and more crushed myrabolans may be exported.

8. An effective coordination must be established between the national and state agencies responsible for production of tannin bearing raw materials, their industrial processing and export.

9. For *katha* manufacture, availability of raw material of required specifications and in quantities within economic lead should be assured over a period. Steps should be taken to take up a more scientific method of production to reduce wastage.

10. To increase the production of gums from existing natural resources, the methods of collection have to be improved. Future availability may be increased by raising new plantations.

11. Apart from adopting better methods of collection of pine resin, the installed capacity of the Government factories should be augmented, so that a larger percentage of crude can be processed. With a view to increasing export of rosin, its quality should be improved by installing modern machinery. The industry should take up diversification of products for import substitution.

12. In order to meet the requirements of different types of vegetable drugs and insecticides, attempts should be made to improve collection of raw materials from forests. A study should be undertaken, and reviewed from time to time, regarding the future requirement of vegetable drugs and pyrethrum. Cultivation of concerned plants should be undertaken in suitable localities in forest areas.

13. The production of good quality *bidi* leaves should be increased and wastage avoided by improving the methods of collection, transport, grading and storage. Research should be initiated or intensified in relation to pruning/pollarding of trees, pest control, rotational working, regeneration, etc.

14. Cultivation, processing and marketing of lac should be considered as an integral industrial venture. The activities concerning lac cultivation and processing should be taken up as parts of both drought prone areas programme and tribal development programme.

15. Wide fluctuations in lac production experienced in the past should be minimised and increase in production to be achieved by :

(i) arranging supply of broodlac to needy cultivators;
(ii) taking suitable extension measures;
(iii) arranging suitable demonstrations; and
(iv) guaranteeing a minimum remunerative price to the primary producers.

16. Arrangements for marketing and storage of the primary products, namely stick lac and seedlac, should be streamlined. There should be an effective link up between state minor forest produce organisations, cultivators' cooperative societies, manufacturers of shellac and exporters.

17. Research on selection and management of host plants, finding out new hosts, etc. for lac should be intensified. Effective control of lac predators, broodlac preservation, improvements in processing techniques, etc. should be subjects of further intensive study.

18. Attempts should be made to take up wood distillation commercially after making a thorough feasibility study, specially in areas from where extraction of fuelwood is uneconomical.

19. Greater attention should be paid to identified traditional markets for each kind of produce. Market intelligence should be collected from abroad. Agmark standards for all important items of MFP should be developed and enforced to ensure confidence in Indian products. A pre-shipment inspection by the national export organisation should be made compulsory.

20. A study of the problems of increasing export of gum *karaya* should be undertaken. Tapping of gum *karaya* on scientific lines should be introduced in all the concerned states.

21. More concentrated efforts should be made to develop the widely varied markets for export of lac products, and to gear their production, quality control etc. Benefit of increasing export prices should be passed on to the cultivators/collectors.

22. Export of *bidi* leaves should be channelised through a national export organisation for forest products.

23. Amongst the non-traditional items, greater efforts should be made for increased export of rosin, gum *ghatti* (obtained from *Anogeissus latifolia* Edgew.), kuth (*san ssuria* lapp a C.B. Cl.) root, nux-vomica (*strychnos nux-vomica* Linn.) dried rape seed, sandalwood chips and dust, palmarosa oil and vetiver oil.

24. The states with sizable resources of a particular product, or groups of products, may each set up a Minor Forest Products Corporation exclusively for collection, processing and marketing of the material handled. In other states, it would be desirable to have a separate forest circle devoted exclusively to this work. Collection should be arranged through normal field staff of the Forest Departments and they should be paid honoraria for the purpose.

25. The actual collection and at least the initial processing of minor forest produce should be done either by direct recruitment of labour or through labour cooperative societies, and the system of intermediaries should be abolished.

26. The development of minor forest produce resources and their utilisation for the benefit of the national economy should be the primary responsibility of the State Forest Departments. The minor forest produce corporations should be manned by competent technical personnel with suitable training.

27. The survey of minor forest produce by the state inventory organisations should aim at collecting data on the distribution, processing, grading, storage, transport, marketing, prices, utilisation, etc. Wherever corporations come to be established, they should promote, and simultaneously extend financial support, for the investigation.

28. Nationalisation should be resorted to in respect of trade in certain products, like *tendu* leaves, sandalwood, gum *karaya*, bamboo, myrabolan, resin, etc. Sandalwood oil industry should also be nationalised.

29. Labour should be trained in proper and methodical collection, quality control and grading. The trained labour should be encouraged to form labour cooperative societies. Forestry personnel should be trained in marketing strategy.

30. The industries processing minor forest products should be located wherever possible near the source of raw material, and provision should be made for proper storage and marketing of the products, including timely transportation to consumer centres.

31. There should be an organisation at the all-India level for tackling different matters connected with export of minor forest produce, particularly for ensuring quality control, undertaking market research and export promotion, and gathering and disseminating information on production costs and sale prices.

32. With proper investments and organisational support on the lines recommended, it should be possible to increase the present employment level of

250 million man-days to 1,000 million by 2000 AD. Such employment should be regarded as alleviation of seasonal unemployment/under employment.

33. Wages should always be paid in cash and linked to production with quality checks by way of sample testing in terms of yield of final product. Incentive plans should be prepared to get higher collection and better quality of products.

Forest Ecology and Wildlife Management

Summary of Recommendations

The more important recommendations made in this chapter are given below :

1. The coverage of preservation plots should be increased to attain a fair percentage of all the recognised subtypes.

2. A list of protected trees in the country should be prepared by the Forest Research Institute, Dehra Dum (FRI) and deficiencies discovered regarding coverage of important species should be made good by joint action of the State Forest Departments and the FRI.

3. The Forest Departments should demarcate a few nature reserves to preserve forest areas and wetlands under virgin or near virgin conditions.

4. Where coppice systems are adopted, environmental considerations should be carefully balanced with silvicultural considerations and convenience of working.

5. In the man-made forestry programme, safeguard against likely environmental ill-effects should be taken by a correct identification of the programme area.

6. It should be possible to plant up in multiple rows the strips on the sides of roads, canals and railway lines for creating better aesthetic effects along with meeting other demands through extension forestry on such lands. Whenever the highways pass through some interesting landscape planting should be adjusted with suitable gaps to make viewing possible. *Ficus* trees, *neem*, etc. should be introduced along with other quick growing species, so that these trees can provide food to the birds, which would otherwise descend on the cultivated fields.

7. Recreation forests should be developed with aesthetic considerations, and alignment and specification of the roads and paths should be made with the idea of creating and maintaining natural forest character.

8. The structures in the forest should be so planned that aesthetics are preserved. The design and siting of all structures in national parks, wild life sanctuaries and nature reserves should be put up for approval by the Indian Board of Wildlife (IBWL) or the State Wildlife Advisory Boards concerned. In particular, care should be taken not to create multistoreyed or large concrete structures that do not merge well with the surrounding forests. In other forest areas, the Forest Departments should generally follow the trends set by the Wildlife Boards.

9. All private advertisement hoardings in the forests should be prohibited, and the signboards of plantation etc. should be small in conspicuous and so fixed as not to obstruct the natural features.

10. The object of habitat management for Wildlife should be to have as large a population and as varied a composition as is compatible with the carrying capacity of the habitat. To coordinate forest management with that of wildlife areas, the forest working plans should recognise the conservation and scientific management of wildlife in all forest areas as one of the general objectives of management.

11. The states which have not adopted the Wildlife (Protection) Act 1972 should be persuaded to do so.

12. There should be a provision in the 1972 Act for constituting the IBWL, with adequate representation of the State Wildlife Advisory Boards in the IBWL. The scope of the functions of the IBWL should be enlarged.

13. The coverage of wildlife preservation areas (national parks and sanctuaries) should also be extended to the following four major forest types, where there are no wildlife preservation areas at present : (a) montane wet temperate forests, (b) sub-tropical broad-leaved hill forests, (c) Himalayan dry temperate forests, and (d) sub-tropical dry evergreen forests.

14. The boundaries of the national parks and sanctuaries should have sufficient buffer zone to cover the range of movement of wildlife in these areas. Grazing and collection of forest produce should be prohibited in the core areas. Habitat manipulation should aim at providing maximum facilities and protection to the local fauna so as to raise the population density to the maximum carrying capacity.

15. The game areas outside national parks and sanctuaries should be divided into convenient shooting blocks or shooting reserves depending on availability of games, etc. Availability of all forms of wildlife in each shooting block should be assessed periodically so that game in excess of an optimum genetically viable number may be fixed for cropping. The bag limits prescribed for each kind should always err on the safe side of the above number.

16. There should be uniformity with regard to game rules and regulations at least in contiguous blocks of

forests if not cover the whole country. The close season should be uniform as far as possible, and the reproductive biology of the game animals should be taken into account for fixing the close season. Model rules should be drafted by the Central Government to cover hunting regulations, payment of fees, etc.

17. All the species threatened with extinction as listed in Appendix 44.1 should be included in schedule I of the 1972 Act. In the case of big game, they should be brought under the list of protected animals for at least 5 years and their exploitation should be only for scientific purposes.

18. In the management of forests, the sequence and arrangement of areas taken up for regeneration fellings should be such that they proceed from the fringe towards the heart of the forest.

19. The state forest corporations should be responsible for development and management of wildlife in areas transferred to their control. Environmental considerations should also guide the corporations' working of the forests. Their requirement of staff for development of wildlife and recreation should be obtained from the wildlife wing of the forest services.

20. For administration, management and conservation of wildlife the State Governments should establish a separate wildlife wing in the Forest Departments directly under the Chief Conservators of Forests as recommended by the IBWL. The strength of the wildlife wing in each state should be adequately built up for effective wildlife conservation in areas inside and outside the forests.

21. There should be a Division of Wildlife under the Inspector General of Forests, headed by an officer of the rank of Additional IGF, who should be assisted by three Directors in the rank of Deputy IGF.

22. The personnel in the wildlife wing should directly manage the national parks and sanctuaries, and dual control by having a separate territorial staff or officer with overlapping wildlife staff should be eliminated. In the rest of the forest areas, the territorial staff should be responsible for wildlife management.

23. There should be a strong publicity machinery to produce popular literature and audio-visual material on wildlife for free distribution and display in educational institutions and rural congregations. The help of spoken and visual media, community centres and village teachers, etc. should be enlisted, and popular literature, journals and magazines devoted towards environmental role of forests should be published. The local bodies, like the *panchayats* should be actively involved in wildlife conservation movements.

24. Master plans to cover at least 10 years should be prepared for wildlife management, including development of national parks, sanctuaries, etc. and the plan allocations channelised on need-based priorities to the schemes so drawn up. It would also be worth while to raise trust by taking donations for financing selected projects of national importance aimed at conservation of selected species likely to become extinct.

25. The Council of Forest Research and Education (CFRE) should select suitable forestry personnel or outside specialists for entrusting them with specific wildlife research projects. The CFRE should set up a strong research cell in the FRI, and in each state there should be adequate wildlife research personnel.

26. The syllabi in biology, physics, chemistry, geography, social sciences and other related disciplines should be suitably modified for incorporating environmentalist ideas. A core of teachers should be trained through short lecture courses in environmental concepts to train further batches of teachers.

27. Post-graduate interdisciplinary courses of study for vocations in the field of natural resources should be opened in more and more universities.

28. All the professional training institutes dealing with land use, e.g., agricultural universities etc., should include in their training programme a course of lectures on environmental conservation. Visiting experts from other institutes and universities should be invited where the teaching faculties do not have the facilities for running such courses. The Forest Research Institute and Colleges, Dehra Dun can be called upon to provide lectures dealing with the role of forestry and wildlife in environmental conservation.

29. Short courses on wildlife and environment should be devised for all levels of forestry personnel. Undergoing such short courses should be compulsory for the personnel to be inducted in the wildlife wing. The staff for this purpose in the FRI should be suitably augmented.

30. The CFRE should organise in collaboration with the Indian Veterinary Research Institute (IVRI) and the agricultural universities a survey on major diseases affecting wildlife for devising preventive measures, and an investigation on the importance of stress in causing or accentuating disease conditions among wildlife.

31. Experienced veterinarians in each State Veterinary Department should be trained in diagnosis and prophylactic treatment of diseases among wildlife and they should be made available to forest authorities, whenever required. Every national park/sanctuary should employ qualified veterinary staff to look after the work of prevention and treatment of

diseases of wildlife.

32. The forest officers concerned with wildlife management should be trained for a short period in the actiology and symptomatology of the commonly occurring infectious diseases of wildlife.

33. A systematic survey of the commonly occurring infectious and deficiency diseases among wildlife animals in captivity should be organised by the CFRE in collaboration with the IVRI and the agricultural universities, for devising suitable preventive measures and curative treatment.

34. For developing wildlife tourism, a few selected national parks and sanctuaries should be taken up for development. More national parks should be set up in special category areas, e.g. marine, mountain and desert, to effectively preserve and display the typical habitat of these areas and their characteristic fauna and flora for the purpose of tourism and research. The state authorities should be actively involved in wildlife tourism development effort.

Forest Protection and Law

Summary of Recommendations

Some of the more important recommendations are given below :

1. Record of forest fires should be maintained by all the states under a uniform classification, types and causes as per proforma prescribed in Appendix 45.1, with a view to planning fire prevention measures.

2. Voluntary associations should be organised with local leadership to support administrative measures for protection of forests from fire.

3. Letters of appreciation and cash rewards should be granted to local *panchayats* and voluntary associations in fireprone areas for their fruitful cooperation and assistance.

4. Publicity for protection of forests from fire should be ensured both among urban and rural groups of population, particularly by an imaginative use of the audio-visual medium.

5. There should be a provision for the award of enhanced punishment in the case of wilful fire damage to a forest, provision for summary trials of offences relating to forest fires may be made either by appointment of special magistrates or by investing gazetted forest officers with magisterial powers. In case of repeated man-caused fires, the Government may suspend rights and privileges of the community in the locality.

6. A network of lookout stations should be built. The practice of engaging local people for detection and suppression of forest fires should be widely adopted, but the employment should be related to performance.

7. A reliable communication and transport system should be built up for fire control. Main roads, subsidiary roads, inspection paths, etc. should be so planned that they become part of a well planned system of fire breaks/fire lines. The benefit occurring due to fire protection should be included for determining the cost-benefit ratio of road projects.

8. Fuel condition for a particular forest area in the form of maps should be prepared for all fire-prone areas previously identified. The maps should show the probable rate of spread of fire and resistance to control. The concept of "fuel types", to guide the mapping, should be developed by the Forest Research Institute, Dehra Dun.

9. There should be well planned fire protection organisation in the states, particularly in those having fire-prone forest areas, specifically, it would be necessary to develop an efficient system of fire protection to safeguard the investment in man-made forestry.

10. Training programmes in fire detection, prevention and suppression should be arranged for all levels of field officers.

11. Research on various topics concerning forest fires should be properly organised. A research project involving the states having fire-prone areas should be evolved and centrally coordinated by the Forest Research Institute, Dehra Dun.

12. *Nistar*, i.e. the rights and privileges in forests, should be regularised in such a manner that on the one hand the deserving people get their essential requirement conveniently and at reasonable rates, and on the other the productivity of the forests is maintained. Wood/bamboos should be supplied after treating them with preservatives, which would result in their distribution at longer intervals.

13. All unclassed and protected forests should be constituted into reserved forest at the earliest possible, in order that *nistar* could be extinguished as far as possible in the manner provided in the forest law.

14. Large scale social forestry programme should be taken up in such a way as to make it possible to meet the needs of rural people for forest produce from readily accessible area and thereby decrease the burden on production forestry.

15. The villagers should not be allowed to collect *nistar* themselves from the forests. Instead, *nistar bhandars* (depots) may be established at convenient places by the Forest Departments for meeting the bonafide requirements of the people, and a change to include the cost of production, transport, depot charges as also a nominal profit should be made.

Ultimately *nistar* should be abolished. The system of commutation, known as *nistar* cess, should also be abolished.

16. Where necessary as an interim measure, as for as possible separate areas of forests should be set aside for meeting the nistar demand. Association of panchayats for protection of nistar forests should be secured. Once nistar forests are demarcated, no rights and privileges should be allowed in forests reserved for production forestry and for conservation of nature of environment.

17. Where disforestation takes place, nistar rights should be proportionately abolished.

18. Wherever the nistar demand is acute, wasteland available nearby should be utilised for producing fuel and hay as also other products considered indispensable by the nistaris.

19. For logging as well as for other forest works, a representative of the village institution (panchayat) should be associated when payments to workers are made.

20. To protect the forests from destruction and unauthorised encroachments, more employment opportunities should be created in forest operations and for that purpose sufficient funds should be allocated for forest development.

21. There should be an all-India Forest Act enacted by the parliament for the sake of uniformity. It should be possible to frame the Act in such a manner that the states are free to make subsidiary rules and regulations under the Act to solve any special situations.

22. The provisions for creating 'village forests' in the Act should reflect the approach regarding creation of forests on waste lands belonging to Government and the community and on parts of degraded forest lands, to meet the requirement of the villages, subsidiary rules and regulations to manage these 'social forests' should be made by the states.

23. There should be provision in the Act for setting up a national/regional agency for rational use of forest resources, both internally and for export.

24. There should be a provision in the Act that no disforestation should be permitted without the approval of the State Legislatures and that where some diversion of forest lands for other uses becomes inevitable an attempt should be made to make up the loss by bringing some other areas under forests.

25. A revised all-India Act should be framed, instead of amending the Indian Forest Act, 1927. Attempt should be made to evolve a consensus in the Central Board of Forestry on a suitable draft, to be prepared by the Central Forestry Commission.

Forest Planning, Research and Education

Summary of Recommendations

Some of the more important recommendations contained in this chapter are summarised below :

1. A survey on the national scale of a more generalised nature should be a pre-condition for deciding priorities for the selection of areas for detailed pre-investment studies.

2. For working plans, particularly in areas where fairly intensive forest management is being practised it is necessary to have maps on 1:15,000 or 1:25,000 scales. For normal forest management purposes, aerial photographs on 1:50.000 scale would suffice. In areas of special interest and for those intensively managed or under man-made forests, aerial photographs should be on 1:20,000 scale.

3. Space photography from Indian Scientific Satellite should be used for rapid forest survey in areas which are little known.

4. A National Forest Survey Organisation should be set up, and its programme should encompass the following elements :

(a) resource analysis, (b) Current and prospective supply of goods and services, (c) current and prospective demand for goods and services, (d) technical support services, and (e) methodological development.

5. For analysing current and prospective supply, some kind of permanent plot system that can be measured in part or in entirety over different periods should be established. Systematic sample and continued use of clustered ground sample should be used. Each unit in a cluster should cover a relatively large area.

6. Adequate information should be collected on growth, mortality, cull, increment and removal rates, as also data for pricing of future timber supplies.

7. Changes and trends in wood use over time, as well as absolute amounts should be determined; and this information should be used along with census data etc. to make estimates of aggregate present and future wood requirement. An iteration between supply and demand at various price levels should be done.

8. A national forest information system should be developed, to act as a data bank in respect of information required for planning, implementation, evaluation and modification, as and when required.

9. While the coverage, accuracy and break up of the data for different levels would be different, there should be a common layout and format so that

data could readily flow from the district or project level to the state and regional level and then to the national level.

10. For building up an efficient national forest information system, the requirements are; (a) national forest inventory, (b) national timber trend studies, and (c) data processing.

11. The standard forms for collection of forestry statistics should be revised and re-grouped into : (a) periodic forestry statistics, and (b) annual forestry statistics. The collection of periodic forestry statistics should be so organised that the data collected prove useful for formulating the five year plans. Annual forestry statistics should be collected from different sources.

12. The chief conservator of forest and the crop reporting authority at the state level should get together and take steps to eliminate the discrepancy in the statistics of area under forests. Clearcut procedures should be laid down for up-dating of the records every year and publication of one set of figures by both the agencies.

13. Production statistics should be improved in quality and their scope enlarged.

14. Movement of forest produce from one state to another should be collected by sample studies undertaken in the concerned sectors of the industry.

15. Steps should be taken for improving in quality and scope, price and cost statistics for forest produce in the manner suggested in the text.

16. Detailed data of labour employment in various forestry activities and forest industries should be collected and assessed.

17. For co-ordination and linking of the forestry activities with other activities in the district, the data from the forest divisions should be collected in such a manner as to enable them to be split or combined by districts.

18. For achieving the national growth goals, there should be three distinct levels in planning—(a) national plan, (b) regional or state plan, and (c) local plan. Planning could be both from the top at the national level or from the bottom at the local or project level. The national production goals should be split into regional targets. The latter in turn should be split into local targets with a view to producing specified products from specified areas. The core industry and its location should be identified in advance, so that the development of forestry production programme through local or project plans could be planned around such a core industry.

19. As far as possible, the area management plan should be replaced by purpose or production or industry oriented project plan.

20. An industry oriented management plan should be designed for the production of fixed quantities of the raw materials of the prescribed specifications to cater to the requirements of the industry or industries with which the plan is linked. Maximum utilisation of the various products and by-products from the same area or the same tree should be an essential feature of the plan. There may be different area coverages for different types of raw materials, when required by the same industry.

21. The satisfaction of the bonafide domestic needs of the local community from the operational areas itself or from separate areas reserved for the purpose should be a part of the industry oriented management plan.

22. Creation of local employment should be specifically taken care of in the preparation of industry oriented management plans.

23. The biological requirement of the species occurring and the species that are proposed to be introduced should be the primary consideration in the formulation of the industry oriented management plans.

24. The provision of financial and other inputs including staff and equipment, should form an integral part of the sanction of the plan by a competent authority.

25. The first phase of the industry oriented management plan should be the optimum utilisation of the existing crop (crop I). The second crop (crop II) need not be a reproduction of the original crop but should be planned for the actual requirement of the existing and projected industries.

26. There should be a Division of Forest Inventory Planning and Evaluation under the Inspector General of Forests, headed by an Additional Inspector General of Forests. The Division should have two wings, each in charge of a Chief Coordinator in the rank of Deputy Inspector General of Forests : (a) national forest survey and (b) planning cell as recommended in the Interim Report on Production Forestry Man-made Forests.

27. National forest survey organisation should be built up by expanding the existing pre-investment survey of forest resources. The entire forest area should be surveyed every 10 years.

28. A pattern should emerge in which the state would be responsible for collection of statistical data sought for by the regional units of the Central Government, who would process and analyse the data and maintain the information bank for feeding the states with the necessary data and assisting them in their planning work. In the states, resource survey and planning organisations should be created

29. There should be an Advisory Council at the Centre to advise on the policy of forest surveys and priority to be assigned and to provide necessary coordination with the concerned industries.

30. There should be regional technical committees, one for each region, to decide the details on technical working, inter-relationships of forest surveys with local plans and connected matters and to suggest priority for surveys.

31. Specific action in the matter on centre-state coordination in forest development planning should be taken as suggested.

32. Statistical organisations should be set up in the State Forest Departments in the manner suggested in the text. The existing statistical unit in the Central Forestry Commission should be developed into a fulfledged statistical division.

33. The regional technical committee, to be set up by the Council of Forest Research and Education for identification of research problems should consider, and give due importance to, the topics of research indicated in broad outlines.

34. Problem-oriented multidisciplinary research centres should be established by the Central Government for research on (a) latosols vis-a-vis forest management practices, and (b) sandal spike disease.

35. The unit of industrial design, the establishment of which has been recommended in the Interim Report on Forest Research and Education, should design machinery for developing economic units for industries, particularly for utilisation of logs of smaller girth by the plywood factories and for the establishment of small economic pulp and paper mills.

36. A collaboration with the Council of Scientific and Industrial Research should be established in utilisation and industrial research.

37. There should be one or two separate college(s) for the in-service education and training of officers recruited to the State Forest Services.

38. The suggested revised pattern of in-service education and training for the higher forest services should be introduced.

39. Facilities for periodical training of officers of different levels on the staff college pattern should be created in the Forest Research Institute and Colleges, Dehra Dun. Normally a person being promoted to a higher post or a higher or a different kind of responsibility, should undergo the staff college pattern training.

Seeds

The Seed Review Team Report (June 1968) should be considered as the base and the recommendations in this chapter should be read in continuation of the Commission's Interim Reports entitled (a) Multiplication and Distribution of Quality Seed pertaining to High Yielding Varieties and Hybrids of Cereals and (b) Potato Seed; the main recommendations are given below.

1. The programme of seed production in the country should be developed in future on commercial lines. The industry could be expanded gradually so as to be able to cater to the needs of other countries also. Even reputed foreign seed firms and scientists could be invited to collaborate in the seed production programme.

2. The Central Seed Committee with the assistance of its State Subcommittees can operate a system of national registry of varieties for the entire country whether released by the centre or states. A suitable registration fee could be charged for this work and inspection on site should constitute an essential step for issuing certificates. Necessary rules and procedures in this regard could be laid down mutually by the ICAR and the Central Seed Committee.

3. The Central Seed Committee, the ICAR and the Governments should evolve a working machinery so that the problems arising from time to time in the implementation of various reports could always be tackled expeditiously. It will be necessary for the Central Seed Committee to constitute separate subcommittees for dealing with specialised group of crops and the National Seeds Corporation could also likewise have specialised wings for crops.

4. In order to ensure full benefit to small participants, they have to be educated and encouraged to form "compact areas" for seed production. Certified seed agencies which will have to depend on small farmers, should be made to undertake directly this programme and the State Governments have to render assistance through all possible financial and administrative measures.

5. Promotional measures like (a) seed crop insurance, (b) exemption from levies operative for grains, octroi, sales tax or local taxes in any other form, (c) timely release of wagons in adequate number, their proper insulation and unobstructed rapid movement, (d) air movement of seed material and concessional air freight for the purpose are all very desirable. Detrimental practices like *sawai* system and sale of uncertified sub-standard seeds has to be discouraged in general and the governments, autonomous institutions and organised seed agencies in particular have to desist from taking recourse to those under all possible avoidable circumstances.

6. The network of processing and storage plants

should be made as widespread as possible so that the facility could be utilised by farmers in all parts of the country. At the same time, their distribution should be compatible with the magnitude of seed industry, which will determine the ultimate economic viability of the project in different places. It will be ideal if all the organised seed agencies and even individual seed growers can be encouraged to form limited concerns on a regional basis to own and construct the seed processing and storage plants. Even packaging can be included in their scope.

7. Seed processing has got to be made compulsory and performed separately from the produce of the commercial crop. In order to cope up with the load, processing equipments and machines have to be manufactured within the country as an ultimate objective. Whatever little is manufactured at present under small scale industries suffers from inadequate supplies of basic materials i.e., steel or various manufactured components like sealed bearings, precise screens etc. and even if the materials are available, these are not on controlled rates. Small scale manufacturers are put to a disadvantage even in procurement, because they cannot afford to pay for the whole wagon load, which is the basis of allotment at present. These bottlenecks have to be removed.

8. The Industrial Development Centre (IDC) of the National Seeds Corporation and the Indian Standards Institution have to collaborate in designing, making specifications for fabricating, processing equipments and machines suited to Indian conditions for the benefit of local manufacturers and testing the same for performance. In order to provide necessary incentive to individuals, a system of prizes and royalties has also to be instituted. In the intervening period, when the country has to depend on imported materials, the centre should liberalise its import policy with regard to the required items.

9. The Seed Technology Division of the IARI, IDC and the Indian Institute of Packaging (Bombay) have to join together in developing materials, methods and designs for ideal packaging to meet different requirements. New innovations like chemical coating of seed as developed in other countries for special crops and ready made 'seed on tape' have also to engage constant attention.

10. Storages for breeder and foundation seed have to be airconditioned (both for temperature and humidity) and those for certified seed could be only damp-proof and free from pest attack.

11. The Central and State Governments should ensure that seed marketing is enforced only through the Seed Inspectors under the Seed Act and not through the marketing staff under the provisions of the Agricultural Produce (Grading and Marketing) Act or under any other law. Clear orders are necessary to operational staff to remove any ambiguity which might be existing in this regard. Further the Seeds Act should be enforced as far as possible through persuasion and educative methods rather than through penal measures.

12. Amending the Seeds Act should be deferred until experience and working with the Act have reached a stage at which a comprehensive bill could be brought forward to make it foolproof and reasonably comprehensive. In the meantime, conventions should be developed within the existing framework of the Act. For the same reason, working arrangements have to be made by the ICAR and Central Seed Committee with various directorates of crop commodities as well as boards of different plantation crops so that common standards could be enforced in all crops on a uniform basis.

13. Some of the aspects related to the Seeds Act which require pointed attention are specified below :

(i) Grow-out test should be made an integral part of seed testing. This job should be entrusted to seed testing laboratories.

(ii) Compulsory certification is desirable in the case of seed material of hybrids and vegetatively propagated crops.

(iii) In order to avoid chances of deterioration in the multiplication of seed at different stages, breeders or breeder institutions should specifically state about the chances of a variety to maintain the varietal standards as needed under certification and the Central Seed Certification Board should specify for each variety the time limit up to which subsequent multiplication can be practised without deterioration of the standards.

14. There is need to undertake research under Indian conditions in almost all fields of seed production, preservation and standardisation. Seed ecology, biochemistry, physiology, pathology, entomology, breeding and cultivation aspects as also the laboratory or industrial aspects require attention, physical constants of seed under various conditions and for various purposes also require to be determined.

15. Congenial areas for seed production for every crop will have to be determined and developed through experiments. In this work special emphasis should be given to the selection of areas remote from the traditional areas of cultivation in respect of every crop. Specialised pockets of seed production already exist in the case of vegetable crops, but the material being produced, pertains to varieties of unknown

purity and performance. In their case, therefore, the need is to educate the traditional growers in the practices of growing quality seed and provide them with the requisite inputs and guidance. Another point for consideration could be whether their own material could not be improved upon rather than introducing new material.

16. Necessary steps to tackle the seed problems of some of the selected crops are suggested below :

(i) Sugarcane—Multiplication of disease free planting material is the prime necessity. It is equally important to multiply sufficient quantity of seed material suitable for every track. Whereas the usual agencies have to be utilised for multiplication of foundation and certified seed, the responsibility for breeder seed should lie with the Central Sugarcane Research Station, Coimbatore. This station should take the assistance of research stations situated in various states in order to get the benefit of multiplying seed for different agro-climatic conditions.

(ii) Fodder crops—Fodder crops are many, and may be classified into legumes and non-legumes. Increased attention should be given to the research and multiplication aspects of all these crops so that adequate quantities of good quality seed become available. State Departments of Agriculture should take direct responsibility in planning and encouraging this work with the help of established foundation and certified seed agencies.

(iii) Horticultural and plantation crops—In the case of fruits, vegetables, flowers and plantation crops, the first necessity is to screen the existing varieties in order to choose the best amongst them and then take measures to multiply the seed material of the chosen ones in adequate quantities. Seed material to fruit growers must pass through known pedigree orchards and for this it is very necessary to establish chain of progeny orchards from breeder to foundation and certified seed stages. The supervision and promotional measures with regard to progeny orchards must be the responsibility of State Governments. It is also very desirable that detailed codes are laid down within the purview of Seeds Act to regulate multiplications and distribution of seed and planting material of these crops through progeny orchards.

(iv) Papaya—Papaya seed requires to be multiplied under controlled conditions through artificial pollination and begging of selected types in order to avoid mixing.

(v) Banana and Pineapple—Clones of improved types of known pedigree are required to be multiplied for the sake of uniform and better production. Multiplication from bits of corn in the case of banana and from small pieces of stem below the flowering shoot in the case of pineapple increase progeny and, therefore, this practice has to be encouraged after due trials.

(vi) Guava—The vegetative propagation through experimentally proven methods such as by air-layering could be tried for multiplication.

(vii) Mango—The important problem is to standardise the stock and scion in the case of mango. Nuclear technique could be utilised to develop uniform root stocks or it can be done through clonal propagation by air-layers. Scions require to be multiplied from varieties whose fruiting performance has actually been verified. Once the parent material has been thus established, veneer grafting could be adopted for mass production.

(viii) Citrus—The most important problem in the case of citrus is to produce virus free planting material for which, nuclear technique could be put to use to the advantage.

(ix) Cashewnut—Vegetative propagation through budding and dis-layering could be tried in multiplication work.

(x) Cardamom—The possibility of grading rhizomes for multiplication purposes in the aphid-free period is worth trying in the same way as applicable to potato.

17. The ICAR should take steps for introducing suitable courses related to seed production methods at the graduate as well as post-graduate levels in all the agricultural universities. Some suitable course in the management aspects of seed business could also be introduced in the existing Indian Institutes of Management to begin with and later on such courses could form part of the curriculum of the specialised management institute with a bias towards agriculture, animal husbandry and rural sciences as envisaged in the Commission's Interim Report on Agricultural Research, Extension and Training. In addition, short term training courses have to be introduced by the State Departments of Agriculture for training of the lower cadres as well as private seed producers, processors, salesmen etc.

18. The Departments of Agriculture at the Centre and in the States should have three distinct wings each dealing respectively with the input aspect, law enforcement and certification work. The Departments of Agriculture/Horticulture have to deal with various other inputs and laws too. It is suggested that separate divisions are created for inputs and law enforcement and aspects pertaining to seed are also looked after by them. Insofar as certification is concerned, the Central Seeds Certification Board together with its State Boards would serve the purpose

of the third wing.

19. The various foundation and certified seed agencies, which will be coming forth in future, will have to be organised in an integrated manner. The National Seeds Corporation could play a leading and purposeful role in this connection. It could create a distinct wing to look after the promotional activities like the establishment of new seed enterprise, training of personnel and the rendering of technical advice to banks and other leading agencies on credit and financial needs of the seed industry.

Fertilisers and Manures

The following is a summary of important recommendations made in the text of this chapter :-

1. Algal fertilisers deserve to be exploited to the fullest extent.

2. For success in modernised farming, specially with high yielding varieties, an efficient and balanced use of fertilisers and manures is imperative. A correct measure of nutrient balance is to be based on the ratio in which they appear in fertiliser recommendations resulting from field trials instead of the ratio of consumption, as is usually done.

3. For making assessment of fertiliser requirement for achieving certain levels of agricultural production the exercise should be more realistic and related to the actual performance in the field.

Factors affecting efficient use of fertilisers : 4. If adequate safety measures are taken, anhydrous ammonia should, under suitable circumstances, replace the solid nitrogenous fertilisers in our country. Before venturing its large scale application, which involves new technologies and techniques both in the field and in handling from the factory to the distribution end, a series of experiments need to be undertaken. Because of the risks involved in handling anhydrous ammonia, its use can preferably be promoted through well organised custom services.

5. High analysis phosphates like the polyphosphates promise certain advantages and, therefore, deserve attention as to their performance under different soil and climatic conditions.

6. Constant watch should be kept in respect of micronutrient deficiencies under intensive agriculture and suitable methods are developed for incorporating them.

7. Methods of application of fertilisers and their efficient utilisation have to be considered in relation to the root systems of crops and their pattern of development in the soil medium. Sufficient information on these aspects is wanting. Appropriate research work should be initiated in this field.

8. Considerable controversy exists in regard to the efficacy of foliar fertilisation with urea and also its economics. As leaf characteristics have a definite role to play in the absorption of nutrients, the physiological behaviour of the plant leaves needs to be studied before coming to a definite conclusion about the efficiency of foliar fertilisation with urea or such other fertilisers.

Soil organic matter and organic manures : 9. Bulk and consequent cost of transport are handicaps in the application of processed organic wastes to the field. Suitable methods of reducing bulk by chemical and microbiological or other methods need to be evolved. Enrichment of organic wastes with nitrogen and phosphates will considerably enhance their manurial value.

10. The programmes of development of organic manures by the Ministry of Agriculture and Irrigation in which urban and rural composts, sewage and sullage etc. are being mobilised are attempts in the right direction. The manner in which the urban wastes are processed determines its manurial value which can be enhanced by suitably treating them with ammonium and phosphatic compounds.

11. Centres for utilisation of sewage and sullage should multiply and develop as a continuing venture.

12. By introducing gobar gas plants the energy requirements of the farmer's household can be met, retaining the manurial value of the dung. Rural population should be given adequate technical guidance and help in making use of this innovation.

Chemical fertilisers and soil amendments : 13. In a vital sector like fertilisers, the shortfall in indigenous production is of disastrous consequences. All available resources should be mobilised to reduce a big shortfall, particularly in the field where the country's technological capability is of no mean order.

14. In selecting coal as feed stock, the question of economics has to be weighed in its totality, in which indigenous availability of coal and returns in terms of employment in related sectors of mining and accessory industries have to be taken into consideration. For a long term plan of developing nitrogenous fertiliser capacity there is no alternative to indigenous production.

15. It would be prudent to avoid, as far as possible, sulphur in the indigenous manufacture of phosphatic fertilisers.

16. There is controversy over the ratio of water soluble to citrate soluble forms of phosphate in regard to efficiency. Extensive field experimentation should be taken up in verification of the efficiency of the above two forms and their optimum ratio in crop

production under varied soil and climatic conditions.

17. Geological explorations should be intensified on an extensive scale in search of new sources of phosphorus.

18. In respect of potash, it is suggested to explore the possibility of utilising bittern of salt industry and of developing chemical processes to make potassium in potash foldspar and mica available for fertilisation.

19. Some kind of recycling process may be exploited to make the locked up phosphate and potash in the soil, both native as well as from added fertiliser sources, available to crops.

20. A Committee of analytical and agricultural chemists drawn from IARI, agricultural universities, State Departments of Agriculture and Fertilisers to suggest suitable methods of analysis for general acceptance throughout the country. This committee will also review the methods at intervals.

21. The fertiliser industry should aim at developing technology for meeting requirements of high analysis fertilisers straight and complex/compound, so that materials of higher efficiency could be made available to the farmers at a low cost.

22. Soil testing data and fertility index map should help in channelising the fertiliser distribution, so that proper grades are available to the farmers in relation to their soils and crops.

23. The recommendations made on quality control of fertilisers in our Interim Report on Fertliser Distribution are reiterated.

24. Necessary facilities for grinding basic slag to proper mesh size should be developed under the auspices of iron and steel manufacturing agencies for making use of this valuable waste material for crop production.

Fertiliser dose : 25. Farmers are found rarely to apply the recommended doses of fertilisers. The reasons for this should be investigated in order to take remedial measures.

26. Two situations are recognised in farming, namely (1) one in which maximum profit per hectare is derived from fertilisation, and (2) another in which maximum return is obtained per rupee invested in fertilisers. The fertiliser trials should be so designed as to enable isolation of these two situations and to make separate recommendations for each.

27. The generalised recommendation of fertiliser doses for different crops in an administrative unit and agroclimatic region would be more useful for programming fertiliser despatch to potential areas of consumption. For a more accurate scheduling of dose from one field to the other in an agroclimatic region, soil tests backed by research experience on crop response should be a better guide.

28. In dry farming areas balanced and judicious fertiliser use is called for in order to utilise efficiently available soil moisture.

29. All coordinated research programmes and projects should lay considerable emphasis on the economics of fertilisers use not only with reference to a particular soil type and a single crop but also to the sequence of crops in multiple crop fertilisation.

Soil testing as a guide to efficient use of fertilisers : 30. The efficiency of soil testing should be improved, so that the predictability of crop response to fertiliser use based on soil tests in enhanced. While recommending fertiliser doses, it should be ensured that they are appropriate for the soil to be used, the crop to be grown and the level of farm management.

31. Necessary steps should be taken to improve the working efficiency of soil testing laboratories by keeping the measuring instruments in order and introducing automatic and time-saving devices.

32. For creating interest in the cultivators and motivating them in getting their soils tested for better fertiliser use, the cultivators should be involved in the service programme.

33. In each state there should be a central laboratory to function as a central laboratory. There should be an officer of high rank at the State headquarters to coordinate the work of the different laboratories and to render necessary help for efficient working of the laboratories.

34. The State Department of Agriculture should continually evaluate the performance of the mobile soil testing laboratories. It should have a close look into the working of the laboratories set up by the fertiliser manufacturers marketing federations and other private agencies so that the developed facilities are not utilised to the detriment of balanced use of fertilisers. The institutional and private soil testing laboratories should demarcate the areas of operation in order to avoid unnecessary overlapping.

35. Attempts to increase the number and capacity of soil testing laboratories should be proceded by a full utilisation of the existing facilities and improvement in quality of service.

36. The demonstrations and trials of fertiliser use based on soil tests being conducted by different agencies should be widely spread out. A Coordination Committee under the chairmanship of the Director of Agriculture may be formed in each state in which all the participating agencies will be represented. This committee will draw up an annual programme, specifying the areas of operation for the different agencies, ensure fertiliser use based on soil tests and evaluate the effectiveness of the programme.

37. Soil test-crop response correlation studies should be a continuing process in order to guide the soil testing laboratories in formulation of more and more reliable and reasonable fertiliser use recommendations. The data collected for various agro-climatic and soil regions should be analysed to draw fertiliser schedules. The officials of the soil testing laboratories should be adequately trained in various aspects of soil testing including interpretation of data so that they are able to make specific fertiliser use recommendations for different crops and soils. There should be a programme of revision of fertiliser schedule as new knowledge develops.

38. The method developed under the International Soil Testing Project of the North Carolina State University may be tried to find out if it could be more efficiently and speedily used in India in recommending fertiliser doses.

39. Soil fertility maps should be prepared by adopting improved methodology. For proper assessment of the fertiliser needs to each administrative unit and efficient fertiliser distribution they have to be superimposed on administrative unit maps.

Plant Protection Chemicals

The following are the important recommendations made in this chapter :

1. Most of the crop are able to recoup from injuries by pest attack incurred early in their growth or away from the critical stage. Such critical stage for each variety of crop should, therefore, be ascertained by careful experimentation.

2. The Institute of Agricultural Research Statistics should examine the available data on various coordinated trials carried out all over India to arrive at an estimate of crop losses by insect pests and diseases. The institute may design experiments to enable valid estimates to be made of crop losses by insect pests and diseases.

3. Research work and field study for the estimation of crop loss under different agroclimatic regions and pest situations should be continued at least for 3-5 years for the purpose of verification. Wherever possible, laboratory work and field testing may run simultaneously to gain time. Crop loss estimates should preferably be expressed on a uniform basis.

4. A close coordination of research work done by different research institutions, agricultural universities and State Departments of Agriculture would be highly desirable. It may be opportune to associate the pesticide industry at a consultative level.

5. All future studies on plant protection chemicals should preferably be correlated with the losses caused by various pests under different conditions and in different regions.

6. With changing cropping patterns, pest surveillance should become an integral part of crop protection. New crop introductions which are likely to bring hitherto unknown pests should be watched cautiously.

7. Pest Surveillance Programme should be continued throughout the year beyond the wheat growing season, particularly in the hills, for getting a clearer understanding of the inoculum potential, perpetuation, survival and movement of rust spores.

8. The *ad hoc* rice survey should be placed on a permanent footing to allow it to carry on "off season" surveys preferably in the endemic areas.

9. There is a need for a thorough re-examination of the techniques and procedures of sampling stated in the FAO Manual, 'Plant Pests Diseases Survey Manual for Plant Protection Workers' for the purpose of improving on them.

10. Surveillance-Forecasting Plant should specially be concerned with the occurrence of major as well as minor insects pests and diseases and the distribution of species, exact time of occurrence, varieties of crops affected, plant growth stage preferred etc.

11. Surveillance project should continually strive to find methods suitable for determining the occurrence of each individual insect pest and disease. This activity should either be a part of the research work being done or the subject of new research projects.

12. A more accurate estimate of the benefit-cost ratio should be obtained by carefully carrying out a large number of field experiments (result demonstrations) which would enable analysis of the data according to crops and treatments.

13. The state departments should review their plant protection set-up, especially the extension unit, and streamline the organisation for increasing farmers' awareness regarding the magnitude of damage caused by pests and that of plant protecting measures needed. It is suggested that the pesticide industry should also undertake intensive efforts to educate farmers.

14. States should maintain a complete yearwise record of all the plant protection chemicals actually being consumed according to a uniform system. These data should not only refer to records kept at the governmental level but should also include those distributed through private and other agencies.

15. In view of the lack of any relation whatsoever between the recommended chemicals in the plant protection schedules and those required and consumed by the states, the present plant protection

schedules should be revised immediately, making it obligatory to revise them every two years.

16. The state surveillance agencies should maintain records of cropwise pest problems together with the time and intensity of attack. In the long run this information would be of use not only to assess more exactly the requirement of chemicals but also to plan control operations more systematically.

17. The state plant protection units should be reorganised to collect and evaluate data on pest problems cropwise and seasonwise and of the pestwise requirement of chemicals. They should accordingly be armed with necessary equipment, machinery, trained personnel and other facilities to fight sudden outbreaks and emergencies.

18. Efforts are needed to develop knowhow for the indigenous manufacture of intermediates, active technical pesticides and their formulations.

19. Research work on naturally occurring pesticides and on products synthesised from them and having desirable stability should be intensified.

20. For introducing fertiliser-pesticide mixtures, studies should be undertaken to find out (a) the conditions for a homogeneous mixture; (b) reactions which effect the efficacy in the mixture of either the plant nutrient or the protection chemicals or of both; and (c) keeping qualities of the mixture in storage.

21. A committee representing the agricultural universities, DPPQ&S, ICAR, IARI, ISI and the fertiliser and pesticide industries should thoroughly study the use of fertiliser-pesticide mixtures in relation to the pattern of future consumption of both fertilisers and pesticides, changes in cropping patterns under various agro-climatic conditions, pest complex, and cost of application.

22. There is an urgent need to monitor especially in areas of intensive use of pesticide, foodstuffs for pesticides residues, which should include, besides foodgrains, vegetables, fruits and milk, meat, oils, fats and animal feeds, waters from rivers, fish ponds, lakes, wells and canals. Tolerance limits for all pesticides used in the country should be ascertained, and also those of the "Acceptable Daily Intake" and residue tolerance of different pesticides under Indian conditions.

23. The need for using multiple analytical procedures to confirm the identity of the components of pesticides residue is necessary. Facilities for more sophisticated techniques like infrared, ultraviolet and mass spectrometry should be made available.

24. Facilities for studies on degradation of pesticides and on residues should be provided and developed at a number of locations in the country.

25. Recognising the upward consumption of pesticides in the country it is necessary to gradually discontinue the highly toxic ones now in use, which have no industrial base, and to find more suitable and safer substitutes. Also, research on and development of less hazardous and superior formulations have to be encouraged and emphasis should be laid on the development of indigenous knowhow of manufacturing pesticide chemicals from indigenous sources. The different plant protection schedules should be re-examined from the point of view of pesticide residues.

26. For adopting integrated pest control, knowledge of ecology, biology and behaviour of pests and their natural enemies, crops and crops complex, and characteristic properties of chemicals is required. In order to minimise pollution hazards, more and more non-pesticidal control methods have to be devised and suitably integrated with chemical methods.

27. Because of their persistence and toxicity, the use, if at all, of DDT, BHC, malathion etc., as storage pesticides should be confined to seeds.

28. All bags containing formulated dusts should be of uniform standards and machine-stitched with metal seals. Other formulated products in metal containers and glass bottles should be made pilfer-proof.

29. The Indian Standards Institution should bring out standards for fertiliser-pesticides mixtures in anticipation of their becoming a part of the future consumption pattern.

30. Methods of sampling and analysis should be uniform throughout the country and brought within scope of the Insecticides Act and the quality marketing system of the ISI. The methods should be periodically reviewed for introducing improvements.

31. The Central Insecticides Laboratory should have arrangements for training the states' quality control personnel engaged in drawing and analysis of pesticide samples.

32. Attention has to be paid to equip mobile soil testing laboratories for carrying out preliminary pesticide analysis.

33. The pesticide analysis laboratories should preferably be located in the campuses of the agricultural universities, so that the latter can assist the laboratories in an advisory capacity.

34. Publicity media should be used in order to educate farmers with regard to the existing facilities available for the testing of pesticides and in distinguishing the standard materials and the spurious ones.

35. Small amounts instead of bulk quantities of pesticides should be made available in tamper-proof containers to reduce risk of adulteration and to enable

small farmers to buy pesticides, which they cannot afford if sold in bulk.

36. State departments should maintain emergency stock of pesticides to guard against natural calamities and unforeseen situations.

37. The distribution centres are generally opened in demand areas and the places which are easily accessible by railway or road. These defects may be remedied if, while issuing licences, equal opportunities are given to all categories of farmers, especially, those of the small ones. The farmers' service society may be entrusted with the task of running inputs, depots, including those of pesticides, so that they become available in time to the members of the society.

38. The same priority as given to fertilisers should be extended to pesticides in the matter of allotment of railway wagons and their movement.

39. The godowns and storage facilities available with agencies like the Fertiliser Corporation of India should be given on a priority basis for pesticide storage.

40. Subsidy for the purchase of pesticides should be discontinued except in the case of small and marginal farmers. The subsidy, however, may be given (a) for transportation charges of pesticides from railway tracks to distribution points for stabilising price, (b) for aerial spray, (c) for appliances, (d) for spraying pesticides in epidemic areas, and (e) for opening more sale points in backward areas.

41. The present state of promotional efforts made by State Governments is not satisfactory. A part of the saving accruing from the withdrawal of subsidy for the purchase of pesticides should be utilised for promotional activities.

42. In conformity with the multifarious activities and responsibilities of the DPPQ&S is the Union Ministry of Agriculture and Irrigation, the status of the Plant Protection Adviser should be raised to that of a Joint Secretary. A similar upgrading is called for in respect of other officers at the central and state levels.

Farm Power

Summary and Recommendations

The aggregate farm power available at the turn of the century will be of the order of 129.62 million hp. which gives an average power availability of 0.86 hp/ha, of this the share of human labour would be 8.40 million hp, draught animals 25.60 million hp, engines and motors 60.00 million hp and power sprayers and dusters 16.00 million hp. The various recommendations given in the chapter are directed towards achieving this goal. The main recommendations are the following :

1. There should be provision for extending loans covering the full cost of draught animals. Advances should be made available in time and if there are any bottlenecks government should so frame the rules that it becomes easy for farmers to get the advances. Credit cooperatives and commercial banks should also undertake advancing such loans.

2. The two-wheeled power tiller which is mainly used at present for puddling operations in paddy fields should also be designed for other light jobs like tillage of minor nature, water pumping and spraying and dusting operations, it should be particularly popularised in hilly regions where other heavy machinery cannot be worked

3. The use of electricity should be popularised as much as practicable in farm activities and stationary indoor jobs.

4. It should be ensured that fuel oil required for farm machinery like tractors and earth moving machinery is arranged on a priority basis.

5. There should be detailed research and analysis to find out the fair requirements of farm power in various agroclimatic zones in the country under irrigated as well as unirrigated conditions.

6. Machines should be utilised only in areas where there is serious shortage of human labour and draught animals. Any tendency to utilise machines in labour surplus areas should be suitably controlled.

7. In the manufacture of tractors, it is desirable to ensure that interchange of the fast moving parts becomes possible between different makes in order to facilitate repairs and replacement. The Government should keep a constant watch on production so that farmers' needs can always be met full and the industry does not face any difficulty in regard to essential raw materials etc.

8. Particular attention should be given to popularise the two-wheeled power tiller and to manufacture them in accordance with the rising demand as explained in the text.

9. Crawler tractors of 150 hp capacity are required to be manufactured specially for heavy earth moving work.

10. Facilities of testing power machinery should be expanded at the Tractor Training & Testing Centres. A testing section should also exist at the Central Institute of Agricultural Engineering, which has been set up recently. Facilities for testing of commerical equipment should also be created at some agricultural universities depending upon need. The Indian Standards Institution should start laying down specifications

for ancillary parts of farm power machinery.

11. Procedures followed by banks should be simplified and rural credit made more liberal than at present in order to make it easy for farmers to purchase agricultural machinery.

12. The agro-industries corporations should undertake manufacture only of such items which are not being manufactured by others or the production of which is not sufficient and, therefore, requires to be supplemented.

13. The agro-industries corporations should assist small and medium scale manufacturers by purchasing their stocks and taking over the responsibility of their sale upon themselves.

14. The agro-industries corporations should offer two kinds of services, viz., (a) custom-service, and (b) workshop facility for overhaul and repairs etc. In order to be able to perform both these functions full-fledged workshops should be established at each taluk headquarters and there should be arrangement for some essential facilities to be made available at a sufficiently dense network of points below the taluk level also. Wherever other entrepreneurs are coming forward, they should be encouraged to open workshops. In other places, particularly inaccessible areas the corporations themselves should take up this responsibility.

15. The agro-industries corporations should encourage creation of community threshing and post-harvesting processing facilities in village. Panchayats could profitably undertake this activity.

16. The agro-industries corporations of major states should extend their activities to their neighbouring smaller states (i.e., Meghalaya, Nagaland, Manipur and Tripura) and Union Territories.

17. The agro-industries corporations should not remain responsible for the training of farmers with regard to handling of farm machinery. The extension work with regard to such machinery should also not be considered as a function of these corporations.

18. A course in agricultural engineering should be introduced in engineering polytechnics as well as in industrial training institutes.

19. Training of farmers in the handling of farm power machinery should be performed by the State Agricultural Departments.

20. The State Departments of Agriculture should organise extension work relating to farm power machinery in an effective manner. For this, they have to provide duly qualified staff at the district, taluk and block headquarters.

21. A research base for producing power machinery suited to Indian conditions is very necessary. The present machinery in use has to be tested with this aim in view and suitable modified types developed. The manufacturers must create their own research and development units. It should be the responsibility of the licensing authority to ensure that they allocate adequate funds for this purpose.

22. Besides conducting its own research, the Central Institute of Agricultural Engineering should bring together agricultural scientists and engineers in order to determine problems and priorities. It should also try to co-ordinate the research activities of the manufacturers and other institutions.

23. With the help of the central state farms, the Central Institute of Agricultural Engineering should undertake studies to determine the optimum levels of mechanisation under different conditions of soil, climate and irrigation and to collect information on related aspects.

Implements and Machinery

Summary of Recommendations

The main recommendations of this chapter are given below :

1. An exhaustive survey should be made to find out the causes for low acceptance of improved types of implements and machinery and the continued preference to wooden plough.

2. Improvement of the wooden plough or its replacement with a more acceptable form of the iron plough and the development of suitable types for different regions should receive due attention in research work. There should be a publicity drive to popularise the improved types.

3. Causes as to why a useful implement like blade harrow is not finding favour in northern alluvial tracts are to be assessed and attempts should be made to introduce it in the existing or modified form.

4. The use of levellers should be popularised both in rainfed as well as irrigated areas to make water management more efficient.

5. More attention is required to be paid to research on the entire system of land preparation in different regions of the country.

6. Extension work to promote improved land preparation implements and their right use is needed. Sale and service network to make these implements more easily available and a system of custom hire service at the village level are also required.

7. Appropriate types of seed drills should be introduced and local artisans trained to manufacture them and farmers to use them. Agricultural universities should intensify research in improving the drills. Suggestions from local artisans and farmers

may be invited in this regard and some incentive rewards offered.

8. The new paddy transplanter developed in Orissa should be tried and improved further for adoption in all paddy growing areas.

9. The use of implements for inter-cultivation should be popularised along with drill sowing or dibbling. The indigenous hoes require improvement. The use of weedicides could also be encouraged to do away with the drudgery of hand operations.

10. Japanese model pedal operated thresher requires to be improved for general acceptance.

11. Every village should be provided with engine-driven stationary theresher-cum-winnower in required number on custom service basis. Attempts should also be made to devise simple reapers for harvesting various crops. Particular attention is required for developing harvesting machines for crops like groundnut, cotton and potato.

12. Efficient water lifting devices which are required to lift water through a few feet only (where use of engines is uneconomical) and which could be operated manually or through bullocks should be developed through research efforts.

13. One or two seed treating drums may be provided in every village. Chaffcutters need to be popularised so that each farmer has one.

14. Intensive research on hand tools is required in respect to quality of metal and design so as to increase their effectiveness.

15. Improved tools of standardised shapes should be made available locally at low price. Steel of desired quality should be made available locally at low price, steel of desired quality should be made available to production centres at fair price through special steel banks.

16. Manufacture of standard tools can be taken up at the taluk or district or even state level through farmers cooperatives or agro-industries corporations. Local artisans can also be trained adequately for this purpose though it is better they are trained more in repair work than in manufacturing. The gram sewak training centres should be activised and more centres set up to train local artisans in repair work.

17. In matters of improving or developing implements and machinery, some observations of the team of specialists of the Michigan State University applicable to mechanization of agriculture in Equatorial Africa and quoted in paragraph 51.2.34 of this report are relevant to Indian conditions also. We recommend that the various authorities concerned with the improvement of agricultural implements give their earnest attention to those observations and apply them to Indian conditions.

18. Design and development of a standard toolbar for multipurpose use with various bullock drawn implements like plough, harrow, drill, inter-culture implements or even with cart is recommended.

19. Village artisans should be encouraged to give suggestions for developing better designs of tools and implements and suitable prizes should be given to them. The existence of this provision should be widely publicised.

20. The agro-industries corporations should undertake the manufacture of improved bullock carts. It should be examined whether solid rubber tyres would not be better than the pneumatic ones for use in bullock carts. The size of the cart wheel also requires to be standardised to facilitate large scale manufacture of tyres.

21. Future design of yokes should be such that they would suit the humps of improved crossbred draught animals.

22. Import of implements and machinery for the development of prototypes should not be resorted to as a matter of routine and the emphasis should be to develop machines typical to the country's own conditions.

23. The development of prototypes of implements and machinery and their feasibility trials before release to the prospective manufacturers should be incorporated in the research programme compulsorily. The institutions which have to be made responsible for this kind of work are : the Central Institute of Agricultural Engineering, IITs and agricultural universities. Adequate workshop facilities should be created with every RTTC for this purpose and necessary funds provided.

24. When testing prototypes, research workers should associate farmers, extension workers as well as manufacturers in order to elicit their views on them.

25. RTTCs which deal with farm machinery and implements must be so strengthened as to enable them to play a prominent and leading role in their sphere of activities. All the RTTCs should be placed under one or the other agricultural universities. The universities must ensure that the individuality of RTTCs is not destroyed and their funds are expended on them only.

26. The ISI standards should be extended to all implements and machines manufactured in any sector—small, medium or big.

27. The testing of the implements made by village artisans should be done by agro-industries corporations, while those manufactured by the medium and large sectors should be done by the RTTCs. In the case of big manufacturers, each machine sold by them should have a performance report.

28. Uniform standards for testing and evaluation of farm implements and machinery should be made applicable throughout the country.

29. The State Departments of Agriculture should undertake to collect data as market intelligence relating to agricultural implements and machinery. The information so collected should be disseminated amongst the manufacturers.

30. The workshops to be set up by agro-industries corporations for maintenance and repair service as suggested in chapter 50 on farm power, should cater to the needs of farmers with regard to sales and service of implements and machines also. Besides this arrangement, the agro-industries corporations should also encourage private parties to undertake these services.

Research

Summary of Recommendations

The following is a summary of the important recommendations made in this chapter :

1. Agricultural universities have generally not been able to undertake fundamental research so far. In the interest of agriculture, it is essential that they should pay immediate attention to this aspect.

2. There is an urgent need to encourage development of specialised centres of fundamental research in different parts of the country which would be capable of tackling problems that are basic in nature. The best places where such centres could be developed are naturally universities in general and the agricultural univerisities in particular. Central institutions of the ICAR are also places where such centres could be developed. One of the ways to encourage universities to develep such centres would be the setting up of professional chair by the ICAR.

3. Some of the state regional research stations should be placed at the disposal of the universities in such a manner that they have at least one such station for each type of climatic regions.

4. The State departments should confine themselves only to adaptive research such as varietal testing, fertiliser recommendation based on soil analysis, water duties, etc., and must not use this freedom to develop parallel research organisation is competition with the universities.

5. There must be adaptive research council in Government departments similar to the research council obtaining in agricultural universities and in these councils the senior university experts should also find a place. The advice of these experts should be given full consideration in planning adaptive research programmes of the Government departments.

6. A system must be evolved in the state departments whereby research personnel have the experience of administration and extension work so that they have the necessary field experience to back up their research.

7. State experimental farms which are meant for demonstration work and for raising seeds etc. should be exclusively under the control of state departments, which can utilise them for adaptive research and extension work. But agricultural universities should not be precluded from using them.

8. The ICAR should, with the help of its scientific panels, undertake to draw up long-term plans of fundamental and applied research, identify gaps in information and assign them for execution to appropriate scientists, universities and research institutes.

9. In dealing with *ad-hoc* schemes, the scientific panels should make themselves more purposive and in this they should be provided with adequate administrative support from the concerned offices of the ICAR.

10. The agricultural and general universities, and especially the former are entitled to a larger share of research grants in those subjects in which they are still deficient. Attempts should be made to sponsor a large number of research schemes on those subjects.

11. The money available for *ad-hoc* research schemes should be more and more diverted to universities and other research institutes wanting in research grants.

12. A fresh and critical examination of matters connected with ICAR publications is urgently called for. Much more imagination and drive would be necessary to give proper shape to this important objective of the ICAR.

13. The research activities in universities which are unable to finance from their own resources are on a low key. In spite of the increasing importance of co-ordinated projects the *ad-hoc* research schemes coming especially from the universities should be liberally funded.

14. Co-ordinated programmes on research problems of both fundamental and applied nature in agriculture which are important from the national point of view should be sponsored by the ICAR. These programmes should be drawn up carefully after a review of the present status of research in that particular field and the gaps needed to be filled in.

15. The all-India co-ordinated research projects should broadly satisfy the following criteria :

(i) The projects should envisage problem-oriented applied research of known knowledge under different broad agro-climatic conditions with marginal short-term basic research;

(ii) the problems to be studied should be of national importance and they may belong to a single discipline or may be multidisciplinary;

(iii) problems should be such as to warrant the concentration of efforts of a number of scientists on a single problem; and

(iv) the projects should aim at developing recommendations in the shortest time for increasing production.

16. Where it is necessary to carry on the relevant research at more than one centre, a coordinated programme, with appropriate arrangements for funds and coordination should be developed without the necessity of having a coordinated research project.

17. The ICAR should lay down the type of coordination suitable to the particular programmes under various schemes financed by it. All research work of local importance should be carried out by the agricultural universities and the state departments through their own organisations and there may be no need for making any institutional arrangements by the ICAR for coordination for such work.

18. An important objective of these projects being to provide additionality and not to replace the research efforts already in hand it is reiterated that the State Governments should not reduce the allocation for research in their development plans.

19. A large part of the research work in agriculture should be conducted outside the purview of the coordinated projects under the coordinated individual programmes.

20. The number of workshops should be reduced by suitably grouping together those of allied disciplines. In case of crop like rice, oilseeds, pulses etc., which are grown under diverse agro-climatic conditions, it would be appropriate to have zonal workshops.

21. As the workshop is the forum to consider the various problems arising from the researches carried out under the projects and as field acceptability is of great importance in the system of research, it would be desirable to associate the farmers, extension personnel, users and the industry also in the deliberation of the workshops at suitable interval so as to get a feel of the field problems.

22. The all-India co-ordinated research projects should include a provision of nonrecurring grant for construction of glasshouses, laboratory facilities etc. This would enable locating the coordinating projects at different universities.

23. The following criteria for selection of locations for coordinated projects centres have been proposed :

(i) importance of a crop or livestock species in the region and specific problems therein;

(ii) existence of central research institutes/ agricultural university/experimental sations;

(iii) quality of research staff already available in the institute/university/experimental stations etc., and availability of contact with high level scientists in various disciplines; and

(iv) availability of facilities (land, irrigation, library, laboratory) at the institute/university/experimental stations.

24. The project coordinator should be a highly competent scientist in the field, possessing qualities of leadership. Mere length of service should not be the criterion for his selection, instead, the quality of his performance as also the capacity to coordinate the work of fellow scientists should be the major criteria.

25. A suggestion has been made that insofar as the post of Project Coordinator is concerned, other scientists in the project should be allowed to hold it by rotation. It is felt that it would be possible only in a coordinated programme and not the coordinated project. Such a rotation would be feasible in case of zonal coordinators. At the same time, we recommend that this may be tried in one or two projects as a trial basis and, if found successful be extended to other projects of long duration.

26. There should be continuous and rigorous assessment of each project. For this purpose, ICAR should develop a system of regular progress reporting on a quarterly basis. The progress reports should be scrutinised by the project coordinator. Unless the coordinator certifies that the work is satisfactory, release of funds should not be made to that project. Further, there should be not only a regular financial audit, but also performance audit of each project, at regular intervals.

27. There should be a suitable system of adjustment through which savings on particular project centres or sub-centres could be allowed to be utilised for other projects where progress has been quite significant. Foreign exchange needed for the import of essential equipment and livestock for various projects should be ensured.

28. Simpler and speedier procedures should be evolved for the sanctioning of the projects especially at the State Department/Agricultural University level. In addition to the necessity of some flexibility in the allocation of funds, there should be a small grant at the disposal of the project coordinator which could be utilised for unforeseen items of expenditure.

29. Large scale testing in our view forms part of applied research which should be taken up by the

agricultural universities, central research institutes on suitable problems of relevance to the areas in which they are located, in close coordination and collaboration with the devlopment agencies. Funding and execution of research problems which are strictly of local nature should be the responsibility of the agricultural universities and state governments.

30. The tendency of establishing divisions on the basis of discipline and of expanding them by introducing limitless sections or units based on species has to be deprecated and stopped at an appropriate and manageable size of the divisions.

31. Research institutes should spread evenly over the different agro-climatic regions. For this purpose, they should preferably be of small and medium sizes having more specific and restricted objectives, so that manageability and viability are assured.

32. Posts of Directors of all the ICAR research institutes should carry the same scale of pay. The salary to be paid to a Director should, however, be in accordance with the merits of the person as a scientist, and be fixed by referring the matter to the body appointed to select him, irrespective of the status of the institute.

33. For the sake of better management of the institutes, the good institutions of achievement audit should be taken seriously and the recommendations made by the committee be effective instruments of improvement.

34. Now that agricultural universities have been established in good number, the training courses in research should be installed in the universities only. The present tendency of research institutes to compete with the universities in awarding degrees will defeat the very purpose of the institutes, and should be done away with.

35. The institutes should refrain from any enterprise of large scale production and distribution of materials, e.g., of seeds (except breeder seed), fertilisers (including bacterial or algal cultures, biological products) etc. They should restrict themselves to the perfection of products of their research work, allowing outside agencies, preferably trained persons from the institutes/universities to commercialise the products.

36. Throughout each institute the spirit of expansion permeates. This defect has originated from the behaviour of the big institutes, and should be checked.

37. Those institutes/divisions which are below the 'critical' size should de strengthene d and those above should be allowed to be dispersed in the best possible manner, or redistributed with suitable administrative changes.

38. Realising the need of developing Animal Genetics in an integrated manner, an Institute for Animal Genetics should be set up. This institute may also deal with the discipline of animal reproduction.

39. The acceptance of the principle of technical assignments of the scientific staff at the ICAR headquarters is in the right direction. We would strongly urge that the principle is rigidly followed, and no one should on any account be allowed to have more than two terms of three years each.

40. Facilities should be created for management training of personnel engaged in agricultural research and technology.

41. The staff research councils of research institute should encourage interdisciplinary research by sanctioning more funds for such projects.

42. For more efficient and effective utilisation of costly and sophisticated instruments the system of pooling the latter and appointing trained technicians to operate them should be encouraged.

43. In the matter of distribution of projects amongst researches equity should be maintained in conformity with the ability of each of research scientists but in no circumstances should even a capable scientist be over-burdened with responsibilities.

44. Each institute should have a competent publication section entrusted with the presentation, language, get up etc. of the publications.

45. In the choise of participants in conferences, seminars and symposia held either within the country or abroad the scientist who has made the major contribution should be preferred even though junior. The choice of a younger research worker is suggested in view of the fact that it would act as an incentive to him. Every scientist who is so selected to participate should be properly groomed, for which the senior scientists having experience should be held responsible.

46. It should be made obligatory on the part of all categories of research workers including the heads of divisions and institutes not to be away except under special circumstances, for more than a week or so from the headquarters for attending meetings, conferences, symposia etc.

47. Triplication of substations being out of question, the most feasible arrangement seems to be to put the substations of central institutes under the control of agricultural universities, but making the facilities available thereto the central institutes and the State Governments either for collaborative or for independent work.

48. The agricultural universities should take up, in their stride for carrying out rssearch work, more and more of basic research related to agriculture, and formulation of such projects as part of their own

research programmes.

49. Because of ready help received, complacency prevails which cuts at the root of self-reliance. The opposite has also happened, though rarely. Because of these possibilities all collaborations should be sought with proper caution and foresight.

50. All the scientists of a laboratory should be familiar with the agency's as well the nation's scientific and technological objectives and country's socio-economic plans. They should also be apprised of the functions of the laboratory to further these objectives.

51. Once the projects are distributed and budgetary allocations made for each project, the scientists-in-charge should be independent of any financial control within the budgetary allocation. They should, however, be accountable for the progress achieved and the expenditure involved at the end of specified periods, which may ordinarily vary from one to five years.

52. Instead of hierarchical system with defined functions and status and seniority consciousness, a collegiate system with appropriate freedom and responsibility and accountability is desirable in a laboratory.

53. There should not be any bar on an outstanding scientist getting a higher emolument than that of the head of the department to which the scientist belongs, or even higher than that of the Director.

54. Gradation of scientists into categories A to F, as, for instance, in the CSIR with overlapping scales of pay commends itself, in contrast to scales having well defined stages commensurate with status as in Government establishment.

55. The procedure for the evaluation of a research scientist on the basis of scrutiny of his self-assessment report is more objective and should be given a fair trial.

56. It is in the interest of the laboratory that its scientists are given opportunities to upgrade their knowledge by occasional training in advanced centres, attending conferences, and participating in seminars and symposia.

57. The writing of monographs, reviews and text-books by competent scientists should be encouraged.

58. There should be arrangements to rotate administrative posts, so that after a lapse of 3 to 5 years a scientist may return to his research work.

59. A scientist should not be attached to more than three projects whether as leader or as associate or both.

60. If a scientist has got a bright idea, which does not even remotely, conform to the objectives of the laboratory either this should be taken up as a special case, or he may be offered facilities in another laboratory either of the same or of another agency.

61. Delegation of powers from the headquarters of the agency to the Director of the laboratory and a similar delegation to the head of a division/section are desirable features in a collegiate type of structure.

62. The Director and divisional/departmental heads may have the option to set out at the end of a tenure if they choose to join the rank of active scientists. The tenure should not exceed two terms of three years each at the ICAR headquarters.

63. At least a block grant or a rolling budget on a five year basis may be quite helpful so that money in one year may be carried over to the next year. The control of expenditure of sanctioned budget for the laboratory should be entirely in the hands of the Director, and similarly for divisions and even projects in the hands of the heads and project leaders respectively.

64. Every teaching institution and research institute should be provided with workshop training and the practice of designing and fabricating equipment.

65. The scientists belonging to the same or different agencies should have scope for free exchange of ideas, expertise and facilities. There should be some regular arrangements for scientists of one agency to work in another agency and derive mutual benefit.

66. A competent administrator should see that men capable of contributing to fundamental knowledge are given opportunity and freedom. "Research originating in the minds of scientists" should form an equally important component of the total research effort.

67. On the one hand, the status and prestige of extension workers should be raised, on the other hand, the research worker must compulsorily go to the field and join hands with the extension workers and see that his research findings are properly applied.

68. For the initial induction the candidates for Agricultural Research Service should possess research experience and evidence of research capability. To attain this competence they should require at least a period of 4 to 5 years after the Master's degree. Maximum age of the candidate should, therefore, be raised to 28 years.

69. In view of the fact that a major reorganisation has been brought about in the ICAR only recently, the impact of the reorganised system should be watched and evaluated over a period of time before any further changes are introduced.

70. The research council of the Agricultural University and the adaptive research council of the State government should identify the priority areas of basic and long term applied researches which are of

importance to the development of agriculture in the state and draw up relevant projects and programmes. The latter being of the direct significance in agricultural development of the state, the State Government should finance them entirely. The two councils should jointly decide upon the more essential programmes and projects and allocate funds accordingly in case of financial constraints.

71. Considering the importance of contributions the agricultural universities can make towards the unliftment of country's agriculture, the Central Government should give such grants to the agricultural universities as would enable them to establish solid research foundations. As the different agricultural universities are at various levels of research achievement it would not be desirable to grant them research funds on a prorata basis. Instead, the grants should have to be determined by the individual requirements so that all the agricultural universities come up to a desired level.

72. One of ICAR's objective being to promote agricultural research, it should identify with the help of experts gaps in knowledge and scope of research in relevant fields, and find institutions and scientists competent to take up the needed research work.

73. For every plan period the centre and the state shall inform the university of the minimum level of funding that the university can expect for research from plan funds annually during the plan period. Funds will, of course, be made available on accepted programmes, but the sum total of such programmes shall not be less than the minimum accepted. Given the will, there is no doubt that guarantee of a minimum at the level of 80 per cent of possible actuals can be given by both the states and the centre. It should then be possible for the universities to plan the recruitment of their research personnel on a fairly long term basis so that at least 80 per cent of such personnel have long term contracts. The 20 per cent of the temporary posts that are unavoidable in any organised system, will take care of the fluctuations in the research programmes.

74. A strong centre of research can only be built around a scientist who has the qualities of leadership and therefore, the creation of professorial chairs and the subjects chosen should depend on the identification of suitable field of research which the university is in a position to promote and the presence of an outstanding scientist who can build up a tradition of research in the particular research field.

75. By creating these professorial chairs and providing for sufficient research grants many of the talented scientists competent to carry out fundamental research can be attracted to join the agricultural universities. While a good number of these chairs may carry a scale of pay of professors available in the universities, a few may be created on a higher scale and designated as Chairs of Excellence to be offered to outstanding scientists who have earned recognition in the field of fundamental research in agriculture or any discipline allied to it. These chairs may also be availed of to enable outstanding Indian scientists serving abroad to return and work in the country. It will also be useful to provide for research fellows, generally three to four in numbers, to work with each professor in the designated subject.

76. In view of the important role of agriculture in Indian economy, R&D funding in the agriculture sector should be raised in a phased manner so that in ten years or so it constitutes about 1 per cent of the contribution which the agriculture sector makes to the GNP.

77. Future research efforts should be directed more specifically to :

(i) Varieties of improved crops requiring intermediate doses of inputs for optimisation of yield ;
(ii) dry farming based on optimum water used ;
(iii) pulses, oilseeds, coarse millets, fodder, medicinal plants, vegetables and fruits ;
(iv) balanced emphasis on animal production, animal health and animal products technology ;
(v) mixed farming and use of a suitable mix of animal and mechanical/electrical power, keeping small size of farms in view ;
(vi) development of intermediate technologies ;
(vii) area development programmes ;
(viii) nutrition *vis-a-vis* food habits ;
(ix) waste utilisation and recycling of wastes ;
(x) development of biodegradable plant protection chemicals based on plant products having pesticidal properties ;
(xi) microbiological synthesis of products as supplementary and complementary to chemical synthesis ;
(xii) increase in the efficiency of solar energy utilisation by means of photosynthetic process ;
(xiii) introduction of nitrogen fixing power into cereals through genetic manipulation and other means, and tissue culture ;
(xiv) study of monsoons ; and
(xv) study of plant roots and their functions.

Education

Summary of Recommendations

The following is a summary of the important recommendations made in this chapter :

1. We reiterate the recommendations of the Education Commission regarding an agricultural orientation at primary and secondary school levels and recommend that the text books on general sciences should be written and the existing ones revised.

2. Education in home science should form an integral part of the general education for all children upto the middle stage.

3. There is urgent need for organising sound vocational and technical training in agriculture for intermediate level workers (men and women) through appropriate non-degree educational programmes.

4. Vocational education should be available more easily to the small and marginal farmers who are hard pressed for land and require greater technological guidance to increase productivity of their farms.

5. For the sake of expediency some of the KVKs for trainer's training may be associated with the research institutes but as a long term policy they should be attached only to the agricultural universities. Some of them may also be operated in consultation with and with the approval of the State government by voluntary agencies having reputation for public service.

6. Each of the Krishi Vigyan Kendras should have academic freedom to develop its own programmes in conformity with the needs of the area in which it is situated. Evaluation should be a built-in component of the Krishi Vigyan Kendra to review, revise and improve the courses in conformity with the need of the region, type of trainees and development programmes.

7. Some programmes of non-formal vocational education suitable for the people of tribal areas should be formulated, which in several respects may have to be different from the ordinary run.

8. As a follow up measure of the training and trainees not absorbed in jobs should be provided with loans, marketing, extension and farm input services, as a step towards self-equipment.

9. For the vocational education infrastructures of existing institutions should be utilised, as far as practicable for the vocational courses meant for women trainees, women teachers should preferably be appointed.

10. For the success of vocational education programmes it will be advisable to give preference to those who have graduated from the polytechnics and vocational agricultural schools and have appreciable farm experience.

11. There should be ample opportunity and provision for continuation and development in academic skill and aptitudes, so that apart from ensuring a flow of skilled operatives for the agricultural services, the best and the most gifted students could continue their training at the higher level.

12. Coordination of non-degree agricultural education programme could best be ensured by an apex body consisting of representatives of the ICAR, Directorate of Extension at the centre, Ministry of Education and Social Welfare (NCERT), Ministry of Labour, Ministry of Health and Family Planning and selected technical heads of the State Departments.

13. The responsibility for follow-up activity, guiding supporting and assisting the field activities in connection with youth programmes and developing non-formal educational activity at the block level should be that of the block authorities.

14. There should be only one agricultural university in a state, having if necessary autonomous campuses in suitable locations. Each of such campuses should have a pro-vice-chancellor as its executive head, having the same powers in the campus as the vice-chancellor of the main university. All such campuses should be under one academic umbrella.

15. The Board of Management of the university should have members who are committed to academic principles and would be prepared to give more of their time and experience for the development of the university.

16. The substandard colleges should be abolished and be reorganised into Krishi Vigyan Kendras or centres of vocational education.

17. The Dean of the faculty/college who is in charge of teaching, Director of Research and Director of Extension should be jointly responsible for an integrated function of the three activities within the overall purview of the subject matter.

18. The inclusion of student representatives with limited participation is the best possible means of getting across students' ideas in the administration of universities in which they are the most vital and important constituent.

19. Universities should provide not only the needed practical training as a part of the curriculum but also some well planned activities of learning by doing, aimed at creating practical competence and confidence. To ensure these activities for students it is necessary to have an organisation of student welfare and services.

20. Undergraduate curricula should be developed

with a core component emphasising fundamental principles with ability to solve problems as they arise, with electives in production oriented areas like crop production, farm management, farm machinery and power, soil and water conservation, agricultural communication etc.

21. Instead of prolonging the training period of under graduates as it happens in internship training, the practical training required for either self-employment or professional employment should be built into the course, except in cases like animal sciences and fisheries.

22. Bachelor degree programmes in basic sciences and humanities need not be started in agricultural universities, post-graduate programmes in selected disciplines in basic science which would provide the necessary support to advance research work in agriculture may be taken up.

23. Periodical checks on the grading by the individual teachers/teaching departments should be enforced for some time to come to remove the doubts about the fairness of internal evaluation.

24. The agricultural universities' staff including those of research and extension should accept, as a part of their academic responsibility, the preparation of suitable text books.

25. It would be desirable for the universities and employing agencies to confer regarding modification of courses or introduction of new ones, keeping an eye on employment opportunities. The agricultural universities may also think of short-term courses to meet the needs of employer.

26. The ICAR should insist on creation of an inter university task group which would study the employment opportunities of agricultural graduates and formulate necessary action programmes.

27. The universities should organise an efficient placement service to provide a link between the graduates and their prospective employers by publishing and circulating directory of their graduates.

28. The universities must have a system of transfer of academic credits from one university to the other.

29. The agricultural university should develop linkages with agencies which supply the necessary inputs to agriculture.

30. The agricultural university should work with the state manpower bodies so that manpower planning may be related both quantitatively and qualitatively to changing employment needs and opportunities. It would similarly be necessary to work with manpower cells of agencies in the private sector concerned with agriculture.

31. For improving the standard of university education and arming the state with adequately trained personnel for developmental work, the universities and research institutes should come together and formulate training programmes and implement them jointly with a clear understanding of purpose and complementarity.

32. Collaboration for improving the standard of post graduates research should be fostered between the agricultural universities and general universities.

33. It would not be proper in the best of university tradition to conduct any commercial enterprises for increasing financial resources.

34. The State Government should fix block grants for the university making a practical and realistic assessment of requirements of the funds for efficient management of its programmes for a period of five years giving complete freedom to the university to regulate the expenditure within the grant without any preconditions. An automatic annual increase of 5-10 per cent in block grant should be allowed on the previous grant for normal rise in almost all the items of expenditure.

35. The State Government should be prepared to give matching grant to take over the entire liability of educational and research programmes financed initially by the ICAR, and to provide separate grant for the maintenance of all facilities namely college buildings, laboratory and library buildings and other physical facilities constructed with the financial assistance of ICAR following State PWD norms and also to provide sufficient 'foundation grants' for agricultural universities.

36. Ten to twenty per cent of the total plan outlay under the agricultural development programmes should be earmarked in the state budget for agricultural education and research.

37. We endorse the guidelines in respect of ICAR assistance as suggested by vice-chancellors of agricultural universities and examined by the ICAR's Norms and Accredition Committee.

38. For education and training of women, educational infrastructure at the middle and lower levels should be developed. The women's training centres should be strengthened and those closed should be revived. This programme should be brought under the integrated department of agriculture.

39. Since the number of VLWs (men and women) and other functionaries needed at the village level is very large, all the Gramsevak/Gramsevika training centres, agricultural schools and other similar training institutes should concurrently run in-service training courses for them. For this purpose the centres of training should be equipped with adequate qualified teachers and uptodate teaching materials.

40. Since modern farming involves managerial skills for efficient use of land, labour, water and other necessary inputs, farm management specialists should be posted at each Gramsevak/Sevika training centre. To impart adequate practical training to VLWs each Gramsevak training centre should be allotted not less than 20 hectares of land with reasonable irrigation facilities. Necessary steps should therefore be taken to provide this facility at centres where they do not exist. Where new centres are to be set up, it would be desirable to locate them a t the available seed farms.

41. It would be desirable for each State Government to draw up a phased programme for deputation of its staff for in-service training. For maintaining quality and imparting uptodate knowledge to the trainees the agricultural universities should be suitably involved either by arranging for classes there or having university experts on short-term deputation to the training centres. A joint training board suitably represented by the relevant training institutions, faculties of universities and State Departments should formulate training programmes, organise the curricula and courses and set norms of evaluation of the trainees. The agricultural universities should be given the responsibility of the training programmes of the trainers.

42. Considering that the in-service training of extension officers is to be repeated after every 3 years, to keep pace with modern technology, it is imperative that all the agricultural universities and colleges should develop appropriate training facilities for officials of all categories.

43. There is need to review the working of the summer institutes and to find out to what extent the intended benefits accrue in reality, commensurate with the financial commitments involved.

44. It may be ensured that the trained persons are retrained where they are most useful.

45. There is lack of adequate and reliable data about current manpower situation, namely, staffing pattern, classification of jobs, number of persons who have received in-service training etc. The concerned subject matter departments/organisations instead of a central agency, should in our opinion, be made responsible for collection and analysis of these data for their own use and benefit. The data may be centrally pooled in the Ministry for purposes of information and for correcting regional imbalances, if any.

46. In regard to division of responsibility for organising training programmes, following recommendation made in our Interim Report on SAARET is reiterated. Joint Training Board may be constituted at the State level with an officer of the rank of a Joint Director as convener to look after the training programmes of departmental junior staff members, field functionaries and farmers, and the agricultural universities should organise periodical training of top and middle level administrators and experts of Government Departments.

47. The expenditure for training should be earmarked and placed at the disposal of training centres with the provision that the same allowances and amenities are enjoyed by the trainees irrespective of the states which they come from.

48. Animal production should be treated as an independent major subject. Veterinary science should also be developed to a high standard simultaneously.

49. Education in dairying should be integrated with the mainstream of educational programme in animal science or organised in agricultural universities. Central Government should grant financial assistance to selected agricultural universities agreeing to initiate such programmes.

50. The National Dairy Research Institute should divest itself of the Indian Dairy Diploma and the Bachelor's degree course training in dairying as soon as possible.

51. For better commercial exploitation of different animal products, education not only is dairy technology but also in technology of other animal products should be developed expeditiously.

52. Educational programmes in animal science should be developed in agricultural universities under a single faculty.

53. Training course in dairy production should be integrated with the educational programme in animal production but dairy technology course should remain separate.

54. In the educational system in animal science, the following Bachelor's degree courses may initially be introduced :

(a) B.V.Sc.
(b) B. Sc. (Animal Production)
(c) B. Sc. (Dairy Technology)
(d) B. Sc. (Meat and Poultry Product Technology), and
(e) B. Sc. (Wool Technology).

55. Duration of study for the proposed Bachelor's degree courses should be more than four years. Additionally, internship or intensive practical training for a fixed period should be introduced.

56. Students in animal production should be provided with choice of elective courses pertaining to a particular species of livestock. Such courses may be pursued during the last six months of the study period.

57. A thorough revision and recasting of curricula and syllabi will be required for introdu ing reorganised educational programmes. The Indian Council of Agricultural Research or the Association of Agricultural Universities should constitute a special committee for this purpose.

58. Senior members of the teaching staff should also take practical classes. Lack of facilities for conducting practical work should be removed.

59. The ICAR should make a thorough and critical evaluation of the facilities for post-graduate education in animal science.

60. Specieswise Master's degree course in addition to the existing disciplinewise degree courses should be developed.

61. Should a student desire a change in the field of study at Master's degree level, there need not be any bar for enrolment provided he first earns the required credits in which he may be found deficient.

62. Central research institutes should undertake only the educational programmes that agricultural universities or other teaching institutions are at present unable to manage effectively.

63. Post graduate certificate and diploma courses should be discontinued in the central research institutes when such programmes or degree courses in coguate subjects have been developed in other teaching institutions.

64. No post graduate diploma should be awarded where facilities exist for award of degree courses in the same subject.

65. To ensure effective utilisation of university level education, apex bodies should be constituted in each state expeditiously.

66. Agricultural universities should re-examine the question of allocation of funds for education in animal science to ensure high standard of education and training.

67. Below-university-level training courses should be periodically reviewed by competent bodies. Provision of competent staff and teaching aids should be given adequate attention in these training programmes.

68. There is a need to establish 'intermediate' level educational programmes in all the three divisions of animal science with openings for subsequent university level education.

69. Schemes should be drawn up and implemented for bettering the promotion prospects of and for providing incentives to the junior staff with below-university-level education.

70. The educational pattern at the Central Institute of Fisheries Education, Bombay, should be reoriented and facilities strengthened in order to cater for degree courses, both B.Sc. and M.Sc. in Fisheries sciences, under the administrative control of the ICAR. The facilities and the staff at the Central Institute of Fisheries Operatives, Cochin, should also be strengthened to make it more effective and useful.

71. As part of agricultural education, fisheries education should be imparted in the agricultural universities. The ICAR may select a few universities for supporting fisheries education, only agricultural universities for inland fisheries on a regional basis, and the universities of Cochin, Bombay and Mangalore college of the university of Agricultural sciences, Hebbal, for marine fisheries. Courses in fisheries at universities should be opened only after careful examination by expert groups constituted by the ICAR. The graduate level courses can develop on a regional basis, depending on the special needs of the region where a university is located, but the post graduate courses should have an 'all-India basis' in order to provide for recruitment, placement and inter-changeability of personnel at senior levels.

72. The B.Sc. degree course in fisheries should be of the same duration as other disciplines in agricultural universities, and should be without any specialisation but with an elective subject in the final year and additional practical training for six months after the completion of the degree course, preferably biased towards the elective subject. In the recruitment of middle level fisheries personnel, preference should be given to graduate in fisheries.

73. The M.Sc. degree course in Fisheries should cover, at an advanced level, all aspects of fisheries as included in B.Sc. (Fisheries), but with specialisation in an elective subject. The admission would ordinarily be open to graduates in fisheries only, but consideration should also be given to graduates in other subjects having bearing on fisheries, with initial compulsory orientation course is fisheries. In the recruitment of higher level personnel and research associates in fisheries, preference should be given to candidates with M.Sc. in fisheries.

74. Training and guiding research work leading to Ph.D. degree in fisheries, should be conducted at the agricultural universities and such general universities as would have fisheries and allied courses.

75. The concerned universities, developing facilities for degree courses in fisheries education, should constitute a committee comprising representatives of the ICAR, UGC, State Governments, fisheries institutes and the fishing industry, to look into the question of entrance requirements, core and elective subjects, duration of study, practical training and internship.

76. The training of middle level extension workers

should receive special attention, since extension has been a weak link in the fisheries developmental activities. The extension centre in inland fish culture at Hyderabad should be suitably staffed and adequately equipped and the proposed extension centre in marine fisheries should be established immediately.

77. Keeping in view the need for assistance in the diversified fields of engineering such as naval architecture, refrigeration, fish farm construction, electronic, electric and mechanical machinery, etc., orientation training biased towards fisheries should be organised at the existing fisheries institutions having the necessary facilities.

78. Provision should be made for the training of field assistants employed in fisheries research, production and utilisation centres at the secondary/polytechnic and at the diploma/intermediate levels, with opportunities to acquire higher qualifications at the degree level.

79. Training for inland fisheries operatives has to be arranged at the regional, and even at the state level so that instruction can be imparted in the local languages. Arrangements for this training should be made at the Krishi Vigyan Kendras (KVKs) and other polytechnics at the state level. Adequate teaching staff and training facilities should be made available through the Department of Fisheries.

80. Training of higher level functionaries in the fisheries organisation should be the responsibility of the Central Government.

Extension

Summary of Recommendations

The main recommendations are as under :

1. The operational procedure of National Demonstration Programme needs to be streamlined. The staff located at each of the research stations of the agricultural universities should be encouraged to conduct the national demonstrations around research stations rather than establishing a separate team of national demonstration specialists in a few selected districts.

2. The demonstration plot should be within easy reach of the farmers who are expected to benefit by them. There is also need for taking up more of commercial crops in various rotations on demonstration plots so as to meet the needs of different categories of farmers.

3. Facilities for mobile soil testing laboratories should be fully utilised for the work of national demonstrations. Agricultural Universities should arrange intensive refresher training programmes for subject-matter specialists in soil analysis so as to make them fully conversant with the latest research in techniques of soil testing. They should also be acquainted with the micro-nutrient deficiency symptoms in the crops.

4. Suitable national demonstration programmes should be developed for new programmes such as dry farming, fodder development, horticulture and plantation crops which should be the responsibility of the research organisations and the technical experts under the state administration.

5. There should be national demonstration on the proper use of cross-bred bullocks in different seasons and on other animal husbandry activities such as improved poultry raising, sheep rearing, swine husbandry etc. National demonstrations in fisheries also will have to be developed mostly on government or institution-owned farms for intensive development of water spreads in the surrounding areas.

6. The aspects relating to water management technology should form part of the national demonstration programmes.

7. Greater emphasis is required on systematic test demonstrations or adoptive trials on the farmers' fields in different areas.

8. Work and experience under the national demonstrations should be evaluated continuously so that lessons of universal nature are disseminated and there is adequate feedback to the agricultural universities and research stations for better organisation of these demonstrations.

9. It is desirable to have adequately large number of demonstrations to ensure sufficient positive results to change people's minds. There should be greater emphasis on intrinsic motivational approach while organising these demonstrations through the educational process rather than through subsidies.

10. Extension workers should be encouraged to organise village meetings and discuss the advantages of new practices in order to motivate the local community. Greater attention should be given to increasing achievement motivation of farmers.

11. There should be close coordination between extension efforts and the availability of agri-support activities for the rapid transfer of agricultural technology.

12. The decisions regarding the format, time and method of dissemination through publicity media should be taken at the district level and made to suit local conditions.

13. The information organisation should have close rapport with the research scientists so that the information to be supplied is in keeping with the latest research findings. The central information unit should

only disseminate important scientific findings to the administration in the states and leave it to them to disseminate what they think is topical and important from the local angle.

14. The films should be topical and of immediate interest and should be properly dubbed in the local language. Films and magic lantern shows should be tuned to the local conditions and requirements.

15. The state departments and the agricultural universities should try to make greater use of the local press for disseminating farm information.

16. It is necessary that the farmers trained under Farmers' Education and Training Programme are involved in the extension process.

17. The farmers' training centres and the gram-sevak training centres should, as far as possible, be located on the same campus and a senior officer should be in charge for coordinating the activities of the training centres and production programmes in the district.

18. In the farmers' training centres in districts where intensive cattle development projects and dairy schemes and poultry and sheep development projects are in operation, special facilities should be created to train farmers in these specific fields.

19. There is immediate need to train farmers and members of farm families to improve their competence in the profitable processing of livestock products.

20. Farmers' education and training programme should include the education of women in the rural areas also. A special curriculum for women should be introduced for the more technical aspects of subsidiary occupations and to change the diet patterns and the production with a view to having better nutrition. Farm women should have appropriate population education. These aspects should be included in the curricula of farmers' education.

21. The present programme of training farm women should be expanded and intensified and a separate wing should be opened at the farmers' training centre with suitable staff for training farm women.

22. Farmers' education and training must include courses on organisation skills, family skills and continuing educational skills.

23. It will be necessary to put across special programmes of broadcasts for women emphasising action points in subsidiary occupations and nutritional guidance and culinary instructions The *mahila samitis* organised under the Applied Nutrition Programme can be suitably expanded to be the discussion forum for this special programme.

24. The Extension Directorate at the centre and the proposed Directorates of Extension at the state level should be more closely involved than at present in the administration of Farmers' Functional Literacy Programme.

25. Particular attention will have to be given to bringing those farmers within the fold of the functional literacy programme who cannot utilise the developmental facilities because they are illiterate.

26. The functional literacy-cum-education campaign should focus its attention on developing decision-making ability of the farmer.

27. The farmers' training should embrace the farmers at the lower socio-economic levels. The scope and concept of farmers' training should be expanded to cater to the needs of different types of farming activities characteristic of a particular area.

28. In the curriculum for training of farmers, farm management including maintenance of farm accounts should be made an essential part.

29. Farmers' discussion groups should be formed in as many villages as possible.

30. The allotment of farmers' training centres should be by the number of blocks. For the present, there should be at least one farmers' training centre for every 15 blocks irrespective of the size of the district.

31. It is necessary to bring the VLWs to the training centres at least once in three years for practical training on new methods and techniques of agriculture.

32. The refresher course for extension personnel should be revised at an interval of two to five years depending on the field covered and pace of advancement in that field. The training course should be of six weeks or so.

33. Agricultural universities can provide facilities for subject matter training to the instructional staff of the various vocational institutes. It is also desirable that some of the senior staff members of the university are deputed for the staff courses organised on regional and all-India basis.

34. The teachers in the agricultural polytechnics or Krishi Vigyan Kendras should be graduates in the various disciplines and suitably trained in extension education.

35. The section of home-science and nutrition education in the Directorate of Extension at the centre should be suitably strengthened so that they can provide a desirable national leadership. All such programmes handled by other Departments and Ministries should be brought into its fold.

36. There should be no control from the centre in the field of extension or training, vocational education or in home science. The responsibilities of each level should be clearly defined so that there is no tendency to overlap.

37. Every effort should be made to have proper

coordination and integration among the various agencies of extension, i.e., normal block agency, extension staff under special programmes, farmers' training centres, national demonstrations and the agricultural universities, so that the farmer is able to take full advantage of them and multiplicity of agencies is avoided.

38. The non-governmental and governmental undertakings like the National Seeds Corporation or the Fertilizer Corporation of India and similar other agencies like cooperatives should provide facilities for the training of farmers, farm youth and farm women.

39. There should be a close relationship between the grāmsevak training centres and agricultural universities.

40. The original concept of the rural institutes as suggested by the University Education Commission, 1948 should be accepted and adhered to.

41. The role of the agricultural universities in extension should be confined to conducting field trials for testing the research findings, development of agricultural technology and demonstrating its practical utility, provision of farm advisory service up to the district level, functioning as a source of agricultural information, development of effective communication media, participation in training programmes etc.

42. The Departments of Agriculture/Animal Husbandry/Fisheries at the state level should have overall responsibility for extension work and should also be responsible for suggesting field problems and formulating new farm technology, conducting field trials and demonstrations, a common information cell alongwith the agricultural university, organisation of training programmes etc.

43. The Central Directorate of Extension will be responsible for coordinating extension and training activity in the country, and laying down the broad principles for the nation in the field in consultation with states. The central agency should also conduct sample assessment of the extension and the training programmes with a view to drawing conclusions of value for improvement of these programmes. It should also maintain up-to-date data of manpower requirements in the context of development programmes.

Credit and Incentives

Summary of Recommendations

The main recommendations are as under :

1. For maximum coverage of small and marginal farmers under the credit system for upgrading and modernising agriculture over the next 10 years, a ground level organisation should be built up fulfilling the criteria of : (a) facilitating conversion of credit into inputs and services and ensuring a fair price for the produce, and (b) operating fully on a commercial basis.

2. The major components of the new credit policy should be (a) to provide an integrated agricultural credit service to facilitate the adoption of new technology, (b) to extend its scope to all aspects of rural development (including livestock rearing, dairying, fisheries, farm forestry, sericulture, etc.), and marketing, transport and processing, and (c) to facilitate linkages between finance and services for current inputs and investments in land improvement, minor irrigation and farm equipment.

3. The first principle of agricultural credit policy should be that the activities financed for individual enterprises or projects, must have actual or potential financial viability. When necessary suitable organisational support should be provided to generate viability. The institutional and public resources used for capital investment and working capital must generate, over a period, adequate income for repayment of loan.

4. There should be a single source of institutional credit for all credit requirements of the farmers. Commercial banks can lend to the small farmers upto 12 years, when such lending is eligible for refinance from ARC or other financial institutions.

5. There should be close integration of financing plans and lending between different agencies operating in the same area in the form of agreed lending norms, broad division of functions and collaboration.

6. Supply of credit should be integrated with the organisation and management of supply of inputs and services. Both should be entrusted to the same agency at the field level.

7. Institutional financial agencies should ensure that necessary credit facilities would be available to medium and large farmers promptly on normal commercial terms for all requirements.

8. In order to enable small and marginal farmers to catch up with the previous lag, weightage should be given to their needs and credit should be extended on preferential terms both in regard to interest charges and quantum of advances.

9. The commercial banks should enjoy the same authority and facilities in terms of statutory rights as financing institutions over defaulting borrowers and power to supervise and give directives to the borrowers for appropriate use of credit, as the cooperative banks vis-a-vis their role of financing primary cooperatives.

10. Necessary facilities should be given so that suspension of credit does not take place because of crop failures or market fluctuations. Adequate

medium-term carry-over finance should be provided in dry farming areas to tide over bad years and the criterion of profitability over a period of years should be built into the system of credit.

11. Effective credit service should help the farmer to reach self-sustaining stage as regards to requirements of working capital.

12. Farmers' service societies should be set up, one for each tehsil/block or any other viable unit of convenient size with as many branches as are required in the area, to provide integrated agricultural credit service to the farmers. This service should be accessible to all small and marginal farmers and agricultural labourers who want to upgrade their technology. The FSS would be a registered cooperative body to ensure autonomy, efficient management and freedom.

13. The FSS should have functions as listed in the paragraph. FSS should take care of all the development needs of the small and marginal farmers and agricultural labourers, village artisans and persons rendering rural services.

14. The working capital of the FSS should be drawn from credit lines from the financing banks and proceeds and charges for services, reasonable trade margin as inputs, commission and fees from marketing organisations, margins on loans, etc.

15. The FSS should develop close business relationship with other bodies such as land development banks and various corporations. Such institutions should play a vital supporting role in offering services to farmers to absorb credit for productive purposes.

16. There should be a union of the FSS at the district level for mutual consultation and coordination of policies. Where the production, marketing and processing of any agricultural produce assume large proportion, separate functional cooperative organisations should be established. A close organisational and functional link-up should be established between the FSS and the functional cooperative organisations.

17. The State governments and the cooperative departments should extend administrative and extension support to the FSS and direct and encourage them. There should be a clear demarcation of functions between the extension services, general planning and development agencies and the FSS.

18. The areas served by the FSS the extension service should be the concern and responsibility of the society. The group of technical experts at the taluk/tehsil level should help the extension cadre of the FSS in technical matters. There would be no need in these areas for a separate departmental agency. FSS should develop its own cadre with various hierarchical tiers so that right type of personnel get attracted for serving the society.

19. The FSS should not restrict itself to land-based cultivation. Diversification of business is important and provision of facilities for developing subsidiary occupations like livestock rearing, dairying, fisheries, farm forestry, sericulture, etc. should be encouraged to benefit particularly weaker sections of the farming community.

20. The experience of the existing societies indicates the need for caution and proper phasing in the establishment of new societies so that by the end of the sixth year 2,520 societies are started on the lines indicated.

21. Forty-five per cent of the 1985 level of "graduated" requirements of short-term loans and 40 per cent of medium and long term loans should be met by the end of the fifth five year plan itself. (The respective roles of commercial and cooperative banks has been indicated in Appendix 55.9—statement VI, of the chapter). During 1975-85 the cooperative will have to almost double both their short-term and medium and long-term credit and the banking system should work towards increasing their agricultural loans from Rs. 1,450 crores in 1978-79 to Rs. 4,050 crores in 1984-85. The Reserve Bank of India and the Government should immediately initiate planning for business and manpower development to equip them to achieve these targets.

22. Storage and marketing system should be developed to keep pace with the expansion of output generated by credit services. Storage development, preferably by the FSS and cooperative sector, should start right at the farm. The negotiability of warehouse receipts needs improvement.

23. Location of new branches of commercial banks in rural areas should be related to concentration of small farmers to ensure reasonable proximity and mutual access. The banks and the cooperatives should give priority to the needs of the non-borrowing members blending credit with services.

24. Previous debts should be scaled down in the light of prevailing regulations regarding debt redemption. Outstanding amounts should be taken care of by the period of repayment being extended and by making production programmes of the farmers so broad-based as to take care of repayment of not only instalments of old loans but also the due instalments of new loans. The FSS can help in observing a discipline so that the genuine cases are disposed off fairly by a convention.

25. The concept of linking specific investments for local agricultural development with locally mobilised savings should be adopted. It should be possible to have specific schemes of a local nature ready for implementation from these resources.

26. Generally subsidies to individuals should be confined only to the weaker sections of the society such as the small and marginal farmers and agricultural labourers.

27. The policies for subsidies should be based upon the principles of selective application and subvention for those classes, sectors and key programmes that need support in the interest of balanced and quick development and in keeping with the objective of growth with social justice. The attempt should also be to use the intrinsic methods of motivation more and more and depend less upon the extrinsic ones i.e., subsidies etc.

28. Subsidies on export-oriented crops should be reviewed periodically and should be discontinued as soon as the purpose has been served and are no longer justified.

29. As demand for the insurance of capital assets can be expected to be greater than for the insurance of crops, this aspect may be examined in detail with a view to evolve a practical approach.

30. Pilot studies should be undertaken for covering more crops under insurance specially foodgrains in the different regions of the country.

31. The premium rates for crop insurance will have to be kept low in areas of low productivity and high fluctuations.

32. The arrangements for ensuring the minimum prices in the case of commercial crops like cotton, jute, etc., should be adequately improved.

33. A system of competitions with a wider appeal should be instituted in addition to the National Award Competitions, under which all those who reach specified yield levels should be recognised.

34. The competitions for crop, fruits, milk, etc., have proved useful and should be continued in future. There should be greater social and community recognition to innovating and enterprising farmers who have distinguished themselves by achieving greater productivity irrespective of their economic status.

Marketing, Transport and Storage

Summary of Recommendations

The main recommendations made in the chapter are summarised below :

1. The existing shandies should be restructured either as assembly or sub-markets depending upon their location, volume of commodities, trade and number of buyers and sellers. At the sub-markets there should be adequate facilities for grading, weighing and storage of all commodities.

2. All assembly, wholesale and terminal markets should be brought under regulation as early as possible.

3. Each regulated market should have a market committee duly constituted to supervise the market in accordance with the rules and regulations as formulated by the Agricultural Produce Marketing (Regulation) Acts. Growers should have major representation in the Market Committee. The chairman and vice-chairman should be representative of growers only.

4. All commodities of crop and livestock origin and minor forest produce should be notified at every market to make the Act really meaningful. The levy of market fee should be on *ad valorem* basis. The market area should comprise of a revenue sub-division of a tehsil or taluk.

5. Each regulated market should have an adequate market yard and an administrative block to accommodate officials of the market committees, market functionaries, post and telegraph office and bank. Each market should have an optimum number of warehouses for storing the produce.

6. A regulated market should have a minimum number of qualified people to operate the market efficiently. The persons who are vital to operate a market are Secretary, Supervisor, Market Intelligence Inspector, Grader and Auctioneer.

7. Sale of produce should be by open auction and/or tender system.

8. All State governments should create a Market Development Fund. This Fund should be utilized for developing weak markets.

9. All State governments should prepare an integrated plan for development of regulated markets on the lines indicated in paragraph 56.1.6.

10. Branches of primary cooperative marketing societies should be established at all the regulated markets.

11. Farmers' service societies should assist the cooperative marketing societies at all markets and perform marketing functions on their own at locations where cooperative marketing societies do not exist.

12. Brokers should be phased out from the markets. The question of making payments to producer-seller from banks at the regulated market needs consideration. State Marketing Authority should issue licences to market functionaries operating in more than one market within the State and DMI should be authorised to issue licences to all market functionaries operating at regulated market in more than one state.

13. All inputs needed by the farmers for agricultural operations should be made available to them through

any of the existing three channels namely, primary cooperative marketing societies, agro-industries corporation and sale depots of the private traders.

14. Research should be done in improving pre-harvest treatment of crops, and to prevent post-harvest losses and also to improve the quality of products intended for marketing. The economics of using mechanical driers to avoid microbial contamination in pepper berries needs immediate attention. There is an urgent need to standardise the drying and bleaching process in case of ginger. Using cow-dung for cooking and use of lead salts to brighten the colour of turmeric should be discouraged. Suitable alternative methods should be evolved.

15. The existing tobacco flue-curing barns should be modified to improve the efficiency of fuel utilisation.

16. Steps should be taken to establish ribboning and decortication centres in jute growing areas and these should be operated either through the village panchayats or farmer service societies.

17. To break the monopoly of the private sector, a chain of efficiently operated processing units should be established in the cooperative sector. To ensure regular supply of raw materials, they should be linked with the primary cooperative marketing societies. Marketing orders and market agreements between growers and processors should be encouraged.

18. Existing sheller mills for paddy should be modernized since they are economical for medium capacity milling. The number of modern rice mills to be established and their location should be decided only after a detailed feasibility study. The price policy of the government should be such as to provide stability to the marketing system and encourage modernizing of rice mills.

19. Traditional *dal* mills should be phased out and instead mills equipped with proved technology based on research findings CFTRI should be established.

20. New type of gins and presses should be installed in future. Local firms should be encouraged to fabricate these in the country. Processing units in the cooperative sector should be established to handle at least 50 per cent of cotton produced in the country in order to break the monopoly of the textile industry and save producers from exploitation.

21. Low cost, small capacity sugarcane crushers should be designed and popularised in the rural areas.

22. Feasibility studies should be conducted before establishing processing units so as to utilize the capacity to the maximum and to operate it at the lowest cost possible.

23. All markets brought under regulation should have facilities to grade all agricultural commodities. Procedure for grading at producer's level should be simplified by laying down one or two recognized quality factors looked for by buyers in the case of each kind of produce at this stage of marketing.

24. Grading Supervisors and Graders working at regulated markets, warehouses of FCI, CWC, SWC and primary cooperative marketing societies should either be employees of the State or Central Marketing Department only.

25. Grading of all agricultural commodities raw as well as processed, intended both for intra-state and inter-state trade should be compulsory. All products meant for inter-state trade should be graded, inspected and certified by the staff of the DMI.

26. All commodities of crop livestock and fishery origin (both raw and processed) intended for export should be graded and inspected before shipment by DMI only acting as an Export Inspecting Agency on behalf of the Export Inspection Council.

27. A committee should be constituted by RBI to examine the credit needs of all agencies performing marketing functions.

28. A Perishable Agricultural Commodities Act to suppress unfair and fraudulent practices in inter state trade of perishable agricultural commodities should be enacted.

29. State marketing department should provide temporary physical facilities for orderly marketing to take place at cattle fairs and also depute their officials to supervise trading practices.

30. Separate space should be earmarked within the market yard for trading in livestock. Arrangements for supervising trading should be provided at small towns, where there are no regulated markets.

31. PCMS or wool boards should assist sheep breeders in assembly, grading, transport and selling of wool.

32. Curing centres should be established in rural areas and also at places near slaughter houses.

33. Poultry farmers associations or cooperative marketing societies should collect, grade, transport and organise sale of eggs in terminal markets on behalf of poultry breeders. They should set up more processing plants in urban areas.

34. Village roads should be improved by Zilla Parishads and roads between market centres to towns by Public Works Department. Market committees should contribute from their revenue towards development of these roads.

35. The conventional bullock cart needs to be redesigned so as to improve technical efficiency and increase the rate of return on capital invested and the

task of redesigning and field testing should be entrusted to the regional research-cum-testing centres set up by Indian Council of Agricultural Research.

36. Construction of all weather roads in hilly areas where fruits and vegetables are grown should be taken up on priority basis and introduction of helicopter service in the inaccessible areas needs consideration.

37. Efforts have to be made by railways to reduce detention time at transhipment points, avoid procedural delays at the time of booking and unloading and increase the number of quick transport services.

38. Sample traffic surveys should be conducted in selected areas to collect data on quantity and type of commodities moved to find out wasteful use of transportation facilities and suggest better methods.

39. Freight structure for fruits and vegetables needs to be rationalized. The number of refrigerated and insulated wagons should be increased. The wagons carrying perishables should be attached to express or mail trains.

40. Special type of trucks should be designed to transport perishable commodities and covered sheds provided at checkposts on highways where the trucks are likely to be detained for some time.

41. Detailed studies have to be conducted regarding the requirement of type of rail vans (insulated, refrigerated van 0°C temp., and refrigerated van at 20°C) needed at each production centre and marketing centre so as to make maximum use of scarce finance available.

42. Research should be conducted to assess the impact of transport on the condition of livestock. Special types of trucks should be designed to prevent bruises and shrinkage during transit.

43. Card board boxes should be used for fruits being despatched to long distances. Similarly, scientific use of paper for wrapping fruits and for padding and lining to prevent losses should be adopted.

44. Improved storage structures needed by farmers should be manufactured by agro-industries corporations and entrepreneurs as per ISI specifications. Research studies on designing improved storage structures using locally available material should be taken up by state agricultural universities.

45. The existing staff at the block level should be trained to conduct demonstration and training of farmers in the method of scientific storage and pest control.

46. Rodenticides and fumigants should be used for controlling loss in storage due to rodents and insect pests.

47. Grains should be properly dried and moisture content brought down to 8 per cent before storing. Fumigation of storage structures and dipping of bags in solutions of malathion or pyrethrum should be done by trained personnel only.

48. Where there are discolouration or signs of bad smell in bulk stored grains, they should be removed and cooled so as to prevent further damage. All bags containing grains should be stacked over dunnage and kept away from walls.

49. The existing all-India coordinated project on grain storage should be suitably modified and instead an all-India coordinated research project on post-harvest technology should be instituted under ICAR, with the coordinator at Hapur and research units at all state agricultural universities.

50. Government should not depend on private agencies to store foodgrains needed for public distribution. The storage capacity of FCI, CWC and SWC should be increased to store foodgrains required in cities, industrial towns, drought prone areas and flood affected areas.

51. The cooperative marketing societies and regulated markets located in cotton growing areas should plan an increase in the capacity of warehouses taking into account the likely areas. CCI should advance money to producers on the warehouse receipts issued by CWC, SWC and PCMS.

52. Cooperative marketing societies have to be organised in jute growing areas, to provide the much needed storage and credit facilities at the assembly points and regulated market complexes.

53. In view of fall in prices of fruits and vegetables, below economic levels, immediately after harvest for lack of storage and transport facilities, adequate measures have to be taken by cooperatives and public sector undertakings to provide cold storage facilities in production areas and terminal markets. The question of fixing maximum rental charges and the possibility of earmarking a certain percentage of cold storage for primary products under Cold Storage Order, 1964 needs examination.

54. FCI should concentrate on construction and maintenance of silos and flat type warehouses to store foodgrains needed for public distribution system and buffer stock on priority basis.

55. Since many quasi-government agencies and cooperatives are engaged in construction and operation of warehouses in each state, a committee consisting of representatives of FCI, CWC, SWC and co-operatives should be set up to co-ordinate the activities of these agencies.

56. Courses leading to a Degree in Agricultural Marketing should be instituted at agricultural

universities.

57. Diploma course in Agricultural Marketing of one year duration, senior level course for market secretaries and grading supervisors course should continue to be organised by DMI. Grades courses for specific commodities should be conducted by the state marketing departments.

58. All-India Co-ordinated Research Programme on Agricultural Marketing may be initiated under the aegis of ICAR.

59. Extension education in marketing should be improved. "Agmark" exhibitions should be held in rural areas. Extension literature in marketing should be distributed through regulated markets, PCMS and FSS to farmers.

60. Enforcement of rules and regulations is vital to prevent malpractices. The DMI should be suitably strengthened to perform the functions. Hence four units each headed by an officer of the rank of Jt. Agricultural Marketing Adviser should be set up at the DMI. The four units are :

1. Grading, standardization, inspection and certification.
2. Market surveys, co-ordination and extension.
3. Training, planning and development.
4. Supervision and regulation.

61. Each state should have a Directorate of Agricultural Marketing. State Agricultural Marketing Boards should be set up in those states where they have not been set up. The Boards should have both advisory and policy functions.

62. A Central Advisory Committee on Agricultural Marketing should be established with Principal Secretary in the Ministry of Agriculture and Irrigation as chairman, and consisting of representatives of departments concerned with different aspects of agricultural marketing and four State Governments by rotation.

Processing and Agro-Industries

Summary of Recommendations

The recommendations made in this chapter are summarised below :

1. In order to build up a good export market in processed fruit and vegetable products, a constant watch should be kept over the kinds of commodities required, the form of preservation preferred and the taste sought for in different countries.

2. In commercial dehydration of vegetables, tuber crops require special attention and among the tuber crops potatoes need particular attention. Big dehydration plants should be installed in the immediate vicinity of markets where wholesale transactions take place so as to avoid delays and save time and money in transport.

3. The plate of low phosphorus content suitable for canning purposes should be manufactured in the country and made available to can fabricators at reasonable cost until local manufacture becomes possible, sufficient imports of this kind of tin plate should be allowed to meet the requirements of the canning industry whether the product is meant for export or internal consumption.

4. The cost of tin cans should be kept within reasonable limits by reducing the charges levied on imports. There is also a case for reducing the ex-factory price of the canned or bottled product through concessions in taxes.

5. Glass manufacturers should be encouraged to produce canning jars of required quality.

6. Research is required to be expedited for producing plastic containers suitable for use in the preservation industry.

7. Sugar should be made available to fruit preservation industry on controlled rates uniformly irrespective of the fact whether the product is meant for export or otherwise.

8. It is necessary to enforce compulsory grading of fruits and vegetables in markets according to the already available ISI standards so that right quality of these items become available to the processing industry.

9. Research is needed to determine whether the processed food articles which are in contact with preservatives and tin or plastic containers are safe for habitual users and if not what type of containers have to be developed. It is desirable to determine the microbial and hygienic standards which should apply to fruit and vegetable preservation industry in the country. It is also necessary to determine at what levels sulphur is injurious in jams and the specifications should accordingly lay down these levels rather than insist upon the product to be completely free of this element.

10. The feasibility of utilizing broilers and culled birds need to be determined for canning industry.

11. There is need to establish in towns and rural areas manufacturing units to produce bakery and confectionery articles of daily use under hygienic conditions.

12. Use of millets and pulses in suitable blends needs to be developed for making bakery and confectionery products.

13. The equipment used in the preparation of various kinds of parched products from cereals and

millets needs to be modernised.

14. Various millet grains could be tried for starch making. These foodgrains could also be utilized for the preparation of glucose syrup. Steep water obtained from the wet milling of maize and jowar requires to be tried as a nutrient medium for the culture of micro-organisms in antibiotics industry.

15. Various foodgrains should be utilized for the separation of certain of their chemical ingredients which have potentialities in industry.

16. The preparation of malt syrup and other malted products requires to be stepped up by establishing more manufacturing units. This equally applies to beer manufacture and for this purpose the indigenous cultivation of hops (*Humulos SP.*) has to be encouraged.

17. Carbon-dioxide which is obtained as a by-product of the fermentation industry could be used for preservation purposes either in gaseous form by providing an inert atmosphere or in the form of dry ice which lowers the storage temperature.

18. The exploitation of pulses for preparing protein concentrates and isolates needs attention. It is also worth considering whether India could not manufacture gum from guar and export the finished commodity rather than trading in the raw material. This recommendation applies to other gum yielding plants as well.

19. The manufacture of golden syrup rich in glucose should be attempted from sugarcane crop of tender age.

20. Soyabean proteins and oil could be exploited for various purposes. The manufacture of vegetable milk from soyabean and groundnut should also engage attention.

21. All tuber crops require to be exploited for the manufacture of industrial starch. Preparation of industrial starch and sago has to be particularly encouraged in all the tapioca growing states because the low keeping quality of this tuber and also because sago has greater potentiality of utilization. It is expected that the cost of starch manufacture would go down with the increase in production in future. When this happens, possibility of exporting industrial starch could be explored.

22. The manufacture of products like garlic powder, alcoholic and non-alcoholic beverages and oil and oleoresius from ginger, flavouring constituents from turmeric rhizomes etc., could be encouraged.

23. Suitable restrictions should be imposed on the export of raw medicinal and aromatic plants. The processing of such material should be encouraged in the country itself and the manufactured product exported.

24. There should be a central laboratory for industrial utilization of agricultural products under the aegis of the ICAR with the status of a national laboratory. The scope of research work of this laboratory should cover all the branches of agriculture and its main objective should be to examine the main products, by products and waste products of each of the agricultural commodities in order to advise the government and industries of their feasibility for commercial exploitation. The laboratory should avoid duplication with other specialised institutes and to achieve this objective, it should maintain proper coordination with them. In order to share its work, small technological units are also required to be created in the agricultural universities and central institutes of the ICAR.

25. The agro-industries corporations should participate in processing and manufacturing activities relating to agro-based products on the basis of common pattern applicable throughout the country. The spheres of activities could be: (a) Agricultural processing industry, (b) Preservation industry relating to perishable commodities and (c) Selected agro-based industries.

26. The agro-industries corporations should not compete with private entrepreneurs or cooperative enterprises but should render all possible help to such units particularly those functioning on a small or medium scale. The corporations should take up those activities which have not been covered by other units. It would be a special responsibility of the corporations to ensure that agro-processing activities spread in inaccessible areas. They should take direct responsibility for establishing such industries in these areas.

27. The agro-industries corporations should shoulder direct responsibility to make arrangements for purchase of the products manufactured by units in small and medium sectors operating under their patronage and the sale thereof.

28. A coordinating body should be set up under the aegis of the Ministry of Agriculture and Irrigation at the Centre to develop and harmonise agro-processing activities and avoid duplication among various organisations like the All India Khadi and Village Industries Commission, the All India Handloom Board, the Handicraft Board, the Central Silk Board and the Coir Board on the one hand and the agro-industries corporations on the other.

Rural Employment

Summary of Recommendations

1. The strategy for creating larger employment opportunities will have to be two-pronged : firstly, all efforts will have to be made to generate additional employment in the various agricultural activities and secondly, the potentialities of employment in the non-agricultural rural jobs will have to be fully exploited in order to accommodate those who cannot find work in the land-based occupations.

2. Estimates of unemployment and the additional employment to be created as a result of the plan programmes should be attempted in aggregates as well as disaggregated estimates.

3. There are potentialities in the different agricultural programmes for providing additional employment opportunities of the order of about 52 million man-years by 2000 AD. Every attempt should be made to ensure that measures required for realising these potentialities are adopted quickly.

4. The rural works programmes are basically meant to provide opportunities for employment to the poorest strata of the rural community or the hard core of the rural poor.

5. Suitable steps should be taken to evaluate the results under the Pilot Intensive Rural Employment Projects (PIREP) with the minimum time lag and the scope of the scheme should be enlarged to cover a larger number of districts.

6. The scope of the SFDA/MFAL agencies could be extended adequately so that similar other employment generating programmes are brought within their purview and employment planning for small and marginal farmers and agricultural labourers is done in an integrated manner.

7. There should be provision for regular dependable employment throughout the year through rural works programme to draw away in certain regions of the country, landless labourers who are mobile and are prepared to accept wage employment outside their village.

8. The rural works programmes should be preplanned thoroughly in order to avoid any non-productive item of work and a shelf of properly planned projects should be readily available to be handled when the demand arises.

9. Labourers opting for more or less permanent employment should first be directed to the various large scale plan works like major and medium irrigation, road works etc., and only after these are saturated, smaller projects should be taken up. Since the mobility of this class of workers is comparatively higher, it should be possible to concentrate such programmes at selected centres and attract the workers to these programmes by providing suitable wage rates.

10. A shelf of small projects of rural works should be kept in hand to be used effectively when the demand for labour rises due to a bad agricultural season and more works nearer the village have to be provided.

11. Production of sophisticated goods and services which is at present concentrated in the urban sector should be decentralised and shifted to the rural areas. Employment opportunities in the production of more sophisticated processed food and processed agricultural raw materials should be reserved for the rural sector as a matter of national policy. Accordingly, activities such as wholesale and retail trade-distribution, packaging and processing, marketing, etc. should be brought within the fold of the rural sector.

12. Review of the list of industries reserved for exclusive development in the small scale sector should be made periodically in the light of the increasing relevance of the agro-based and rural industries and the principle of reservation extended to all these items which fulfil the criterion laid for the purpose.

13. It should be our objective to remove children from the field of rural workers seeking employment and prepare them sociologically through education and training for taking up more remunerative and skilled employment in the rural sector.

14. There potentialities in the non-agricultural rural sector for providing employment to about 30 per cent of the total rural labour force as in 2000 AD. Every attempt should be made to ensure that measures required for this change in the occupational structure are adopted as a national policy.

15. A reasonable level of minimum wage should be ensured along with better employment to enable the class of agricultural labourers to move above the poverty line. The minimum wage for agricultural labour should be fixed periodically so that it fits in with the prevailing productivity levels in the agricultural sector.

16. Creation of employment should not be left to a few *ad-hoc* employment programmes. The entire rural development plan should be reoriented towards larger employment. There should be proper coordination in the creation as well as utilisation of employment opportunities in the various agricultural and non-agricultural programmes.

17. Detailed employment planning should be done at the micro-level. Regional characteristics of unemployment should be taken into account and the areas having higher incidence of unemployment should be given priority in the allocation of resources.

18. There should be proper phasing of the employment programmes over time so that the labour force rendered surplus under one programme could be utilised under other programmes.

19. The programmes selected for creation of employment opportunities should have a sound economic basis and should not be in the nature of relief works or remedial measures. The object should be to raise the productive capability of the agro-based sector on a permanent basis.

20. Attempt should be made to utilise those factors of production which are plentiful in rural areas but are under-utilised. Accordingly, efforts should be made to concentrate on such sectors and programmes where the labour requirement can be clearly identified.

21. The district planning organisation, suggested in the chapter 62 on Administration, should be suitably equipped to collect information on the nature and incidence of unemployment and to assess the experience of the working of the various employment generating programmes.

22. The strategy should be to restrict unhealthy migration from rural to urban areas by providing more employment alongwith better amenities and services in the rural areas.

23. The institutional facilities for training as well as research for further development of the skills required in connection with greater employment in the rural areas will have to be adequately strengthened.

24. The object should be to avoid shortages of trained manpower even if this results in unemployed manpower on hand in some cases.

Special Area Development Programmes

Summary of Recommendations

The following is a summary of important recommendations made in this chapter :

1. An integrated area development should be the basic approach to be adopted for the development of backward and underdeveloped regions in the country.

2. **Hill Areas—Himalayan Region :** Resource development programmes in the hill areas should be adequately supported by essential infrastructural facilities and minimum social development programmes. Generation of indoor employment opportunities during winter months should receive high priority.

3. Due note should be taken of the economic constraints of the environments and productivity should be maximised directly by crop production and supplemented by suitable subsidiary occupations which the environment can support.

4. A change in the pattern of production to optimise economic return should be followed by arrangements to provide foodgrains through controlled channels from other parts of the country as a national responsibility.

5. Soil and moisture conservation measures should be an important strategy of development and include complete land management to ensure efficient use of soil. Production of field crops should preferably be confined to such areas where soil erosion is minimum and can be checked effectively.

6. Shifting cultivation in the north eastern region should be controlled and ecological balance restored by encouraging permanent cultivation and tree growth.

7. Irrigation should be developed through minor lift schemes and ground water utilisation, wherever feasible. Steps should be taken to ensure that all the farmers with the command of a kulh receive a share of its water.

8. Power development should be an integral part of the hill area development programme.

9. Production in the north eastern region should preferably be planned for food self-sufficiency because of transport and communication difficulties.

10. In order to improve the hill economy as well as for soil conservation, greater emphasis on horticultural development is necessary.

11. Production of many types of cash crops like soyabean, sunflower, mushroom, hop, many temperate climate vegetables and the production of seed of many temperate vegetables like cauliflower, beetroot and sugarbeet which do not produce seed in the plains need to be popularised in the northern hills.

12. In the north eastern region plantation crops like tea, coffee and rubber should be encouraged in suitable areas.

13. Production and marketing of floriculture should be organised and expanded. Research needs to be strengthened for the improvement of indigenous flowers including orchids on the lines indicated in Chapter 23. Orchid Sanctuaries should be created in all the natural habitats and the exploitation regulated. Hill areas can specialise in aromatic and medicinal plants.

14. The strategy of development in the hill areas should include a well-laid out livestock programme and measures should be taken for the improvement of livestock for better yields and higher income to the farmers.

15. The productive animals of *gujjars* should be provided grazing facilities in the forests but under strict control as explained in the text. The milk plants

at Almora and Haldwani should make suitable arrangements for the collection of milk from them.

16. Milk production programme should be organised in selected hill districts by taking up intensive programmes of crossbreeding. Programme should be supported by animal health cover to ensure its success. In the Himalayan region even pure bred exotic cattle can be raised provided adequate nutrition and health cover are ensured.

17. A programme of development of pastures with promising varieties of grasses and fodder should be taken up in each of the hill states simultaneously with the introduction of measures to improve the cattle.

18. Sheep development, for which there is scope in the western and central Himalayas, should be organised in selected hill districts on the lines recommended in the Interim Report on sheep, poultry and pig production.

19. For the maintenance of sheep, pastures should be developed and grazing controlled according to their carrying capacity. More grazing areas in the hills should be identified, seeded, fertilised and brought in rotation.

20. While the number of goats in the hills should be contained, their quality must be improved to get more milk and meat.

21. Special programme should be taken up for increasing the production of pashmina in Ladakh and Mohair in the hilly areas of Uttar Pradesh and Himachal Pradesh.

22. An integrated development of piggery should be undertaken in the north eastern region as recommended in the Interim Report on some aspects of livestock production in the north eastern states. In other regions of the Himalayan hills piggery development should be on the lines recommended in the Interim Report on poultry, sheep and pig production.

23. Poultry in the hill areas should be improved through crossbreeding.

24. In high altitudes, cold water fisheries should be developed both for commercial and sport purposes. In low regions of the hills, many ponds, tanks and *beels* will have to be suitably reclaimed for developing culture fisheries of major carps with emphasis on better pisciculture practices. The collection of data in respect of ecological and biological conditions, hydrographic surveys of water areas suitable for pisciculture and the training of officers and fishermen in the techniques of cold water fisheries should be organised.

25. There is need for an aggressive programme of production forestry in the hill regions and opening up inaccessible forests as recommended in the Interim Report on Production Forestry—Man-made Forests.

26. In improving the quality of the forests, the improvement of natural meadows should become a specific objective of the working plan of the Forest Departments and it should be linked integrally with the requirements of an intensive livestock development in the hill areas.

27. The scope for developing different kinds of sericulture like mulbery silk *tasar* and *muga* in the hill areas should be exploited on the lines indicated in Chapter 26 on Sericulture. The possibilities of taking up tasar culture throughout the oak belt of the Himalayas should be explored.

28. The scope for improving honey yields in the hills through organised agriculture as recommended in Chapter 27 on Apiculture should be exploited and a detailed survey of the vegetation of forests with regard to the floristic composition undertaken in all the hill areas.

29. The production of fruits and vegetables should be in line with the pattern of internal and export demands. A systematic changeover to different varieties which will be best for marketing will require continuous assessment for planning production and marketing in future.

30. Detailed studies should be made of the problems of cold storages at the producing and consumer centres. The development of refrigerated transportation facilities should be given attention.

31. There should be an integrated approach linking up production and processing and the processing facilities developed accordingly.

32. As livestock production improves, appropriate arrangements for collection, storage, processing and marketing of the products should be organised.

33. The development of cottage wool industry should receive encouragement, special attention should be paid to the development of home industries including rural crafts to provide indoor employment especially in high altitude area where in winter months no out-door work is possible.

34. Apart from locating wood-based industries, arrangements should be made for the processing of various minor forest produce near the sources of raw material and their proper storage and timely transportation for marketing.

35. Construction of feeder roads linking production centres and villages with the main roads should be given a high priority. The possibilities of ropeways should be explored in difficult areas.

36. Extension education should form part of the integrated programme of development and the technical staff of all categories should be trained and

oriented to the special problems of hill areas.

37. **Hill Areas—Southern Hills :** In the strategy of development of hill areas in the Western Ghats, the order of priority should be forestry, plantation and livestock development.

38. An aggressive programme of production forestry should be taken up in these areas on the lines recommended in the Interim Report on Production Forestry—Man-made Forests. Intensive fodder development should also be undertaken to support a commercially viable animal husbandry programme.

39. In the upper reaches of the southern hills, the accent should be on plantation crops and wherever irrigation is available, the area under plantation should be extended in preference to other crops.

40. Intensive work should be done to improve land utilisation under plantations, wherever possible. Low yielding plantation crops, particularly in small plantations, should be replaced by plantation crops with higher yield potential. The anomalies resulting from raising unsuitable varieties or from wrong siting of plantations should be rectified. In Malnad of Karnataka, an area programme could be developed for coffee cultivation. The possibility of extending pepper and rubber cultivation to suitable areas should be explored. The area under cashew plantations should be increased. Cashew plantations in Kerala should be shifted from unproductive to more promising areas.

41. Suitable programmes should be taken up for developing milksheds in selected hill districts on the lines recommended in our Interim Report on Milk Production. Production and rearing of crossbred heifers upto the age of weaning for supply to the milkshed areas in the plains should be encouraged.

42. Sheep development should be taken up only in selected districts where rainfall is not heavy. In the identified districts, pasture development at appropriate locations should be undertaken for promoting sheep development. Poultry and pig production should also be developed in the districts identified for the purpose.

43. **Tribal areas** : In designing programmes, due note should be taken of the capacity of the tribals at their present level of development to absorb and practise improved methods of production and management. Adjustments in their cultural and traditional life should be gradual.

44. In formulating programmes for tribal development a distinction should be made between areas which are easily accessible and already exposed to market economy and areas which are not easily accessible, lack market economy and have yet to be opened up.

45. The existing laws and rules should be reviewed to give adequate protection to the tribals against land alienation. Immediate action should be taken to prepare reasonably authentic land records and give rights to the tribals.

46. Tribals having cultivable lands should be helped with an intensive programme of crop production. In the initial stages, production of food crops should be emphasised particularly in the interior areas. In areas which are close to the markets, production of cash crops could be emphasised depending on marketing possibilities.

47. The tribals practising shifting cultivations should be weaned away from it and permanently settled. Past deficiencies in land colonisation should be taken note of in developing the settlement programme.

48. Debt redemption should be a priority programme. As a follow-up of the moratorium declared on existing debts of the weaker sections, the project authorities should set up itinerant courts for settling disputes regarding both debts and land rights on the spot. Debts which are not liquidated should be paid off by the project authorities from a suitable fund and treated as an interest free loan to be recovered from the tribal family over a reasonable period. The recovery should be through the agency of cooperatives.

49. Arrangements should be made for the rehabilitation of labourers freed from their bondage including settling them on land.

50. As stressed in Chapter 41 on Forest Policy, there is need for developing a symbiotic relationship between the forest and the tribals.

51. In forest areas where intensive harvesting of forest resources is being undertaken, the socio-economic impact on the tribal economy should be kept in view.

52. The Forest Department should be fully involved in the planning and execution of tribal development programmes. The Forest Department should establish processing units or encourage cooperatives to do the same in the vicinity of forests. The tribals should be trained for employment in these units.

53. In areas which have a market economy, commercialisation of livestock production can be attempted based on adequate measures for breed improvement, health cover and adequate processing and marketing arrangements.

54. Tribal skills in traditional handicrafts and village industries should be identified and developed through necessary training.

55. Construction of arterial roads and link roads and opening up interior forest areas should constitute

an important programme for tribal area development.

56. Officers fully committed to the welfare of tribal population should be posted to these areas and adequately trained for work by giving additional incentives for working in difficult areas. There should be a state level committee to ensure multi-disciplinary support and to monitor and evaluate programme performance.

57. While the present approach to the provision of credit, marketing and other services through a unified credit-cum-marketing organisation is commended, the societies at the primary level should, for the time being be officially sponsored and managed.

58. **Drought Prone Areas** : All the factors taken into account and those recommended by the Irrigation Commission need to be considered before an area is regarded as drought prone and hence requiring special assistance. Since the factors are continuously changing, the existing coverage of the special programme of DPAP be reviewed from time to time.

59. There should be a comprehensive 15 year integrated programme for the economic development of the desert area paying simultaneous attention to the development of water resources, forestry, animal husbandry and pastures.

60. The Rajasthan Canal Project should be recast to take water deeper into the desert with a view to bringing in more areas under irrigation and extending the benefit to a larger section of the community.

61. To maximise the utilisation of the scanty rainwater, suitable water conservation techniques should be adopted on a larger scale.

62. As water becomes available in the command areas of a canal, a large-scale programme of tree plantation, raising of shelter-belts and wind-breaks and rejuvenation of vegetal cover should be undertaken.

63. The economy of the desert area should continue to be mainly animal husbandry oriented. A major thrust of the programme should be to reduce the nomadism among cattle breeders and sheep owners.

64. The number of animals in the desert area should be contained and breeding programmes, through provision of facilities and services, should be designed to improve the quality and productivity of cattle and sheep.

65. In the canal command areas, dairy development through setting up of additional milk collection and milk chilling centres and milk product factories should be undertaken.

66. In the arid areas outside the canal command, the major emphasis should be on sheep development. Apart from improving the quality of sheep, wool shearing and grading centres should be established and arrangements made for wool and meat marketing. Processing of the wool locally should be encouraged to create more employment.

67. Attention should be paid to large-scale development of pastures, regulated grazing to prevent over-use and creation of grass reserves and fodder banks for supply of hay in scarcity years. In canal command areas, the cropping pattern should be adjusted to bring 30 per cent of the area under fodder crops in mixed farming.

68. The entire programme should be phased over three plan periods and adequate organisational support arranged for timely and effective implementation.

69. In drought prone areas improvement of existing irrigation works and completion of the projects under consideration should be accorded high priority.

70. Investigations should be made into further possibilities of irrigation in these areas by both surface and ground water and irrigation developed, wherever feasible on a priority basis. The special programme of DPAP need not be continued in areas where irrigation improves substantially.

71. The diversion of water from other parts of the basin or other river basins to supplement local availability and give a minimum support to drought affected districts should be viewed as a national requirement.

72. The limited quantity of available ground water should be equitably distributed by operating the irrigation source on cooperative or community basis.

73. Water being scarce, the approach should be to maximise the return per unit quantity of water used by taking crops requiring less water or by growing fodder in milkshed areas.

74. Land management should be on complete watershed basis; and the vegetative cover should be improved in the entire catchment area including hill slopes and uplands for soil and moisture conservation.

75. Wherever irrigation facilities do not exist, the land use pattern should aim at reducing the area under arable cropping and increasing it under permanent vegetation.

76. An intensive programme of mixed forestry should be undertaken in the drought prone areas as a soil and moisture conservation measure and for providing fuelwood, timber and fodder. Where available lands are not fit for cultivation, pasture and development should be taken up.

77. Where the present centres set up under the

All India Coordinated Research Projects for Dryland Farming do not cover some types of soils and pattern of rainfall, additional centres should be opened for formulating the cropping patterns appropriate to such areas.

78. Since the rearing of livestock provides a much more stable economic base than crop production in the drought prone areas, due emphasis should be placed on animal husbandry programme in the development strategy.

79. Where irrigation is available and fodder production possible, a planned cattle development programme should be undertaken for milk and dairying if such area is within a milkshed.

80. Programmes for the development of sheep, poultry and pig production should be undertaken in the identified districts.

81. The scope for processing activity should be assessed in each area and processing units located where appropriate. Marketing arrangements should be planned for processed and semi-processed products.

82. **Cold Arid and Semi-arid Areas :** A comprehensive research should be taken up early in the cold arid and semi-arid areas by the ICAR to provide the basis for formulating a viable economic development programme for these areas.

83. **Rann of Kutch :** The feasibility of bringing the Narmada waters to the Little Rann to control salinity for brackish-water fish culture should be considered.

84. A study in depth should be made of the possibility of fish culture in the Little Rann. To start with, preinvestment survey in selected areas should be undertaken.

85. **Sundarban :** An integrated development programme simultaneously covering scientific crop production, fisheries, animal husbandry and forestry and providing for improvements in infrastructural facilities including communications and supply of potable water will be necessary for the development of the Sundarban area.

86. For the protection and development of land and for increasing the availability of fresh water for agricultural and drinking purposes, engineering and other measures, as envisaged both in the interim plan of development of the Sundarban and in the Sundarban delta project and as explained in the text of this chapter should be taken. In view of the limitation of fresh water, industrial development should be restricted to such agro-based industries as do not aggravate the problem.

87. The land use pattern defining areas for raising crops and developing fisheries should be determined after a proper survey and adhered to.

88. Due importance should be given to the utilisation of suitable portions of land in the command areas of the proposed reservoirs for the development of fresh water fisheries to compensate the loss of brackish water fishery in the delta project area. If need be, there should be appropriate legislation to ensure the utilisation of earmarked land area for fishery development. Brackish water fish farming units should be located in some of the suitable forest swamps outside the project area.

89. Investigations should be made into the problem of an assured supply, at an economic rate, of wood suitable for pulping. Extensive industrial research and feasibility studies for the establishment of industries in urban areas should be made.

90. Research to evolve techniques for ensuring natural or artificial regeneration of forests should be intensified.

91. The development of livestock leading to increased production of milk, egg and meat should be supported by adequate transport and marketing arrangements.

92. As an integral part of the overall development of the region, river, road, and rail transport facilities should be considerably improved. Electrification should be extended to the area to support development.

93. **Small and Marginal Farmers and Agricultural Labourers :** An area development approach should be adopted by covering both small farmers and marginal farmers in each programme area and the distinction between the two programmes of SFDA and MFALDA should be done away with.

94. The main accent of the SFDA programme should be on improving the capability of the farmers for increasing crop production.

95. The coverage of the programme should be extended as much as possible to rainfed areas having fairly assured rainfall, where the State should take up substantial works of water harvesting, soil conservation and land shaping on area basis.

96. Since farmers with a very small land holdings may not be able to derive sufficient income from crop production, subsidiary occupation programmes should be superimposed as separate programmes in those programme districts which coincide with the districts identified for special subsidiary occupation programmes in different Interim Reports on the subjects.

97. The SFDA programme should be extended to 160 agency units in all, each unit covering preferably the area of a district and an average of 70,000 families.

98. Small farmers and marginal farmers with land

holdings below 2 hectares and one hectare respectively should be eligible for special assistance under the SFDA programme. In irrigated areas, a lower limit could be set.

99. The SFDA programme need not be extended to drought affected districts in which a separate programme (DPAP) has been taken up.

100. In view of the special circumstances in the desert districts, the limit of land holdings for eligibility for special assistance should be kept flexible in order to bring a certain number under the special assistance programme. The minimum should be 20,000 cultivating and agricultural labour households, where the number of cultivating households having holdings of 2 hectares and below is more, the existing definition should apply.

Planning

Summary of Recommendations

The main recommendations are given below :

1. Plan formulation process has to commence from below, making optimum use of resources available locally, for the development programmes to be realistic and feasible.

2. At the district level, there should be an effective set up, both for drawing up integrated plans and budget for agricultural development and coordinating the implementation of various agricultural programmes at the field level.

3. Planning efforts at water-shed and regional levels, in regard to both formulation and implementation should be effectively coordinated and integrated with such efforts at the district and the state levels.

4. The concept of whole-village development needs to be tried seriously on a pilot basis. This concept requires a strong and devoted leader who can counter initial reactions of the vested interest to the programme of social justice inherent in it.

5. Alternatively, a plan based on an area approach taking a village and developing to a large watershed should be tried. Farmers' participation in such a plan has to be mobilised by the agricultural extension organisation with necessary help from other field organisations. The farmers' service society recommended by the Commission can deal with both credit problem on an area basis and provide responsible extension organisation under the control of the society.

6. A district should ordinarily be the unit of planning for agricultural production except for irrigated agriculture where the unit would be the command area. Where the planning unit extends over more than one district, there should be close coordination between the district units concerned.

7. It is necessary to assess the total financial resources likely to be available for agricultural development in the form of plan allocations and committed non-plan funds and those from institutional resources. Programmes for agricultural development should be drawn up on the basis of such an assessment.

8. There should be a closer coordination and understanding on methodology, approach and basic assumptions for formulation of plan proposals among the various working groups at the centre and in the states. There should also be a greater involvement of representatives having field experience from states as well as non-officials (e.g. agricultural economists, scientists and progressive farmers) in these working groups.

9. The procedure for farmulation and administrative approval of centrally sponsored schemes needs to be simplified. Larger discretionary powers should be given to the Ministry of Agriculture and Irrigation in issuing administrative approval and expenditure sanctions to approved centrally sponsored schemes. The State Governments should also be given freedom to adjust the details within broad objectives of the model schemes.

10. Plan schemes should be drawn up in sufficient detail so that they could be taken up as soon as the plan is approved for implementation by concerned authorities.

11. Greater decentralisation of powers and delegation of authority are necessary for effective implementation of plan projects. A careful review has to be made of the current procedures and as far as possible the power of decision-making should be decentralised.

12. An effective evaluation system is essential to keep a watch on the progress of schemes and for keeping the implementation agency adequately and promptly informed about their progress. Apart from proper evaluation and appraisal of projects by government departments, evaluation through independent autonomous bodies like the agricultural universities and research institutions should be encouraged.

13. Suitable information and reporting systems need to be evolved so that those responsible for implementation can anticipate difficulties, judge the progress and performance of these programmes in relation to pre-determined targets with a view to take necessary corrective measures.

14. A strong and well organised Planning Division

should be set up in the Ministry of Agriculture and Irrigation combining the functions of planning, administrative coordination and concurrent evaluation.

15. The present system of periodic reviews at the centre in respect of central and centrally sponsored schemes should be supplemented by integrated sectoral reviews as well as reviews of the total agricultural sector with the support of the proposed evaluation units.

16. There is need for setting up planning units at district level and corresponding units at the block level which should be responsible for formulating agricultural plans and keeping a watch over their progress. The functions of these units are given in paragraph 60.6.17.

17. The methodology for formulating projections of demand should be constantly reviewed and improved upon. Apart from economic considerations other considerations such as attaining desirable and feasible nutritional levels of diet, changes in tastes and preferences etc. have also to be taken into account in making demand projections.

18. A careful assessment of the production potential has to be made in respect of different agroclimatic regions. The conditions in different regions have to be carefully analysed for improvement of biological productivity. Even within the same agro-climatic region there are differences in productivity which require a careful appraisal for a complete restructuring of cropping patterns on agro-climatic considerations.

19. The yardstick should be fixed separately for relatively homogenous group of farms (or at least for relatively homogenous agro-climatic regions) and for different crops. These should be reviewed at the end of each plan period to take account of technological changes that have occurred during the period.

20. Specific targets of production should be indicated down to the district level which is the crucial level of plan implementation.

21. Targets of production in respect of essential commodities might be fixed not in terms of a single figure of final output but in terms of range of output or aggregate output during the plan period.

22. The concept of yardsticks and production potential should be extended to animal husbandry and fisheries sector.

23. A systematic identification of areas with low productivity and factor leading to it is a necessary prerequisite for suggesting measures for improvement of productivity.

24. Agricultural planning has to be a comprehensive effort starting with an assessment of the potential for production, drawing up of development programmes to tap this potential and creating the necessary infrastructure to ensure the availability of inputs credit and marketing facilities needed by the farmers to translate these programmes into practice.

25. The data base for agricultural planning should be improved on the lines indicated in paragraph 60.7.13 to 60.7.17.

26. The objective of agricultural development should not be merely one of maximising production in overall terms but should also include considerations of regional balance, economic stability and growth with social justice.

27. In the ultimate analysis detailed work of regional planning would essentially have to be done by district planning cells. Where a region covers two or more districts, a coordinating committe could deal with the problems on an *ad hoc* basis. The regional agricultural development plans would also have to be tied up within the framework of overall national and state planning.

28. The evolution of appropriate location specific strategies based on careful identification of the causes of backwardness as well as the potential for development is an essential pre-requisite for accelerated development in backward areas. Appropriate techniques for regional planning should be developed to minimise the possible conflict between the criteria of efficiency and equity.

29. There is need for introduction of programmes designed to benefit the weaker sections of the population through development of animal husbandry, poultry, fisheries, horticulture, forestry etc. in areas where the potentialities for development of crop production are low due to poor resource endowment.

30. Identification and removal of inadequacies in the matter of infrastructural development is basic to the development to various backward regions. Such programmes have to conform to a long term policy within the available financial resources. It is also important that in such areas other development programmes are also undertaken simultaneously with infrastructural development.

31. The planning cell under the Agricultural Production Commissioner should undertake the detailed perspective planning for the various agro-climatic regions in the state. Agricultural universities and other scientific organisations and technical departments should be fully associated with this process of formulating a detailed plan.

32. After a perspective plan for development of regional resources is drawn up by the state, the district planning cells have to examine how far under

the socio-economic conditions prevailing in the district and in the existing state of infrastructure, the changes postulated can be carried out and in what time frame. District planning cells can also refer to the Planning Division in the Ministry, through state planning cell, the problems that may have to be faced in detailed planning for lack of infrastructure or socio-economic restraints.

33. The Agricultural Planning Cell at the state level should build into the state plan the necessary correctives on the basis of the feed-back by the district cells about existing infrastructure and socio-economic constraints. The problems that cannot be resolved at the state level will have to be passed on to the Planning Division in the Ministry of Agriculture and Irrigation to be examined in the perspective of the national plan.

34. Planning of certain aspects like irrigation, communications, marketing and socio-economic changes have to be done at the macro (national) level. Water-use planning and the developing of a suitable infrastructure therefor has to be done at the state and national levels. Increasing the productivity of backward areas like north-eastern part of the country and Himalayan hill ranges, requires national planning of communications, both roads and rail. Exploitation of seas for marine products has to be nationally planned for maximum productivity.

35. Detailed work of regional planning would involve intensive training in the analysis of available data, identification of constraints on development etc. and would also call for inter-disciplinary coordination between the scientists and planners in the relevant fields. This work could be undertaken under the auspices of the planning units at different levels.

36. The procedures for finalization and sanctioning of different types of plan schemes should be streamlined to make them less time consuming.

37. Formulation of regional/agricultural plans would require collection of basic trend and inter-related data and selected data based on surveys and investigations.

Statistics

Summary of Recommendations

Important recommendations for the improvement of agricultural statistics made in this chapter are indicated below:

1. The coverage of land utilization and crop statistics should be extended to the entire geographical area of the country by 1978-79 at the latest. *Ad hoc* estimates of land utilization should be prepared in respect of the non-reporting areas on the basis of aerial photographs, broad topographical survey and other available information.

2. The patwari agency should continue to be responsible for collection of basic agricultural statistics. The jurisdiction of the patwari should be reduced whenever it is excessive. Intensive supervision through normal revenue and statistical staff should be organised over his work of area edumeration.

3. The method of complete enumeration for collection of basic agricultural statistics should be introduced in the states of West Bengal, Orissa and Kerala in a phased manner.

4. Refresher training should be imparted to the patwaris and the kanungos in the methods of collection of agricultural statistics, at periodic intervals.

5. The states should adopt the revised basic and abstract land record forms and concepts and definitions and the procedures for recording of area under mixed crops recommended by the Committee on Improvement of Agricultural Statistics.

6. Crops like soyabean and sunflower which have been introduced in recent years should be included within the scope of crop estimation system.

7. The sampling design for crop-cutting surveys should be reviewed with a view to introducing stratification according to irrigated and rainfed areas and according to high yielding and local varieties of crops.

8. The Timely Reporting Scheme, which is in operation in 17 states, should be extended to the remaining states by 1976-77. The Directorate of Economics and Statistics (DES) should try to ensure the quality of the field and supervisory work done in the states under the scheme.

9. Each state should review the sowing and harvesting seasons of different crops, at the district level and revise the period of crop inspection where necessary so that all crops including late sown summer crops are covered.

10. Steps should be taken to reconcile the variations between the different sets of estimates for crops like cotton, tobacco, pepper, cashewnuts, etc. issued by different agencies.

11. The DES should prepare qualitative reports on crops and weather conditions on the basis of reports from Block Agricultural Development Officers at the block level and Chief Agricultural Development Officers at the district level, which could be later developed into advance estimates of crop production.

12. The scope of the pilot investigations being carried out by the IARS for developing advance

estimates of crop production on the basis of biometric measurements of the crop during its growth should be extended to other crops and the results utilised on a field scale as soon as the requisite techniques are evolved.

13. The Committee on Improvement of Agricultural Statistics (CIAS) should be activated to consider new proposals for improvement of agricultural statistics and to review from time to time the action taken on its recommentions. The scope of the committee should be widened to cover livestock, fisheries and forestry statistics also.

14. At the present stage of development of remote sensing techniques, their use in crop estimation has certain limitations. The DES should however keep in touch with the developments in the field.

15. Situation and outlook reports covering area, production prices, market arrivals, internal and external trade, stocks, etc. should be prepared and issued in respect of principal crops.

16. Adequate arrangements should be made in each state for collection of statistics of area under important fruits and vegetables.

17. A census of fruit trees should be conducted once every five years.

18. Sample surveys for estimating the yield rates and production of fruits should be conducted for one or two crops every year in rotation in accordance with an all-India programme. For vegetables, pilot investigations should be conducted by the states and IARS in important growing areas.

19. To collect the data on prices and arrivals of fruits and vegetables, full time staff should be provided in all the important city fruit markets.

20. Methodological investigations should be carried out to standardise the data collection techniques for estimating cost of cultivation of fruits.

21. Statistical units should be created in the State Horticulture Departments or agricultural statistics sections to look after the work of horticulture statistics. A separate cell may be created in DES to coordinate the data collected by the states.

22. Standard concepts and definitions of terms used in irrigation statistics should be adopted uniformly. Reconciliation of the figures reported in LUS and Irrigation Progress Reports should be done by the planning unit at the district level.

23. Source-wise classification of irrigated area should be amplified to give separate figures for major, medium and minor sources and from surface and ground water sources.

24. A census of irrigation sources should be undertaken along with the agricultural census once in five years. Special irrigation surveys on the number of wells and their utilisation may be undertaken by other states.

25. Annual administration reports of State Irrigation Departments should be published every year together with comprehensive statistical data in standard performas. These data should be consolidated at all-India level and published annually.

26. Statistical units should be provided in the State Irrigation Departments for collection and analysis of irrigation statistics.

27. Livestock census should be undertaken simultaneously in all states and union territories. While the complete enumeration census may be confined to the broad classification of cattle and other livestock and poultry, details regarding breeds, sex, etc., should be obtained through sample surveys. The practice of having a post-enumeration check by an independent agency should be revived.

28. Advance reports on the livestock census results should be brought out within a few months of its completion on the basis of advance tabulations on sampling basis.

29. The methodology of integrated surveys for obtaining estimates of output of livestock products and numbers spread over a period of five years should be finalised quickly. Till then, sample surveys for estimation of production of milk and other livestock products should be conducted on a priority basis. A system of periodical release of all-India and state estimates of livestock products should be introduced.

30. Weekly wholesale and retail prices of livestock, livestock products, livestock feed and fodder, market arrivals of major livestock products, and monthly production of livestock feed should be collected regularly.

31. The Directorate of Marketing and Inspection should carry out fresh surveys to collect uptodate information on marketing of major livestock products and proportions of these products converted into various indigenous products such as butter, ghee, cheese, etc.

32. Standard proformas for collection of information on various items in respect of dairy plants, slaughter houses, bacon factories, poultry dressing plants, feed manufacturing plants, bone digesters, etc., should be prescribed.

33. Quarterly district livestock situation reports containing information relating to season, incidence of disease, availability of animal feed and fodder, etc., should be developed.

34. The District Animal Husbandry Officer should have the help of requisite computational and other staff, to help him in the collection, compilation and submission of various types of livestock statistics.

At the state level, the Director of Animal Husbandry should have a full fledged statistical division for collection, compilation, analysis and dissemination of all animal husbandry statistics. This division should be under the charge of a fairly senior statistician not below the rank of Joint Director of Animal Husbandry. An economist of a suitable rank should also be provided in this division for economic analysis of various projects and undertaking evaluation studies.

35. The major dairy plants should have an economist on their staff to render advice on economic problems.

36. At the central level, the statistical unit in the Animal Husbandry Division of the Ministry of Agriculture and Irrigation should be considerably strengthened. An economist should also be provided in this unit.

37. The IARS should continue to handle methodological research and pilot investigations in the sphere of livestock statistics. Similar methodological studies should also be taken up by agricultural universities with financial assistance from the centre.

38. An integrated survey should be designed to enable all-India and statewise estimates of marine fish catches to be obtained with a reasonable degree of precision.

39. Appropriate methodology for estimation of inland fish production including catches from captive fishery resources should be made available to the state governments for implementation.

40. Data on fishermen population, fishing craft and tackle, inland water resources, biological and research statistics, prices, etc., should be collected regularly.

41. Census of fishing craft, tackle and nets should be conducted independently of the livestock census by the state fisheries departments under the overall technical control and guidance of the Fisheries Division of the Central Ministry of Agriculture and Irrigation.

42. Inland fisheries resources should be surveyed periodically, specially with reference to geographical, physical, chemical and biological factors and classified accordingly.

43. A continuous survey of marine fisheries resources should be undertaken to collect information on various biological characteristics such as growth, recruitment, mortality etc.

44. Registration of small mechanised boats below 25 GRT should be introduced to enable maintenance of uptodate statistics of number of such boats in operation as also to keep a watch on the growth of mechanisation of boats.

45. In the case of larger vessels above 25 GRT data regarding operational details and performance should be collected and analysed systematically.

46. State Departments of Fisheries should collect reliable estimates of seed fish on a regular basis.

47. Data on producers' wholesale and retail prices for standard varieties and predetermined specifications and other market intelligence in regard to fish should be collected.

48. Every state should have a strong statistical unit in the Fisheries Department to deal with all aspects of fisheries statistics. At the central level the fisheries statistics unit in the fisheries division should be strengthened. An economist should also be added to this unit at the central and state levels.

49. The statistical units in the central fisheries institutes like the Central Marine Fisheries Research Institute, Central Inland Fisheries Research Institute and Central Institute of Fisheries Technology should be strengthened. For the work of economic evaluation etc. the assistance of an economist should also be provided to these institutes.

50. Efforts should be made to reconcile the differences in the two sets of forest area figures available from land utilization statistics. The states should adopt modern classification in the collection of forestry statistics according to functional classification.

51. Suitable procedures should be devised to frame estimates of unrecorded production through sample surveys or otherwise atleast once in five years. The possibility of collecting data on timber and fuelwood from agricultural lands through the periodical agricultural censuses should be examined.

52. There is need for verifying the reported figures of output of forest produce in respect of coupes auctioned in standing position through sample checks.

53. The concept of value of outturn of forest produce should be clearly defined and should relate to the value at the first point of sale by the Forest Departments.

54. Wholesale price of major and minor forest products should be collected regularly at fortnightly or monthly intervals and should be included in the scope of index numbers of wholesale prices.

55. Careful analysis of costs of various operations from the stage of plantations to the actual marketing of timber on the basis of economic concepts and usual principles of costing is necessary.

56. Regular data on various aspects of labour employed in forestry should be collected according to uniform concepts and definitions.

57. A whole-time Forester (statistics) should be provided in each range for collection and compilation of forestry statistics. At the divisional level, the

Divisional Forest Officer should be assisted by a Range Forest Officer (Statistics) and junior statistical assistant for statistical work. At the circle level the statistical unit should consist of a class II statistical officer assisted by requisite complement of statistical assistants and clerks. At the State Headquarters, the Chief Conservator of Forests should be assisted by a Director of Forest Statistics. He should be assisted by requisite number of statisticians.

58. At the centre the existing statistical unit in the Central Forestry Commission should be developed into a full-fledged statistical division and put incharge of a statistician in an appropriate scale.

59. Data on consumption of fertilisers by crops and by size classes of holdings, etc., should be collected through the comprehensive scheme for cost cultivation of crops or through special surveys.

60. Data on seed production and distribution and seed rates of different crops/varieties should be collected and compiled regularly.

61. Data on quantities of pesticides produced, distributed and applied to different crops should be collected systematically.

62. Scope and coverage of foreign market intelligence should be reviewed in consultation with the Ministry of Commerce and adequate arrangements should be made for their systematic collection.

63. The agricultural census with 1976-77 as the reference period should be carried out as proposed by the Ministry of Agriculture and Irrigation. The results should be made available by the end of 1978 at the latest.

64. For meeting the minimum data needs in the sphere of agriculture, an integrated system of agricultural surveys, covering both the current agricultural surveys and the periodical agricultural and livestock censuses, should be devised. Various integrated surveys should continue to be carried out by the agencies responsible for the different subjects as at present. There should, however, be adequate arrangements for technical coordination and guidance. The governing council of the NSSO should examine this question further.

65. The scope of the assessment surveys on high yielding varieties programme being conducted by the IARS should be extended to provide information on the local factors and problems contributing to low or high yields in different regions to serve as the basis for accelerating the pace of agricultural development.

66. The work regarding the determination of optimum dosages for fertilisers for different crops in different regions already being done by the IARS should be expanded.

67. The IARS should be suitably strengthened to tackle the various research problems, to coordinate and supervise the programmes of statistical surveys and to expand the programmes of training in agricultural statistics.

68. Revised series of all-India index numbers of area under crops, net area sown, crop yields, agricultural production etc. should be issued for all the states. The all-India and state series of these index numbers should be published every year with the minimum possible time lag.

69. The new series of index numbers of harvest (producers) prices as recommended by the Technical Committee on Index Numbers should be initiated as early as possible.

70. The compilation of the revised series on index numbers of parity between prices received and prices paid by the farmer should be taken up by all the states.

71. Statewise and district-wise studies on growth rates in agriculture should be undertaken at more frequent intervals.

72. Technical coefficients for input-output relationships should be worked out on the basis of the data collected during the comprehensive scheme on cost of production of prinicipal crops.

73. The scope for use of computers in the collection, compilation and analysis of agricultural statistics needs to be carefully examined. A beginning in this regard should be made by transferring the basic data for past years to magnetic tapes for depth studies, easy and timely retrieval and accuracy of tabulation. If found useful this could be followed up to cover current data also.

74. To reduce the time-lag in the availability of agricultural statistics the concerned departments should be provided with printing facilities of their own or a Government Printing Press should be reserved for the purpose.

75. A bibliography of all printed and cyclostyled reports on different aspects of agriculture including those intended for limited official use should be brought out regularly by a central agency.

76. One statistical supervisor should be provided in each tehsil to supervise the field work of different censuses and surveys, etc. This supervisor should work under the tehsildar. To improve the accuracy of tabulation, one hand operated calculating machine should be provided for each tehsil.

77. A statistical unit consisting of a District Agricultural Statistics Officer assisted by one Statistical Supervisor/Assistant and one junior clerk/computer should be provided at the district level. He should work under the proposed Chief Agricultural

Development Officer at the district level. Two hand operated calculating machines should be provided to this unit

78. At the state level, the existing organisation for agricultural statistics should be strengthened. The Head of the state agricultural statistics organisation should be a qualified statistician with adequate experience, in an appropriate scale. The Agricultural Statistician should be administratively under the Agricultural Production Commissioner and should be physically located in the same office. He should be assisted by an adequate number of Statisticians, Assistant Statisticians, Economists, and lower staff.

79. At the centre, the Agricultural Intelligence Division of the Directorate of Economics and Statistics, the National Sample Survey Organisation and IARS should be suitably strengthened.

80. Suitable training courses should be developed for periodic training of statistical staff employed in the state and central offices.

81. For rationalisation of agro-economic research priority areas of research have broadly been spelt out. Institutions having field level staff like the agro-economic research centres etc. can be entrusted with the type of studies which need collection of information from micro level units. Studies based on secondary data could preferably be arranged at postgraduate centres of research.

82. Postgraduate students of the agricultural universities should be involved in the process of economic investigations, data collection and analysis by including investigational work in the field of agricultural economics as an integral part of the curriculum prescribed for M.Sc. students in agricultural economics, applied statistics, etc.

83. Research scholarships or fellowships may be arranged at specialised institutions for systematic analysis of the information collected during the village surveys by the agro-economic research centres so as to provide an insight regarding the growth and development process of Indian economy. The cadre authority administering the Indian Economic Service and Indian Statistical Service should, in consultation with the Ministry of Agriculture and Irrigation, select eligible and competent candidates for these fellowships.

84. Farm management studies provide a lot of useful information and should be continued.

85. All important institutions engaged in agro-economic research should be represented on the coordination committee for organisation of micro-economic studies in the field of agricultural economics.

86. The Research Division and the Economic Policy Cell of Directorate of Economics and Statistics should be strengthened.

Administration

Summary of Recommendations

The main recommendations are as under:

1. The village level workers should continue to be multipurpose workers but they will deal with different disciplines of crop production, animal husbandry, fishery and farm forestry only. Of the 10 VLWs in the block in the general pattern, 8 should be allotted for this work and 2 might look after extension work in spheres other than agriculture.

2. Ordinarily there should be a direct hierarchical control from the VLWs to the District Officer and to secure cooperation and participation from people in agricultural development programmes the technical organisations should work in close association with the elected representatives. Where the Zila Parishad is active and effective, the district field organisations may be put under its control but even then, the link-up at the taluk/block and village level technical organisations with the corresponding panchayat samiti organisation and village panchayat, if any, will have to be severed so that there is unified technical and administrative control at the district level.

3. Coordination in the agricultural sector should be achieved through a senior technical officer belonging to one of the agricultural disciplines. The District Collector should not have administrative control over the district officers in various subjects in the sphere of agricultural development and should not be concerned with their detailed working. For ensuring coordination at the district level, there should be a Chief Agricultural Development Officer (CADO) in each district. However, all the district level officers under the different departments will continue to function independently as at present under the respective departmental heads at the regional/state headquarters. The CADO should not interfere with the working of the technical officers except what is required for the purpose of planning, coordination and progress evaluation.

4. The team of subject matter specialists at the district level will have to be adequately strengthened to include an agricultural economist and a farm management specialist.

5. For facilitating coordination and consultation, all the different branches of the district level organisations may be located in the same building or on the same campus offering full opportunities for mutual discussions and exchange.

6. There should be a separate planning and coordination unit for agriculture at the district level which should also deal with progress and evaluation. The unit should be placed under the CADO.

7. Subject to eligibility and competence, officers of the different agricultural departments should be given their due share in the pool of officers from which the selection of the CADO is to be made.

8. There should be a District Agricultural Coordination Council on which the various non-official and autonomous bodies operating in the field of agriculture as well as the district level specialists/district officers concerned with various disciplines should be duly represented. The Council should be an advisory body under the chairmanship of the CADO. It may be supported by consultative groups for different areas of development under the CADO.

9. There should be a Block Agricultural Development Officer (BADO) at the block level who should be directly responsible to the CADO and should have the same role of coordinator as the CADO, at this level. The present BDO should deal only with the development in the non-agricultural sectors.

10. At the block level there should be a unit under the BADO to watch the progress of agricultural development programmes.

11. On the pattern of the agricultural coordination council at the district level there should be a block agricultural coordination committee.

12. The norms regarding staffing pattern and the strength of extension workers would differ from area to area and should be worked out separately for different areas.

13. There should be separate secretarial department at the state level at least for agriculture, animal husbandry, fisheries and forestry in all the major states depending upon the importance of the different subjects in the state and the workload in each subject.

14. There should be a single officer of the status of Agricultural Production Commissioner cum-Principal Secretary to the Government to plan, direct, guide and coordinate the various subjects within agriculture and those states where the APCs have not been appointed should take immediate steps for appointing one. The APC should be in rank only next to Chief Secretary to the state.

15. A senior Cabinet Minister who should be Deputy Chief Minister in the state cabinet should be entrusted with the overall responsibility for all the subjects in the sphere of agricultural development. There could be Ministers of State in charge of different departments, the number and grouping of subjects depending on the workload and their inter-relationship.

16. Where there are several technical directorates in the sub-sectors relating to agriculture/animal husbandry, the seniormost Director who may be designated as Director-in-Chief, could be entrusted with the responsibilities at the state headquarters for coordination. Similar arrangements should be made for fisheries where there are separate directorates for inland and marine fisheries.

17. There should be a separate technical directorate for extension and training at the state headquarters.

18. There should be a unit for planning, coordination and evaluation under the APC which will be the main instrument with him for coordinating the activities of the different secretariat departments, technical directorates and other organisations effectively. The level of expertise in the unit should be adequately high. The planning unit must work in close harmony with budget and finance unit.

19. Strong planning, coordination and progress analysis cells will have to be organised under the different integrated directorates also.

20. There should be a budget control unit under the APC to have overall supervision over utilisation of the budget provisions. Also each department/directorate must have its own budget cell.

21. There should be joint councils at the state under the respective departments comprising the subject-matter specialists under the department and the top level subject-matter experts in the various faculties in the agaicultural university in the state. The coucils may make periodical assessment of the state of science and advise on technical matters having policy implications.

22. In order to maintain technical competence in State Departments, provision should be made for exchange of staff at appropriate level between the universities and the departments on deputation basis.

23. There could also be adoptive research cells at the level of technical directorates which could function in close liaison with the agricultural university.

24. Supply and service functions should be entrusted to institutional agencies and other alternative systems of supplies outside the departmental purview.

25. The extension staff of the department attending to agricultural development and promotional work should not be asked to attend to the regulatory work.

26. The cadre of the department concerned with agricultural development should be built on a stable basis taking into account a total and long-term view of the additional requirements of developmental staff.

27. The divisional level of administration is justified

only in the case of large states with a very large number of districts and regional homogeneities. Such cases, however, should be exceptional and even where divisional level is introduced, its functions should be limited to regional planning and coordination.

28. The secretariat or state headquarters organisations should be comparatively small and compact by due decentralisation of authority to the field level organisations.

29. Top management posts in the secretariat at the state level including those of secretaries and joint secretaries should be held by the technical officers of the various directorates and executive departments. The post of APC should be filled from the secretaries of the departments. A technical officer should be preferred for this post.

30. Technical officers should be provided the maximum opportunity for manning senior positions of management of agricultural development corporations, agencies, boards etc.

31. The heads of technical directorates should be granted suitable ex-officio secretariat status in order to facilitate quicker decisions.

32. The various directorates connected with agricultural development should be specifically declared as technical organisations and a provision to the effect that the post of directors of these directorates should be held by technical officers alone, be incorporated in the recruitment rules.

33. All states should follow uniform pay scales and prospects for the agricultural cadres which should be comparable to those in the administrative service.

34. All central technical posts should generally be filled by deputation from the states. The period of tenure should not be too short and may be fixed at five years. In the selection of these officers on deputation their position in the cadre and their competence rather than their pay scales should be the criteria.

35. An All India Agricultural Service should be formed immediately. This service should have different wings dealing with agriculture, animal husbandry and fisheries. There should, in addition, be State Agricultural Services, Junior and Senior, with provision for inducting competent persons from the senior state services to the all-India service on a quota basis.

36. There should be an Agricultural and Rural Development Council at the state level under the chairmanship of the Chief Minister/Deputy Chief Minister. It will be an advisory body and will consider the basic approaches and policy issues and review the general progress of the plan. The APC may act as the Secretary of the Council.

37. Separation of cooperative agricultural marketing of the NCDC from the Ministry of Agriculture and Irrigation is not justified. A service division like credit and marketing should be placed under the Department of Agriculture.

38. Minor irrigation and the Central Ground Water Board (CGWB) which are at present under the Department of Agriculture should be transferred to the Department of Irrigation in the interest of integrated development of surface and ground water irrigation sources.

39. All developmental activities in the field of fisheries should be handled by the Department of Agriculture.

40. Research activities handled at present by the Boards for Tea, Coffee, Rubber and Cardamom which are under the control of Ministry of Commerce should be transferred to the ICAR, considering the need for a strong organisation of extension and development in respect of all these commodities, the extension activities also should be brought under the agricultural set-up. The Ministry of Commerce may handle the marketing aspects including exports.

41. The different departments under the Ministry of Agriculture and Irrigation at the centre should be the Departments of Agriculture, Crop Production, Animal Husbandry, Fisheries, Foresty, Irrigation, Rural Development, Research and Education and Food.

42. There should be a Principal Secretary in the Ministry of Agriculture and Irrigation who, besides playing the role of a coordinator should also be in charge of the Department of Agriculture which will deal with planning, budget and finance, area development programmes, agricultural credit, economics and statistics, foreign aid etc. The post of Principal Secretary should be filled by the best man available for the job irrespective of whether he is a generalist administrator or a technical expert.

43. The Secretaries of the Departments of Crop Production, Animal Husbandry, Fisheries, Forestry, Irrigation and Research and Education should be scientists specialised in their respective fields.

44. For coordination between research and development at the central level, there should be a joint council consisting of secretaries of development departments and the Department of Agricultural Research and Education with the Extension Commissioner as the convener. The group should be presided over by the Principal Secretary of Agriculture. The joint council should also function as an agency for consultation, evaluation and coordination between the production divisions and extension organisations.

45. There should be a well organised Planning Division under the Department of Agriculture dealing with formulation, coordination and evaluation of the plans. The Planning Division as also the budget and finance Division which will work in close harmony should be placed under the Principal Secretary of Agriculture.

46. High level committees may be constituted wherever the need arises for policy coordination amongst Ministries and Departments.

47. It is necessary to form similar *ad-hoc* groups of implementation under the different departments of the Ministry of Agriculture and Irrigation in order to expedite executive actions.

48. The division for land reforms and land management legislation under the Department of Agriculture should be entrusted with the study of agrarian legislation and regulatory acts etc. with a view to identifying deficiencies of the existing legislation and creating consensus for model legislation.

49. The Directorate of Extension at the centre which should be the source of technical guidance and advice regarding extension organisation, training and communication should be strengthened and placed in the Department of Agriculture under the Principal Secretary. The Extension Commissioner should be a technical officer at the rank of an Additional Secratary.

50. There should be ultimately a full-fledged Division in the Ministry of Agriculture and Irrigation under the Department of Agriculture to look after women's programmes. To begin with the existing Home Science and Nutrition Education Science unit in the Extension Directorate should be converted into full-fledged Directorate of Women's Programme and placed under the administrative control of the Extension Commissioner.

51. Decentralisation of powers to the Directorates and the executive organisations under the Ministry of Agriculture and Irrigation should be carried out fully so that the experts in the central departments are able to devote their entire time to professional guidance and overall direction.

52. There should be a Standing Consultative Council at the central level for facilitating decisions on key issues having overall importance. The heads of departments or divisions or the secretaries in-charge of Agricultural departments and the representatives of the State Governments should be associated with the Council. The Council should be presided over by the Minister of Agriculture and Irrigation. Besides, there may be separate consultative groups for agriculture, animal husbandry, fisheries, forestry, etc.

53. The system of multiple technical-cum-administrative hierarchies in which papers have to pass through several stages before a final decision is taken must be changed and an officer-oriented system introduced in which responsibilities are clearly fixed at each level. Disposal of any case should not generally involve more than two levels.

54. The Agricultural Commissioner, the Animal Husbandry Commissioner, the Fisheries Commissioner and the Inspector General of Forests should be Secretaries of the concerned departments. The Agricultural Marketing Adviser and the Plant Protection Adviser should be given the ex-officio Joint Secretary's status. The Extension Commissioner should be given the ex-officio status of Additional Secretary and the Economic and Statistical Adviser should enjoy the status of a Joint Secretary. The entire Ministry of Agriculture and Irrigation should mostly consist of technocrats with necessary administrative and management training.

55. The posts of Commissioners of Agriculture, Animal Husbandry and Fisheries and Inspector General of Forests-cum-Secretaries to the respective departments should also be filled on a tenure basis from amongst the competent and senior officers in the states and the centre. Ultimately when the All-India Agricultural Service is formed, senior officers from the service will be eligible for appointment to these posts. Further in the case of the Animal Husbandry Commissioner, the post should not be a close preserve of any one field; the recruitment should be made from amongst the outstanding scientists in the disciplines of veterinary science, livestock production or dairying.

56. It will be desirable to have a smaller number of compact advisory bodies covering homogenous groups of subjects with strictly laid down drill of meetings, reviews and follow-up action.

57. There should be closer working relationship between the field units under the Central and the State Organisations. As a general policy, the continuance of pilot projects, model farms, etc. under the central organisations should be reviewed from time to time and those which could be transferred to the state sector should be done so immediately.

58. The development corporations at the central level should not be isolated from the general development and extension set-up at the state level and the attempt should not be to duplicate the state staff and organisation. However, the Ministry of Agriculture and Irrigation should not be directly involved in any operation of commercial nature.

59. The working of the administrative set-up

should be reviewed periodically.

60. Training in agricultural administration and management should be given at the point of entry into the service both for recruits to the proposed Indian Agriculture Service as well as to the incumbents of other posts in the central and state agricultural departments. Provision should also be made for in-service training which should be given to all within a certain period of service, say 5 to 7 years after an officer has joined duties.

61. Fresh recruits to the All India Agricultural Service should be given training in the same way as the recruits to the IAS and other all India services, at a central agricultural administrative college which may be called the All India Institute for Agricultural Administration and Management. Similarly, new entrants to the State Agricultural Services should be given training at staff colleges at the state level.

62. For the purpose of in-service training the state level technical officers from agricultural assistants to the top level posts at the state level may be graded into four categories in accordance with their scale of pay, position and functions. The training courses and content may be formulated keeping in view their functions and responsibilities. Except for the officers of the rank of Joint Director and above, facilities for training of officers should be provided by the State Governments. The officers of the rank of Joint Directors and above should be provided training at the All India Institute for Agricultural Administration and Management.

63. The technical officers at the central level also should be similarly classified for providing the training facilities and the training programme and content should be decided taking into account their duties and responsibilities. The senior officers should be trained at the All-India Institute for Agricultural Administration and Management whereas the junior officers could be trained at one of the state institutes.

Farmers' Organisation

Summary of Recommendations

The important recommendations made in the text of this chapter are given below :

1. A farmers' own organisation can further the interests of agricultural development as well as those of the farming community more effectively than a Government organisation. It will be desirable if the farmers' organisation operates in two separate but complementary wings, one dealing with economic and service functions and the other with promotional and welfare activities. For the former, we have recommended in Chapter 55 on Credit and Incentives the setting up of farmers' service societies. For the latter, we recommend the setting up of FU or Krishi Sabhas.

2. At the primary level, the Farmers' Union (FU) will cover the same area as a Farmers' Service Society (FSS), i.e. a block or a circle with a population often to twelve thousands, to begin with. The membership of the FU will be open to all farmers, artisans and agricultural labourers who are enrolled as members of the FSS.

3. The main functions of the FU will be to motivate all members towards planned economic development, disseminate information on modern farm and other production practices, organise training in improved methods and techniques of production and help achieve the objectives of the various development programmes and the targets laid for the various development programmes and the targets laid down therein. It will also undertake welfare activities, such as running adult literacy classes, youth clubs, consumer stores etc.

4. The finances of the FU will comprise a graded membership fee collected annually from all its members, a contribution made by its counterpart FSS and, if necessary, a levy on the produce marketed through the societies.

5. When a minimum of 15 farmers' unions are formed in a district, they will federate into a District Farmers' Union (DFU). The main functions of the DFU will be to establish a regular channel of communication between the village community, as represented by it, and the district planning authorities, assist the latter in programme planning, organise training courses for farmers and other interest groups and help implement the various development programmes through its constituent units.

6. The finances of the DFU will consist of an annual contribution from the farmers' service societies in the district, a levy on agricultural produce marketed through the FSS, grants from regulated market committees in the district and a matching grant from the government.

7. In order to safeguard the interests of the weaker sections of the community like women, agricultural labourers, scheduled castes and tribes and the special interest group of artisans, they should have their representatives in the executive committee of the Farmers' Union and the District Farmers Union through cooption, if they are not represented among the elected members of these bodies.

8. The executive committee of the FU will be same as the elected members of the Managing

Committee of the FSS, about two-thirds of whom will be from the small and marginal farmers. Consequently, these classes will have a majority in the District Farmers' Union as well. It has, thus, been ensured that the proposed Farmers' Organisation will largely represent the interests of small and marginal farmers and other weaker sections of the village community.

9. After a sufficient number of District Farmers' Unions are formed in a state, they can form a State Farmers' Union (SFU). The main function of the SFU will be to apprise the State Government of the needs, expectations and opinions of the people in the rural areas in respect of the development of agriculture, general rural development and welfare measures and to assist the State Government in formulating a proper policy for rural development, with special emphasis on agriculture.

10. The farmers' organisation at the all-India level will take the form of a National Farmers' Union analogous to that of SFU. It will have an advisory and consultative role in the formulation of national policies with regard to general rural development, development in agriculture and progressive welfare measures like rural housing, debt redemption, etc.

11. Since the national and state farmers' unions will function mainly in an advisory and consultative capacity, it will be expedient if they are represented also in other organisations engaged in promoting the development of agriculture and related fields of the economy, such as the Food Corporation of India, National Seeds Corporation, the Central Warehousing Corporation, etc. at the national level and the state agro-industries corporation, state electricity board, state land mortgage development bank, etc., at the state level.

12. The main job of the representatives of the farmers' organisation in the aforesaid bodies will be to apprise their managements of the needs and expectations of the people in the rural areas and of the possibilities that exist there in respect of the development of agriculture and related fields of the economy and help evolve proper policies for framing and scheduling their programmes.

International Cooperation

Summary of Recommendations

The main recommendations in the sphere of international cooperation are briefly given below :

1. In view of the availability of a very large range of plant material to the modern plant-breeder, it is necessary for the Indian breedr to keep himself abreast of the latest developments. For this purpose, international and inter-regional cooperation in plant breeding through multi-disciplinary research in specific crops and seed exchange programmes will be required. The existing arrangements in this field need to be strengthened.

2. Foreign assistance will be necessary for the purchase of sophisticated laboratory, seed testing and cleaning, storage and disinfestation equipment which is not available in India.

3. There is need to further foreign assistance for the import of fertilisers and pesticides (technical grades) not manufactured in India and of raw materials, plant and machinery required for the manufacture of these inputs till we are able to achieve self reliance. Foreign assistance will also be needed for research on the most effective and/or economical use of material and formulations and forecasting and control of pests and plant disease.

4. In the field of animal husbandry, it would be useful to have further foreign collaboration to build up animal husbandry on scientific lines. The areas where foreign collaboration is needed are the setting up of plants to manufacture foot-and-mouth disease vaccine, and supply of high-producing milch-animals, equipment for the establishment of frozen semen stations, fine wool and mutton breeds of sheep, high quality foundation breeding stock of pigs and the pure live poultry-breeding stock.

5. In the field of fisheries there is still need for development of purseining and other methods of pelagic fishing. Technological advice and assistance are also required for mid-water trawling and tuna fishing.

6. Since the available sources of bamboo in India cannot alone provide the range of fibres required for the pulp and paper industry, part of the future long-fibre needs will have to be met both from the existing coniferous forests and by establishing tropical pine plantations for meeting the requirements of this industry. India's experience in this regard being limited, bilateral and/or multilateral assistance for the supply of seeds and trial of tropical pine species will be required.

7. Development of wild life is another area where advantage can be takan of the expertise available with international agencies, like the FAO, world wild life fund, the international union for the conservation of nature, etc.

8. A greater use of latest development in remote sensing and infra-red photography will be useful for detecting plant disease and assessing soil characteristics. This will need import of sophisticated equipment and foreign expertise for guiding and training Indian

personnel·

9. India's future need for foreign expertise will be mostly in the fields of advanced production technology, research and training. The foreign experts will, however, be needed more as consultants than as regular, whole-time advisers.

10. International cooperation need not necessarily be in one direction only. India can also contribute significantly both the agricultural research and production. In the field of crop production, it should be part of India's policy to provide seed to other countries where needed. In respect of fertilisers and pesticides, India can provide experts and training facilities.

11. In the field of irrigation, India is in a position to assist in conducting feasibility studies and preparation of project reports, provide consultants, depute irrigation engineers and offer fellowships for training in India. India can also undertake turn-key jobs for constructing Irrigation projects.

12. In respect of animal husbandry India can render assistance in establishing biological production stations for the manufacture of vaccines and diagnostic agents, disease investigation laboratories, animal science teaching and research institutions, installing dairy and feed mixing plants on turn-key basis and setting up livestock farms.

13. As the largest fishing nation in the Indian ocean area, India should undertake cooperative research and investigations with the neighbouring countries in subjects of common interest. Research institutions in marine fisheries and oceanography should also be fully equipped to handle this task.

14. In forestry, India can continue to provide facilities for education and training to students from other countries. In addition, India can offer assistance in the form of experts for field posts and teaching in tropical forestry.

15. In agricultural research there is need for worldwide collaboration programme through arrangements with international organisations, institutions, foundations and bilateral agencies, whereby foreign scientists could work in Indian research institutions and Indian scientists in the research institutions abroad.

16. Close relationship should, in particular, be developed with International Research Institutes on wheat and maize in Mexico, rice in Philippines, potato in Peru and tropical agriculture in Columbia and Nigeria.

Summing up of Tenancy Reforms

The specific features of tenancy legislation in India arise from the basic framework of land reforms policy adopted by the law makers, which favoured neither the wholesale expropriation of landlordism in the interest of tenant cultivators nor the wholesale expropriation of tenant cultivators in the interest of large scale farming by big landlords. A middle course was adopted and successive five year plans and the panels and committees for land reforms set up. The Central Government laid down the objectives of tenancy legislation as follows :

(i) Security of tenure to be conferred on tenant cultivators in the interest of social justice and agricultural production;

(ii) fair rents to be fixed for tenants;

(iii) landowners to be permitted to resume land for self cultivation upto a limited area; and

(iv) on non-resumable areas, landlord-tenant relationship to be ended and the tenant cultivators on those areas to be brought into direct contact with the state as peasant proprietors.

A survey of the tenancy legislation enacted during the last two and a half decades would show that while considerable progress has been made in the field of tenancy reforms many serious deficiencies and loopholes in law still persist which impede the full realisation of the above mentioned objectives. The following outstanding drawbacks in the present structure of tenancy reforms can be identified.

Firstly, the definition of the term "tenant" generally excludes the share croppers who form the great bulk of tenant cultivators in all parts of the country and who also constitute one of the most vulnerable sections of rural society. The share croppers as such were not treated as tenants in West Bengal, Assam, Bihar, Orissa, erstwhile Travancore, Cochin, Punjab and Haryana. Besides, by practice and custom, persons employed as partners (sajhis) by the landlords on terms of payment of a share of the produce were not treated as tenants in some states and no tenancy rights accrued to them, e.g., in Uttar Pradesh. In Kerala and Maharashtra the term tenant has now been defined to include informal share croppers. Not only are the share croppers kept outside the area of protection provided by tenancy legislation in many states, but in some states, as in Uttar Pradesh and Madhya Pradesh where leasing out of land is legally prohibited, the very existence of share croppers is not recognised, and the tenancy law takes no cognisance of them. A fiction is maintained there that since the law does not permit subletting of land, there are no sharecroppers and the question of giving them any protection, therefore, does not arise. The reality, on the other hand, is that in all states most leasing out is done in the form of share cropping and the exclusion of share croppers from the scope of tenancy legislation deprives millions of real tillers of the soil of the protection and rights provided for tenants under tenancy reform measures.

Secondly, ejectment of tenants from their holdings is still permissible on many grounds and this is essentially a continuing hangover of feudal tenancies. Total eviction from land is one of the besetting evils of the present tenancy system, which weakens very seriously the position of the tenant vis-a-vis the land owner.

The Report of the Panel on Land Reforms of the Planning Commission, 1958, clearly recommended that pending the enactment of comprehensive legislation for tenancy reforms, the following steps should be taken with immediate effect :

(i) "Ejectment of tenants or sub-tenants should be stayed. Ejectment on grounds of non-payment of rent or misuse of land may be permitted through the due process of law.

(ii) Tenants who have been dispossessed of their lands in recent years should be restored except where ejectments were made through the courts for non-payment of rent or misuse of land. 'Voluntary surrenders' result mainly from landlord's influence and the tenants low bargaining power. All such surrenders should be treated as cases of ejectment and restoration provided for.

(iii) All tenants should come into direct relation with the state which should undertake the obligation to recover fair rents from the tenants and pay it to the landlord after deducting the cost of collection."

The grounds of termination of tenancy as land in the tenancy laws of various states make a very long list. The main grounds found to be used for termination of tenancy are : (a) non-payment of rent; (b) failure of payment within a given period; (c) faiture to deliver share produce within a given time; (d) failure to comply with any order of a court; (e) failure to deposit arrears within 15 days or within given time; (f) failure to pay balance, if any, of fair rent after it is determined within a specified period; (g) failure to pay rent regularly without reason; (h) sub-letting, sub-leasing or otherwise illegally transferring the land; (i) sub-dividing the holding; (j) failure to cultivate properly; (k) failure to cultivate personally; (l) failure to cultivate in the manner and extent customary; (m) use of land in an unauthorised manner; (n) keeping the land fallow continuously for two years; (o) using the land for non-agricultural purposes; (p) failure to execute agreement; (q) expiry of the term of lease; (r) land is required or reserved for personal cultivation of the owner; (s) land in possession of the owner is below the permissible limit; (t) land in possession of the tenant is in excess of the permissible limit; (u) breach of conditions of a tenancy contract; (v) denial of land owner's title; (w) failure to give notice of harvesting; and (x) removal of produce before division.

While many of the above reasons for termination of tenancy could be maintained in one context or the other, there is no reason why tenancy should be terminated on the following grounds; (a) failure to give notice of harvesting (Tamil Nadu); (b) removal of produce before division of crop (Tamil Nadu); (c) failure to execute agreement (Punjab & Haryana); (d) failure to cultivate land properly (Orissa); (e) failure to cultivate in the manner and extent customary (Punjab and Haryana); (f) keeping the land fallow for two years (Assam); (g) failure to deliver share of the produce within specified time (Assam, Andhra Pradesh—Andhra Area); (h) failure to deposit arrears of rent within 15 days of the final order in cases of disputes (Andhra Pradesh, Maharashtra—Marathwada, Vidarbha areas) and Gujarat (Cutch area).

Thirdly, provisions regarding 'voluntary surrenders' have become the biggest instrument in the hands of the land owners to deprive tenants of their due protection. The so called 'Voluntary Surrenders' are hardly ever voluntary. Land owners resort freely to pressures and even coercion to secure surrenders in order to get their tenanted lands vacated. Experience has shown that implementation of tenancy laws has everywhere been accompanied by large scale 'surrenders' of tenancies which defeat the very purpose of tenancy legislation.

The Third Five Year Plan sought to plug this loophole by the suggestion that (a) 'Surrenders' should not be regarded as valid unless they were registered with the revenue authorities, and (b) even where 'surrenders' were held to be valid, the landowner should be allowed to take possession of land only upto the right of resumption permitted. These provisions were included in the tenancy laws of certain states but even that did not bring about any material change in the situation. As long as the landowner could derive any advantage from surrenders he could maneouvre to get them registered and even approved by the local land revenue authorities. The Fouth Five Year Plan, therefore, suggested that the land owner should not be allowed to regain possession of the surrendered land and that the Government should allot such land to other eligible persons. This suggestion has, however, not yet been incorporated in tenancy laws of most of the states. There are no provisions for the regulation of surrenders in Tamil Nadu, Punjab,

Haryana and Uttar Pradesh. Provision for the scrutiny of surrenders by revenue authorities has been made in Andhra Pradesh, Assam, Bihar, Gujarat, Himachal Pradesh, Karnataka, Kerala, Madhya Pradesh, Maharashtra, Manipnr, Orissa, Tripura and West Bengal. The suggestion of the Fourth Plan that the land-owner should not be allowed to regain possession of the surrendered land and that every surrender should be in favour of the Government has been accepted and acted upon in Kerala, Gujarat, Himachal Pradesh, Orissa, Karnataka and West Bengal.

The fourth major provision which has worked to the detriment of the potential beneficiaries of tenancy legislation is the law regarding resumption of land by landowners.

After the abolition of Zamindaris, the land-owners were not permitted to resume any tenanted land in Uttar Pradesh and West Bengal. But a limited right of resumption was permitted in all other states. The right of resumption was allowed to be exercised within a limited period in Madhya Pradesh, Maharashtra, Kerala, Gujarat, Karnataka and Orissa. In all these states the time limit has expired. Land-owners were allowed to resume land upto the ceiling limit in Bihar, Haryana, Assam, Punjab and Orissa. In other states the maximum area that could be resumed was fixed below the ceiling limit. In many states the resumption law provided for leaving a certain minimum area with the tenant. Tenancy laws in Kerala, Gujarat, Himachal Pradesh, Maharashtra, Tamil Nadu and Karnataka provide for leaving half of the land with the tenant on resumption. Bihar provides for leaving half the leased out area or 5 acres (2.02 ha), whichever is less, in the case of land-owners having land more than the ceiling area. In West Bengal, the land to be left with the tenant or share cropper on resumption is one hectare or the actual area under cultivation, whichever is less. In Punjab, Haryana and Assam, aminimum area is to be left with the tenant until an alternative piece of land is provided to him by the Government.

The right of resumption has been sought to be justified on the ground that it would help to convert non-working and rent receiving land owners into owner cultivators who could step up agricultural production. The accent in the concept of resumption is on 'personal cultivation'. However, the term 'personal cultivation' has been so defined as to cover cultivation through hired labour, paid in cash or kind but not in a crop share. Even personal supervision by the land-owner or his family is not treated as an essential requisite of personal cultivation.

With this definition of 'personal cultivation' right of resumption has become an instrument in the hands of unscrupulous land-owners for land grabbing and unwarranted eviction of tenants. This provision has, in fact, indirectly created an atmosphere for the growth of informal, oral and concealed tenancies under which the actual tenant is characterised as a farm servant or an 'agricultural partner'. It has also encouraged absentee landlords to resort to rotation of tenancies from plot to plot. The highly defective state of land records facilitates the continued prevalence of such tenancies. Furthermore, in the absence of clearcut provisions for the demarcation of non-resumable areas on which the tenants could exercise their right of purchase, the big land owners can easily defeat the objectives of legislation by resorting to resumption in an indiscriminate and very often fraudulent manner.

The right of resumption is a continuing right in several states such as Andhra Pradesh (Andhra Area), Assam and Tamil Nadu. In West Bengal, this right would automatically end with the implementation of the ceiling law. In Karnataka (Mysore) a continuing right of resumption has been accorded to land-owners holding less than 4 standard acres (1.61 ha) of land. No provision has been made for resumption for personal cultivation in Uttar Pradesh. In case of Haryana and Punjab, the right of resumption had to be exercised within a period of one year from the commencement of the President's Act by land-owners in the Armed Forces of the Union and within a period of six months by other land owners. In Madhya Pradesh the right of resumption has expired and the tenants have been conferred ownership in respect of non-resumable areas. In Kerala, application for resumption in respect of tenancies existing on the commencement of the Kerala Land Reforms Act, 1963 (as amended up to 1973) were to be made within one year of such commencement.

Fifthly, tenancy legislation has not yet been able to regulate rents as recommended by the five year plans, that is, at one-fifth to one-fourth of the gross produce. All states have passed laws fixing rent of cultivating tenants but fair rents have not been defined uniformly. In fact in certain states they have been fixed at a higher level than what was recommended in the plans. In Punjab and Haryana, for example, fair rent is fixed at one-third of the gross produce. In Tamil Nadu it is 40 per cent of the gross produce in irrigated areas and one-third in other areas. In Andhra Pradesh (Andhra Area) the fair rent has been fixed at 30 per cent of gross produce for irrigated and 25 per cent for dry lands. In Jammu and Kashmir it has been fixed for tenants of land owners holding above 12½ acres (5.06 ha) of land at one-fourth of the gross produce for wet lands and one-third for dry lands. For tenants of landlords owning less than 12½ acres (5.06 ha) fair rent has been fixed at one-half of the gross produce. In other states fair rents have been generally fixed at one-fifth to one-fourth of the gross produce.

In view of the fact that the fixation of rent in term of gross produce is a cumbersome and protracted process, some states have fixed rents as multiples of land revenue. In Gujarat and Maharashtra it has been provided that fair rent is not to exceed one-sixth of the gross produce or 3 to 5 times the land revenue, whichever is less. In Rajasthan fair rent is not to exceed one-sixth of the gross produce or twice the rate of land revenue. In Madhya Pradesh fair rent has been fixed at 2 to 4 times the land revenue depending on the quality of land.

The point is that it is extremely difficult to get the provisions regarding fair rents enforced in the case of share croppers and other tenants not enjoying any security of tenure. For any demand or litigation on the part of such tenants for the fixation of fair rents leads to their ejectment from land. The outstanding example in this respect is that of West Bengal where despite the fixation of the rent of share croppers (bargadars) at 25 per cent of the gross produce in kind, the prevailing share of the land-owners is no where less than 50 per cent. In fact this rate prevails almost throughout the country in the case of share croppers and other categories of unprotected tenants.

One of the principal aims of tenancy reforms was to convert tenants into owners of lands they cultivated. But the rates of compensation to be paid by the tenants for acquiring ownership rights were generally very high and beyond the paying capacity of tenants. Therefore, the objective of conferring occupancy rights, on as large a body of tenants as possible, could not materialise. Besides, the purchase of ownership was optional in certain states. In view of the financial weakness of the tenants and intimidation by land-owners the results proved to be far from satisfactory.

One of the major weak spots of tenancy legislation has been the provision which entitles a tenant to acquire occupancy right provided he can prove continuous occupation of his holding for a number of years. This provision totally negates the spirit of the principle of 'land to the tiller' because under the peculiar character of landlord-tenant nexus obtaining in India it is virtually impossible for an ordinary tenant to prove continuous occupation for a number of years. In fact the landlord takes good care that the tenant is unable to do so by manipulating land records, by not issuing rent receipts and by rotating tenancies *yearly* from plot to plot. The burden of proof being on the tenant, the law thus becomes virtually ineffective.

It is only the very influential tenants who are in a position to establish their rights on that basis of continuous occupation. In order to give protection to the mass of tenants it should have been provided that once a tenant puts forward his claim to occupancy right under the law, the burden of proof to the contrary should be on the landlord.

Summing up of Ceiling Legislation : On an evaluation of the post 1972 ceiling legislation, it can be said that ceiling legislation has been improved, rationalised and put on a more or less uniform basis throughout the country. The National Guidelines, on the basis of which this has been done, represents a national consensus on the question and marks a considerable advance on the situation that prevailed earlier. The main question now is how to get the amending legislation effectively implemented. The tasks in this respect are—

(i) to detect 'benami' or clandestine transfers of property made to relatives, friends or other persons, real or imaginary, through ficticious or collusive transactions;

(ii) To secure correct records of land-owners of more than ceiling;

(iii) to take possession of the land vested in the state after the completion of the administrative process; and

(iv) to distribute the surplus land among the beneficiaries as provided under the law.

The biggest constraint in this process is the date of retrospective effect. The reality is that transfers, partitions, sales, gifts etc., on a large scale were deliberately effected by the big land owners earlier than retrospective date provided in the National Guidelines i.e., January 24, 1971, in anticipation of ceiling legislation. The issue boils down to the question whether any further amendment of the ceiling legislation is to be made in order to advance the date of retrospective effect

Summing up of implementation : The foregoing analysis brings out the fact that, with all the moderate stance of land reforms legislation in India, the performance by and large has been disappointing. In fact, the tragedy of land reforms in the country lies essentially in the manner and method of implementation. What is clearly noticeable is a widening gap between the declared objectives of land reform legislation and its actual achievements in terms of institutional and structural changes for mass welfare.

It is time to take a hard look at the prevailing situation. The question is, who has failed ? Is it the legislator or the administrator ? In a measure both have failed. However, the major responsibility lies on the shoulders of the enforcement agencies, that is to say, the administrative set up entrusted with the task of implementation. The question then arises, when the same administrative machinery can do excellent work at the time of the general elections or for managing any emergency whether it is civil commotion or drought and flood relief, why does it fail to deliver the goods when it comes to implementing land reforms. The answer to this question lies in the fact that since land reforms involve certain basic structural changes in rural society affecting property rights in land, the officials cannot on their own function as a change agency in this field. In fact the official machinery has not been conditioned to act as such; on the contrary, it has been trained and conditioned to function as the custodian of status-quo and the defender of existing property relations. It is, therefore, clear that without a powerful will of the state, explicitly defined and forcefully asserted from above, land reform programmes in the hands of the officials alone would continue to flounder on the rocks of conservatism and defence of status-quo and the defender of existing property relations. Land reforms implementation has to be a continuing process with ingredients ranging from the assertion of will of the state, to the interpretation and enforcement of law in the correct spirit and the carrying out of multifarious practical tasks at the field level for delivering the goods to the beneficiaries. In this situation the enlistment of popular cooperation, particularly in the form of participation of the potential beneficiaries in the practical process of implementation assumes even greater significance.

The recent assertion of a political will for land reforms in a development of crucial importance comparable to the post-Independence determination which resulted in the abolition of the *Zamindari* system. The effectiveness of implementation would, however, depend on the extent to which this political will can be transmitted to the administrative machinery in term of concrete acts of enforcement of the multifarious provisions of land reform laws. It is important, under these circumstances, to formulate time-bound programmes, to strengthen the organisation and streamline the procedures for implementation, having in mind the need to overcome (a) the legal and administrative constraints, (b) the rigidity of existing administrative system, and (c) the opposition of vested interests.

We have analysed above the provisions of land reform legislation and evaluated its implementation. The impact of land reforms on the emerging agrarian structure with their bearing on agricultural productivity, economic growth and social justice is discussed in the following chapter.

Consolidation of Holdings

Summary of Recommendations

The main recommendations are as under :

1. The advantages of consolidation of holdings are likely to be neutralised over a period of time if curb on fragmentation is not imposed. The partition of holdings, if it results in fragmentation, should be prohibited and alienation by sale, gift and mortgage may be permissible in favour of contiguous tenure holders in order of preference as follows :
   - (i) to the collateral contiguous right-holder if one exists and if there are more than one contiguous collaterals, the preference will be in order of preference of succession as prescribed by the Hindu Succession Act; and
   - (ii) In all other cases the preference will be in the ascending order of holdings' size of the contiguous right-holders.

In order that such restrictions do not peg the price to the detriment of the alienator, some mechanism for the fixation of fair price should be considered. The State Government should also assume the right of pre-emptive purchase.

2. In some states as a result of consolidation, holdings with two or more blocks have been created. Land holdings in such states be reconsolidated to create one block holdings if the underground water potential is fit for irrigation and the area is plain.

3. As voluntary scheme for consolidation of holdings, wherever introduced, did not make much headway on account of reluctance of right-holders to part with their ancestral land and opposition by vested interests who are always placing obstacles to retard the progress, the scheme should be made compulsory in all areas of the country fit for consolidation.

4. While framing a legislation of consolidation, the main criteria that should be kept in view are that
   - (i) the legislation is independent of other central or state measures governing the ownership, possession, title to holdings and disposal or other treatment of agricultural land; and
   - (ii) the legislation should clearly provide for determination of value of land, draw-up of

scheme and reservation of areas for common village needs in consultation with the people and the advisory committee, measurement and preparation of record of rights by the field staff and checking thereof.

5. The consolidation operations should not be allowed to linger on inordinately. A time limit should be fixed for completion of every stage of consolidation proceedings including the disposal of cases and transfer of possession depending upon the area of the village. The consolidation law should not envisage more than two remedies against the court of first instance.

6. To speed up progress of consolidation, the disposal of writ petitions within six months of the date of presentation is an essential requisite. The State Governments may request the High Courts to assign one or two judges, as may be necessary, exclusively for hearing such writs.

7. In area under consolidation, cases relating to right in or title to land, if continued to be tried and decided by Civil or Revenue courts, would entail inordinate delays in the matter of transfer of possession and completion of consolidation proceedings. All such cases, other than writ petitions, pending in any court of law whether at trial, appeal or revision stage, should abate and be allowed to be subsequently tried by consolidation courts which alone should have jurisdiction to decide such cases till the operations last.

8. To associate right-holders in the consolidation of their land-holdings advisory committee be formed at state, district and village levels. These should represent the interests of land-holders and landless labourers particularly those who directly or indirectly draw their livelihood from land income. The village committee will play an important role in the evaluation of land, carving out of blocks, reservation of areas for common purposes and homesteads. The committees at state and district levels will have advisory functions.

9. Three different methods, one based on productivity, the other on market value and the third on rental value, are adopted in the country for determination of the value of the land. Market value method of valuation based on rental value is found to be out-moded. The first method, which also takes into account the evenness of the surface, type of soil, facility of irrigation, proximity to inhabited site of the village, market or road and similar other factors, is very popular as the farmers can avail to their age-long experience of observing crops sown in the field for assessing their values. It should be uniformally adopted in the country. The determined values of fields, trees, tanks, wells and buildings on land should be communicated to farmers in writing through pass-books prescribed for the purpose.

10. For the replanning and development of villagers, reservation of land for complusory common-purpose like roads, extension of *abadi* sites for proprietors and non-proprietors, water courses, tanks, manure pits, schools, play grounds, panchayatghar, public latrines etc., should be made. Reservations should also be made for fuel plantations, worshipping places, grazing grounds, threshing and winnowing grounds, rural dispensary, road-side vehicle stand, storage for fuel and fodder, fair and festival grounds and other allied purposes on option basis. Since such reservations are essentially required for the convenience, use and improvement of living conditions of residents, these should form an unfailing feature of all consolidated villages.

11. To avoid waste of time and labour, it would be desirable to align the soil conservation programme with consolidation for which joint scheme be drawn up and soil conservation works started only after the completion of consolidation of holdings operations.

12. It is noted that there is a tendency among the influential sections of the villages to oust forcibly the weaker sections from the areas allotted to them as homestead sites. Restoration of possession through courts of law entails financial hardship beyond their means. It is, therefore, recommended that revenue authorities may be empowered to restore the possessions of land to such allottees.

13. The rectangulation of land provides right-holders with fields of uniform shape and size, convenience for irrigation and cultivation. With straight water courses there is great convenience and much less waste in the use of water. Boundary disputes and the consequential litigation is almost eliminated. Seasonal crop inspection is made easy and supervision is rendered effective and efficient. The process of planning for the tract becomes much easier particularly when new village roads are to be aligned and water-channels dug. These considerations should be kept in view while suggesting the adoption of rectangulation in plain areas to be brought under consolidation.

14. Legal significance attached to the new records of rights prepared as a result of consolidation is exaclty the same as that attached to those prepared during regular settlement. Regular settlement operations, where due, should be commenced immediately after the consolidation is completed as it would reduce the settlement cost.

15. The scheme of consolidation is not to be spread over the entire state all at once. To provide

publicity and experience to the staff, a pilot scheme covering a compact group of villages in a tehsil should be undertaken and thereafter it should be extended to other areas.

16. The consolidation scheme when in full swing needs undivided attention at the state level. To implement it, officer with experience in revenue work, may be appointed as Head of the Department.

17. Sometimes the office of the settlement officer is away from the area of operation. To enable him to exercise proper supervision over the staff working under him, the headquarters of the settlement officer should be at the district headquarters in which the work is being done.

18. In order to maintain a close watch over the progress of consolidation work and to ensure achievement of targets, a suitable norm of performance should be fixed for each Patwari.

19. There is scope for malpractices and corruption among the consolidation staff. The standard of integrity can be raised through closer supervision, rigid control, surprise checks, appreciation of good work and strict disciplinary measures. The staff for consolidation of holdings should be taken on deputation so that there is no difficulty about its absorption after the completion of the consolidation programme. Flying squads headed by a Consolidation Officer should be set up and attached to the head of the Department. They should make surprise raids to go into complaints of corruption and make suitable recommendations for action against guilty officials.

20. To keep a watchful eye on the working of the staff, their behaviour towards public and to prevent malpractices it is necessary to have a watch-dog committee.

21. The revenue staff needs training in consolidation procedures and practice. Training centres of short duration, should be set up for this purpose. The officers of the rank of Assistant Consolidation Officer and above should also be imparted practical training in consolidation under the direct control and supervision of the Director of Consolidation of Holdings so that they may be able to guide properly the staff working under them.

22. For an effective management and to increase the income potential, village common lands which at present are scattered over a large number of pieces, should be consolidated as far as possible in one block. Land reserved as homestead sites for harijans and landless labourers should be earmarked for individuals and not set apart as a common plot for the entire community to be subsequently divided among them by the village panchayat or other agencies. This is necessary as it would facilitate securing of loans and would not delay the construction of houses.

23. In some districts of the state of Kerala, the problem of fragmentation is much more serious than in others. In such areas a pilot scheme of consolidation of holdings should be tested. Once it succeeds there it could be tried in other areas of the state.

24. Absence of uptodate revenue records and complexity of tenurial system should not present much difficulty in the adoption of the scheme as the former can be brought uptodate by the concerned revenue agency and the latter can be simplified through land reform measures.

25. The rainfall in the dry areas is low, erratic as well as sporadic. The topographical and soil characteristics of holdings in the same locality may vary greatly. The difficulties experienced in the districts of Mohindergarh and Bhiwani of Haryana State have since been successfully resolved. There was good response from the farmers benefited by the consolidation. In view of the undoubted production benefit and operational economy accruing from the consolidation of holdings, the programme should be taken up in dry and arid areas of the country also.

26. Consolidation should not be attempted in hilly areas where terrace cultivation is practised and scope of exchange land is limited.

27. The practice of treating apple orchards, coffee and tea gardens etc., as separate blocks during consolidation operations is rational and necessary. This practice should continue.

28. The cost of consolidation can be reduced if the consolidation is done on a compulsory basis in a compact unit inhabited by progressive farmers and without abandonment of proceedings at any stage. The staff to be deployed should be well trained, honest and efficient. Targets should be achieved through strict supervision and frequent inspection. Possession should be transferred quickly to avert writs for revocation of repartition.

29. The cost of consolidation depends upon different factors like topography, extent of fragmentation, social awareness of the people and level of prevailing technical 'know-how' and several other related factors. Therefore, no uniform rate can be fixed for the country as a whole. Reasonable charges should be realised from the beneficiaries to reduce the financial burden of the State Governments. The small and marginal farmers should be exempted from the payment of cost of consolidation of their land. Twenty-five per cent central financial assistance in the form of grant should be paid to the State Governments on account of expenditure on the programme undertaken on the land of small and marginal farmers.

30. There should be an effective machinery for

periodic assessment of progress of consolidation programme.

Agricultural Labour

Summary of Recommendations

The principal recommendations for improving the conditions of agricultural labourers are given below :

1. Under the Minimum Wages Act of 1948, many states have fixed minimum wages to be paid to agricultural labourers. But most of the provisions of the Act have remained on paper. To be effective, the policy for minimum wages for agricultural labourers calls for planned and concerted efforts for enforcement in selected priority areas.

2. There should be a small body at the state level making a review of the implementation of the provisions of the Minimum Wages Act. It is of utmost importance to arrange for constant and vigilant supervision over implementation.

3. The minimum wage legislation should work for a progressive increase in the minimum level through positive programmes to eliminate 'poverty of agriculture, and through gradual strengthening of the enforcement machinery. The long term target of the legislation should, of course, be to ensure the need based minimum for all agricultural labourers.

4. Enforcement of minimum wages by the *panchayat* under the guidance and supervision of a watchdog committee would bring in substantial and enduring benefits to agricultural labourers. It should be the responsibility of this committee to lay down the working procedure for enforcement and to function as an appellate body to look into the grievances arising in the process of enforcement.

5. It is no less important to strengthen the official machinery for inspection, conciliation and enforcement. The modified enactments in this regard now being implemented by the Government of Kerala and Maharashtra should be studied by the other State Governments with a view to introduce similar provisions in the minimum wage laws, wherever necessary.

6. A long term solution of the enforcement of minimum wages would lie in the effective unionisation of agricultural labourers. The supporting role that the state can play in this respect should receive careful consideration.

7. As the direct enforcement of minimum wages would take time to be effective, the policy on minimum wages needs to be integrated with the 'employment creating' programmes, such as rural works programme, to influence wages indirectly by offering alternative employment. However, the objective should not be to assign a relief-cum-welfare role to rural works programmes.

8. While distributing surplus land made available as a result of ceiling on land holdings, priority should be given to agricultural labour. It would be desirable that surplus land is allotted in compact blocks to facilitate the management of land on cooperative basis. Such a step would facilitate the adoption of a policy of directing the flow of future public investments in irrigation and land development for the benefit of the under-privileged.

9. Certain lines of production like printing of textiles and weaving of multi-coloured textiles should be reserved exclusively for the 'household and small producer sector not using power'. This would provide a major impetus and scope for classes like agricultural labourers to adopt these lines as main/subsidiary occupations.

10. The strengthening of land base would, in our view, be the most important single measure in promoting subsidiary occupations like dairying, poultry, vegetable-gardening, etc. among the agricultural labourers, small and marginal farmers and agricultural labourers should be given all help like access to an artificial insemination centre, milk collection centre, and availability of veterinary facilities to induce them to take to dairying. Second priority should be given to development of poultry, horticulture and fishery, depending on the availability of land, skill and willingness of the labourers. Arrangements for marketing the products of these activities should also be made.

11. There should be a regular programme of enrolling rural youth for vocational training in special institutions. After such training, they should be given facilities to set up workshops or workplaces to cater to the needs of the village either on individual or group basis.

12. The requirements of land needed for constructing shelters to live and sheds to work for each household belonging to agricultural labour, scheduled castes, scheduled tribes, village artisans and other weaker sections, should be worked out by each village.

13. Attempts should be made to bring together the surplus lands given to agricultural labourers, the house-sites allotted to them and the land acquired by the state for this purpose in a contiguous block. A redevelopment plan of the area thus consolidated should be prepared providing for drainage, sanitation, paved streets, community drinking water sources and electricity.

14. Once the house-sites/additional land over the

existing sites have been made available, programme for mass construction/improvement of houses on such sites including sheds for subsidiary occupations should be organised. This programme should be organised on aided self-help basis. It would be desirable if this phase of the programme is made a part of the rural works programme.

15. In designing the programme for agricultural labourers the highest priority in the initial phase should be accorded to rural works programme, an effective net work for distribution of 'foodgrains at fair prices, and the welfare programmes for education, health and housing in order to provide quick and substantial relief to agricultural labourers and to raise their level of living to ascertain minimum specified level. These should be implemented with specified time-bound targets.

16. After sufficient progress is achieved in imparting certain minimal economic strength to the class of agricultural labourers, conditions will be ripe for legislative measures for social security programmes like provident fund, unemployment and sickness insurance etc.

17. The rule of law which has so far not been very effective should be restored in the areas where bonded labour prevails. The state should make its presence manifest on the side of this class of people and take drastic and punitive measures against landlords and money lenders and other traditional exploiters to loosen their hold on land, rural finance and trade. Only such officials who have an understanding of tribal problems and genuinely work for them should be posted to such areas.

18. A vigorous propaganda campaign should be launched among the bonded labour to convince them of the sincerity of these measures and enlighten them on their rights and of the new opportunities for a better life. The farmers among the bonded labour should be given interest free loans to buy inputs and implements at concessional rates while their children should be granted special scholarships.

19. The present rudimentary system of collection and compilation of data on agricultural labourers needs thorough revision, strengthening and extension to improve the information output along all its major dimensions. Immediate action should be initiated by the state governments to see that every local authority should maintain a register of agricultural labourers residing within its jurisdiction. This information will be of prime importance in planning and implementing the wide range of programmes intended for this class.

20. The country still lacks reliable statistics and data to assess the changing economic conditions of agricultural labourers as reflected in levels of wages, employment, income, indebtedness etc. A special cell in the Ministry of Labour or Ministry of Agriculture and Irrigation should be entrusted with the task of collection, compilation and expeditious publication of basic statistics relating to agricultural labourers on a continuing basis.

SUGAR INDUSTRY ENQUIRY COMMISSION, 1970—REPORT

New Delhi, Manager of Publications, 1974. 2 Vols (bound in one) 392p.

Chairman : Justice V. Bhargava (who replaced Justice Deep Narain Sinha who passed away in June 1971 due to illness).

Members : Shri J.C. Dikshit; Shri B.N. Khosla; Dr. Dharam Narain (resigned in Sept. 1971 and replaced by Dr. V.S. Vyas; Shri Vasantrao Patil (resigned in March 1972 and replaced by P.S. Rajagopal Naidu); Shri Fazlur Rahman; Lala Bansidhar; Shri A.C. Bose.

Member-Ex-Officio : Shri S.C. Gupta (retired in July 1971 and was replaced by Shri L.S. Saxena in May, 1972).

Member-Secretary : Shri R.H. Chistie.

APPOINTMENT

The Sugar Industry Enquiry Commission was set up in September 1970 by the Ministry of Agriculture, then known as Ministry of Food, Agriculture,

Community Development and Cooperation under Notification No. S.O. 3180 dated 28th September, 1970.

For the immediate background of the setting up of the Commission, reference may be made to a debate on the question of nationalisation of the Sugar Industry which took place in the Rajya Sabha and the Lok Sabha in December, 1969. During the course of the discussion in the Lok Sabha, Shri Jagjivan Ram, the then Union Minister of Agriculture, made the following statement on 15th December, 1969 :

"The Sugar Industry is over 30 years old now and many developments have taken place during these years. It is, therefore, an opportunate time to appoint a Committee to study the working of the Sugar Industry in the context of the demand for nationalisation of the Sugar Undertakings in certain areas. The scope of the enquiry would be left sufficiently wide to enable an enquiry being made into the causes underlying the present demand for nationalisation of the Sugar Industry and the manner in which the various problems relating thereto may be tackled. The Committee may go into the factory-grower relationship, the payment of cane-prices, returns to the factory, their working and performance, the condition of plant and machinery and other relevant matters. In dealing with sick mills, the Committee can suggest steps which will help improve the working of these mills. In dealing with the sugar industry in general and with the sick mills in particular, the Committee should assess the financial, administrative and managerial problems involved as also the organisational structure necessary to implement the recommendations of the Committee. I propose to set up this Committee very quickly to go into the entire question of the sugar industry and to make recommendations".

TERMS OF REFERENCE

1. To study the working of the sugar industry in all its aspects, with particular reference to its performance during the last ten years and the condition of plant and machinery in different sugar mills;

2. To identify the inadequacies in the performance of the sugar industry and the causes thereof;

3. To study in detail the causes for the existence of a large number of sick sugar mills;

4. To study the progress and the working of sugar mills in the cooperative sector;

5. To make suggestions, in the light of such studies, for a rational and efficient organisation of the sugar industry in different parts of the country, in order to improve its working and performance, and to suggest measures for solving the problem of sick sugar mills, in the context of the demand for nationalisation of the sugar industry;

6. To study the relationship between sugarcane suppliers and the owners of sugar mills, with particular reference to the supply of cane and the payment of cane price and to make suggestions for improvement in the present laws and practices in this behalf;

7. To study the problem of large fluctuations in sugar cane production, of its processing into gur, khandsari and sugar and to make suggestions for securing stable conditions with a view to achieving a balanced development in these fields; and

8. In the light of the foregoing studies, to suggest a blue-print for the development of the sugar and allied industries over a period of next ten to fifteen years.

CONTENTS

General Questionnaires were issued and with whom Commission held discussions; (E) List of Sugar Factories visited by Commission and its Officers; (F) Introduction to Second Interim Report; (G) Introduction to First Interim Report.

RECOMMENDATIONS

The following norms should be adopted for assessing the technical performance of Sugar factories :

Particulars	*Norms*
Sugar per cent bagasse	3.0
Total Sugar Losses per cent Cane	
(a) for carbonation factories	2.3 to 2.5
(b) for Sulphitation factories	2.3 to 2.7
Reduced Mill extraction	93
Reduced boiling house extraction	90
Reduced overall extraction	84

The break-up of the total sugar losses is as follows :

(i) Loss of sugar in bagasse per cent cane	0.9 to 1.1 depending upon quality of cane
(ii) Loss of Sugar in press-cake per cent cane	0.1
(iii) Loss of Sugar in Molasses per cent	1.2 to 1.4 depending upon quality of cane
(iv) Undetermined loss of Sugar per cent cane	0.1

The requirement of fuel depend on the type of equipment, its maintenance, process adopted and the efficiency of operation. In well maintained and well operated modern factories having steam economy measures, the fuel requirement in terms of bagasse is about 26-28 per cent on cane. In carbonation factories where the consumption of steam is higher, a further 2 per cent bagasse on cane is needed. In the case of well balanced old plants having fuel and steam economy measures, the consumption of bagasse per cent cane should be 30.

The norms laid down relate to the present conditions existing in the industry in the country. The norms may have to be improved or revised from time to time in the light of research and technological development and marked change of conditions. The technical performance of a factory can hereafter be an important criterion in assessing the success or failure of a factory.

Rational and Efficient Organisation of Sugar Industry

(i) There should be a statutory provision for membership of a representative each of labour and canegrowers on the Board of Management of each sugar factory.

(ii) The Units, which have failed to observe even the minimum norms to be indicated to judge the performance in respect of financial and technical management, deserve to be looked into more carefully and if the charge of failure is established due to factors within the control of the management, they should be acquired by the Central Government. A statutory provision should be made to enable the Government to acquire all such units. Such units could be termed as sick units.

(iii) Good units, operating as private limited companies, proprietory or partnership concerns, should be converted within a stipulated time into public limited companies. If such units do not comply with this requirement within the time allowed, they should be taken over and nationalised.

(iv) A statutory provision should be made for constitution of a National Sugar Authority (N.S.A.).

(v) The National Sugar Authority should be a well-knit body of eleven to fifteen persons nominated by Government of India. It will include five whole-time persons viz., the Chairman, the Managing Director, a Technical Member, a Financial Member and an Economist. The other members will be nominated on the basis of their knowledge of Sugar industry including persons who will represent interests of canegrowers, labour and factories. All policy decisions will be taken at the meetings of the NSA. The day-to-day administration will be in the hands of an executive of five persons viz., the Chairman, the Managing Director, the Technical Member, the Financial Member and the Economist Member. The status of the Chairman must be fairly high corresponding to, say, a Senior Secretary in the Government of India.

(vi) In each sugar producing state, there can be a regional body or statutory corporation, either for whole state or co-terminus with sugar zones, members of which may be nominated by the State Government concerned in consultation with NSA. This regional body or corporation will be directly incharge of running the public sector factories in its region and will also be responsible for other functions to be delegated by the N.S.A.

(vii) The functions of the National Sugar Authority will be :

1. To assess the demand for sugar for domestic requirement and for exports.
2. To arrange for the production of sugar through factories in the corporate, cooperative and public sectors and arrange for its marketing in an orderly manner.
3. To build and operate a buffer stock of sugar

with the objective of stabilization of prices.

4. To acquire sugar processing units and to run them directly or through regional subsidiary bodies.
5. To plan production and assist in development of cane in different regions of the country.
6. To ensure technical efficiency of factories by way of regular technical audit, and to maintain Research and Development Divisions at the Central and regional offices.
7. To arrange for efficient utilization of by-products directly or through subsidiary organisation.
8. To regulate marketing of other sweetening agents.
9. To arrange for equitable distribution of sales realisation on a pre-arranged basis; and
10. To act as spokesman of the sugar industry at international forums.

(viii) The National Sugar Authority will have the authority to permit higher prices in particular areas than those recommended to overcome difficulties in the procurement of cane. A limit to these prices can be suggested on the basis of the opportunity cost of cane in the manufacture of gur and Khandsari in areas where they offer stiff competition to the sugar units.

(ix) Factories in all the sectors will conform to the guidance and supervision of the N.S.A. and the N.S.A. can recommend take over or acquisition of defaulting units.

(b) Recommendations from Chapter VII

(i) The entire private sector of the sugar industry, other than the cooperative sugar factories should be nationalised;

(ii) The marketing of sugar upto the level of wholesale trade should be completely nationalised;

(iii) Provision should be made for adequate representation of labour and cane-growers in the nationalised sector and in the cooperative sugar factories at all levels;

(iv) For formulating and executing policies in regard to the entire sugar industry (public sector and cooperative sector) and for the administration of the public sector of the sugar industry, the following statutory bodies and organizations should be set up :

1. A National Sugar Commission (NSC); and
2. State Sugar Corporations.

The National Sugar Commission should have the power to fix the prices of sugar and sugarcane in consultation with such organisations and experts as it may deem fit or may be required. It should lay down the policies for the marketing of sugar and the regulation of the working of sugar industry in its various aspects. It should build up and operate a sugar buffer stock. It should carry out technical, financial and other inspections and audits of the different sugar factories in the country. It should develop professional management. It should plan and implement the plans for the growth of the industry to meet the current and future requirements particularly as regards finance, sugarcane development, plant and machinery, better utilisation of by-products and quicker realisation of the socio-economic obligations of the sugar industry. For these purposes, the National Sugar Commission may utilise existing agencies or may create new agencies with the approval of the Government. The National Sugar Commission should be a well-knit body and have on it representatives of canegrowers, workers and cooperative factories.

Every State Government may set up one or more Corporations to run the sugar factories in the public sector. The Management Boards of the State Corporations will have on them representatives of the workers and canegrowers. The National Sugar Commission will have the power of giving directions to the State Sugar Corporations for the efficient working of the factories and for the marketing of sugar through the Food Corporation of India and Cooperative Societies.

(v) At every sugar factory, there should be a Managing Committee on which canegrowers and workers should be represented.

The organisation should essentially be a two-tier system with the State Sugar Corporation entrusted with the actual management of the required units and the central organisation acting as an apex organisation at the central level.

The organisation at the central level will be a stautory body established by an Act of Parliament. The basic structure of the Central Organisation will be as follows :

(a) It will consist of a whole time Chairman, 4 whole time members and 10 part time members.

(b) The chairman and whole time members should have among themselves special knowledge, experience and expertise in administration, finance ond economic affairs, agriculture, sugar technology and engineering and marketing. They should also have adequate practical experience in their particular fields as head of an organisation or institution or department. This is necessary as, apart from participation in policy making, they will have to implement and execute the policies and administer the various programmes and schemes relating to the function and work of the Commission.

(c) The part time members may consist of the following :

(i) Director, National Sugar Institute, Kanpur, ex-officio;

(ii) Two representatives of State Corporations and Government of States where there is no State Corporation;

(iii) A representative of the public sector;

(iv) A representative of the private sector (if private sector exists);

(v) A representative of the cooperative sector;

(vi) A person who, in the opinion of the Central Government, is capable of representing the interest of the canegrowers;

(vii) A person who, in the opinion of the Central Government, is capable of representing the interests of the workers; and

(viii) Two other persons having knowledge and experience of the sugar industry.

(d) The term of the Chairman and the whole time members may be 5 years at a time; the term of the part time members may be 3 years, except in the case of the ex-officio member.

(e) There shall be an Executive Board consisting of the Chairman and the whole time members. Each whole time member will be placed in charge of work and functions of the Central Organisation for which he may be best qualified or may be found suitable. The Chairman besides being in overall charge of administration and coordination of the work of the Commission, will be in charge of nationalisation and acquisition of Sugar Mills in the future (if the organisation functions as N.S.A) fixation of prices of Sugar and Sugarcane (if the organisation functions as N.S.C.); and such other work as he may like to deal with.

(f) The Central Oraganisation will have the power to set up standing committees and *ad-hoc* committees to deal with such matters and responsibilities as may be entrusted to them by it. Each standing committee/ *ad hoc* committee may consist of some members of the Commission and others, including experts.

(g) One of the standing committees may consist of the Chairman and some or all the members of the Central Organisation and the Chairman of State Corporations and the representatives of Governments of States which do not have a State Corporation. The representatives of a State Government will be the officer appointed for controlling and supervising the management of the sugar factory/factories of the state.

(h) The Central Organisation will have the power to nominate one Director on the Board of Directors of every State Corporation.

(i) All central assistance to State Corporations for rehabilitation of sugar factories and for other purposes will be channelled through the Central Organisation.

(j) The Central Organisation will have power to issue directions to State Corporations on matters of general policy.

(k) The role of the Central Organisation *vis-a-vis* Central Government will essentially be advisory except in so far as fixation of sugar and sugarcane prices is concerned when functioning as N.S.C. However, as the principal authority responsible for the regulation and development of sugar and allied industries, it will have important executive functions also.

(l) The Central Organisation will be the spokesman of the sugar industry as a whole at the national and international forums.

(m) The Central Organisation will have two wings—(a) secretariat, and (b) functional divisions/directorates dealing with specific fields of activities of the Central Organisation.

(a) A State Corporation may be a statutory body created by State legislation or may be a Government company within the meaning of section 617 of the Companies Act, 1956. It will work as an autonomous legal entity subject to the overall supervision of the State Government and the general directions of the Central Organisation (N.S.A./N.S.C) on policy matters.

(b) It will have a whole time Chairman-cum-Managing Director and a number of whole time and part time officials and non-officials as its Directors. One Director will be a person capable of representing the interests of workers and one Director capable of representing the interest of canegrowers. One of its Directors will be nominee of the Central Organisation. Subject to the above conditions, the constitution, powers and functions of a State Corporation may be drawn up more or less on the lines of the Uttar Pradesh State Sugar Corporation. The State Corporation will have the requisite financial, technical and other staff.

(c) A State Corporation may manage 5 to 10 factories and there may be more than one Corporation in a State. Where there is no State Corporation, the State Government will appoint a suitable officer for controlling and supervising the management of the factory or factories in the State. This officer will represent the State Government on the standing committee.

(d) The State Corporation will, inter alia, plan and carry out the rehabilitation of the sick mills in its charge and secure funds for the purpose from the State Government and other agencies.

(e) There shall be a nominee of the Central Organisation on the Board of Directors of every State Corporation.

(f) The State Corporation shall carry out the directions of the Central Organisation in matters of general policy.

(a) There shall be a Board or Committee of management at each nationalised unit.

(b) It may consist of the General Manager of the factory and 4 or 6 other members of whom one shall be a representative of the factory canegrowers and of one of the factory labour.

(c) The Board/Committee will work under the general supervision and guidance of the State corporation or the officer concerned and will look after the day-to-day management of the factory and take decisions on the matters within its scope as may be laid down by the State Corporation.

The annual cost of the Central Organisation will be Rs. 20 lakhs to Rs. 25 lakhs. The cost will be borne entirely by the Central Government.

A State Corporation will cost Rs. 6 lakhs to Rs. 8 lakhs annually. The cost will be borne by the State Government and the factories concerned.

The sugar marketing transactions carried to some extent towards the expenditure on the central organisation, if any part of sugar is sold at prices higher than levy prices.

A factory Board/Committee of management will cost about Rs. 10,000 to Rs. 15,000 per year. Its cost will be met from the earnings of the factory.

The Sugar Development Council set up under section 6 of the Industries (Development and Regulation) Act, 1951 should function in close association with, preferably as a wing of the Central Organisation. The Chairman of the Central Organisation may be nominated as Chairman of the Sugar Development Council and some members of the central organisation also may be nominated on the Council.

The Sugarcane Development Council set up by a Govenment Resolution may be converted into a Standing Committee set up by the Central Organisation under its own powers with the same functions and constitution.

Action for selection of officers for appointment to the various managerial posts of Central Organisation; State Corporations, Factory Boards/Committees of Management, etc., should be started immediately.

Government should invite applications for the managerial posts from the General Managers/Managers by a general circular/notification. Selection may be made from the applicants for temporary appointments but they should be assumed in advance that they will be considered for regular appointment in the public sector if they fulfil the qualifications and conditions which may be prescribed for recruitment and appointment to the services in the public sector on a regular permanent basis.

The training of the selected officers should begin without any loss of time. The selected officers should be given an intensive training for 12 weeks or more depending on the time available before they are placed incharge of sugar factories. Their practical training may include training at the National Sugar Institute, Kanpur for one month and at the Indian Institute of Sugarcane Research, Lucknow for a fortnight. For another month and a half the officer should be placed for training under competent and experienced Managing Directors/General Managers of selected factories.

Officers who have had previous experience of running sugar factories as receivers/authorised controllers should be appointed straightway as General Managers/Managers etc.

Government should start on the work of creating a pool of officers who are trained and qualified for working as Chairman-cum-Managing Director/General Manager/Manager, etc., of sugar factories as their regular and permanent career.

The practice of deputing officers from the administrative and executive services to the posts of Managing Director and General Manager etc., should be stopped as soon as possible.

If it is at all necessary to fill these posts by officers from administrative and executive cadres, the officers should be given intensive training in theory and practice of management of sugar factories before they are put in charge of the factories and they should continue there for a reasonable period, say, four to five years.

Every State which has or expects to have in the near future 5 sugar factories should create a sugar industry management cadre. The industrial management cadre of the State should be adequately strengthened by increasing the number of the posts in the cadre to the extent required for manning posts in the State Corporation(s) and sugar factories in the State.

The scales of pay and conditions of service of officers in these cadres should be laid down. As far as possible the classification of posts and the scales of pay should be the same in all the States.

A meeting of the representatives of the State Governments should be called at an early date to discuss and decide the matters relating to the cadres.

A small Committee should be set up to work out

the strength of cadres, conditions of service, qualifications etc. In drawing up the rules of service, the modern trend of giving opportunity to the junior most member of the staff including technical staff of an organisation, to rise by promotion on ground of competence from one rung to another right upto the highest post in the organisation, should be kept in view.

The State Public Service Commission should be requested to recruit the requisite number of candidates for the various posts urgently.

Alternatively an *ad hoc* Selection Board may be set up early by the Central Government in consultation with the State Governments. The Board should make selections separately for different States, maintaining a uniform standard of selection.

It is desirable that there should be a central cadre also, not only to work at the Centre but also sometimes in the States, particularly those states which do not have a cadre of their own.

A small committee of experts should also be set up straightway to prepare a syllabus for the training—theoretical and practical—of the selected candidates.

Candidates for the posts of Chairman-cum-Managing Director/General Manager, etc., should be recruited through State Public Service Commission Selection Board. The selected candidates should be appointed on probation for a period of two years and should be given intensive training, both theoretical and practical, for one year. The officer should then be put in charge of sugar factories on posts for which they have been recruited and are qualified and their performance should be considered in deciding upon their confirmation.

A committee should work out details of pay and scales of pay for different levels of technical personnel which could be offered to the technical staff straightway on taking over of factories, if possible. The technical and other qualifications should also be laid down.

While in conditions existing at present, the scheme drawn up by the National Sugar Institute, Kanpur, for linking the prices of sugarcane supplied by a canegrower or a group of canegrowers to its quality cannot be enforced on an all-India basis or even on a regional basis it might be found workable in a few selected factories where favourable conditions exist. Such factories should be identified and, if necessary, special schemes suitable for them prepared, keeping in view the main objective of the scheme. The scheme or variations of it may be tried in the selected factories in consultation and agreement with the cane growers and with full backing, moral and legal, of the Central Government and the State Government concerned so that it may be possible for these factories to pay cane prices to canegrowers on quality basis. The ultimate aim should be to pay to every individual canegrower a price which corresponds to the quality of his cane.

There is very limited room for an increase in the net cultivated area in the country. Even if the all India present average yield of cane is increased by about 25 per cent by 1985-86, as a result of intensive cultivation, technological advancement, use of better seeds, adequate fertilizers and more irrigation, it will not be possible to increase the production of sugarcane to an estimated 236 million tonnes required by that time. The area under sugarcane will, therefore, have to be increased during the next 10-15 years. But for the next few years our efforts should be directed to get the most from the existing area. Extension of area need take place only when a level of yield per hectare is reached which leaves only a marginal room for further increase in yields and when there is no escape from extension in cane area.

For meeting the increasing requirements of sugarcane in the years to come, there is need not only to intensify cane development to increase sugarcane yield but also to bring more area under sugarcane. It is, therefore, essential to fix a remunerative price for sugarcane, which has an edge over the parity prices for other competing crops.

The statutory minimum cane price should be so fixed that the return from cane is better than from other alternative crops, in which technological break through has already been achieved, and should be varied from year to year in the future in proportion to the changes in the return from other competing crops.

The statutory minimum cane price should be so fixed that it fully covers the cost of cultivation in the major cane growing regions.

For purposes of fixing cane prices, the data on cost of cane cultivation and return from sugarcane and alternative crop should be collected and kept up-to-date.

The basic level of recovery to which the minimum cane price is linked, should be fixed at 8.5 per cent.

In areas in which the average sugar recovery is below 8.5 per cent, special efforts should be made by the Government, the factories and cane growers to improve the quality of cane.

The suggestion of the Indian Sugar Mills Association for separate basic recoveries for the North and some of the Southern States is not acceptable. The acceptance of the principle of having more than one basic recovery on an all-India basis will open the doors to demands from other States/regions for a basic recovery specially suitable for their areas.

The premium for every 0.1 per cent increase in recovery over the basic recovery should be calculated on proportionally basis. This will mean a marginal increase in price of cane and a consequential increase in the price of sugar. This aspect can, however, be kept in view while fixing the basic minimum price for cane.

The adoption of the principle of proportionality in fixing the sugarcane price for individual sugar factories will prove beneficial to the industry as a whole and will provide a further incentive to canegrowers to improve the quality of cane.

In calculating statutory minimum cane price for individual sugar factories on the basis of the average sugar recovery of the optimum period of the preceding season, the figures for sugar recovery is rounded up to the first place of the decimal. This system of rounding is inequitable. The rounding may be done upto two decimal places. For this purpose, the recovery should be calculated upto three places and the figure at the second decimal place may be increased by one if the figure at the third decimal place is other than zero.

The average sugar recovery of the normal crushing period, instead of the average sugar recovery of the optimum periods, of the preceding season should be taken into consideration for the purposes of fixing the statutory minimum cane price payable by individual sugar factories.

The Government of India may fix and announce the normal crushing period for different factories in the place of the optimum period after consultation with the experts, growers and processors.

The statutory minimum cane price for a crushing season should be announced by the Central Government before the sowing of cane that will be crushing in that season—latest by early september each year.

The erratic supply of cane to factories can be greatly stabilised if canegrowers could be held to their agreements for supply of cane in years of shortage and bonding of cane could be restricted to the requirements of factories in years of excess production of cane.

Incentives should be provided to persuade cangrowers to enter into agreements and to fulfil their contracts, and disincentives to discourage canegrowers from committing breaches of contract. A monetary incentive will produce better results than coercive measures.

Where canegrowers supply came through a canegrowers' society, tripartite agreements for supply of cane should be executed to which the factory, the society and the individual canegrower concerned should be parties.

A scheme for stabilisation of cane supplies to sugar factories has been suggested.

Sugar factories should estimate the requirement of the cane on the basis of the normal crushing period and should enter into agreements with canegrowers or canegrowers' societies for supply of cane upto their full requirements.

Both bonded cane and unbonded cane will be paid the same prices before and during the normal crushing period, but after the normal period unbonded cane will be paid a lesser price than bonded cane.

An additional price shall be paid to canegrowers who are entitled to it under the scheme. The additional price payable to the canegrowers out of extra realisations should be announced in October, so that it may influence sowings of cane and execution or agreements for supply of cane.

The amounts realised by a Sugar factory from canegrowers and canegrowers' societies as penalty for breach of contracts for supply of cane will not go to the factory but will be merged with the canegrower's share from extra realisations for payment as additional cane price.

The principle of factories sharing extra realisations from sugar with canegrowers must be revived and reintroduced.

Extra realisations from sugar should be divided between a factory and the canegrowers in the ratio of 50 : 50.

Every factory should issue to every canegrower supplying cane to it, a pass book containing information about area under cane with the canegrower, quantity of cane to be supplied by him, progressive supply of cane, payment of cane price, etc. In the case of a canegrowers' society, the society will issue a pass book to its members.

Clause I of the scheme regarding the sharing of extra realisations by canegrowers and factories will not apply to factories which pay to canegrowers prices higher than laid down under the scheme.

Most of the future requirements of sugarcane have to be met by higher tonnage and sugar per hectare so that the need for expanding cane area is reduced to the minimum.

It is necessary to plan ahead for meeting the developing situation so that the country may have at any given time enough new cane varieties available to replace the comparatively inferior ones as well as to replace the deteriorated varieties and to meet the future large requirements of improved varieties of sugarcane.

(a) The Pusa Institute in Bihar and Padegaon Institute in Maharashtra should be strengthened;

(b) Sugarcane breeding Institute at Coimbatore should be enlarged and strengthened;

(c) One more Central Sugarcane Breeding Institute should be established. The new institute should start as a branch of the Coimbatore Institute as that will help considerably in the initial stages of its organisation. Later say, within 5 to 10 years, it should become an independent institute; and

(d) It will be necessary to make a detailed study for deciding upon the location of the new breeding institute. The Government should set up an expert committee to go into this question and to give its view about the location of the institute. It should also plan a project for the establishment of the institute at an early date and for training the technical staff that will be required for the institute. The institute will take several years after its establishment to be in a position to make any significant impact on the availability of new varieties of sugarcane. In the circumstances, the earlier a project is planned and executed, the better it will be.

The country is so vast and the problems of sugarcane in the tropical and sub-tropical regions are in some respects so different that it is necessary to have a separate Sugarcane Research Institute located in the tropciai region for closely attending to the problems of sugarcane in the tropical region. A Central Sugarcane Research Institute in the tropical region should be established on the same lines as the Indian Sugarcane Research Institute, Lucknow. In this case also, the new Sugarcane Research Institute should start as a branch of the Lucknow Institute to develop later into an independent institute.

The scope and facilities at the National Sugar Institute, Kanpur should be enlarged so that the institute may undertake and discharge its various responsibilities connected with training, research, advisory and extension services satisfactorily in the context of the expanding production and the growing responsibilities it will have to shoulder.

Sugar Industry has been fast growing with increasing shift towards the south. Another sugar technological institute in the south should be set up on more or less the same lines as the Kanpur Institute.

Research on sugarcane breeding and cultural techniques and sugar manufacture has to be strengthened if the sugar industry has to play its expected role in the national economy. Sugarcane and sugar research has not received the attention that it deserved, Neither the sugar industry nor the Government has provided adequate resources for carrying out sugarcane research on the scale that is necessary. Allocation of funds for sugar and sugarcane research, which is at present very low, should be increased immediately at least to one per cent of the total revenue earned by the exchequer and should be progressively and steadily raised year by year so that within the next 10 to 15 years, it reaches about 2 per cent of the total revenue realised from sugar and sugarcane. Sugar industry should also contribute literally to the organisation and execution of research programmes.

At present, there is insufficient contact between the sugarcane research stations and the Sugar Institute at Kanpur. There is also very little coordination between the two wings of research--research on sugarcane and research on utilisation of sugarcane. The senior experts of one institute should visit the other institutes carrying on research in related fields. It is not only desirable but necessary that the experts carrying on research on utilisation of sugarcane should remain constantly in touch with the experts carrying out research in breeding and production of sugarcane. There should also be half-yearly or annual meetings of senior sugarcane and sugar experts of the centre and state research institutions and centres and the universities and of the national institutes for a joint study of the problems facing the cane-growers and the sugar industry.

Research work is impeded on account of considerable delays which occur in obtaining financial sanctions from higher administrative authorities for research programmes. There should be freedom for the research worker to work in his own way without undue outside constraints. There is need for greater autonomy to the research institute and scientists, which should have far-reaching and beneficial effects on the progress and results of research.

Sugarcane crop competitions should be held both on the basis of quality and yield of cane, the criterion being the total sugar (tonnes brix) per hectare.

The very low and halting progress in cane yields and near-stagnation in sucrose content during the last 10 to 12 years is a matter of concern. For improving the cane yields and the sucrose content, adequate irrigation, good seed, sufficient and suitable fertilizers and drainage facilities, plant protection services, etc. are to be provided. These are basic and elementary measures which must be taken. It is here that factories and other organizations and agencies concerned with cane development can provide necessary help to canegrowers.

Active and direct participation of factories in cane development will be an effective means for achieving rapid cane development in the country. Factories should be given an effective voice in the cane development councils. A council should constitute of 7 members—3 members from the factories, 3 from canegrowers and 1 government official. Where cane growers' union exist, the representatives of canegrowers' unions should be members of the council concerned. Otherwise, they should be nominated by the State Government or by a subordinate authority empowered to do so. A senior executive of the factory should be its chairman. The secretary of the council should be a regular employee of the council.

Competent and qualified agricultural experts should be employed and maintained by the factory for extension services.

The funds of the council should be augmented considerably. A factory should contribute to the funds of the council of its area at the rate of five paise per quintal of cane purchased by it. This amount should not form part of the sugar price but should qualify as development expenditure for the purposes of exemption from corporate/income tax. Canegrowers should contribute to the funds of the council at the rate of two paise per quintal of cane. The central and the State Governments should each contribute at the rate of ten paise per quintal. In addition to the above, the council should receive, as at present, its share from the commission payable by a factory on cane purchased by it, which is seven paise per quintal.

Cane development councils should be established in those states also where they do not exist at present so that cane development work is carried out with active collaboration of the factories and the canegrowers.

There is need for a direct link between the factories and the cane growers even in areas where canegrowers' union exist. In the case of cooperative factories, however, there is no need for having separate canegrowers' unions.

Deterioration of varieties occurs primarily due to virus infection of which the major source is the diseased or infected cane setts used for planting. Heat treatment of cane setts eliminates or minimises the infection. This treatment technique should be adopted for which adequate facilities should be provided by research centres, factories, government departments etc.

The problem of propagation of the seed of newly evolved varieties and multiplication of good quality of seeds of existing varieties requires an effective and urgent solution, if the life of the improved high-yielding varieties with high sucrose content is to be prolonged and the standard of sugarcane crop all over the country is to be raised. The best solution to this problem lies in the setting up of sugarcane farms by sugar factories for this specific purpose. Each sugar factory should maintain a farm or farms in its areas with a total acreage sufficient to produce seed to meet the requirements of its area under a scheme of seed propagation and multiplication. The total area of the farm or farms should be about 40 hectares, which is minimum required. An exemption from the land ceiling laws should be granted in respect of factory farms.

The factory farm will function as a primary nursery to produce sufficient healthy seeds to serve the secondary nurseries to be maintained by progressive growers. The seed from the secondary nurseries should be supplied to cultivators at subsidized rates. The subsidy should come out of the funds of the development council. The cane development staff should ensure that the healthy and improved seed actually supplied goes for planting and that the farmer who can obtain healthy seed from or through the factory, does not use inferior and unhealthy seed.

There should be a soil testing laboratory as an integral part of the farm where farmers may get their soils tested free of cost or on payment of a nominal fee and obtain advice regarding the kinds and doses of fertilizers to be used in their fields and on other relevant matters.

A small workshop for repairing agricultural implements commonly used in the area may also be set up as an adjunct to the factory farm.

Arrangements should be made for sale of fertilizers from deposits located in the factory farm premises.

Various experiments on healthy cane cultivation should be conducted by a factory on its farm and demonstrated to the canegrowers.

Agricultural credit to canegrowers should be made available primarily by sugar factories and canegrowers' union instead of through the village credit societies.

One of the main reasons for slow progress in cane development has been the lack of adequate credit facilities to the canegrowers. Adequate agricultural credit must be made available to the growers for cane development. This is possible only if the factories which have adequate bank credit facilities are actively involved in this matter. Every factory should be under obligation to advance loans or arrange for loans (in cash or kind or both) for cane development to the canegrowers of its area when the canegrowers enter into tripartite or bipartite agreements, as the case may be. The amount of loan which a factory should advance or arrange for, should be not less than 40 per cent of the value of the cane agreed to be supplied.

It should be the responsibility of the factory to ensure that the canegrowers of its area get cane production loans. To facilitate factories granting loans to the canegrowers, it is necessary that they should be allowed and enabled to recover the loans through deduction from cane price.

The payment of cane price should invariably and in all cases be made by factories directly to canegrowers, even in respect of canegrowers who supply cane through canegrowers' union.

Provision of adequate irrigation facilities is of the utmost importance for cane development. The Central and State Governments should extend and intensify the creation of irrigation potential by providing large tubewells, construction of canals, etc., to produce a significant impact on the irrigation situation in factory areas. Cane development councils and factories should launch minor irrigation schemes in their areas on a significant scale.

While establishing new factories, provision should invariably be made for developing minor irrigation facilities, within a radius of 10 to 15 kilometres of a factory.

In areas which are subject to floods and waterlogging, the provision of drainage facilities is necessary. Construction of tubewells and surface wells in such areas has helped in lowering the water level and in providing drainage. The Central and State Governments should attend to the drainage problem. To a small extent and in limited areas, the development councils should also help.

Development councils and factories should evolve schemes for providing required quantities of balanced fertilizers to canegrowers at appropriate times and, if possible, at subsidised rates.

There is need for augmenting research on biological control of sugarcane pests. A section for research on biological control should be added at the Lucknow Sugarcane Research Institute.

Sugarcane should be included in the Endemic Area Schemes and Epidemic Area Schemes of the Central Government. More funds should be made available to the State Governments for plant protection of agricultural crops including sugarcane.

Development councils and factories should also participate actively in the control of pests and diseases in the sugarcane crop areas. Factories should maintain on their staff a qualified plant protection officer, whose duty should be to guide the canegrowers in maintaining their crop well. Suitable pesticides should be supplied to canegrowers at subsidised rates. Spraying equipment should be maintained by the development councils and factories and given to the canegrowers at normal hire rates.

Harvesting and transport of cane by factories ensures fresh cane supplies to factories and leads to better sugar recovery. Where conditions are favourable, factories should endeavour harvesting and transport of cane, in consultation with and cooperation of canegrowers and canegrowers' unions of their areas.

The need for improvement of existing roads and the construction of new roads in factory areas is urgent. State Governments concerned should pay early attention to this problem.

As the condition of roads is generally poor and transport of cane over longer distances by bullock carts is difficult and time consuming, no canegrower should have to transport his cane over a distance of more than 8 kilometres. More out-station centres should be established wherever necessary.

Canegrower is to be educated about the cane and attention to be paid to the ratoon crop and about its advantages. Development councils and the factories should launch schemes to demonstrate in factory areas in the field of progressive farmers, how good ratoon crop can be obtained by adopting proper techniques.

Factories and cane growers' unions should adopt maturity-wise harvesting. Maturity-wise harvesting schedules should be drawn up on the basis of the brix data of sugarcane crop in different fields.

To achieve the target of production of 2360 lakhs tonnes of cane by 1985-86 the per hectare yield has to increase from 47.7 tonnes (1971-72) to 63 tonnes. The research institutes, the state governments, the factories, cane development councils and the growers will have to make concerted and coordinated efforts to obtain this increase in yields. These efforts are specially called for in the sub-tropical regions where the yields are generally low and where a large potential for increase exists.

For reaching the target production of 95 lakh tonnes of sugar by 1985-86 large scale finance and detailed and careful planning both at the central and the state levels and close cooperation of all concerned—the industry, canegrowers, workers, government etc. are required.

To achieve sugar production target, the daily installed cane crushing capacity has to be increased from 3.16 lakh tonnes (1971-72) to 6.24 lakh tonnes by 1985-86. The emphasis should be on utilization of the installed machinery over a longer period.

The present policy of licensing expansions to all factories irrespective of the sector to which they belong and preference to cooperatives in the matter of new units should continue.

Dispersal and location of sugar factories all over the country in suitable areas will be in the interest of overall development of the rural economy and the mechanism of licensing should be utilised to this end.

While issuing licences to new sugar factories, the cane availability position should be very closely examined and licences should be issued for setting up of sugar factories in those areas only which have cane and which can grow more within a year or two of a factory coming into production. The setting up of new factories in areas where there is very little cane potential should be severely discouraged. A sugarcane expert should be associated in the study of this point and the screening committee may be strengthened by including a sugarcane expert.

Expansion is cheaper and quicker than the setting up of a new factory. All sugar factories should be exempted from the licensing restrictions in respect of expansion upto 2,000 tonnes of cane per day.

Licensing of additional capacity by way of new units has not been properly phased. Government should work out a long term plan and should issue licences in a phased manner.

Most of the existing sugar factories will have to be expanded sooner or later, say, upto 3,000 to 4,000 tonnes. This aspect has to be kept in view while sanctioning new units in the vicinity of the existing factories. In the future a new sugar factory should not ordinarily be set up within 50 kilometres of any other factory.

Sugar factories should be established in all regions which have adequate potential for sugarcane production and not be limited to any particular region or regions on considerations of productivity alone.

The future annual requirements of sugar machinery have been estimated at more than 26 units. The present capacity in the country is 20 plants per year. There is need for installing additional sugar machinery manufacturing capacity. The Government may take suitable action for setting up one or more sugar machinery manufacturing units.

The additional capacity may be given to entrepreneurs outside the existing sector with a view *inter alia*, to providing healthy competition between the existing machinery manufacturers and the new manufacturers in respect of cost and quality. A part of the additional capacity can be obtained by expansion of the existing units.

For a proper planning of production of sugar machinery by sugar machinery manufacturers, it is essential that there should be regular and even flow of orders on the manufacturers. This will be facilitated if the grant of licences is evenly phased keeping in view the manufacturing installed capacity of the sugar industry and also the capacity of the sugar machinery manufacturers.

One of the reasons for the delay in the setting up of the cooperative sugar factories was due to difficulty in raising substantial amounts of money towards the share capital from canegrowers residing within a limited area. State Governments should contribute to the share capital to the maximum extent they can without waiting for a canegrowers, towards the share capital of a cooperative factory. This will enable the cooperative factories to place orders for plant and machinery more quickly than has been the case so far. Apart from the contribution which the State Governments make to the share capital from the funds placed at their disposal by the National Cooperative Development Corporation, they should also find funds from their own resources.

To avoid delay in the manufacture of sugar plants, the required quantity of steel may be earmarked for manufacture of sugar machinery and placed at the disposal of the Central Organisation (NSA/NSC) which would make allotments to the sugar machinery manufacturers. In case sufficient steel cannot be allocated from the indigenous production, the manufacturers should be allowed to import the required quantities of steel.

The cost of plant and equipment of a sugar factory has been going up rapidly. The Bureau of Industrial Costs and Prices may be asked to find out the cost of standard plant and major components.

If the requirements of the plant and equipment needed for the future development of the sugar industry are to be met, it is necessary that the entire sugar machinery manufacturing capacity should be available to and utilized for manufacture of sugar plants and machinery. It is necessary to exercise some supervision and control over the working of the sugar machinery manufacturers.

It is necessary to maintain a high standard of quality of production not only from the point of view of indigenous requirements but also from the point of view of export. The Technical Wing of NSA/NSC should have the authority and the responsibility for supervision over sugar machinery manufacture and quality control of sugar machinery. Alternatively, the National Sugar Institute, Kanpur may be entrusted with the responsibility for quality control.

Intensive and continuous research on design of sugar machinery is called for. The facilities of the Design and Development Section in the National Sugar Institute should be strengthened for this purpose.

Intensive research should be undertaken to design and manufacture a furnace which should be capable of working primarily on coal but could be run efficiently on bogasse also, should coal be not available.

There is a good scope for earning foreign exchange by export of sugar and it will be in the interest of both the industry and the nation to increase export.

So far India's exports have fluctuated widely from year to year. Under such conditions it becomes difficult for the importing countries to rely on India for meeting their import requirements. If these conditions were to continue, it would greatly damage the prospects of expansion of sugar exports. For building up and sustaining our export market, it is necessary to evolve a definite long term policy.

The pattern of meeting export losses in India has been different from year to year. There is no fixed procedure for meeting the export losses. It is unfair to expect the industry only to bear the entire loss in transactions which are carried out to earn foreign exchange in the interest of the country as a whole. Government, therefore, should also share the losses. As a long term policy, the export under the preferential quota should be on the industries account and the export under the International Sugar Agreement Quota, on the Central Government Account. In regard to the sharing of profit or loss, the arrangement should be as follows. If profit is made under one quota and loss is incurred on export under the other quota, the profit of the first should be utilized for offsetting the loss and only the balance of profit, if any, should be retained by the former.

If the entire sugar trade is taken over by the Government, a provision for export losses may be made in the sugar price and funded separately. The loss in exports, if any, may be met from this fund. Any savings in a year could be utilised for supporting export in other years.

When exports are made under the provision of Sugar Export Promotion Act, the system of apportionment of sale proceeds from exports is not reasonable. Section 9 of the Act should be suitably amended so that the losses are distributed in such a way that the loss per tonne of sugar will be the same for all factories.

Government should make use of the condition existing in the licences for expansion of setting up of new units issued after 1964-65 (the condition being that sugar factories, if required by Government, shall manufacture and supply raw sugar for export purposes) and ask selected factories to manufacture raw sugar for which payment may be made at the price not of white sugar but of raw sugar according to cost schedules which may be worked out from time to time. This would reduce the export losses to some extent.

A few factories of large capacity may be set up in public sector in Gujarat in particular and also in Maharashtra, Tamil Nadu and Andhra Pradesh for producing sugar for export.

The possibility of setting up and developing sugar industry in suitable areas of the Andaman Islands, for manufacture of sugar for export purposes should be fully explored.

Bagasse because of its high cellulosic content has great potential for use in the paper industry. There are several difficulties in setting up paper mills based on bagasse as primary raw material. A paper mill cannot possibly be run on the basis of 'saved' bagasse only. It will be necessary for a paper mill to secure from a sugar factory or a group of factories suitable situated in relation to it, the whole or substantial part of the bagasse of the factory or factories concerned. This will necessarily entail the conversion of bagasse furnace into coal furnace. To induce sugar factories to change over to coal firing with a view to diverting their bagasse to the paper industry, it will be necessary for the Government and the paper industry to give them adequate incentives.

As the national need for development of paper industry is immediate, the Central Government itself should initiate early action to set up a paper-cum-sugar factory complex in the public sector. It will be advisable to establish a sugar mill of about 5,000 tonnes capacity in an area having adequate cane potential. The boilers of the sugar factory should from the very beginning be based on coal and the entire production of bagasse should be utilized for paper.

The techniques and equipment required for fuel and steam economy resulting in savings of bagasse are available. Sugar factories should take recourse to these techniques and equipment and reduce the consumption of bagasse to the minimum. Bagasse saved by factories should be converted into paper pulp by installing suitable equipment and by transporting the pulp to a central paper factory. For this purpose, sugar factories should be given suitable incentives.

In the sugar-cum-paper project furfural should be manufactured from the pith separated from the bagasse before using the latter for paper manufacture.

In regard to the other uses of bagasse especially on sacharification, production of vanillin from lignin etc. the available information is inadequate. Research on these uses of bagasse should be intensified.

There is a definite need for increasing the price of molasses. A substantial part of alcohol produced from molasses is utilized for manufacture of potable liquors. It should not be difficult to work out the quantity of molasses corresponding to potable liquors manufactured. The price of that quantity of molasses should be fixed at a much higher rate.

It is in the national interest to preserve the valuable bye-product molasses from deterioration and wastage. Factories not having adequate and suitable molasses storage tanks should be encouraged to instal them.

The cultivation of beet should be taken up with caution and only in areas where enough sugarcane of reasonable quantity cannot be grown and there is absolute certainty that the entire beet crop will be utilized for sugar production. To this end, it will be necessary to plan and regulate sugarcane production also. In addition to the Government schemes now in progress research and development activities should, therefore, be oriented towards developing—

(a) Coordinated programme for cane and beet cultivation;

(b) procedures for reducing the fuel consumption in factories processing cane and beet; and

(c) procedures for proper utilization of by-products, particularly beet pulp.

Work on the above aspects should be taken up at the National Sugar Institute, Kanpur in collaboration with the Indian Institute of Sugarcane Research, Lucknow and some sugar factories.

Firm and reliable data on production of gur and khandsari are not available. In all the important gur and khandsari producing states, data on production and other essential aspects of these sweetening agents should be collected and correlated regularly and maintained properly. Suitable agencies should be made responsible for this.

The production of gur and khandsari is inescapable and will have to continue as an important economic activity in the forseeable future.

There is paramount need for improving the techniques of gur production. Losses of sugar should be reduced and gur of better quality should be manufactured. Improved types of roller crushers, capable of giving 80 per cent extraction and increasing recovery of gur from 10 to 12 per cent should be popularised. Easily understandable literature, which even neo-literates may follow, on the subject showing the technical and economic advantages of the crusher should be brought out. Demonstrations in important gur producing areas should be organised. If cane growers are convinced of its satisfactory performance —from technological as well as economic angles--it could be set up by village level cooperative societies for processing canegrower's cane into gur.

Gur production in the vicinity of sugar factories through power crushers must be regulated and controlled as such crushers are generally used for production of gur for commercial purposes.

The demand of the sugar industry for keeping khandsari units outside the factory area is a reasonable one. New khandsari units should not generally be allowed in factory areas. Inducements should be offered to khandsari units to shift away from the sugar factory areas.

As gur and khandsari industries must also continue and have cane for crushing suitable arrangements should be made by legal and executive measures to coordinate cane supplies to them and to the sugar industry.

Gur prices can be maintained by building up and skillful manipulations of a buffer stock of sugar. Maintenance of gur prices at a reasonable level will in due course lead to a narrowing of the range of fluctuations in the area and production of cane and stabilization of cane supplies to each of the sugar, the gur and the khandsari industries.

There is need for improving techniques of gur storage so that gur can be stored over comparatively long periods without loss in weight, quantity and colour. Research for the same should be intensified.

There should be a department or a directorate at the centre to initiate and coordinate policies and programmes for the proper development of gur and khandsari industries. The existing Directorate of Sugar and Vanaspati should be enlarged so as to deal with the gur and khandsari industries also. When the central organisation is set up, it will take over these responsibilities.

Factory should employ specialists such as entomologists, agronomists, plant protection officers etc. to attend the special problems of cane cultivation in their areas.

Cane development officers may undergo short course in Management in Agriculture. Facilities available for such a course at the Indian Institute of Management, Ahmedabad or any other organisation may be utilized.

The Sugarcane Research Institute to be set up in the South should undertake the training of the Cane Development Field Staff.

The various State Sugarcane Research Stations' Centres should take up the training of Field and Extension Staff of Government, Factories and Canegrowers' Unions. State Governments should provide funds and adequate facilities for this purpose at their Research Stations/Centres.

The annual requirement of Sugar Technologists and Sugar Engineers will be of the order of 100 each. They should be trained according to a planned programme, so that the needs of the new factories and the additional needs of the old factories after expansion could be met.

The proposed new Sugar Technological Institutes in the South should impart training in Sugar Technology. The facilities at the Kanpur Institute should be increased at an early date and utilized to the maximum.

Necessary steps should be taken immediately for augmenting training facilities for sugar engineers. This can be done in number of ways. First, the number of seats at the Kanpur Institute should be increased considerably. Secondly, the other Technological Institute to be established in the South should have larger facilities for such training. Further, some of the Indian Institutes of Technology in the country should be requested to start special courses in sugar engineering.

The engineering staff already working in the sugar factories and not posseessing the required qualifications should be given preference in admission so that they also get qualified quickly.

Regarding the under-graduate staff required for Technology and Engineering Wings of the industry, the training facilities will have to be expanded on a large scale. State Governments of all major Sugar Producing States should select one or two polytechnics in their states and institute courses for training suitable number of technicians.

A majority of the existing managerial personnel of sugar factories need training and the purely technical staff should also be given some basic knowledge of scientific management. Arrangements may be made with the various management institutes in the country to organise Short Term Courses. The facilities available for Business Management Training to senior executives at the Hyderabad Staff College may also be utilised. The personnel at lower levels may be given training for a longer period.

Officers promoted from lower to higher levels in the managerial cadre should be given orientation course to equip themselves for higher responsibilities, particularly when their duties change i.e., from purely technical control to say. man-management.

Not only the managerial personnel at the poly level (such as Managing Director/General Manager, etc.) but also the technical personnel in key post in a factory e.g., Chief Chemist, Chief Engineer and Chief Accountant, should be given some training in modern management and techniques.

There should be provision for periodical refresher courses (including seminars, workshops, etc.) to enable them to keep abreast of the latest developments in their own respective fields of responsibility.

The annual de novo consideration and issue of reservation orders is a very disturbing factor. It will be advantageous to reserve areas for a period of at least five years with the stipulation that the reservation orders can be revised any time to meet special situations. The special situations should also be clearly specified such as the establishment of a new factory in the neighbourhood, the expansion of the capacity of the factory, exceptionally high or low production of sugarcane in reserved areas, and so on.

The law, the rules and the orders on the subject of reservation of areas should be amended so as to make it obligatory on the competent authority to pass orders for reservation of areas for a period of not less than five years. Even if such provision is not made in law the State Government should, under the existing law, reserve areas to sugar factory for at least five years at a time.

State Governments which do not at present pass Statutory Reservation Orders under the provisions of any law should also fall in line and pass reservation orders under the Central Sugar Cane (Control) Order Bill they have their own legislation in this regard.

Purchase of cane from free areas should be strictly regulated so that they do not unduly reduce cane purchases from the reserved areas at any time.

To ensure that the legal provisions and restrictions that may be made and imposed are not contravened, an effective inspectorate should be set up.

The absence of obligation on the canegrowers of the reserved areas of a factory to sell any part of their cane to the factory creates uncertainty in the working of the factory and results in wide fluctuations in cane supplies from year to year. A canegrower in the reserved areas of a factory should also be under obligations to supply cane to the factory. A pre-condition for this should be that the minimum price of cane intended for use in sugar factories should be notified by the Central Government well ahead the cane sowing season every year.

State Governments should effectively use the legal powers which they already have under their own existing legislation or under the Sugar Cane (Control) Order, 1966, to require each canegrower of the reserved areas to supply a specified quantity or percentage of cane grown by him to the factory concerned directly or through the Canegrowers' Union, as the case may be.

To give effect to the scheme relating to the agreements for supply of cane by canegrowers to factories and to arrange for agricultural credit being made available by factories to the cultivators for cane production, it will be necessary to make suitable statutory provisions either in State Act or a Central Act. They must include the following:—

(i) Every factory shall enter into agreements with canegrowers of its area for supply of cane upto its full requirement for a normal crushing period;

(ii) When canegrowers supply cane through a society, tripartite agreements for supply of cane should be executed to which the factory, the society and the individual canegrowers concerned should be parties;

(iii) The agreement shall specify the quality of cane to be supplied by the cultivator to the factory and the area and the particulars of the plot or plots, the crop of which will be supplied to the factory;

(iv) On execution of the agreement for supply of cane by a cultivator to the factory, the factory shall be under the obligation to advance loan in cash or in kind or both to the canegrowers for the purpose of production of cane;

(v) The amount of loan shall not be less than forty per cent of the value of the cane agreed to be supplied, calculated at the minimum price for the cane fixed by the Government;

(vi) In the alternative to itself advancing the loan as mentioned in clause (iv) the factory shall arrange for the advance by a Bank of the stipulated amount of loan to the canegrower by guaranteeing or/and under-writing such loan;

(vii) On execution of the agreement and payment of the loan the factory will be entitled to recover the loan and the interest thereon through deduction from the cane price payable to the canegrower concerned;

(viii) In case of a wilful default by the factory in arranging for the loan as stipulated in clause (vi), the agreement shall be voidable at the option of the cultivator, if the cultivator does not declare the agreement as void, he may apply to the appropriate authority for specific performance of this term and the said Authority may require the factory to advance the stipulated amount to the canegrowers. The order of the appropriate authority shall have the force of a decree of a court and shall be executable as such;

(ix) The factory shall not charge interest at a rate higher than the rate charged by the bank for advances for sugarcane cultivation and shall not realise from the canegrower any part of service charges incurred by it on the disbursment and recovery of the loan.

Besides these changes in the laws, amendments will have to be made in the laws and agreements to incorporate the recommendations made in chapter III, part II. In addition, the following two terms should also be contained in each agreement:—

(i) On receipt of the loan granted (in cash or in kind or both) the cultivator shall utilize it exclusively and only for the purpose of cane production in the area and in the plots specified in the agreement; and

(ii) In case of breach of the above clause by the canegrower, he shall also be liable to pay penal interest at a rate not exceeding twice the rate of interest at which the loan has been given.

The penalty for deliberate default on the part of the canegrower should be equivalent to 50 per cent of the price of cane in deficit and on the part of a factory equivalent to the full price of the cane in deficit.

The form of offer to sell and form of agreement to sell and purchase cane should clearly indicate the plots whose cane will be supplied to the factory.

In fixing the credit limits for the sugar industry as a whole and for individual factories and in determining the margins for the purposes of advancing money against pledged stocks of sugar, due consideration should be given to the requirements of funds for payment of cane price and the need for its prompt payment.

There should be uniformity in the laws and rules relating to the payment of cane price and also interest in default of payment of cane price within the prescribed period.

A factory should be under obligation to make payment of cane price immediately on demand and in any case not later than 24 hours of demand after delivery of cane, at the gate of the factory. For outstation Purchasing Centres the payment should be made not later than 72 hours of demand after delivery of the cane at the Centre. State Government or an authority empowered to do so may extend the period of 72 hours in respect of Out Sation Purchasing Centres where he is satisfied that payment of cane price within this period is not feasible. The relevant provisions of the State Acts and Rules and the Central Sugarcane (Control) Order should be amended accordingly.

The only way in which prompt payment even immediate payment can be arranged is to make the factories responsible for payment of cane price directly to canegrowers irrespective of whether they are direct suppliers or suppliers through a Canegrowers' Union or Society, provision should be made in the laws, rules and orders relating to the payment of cane price accordingly.

For expediting cane price payment, the pass books issued to canegrowers should contain *inter alia*, all the relevant information about the canegrowers' ledger and account number, the amount of loan advanced, the number and amount of instalments in which it has to be recovered, the deductions made from time to time and so on.

Canegrowers should be encouraged to open their accounds with banks as that will facilitate the payment of their cane price into their account immediately it becomes due. When a canegrower requests for payment of his cane price by cheque, the factories concerned should made arrangement for payment by cheque. This will encourage banking habit among canegrowers.

In the case of a cooperative factory, the constitution of the Development Council will be adjusted to the extent that canegrowers will be nominated by the Board of Directors of the cooperative factory and may be the directors of the Board.

A uniform set of functions should be prepared for development councils all over the country. A suitable provision should be made in the relevant States Acts, Rules and Orders and in Central Sugarcane (Control) Order.

Necessary provision should be made in the Central Sugarcane (Control) Order giving statutory sanction for sharing extra sales realisations between factories and the canegrowers. Provision should also be made in the said Order that only those canegrowers who enter into contract for supply of cane during a season and fulfil their contracts will be eligible for sharing the extra sales realisations with the factories. A suitable machinery should also be set up having adequate powers under the law to verify the extra sales realisations from sugar and to enforce the sharing of extra realisations between factories and canegrowers and their distribution among the eligible canegrowers. It should also be laid down that penalties realised from defaulting canegrowers will be proportionately distributed to canegrowers who fulfil their agreements to supply cane in each year. Provision should also be made for the submission by factories of fortnightly or monthly returns of sugar sales and the prices obtained by them and for their checking from time to time. Proper forms should be devised in consultation with financial experts.

Suitable provision should be made in the relevant Acts requiring managements of factories to have on their Boards of Managements/Directors at least one representative of labour who should be a worker-employee of the factory concerned. Factories other than cooperative factories should also provide for the inclusion of a canegrowers' representative on their Boards of Management. Pending formulation of rules and procedure for the election of the representatives of workers and canegrowers, they should be nominated by the State Government concerned or by an authority empowered to do so.

The recommendations relating to the reservation of areas, obligation of canegrowers and factories to sell and purchase cane grown in the reserved areas, would not apply to cooperative sugar factories and the canegrowers of their areas, inasmuch as the areas of their operation are defined by their bye-laws and the relations between them and their shareholder-canegrowers in regard to production and supply of cane, payment of cane price, etc., are governed by their bye-laws.

There should be a statutorily reserved area for every cooperative factory, generally co-extensive with its area of operation as defined in its bye-laws. The general law precluding a factory from purchasing cane from the reserved areas of another factory should apply to cooperative factories also.

The canegrowers of the areas of cooperative factories who cannot become members should have the right and the opportunity to sell their cane to other factories and the latter to purchase the cane.

The law and rules relating to immediate payment to cane price should apply to cooperative factories in the case of non-member canegrowers from whom they purchase cane. The cooperative factories should also be under obligation to grant agricultural credit facilities to all canegrowers with whom they enter into agreement for purchase of cane.

The bye-laws of the cooperative factories do not contain a clear indication of the objectives which a cooperative factory should have in view and should aim at—for instance, socio-economic development of its area and rendering services to the vulnerable and weaker sections of the community. The aims and objects of every cooperative factory should include the social objectives.

The bye-laws of cooperative factories should be revised where necessary with a view to broadening the base of the cooperative factories so that with every increase in the capacity of the factory, new members also should be enrolled from amongst cultivators who want to become members of the cooperative factories.

Sugar factories can play an important role in the socio-economic development and in helping to improve the lot of the weaker sections of the community in their areas. Sugar is the largest rural-based industry. Sugar factories should not confine themselves purely to production of sugar as they are in the best position to look after the socio-economic development of rural areas around them.

RESERVE BANK OF INDIA, WORKING GROUP ON FINANCING OF INDUSTRIAL ESTATES, 1970, REPORT

Bombay, Reserve Bank of India, 1972. 154 p.

Chairman : Shri K. N. R. Ramanujam.

Members : Shri L. N. Renu; Shri J. R. Joshi; Shri H. E. Chatelier (replaced by Shri J. S. Varshneya); Shri J. J. Khambata; Shri M. S. Palnitkar; Shri N. H. Shah (ceased to be the member and replaced by Shri H. R. Patankar); Shri O. Swaminatha Reddy; Shri D. V. Narasimhan (ceased to be the member); Shri K. C. Pandeya (ceased to be the member); Shri Anwarul Hoda; Shri B. S. Lulla; Shri P. M. Mathai.

Member-Secretary : Shri Philip Thomas.

APPOINTMENT

One of the subjects discussed at the Fourteenth Conference of representatives of the State Financial Corporations, held in Bombay in March 1970, was the financing of industrial estates. While it was recognised that industrial estates could play an important role in the development of small-scale industries and that it was necessary to locate additional resources for setting them up, it was also realised that unless adequate attention was paid to the conditions determining the successful functioning of industrial estates, it would not be prudent for the financial institutions to expand their loan assistance to these ventures. The Governor of the Reserve Bank, who inaugurated the Conference, observed in his Inaugural Address that some of the industrial estates had remained "empty shells". The Deputy Governor of the Bank, who presided over the sessions of the Conference emphasised the need for the financial institutions coming forward with concrete suggestions for augmenting the resources available for financing industrial estates and ensuring that the resources are utilised properly and not frittered away in the construction of estates based on political or other considerations, resulting in the entire expenditure becoming infructuous. It was, therefore, decided at the Conference that a Working Group should be appointed by the Reserve Bank to go into the problem of financing of industrial estates in all its aspects and to make recommendations for consideration by the lending institutions. Accordingly the Reserve Bank constituted the Working Group on Financing of Industrial Estates in October 1970.

TERMS OF REFERENCE

(i) To study the economics of establishment and operations of industrial estates owned by Government, public sector organisations/bodies, Co-operative organisations and private parties and suggest suitable criteria for the establishment of such estates by public sector organisations/bodies and private parties and appraisal of their working ;

(ii) to examine the present pattern of financing of industrial estates by banks, term lending institutions and the Life Insurance Corporation of India and evolve guidelines for financing them by banks, term lending institutions and the Life Insurance Corporation of India ;

(iii) to consider any other matter incidental to and arising from the above.

CONTENTS

Introduction ; The Programme of Industrial Estates, Its Broad Dimensions and Results ; The Origin and Objectives of the Industrial Estates Programme and the Evolution of Governmental Policies; Working of Industrial Estates—Evaluation Reports ; Sample Survey of Industrial Estates ; Private Industrial Estates—Some aspects of their Establishment and Operation ; General Policies of the State Governments regarding the setting up and Management of Industrial Estates ; Suggestions regarding setting up of new Industrial Estates and their Operations ; Proposed Arrangements for Financing Industrial Estates by Financial Institutions ; The Role of LIC in the Financing of Industrial Estates ; The Role of the State Financial Corporations and of Commercial and Co-operative Banks in the Financing of Industial Estates ; Guidelines to be followed by Financial Institutions for considering Loan Proposals for setting up Industrial Estates ; Summary of Conclusions and

Recommendations ; Annexures, Appendices ; Statements.

RECOMMENDATIONS

Although the programme of industrial estates has made good progress during the last two decades or so, certain deficiencies in its implementation were observed. Of the total number of sheds completed in 455 estates, as high a proportion as 38 per cent was not utilised. The average utilization of sheds in completed estates was 64 per cent. The rate of utilization was the highest in urban estates (74%), followed by semi-urban estates (56%) and rural estates (42%).

By and large, the extent of use of sheds in the co-operative estates in Andhra Pradesh, Gujarat and Madhya Pradesh was generally higher but in Rajasthan, Tamil Nadu and Uttar Pradesh it was lower than that in other estates.

The magnitude of utilization in private industrial estates was relatively high, irrespective of the area of location.

The evaluation studies on the working of the industrial estates undertaken by a few State Governments revealed several defects, such as improper selection of sites, inadequate attention to the provision of infrastructure facilities and lack of leadership on the part of management to attract entrepreneurs.

A field study of a sample of industrial estates and the units located therein revealed that (i) the estates which had been set up after careful techno-economic surveys proved to be successful, irrespective of whether the estates were located in urban, semi-urban or rural areas; (ii) proximity to markets and adequate transport links to the markets were important pre-requisites to the success of estates; (iii) the utilisation ratio (i.e., the proportion of the number of sheds occupied by units in production to the number of sheds constructed) was generally higher for urban estates than for the rural estates; (iv) the time taken for acquiring land was generally about a year or so and, for development of land and the provision of infrastructure facilities, about two to three years; (v) the proportion of rentable area to the total developed area was generally lower for rural estates than for the urban estates, mainly because in the former estates, a larger proportion of the developed area was occupied by roads, open space, etc.; (vi) the cost of development of land and provision of infrastructure seemed to be generally higher in the rural and semi-urban areas than in the urban areas; (vii) the cost of setting up the estates was lower for those set up by co-operative societies than for those set up by Government; (viii) the ratio of the cost of acquisition and development of land and provision of infrastructure facilities to the total cost of setting up the estate generally ranged between 25% and 35%; this ratio was generally higher in respect of estates set up in rural areas than those in urban areas; (ix) almost all the units located in the estates belonged to small industry sector and most of these were new units; (x) barring the estates in Gujarat, Maharashtra and Uttar Pradesh, where plots/sheds were acquired on hire purchase terms, in other States, where Government estates predominated, the sheds were occupied mostly on a rental basis; and (xi) about two-thirds of the units in the estates were purchasing raw materials or selling their finished products from/to centres situated beyond a radius of 100 miles.

In most of the States, the industrial estates programme was exclusively concerned with the development of general purpose estates.

In Gujarat and Maharashtra, the programme of industrial estates has been relatively successful; in the former State the programme of Governmental industrial estates is administered by Government-owned Corporation (GIDC) while in the latter State, co-operative industrial estates predominate. In Tamil Nadu, where also the programme has a record of good performance, it is implemented by the State Industries Department.

The choice of location and meticulous care in the implementation of programme are as important for the success of the industrial estates as the general climate for industrialisation.

Past failures of some of the industrial estates should not be regarded as an undue deterrent for setting up new estates in as much as the failures are due to clearly identifiable defects, both in the formulation and in the implementation of the programme, and if care is taken to avoid them, there is no reason why industrial estates could not be a successful aid to industrialisation.

The failure of the industrial estates programme in rural and backward regions is attributed to (a) the general failure to bring about dispersal of industries ; (b) wrong location of the estates ; (c) faulty planning of the estates and poor execution and (d) lack of an effective machinery to supervise the day-to-day operations of the estate. Some of these defects can be avoided through a better programme of pre-planning of the estates and its more effective implementation.

There is considerable scope for setting up new industrial estates in the vicinity of urban and semi-urban centres or what may be alternatively termed as growth centres and potential growth centres.

Barring functional or single trade estates in urban and semi-urban areas, in the formulation of a programme, attention should generally be devoted to the development of land and the provision of infrastructure facilities because in most instances, the type of industrial units which are to be allotted sheds, which may be in different dimensions, cannot be visualised in advance. Further, sheds of a general type would not necessarily suit the requirements of different industries. In States, such as Bihar and Orissa, where the programme of industrial estates has not developed to any significant extent, a minimum number of sheds of standard size may be constructed on a part of an estate and some plots kept vacant for meeting the requirements of individual units to be set up at a later stage.

At least for the next few years, co-operative and private industrial estates are likely to be confined to a few States, such as Gujarat and Maharashtra which have already made much headway in establishing co-operative and private estates and also in some others, such as Andhra Pradesh, Tamil Nadu and Mysore which have made a beginning in these fields. In the remaining States, the Government concerned will have to take an active and direct part in setting up and running the estates.

State Governments should play a crucial role in encouraging the establishment of new industrial estates in urban and semi-urban areas. This should comprise the identification of industrial areas, advance planning of the prospective centres for industrial growth and zoning of industries in the centres, prompt and adequate arrangements for the supply of infrastructure facilities and the establishment of an efficient machinery to co-ordinate and guide all these activities.

Taking into account the various stages in the industrial development of the States and the differing patterns adopted by State Governments in the management and implementation of the programme of industrial estates, no standard arrangement for setting up industrial estates in all the States is recommended. However, it is evident that Government Departments with rigid rules and procedures do not seem to operate them with the necessary flexibility nor do they appear to possess the expertise to implement the schemes successfully.

While the Group endorses the suggestion by the Government of India that steps should be taken to set up co-operatives to take over and manage Government estates, it is felt that this programme will take a long time particularly in the States where co-operative movement itself has not made any significant progress.

The States in which the programme of industrial estates has not developed adequately, might consider handing over the management of the existing industrial estates as well as establishing and managing new estates to Corporations, namely, the Industrial Development Corporations (IDCs) which should run them on business lines and be responsible for all the aspects of their growth and expansion. The Development Corporations may be set up to function on the lines of the Maharashtra Industrial Development Corporation or the Gujarat Industrial Development Corporation.

Local bodies, such as municipalities, city improvement trusts, etc. should be increasingly involved in establishing industrial estates in the areas falling within their jurisdiction. If need be, the statutory regulations governing the operations of municipalities or other local authorities may suitably be amended so as to enable them to play their part in the industrial estates programme. The funds for setting up industrial estates should come partly from their budgetary allocations and partly out of funds made available by the financial institutions, particularly the LIC.

With a view to facilitating the setting up of industrial estates by private parties, for all the major centres of prospective industrial growth there should be area plans with plans for industrial zones.

The exemption under Section 80J of the Income-tax Act, 1961, should be extended to private industrial estates to be set up after April 1, 1972. This exemption should also be made applicable to such Industrial Development Corporations as have share Capital of their own and have been entrusted with the programme of management of industrial estates.

The State Governments should examine the scope for a reduction in the stamp duty chargeable on land acquired by the co-operatives for setting up industrial estates.

Industrial estates should have a whole-time supervisor to look after the administration as also to attend to the difficulties faced by the units. State Governments should set up Regional Advisory Committees to review periodically the progress made and the problems faced by the industrial estates in the respective zones.

The main scope for the financing of industrial estates by the financial institutions will be in respect of estates in urban and semi-urban centres. Industrial estates in rural areas will generally require not only finance on soft terms but also a number of other concessions and facilities for development ; the responsibility for setting up or assisting such estates should be largely that of the respective State Governments. Financial assistance on the normal terms applicable to investment proposals from small-scale units in the area concerned should be made available, provided a prior techno-economic survey of the area has been conducted and the project is sponsored by adequate number of entrepreneurs.

For estates set up/managed by the Government Departments/local authorities the funds for development of land and provision of infrastructure would have to come from their budgetary allocations.

As regards the estates set up and managed by the Industrial Development Corporations, it will be appropriate if the two types of operations, viz., those covering the provision of infrastructure facilities and those of construction of sheds, are separated, and the requirements for finance for the two types of activities are met through separate arrangements. While the construction of industrial sheds can be financed by banks and term-lending institutions at the normal rates of interest applicable to industrial loans, the investment in infrastructure facilities will have to be financed appropriately by long term loans at relatively low rates of interest. These Corporations will have to add to their borrowing rates, a spread to enable them to meet their administrative costs, make a provision for bad debts and make profits to pay dividends on capital and transfer to reserves. Hence, their lending rates may be around 8-8½ per cent. If the State Governments propose that a still concessional lending rate should prevail, they should subsidise the difference between the normal lending rates and the concessional rates to be charged by the Corporations. Alternatively, resources required by the Corporations for financing infrastructure might be raised by way of loans from the State Governments at a concessional rate of interest. The Corporations should adopt an appropriate policy for pricing their products and services.

For co-operative and private estates, finance for development of land and the provision of infrastructure could come either from State Government and IDC and/or from financial institutions like the LIC and finance for construction of sheds could be provided by banks and SFCs to industrial units to enable them to put up sheds. Banks and financial institutions should have appropriate arrangements for financing industrial estates in urban and semi-urban areas to be set up by co-operatives, private parties and agencies of the State Governments, such as Industrial Development Corporations.

For relatively small projects involving loans of not more than say Rs. 20 lakhs, the appraisal and financing may be done by the SFCs and where the project costs not more than Rs. 25 lakhs, by the commercial banks having deposit resources of less than Rs. 300 crores. No such ceiling on loan amount need operate for banks with a larger deposit base than Rs. 300 crores.

Until such time as the IDBI is not in a position to mobilise savings from the public, say to the extent of at least half of its net outlay in any year it may not be desirable for it to provide refinance on loans by financial institutions and banks for the setting up of industrial estates. The IDBI Act may be suitably amended to enable the Bank, in future, either to lend directly or to refinance loans extended by banks and financial institutions for the setting up of industrial estates.

Advances granted by banks and SFCs to co-operative societies of technician-entrepreneurs for the purpose of setting up industrial estates for their use may be made eligible for cover under the guarantee scheme of the Credit Guarantee Corporation of India Ltd., provided that the estates are meant to be used exclusively by small-scale industrial units.

Estates which cater to the different size categories of industries are more likely to be successful than those which are exclusively meant for small-scale units. But, since the programme is meant essentially to help the small entrepreneurs, it should be ensured by banks and SFCs that the industrial estates cater mainly to the needs of small units.

Institutional finance to develop industrial estates may be provided to private parties who may own land which they might like to develop into industrial estates; in such instances, the lending institution should ensure that at least 75 per cent of the sheds financed are firmly committed to be sold/rented/leased out to genuine small-scale industrial units on reasonable terms.

The LIC may continue its present arrangement for financing the setting up of industrial estates against the guarantee provided by the respective State Governments.

The LIC should lend to IDCs against the mortgage of their fixed assets at around 7½% p.a. To the extent that there is a shortfall in the value of assets to be mortgaged at a margin of 50 per cent the LIC could accept State Government's guarantee and the rate of interest on the amounts to be guaranteed by the State Governments could be around 7 per cent.

The LIC might also grant loans to the municipalities and other local authorities to enable them to participate in the programme of industrial estates. These loans may be given by the LIC against the State Government guarantee on the same terms and conditions as those stipulated for loans to co-operative societies/joint-stock companies.

The LIC could make larger resources available for financing of industrial estates through participation arrangements with SFCs and banks. The participating bank/SFC may take up earlier maturity say, upto 7 years of the promissory notes/participation certificate arising out of the conversion of the original loan, the remaining period of maturity being taken over by the LIC. The rate of interest to be charged by the LIC may be 8 per cent and that by the SFC 9 per cent. Since commercial banks would find it difficult to lend at a rate below 10 per cent, the State Government may, bearing in mind the type and location of estates, subsidise the difference between the rate of interest normally charged by banks and the concessional rate which the Government deems it desirable to be charged by banks. The participation agreement should provide that both the institutions will bear losses, if any, arising out of defaults in the repayments during the entire currency of the loan in the same proportion as the amounts lent by them and that this should hold good even after the loan amount granted by the bank/SFC has been repaid in full during the earlier period of repayment of the advance. For the contingent liability incurred by the bank/SFC during the later period of loan maturity it may levy on the borrowers a commission at a concessional rate of ½ to 1 per cent per annum on its proportionate share in outstanding balance of the loan. The bank/SFC which would be acting as an agent of the LIC for the recovery of the loan should be paid a small commission, say upto ½ per cent by the LIC on the amount of the loan outstanding during the later period of the advance.

Yet another method for the LIC to make larger resources available for financing of industrial estates and particularly the worksheds which may be set up in the rural areas, would be for the Corporation to lend to the estates after the projects are appraised by credit institutions which would also guarantee repayment of the loan and payment of interest. While these loans would have to come out of the funds earmarked for unapproved investment of the Corporation, it will be necessary to suitably amend the State Financial Corporations Act, 1951 so as to enable SFCs to give guarantees to the LIC.

The SFCs and commercial banks, barring the bigger banks, should confine their credit to financing the setting up of small and medium estates and financing of industrial sheds. As a matter of general policy, proposals for any loan exceeding Rs. 25 lakhs to an industrial estate should not ordinarily be entertained by commercial banks, with deposit resources less than Rs. 300 crores. Such proposals, however, may be taken up by such a bank in participation preferably with a State Financial Corporation. For SFCs, a ceiling limit should be imposed on the financing of industrial estates so that the total amount of loans for the purpose does not exceed 10 per cent of the total loans sanctioned by it during a year.

The co-operative banks should confine themselves to (a) financing medium and small co-operative estates in urban and semi-urban areas in participation with commercial banks/State Financial Corporations and (b) financing individual members of the societies for construction of sheds.

The amount of loan assistance required for the construction of sheds would be Rs. 10 crores per annum for the next few years, of which the share of the LIC may be put at Rs. 5 crores, that of SFCs at Rs. 3 crores and of banks at Rs. 2 crores.

INDIA, FUEL POLICY COMMITTEE, 1970—REPORT

Delhi, Controller of Publications, 1975. 139p.

Chairman : Shri R. Venkataraman (replaced by Shri S. Chakravarty).

Members : Shri M. Dutta Chaudhury; Shri A. K. Ghosh (replaced by Shri N. Tata Rao); Dr. M. G. Krishna; Dr. A. Lahiri; Shri R. Lall; Shri B. S. Negi; Dr. Kirit Parikh; Dr. B. Ramamurti (later resigned); Shri K. Vaidyanath (transferred and replaced by Shri H. M. Chatterjee who also retired and replaced by Shri N. N. Tandon); Shri Rasiklal Worah; Shri V. N. Meckoni; Shri R. G. Mahendru.

Secretary : Shri T. L. Sankar.

APPOINTMENT

The Fuel Policy Committee was appointed by the Government of India, Ministry of Petroleum and Chemicals and Mines and Metals (Department of Mines and Metals) vide its Resolution No. CI-13(11)/70 dated

October 12, 1970.

TERMS OF REFERENCE

(a) Undertake a survey of fuel resources and the regional pattern of their distribution ;
(b) Study the present trends in exploitation and use of fuels;
(c) Estimate perspective of demand by sectors (in particular transport, industry, power generation industry and domestic fuel) and by regions;
(d) Study the efficiency in the use of fuel and recommend :—
   (i) the outline of a national fuel policy for the next fifteen years;
   (ii) a pattern of consumption and measures, fiscal and otherwise, which would help the best use of available resources; and
   (iii) the measures and agencies, to promote the optimum efficiency in use of fuel.

CONTENTS

Chairman's letter forwarding the Report; Names of Chairman and Members of Fuel Policy Committee; Names of the Secretariat of the Fuel Policy Committee; Abbreviations; Introduction; Trends in Energy Consumption ; Forecast of Energy Demand ; Fuel Resources of India ; Regional Distribution of Demand for Energy ; Perspective of Long Term Energy Problems; Coal Policy; Oil Policy; Policy for Power Sector; Policy for Energy Supply to Domestic Sector; Costs and Prices in Energy Sector; Technology Plan for Enery Sector; Summary of Recommendations; Annex Tables II. 1, II. 2, II. 3, II. 4, II. 5, III. 1, III. 2, XII-1.; Technical Note II. 1, II. 2, VIII-1.

RECOMMENDATIONS

Demand for Energy : In estimating the demand for fuels the Committee took note of the "Long Term Perspective" of the Indian Economy set out in Fifth Five-Year Plan. The Committee has estimated three levels of demand for energy, viz.—

Case—I : assuming that the relative prices of fuel will continue to be the same in future and that technology shifts would follow the same trends as in the past*;

Case—II : assuming an intermediate level between Case-I and Case-III which is considered possible of achievement under most of the foreseeable set of conditions; and

Case—III : assuming that the relative price of oil products and other fuels will continue to be in the same state as in the first quarter of 1974 and that the measures indicated in the report for increasing fuel efficiency and for substituting oil products by other fuels in areas which are viable and desirable on techno-economic considerations are implemented as suggested.

Case-II has been referred to as the normal case while discussing policy issues relating to specific fuels, but the Committee's recommendations are that efforts should be made to bring the demand in line with the estimates made in Case-III. The requirements of the different commercial fuels as estimated by the Committee are indicated in the Table see on next page.

Reserves of Coal. A summary of the total gross reserves of the different varieties of coal is given below :

Summary of reserves of coal available in India

(In million tonnes)

	Total Gross Reserves	*Proved Reserves*	*Indicated Reserves*	*Inferred Reserves*
1. Cooking Coal				
Prime cooking coal	5650	3650	1540	460
Medium cooking coal	9431	3850	4309	1272
Semi to weekly cooking coal	5073	1559	2600	914
Total cooking coal	20154	9059	8449	2646
2. Non-cooking coal				
Non-cooking coal	59968	12306	22310	26180
Tertiary coal	828			
3. Lignite				
Lignite	2025	1795	202	28
Grand Total	82975	23160	30961	28854

Our cooking coal reserves will be able to sustain the growing requirement of the steel industry for a period of about 40 years only. On very rough calculation, it

* With certain adjustments in the trends of consumption of fuel oil, to correct for the increased use of fuel oil in the early seventies due to lack of coal supplies.

Estimated requirements of the different commercial fuels

Consuming Sector		*Coal (Million Tonnes)*			*Oil Products (Million Tonnes)*			*Electricity (Million kWh)*		
		CASE			*CASE*			*CASE*		
		I	*II*	*III*	*I*	*II*	*III*	*I*	*II*	*III*
					1978-79					
Energy use	—	132.0	137.8	142.8	26.7	24.5	22.7	120	124	128
Non-Energy use	—	3.0	3.0	3.0	7.7	7.7	7.7	—	—	—
Total	—	135.0	140.8	145.8	34.4	32.2	30.4	120	124	128
					1983-84					
Energy use	—	195.0	203.8	210.4	37.0	33.2	29.9	199	205	211
Non-Energy use	—	6.0	7.0	8.0	10.8	9.4	9.0	—	—	—
Total	—	201.0	210.8	218.4	47.8	42.6	38.9	199	205	211
					1990-91					
Energy use	—	330.0	342.0	352.9	61.0	52.5	44.6	385	392	398
Non-Energy use	—	9.0	10.5	12.0	16.5	14.2	12.2	—	—	—
Total	—	339.0	352.5	364.9	77.5	66.7	56.8	385	392	398

The estimates of demand for non-commercial fuels are as follows :—

Fuel		*1978-79*		*1983-84*		*1990-91*	
		In mt	*In mctr*	*In mt*	*In mctr*	*In mt*	*In mctr*
Firewood and Charcoal	—	132	125	131	124	122	116
Dung cake (dry)	—	65	26	65	26	53	21
Vegetable waste	—	46	44	46	44	46	44

may be stated that the reserves of non-coking coal that have been categorised so far would last for about 100 to 150 years.

Oil reserve : In the oil prospect map of India, 27 basins have been delineated on land and off-shore covering a total sedimentary area of about 1.41 million sq km on land and about 0.26 million sq km lying with the 100 metre isobath of shelf-zone in the Indian off-shore. The well studied oil bearing area constitutes about 4 per cent of the total area of the Indian sedimentary basins which could be the habitat for oil. The proved reserves of crude oil and natural gas are shown in Table below :—

Reserve of Crude and Natural Gas

Area	*Crude Oil (In million tonnes)*	*Natural Gas (In billion Cubic Metres)*
Gujarat	56.38	19.66
Assam	71.46	42.82
Total	127.84	62.48

Hydro-electric potential : The economically usable hydro electric potential estimated for each of these river systems and its State-wise distribution is given in Table below :—

Statewise Distribution of Power Potential

State	*MW at 60% LF*
1. Andhra Pradesh	2,476.5
2. Assam (including Meghalaya, Nagaland, Mizoram)	11,599.4
3. Bihar	600.7
4. Gujarat	677.0
5. Jammu and Kashmir	3,590.5
6. Kerala	1,539.5
7. Madhya Pradesh	4,582.3
8. Madras	708.2
9. Maharashtra	1,909.6
10. Mysore	3,372.8
11. Orissa	2,062.0
12. Punjab and Haryana	1,360.5
13. Rajasthan	148.0
14. Uttar Pradesh	3,764.0
15. West Bengal	22.0
16. Himachal Pradesh	1,867.5
17. Manipur	865.0
Total	41,155.5

Source : Central Water and Power Commission.

The Power Economy Committee expressed the view that "on the basis of the latest information regarding hydel energy resources and their economics of development, it would be possible to instal about 80 to 100 million kW of hydel capacity on our river systems during the next two to three decades...." In the absence of details this Committee has taken note of the hydel potential as indicated by CW and PC. The Committee would recommend that a more systematic delineation of our hydro-electric potential should be taken up as soon as possible.

Uranium reserves : The reasonably well assured uranium resources in India are about 22,000 Te U_3O_8 with an additional inferred reserves of 24,000 Te U_3O_8. Once these fast breeder reactors come on line by 1985-90, they will produce more plutonium than they would burn, and then the uranium resources available in India would be able to support about 600,000 to 10,00,000 MW of installed capacity for a life time of 30 years. Thus, the potentially available energy from the presently known uranium deposits in India would amount to 120×10^3 to 200×10^3 billion kWh of electricity.

Energy perspective beyond 1990-91 : The considerations described above suggest that the rate of growth of energy demand in the period beyond 1990-91 may not be as high as the projected rate of growth of energy demand upto 1990-91 and certainly not as high as the growth rates observed over the past two decades.

Regional energy policy : If the objective is to achieve a more balanced per capita total commercial energy consumption by 1990-91, there should be a well conceived policy towards regional development which will take note of the divergences in resource endowments. The region-wise energy policy should be a part of a well conceived regional development strategy.

Review of policy : It is necessary to keep the energy policy under periodic review and to effect changes where-ever necessary. If the energy plans and policies are to be operationally meaningful, they should be reviewed periodically at least once in three years and the planning horizon extended at each time to 15 years.

Organization to implement a coherent fuel policy : The implementation of the recommendations of the

Fuel Policy Committee which call for co-ordinated action by several Ministries and agencies of the Government. An ideal organizational arrangement for this will be the setting up of an Energy Commission clothed with adequate powers and manned by suitable talents which can be entrusted with the responsibility for the periodic review of the energy situation and for planning for optimal production and distribution of the different fuels. However, it is recognised that such a Commission will have to take over the functions which are now dealt with in several Ministries like the Ministry of Irrigation and Power, the Department of Mines, the Department of Petroleum, the Railway Board and the Planning Commission. It is also to be recognised that the scope of work of the Commission will become very large and some of the problems associated with large organization will have to be faced by the Commission. The need, however, to coordinate the activities of the different agencies of Government dealing with energy is very urgent. The Committee considers that it would be appropriate to immediately set up an Energy Board consisting of the Ministers of the concerned Ministries supported by a suitably structured Secretariat to assist this Board. Such a Board would be somewhat different from a Cabinet Committee as the Board would have a Secretariat which would initiate or undertake studies and analysis relevant for the review or revision of the fuel policy and would not depend entirely on the administrative Ministries for such studies.

Studies on energy policy : Whether a separate Institute of Energy Studies is set up or the proposed Energy Board takes up the work, the working of the agency entrusted with Energy studies, should be oriented more towards the arranging for the studies to be conducted by different institutions and agencies in existence now and coordinating the research projects. Any attempt to centralize the research efforts relating to energy problems which extend over a very large area of economics, science and technology under a single institution may prove counter-productive.

Coal resources : Coal should be considered as the primary source of energy in the country for the next few decades and the energy policy of the country should be designed on this basic premise.

The locational aspect of the coal deposits in the country underlines the need for developing an efficient and adequate transport system which would ensure the flow of available fuel resources from the points of availability to the points of requirements.

As the prime coking coal resources may get exhausted in about 40 years' time and the medium coking coal after some more time, it is necessary that all efforts are taken from now on for the conservation of prime coking coal, in particular, and of coking coal, in general.

Detailed investigations should be aimed at providing sufficient mineable deposits for the requisite level of production related to the demand for coal estimated for 1990-91.

Production planning : A careful perspective of coal production should be planned on the basis of the information available and suitable action for exploitation and mine planning taken in advance in the different coalfields. This perspective plan should be followed by preparing a shelf of project reports well in advance of each plan period. The recently set up Central Mine Planning and Design Institute should participate in all activities connected with the formulation and implementation of the perspective plan for coal including exploration and investigation (in association with the Geological Survey of India and Mineral Exploration Corporation) of promising areas assessment of their potential over a period of 20 to 25 years, suggestion of priorities for development and preliminary feasibility studies of the projects.

Steps should be taken urgently to ensure adequate and uninterrupted power supply to the collieries and washeries.

Production of the different grades of coking coal in future will need to be planned in accordance with the proportion in which they are needed in the steel plants and adequate crushing and preparation facilities have to be installed in all steel plants. In future, the planning of metallurgical coal mines and the construction of steel plants should be carefully synchronised.

Coal conservation : There are several technical possibilities of conserving coking coal. It is necessary that research and development activities in this regard are speeded up from now on.

The possibility of projecting large scale mechanised open cast mines in Jharia coalfield with much higher over-burden to coal ratio needs to be studied in depth.

Arrangement for stowing crushed stone locally available should be made so as to permit underground mining of coal from thick seams.

Coal preparation : In future, there should be only three product washeries.

It is necessary to undertake research for evolving suitable designs for washeries which are best suited for washing Indian coal and which would reduce the cost of washing.

In future, there will be need to wash even non-coking coal. As the washing of non-coking coal is a costly process, other methods of improving the quality of coal like simple high specific gravity washing, hand picking of better grades and proper sizing by screening etc. should be explored and the choice of beneficiation decided with due regard to consumer requirements, available grades of coal, the scale of the required operations etc.

The coal industry should accept the responsibility to supply on a long-term basis the required grade of coal, if necessary, by changing the source of supply from time to time or by blending different grades of coal to make up the required grades.

Coal for power generation : The Linkage Committee should consider the loading arrangements at each end and give suitable suggestions for loading and unloading as part of the linkage.

The Electricity Boards should give greater attention to the problems of coal handling and storage; optimal stock levels for each plant should be worked out with reference to the source of coal supply, its distance from the power plant, reliability of the rail link, the seasonal variations in these factors and in the demand.

In the major power plants, it would be desirable to have arrangements for sizing and preparation of coal before feeding into the boilers as this would make it possible to deal with possible changes in the quality of coal received.

It is necessary to have a suitable pricing policy for the use of middlings for power generation, if such use is to increase as estimated in the Report, to about 21 million tonnes by 1990-91.

Meaningful plants for thermal power generation have to be drawn up from now on in a coordinated manner with the plans for coal production, especially in respect of the southern region. The detailed investigation for coal mines to supply the requirements of the power stations should be taken in hand immediately.

Coal dumps for industrial consumers : If the increasing coal requirements of the industrial consumers is to be met satisfactorily, coal dumps will have to be set up in all the major industrial regions.

The setting up of coal dumps in major industrial areas will call for coordinated planning for movement of coal from the dumps to the consumer points by road alongwith the plans for moving coal from the mines to the dumps.

A five-fold increase in the next two decades in the requirement of coal for industries calls for detailed industrial location planning from now on and the locational plans regarding industries should be consistent with the plans for the production and movement of coal.

Coal for the domestic sector : A plan should be drawn up for increased movement of soft coke from the Bengal-Bihar region to the urban centres in the country.

Coal for exports : Separate plans for opening up export-based coal mines near the ports of Haldia and Paradeep may be drawn up, and possibilities of exporting this coal to Bangladesh and Burma and countries in the Pacific region will have to be considered without affecting domestic requirements.

Productivity : Studies should be initiated immediately for the optimal use and maintenance of machines and for training coal mines workers in the use and maintenance of equipment.

Transport : The studies made by the Committee indicate that Railways constitute the most economic way of moving coal for most of the consuming classes and consumer locations in India. Adequate attention should be paid to rail transport planning in regard to development of additional line capacity, yard capacity and signalling and communication which would facilitate speedier turn-round of wagons as well as augmentation of the wagon fleet.

Serious consideration should be given to the problems of coal movement in the Bengal-Bihar area and for removal of the factors which limit the capacity in the Bengal-Bihar region for movement in specific sections towards the northern, western and southern regions.

The Central Water and Power Commission should prepare a feasibility study for the transportation of coal by pipeline for a super thermal power station of more than 1,000 MW capacity.

Use of inland waterways : It would be useful to make a careful study of the techno-economic feasibility of transport by river to selected towns like Varanasi, Allahabad etc. We would, however, emphasise that for the scheme to be successful, large scale river training schemes will have to be taken in hand and a navigable channel marked throughout the course. Aids for night navigation may also have to be provided if the turn-round-time has to be kept within economic limits.

Coal gasification : It is difficult to foresee any large-size gas plants located at the pithead transporting gas for industrial or domestic users far away from cities; but in major cities like Bombay and Calcutta, gas plants located near the cities with smaller capacities may be a viable proposition.

Research and development should be continued on the techno-economic aspects of gasification and specific possibilities should be investigated for using poor quality coal for gasification and for use in industrial locations.

Machinery : A Committee of representatives of the concerned Departments and organisations should make an assessment of the indigenous capacity for the manufacture of coal mining machinery, suggest increases in capacity and fix import requirements for the period till the indigenous capacity catches up with the demand. This Committee should also take up the task of standardising the equipment. It may be made obligatory for the equipment manufacturers to produce a certain quantity of spares for the machines every year.

Choice of technology : The selection of the optimal technology should be made on economic grounds using appropriate weightages for machine utilisation under Indian conditions and for the availability of abundant labour force.

Lignite : It is strongly recommended that the second mine cut at Neyveli be taken up and the capacity of the power plant be increased to 800 MW.

The possibility of manufacturing bucket wheel excavators in the country should be examined and the manufacture of the required number of excavators taken up in a coordinated manner.

In view of the location of Neyveli lignite deposit in relation to other fuel sources, inspite of the heavy investment, the Committee is inclined to recommend the opening of additional mines at Neyveli and increasing this production to a level of about 20 mt.

Oil

Oil policy : India's Oil Policy should be based on an understanding of the international oil situation. It should be designed with the specific objectives of :

(a) reducing the quantity of oil products to be imported,

(b) reducing the total foreign exchange expenditure, and

(c) improving the security of supplies of crude and oil products required from sources outside the country.

Oil exploration : Oil exploration in India should be given priority attention. The exploration activities particularly in the off-shore areas and selected on-shore areas should be speeded up. There is urgent need to augment the capabilities of the ONGC by providing them with more modern equipment.

The following steps may have to be taken in oil exploration :

(i) Expedite the exploratory drilling in the Bombay High region.

(ii) Undertake a large volume of exploration drilling operations in the Tripura and Cachar areas and in the South-Eastern border of the Upper Brahmaputra Valley.

(iii) Re-survey some already explored portion of the Cambay basin and the Upper Brahmaputra Valley region of the Assam Basin using sophisticated geophysical techniques, and intensive exploration drilling operations in such portions, to locate additional traps in particular stratigraphics which might have been missed in the course of the exploration work conducted earlier.

(iv) Extend the exploration operations to the portions of the Cambay Basin and the Upper Brahmaputra Valley region of the Assam-Arakan Basin which had not been explored so far.

(v) Conduct extensive seismic surveys in all the areas and follow up the results by drilling of exploration wells. Poriority to be assigned to the continental shelf in the Arabia Sea adjoining the area already covered, the continental shelf area south of Sunderbans and the continental shelf area of the Andaman Islands.

(vi) Test by deep drilling already known structures in the Shiwalik foot hill belt of Jammu and Kashmir, Punjab and Himachal Pradesh.

(vii) Intensify the exploration work, including seismic surveys and drilling operations, in the Ganga valley in the West Bengal, Saurashtra and Jaisalmer area.

(viii) Intensify the exploration work, including commencement of exploration drilling, in the land area of Andaman and Nicobar islands.

All attempts should be made to take advantage of the complementaries of the resource endowments of India and the oil exporting countries and meaningful bi-lateral arrangements including participation in crude production in other countries entered into.

Crude stocking : With a view to providing an insurance against short-run breakdown in the supply of crude to the country, there is need for building up a stock of crude within the country. We should explore various ways of building up our stocks consistent with our resources.

Refinery planning : In each plan period, there should be a careful examination of the refinery locations, the product mix required in each refinery, the extent of secondary process to be established and the feedstock choice in the fertilizer industry.

Oil products supplies and pricing : While the potential for export of oil products should be kept in view, adequate care should be taken to analyse the long-term prospects for the product before investment options are approved.

Naphtha : Since light distillates will be in short supply right upto 1990-91, Naphtha demand will have to be regulated by proper licensing of fertilizer and petrochemicals projects and it will be necessary to price the naphtha product within the country appropriately.

HSDO : The price of HSDO and kerosene should continue to be kept at par with each other. If, at any time, it becomes necessary to tax the consumers of HSDO and kerosene at different rates, tax should be levied on the consumers of HSDO by suitable levies on other products which they use like tyres, tubes or spare parts.

Road-rail coordination : The Committee recommends that immediate action be taken to coordinate the road and rail transport in all optimal manner in order to manage the HSDO demand to levels indicated in the report. Long distance movement of commodities by road should be discouraged while simultaneously increasing the capability of rail transport.

Dieselization in railways : It has been estimated that 1,800, 3,000 and 4,000 Km of railway track will be electrified during the Fifth, Sixth and the Seventh Plan periods, which would take the total electrification to 12,800 Kms. With electrification of track increasing to that extent, it is anticipated that the railways can maintain the stock of diesel locomotives at a constant level of about 2,600 (which will be reached by 1978-79) and the consumption of diesel at 0.8 mt per year from then on. In other words, diesel consumption which was 0.5 mt in 1970-71 will increase to 0.8 mt by 1978-79 and stay at that level from then on. Though the stock of diesel locomotives will remain the same from 1978-79 onwards, the areas in which they operate will change from time to time. The diesel traction will be introduced in the areas where the steam traction will be unable to handle the increasing load traffic but electricity could not be extended for want of adequate traffic.

Fuel oil : Fuel oil being a valuable raw material for the production of high cost petroleum products which have good export potential or can serve as import substitutes, large quantities of it should be earmarked for the production of high value products like lubes, bitumen, petroleum coke and wax.

The Committee recommends that even at the stage of licensing new industries, the use of fuel oil in furnances should be prohibited and the nationalised coal industry should be asked to take immediate steps to set up coal dumps in all the industrial centres of the country.

The Committee recommends that the Government should take immediate steps to improve the design of indigenous thermal equipment with the specific objective of reducing the technological requirements of oil in the thermal plants.

Coal and fuel oil as fertilizer feedstock : The Committee is of the view that new fertilizer projects should be designed to make use of coal as the feedstock. However, in the refineries, even when the surplus heavy-end products are subjected to secondary processing, there will be some quantities of heavy residual material which cannot be used for any purpose except for burning as a feedstock for fertilizer production. Such material should be used as feedstock in preference to their use as fuels.

The Committee is of the view that even if in view of the lack of operating experience of large scale fertilizer production based on coal and the need to complete quickly a few more fertilizer projects within the country to meet the shortage of fertilizer a few projects based on fuel oil are taken up during the Fifth Plan, these projects should have adequate provision to switch over to the use of coal at a later date.

Recent explorations, inland and on-shore, indicate the possibility of discovering substantial quantities of natural gas. The production of fertilizers, methanol and other chemicals based on natural gas will have to be given preference over the use of natural gas a mere fuel.

Electricity

Installed capacity : The installed capacity requirements for different years in future to meet the energy requirements corresponding to the Case-II estimates are indicated below.

Installed capacity requirements for power generation in 1978-79, 1983-84 and 1990-91.

Year		*Forecast of energy consumption (b kWh)*	*Forecast of energy requirement (b kWh)*	*Installed capacity needed (m kW)*
1978-79	..	*100.3	116.4	33.6
1983-84	..	167.7	193.6	53.0
1990-91	..	320.4	370.7	87.3

*at the bus-bar, i.e., consumption plus line losses.

Note :—(1) On the basis of the calculations for 0.48 plant factor and 90 per cent availability the installed capacity required in the year 1978-79 would be 30.7 million kW. However, as there is a large spillover of works from the Fourth Plan and due to bunching of new projects the capacity coming on stream into the final year of the Fifth plan is very large. But as many of them would be operative only in the second half of the final year, only half of the benefits have been counted towards the Fifth Plan and hence the increased provision of installed capacity.

(2) For the year 1983-84, on the basis of 0.495 plant factor and 92 per cent availability the installed capacity should be 48.5 m kW. This is, however, being assumed as 53.0 m kW for reasons which are similar as in the case of 1978-79.

(3) The figure of installed Capacity has been arrived at 87.3 mkW on the basis of 0.51 plant factor and 95 per cent availability.

Power system planning : The Committe would strongly recommend that rational measures should be initiated in planning and operating the power systems so as to ensure gradual improvement in the plant factors of operation of power system.

Improving load factor of operation : The Committee recommends that during the Fifth Plan period, efforts should be made to develop a more optimal load structure :

(1) by setting up more pumped storage schemes as such schemes would improve the system capability at minimum cost;

(2) by identifying industries which are intensive users of electricity and are also capable of organising their production schedule in such a way that their peak demand would occur during the system off-peak period and by giving to such units adequate incentive through specially designed tariff to encourage them to reorganize their production;

(3) by general pricing of the industrial tariff and agriculture tariff to provide incentive for use of more electricity during off-peak hours.

Hydro-electricity : In order to achieve the objective of maximising the generating capacity with the funds available and to generate cheap power, it is recommended that during the Fifth and Sixth Plans the level of new generating capacity to be added should be derived from hydro stations, both of the energy intensive and peaking categories.

The Committee would urge that during the Fifth Plan, a very strong effort should be made to complete as many as possible of the hydel stations under construction.

The Committee would strongly urge that a detailed investigation of the specific projects which could be set up to utilise the hydro-electric resources should be drawn up within the next two years and the scheduling of different hydro projects should be determined with reference to the cost of the projects, the characteristics of the projects and their locations. On this basis, a detailed hydro-electric power development programme should be drawn up for the future upto 1990-91 or even 2,000 A.D.

Nuclear power : The capacity of the nuclear power stations is estimated to be as follows :—

1978-79 — — —	1020 MW
1983-84 — — —	1900 MW
1990-91 — — —	8620 MW

The Committee would like to endorse the view of DAE that nuclear power capacity, if possible, should be increased to the maximum extent possible by 1990-91. It would recommend that a review of nuclear programme should be made by 1978-79 in the light of the pace of construction of nuclear power stations in the Fifth Plan period, the preparedness of the DAE in respect of designs for 500 MW nuclear power plants and the progress made by them towards the commercialisation of the Fast Breeder technology.

Source-wise possible generating capacities has been suggested as follows :—

(Million kW)

Year, Mode of generation	*1978-79*	*1983-84*	*1990-91*
Hydel —	13.00	20.00	28.40
Nuclear —	1.02	1.90	8.62
Thermal —	19.55	31.10	50.30
Total —	33.57	53.00	87.32

Note :—Thermal stations include coal and lignite power stations.

Plant size : The Committee would recommend that immediate studies should be undertaken to determine the optimal plant size for different regions of the country.

During Fifth Plan period, the design capability should be developed and operational norms for a 500 MW set should be studied by setting up an R and D plant of MW capacity.

Locations : The Committee feels that in the overall interest of the economy and environmental considerations more and more of such power stations should be located at pit-heads. Depending on the local conditions, however, construction of power stations at load centres can be considered on merits as a special case.

Transmission : The Committee would very strongly

urge that the schemes for setting up of regional grids and regional load despatch centres should be vigorously pursued: simultaneously procedures for the integrated planning and operation of power systems based on system studies should be introduced.

Rural electrification : Procedures should be found for a proper evaluation of the relative social benefit cost of electrifying different areas with reference to the ground water potential, the possibility of increasing production in that area, the other non-agricultural production that might be triggered off in the area etc. The correct approach to rural electrification should be through the formulation of an integrated rural development programme for clusters of villages in which the supply of electricity would be one of the inputs arranged by the Government.

The Committee recommends a proper pricing policy for the power supplies to the agricultural loads so as to encourage the consumers to use the optimal size of pumpsets and for drawing supplies during the system off-peak hours.

The Committee would recommend that rural electrification should be pursued on lines which would ensure the electrification of almost all houses in the villages to which electricity is extended.

Captive power generation : The Committee feels that in the overall national interest and in order to achieve the target through the limited resources available, the setting up of captive power stations should not be encouraged. Efforts should be made to increase the capacity of the power utility system to meet all the demands with high reliability.

Nuclear power programme : Apart from the necessity of getting the projects sanctioned and executed in time, the realisation of the nuclear power programme depends on uranium production. Uranium mining from other uranium deposits will have to be taken up. At the same time exploration work to locate additional uranium deposits would also be essential to meet the long-term requirements of the nuclear power programme.

The realisation of the projected nuclear power programme will also depend upon the indigenous industrial back up that could be built up during the next few years. The Indian manufacturers will have to develop their capabilities to produce many of the sophisticated any heavy components as well as special pumps and instruments required for the nuclear power programme.

The Committee would recommend that, if possible, the nuclear capacity should be increased in the years beyond 1983-84. This should be based on a re-appraisal of the nuclear power programme on the lines suggested.

Domestic Sector

Firewood : A fairly generous estimate of the forest fuel resources puts the availability of forest fuels in 1978-79 to be around 94 mt as against our estimate of demand of 132 mt (equivalent of 125 mtcr). The solution to this problem lies in taking up programmes of afforestation especially with wood species which are quick growing and are capable of yielding wood for fuel purposes.

The social forests can be a supplement to the other measures for supplying the fuel needs of the rural population. The Committee recommends that consideration be given for the programme of tree plantation on the road sides, canal sides and railway sides to increase the availability of firewood.

Cow dung : The Committee would strongly recommend that all the efforts should be made to intensify the popularisation of 'Gobar Gas Plants' in suitable areas where the pattern of ownership of cattle will help in its easy implementation in view of the social benefits of the nutrient production, pollution abatement etc., possible from these plants.

Soft coke : The Committee urges that the possibility of setting up plants for the manufacture of solid domestic fuel to suit the requirements of different urban centres should be studied further.

The possibility of reducing the cost of soft coke to the consumer by subsidising the transport and trading margins or by raising the required funds through a surcharge on the price of kerosene should be examined.

The Committee recommends that all efforts should be made to increase the level of usage of soft coke as high as possible.

Efficiency : The Committee recommends that Research and Development should be undertaken on the design of heating appliances in the domestic sector and also other administrative action be taken to ensure that the appliances marketed conform to the design requirements.

Major implications : The Committee would like to draw attention to the fact that the problem of substitution of non-commercial fuels by commercial fuels in the domestic sector has to be considered with due regard to the overall economic implications of the use of different fuels in this sector and the pricing and distribution policies should be based on a full understanding of the social cost of the use of different fuels.

Costs and Prices

Price policy : A proper price policy for the fuels will have to be based on an adequate appreciation of the production cost of each fuel over time. The price policy should take into account the interest of the producer, the consumer and the nation.

The Committee feels that the Government should indicate a reasonable rate of return to be fixed for the fuel industries as a whole which would serve as a guideline for any Committee which is entrusted with the task of price fixation for any fuel.

The Committee would like to endorse the view, taking note of the objectives of a rational price policy in the energy sector, that the price fixed for any fuel, coal, oil or electricity should be such that the particular fuel industry, as a whole, is enabled to earn a return of at least 10 per cent on the investment made in the industry.

Price policy for coal sector : The Committee would recommend the following principles to govern coal prices :—

(1) Coal prices should be fixed with reference to the geographical area from which coal is mined.

(2) Price fixed for the coals produced in each area should cover the total costs of production and should yield a net return of at least 10 per cent on the capital invested in producing coal in that area.

(3) Differential price fixed for coal of different qualities should adequately reflect the value of the specific qualities to the consumer as well as the relative scarcity of coal of different qualities.

Price policy for oil sector : The Committee considers that the producer price of crude produced in India should at least be equal to the long-term cost of producing crude in India and the difference between such a price and the prevailing international market price at any point of time should be collected by the Government as a tax. In effect, the refineries should get Indian crude at prices equal to the international price of similar crude.

The Committee considers that there is no particular advantage in maintaining the "price parity" formula for fixing ex-refinery prices, in view of producing most of the products by refining of crude within the country, in the coming years.

The Committee would like to suggest that there should be a serious examination of the need to continue the import parity formula for product pricing and to evaluate other possible methods of fixing prices which will best subserve the national interest.

Price policy for power sector : The Committee would like to emphasise the inadequate returns from electricity industry will seriously affect the power programme and recommend strongly that the electricity tariff should immediately be revised in all the States so as to give the rates of return as suggested by the Venkataraman Committee. The Committee would like to recommend that the returns on investment in electricity should be 10 per cent in keeping with the rates of return from other energy producing industries. The basis of pricing suggested here should be applicable not only to State Electricity Boards but also to other power generating agencies like the Department of Atomic Energy, Central Electricity Authority, DVC etc.

The Committee recommends that the electricity tariff should be designed so as to discriminate adequately between the use of power during the peak periods and during off-peak periods. As the difference in the peak demand and off-peak demand is very large in this country, the tariff should include a penalty for use of power during the peak hours so that at least over a period of time the load curves of demand are flattened to a more reasonable level. This would bring about substantial savings in the investment cost in the power sector.

The committee is of the view that there is generally no case for subsidizing the cost of power supply to any industry.

The Committee considers that the tariffs introduced earlier need correction, in view of the fact that at present when the demand for power from the agriculture sector is a substantial portion of the total demand and when there is no longer any need for a promotional campaign to encourage the use of power in the agricultural sector (except perhaps in certain selected pockets in the country). The Committee would strongly recommend that the agricultural loads should be charged with due regard to the cost of supplying power to the agricultural sector. At the same time, all measures should be taken to bring about a better utilization of the connected loads in the agricultural sector (like roastering of agricultural loads) which would enable the reduction of the cost of power supply to the agriculturists.

Technology

Fuel efficiency : The Committee recommends that a National Fuel Efficiency Service with centres at the regional sector and industry levels and armed with adequate authority to ensure that their views on selection of fuels and on the level of efficiency are accepted by the consumers, should be instituted as early as possible.

The Committee would like to emphasise that, besides organisational arrangements, there is need for setting up facilities for training operatives who deal with fuel burning equipment.

A well-designed fuel efficiency training scheme should be worked out immediately, taking advantage of the surplus engineering talents available in the country today.

Reduction in investment costs : Suitable design and construction norms for reducing the costs of rural electrification and for meeting the agricultural pumpsets should be evolved.

Efforts should be mounted with the cooperation of the various institutions to implement a time-bound programme of increasing the efficiency of utilisation of oil in the transport sector.

The Committee recommends that the design, development and manufacture of 500 MW generating unit should be entrusted to an Indian agency with a time-bound programme to get the commercial production of such sets started in the early Eighties.

While agreeing with the strategy implied in the NCST recommendation for mounting a serious R and D effort for developing MHD process in India, the Committee would like to emphasise the need to concentrate work first on laboratory and higher scale in the critical areas.

The Committee would recommend that research and development in the areas relating to combined gas turbine-steam turbine plants which would increase the overall efficiency of coal utilisation in thermal power stations should be intensified.

Research and development must be taken up to evolve boilers designs which will avoid the use of oil support even when the load on the boiler is as low as 20 to 30 per cent of its capacity.

Conservation of coking coal : The Committee recommends that a time-bound programme for the development of a formed coke process based on non-coking coals should be drawn up and the project should be carefully followed.

Secondary conversion processes : Development work on hydro cracking should be speeded up so that the designing, manufacture of suitable catalysts, construction and efficient operation of secondary processing plants could be managed with indigenous skills.

Conversion of coal to oil : It is necessary that in the context of the latest review of our energy situation, the rising demand for oil products, the limited success in our oil exploration efforts and the increasing price as well as insecurity of obtaining oil from the international market, a well thoughtout long-term programme for development of coal-oil conversion technology should be drawn up. This should be based on a review of the success achieved in following the diverse routes for coal-oil conversion by various agencies in other countries as well as in our country and the product mix that would be relevant to our long-term demand and supply situation in respect of oil products.

A competent group should be formed to select possible areas for future work, assign this work to different organisations and to monitor the entire R and D effort in coal-to-oil conversion technology.

Coal gasification : The Committee recommends that R and D work on coal gasification and pipeline transport of coal gas should be undertaken from now.

It is necessary to immediately chalk out a comprehensive programme for intensive development work in the optimization of design of cooking and heating appliances manufactured in the country.

Non-conventional energy forms : Research and development in the areas of non-conventional energy should be kept up.

Solar energy : R and D on solar energy in India may be concentrated on—

(a) the development of thin-film technology to produce cooled surfaces which could be used as collectors and concentrators of solar radiation, thus reducing the costs ;

(b) the possibilities of using solar energy to convert animal waste, agricultural waste and algae into gaseous fuels and methane ;

(c) developing low cost solar water heaters ;

(d) developing solar distillation and desalination units for use in arid rural areas.

(e) developing techniques for the optional use of solar energy for drying and strorage of grain, wood and hay and air-conditioning.

Tidal power : The collection of more data on tidal movements and the preparation of feasibility reports with regard to specific coastal locations is recommended.

Chemical sources of energy : Development work on battery powered light vehicles is recommended.

Further work on Fuel Cell Technology for use in remote villages will be of use.

Priorities : Among the other options the important ones are the following :

(1) Development of Fast Breeder Reactor.

(2) Development of Boiler Designs to reduce oil consumption in thermal power generation plants.

(3) Fluidised bed technology/Development of commercial power generating plants based on this.

(4) Development of SNG production and transport technologies suitable for Indian conditions.

(5) Development of technologies for manufacture of cheap smokeless fuels for use in the domestic sector.

Coordination of R & D efforts in energy sector : It is of course necessary to have a competent group to coordinate the R and D efforts in the energy sector which will keep under review the progress registered in the different areas and adjust the priorities from time to time to enable the best results to be obtained.

INDIA, EXPERT COMMITTEE ON THE NATIONAL COOPERATIVE DEVELOPMENT CORPORATION, 1970—REPORT

New Delhi, Ministry of Agriculture (Department of Cooperation), 1971. 226p.

Chairman : Shri B. Venkatappiah

Members : Shri G.R. Kamat; Shri P.N. Damry; Shri P.S. Rajagopala Naidu; Shri V.N. Puri; Shri S.B. Kazi; Shri L.N. Bongirwar; Shri M.S. Chaudhary.

Member-Secretary : Shri K.S. Bawa.

APPOINTMENT

The National Cooperative Development Corporation was set up in 1963 under the National Cooperative Development Corporation Act, 1962 with the object of planning and promoting programmes for the production, processing, storage and marketing of agricultural produce and notified commodities through Cooperative Societies. It is a successor organisation to the National Cooperative Development and Warehousing Board which was set up on the recommendations of the All India Rural Credit Survey Committee. The Public Accounts Committee, in their Hundred and Sixth Report, have observed that "they have reasons to doubt whether the existence of an official organisation like the National Cooperative Development Corporation in the cooperative sphere, besides the Department of Cooperation is at all necessary" and have made the following recommendations :

"The Committee would like Government to remit the foregoing consideration for detailed expert study and come to a decision on the necessity for the continuance of the National Cooperative Development Corporation. In any case even if there is justification for the organisation, the present system of channelising Central assistance to the States through the Corporation does not appear to be necessary."

In pursuance of the above recommendation of the Public Accounts Committee, Government have decided to set up an Expert Committee to examine this and other connected matters in all their aspects. The Expert Committee on the National Cooperative Development Corporation was constituted by the Ministry of Food, Agriculture, Community Development and Cooperation (Department of Cooperation) Vide its Notification No. L. 12015/8/70-Misc. dated October 15, 1970.

TERMS OF REFERENCE

(1) To review the working of the National Cooperative Development Corporation, with a view to assessing to what extent the objectives for which it was established have been achieved;

(2) To examine whether there is need for the continuance of the Corporation; if so, to suggest modifications, if any, in the scope of its existing activities as provided under the N.C.D.C. Act, 1962 and to recommend legislative, administrative and financial measures for enabling the Corporation to suitably strengthen its organisation in order to fulfil effectively its present functions as well as such others as may be recommended by the Committee;

(3) To examine whether the present system of channelising Central assistance to the States through the Corporation is necessary and to suggest any change, modification or improvement therein.

CONTENTS

Introductory; Historical Background; Assessment of Performance; Scope, objects and functions; Financial arrangements; Future set up; Routing of Central

Assistance for State Plan schemes through N.C.D.C.; Legislative Measures; Conclusion; Summary of Recommendations; Annexures from I to XVIII.

RECOMMENDATIONS

Assessment of Performance

Basis for assessment : In terms of its charter, the principal responsibility of the N.C.D.C. is to promote planned development of marketing, processing and storage of agricultural produce and distribution of essential requirements of farmers through cooperative societies and, to this end, provide financial assistance for these activities through the State Governments. To assess the N.C.D.C.'s performance, a broad analysis was undertaken of the record of progress of various programmes with which the Corporation is concerned and its own specific contribution examined with reference to promotional initiative, financial assistance, technical guidance and overall supervision. The conclusions emerging from the field studies organised in eight States on different aspects of the functioning of the N.C.D.C., the replies received to the questionnaires issued to the State Governments, Registrars and national and state level federations, statistical data available in the publications of the Reserve Bank, the Government of India and the N.C.D.C., and the detailed information furnished by the N.C.D.C. form the basis for evaluating the overall role of the N.C.D.C.

Overall progress of programmes : As now constituted, the N.C.D.C. was set up in 1963 (in pursuance of legislation passed in 1962) as successor to the erstwhile N.C.D. and W. Board established in 1956. Since the inception of the N.C.D. and W. Board and more so since 1963, the different programmes with which the N.C.D.C. is concerned, have registered striking progress. The value of agricultural produce handled by cooperatives increased from about Rs 175 crores in 1961-62 to nearly Rs. 600 crores in 1969-70; during the same period, fertilisers distributed by cooperatives registered a sharp increase from Rs. 32 crores to Rs. 232 crores; the share of cooperatives in the total production of sugar in the country rose from 1.5% in 1955-56 to 33.1⅓% in 1969-70; the owned storage capacity available with cooperatives to facilitate marketing and distribution functions expanded from 7.5 lakh tonnes in 1961-62 to 2.7 million tonnes in 1969-70. The principal targets fixed for co-operative marketing and processing in the Third Plan were either fulfilled or exceeded. The Third Plan envisaged that co-operatives would handle agricultural produce worth Rs. 360 crores in 1965-66; the co-operatives fulfilled this target. The Third Plan envisaged organisation of 680 processing units; the achievement was 1021.

While reviewing these programmes, it is important to note that co-operative marketing, processing and storage programmes constitute a relatively new field in the co-operative sector as compared with co-operative credit. Conscious efforts to develop these programmes on a planned basis was taken up only since 1955-56 when the erstwhile N.C.D. and W. Board was established.

Recent trends : The last few years have witnessed significant diversification of the activities of the co-operatives. Co-operative marketing was, till recently, confined to marketing of commercial crops, particularly sugarcane and cotton. Co-operatives have now entered the foodgrains trade in a big way. The value of food-grains handled by cooperatives in 1961-62 was Rs. 32 crores; in 1968-69 it was Rs. 222 crores. The indications are that cooperatives will progressively improve on their past performance. To illustrate, the total quantum of wheat procured by cooperatives in 1970 season was about 7.00 lakh tonnes; it has exceeded 2 million tonnes in 1971. Another encouraging development is the expanding inter-state trade for the sale of produce in terminal markets so as to secure better prices. The value of inter-state business was only of the order of Rs. 1 crore in 1962-63; in 1968-69 it exceeded Rs. 56 crores. Cooperatives are taking up the secondary and tertiary stages of the processing of agricultural produce. Agro-industrial complexes are coming up in the cooperative sector. There is a large network of cooperative retail depots for the sale of fertilisers. Cooperatives are now equipping themselves to streamline their distribution system to cope with keen competition.

N.C.D.C.'s Contribution

N.C.D.C.'s role : In assessing the contribution made by the N.C.D.C. to the implementation of various programmes, it has to be noted that the direct responsibility for implementation of programmes vests in the State Governments; the Corporation is to operate through, and in collaboration with the State Governments. The N.C.D.C.'s role, therefore, is to be assessed with reference to the planning, financing and overall strategy connected with the development of these programmes, as also by the contribution it has made or impact it has had in various contexts such as policy formulation of Central Government and public corporations *vis-a-vis* cooperatives; provision of expert guidance and assistance in the formulation of different programmes, and constructive supervision over and periodical review of the programmes.

Contribution to different programmes: A study of the various aspects mentioned above, points to the useful role played by the N.C.D.C. in planning and developing a strategy for expansion and diversification of cooperative activities. In the field of cooperative marketing the emphasis of the N.C.D.C. has been on the structural improvement of cooperative marketing societies, forging an effective link between cooperative marketing and credit on the one hand, and also among different levels of marketing societies on the other, so that an integrated system of cooperative marketing is developed for the benefit of the farmer. To improve the operational efficiency of the cooperative marketing structure, the N.C.D.C. has been pursuing with state marketing federations and State Governments the question of creating common cadres of key personnel. It has also been assisting in arrangements for the training of personnel at different levels. In regard to processing, case studies indicate that N.C.D.C.'s initiative and support contributed substantially to the large scale expansion and modernisation of rice milling industry in the cooperative sector and the growth of cooperative agro-industrial complexes in the country. In fertilizer distribution, the N.C.D.C. has been directing its efforts to the streamlining of the cooperative distribution arrangements so that various marketing federations, the primary marketing societies and the primary credit societies function as an integrated system for providing efficient service to the farmers in the new context of free trade in fertilizers. The Corporation is assisting the cooperatives in sorting out their problems with fertilizer manufacturers. It is also providing assistance from its own funds for the setting up of granular fertilizer mixing plants and also for soil testing laboratories. The case study of cooperative storage in U.P. shows that "the planning for storage programmes in the State (U.P.) actually started with the initiative and financial assistance of the Corporation."

Liaison with public sector organisations: With the increasing social control over trade in foodgrains and other commodities and the emergence of public sector business and manufacturing organisations like the Food Corporation, the Cotton Corporation and the Fertilizer Corporation, there has arisen the need for an effective link between cooperatives on the one hand and these public sector organisations on the other. At the all-India level, the N.C.D.C. maintains contacts with the Corporations and seeks the help of the Central Government in order that due weight is given to the cooperative sector and due consideration to its problems in the formulation of policies and procedures. The N.C.D.C. also serves a useful purpose in placing the financial requirements of marketing and processing cooperatives before institutions like the Industrial Finance Corporation and the Reserve Bank.

Role of the N.C.D.C. in overall planning: The N.C.D.C. has not only associated itself at the all-India level with the formulation of policies and programmes relating to cooperative marketing, processing, storage, etc., for the Fourth Plan, but has also guided the State Governments in the formulation of these programmes.

Inherent Limitations

Lack of funds: The N.C.D.C. Act has introduced a radical change in the mode of financing of the Corporation. Under Section 11 of the Agricultural Produce (Development and Warehousing) Corporations Act, 1956, the Central Government was required to provide the entire assistance required by the erstwhile N.C.D. and W. Board in the form of grants, even though the Board was expected to utilise the money for grant of assistance to State Governments both by way of loans and grants. But, under section 12 of the new Act, the N.C.D.C. receives Central assistance both by way of loans and grants according to its requirements. The 1956 Act incorporated the basic principles suggested by the Rural Credit Survey Committee that this all-India organisation should have funds of its own for developing different programmes under its purview, and also the freedom to determine the terms and conditions governing its assistance to State Governments for different cooperative activities. The entire assistance from the Government of India was to be in the nature of non-lapsable grants so that this organisation could build up a revolving fund of its own for promoting different programmes coming under its purview. This basic principle has been given up in the new N.C.D.C. Act which provides that funds required by the Corporation for giving subsides to the State Governments should be given as subsidy, while the funds required for giving loans should be given as loan. A significant feature emerging from the case studies of the cooperative processing programmes in Maharashtra is that the financial assistance provided by the N.C.D.C. has not been adequate to meet the requirement of the progressively expanding cooperative sector in that State. Some of the State Governments, in reply to the questionnaire, have also indicated that the financial assistance received from the N.C.D.C. has not been adequate.

Lack of autonomy: Funds are now provided by the Central Government to the N.C.D.C. under various schemes like the centrally aided plan schemes, central sector schemes and centrally sponsored schemes. The N.C.D.C. has, however, no discretion to divert funds from one scheme to the other. In respect of the centrally aided plan schemes under which Central assistance is routed to State Governments for certain cooperative programmes through the N.C.D.C., the ceilings of assistance for each State as also the pattern of assistance to be provided are determined by the Central Government. In such a situation, the N.C.D.C. becomes only a channel for routing Central assistance for those schemes. The N.C.D.C. is neither equipped with funds of its own adequate to meet the requirements of the various programmes nor does it enjoy financial autonomy in respect of the funds received from the Central Government.

Lack of staff: The erstwhile N.C.D. and W. Board was organised as a high-powered body with a Cabinet Minister as Chairman, Deputy Governor of the RBI, Secretaries to the Government of India and prominent cooperators as members. But there was hardly any administrative set up to service this high-powered organisation. An officer of the rank of a Deputy Director in the Government of India officiated as the chief executive of the organisation for nearly 6 years from August, 1957 till 1963. Even after the setting up of the present N.C.D.C. in 1963, the work relating to the planning and promotion of programmes of cooperative marketing, processing, etc., continued to be done mostly in the Union Department of Cooperation. It was only in September 1964, that the entire work relating to the planning and promotion of these programmes was transferred to this Corporation. It was as recently as in 1969 that the Corporation opened two regional offices. Technical experts were appointed by the N.C.D.C. for the first time in 1970. The case studies as also the comments of the various State Governments and Registrars point to the inadequacy of the technical guidance and overall supervision available from the N.C.D.C. This is to be imputed mainly to the absence of adequate staff.

Areas of weakness: While the N.C.D.C.'s role in terms of initiative, promotion and coordination has been of considerable importance, the same cannot be said of the part played by this institution in certain other spheres. The data before the Committee including case studies and replies indicate that the N.C.D.C. has not been in a position except in a few contexts, to provide the range of expertise necessary for the technical formulation of plans and projects. It is now trying to make good to the extent practicable this hiatus in its organisation. Similar lack of staff has prevented its follow-up action on the implementation of various programmes being as effective as it could otherwise have been. The financial support extended by the N.C.D.C. was significant and very often crucial; but here again it fell far short of the expanded requirements. Further, while the overall progress is striking, it is unevenly distributed between different States and between different areas within the same State. This of course is a common feature of practically all development programmes in the country and not merely those with which the N.C.D.C. happens to be associated. Even so, no concerted effort has till recently been made by the N.C.D.C. to promote programmes for backward areas on a priority basis. The N.C.D.C. has, however, now taken a decision to pay special attention to the development of certain cooperative programmes in backward areas and also strengthen its administrative machinery for this purpose.

Assessment by others: The Dantwala Committee on Cooperative Marketing (1966), the Study Group of the ARC on Centre-State Relationships (1967), the Working Group on Cooperation set up by the Administrative Reforms Commission (1968) and the All India Rural Credit Review Committee (1969) have all appreciated the contribution made by the N.C.D.C. to different programmes with which it is concerned.

The need for the N.C.D.C. besides a separate Department of Cooperation as also the question of duplication of functions between the N.C.D.C. and the Union Department of Cooperation were carefully examined by the Government before the present N.C.D.C. was set up. This examination was undertaken by the Government in pursuance of the recommendations of the Estimates Committee (1960-61). The Estimates Committee also agreed with the views of the Government that there is need for the N.C.D.C. besides the Union Department of Cooperation.

The Union Department of Cooperation deals with agricultural credit and indebtedness in the cooperative sector, cooperation in the agricultural sector, matters relating to national cooperative organisations, administration of the Multi-Unit Cooperative Societies Act, training of personnel of cooperative departments and cooperative institutions and consumer, labour and non-agricultural cooperatives. Besides, the Department is also responsible for basic cooperative policies and for coordinating cooperative activities in all sectors. In so far as the N.C.D.C. is concerned, the Union Department of Cooperation concerns itself mainly with policy matters and policy directives as well as with Parliament work in relation to the Corporation and its activities. The nature of the functions of the N.C.D.C. is also different from that of the Department. The Corporation is a promotional and financing agency. The major responsibility of the N.C.D.C.—particularly in the context of the role now envisaged for it—is to formulate, in conjunction with the appropriate Departments of

State Governments and cooperative institutions programmes of cooperative processing, storage, marketing, etc., assist in the assessment of technical feasibility and economic viability of the schemes, assume the role of a coordinator for financing the programmes from various sources including its own funds, help in obtaining, wherever necessary, requisite and prompt policy and other support from the concerned Ministries of the Government of India and all-India public sector organisations, provide constructive supervision over the implementation of the programmes and undertake their periodical evaluation. The N.C.D.C. is thus an executive organisation whose activities are field-oriented and programme-based. The Department's activities belong more appropriately to the realm of policy making. The N.C.D.C. could help the department in shaping policies relating to the programmes with which it is concerned. The Government could issue policy directives to the N.C.D.C. in relation to its activities, and lay down priorities for implementation of the programmes. Thus a clear demarcation of functions emerges between the N.C.D.C. and the Union Department of Cooperation. While the Union Department of Cooperation is responsible for enunciation of policies in relation to the Corporation and its activities the Corporations' responsibilities mainly relate to the formulation, execution and financing of the programmes. The N.C.D.C. is thus not rendered redundant by the existence of the Union Department of Cooperation.

Does the N.C.D.C. prejudicially affect the prospects of de-officialisation : The basic objective of the N.C.D.C. is to provide, at the national level, a forum for non-official leadership, State and Central Governments, public sector financing and commercial organisations, and be the focal point for the planning, initiating, developing and financing of a nation-wide cooperative programme for processing, marketing, etc. The national and State level cooperative federations which were consulted have expressed the view that the existence of the N.C.D.C. has never been a dis-incentive to non-official participation in the cooperative movement; many federations have in fact emphasised that the existence of the N.C.D.C. has helped in non-official participation in the movement.

Scope, Objects and Functions

Core activities : One of the principal grounds on which the Committee recommends the continuance of the N.C.D.C. is the promise it holds out of being able to create increasingly effective facilities in the cooperative sphere for supporting the rising tempo of agricultural production. The N.C.D.C. should continue to concentrate on agricultural and, within the sphere of agriculture, focus its attention on cooperative marketing, processing and storage of agricultural produce and supply of agricultural inputs.

Other functions : Dairy, poultry and fishery are important activities which provide income and employment opportunities to the vulnerable sections of the rural community, and therefore, call for large cooperative programmes for these activities. Their promotion, however, require technical know-how and expertise. Specialised institutions like the National Dairy Development Board have been established in the public sector for these activities. In this connection, the Agricultural Refinance Corporation has also begun to finance dairy, poultry and fishery projects formulated on an integrated basis and linking the provision of credit to individuals with extension services, processing, storage, transport and marketing of products. In areas specially suited for these activities and also in areas covered by special programmes like S.F.D.A./M.F.A.L. designed for assisting weaker sections, the N.C.D.C. should help promote these programmes in the cooperative sector. In formulating such programmes, the N.C.D.C. might draw upon the expertise available with specialised institutions.

As far as forestry is concerned, the activities of the N.C.D.C. might be restricted to helping the tribal people in collection, processing and marketing of minor forest produce through appropriate cooperatives, specially organised for them.

Notified commodities : In terms of existing charter of the N.C.D.C., its activities extend to notified commodities, that is, commodities coming under the purview of Entry 33 of the Concurrent List. The activities of the N.C.D.C. may continue to extend to such commodities as may be notified by the Government from time to time.

N.C.D.C. to give up work relating to cooperative credit and rural consumers : The N.C.D.C. is not directly associated with cooperative credit programmes. Its present role in merely to route Central assistance to State Governments to enable them, in turn, to extend managerial assistance to cooperative credit institutions. The Corporation may give up this function.

The Corporation is now dealing with rural consumer activities. The urban cooperative consumer movement is dealt with in the Department of Cooperation. The N.C.D.C. has no special role in developing the consumer movement in rural areas through primary credit or marketing cooperatives. As a functional activity, it would be an advantage if both urban and rural consumer programmes are dealt with in a single organisation. The Department of Cooperation may deal with rural consumer programmes also.

Promotional and developmental role of N.C.D.C. : The N.C.D.C. is mainly a promotional and developmental organisation. The main features of this role are : development of processing, storage, marketing and supplies in the cooperative sector to back up programmes for increasing agricultural production ; promotion of area and project approach entailing pre-investment surveys, assessment of cost-benefit and investment-return ratios, integration and proper phasing of all factors including credit, marketing etc., relevant to cooperative programmes in compact areas ; stimulating flow of institutional finance to cooperative projects from institutional agencies ; and evolving special programmes for tribals and other weaker sections as also for backward areas.

The promotional and developmental role of N.C. D.C. would also cover the following aspects relating to initiation, coordination, and evaluation of programmes :

(i) Coordination of activities of various agencies for implementing area development programmes through cooperatives.

(ii) Liaison with various Ministries and organisations like the FCI, the Central Warehousing Corporation, the State Trading Corporation, the Fertiliser Corporation, the Cotton Corporation, the Jute Corporation and other commodity organisations with a view to creating favourable conditions for strengthening and expansion of business activities of cooperatives in the rural sector.

(iii) Initiating cooperative pilot projects in strategic areas of agricultural development and providing technical and financial support for such projects.

(iv) Provision of technical guidance, consultancy service and arrangements for training and research.

(v) Periodical evaluation of various cooperative programmes.

Financial role : The financial role of the N.C.D.C. emerges from its promotional role. The efforts of the N.C.D.C. will be mainly to equip cooperatives with the requisite risk capital and margin money and thus enable them to have access to funds from institutional agencies for expanding their business operations and for investment on plant, machinery and buildings for processing and storage programmes. The N.C.D.C. should provide assistance to cooperatives in the States only through, or on the guarantee of, the State Governments. Its direct assistance will be restricted to national and regional level federations.

Autonomy of the corporation policy—Directives by Government : Autonomy in its operations is vital to the effective functioning of the N.C.D.C. At the same time, being a public sector organisation in which public funds are involved, the Corporation should be accountable to the Government and through the Government to the Parliament. The autonomy of the Corporation should, therefore, be subject to the overall policy directives and priorities laid down by the Government from time to time. The policy directives may be as follows :

(a) The main responsibility of the Corporation shall be to promote and develop a country-wide programme of cooperative activities for processing, storage, and marketing of agricultural produce for the benefit of the farmers and in support of agricultural programmes, as also the supply of inputs for such programmes. The Corporation shall endeavour to concentrate its attention on the priorities that may be laid down by the Government from time to time in the overall context of agricultural development.

(b) In performing its functions, the Corporation shall operate in consultation and close association with the State Governments.

(c) In assisting programmes for cooperative development, the Corporation shall establish sound financing policies and procedures and, generally, take such measures as facilitate the flow of institutional finance for these programmes.

(d) In formulating its financing policies and procedures, the Corporation shall lay down and apply criteria for, and establish priorities regarding the choice of programmes and schemes mainly on the basis of consideration of economic viability of the schemes. The Corporation shall also lay down appropriate stipulations in regard to the technical, economic, financial and managerial aspects of each programme, as a condition for providing financial assistance.

(e) The Corporation shall direct its efforts to promote as far as possible, 'project' and 'area development' approach to cooperative programmes.

(f) The terms and conditions of loans to be advanced by the Corporation and the subsidies to be granted by it shall be related to the economic of the scheme financed.

(g) The Corporation shall pay special attention to evolving suitable economic programmes for assisting tribals, small farmers and other weaker sections of the rural community as also for relatively backward areas in the country.

(h) For assisting special programmes for weaker sections and backward areas, the Corporation may, with the prior approval of the Central Government adopt patterns of assistance different from those applicable to other programmes.

(i) The Corporation shall for the efficient discharge of its functions equip itself with adequate expert staff.

Financial Arrangements

The main conclusion is that, in order to render the N.C.D.C effective in the performance of its functions which includ the high priority objectives of helping the weaker sections and stimulating economic growth in the more backward areas, it should be equipped with adequate funds and endowed with autonomy in its operations subject, however, to the broad policy directives that may be given by the Central Government from time to time. The financing role of the N.C.D.C. emerges essentially from its promotional and developmental role. The N.C.D.C.'s assistance should generally provide a base for attracting institutional finance for various schemes assisted by it. As the responsibility for implementing cooperative programmes rests with the State Governments, the Corporation should route assistance to cooperatives through the State Governments or provide assistance to cooperatives only on the guarantee of the State Governments concerned. The N.C.D.C.'s assistance to State Governments should be additive to State Plan resources and should not be at the cost of normal Central assistance to which the State Governments are eligible for their plan schemes. The Corporation will, however, provide direct assistance to the national federations.

Suggested Financial Role of the N.C.D.C.

Equipping cooperatives with margin money : The programmes of cooperative processing, storage and marketing and supply of inputs need to be substantially stepped up to cope with the increasing agricultural production. Cooperatives will have to be financially equipped for intensifying their activities. Increasingly greater reliance has to be placed by them on institutional finance for various programmes. To enable cooperatives to have access to institutional sources of finance, they should be equipped with equity capital and margin money. While cooperatives themselves should direct their efforts to the mobilisation of additional resources from their members, their efforts cannot be commensurate with the rapidly increasing requirements. A large programme of planned participation in the share capital of marketing and processing cooperatives through the State Governments, therefore, becomes a necessity, and the N.C.D.C. should be equipped to provide the necessary assistance to the State Governments. Implicit in the function of providing margin money for different cooperative economic activities is the N.C.D.C.'s role as financial coordinator. It will help in arranging for funds from institutional agencies like the Industrial Finance Corporation, I.D.B.I., etc.

Weaker sections and backward areas : The N.C.D.C. should sponsor special programmes designed to benefit small farmers and other weaker sections of the rural community, and also stimulate the growth of cooperative activities in the agricultural sector in the relatively under-developed areas. These would call for provision of funds by the N.C.D.C. on more liberal terms and also imply a larger element of subsidy to render the schemes economically viable. The Corporation should, therefore, have the necessary degree of automony and flexibility in its financial operations to ensure effective implementation of such special programmes. The autonomy of the N.C.D.C. should, however, be subject to the overall policy directives that might be given by the Central Government.

Project and area development : There are two important lines of approach to planned cooperative development. The first is to promote cooperative marketing, processing and storage as package activities for developing agricultural resources in a given area and linking these activities to agricultural production programmes including supply of credit and other inputs. The second is to promote specific agro-industrial projects based on survey of potentialities of various areas. The N.C.D.C. should assume special responsibility for promoting area development and project programmes and also arrange for their financing by institutional agencies.

Utilisation of N.C.D.C.'s Funds

Purposes : The N.C.D.C.'s funds should be utilised :

(a) for advancing loans to State Governments for giving loans to, or investing in, the share capital of cooperative institutions ;

(b) for participating in the share capital of and providing loans and grants to the national and regional cooperative institutions ;

(c) for providing finance/refinance to other types of cooperatives on the guarantee of the State Governments concerned ; and

(d) for providing grants to State Governments for cooperative programmes.

State governments to be involved : The N.C.D.C will not deal direct with individual cooperatives, with the sole exception of national and regional cooperative institutions. The Corporation should operate only through, or in close association with, the State

Governments who are, under the Constitution, primarily responsible for 'Cooperative Societies' registered under the respective State Cooperative Societies Acts.

Resources for the N.C.D.C.

Non-lapsable grants from Central Government : To enable the N.C.D.C. to finance programmes of cooperative marketing, processing, storage, etc., the Central Government should provide a non-lapsable annual grant of Rs. 10 crores upto the end of the Fifth Plan (1978-79) and the position reviewed thereafter. The N.C.D.C. should utilise these funds for giving grants or loans or both, appropriate for different programmes.

The Central Government are now making available funds to the N.C.D.C. for certain centrally sponsored and central sector schemes. Besides the minimum non-lapsable grant of Rs. 10 crores suggested above, the Central Government may continue to provide funds for these schemes during the remaining period of the Fourth Plan after which the need for raising the minimum grant might be considered in the context of the requirements of the N.C.D.C. for various programmes sponsored by it.

Re-scheduling of existing loans to central government : On 31st March, 1971 the Corporation owed to the Central Government a sum of Rs. 40.45 crores under various loans received for different plan schemes in different years. These loans are normally repayable to the Central Government over a period of 14 years. The loans may be consolidated into a single loan as on 31st March, 1971, and their repayment by the N.C.D.C. to the Central Government rescheduled. They may be made interest-free and repayable in 15 annual instalments commencing after the expiry of 15 years. Section 19 of the Agricultural Refinance Corporation Act provides for loan assistance for 30 years by the Central Government to the Agricultural Refinance Corporation.

National industrial credit (LTO) fund of the Reserve Bank of India : As the objectives of the National Industrial Credit (LTO) Funds of the R.B.I. is to provide support to industrial development in the country and as one of the major functions of the N.C.D.C. will be to promote the agricultural processing industries in the cooperative sector, the N.C.D.C. should be enabled to obtain assistance from this Fund. To make this possible, the Central Government may notify the N.C.D.C. as a financing institution for the purpose of drawing assistance from the I.D.B.I. under Section 46-C of the RBI Act. The N.C.D.C. would require soft loans to enable it to provide assistance on liberal terms to cooperatives towards risk capital and residual block capital. The Central Government may, therefore, examine whether the N.C.D.C. should not be allowed to have direct access to the Long Term Operations Fund and also consider the need for amending the RBI Act.

Assistance from International Financing Agencies : The N.C.D.C. should formulate suitable programmes on the basis of which it may avail itself of assistance from the World Bank and other international financing agencies. The programmes for construction of godowns, establishment of cold storages and setting up of agro-industrial complexes and modernisation of rice mills in the cooperative sector are suitable for attracting assistance from international financing agencies.

Market borrowings : The N.C.D.C. may be enabled to resort to market borrowings through debentures which may be guaranteed by the Central Government. The N.C.D.C. should also endeavour to muster resources from cooperative institutions like cooperative sugar factories.

Exemption from Income Tax : As the N.C.D.C. is a non-profit making, developmental and promotional statutory organisation, it may be exempted from payment of Income Tax and other taxes on income.

Funds : Today, the Corporation maintains a single fund called the 'National Cooperative Development Fund', from which all assistance given by the Corporation as well as administrative and other expenses incurred by it are met. It is, however, important to distinguish between different aspects of the financing role of the N.C.D.C. The first is the financing of specific projects involving the creation of assets such as cooperative processing units and cold storages and cooperative godowns. This involves careful planning of individual units, detailed preinvestment surveys and the insistence on certain standards and criteria, including a minimum net return on the estimated investment. The second is the provision of finance for cooperative institutions which undertake commercial operations of which the main items are the marketing of produce and the distribution of inputs. The third is the provision of subsidy for various programmes as a promotional measure. The Corporation may be required to maintain different accounts or even different funds for these different purposes. It may not be necessary to provide in the Statute itself for the creation of these funds. The Statute may merely provide for creation of such funds by the Corporation as may be notified by the Central Government. The allocation of resources for the funds and the utilisation of the amounts from them may be left to the determination of the Central Government in consultation with the Corporation.

Future Set Up

Essential features : In examining the future set up of the N.C.D.C. the main aspects to be considered are the composition of the membership of the Corporation, its management, appointment of chief executive officer, staff development with field orientation, building up of expertise for the various programmes and relations with the Government. An important feature to be recognised in considering the administration of the N.C.D.C. is its automony. The N.C.D.C. should be allowed to function as an independent and autonomous organisation and not as a mere 'wing' or an 'attached office' of the Ministry of Agriculture. This is not, however, to ignore the responsibility of the Ministry which provides funds to the N.C.D.C. and is responsible to the Parliament. The Ministry should have the right to give policy directives to the Corporation.

A two-tier organisational set-up is recommended for the N.C.D.C. There should be a General Council in which the supreme authority will be vested. Its membership should be broad-based in order to give representation to various related organisations. The second tier will be a Board of Management consisting of a small group representing a cross-section of the members of the General Council. The Board will function under the general direction, control and superintendence of the General Council. The day-to-day administration of the Corporation should be the responsibility of the chief executive. To build into its organisation requisite expertise for various types of programmes, the N.C.D.C. should have Advisory Committees which would include experts drawn from academic and research organisations, industry, government and cooperatives. The General Council, the Board of Management, the staff of the Corporation and the Advisory Committees together should make the Corporation an expert and representative body.

General Council : The supreme authority in the Corporation should vest in a General Council. The Council will function subject to the overall directives of the policy issued, and priorities laid down by the Central Government in the Ministry of Agriculture. The Council should normally meet twice a year. The main functions of the General Council will be :

(i) to lay down broad guidelines for achieving the objectives of the Corporation;

(ii) to ensure that the policy directives issued by the Central Government and priorities laid down by them are implemented;

(iii) to review periodically the implementation of various programmes sponsored by the Corporation; and

(iv) to approve the annual budget of the Corporation.

The General Council may be composed of the following :

(1) President to be nominated by the Central Government.

(2) Vice-President to be nominated by the Central Government.

(3) Chairman of the Board of Management to be nominated by the Central Government.

(4) to (11) Eight representatives of Economic Ministries to be nominated by the Central Government, by virtue of their office.

(12) The Deputy Governor of the Reserve Bank of India in charge of Rural Credit.

(13) to (15) Managing Directors of the State Bank of India, the Food Corporation of India and the Central Warehousing Corporation.

(16) Chairman of the Industrial Finance Corporation.

(17) A representative of commercial banks to be nominated by the Central Government.

(18) to (22) Chairman of the National Cooperative Union of India, the National Agricultural Cooperative Marketing Federation, the National Federation of Cooperative Sugar Factories, the All-India Cooperative Spinning Mills and the All-India State Cooperative Banks Federation.

(23) to (31) Nine representatives of State Governments (Development Commissioner or Agricultural Production Commissioner or Secretary to Government in charge of Cooperation), to be nominated by the Central Government.

(32) to (40) Nine Chairmen of State level cooperative federations to be nominated by the Central Government from States other than those represented under items (23) to (31) above. Chairmen of State level federations in Union Territories will also be eligible for nomination.

(41) to (44) Four persons having special knowledge of, or practical experience in, agricultural cooperative development, to be nominated by the Central Government.

(45) Managing Director of the N.C.D.C.

Of the 45 members of the General Council, 19 will thus be permanently represented by virtue of their office—8 representatives of the Central Government, representatives of the Reserve Bank of India, State Bank of India, Central Warehousing Corporation, Food Corporation of India, Industrial Finance Corporation and five Chairmen of national level federations and the Managing Director of the N.C.D.C. The term of office of the other 26 could be fixed in the Rules to be framed under the Act, as at present, at three years. The Rules may also provide for the different Economic Ministries to be represented on the General Council, nomination of representatives of State Governments and Chairmen of State level federations, and for the nomination of the President and the Vice-President of the Corporation.

President : In the light of the suggestions for extending the scope of activities of the N.C.D.C. to new and difficult fields which call for closer coordination of the policies and programmes of the N.C.D.C. with those of the State Governments, financial, business and policy support from different Economic Ministries of the Government of India, central financing institutions and public sector undertakings, the N.C.D.C. should have the necessary commanding stature and, for this reason among others, it is recommended that the Union Minister of Agriculture should be the President of the General Council and of the Corporation.

Vice-President : The Minister of State in the Ministry of Agriculture might be the Vice-President of the General Council.

Chairman of the board of management : The Chairman of the Board of Management of the Corporation should be a non-official to be nominated by the Central Government and, in this capacity, he should be a member of the General Council of the Corporation.

Representatives of central and state governments : Representation on the General Council may be given to the Union Departments of Agriculture, Cooperation and Food, Planning Commission, Ministries of Foreign Trade and Supply, Finance, Industrial Development and Internal Trade. As the N.C.D.C. is a high-powered organisation, it is expected that Secretaries in charge of different Ministries/Departments would be nominated to the General Council so that they could provide positive direction and support to the policies and programmes of the Corporation. Regarding State Governments, normally, the Development Commissioner or the Agricultural Production Commissioner of the State Governments may be nominated on the General Council; if, for any reason, this is not possible, Secretaries to the State Governments in charge of Cooperation may be nominated.

Board of management : The Board of Management will consist of a Chairman to be nominated by the Central Government and selected members of the General Council. The functions of the Board will be :—

(a) to implement the guidelines laid down by the General Council;
(b) to lay down subsidiary policies;
(c) to prescribe criteria, conditions and patterns in respect of financial assistance for various programmes;
(d) to sanction specific projects involving larger assistance from the N.C.D.C.;
(e) to undertake review and supervise implementation of various programmes;
(f) to deal with general matters relating to staff and general administration of the Corporation;
(g) to determine the lines of investment of the funds of the Corporation; and
(h) to frame detailed regulations for the conduct of business of the Corporation.

The Board of Management of the Corporation may consist of the following 11 members :

(i) Chairman to be nominated by the Central Government.
(ii) to (iv) Three representatives of the Central Government on the General Council to be nominated by the Central Government.
(v) Deputy Governor of the Reserve Bank of India.
(vi) One Chairman of a national level cooperative institution to be nominated by the Central Government from among those in the General Council.
(vii) & (viii) Two representatives of State Governments to be nominated by the Central Government from among those in the General Council.
(ix) & (x) Two representatives of State Level Cooperative Federation to be nominated by the Central Government from among those in the General Council.
(xi) Managing Director.

Advisory Committees : The Corporation may set up the requisite number of Advisory Committees. It is suggested that it may have Advisory Committees on (i) Cooperative Marketing and Storage including Cold Storages, (ii) Agricultural Inputs and Supplies, and (iii) Agricultural Processing Industries. The non-official members of the Corporation who have experience in the respective fields may be appointed as Chairmen of these Committees. The emphasis should, however, be on association of experts with these Committees. Technical officers belonging to the organisation of the Agricultural Marketing Adviser to the Government of India should be associated with the appropriate Advisory Committees. This would also ensure a closer coordination between the N.C.D.C. and the A.M.A.'s organisation.

Chief executive : The chief executive of this high-powered Corporation has a pivotal role. At present, the chief executive is called 'Secretary'. He may be redesignated as 'Managing Director'. The Office of Managing Director would involve large responsibilities —both administrative and financial—and also close association with various Ministries and all-India organisations at the policy making level. The chief executive should be an officer equal in status to that of an Additional Secretary to the Government of India. He should be chosen for outstanding competence, wide knowledge and experience of cooperation. The choice need not be confined to any one 'service'. He should be a member both of the General Council and of the Board of Management of the Corporation.

Technical and other staff : The Corporation should strengthen itself with adequate staff with the requisite technical knowledge. Besides, it should also maintain panels of qualified technical and consultancy personnel to undertake feasibility studies, to prepare project reports and also to provide technical know-how to the cooperatives.

Research and development cell : Statistics and evaluation constitute a weak link in the administrative set-up of the N.C.D.C. The Corporation should set up a Research and Development Cell, the functions of which will be as indicated in para 6.27.

Regional offices : The present staffing pattern of the regional offices of the N.C.D.C. is inadequate for the discharge of the functions envisaged for the Corporation. Regional Offices should be equipped with the requisite field and technical staff. These offices should function in close coordination with the regional offices of the Reserve Bank of India in the States.

Cadres and panels for cooperatives : In view of the vital importance of staff development for the operational efficiency of the cooperatives, the Corporation should assist the State Governments and cooperatives in building up cadres of key personnel for marketing, processing, supply and storage activities. As the cooperatives find it difficult to locate suitable technical and managerial personnel, it would be of considerable assistance to them, if the Corporation maintains panels of suitable qualified personnel for employment in cooperatives.

Routing of Central Assistance for State Plan Schemes Through the N.C.D.C.

Should central assistance be routed through the N.C.D.C. ? In terms of the existing scheme of release of central assistance to State Governments for State Plan schemes, the N.C.D.C. merely disburses certain amounts to which the State Governments are entitled according to a pre-determined formula. The existing procedure leaves no discretion to the N.C.D.C. to alter the amounts of such assistance or vary the pattern of assistance or determine the individual programmes to which this assistance should flow. In this situation, the N.C.D.C.'s role is more in the nature of a pay office of the Central Government for disbursement of centra assistance to State Government than that of an agency for financing programmes sponsored and promoted by it. No purpose is, therefore, served by routing Central assistance for State Plan scheme through the N.C.D.C. As in the case of other important programmes relating to different Ministries, assistance may be released by way of block loans/grants by the Ministry of Finance for the N.C.D.C.'s schemes also.

Earmarking of funds for cooperation : The outlays on N.C.D.C.'s schemes should not, however, be taken out of the purview of the 'earmarked' sector. The schemes coming under the purview of the N.C.D.C. as also those relating to the Union Department of Cooperation may be grouped together as one unit of the 'earmarked' sector so that the outlays on the inter-related and important programmes of cooperative credit, marketing, processing, etc., are earmarked as a group. The N.C.D.C., through its administrative machinery, should keep itself closely in touch with the preparation of State Plans and also assist the State Governments in the formulation of programmes relating to cooperative marketing, processing, storage, etc., and advise on the outlays to be provided in the State Plans for these schemes. While considering the overall resources for financing these programmes and determining its share of assistance to them, theN.C.D.C. should take into account the provisions made in the State Plans for these schemes.

Legislative Measures : The legislative measures suggested for enlarging the scope of objects and functions of the N.C.D.C., broad-basing the composition of the Corporation so that it functions as a representative and expert body, and for equipping the Corporation financially for its tasks, are :

(i) Besides 'agriculture produce' and 'notified commodities' the scope of the N.C.D.C. Act may be extended to cover dairy, fishery, poultry, forest produce, salt, tobacco, etc. The Central Government may examine whether, within the framework of the Constitution, it is possible to extend the functions of the N.C.D.C. to these activities mentioned above. In this connection, the Central Government may also examine the need for relating the functions of the N.C.D.C. to Entry 33 in the Concurrent List, particularly in the light of the considerations mentioned in paragraphs 8.8 to 8.13.

(ii) The principle that the N.C.D.C. should have its own funds may be incorporated in the Act. For this purpose, provision should be made for annual non-lapsable recurring grants from the Central Government.

(iii) To strengthen the resources of the Corporation, provision may also be made for consolidation of existing loans due from the Corporation to the Central Government and re-scheduling of its repayment; ad-hoc loans and grants from Central Government; borrowings on the guarantee of the Central Government; and availing of assistance from the international financing agencies.

(iv) The N.C.D.C. may be exempted from payment of Income Tax and other taxes on income.

(v) The N.C.D.C. may be notified as a financing institution for obtaining assistance from the IDBI under section 46-C of the RBI Act relating to National Industrial Credit (L.T.O.) Fund. The need for amending the RBI Act to allow N.C.D.C. direct access to this Fund may also be considered.

(vi) Provision may be made on the lines indicated in para 8.16 regarding utilisation of funds by the N.C.D.C.

(vii) The N.C.D.C. may be required to maintain such funds as may be prescribed by the Central Government in consultation with the N.C.D.C.

(viii) Suggestions regarding constitution of a General Council with 45 members, a Board of Management with 11 members and also appointment of President, Vice-President and Chairman of the Board of Management, Managing Director and constitution of Advisory Committee may be incorporated in the Act on the lines suggested in paragraphs 8.18 to 8.21.

(ix) The N.C.D.C. Act may be extended to the State of Jammu and Kashmir.

INDIA, CONSTRUCTION PLANT MACHINERY COMMITTEE, 1970—REPORT

Delhi, Controller of Publications, 1976. 2 Vols.

Chairman : Shri S.P. Chugh

Members : Shri Jagman Singh; Shri Gopala Rao; Shri J.N. Srivastava.

Member-Secretary : Shri M.C. Praharaj

APPOINTMENT

In October, 1953, the Government of India appointed a Committee of engineers to visit some of the projects then under execution and submit its report on the economic and efficient operation and maintenance of the plant and machinery used in construction work of River Valley projects in the country. The Committee submitted its report in February, 1954. Since then a good deal of equipment has been imported but satisfactory utilisation thereof has been hampered for want of spares etc. It is considered necessary to take stock of the position in regard to the equipment available in the country and its optimum utilisation. Accordingly Government of India, the Ministry of Irrigation and Power appointed the Construction Plant Machinery Committee Vide its Memorandum No. 6(5)/69-Policy/Mat. dated October 31, 1970.

TERMS OF REFERENCE

(i) Appraisal of the Construction Plant and Equipment in the country ;

(ii) Assessment regarding level of utilisation of available equipment;

(iii) Reasons for low utilisation of equipment and low efficiency in operation;

(iv) Procedure, system and methods of procurement of spare parts and inventory control;

(v) Remedial measures necessary for improving efficiency in the operation of equipment and for optimum utilisation thereof;

(vi) Requirements of equipment in the Fourth Five Year Plan, import substitution and standardisation;

(vii) Inter-departmental co-ordination in matters

relating to Construction Plant and Equipment with emphasis on inter-departmental transfer of surplus equipment;

(viii) Training of operators and mechanics—Review of adequacy of present arrangements etc.;

(ix) Data on performance of different items of equipment of various categories/makes;

(a) Technical assessment;

(b) Norms for schedules of working hours and life of equipment of various items;

(c) Actual performance of various items of equipment in different projects in various sectors in terms of average annual utilisation and the life usefully spent on different jobs over given periods;

(d) Major repairs and field repairs—Charges over the last ten years, in respect of various items of equipment in terms of;

(1) Spare parts; and

(2) Labour.

(x) Hire charges of equipment;

(xi) Maintenance procedures;

(xii) Organisational set-up, including workshop facilities, stores and warehouses etc.

(xiii) Organisation and functioning of Central Mechanical Units in Irrigation and Power sector and similar other establishments in other sectors;

(xiv) Accounting for the ownership and operating cost per plant hour;

(xv) Recommendations for management, operation and utilisation of construction plant and equipment.

CONTENTS

RECOMMENDATIONS

Planning

Project Planning : Technical approval of a project estimate should be followed by finalisation of design details, financial estimates and scheduling of the programme of work itemwise and in an integrated manner. For this to be properly accomplished, there should be a time interval between the approval of a project estimate and the commencement of work. A minimum period of one year should be provided on this account. A very clear view be taken initially of properly coordinating and integrating all resources for planning and scheduling of work.

All technical details relating to work should be finalised in a thorough manner at the inception of the job. This should include job specification requirements individually for items of works involved, considering the climatic conditions—length of construction season or operational season, topography, characteristics of the materials to be handled.

The mode of execution of work—either departmentally or through private agencies, should be clearly decided upon in advance.

Plant Planning : The task of plant planning should be as detailed and meticulous as the project planning.

A master plan of borrow areas and haul roads be prepared initially treating this subject as important as the basic plant planning exercise, so that safety of operations and minimum cycle time of operations by motorised equipment on production job can be ensured.

Adequate provision should be made for the construction plant and facilities for execution of the work according to the planned/phased programmes, as scheduled.

The complexity and character of the work to be performed should be carefully considered, so that radical changes are not necessitated in the course of execution of work as it progresses.

Selection of equipment, by type and numbers, should be based on economy in methods of work relative to job conditions and intensity of use, maintenance and repair costs, facilities required, standardisation etc., etc.

Scaling of requirements of equipment should be based on rational factors of availability and utilisation.

Provision of standby equipment, assemblies, sub-assemblies and components should also make an important consideration, both for determining the total quantum of equipment to be employed on the job and the facilities to be created for maintenance and repairs. The main guiding factor should, however, be least investment, optimum utilisation and maximum possible productivity of machines for economy in production cost.

On the plant planning exercise initially completed, a second opinion should be taken before the financial estimate is prepared.

Plant drawings should be prepared in proper details in designing the lay-out. As far as possible, these should be prepared on standard sized sheets properly titled, dated and numbered, to facilitate reference.

Design criteria and structure design calculations shall be recorded and preserved.

Workshops and Facilities : Adequate provision should be made in the project cost estimate to meet the cost of workshops—buildings, equipment and facilities.

Initial planning of workshops at the stage of formulation of project reports should cover all details regarding items and types of work to be done, the maximum work load possible to arise in respect of each, the pattern of maintenance and repair of equipment whether centralised or an area maintenance basis or a combination of both, and the extent to which work will be got done by outside agencies and the amount of investment that can be made.

A clear plan should be developed of the lay out of the shops by listing out the type of repair work, servicing and maintenance operations to be assigned to shops commensurate with the number and type of machines, plant and equipment to be maintained and serviced, and the load of manufacturing activities. Further room for expansion and flexibility of operation inside the shops should be provided for.

The type and sizes of the workshop buildings should be decided upon with due consideration to climatic conditions, geographical location etc. Clear provision should be made for drainage facilities, parking spaces, storage of raw materials, equipment awaiting work in the shops, repaired equipment awaiting delivery to the users etc.

Adequate material handling facilities should be provided both inside the shops and the open space outside.

The location of the shops should be decided upon by preparing a clear plan of the operational activities which will be served thereby.

Size of the shop should be determined by the type of equipment, components, assemblies that will be put to repairs. Provision should also be made for storage of the components, parts and assemblies and for the fitters'/Workmen benches. There should be no congestion of the work space.

Properly laid service roads, stabilized shop floors to suit the type and size of the equipment that will move over it, should be provided.

The area maintenance shops should be located as near to the scene of operation as possible. Good access roads should be provided.

Creation of adequate facilities in advance for maintenance, repair, storage and care taking of the equipment in the interim period, between the time of its receipt and actual commissioning on the job, should be a prerequisite.

Plant equipment assembly yard should be provided for, as near as possible, to the main workshops for assembly and initial commissioning of all plant and equipment, except those which, by virtue of their type, size, mobility etc., have to be assembled/commissioned on the job as close as possible to the point of application.

Stores and warehouses : Store room and warehouse facilities should be located adjoining the maintenance shops.

Receiving areas in the warehouses should be provided separately with sufficient space to accommodate mechanical handling and loading and unloading operations.

Specific attention should be paid to provide a proper building for storage of tyres, tubes and other rubber materials.

Slow moving and heavy parts which are treated with preservatives, or on which weather has no adverse effect, should be stored in the open.

Procurement of equipment and spare parts : The programme for procurement of equipment should be so planned that it would be physically available for production work on schedule. However, the time table should be so framed that the equipment does not have to lie idle for long for want of work.

Initial supply of spare parts, sufficient for running and maintenance of the machines for 2000 to 3000 working hours should be ensured. Procurement action should be suitably finalised for this to be so.

Supply of filters for maintenance of the machines should be arranged with the machine for a minimum 2000 hours work.

Information on scale of consumption of spare parts

relative to the type, make and category of machine/s to be purchased, should be obtained from projects/departments where such equipment had been in use previously, unless such information is available otherwise. This should be used for a guide line for procurement of spare parts for initial supply.

The procurement of spare parts and provisioning should be done with due consideration to the population of equipment of one type, make and category, and its intensity of use, whether single shift or multi-shift operations.

Operation

Schedules : In defining the annual schedules for operation of equipment, the effort should not be to scale down the figures because of certain persistent occurrences, which take away a part of the available working time; but instead corrective action should be planned for minimising such losses in time.

The working conditions shold be under constant examination and review in order that the operational efficiency of the machine is not impaired.

Requisite conveniences and facilities which help promote efficiency of Operators, should be provided in a liberal manner.

Unless certain physical limitations come in the way of working the schedules of working hours should be framed on the basis of two shifts or three shifts per day.

Utilisation : Utmost efforts should be made for optimum utilisation of equipment. However, maximum utilisation should not be taken as an index of maximum productivity of machines. Progressive review should be made of cycle time of operation of each type of equipment on the job, through organised 'time and method studies' so that the delay factors are removed from the cycle time, the minimum possible and the production the maximum possible. This should set the level of utilisation expected from the machines.

The aim for level of utilisation should be set at a minimum of 70 per cent of scheduled hours.

For improvement in utilisation of equipment, the defect analysis (the defects which account for downtime of equipment) should be made and corrective actions taken to reduce the incidence of breakdowns.

Transport and Communication System : Meticulous attention should be paid to haul-road constructions and maintenance. Sufficiently wide roads, with proper subgrades, smooth surface—properly moist, easy gradients and easy curves and bends, should be provided for attaining safe maximum speeds by motorised equipment.

For excavating equipment, the borrow areas should be made even and clean with the use of proper equipment.

For convenience of expeditious communication, wireless sets, radio net work, telephone lines etc., should be provided where motorised equipment is spread over a fairly wide expanse of area under operational activity.

Maintenance

The work of maintenance of equipment should be assigned to a senior, qualified and experienced officer, who is fully acquainted with the machines to be maintained. The organisation under his charge should similarly include experienced and skilled hands.

Competent senior operators with long-standing experience in operation of the machines on the job, should be employed on maintenance work.

Unskilled labour strength should be brought to the minimum and inefficient maintenance staff removed from the maintenance activity based on proper evaluation of maintenance effectiveness (in terms of availability of equipment and cost incurred on maintenance).

A minimum number of brands and grades of greases and oils should be put to use for the lubrication of various machines at the site of work.

Maintenance charts be displayed at suitable locations in the maintenance area based on recommendations made in the operation and maintenance manuals relative to the machines in use.

Printed forms based on recommendations made in the manuals, stipulating the tasks to be performed at defined intervals of time such as 50 hrs., 100 hrs., 200 hrs., 250 hrs., 500 hrs., 1000 hrs., etc., should be used for recording the maintenance activities performed.

Adequate facilities should be created for maintenance and repairs to equipment. Provision of hand tools and other handling facilities, which would cut down the overall time in maintenance/repair of equipment should be provided.

Preventive maintenance : Preventive maintenance should be given the prime attention and the importance it deserves. The responsibility for preventive maintenance should be assigned exclusively to a senior officer.

Record keeping : Proper record keeping should be organised. This should be looked after by senior persons—engineers, and should not be left entirely to the clerical staff.

Compilation of performance data on production and costs, shall be made by creating proper records under the direct supervision of an engineer, so that corrective actions, if any necessary (based on analysis of the information so recorded), can be taken for improvement in utilisation, productivity and reduction in costs in various segments of work.

Procedures : For effective control in execution of the maintenance work, a clear chart shall be prepared defining "Who", "What", "Where" and "How" of the maintenance activity to be performed.

Wherever the total spread of equipment and the number of machines to be maintained in a given span of time so warrant, mobile/field servicing/maintenance units should be provided.

Training : Periodical refresher courses for the operators, mechanics and maintenance crews should be conducted and systematic training programme for the new recruits will be organised.

Repairs

The work in the main repair shops should be subdivided according to the functional requirements so as to accomplish concurrent repairs of components and assemblies for expeditious completion of the repair of any given machine.

Where major repairs are to be carried out at the site of work, functionally designed mobile repair shops mounted on trucks and equipped with full complement of tools etc., should be provided.

(a) In the process of repairs to equipment, the disassembling and reassembling of the parts/components from sub-assemblies, main-assemblies and the machine should be done according to instructions given in the shop manuals for the particular item of equipment under repairs.

A blue-print showing the important measurements, fits and tolerances to be observed in re-assembling of parts/compnents in sub-assemblies, and main assemblies should be prepared and displayed at suitable locations, in the repair shops for reference by the repair crew, the Chargemen and the Foremen inspecting the work.

(b) Printed Check Lists, listing items of check at stage inspections by supervisors, should be used. These should be recorded in the History Book of the machine/assembly/sub-asssembly etc.

(c) Observations should be recorded after inspection of the machine/assemblies/sub-assemblies at the time of overhaul of machines and comparative study made with similar observations made on inspection of the machine at the time of preceding overhaul.

(d) Such record should be created and maintained by competent hands of the rank of Foreman/Assistant Foreman and should be continually reviewed by the engineer in charge.

(e) Special notice be taken of repetitive type breakdowns and premature wear on components indicated by analysis of information in the Inspection Sheets and corrective actions taken to reduce the incidence in future.

(f) Cost of repairs should be evaluated and recorded after every repair/overhaul; and this should also be subjected to regular review at periodical intervals, from standpoint of economy.

(g) Arrangements for testing of individual assemblies and sub-assemblies after repair and overhaul should be organised where the volume of work involved is heavy.

(h) Tests and trials of repaired equipment should be assigned to a competent hand and all necessary adjustment, in various systems of the machines properly made before the equipment is recommissioned on the job.

(i) Only skilled, qualified and trained persons should be assigned the repair work. The unskilled labour should be employed for handling work only.

Spare Parts

Indenting : Indents/Requisitions for procurement of spare parts should be prepared by experienced engineers who are well acquainted with the technical design and construction features of the machines, their operation, maintenance and repair.

Scaling of requirement should be based upon the record of consumption in the past, the history of performance, of machine/s, the immediate requirements based on observations after inspection regarding wear and tear of the parts and components etc., and the period of time—stage in the age of the machine; for which the spare parts would be required.

For indents to be processed through DGS and D, a clear scrutiny be made of the questionnaire in the Check List to make sure that all the information has been included/given properly in the prescribed indent form to avoid any back reference from the DGS and D.

Procurement : (a) To ensure timely availability of required spare parts, forward planning should be done with due consideration to the lead time involved in procurement—the total time from the stage of framing of the requisition to the point of physical delivery of the spare parts in the stores.

(b) Processing of requisitions/indents for procurement should be done at regular intervals of time—preferably on half-yearly basis.

(c) In processing the indents/requisitions, details of items and quantities on order and the stock position in respect of each, should be first checked up and accounted for and procurement action then taken for the balance items/quantities.

(d) For procurement against DGS and D Rate Contracts, proper evaluation should be made initially of the items that shall have to be imported by the supplier, so that delivery schedules can be suitably fixed and necessary arrangements made for obtaining the Actual Users' Import Licence in case the import is not against the suppliers' own licence.

(e) For time bound programmes of construction work, the project estimates should indicate the cost of spare parts which will be purchased in the service life of the machines thereon.

(f) Annual budget estimates should be framed for purchase of spare parts covering requirements of the period corresponding to the lead time of procurement.

Rate contracts : (a) The DGS and D may examine the reasons why the Rate Contract holders cannot stick to the delivery schedules, furnish price-lists of goods ordered against rate contracts and expedite finalisation of rate contracts.

(b) In verifying the competence of any firm in respect of rate contracts for indigenous items, a more meticulous check may be exercised in indentifying the established facilities, technical know-how on part of the manufacturing concerns, the research, development and design setup available with them, and the goods being actually manufactured by them at the time of the new items of spare parts are planned for manufacture by them.

(c) The DGS and D may consider to introduce a system of review of performance of rate contracts based on annual drawals. If the value of such drawals is below a certain expected minimum, the reasons for such performance may be gone into; and, if necessary, continuance or otherwise of the rate contract in operation should be examined, in case the reasons indicate any serious drawbacks in the quality of goods, service of the rate contract holder etc., etc.

(d) The consignee's copy of the invoice or despatch note should include the unit price and the total value against each item covered therein.

Inventory control : (a) Each major user of equipment should establish a scientific inventory control system. A separate Cell should be created for effective implementation thereof.

(b) Scale of consumption of items of spare parts other materials should be developed and established for guidance of the indenting departments.

(c) For convenience of inter-departmental and intra-departmental coordination in matters relating to equipment and specially that relating to exchange of information on availability of spare parts for different items of equipment, a codified list should be developed for classifying like items of equipment for preparation of inventories of spare parts atleast for high value items.

Scale of provision : (a) Based on the guidelines given in Appendix 8.7 a scale of provision (by value) of spare parts for given types, makes and categories of machines should be lined out taking into account the intensity of use of equipment and the job severity factors.

(b) Until such time there is larger population of indigenous epuipment in the country and the imported equipment ages out to the point of its replacement by indigenous equipment, liberal sanction of foreign exchange be issued for importing maintenance and repair parts.

Obsolescence : In framing a value estimate for the total cost of spare parts for the service life of the equipment on the job, provision should be made upto 5.7 per cent of the value figure towards likely cost of obsolete/ dead stock items of spare parts which may not find any use or resale ultimately.

This provision should also be taken into account in evaluating the inventory holding costs for purposes of determining the issue rates, wherever this system is in use.

Review of inventory of spare parts : Perpetual review of inventory of spare parts should be made a normal feature of the work with the stores organisation. Action to discard items which are physically deteriorated and useless, and disposing of items which are surplus to the requirements, should be taken after such review.

Foreign Exchange : Timely arrangements should be made by the sponsoring authorities for foreign exchange allocations so that import of spare parts is not delayed on this account.

The users of equipment should ensure timely processing of import licence applications, completing these in a satisfactory manner so as to avoid back references from the application processing authorities.

Value limit for import of spare parts against emergency licence should be increased from 0.1 per cent to 1 per cent of value of equipment.

Manuals/catalogues of spare parts : (a) Care should be taken to have a master record of all spare parts catalogues at a central place for all makes and models of machines/plant in use. Besides the central holding, the spare parts catalogues should also be available with each Division/sub-Division in charge of the items of machines.

(b) Arrangements should be made with the suppliers of equipment/manufacturers to supply copies of bulletins/service sheets indicating changes in part numbers or additions and alterations in the original parts catalogues in relation to particular makes and models of machines. Copies of manuals/catalogues should be complete and kept updated all the time.

Accounting

Itemised costs : (a) To simplify the procedure of accounting, a list should be developed giving Code Numbers for the items of expenditure in relation to ownership and operating costs of machines. To develop such a list for the benefit of those who are not already using the system, help should be taken from the management institutes in the country.

(b) The items of expenditure should be properly identified so that accounting thereof helps directly in estimation of costs of future works, evaluating the actual costs for purposes of job control and subsequent estimation, and provides necessary data and analysis relative to subject of 'Equipment Economics'.

Cost evaluation : (a) Grouping of items of expenditure should be so arranged that it facilitates assessment of the unit cost of work and a comparative study of the estimated cost and actual cost not only of the work as a whole, but of the individual items of cost also.

(b) Figures of annual expenditure and cumulative expenditure (1) maintenance and repairs and (2) depreciation cost, for a machine/group of machines of the same make and model, should be readily available through accounts records.

Method of accounting : With the exception of depreciation which should be accounted for as an item of ownership cost, all other elements of the cost of machines should be treated as operating costs or running and maintenance costs.

Repair costs should be classified under one head only without making a distinction between field repairs/running repairs/minor repairs and major repairs.

To gauge more accurately the costs of repairs to the machine, the machine should be broken up into systems/components—power unit, clutch, transmission, final drive, crawler tracks, etc. The intensity of wear and tear on parts, in individual components/systems, can be sized up better by such analysis.

Depreciation costs should be accounted for annually based on 'Declining Balance Method of Depreciation'. The life of equipment for depreciation purposes should be fixed in number of years and the rate of depreciation should be selected commensurate with the pattern of work in one shift, two shifts, or three shifts per day.

(a) The item of 'Spare Parts' should be distinctly identified by a proper classification in a separate sub-head under head 'Stock Suspense'.

Reserve limits for stocks should be defined on annual basis at the beginning of each accounting year.

(b) For commercial undertakings and public enterprises, spare parts should be classified under a separate head distinct from general stock items.

There should be no arbitrary shifting of costs from items showing cost over-runs to items showing cost under-runs, to present apparent balance with 'Control Estimate'.

Arbitrary advance lump-sum distribution of expenses which tend to minimise accounting efforts, but distort current cost accounts by over-writing the cost of items not yet used on works, or to reckon amount of expenditure on national basis, should be avoided.

Meticulous care should be taken to maintain proper records in relation to costs, consumption of POL and materials and expenditure on labour.

Preparation of the record and analysis of costs should be done by competent hands and in time. Delay in accounting for the cost of different levels, would always give a distorted picture hence, promptness should be ensured in accordance with a predetermined time-table.

Hire charges : To safeguard against the burden of idle depreciation due to machines lying idle for certain periods without being given on rent, practice as indicated in Chapter 9 should be adopted to provide for the additional charges.

There should be uniformity in the basis of assessment of rental rates or hire charges of earthmoving machines and construction equipment.

Straight-line Method of Depreciation should be adopted for calculating the hire charges. No salvage value is to be considered in such cases.

To safeguard against idle depreciation due to under-utilisation of machines given on hire, basic minimum charges for defined periods of loan of equipment should be fixed.

Training

Enrolment of trained operators and mechanics for operation, maintenance and repair of equipment, should be pre-arranged, so that the machines are not assigned to unskilled hands or those do not have to wait idle for want of skilled personnel.

In-service training programmes for training of maintenance and repair crew should be organised.

Uniformity should be introduced in the syllabi of training in all training establishments and institutions.

Recruitment of trainees for operators and mechanics should be made from amongst the I.T.I. qualified personnel, or Diploma holders in Mechanical Engineering.

A Governing Body be constituted, comprised of representatives, one each from the Mining Sector, Irrigation and Power Sector, the rest of the users of equipment, Planning Commission, Directorate General of Employment and Training (Ministry of Labour,

Employment and Rehabilitation) for formulating and directing the training programmes of the training establishments and institutions.

In order to make the project/States authorities in the Irrigation and Power Sector partners with the CW and PC/Ministry of Irrigation and Power, in the matter of organising the training programmes, provision should be made in the project estimates from one-fourth of one per cent to one-half of one per cent, of the estimated cost of the project, for training purposes. 50% of this provision could be used for in-service-training on the project and the balance could provide funds for contribution to the Technical Training Centres for training the sponsored nominees of the projects/States.

The Training Centres should be manned by persons of the rank of Joint Directors and engineers, assisted further by skilled Foremen and Mechanics.

The Equipment and facilities in the existing Technical Training Centres of the CW and PC should be suitably remodelled so as to have equipment of more recent origin, the like of which is currently in use on projects. The method of training should be suitably reoriented by introducing short-term courses (of 3 months' duration) for operators' training (Specialised Operator for individual categories of machines) and long-term courses (of 12-15 months' duration) for training mechanics.

The personnel supervising the operations of equipment should be suitably trained. The training of the executives should be such as to make them clearly understand the functions of planning, execution and review, in relation to specific positions held by them. The Foremen, Chargemen, Supervisors and Overseers should also be similarly trained so that the 'How', and 'Why' of a job can be clearly understood by them.

Senior officers managing equipment operations and utilisation shall be trained in net work techniques so that planning and scheduling of construction programmes and operations and utilisation of equipment could be properly achieved.

Supervisors and executive officers should be deputed by various organisations making intensive use of construction plant and equipment for training in "Construction Plant Planning, Administration and Maintenance "on major projects in the country. This training shall be on the same lines as was programmed in the past under the US AID Participants' Programme of training in U.S.A.

For this purpose, about six major projects where the work is being performed efficiently (this will include irrigation and power projects, mining projects and road construction projects) should be identified from time to time and the list circulated to all major users of equipment (Central/State Government Departments, commercial undertakings and public enterprises etc).

The syllabi prescribed for Engineering Courses in the Technical Institutes and Universities should additionally cover the following subjects :

(a) Construction methods and techniques.
(b) Selection of equipment for given job applications.
(c) Planning of equipment for better production and economy in end cost.
(d) Maintenance Engineering.
(e) Equipment Economics.

Standardisation

The term "Standardisation" should be given the required amount of importance it deserves. The economy resulting from standardisation should be properly evaluated not only relative to the selection of equipment for its first purchase, but also to all other aspects which get involved in management, operation and utilisation of machines.

A clear policy about the makes and sizes of machines in different categories and makes of their power units should be laid down at the time of first bulk purchase of equipment for the project in the event of procurement in stages.

Bulk purchase of equipment of new makes should be resorted to only after (i) proper tests and trials are conducted initially on these machines by importing a small number into the country and (ii) the technical modifications on the design and construction features that may be indicated by the tests, are properly carried out.

Coordination

For proper management of construction plant and equipment working on a number of projects, in a State, in a sector, or in a given public enterprise, a central organisation/coordinating agency be established for pooling and controlling the resources and to collect, compile and disseminate important information on equipment, with a view to promoting higher standard of efficiency and better utilisation.

For this to be achieved, these coordinating agencies be actively associated with the functions of, planning the overall requirement of construction plant and machinery; procurement of machinery; introducing inventory control methods; creating a proper record of census of machinery; history of performance; cost evaluation; norms and standards of production by equipment; consumption of materials; planning for major repairs and reconditioning of equipment; transfer of machinery from one project to another within the organisation or outside; establishing liaison and coordination with other coordinating agencies in different departments/sectors in the matter of record of performance of equipment; scale of consumption of parts, methods of work with machines, recruitment and training of operating and maintenance staff etc.

(a) A Standing Committee for Equipment Planning be constituted under the aegis of the Ministry of Irrigation and Power with representatives of major users of construction plant and equipment in the country as members, to coordinate with Departments/Ministries concerned with important matters of common interest, such as import substitution, indigenous manufacture of equipment and spare parts, Import Trade Control policy and procedures, procurement/purchase of equipment and spare parts, etc.

The Committee shall function as an associate technical body for the Plant Planning Committees of major projects/sectors making large scale use of construction plant and equipment.

The Committee shall review periodically, the performance data of equipment, norms and standards for life of equipment, maintenance and repair costs and other cost elements for study of Equipment Economics, and framing equipment replacement policies.

(b) For the function of plant planning, the Plant Planning Directorate of CW & PC will be represented on the Committee and will provide the secretariat service.

(c) For the function of data evaluation and cost evaluation etc., and for other matters of common interest to all users of equipment, the Coordination Cell of the CW & PC will provide necessary assistance to the Committee.

In the Irrigation and Power Sector, the States where the Central Mechanical Units have not been established, or where these are operating as nucleus organisations, should take necessary steps to establish fulfledged units at the earliest.

In order that the Central Mechanical Units perform the assigned functions in an effective manner, considering the amount of equipment working in individual States as at present (barring a few), the officer/s manning the Central Mechanical Units in major States should be of the rank of "Chief Engineer". The functional distribution of work would generally be on the pattern given in Appendix 12·5.

To provide a proper forum for exchange of views on part of major users of equipment in various sectors, on important matters relating to equipment selection, operation, maintenance, utilisation, cost evaluation etc. Equipment Seminars should be organised on annual basis by the Equipment Planning Committee.

Disposal Rehabilitation of Surplus Equipment and Spare Parts

Equipment should not be retained longer than necessary on projects/works. Advance planning should be made for rehabilitation/disposal of surplus equipment.

The Central Coordinating Agency for a State in a sector, or in an Undertaking, should be assigned the work of rehabilitation/disposal of surplus equipment. Prior clearance should be taken from this Coordinating Agency regarding non-availability of the required items before these are purchased from the open market.

Import Substitution

Equipment : The manufacturers should augment the manufacturing programmes under execution or projected to be executed, so that imports of the machines covered by the programme do not become inevitable.

To give an impetus to import substitution, timely forecast of requirements of equipment by the needy users in the country is necessary. They should help the equipment manufacturers by placing their indents of equipment on them at least 12 to 18 months in advance of the actual requirement on the job.

In relation to inevitable imports of equipment resulting from imbalance between demand and supply, specially when emergent/urgent requirements of equipment arise, it should be the policy to import equipment which is similar or identical to the equipment being manufactured in the country. This will help at least in conserving a part of the foreign exchange required to import subsequently the spare parts etc., for maintenance and repair of equipment.

(a) The manufacturers and the users of equipment should coordinate with each other in enhancing the scope of manufacture, by identifying additional items of machines for which the generated potential of demand is substantial.

(b) The Standing Committee on Equipment Planning (defined at 99(a)—Coordination) should be the liaison agency for all major users of equipment and the manufacturers for market survey to determine the potential of requirement of new items of machines.

Spare Parts : To promote import substitution in respect of spare parts, the Co-ordinating Agencies in various Sectors/with various organisations, should work together in identifying the particular items which do not involve complex processes of production—technically or metallurgywise and for which the potential of requirement is substantial for economy in production costs.

Until such time a major portion of the available imported equipment in use in the country is discarded from operational activity, annual sanctions of foreign exchange for import of spare parts for equipment should be sustained at adequate level.

(a) The DGTD, the DGS & D and the Coordination Cell in CW & PC should work together in identifying the manufacturers who would undertake the manufacture of defined items of spare parts identified for import substitution.

(b) Similar effort should be made by the major users of equipment and their Central Coordinating Agencies to which they are affiliated.

(a) While planning the manufacture of spare parts on private firms, a clear evaluation be done of the resources, facilities, technical know-how and the experience on their part so that the resultant product is of standard quality acceptable to all.

(b) Even if in some cases, working drawings and specifications of the items to be manufactured are to be obtained from the primary manufacturers abroad on payment, this should be arranged provided the potential of requirement is large enough to warrant such payment.

Indigenous manufacture—Equipment : Unless the items of equipment selected for manufacture are those, which have been previously in use in the country and whose performance has been found to be satisfactory, a prototype should be imported for rigorous tests and trials for technically evaluating its standard of performance before it is accepted for manufacture in the country. Such selection of equipment for indigenous manufacture may be done in association with the Standing Committee for Equipment Planning.

For optimum utilisation of equipment within the very first two years of its commissioning on the job, adequate supply of spare parts should be ensured by the indigenous manufacturers. Since this will also involve imported items of spare parts, restrictions on the import of such parts for initial supply with the machines should be relaxed as far as possible, unless the indigenous sources are clearly identified to have been properly established and in production by the manufacturers or by the ancillary industry.

Indigenous manufacture—Spare parts : The spare parts catalogues should clearly identify either the imported items or indigenous items to facilitate expeditious processing of indents/orders for spare parts.

The service organisations of the manufacturers should develop a system of collection of information from the users of their equipment regarding scale of consumption of atleast high value items of spare parts, commensurate with the size of fleet of equipment in operation at individual locations to afford guidance in sizing up the indents of spare parts on forward planning basis in a more precise manner.

After-Sales-Service : The manufacturers of equipment, through their service organisations, should organise dispensing of spare parts on 'stock and sale' basis. This alone will help in reducing the size of the inventory of spare parts for indigenous equipment with individual users and thereby curtail the amount of investment blocked up in slow moving items in the inventory.

They should establish a scientific inventory control system for sizing up the inventory of spare parts for stocking purposes.

The service organisations of the equipment manufacturers should be properly developed to help the users of equipment to sort out their problems with respect to operation and utilisation of equipment.

Research and Development : The manufacturers should evolve an effective system for 'feed-back' of information relating to performance of equipment, assemblies, sub-assemblies, components and parts. They should establish close liaison between the service organisation and production department through the Research and Development Section.

The research and development organisation of the manufacturers of indigenous equipment, besides making research for improvements in the design-system of the machines based on experience of the equipment users in the field, should also make a continuous advancement in the technical front to make the machines more productive at lesser maintenance and repair costs.

Management

Organisation : Management of operation, maintenance and utilisation of equipment should be so organised that the planning and execution of work is a smooth and coordinated process for effective control on production and economy in cost. The organisation should be well-knit for a coordinated effort and frictionless working amongst all levels of management on the job.

For proper management, operation and utilisation of equipment, the functional control on operation, servicing, repair etc., of equipment shall be assigned to one suitable organisation only on unitary control basis, under an Equipment Manager.

An efficient maintenance materials management organisation should form a vital part in the whole organisation so that equipment is not laid off in absence of some vital supply of parts etc.

The size of the organisation and the type of administrative control (defining the line of heirarchy) shall be determined by the size of the fleet of equipment value-wise.

For functional control of large-sized fleets of equipment concentrated at single locations, the distribution of work will be so made that specialisation and economy in investment costs can be achieved besides ensuring least expenditure in repairs and better quality of repair and maintenance work.

Improvement methods : For evolving methods of improvement in operation, utilisation and productivity of machines, a separate Cell for carrying out 'Time and Methods' studies should be organised by every large scale user of equipment well in advance.

For proper planning and scheduling of works, use of 'CPM' and 'PERT' which make the modern methods of planning, should be extensively made.

The progress reporting system should be so laid down that review of performance is made for introducing improvements in operations and achieving cost effectiveness.

Incentives : Suitable incentive schemes be introduced for increase in production simultaneously ensuring the proper upkeep, maintenance and repair of equipment on sustained basis. The benefits of the incentive schemes should cover and accrue to every person who is a member of the team, contributing increments in production and safe, continuous and economic working of equipment.

Where the job is of large magnitude entailing employment of large fleet of equipment and heavy investment, use of computors electronic data processing equipment should be considered.

To broaden the perspective and keep abreast with the latest trends in respect of construction jobs, plant and machinery in use, improved techniques of maintenance and operation in advanced countries, a joint team consisting of senior engineer-managers from the Irrigation and Power Sector, Mining Sector, principal manufacturers, should be sent abroad periodically.

INDIA, COMMITTEE ON UNEMPLOYMENT, 1970—REPORT

Delhi, Controller of Publications, 1974. 410p.

Chairman : Shri B. Bhagavati.

Members : Shri Jyotirmoy Bosu; Shri V.L. Gidwani; Shri Man Mohan Singh; Shri K. Balachandran; Shri M. Anandam; Shri Ashok Mitra; Shri Gautam Mathur; Shri R.K. Sinha; Shri J.S. Tilak; Shri Charanjit Yadav, Shri J.C. Mathur replaced by Shri M. Ramakrishnayya. He too was replaced by I.J. Naidu; Shri D.N. Banerjee was replaced by Shri B.C. Ganguli and he too was replaced by M.M. Kasuri who was also replaced by Shri J.C. Talukdar. He too was replaced by Shri B.R. Gupta; Shri N. Sundaram was replaced by Shri G.L. Shukla who was also replaced by Shri N.V. Krishnan.

Member-Secretary : Shri N. S. Pandey.

APPOINTMENT

The problem of unemployment and under-employment in the country has been causing serious concern to the Government in recent years. Great concern was expressed in Parliament and outside at the deteriorating situation in the country in respect of unemployment, particularly in the wake of the unprecedented severe droughts of 1965-66 and 1966-67, and of the subsequent serious industrial recession which afflicted the economy during two years (1966-68). During discussions on a non-official resolution brought by Shri Jyotirmoy Bosu, M.P. in the Lok Sabha in November, 1969, the Government of India indicated its intention to appoint a Committee to assess the extent of the problem in all its dimensions and facets and to suggest suitable remedial measures.

The Committee was accordingly appointed by the Government of India with the Department of Labour and Employment Resolution No. M.P.-10(110)/69 dated December 19, 1970, to assess the extent of unemployment and under-employment and to suggest remedial measures.

TERMS OF REFERENCE

(i) To assess the extent of unemployment and under-employment in all its aspects, taking into account the recommendations made by the Committee of Experts on Unemployment Estimates set-up by the Planning Commission under the Chairmanship of Prof. M.L. Dantwala;

(ii) To recommend the directions in which the programmes included in the Fourth Five Year Plan could be made more employment oriented in their implementation, with due regard to their timely execution, economy and productivity and to the requirements of rapid economic development;

(iii) To suggest suitable strategies for employment generation, both short-term and long-term, including technical, financial and fiscal measures in respect of different sectors of the economy, taking into account the mobility of labour and the openings for employment and self-employment in the tertiary sector as a result of implementation of plan programmes and various measures initiated by the Government for activating the economy ;

(iv) To suggest specific programmes for promoting productive employment and self-employment of the educated unemployed in general and the unemployed technical personnel such as engineers, technicians, etc. in particular and to suggest measures to rectify the imbalance between the outturn of educated and technical persons on the one hand and the available employment opportunities on the other and

(v) To suggest a suitable machinery at the Centre and State level for a continuous appraisal of the changing employment and manpower situation and assessment of long-term demand and supply.

CONTENTS

Introduction; Background of the Problem; Some Basic issues; Dimensions of the Problem; Plan Programmes; Strategies for Employment Generation; Agriculture and Allied Occupation; Industry; Education and Training; Machinery for Continuous Appraisal; Summary of Main Conclusions and Recommendations —Minutes of Dissent and Supplementation; List of Abbreviations; Appendices from I to XXXII.

RECOMMENDATIONS

The dimensions of the problem

The concepts and definitions of employment and unemployment which are in use in the 27th round of the NSS conform as closely as practicable to the recommendations of the Dantwala Committee on this point and they may be sufficient for our present needs. We would, however, emphasise that in a dynamic situation there can be no finality about the concepts and definitions of employment, unemployment and under-employment and the subject has to be reviewed at suitable intervals, so that while comparability is maintained as far as possible, the changing conditions and requirements of the users of data can be taken note of and satisfied by suitable modifications in the concepts where considered necessary.

It will be useful to lay emphasis, in any scheme of disaggregation of estimates relating to different aspects of the labour force, on the social, cultural and economic factors affecting the population as also the aspirations and job preferences of the unemployed and under-employed.

There is scope for further and more frequent studies to determine various characteristics of the labour force, for example, the following :—

(i) the demographic characteristics of different segments of the labour force;

(ii) the educational attainments and other professional and technical training or experience;

(iii) their present state of employment and its assessment with reference to the above background; and

(iv) their attitude towards employment, the cultural conditioning and inhibitions, if any.

For obtaining some of the data required for disaggregated estimates of employment and unemployment, it will be necessary to undertake special type studies. A few suggestions which could be taken note of in organising such surveys and studies have been made.

There is a need for assessing the impact of changes in socio-economic conditions and the emergence of new technology on unemployment and under-employment so as to formulate the programmes of employment on a more realistic basis.

Preparations should be made to face the situation resulting from changes in technology as it develops through the institution of short-term orientation courses which could be organised on the basis of needs as indicated by local studies, so as to enable a large majority of the affected workers to become absorbed into new types of employment.

There is a need for more specific and extensive studies regarding the casual factors which influence the participation rates of different groups of the population.

We consider that the decennial census with its countrywide organisation and its long traditions is an important source of data and that it should continue to be utilised to the extent possible, particularly in view of the importance of obtaining adequate data on the problem of unemployment.

We have combined the data on 'workers' and 'perons seeking work' from the 1961 Census and compared them with the total of the three groups, namely, 'workers', 'non-workers' with secondary activity and 'other non-workers' from the 1971 Census which taken together may reasonably represent those persons who constitute the labour force. It is seen that the percentage of the labour force to the total population estimated on this basis for the country as a whole was 34.6 in 1971 as against the corresponding percentage of 43.3 according to the 1961 Census. This difference includes partly the real change over the decades as well as the variation due to the different concepts and definitions adopted in the two censuses.

Sample studies on the registrants on the live registers of employment exchanges in association with the NSS enquiries can give valuable information for the assessment of unemployment from these live register data, since the technical ratios estimated in this behalf through an earlier survey undertaken by the DGE & T in 1968 cannot be used now with confidence because of the limitations of these ratios including the coverage, the limited size of the sample and the lapse of several years during which the coverage and popularity of registration have increased considerably.

We feel that the persons who work for less than 14 hours a week could appropriately be treated as requiring full-time employment. In our view, therefore, the estimates of the unemployed should include the persons who are wholly unemployed as well as those who have work for less than 14 hours in a week. From the NSS data in respect of the 19th round, information regarding the percentage of the unemployed as well as that of the workers having less than 14 hours of work per week is available. Applying these percentages to the 1971 population, we are of the view, that the likely number of unemployed persons in 1971 may reasonably be taken as 18.7 million, including 9.0 million who are unemployed and 9.7 million who work for less than 14 hours a week and who may be treated on a par with the unemployed. These would include 16.1 million persons in rural areas (7.6 million males and 8.5 million females) and 2.6 million persons in urban areas (1.6 million males and 1.0 million females). These figures can only very roughlyindicate the dimensions of the problem.

The following suggestions for a few measures which will be of help in a better assessment of unemployment and under-employment have been made :—

(i) The decennial census of the population should attempt to obtain broad data on employment and unemployment according to meaningful concepts so as to provide base line information about the working population and its distribution by sex, education, industry, occupation, etc. including the availability for work of those who are currently not working, as well as its classification by other socio-economic conditions.

(ii) While there may be no finality with regard to the concepts and definitions of employment, unemployment and under-employment efforts should be made to keep the main concepts reasonably stable and to maintain the comparability of the results as far as possible by adopting a suitable classification of the data collected so as to reflect the changes in the concepts.

(iii) The NSS should undertake every five years, full scale surveys into employment, under-employment and unemployment, including data on the per capita income and expenditure levels of house-holds, so as to assess the employment situation in relation to suitably disaggregated segments of the population. In the intervening years supplementary surveys or studies should be attempted on particular aspects of the problem.

(iv) A large number of research agencies in the field are taking up studies on their own. These are useful for specific purposes but they could be made more useful if a suitable mechanism is established through a central agency for effecting co-ordination of such studies in respect of their subject coverage, sectoral and regional coverage, study designs, etc.

(v) Despite large collection of data through different sources, their are serious gaps in the information with regard to geographical coverage as well as coverage of specific population groups and subject matter. We feel that the central agency suggested above should take steps to ensure that these gaps are covered as soon as possible by allocating the areas of work appropriately.

(vi) It is observed that considerable data collected by different agencies in different areas remain sometimes unprocessed or unpublished due to various reasons. The cenrtal agency suggested above should therefore, co-ordinate, the work of various agencies so that the data become available without undue delays.

(vii) We feel that it is desirable that efforts should be made to improve the employment exchange data as far as possible in regard to their range and coverage and that studies should be undertaken for interpreting the data from time to time both at the national and the state levels. The employment market information should also be improved so as to give information about the absorption and displacement of persons in various occupations and industries as well as regarding their educational qualifications. The coverage of the EMI should also be extended to include the smaller establishment on a sample basis to the extent possible.

Plan Programmes

The institutions providing credit to the smaller and marginal farmers and agricultural labourers should attempt to develop an integrated agricultural credit service along with provision of credit on the lines of the suggestions made by the National Commission on Agriculture. Such integrated service should include the organisation of facilities for the conversion of credit into inputs and services required by farmers. It should also look after the credit needs for ancillary occupations like animal husbandry, dairying, fisheries, forestry, etc.

We feel that it is necessary to identify on a wider scale all the other districts in the country in which the SFDA and MFAL schemes would be useful for improving the viability of small farmers and assisting the marginal farmers and agricultural labourers to improve their incomes and earnings. Both the schemes could usefully be amalgamated in a large number of areas and operated in an integrated manner so as to benefit both the categories of beneficiaries in the same areas. The extended coverage of the schemes should be brought into effect as early as possible and adequate provision made in the Fifth Plan for this purpose.

(i) The state governments and administrations of union territories should facilitate the task of the SFDA and MFAL agencies by taking steps to get their land record surveys completed speedily. For this purpose necessary funds should be provided as part of the Plan outlay.

(ii) These agencies should indicate to the state governments, etc. the selected areas where ground-water surveys should be undertaken on a priority basis and should also assist the state governments in providing soil-testing kits to extension workers and training facilities to the participants of the programmes, to the extent possible, out of the agencies' funds.

We consider that for the proper and speedy implementation of the SFDA and MFAL programmes, it is necessary to develop suitable criteria which can be applied in an objective manner so as to reduce the scope for subjectivity in the identification of the beneficiaries. As far as possible, small compact areas or blocks suitable for particular programmes should be selected.

It is desirable to extend the benefit of credit under these programmes to those small and marginal farmers who have operational holdings including some part of leased land. For this purpose it should be ensured that such leased land is within a certain reasonable proportion of the total holding and that the person has got some continuity of operation in relation thereto. This would be particularly desirable in those areas where such tenancies have been protected according to local laws.

In order to ensure that the implementation of these schemes is properly coordinated, overseen and supervised, high level officials should be invited occasionally to attend the meetings of the agencies. At the state and regional levels, meetings of the heads of departments could be held to sort out operational problems.

The state governments should attach greater importance to the coordination of the SFDA and MFAL programmes with other related programmes in the areas, e.g., groundwater surveys, land record operations, consolidation of holdings, rural electrification, etc.

In order to meet the difficulty experienced by the agencies in extending assistance to sharecroppers due to the absence of records showing their rights or interest in land, the state governments should take steps to prepare the basic record of rights in land. As suggested in our Interim Report, the agencies should take steps to persuade the banks to advance short-term and medium term loans to share-croppers for cultivation as well as for subsidiary occupations. It may be necessary for the agencies to subsidise such loans and impress upon the financial institutions the need of not insisting on sureties from share-croppers and oral tenants.

Under the CSRE and other programmes, the payment of the part of wages in the form of suitable foodgrains would be very useful in meeting the requirements of the persons employed in the programmes. Alternatively, the availability of such foodgrains at reasonable prices should be assured through fair price shops or other approved dealers in the vicinity.

(i) As suggested in our Interim Report the allocation of funds under the CSRE for each district should be suitably determined after taking into account all relevant factors, such as, its population, state of agricultural development, etc.

(ii) It is necessary to have a number of different types of projects so as to provide a project-mix which would meet the various requirements of areas in which the scheme is being implemented. Such project-mix should contain a larger proportion of works which are productive. It is also necessary that there be kept ready a shelf of programmes conforming to local planning which could be taken up whenever necessary so as to provide, as far as possible, continuous employment to the rural labour.

(iii) Arrangements for identifying the persons who are eligible to be employed could be made through surveys, etc., by the village extension officers.

The scheme known as the Rural Employment Guarantee Scheme, being implemented by the Maharashtra Government has several salutary features which would help in tackling the unemployment problem and also in making a wholesome impact by providing assurance of work to the weaker sections of the people at the time when it is most needed. For these reasons this scheme merits the attention of the Government and should be extended to other states also.

(i) In order that the scheme for agro-service centres may be feasible for technically qualified persons, it is necessary that suitable and convenient terms of finance for them should be arranged with the banks and that the procedures of the latter be streamlined.

(ii) The State governments and agro-industries corporations may consider giving priority for allocation of tractors to the selected technical persons desiring to set up such centres. Special training facilitices in the actual operation and maintenance of the tractors, etc., as well as in business management and public relations should be provided to the young entrepreneurs in charge of these agro-service centres.

(iii) The state governments and agro-industries corporations should assist the entrepreneurs running these centres in obtaining dealerships/distributorships of products like fertilisers, fuel and lubricants from the manufacturers/suppliers concerned.

(iv) We recommend that the above mentioned issues might be considered by the Ministry concerned in order to facilitate the implementation of this scheme.

*The scheme for the creation of planning and design units for the preparation of rural water supply schemes in the states should be taken up along with groundwater investigation in all states.

In making allocations out of the provisions of Rs. 100 crores made in the Central Government's budget for the year 1973-74 for programmes to generate employment opportunities for half a million educated persons in various fields, the need for widespread diffusion of the benefits of the scheme should be kept prominently in view and in particular the needs and requirements of the backward areas and tracts of the country should receive adequate attention.

We feel that the benefits accruing from some of the employment-oriented programmes initiated during the Fourth Plan such as SFDA, MFAL, CSRE, etc. should continue to be available to the people in the rural areas during the Fifth Plan period. For this purpose the question of continuance during the the Fifth Plan of such of these schemes as are found to have sufficient potential for employment generation, should be considered, either as specific programmes or as part of some other Plan programme.

(i) We feel that adequate provision of funds should be made for the continuing major and medium irrigation projects form year to year so that they are completed according to schedule and the benefits expected from them begin to accrue without delay to the regions concerned.

(ii) We consider that in formulating and preparing the project reports, etc., of the major irrigation schemes to be taken up in future as well as in reviewing the existing projects under construction, the necessary policy decisions regarding socio-economic as well as technical matters relating to important aspects of the projects should be taken in time.

We feel that during the Fifth Plan period efforts should be directed towards the completion of all the major and medium irrigation projects already taken up and also the execution of new projects, so as to create an additional irrgation potential of about 6 to 7 million hectares by the end of Fifth Plan.

Government should consider the desirability of undertaking detailed surveys for assessing the technical feasibility of the National Water Grid Scheme as early

*See also item (iii) below,

as possible.

We feel that area development programmes need to be taken up in the command areas of all the major and medium irrigation projects which have been completed so far as well as of those which are under construction or may be taken up in future. Such programmes should, however, be initiated sufficiently in advance of the irrigation works so that the development of irrigation and other facilities can be fully utilised within as short a period as possible after the completion of the projects.

More studies in depth would be required for assessing the impact of the programmes of rural electrification on employment in the rural areas. A further evaluation of employment generation through rural electrification since 1965 might be undertaken by the Programme Evaluation Organisation of the Planning Commission.

(i) To ensure adequate availability of power for agriculture and industry it will be necessary to provide for some cushion in the generating capacity of our power units.

(ii) We feet that it is desirable that the programme of power generation should be so planned that a sufficient proportion of the total capacity is created in the form of thermal power stations in different parts of the country. In this connection, the feasibility of setting up large thermal power stations at the pit-heads in the coal belt areas needs to be examined.

(iii) While planning, emphasis should be laid on schemes of power generation and acceleration of rural electrification programmes particularly in the backward areas so as to bring them into line at least with the national average. In a long-term perspective the objective should be to reach almost all the villages in the country within a reasonable period of about 10 to 15 years.

We consider it of importance that the programmes of the Railways for new railway lines, the doubling of the existing track and the conversion of narrower into broader guages should be undertaken on a larger scale in future years and a higher priority should be accorded to them.

The existing network of railway lines should be strengthened over those sections where at present the traffic carrying capacity is inadequate; so as to facilitate the transport of the increasing volume of raw materials and finished products.

In view of the importance of road communications as an essential part of the infrastructure for socio-economic development, we feel that efforts should be made to adhere to the programme for completion of the construction of roads worked out in the Chief Engineers' Plan. In order to attain the total expenditure of Rs. 3,920 crores on main roads as envisaged in that Plan, and taking into account the total estimated expenditure of Rs. 1,520 crores till the end of the Fourth Plan, it would be necessary to undertake a programme of the order of Rs. 2,400 crores for the construction of such roads in the years up to 1980-81. We, therefore, suggest that a suitably phased programmes over the seven year period from 1974-75 to 1980-81 may be undertaken.

We feel that in regard to 'rural roads' (comprising 'other district roads' and 'village roads') the tempo of construction needs to be stepped up so as to complete the programme envisaged in the reappraisal by the Sinha Committee by the end of the Sixth Plan, i.e., by 1983-84. We would, therefore, suggest that the outlay on such roads during the Fifth Plan may be of the order of Rs. 650 crores while that during the Sixth Plan may be Rs. 780 crores.

We feel that while a larger outlay for the development of roads is essential, the question of constituting a new non-lapsable fund, as suggested by our Working Group on Plan, would not be free from difficulties. A possible approach might be to consider the augmentation of the resources of the existing Central Road Fund by transfer of a larger share of the revenues from the customs and excise duties on motor spirit.

The development of road transport and of the connected industries could have a large employment potential over the years. The expansion of road transport has a multiplier effect not only on the economic activities directly connected with it like the manufacture of automobiles and commercial vehicles, but also on other services and activities like tourism, the development of trade, greater mobility of the people, etc. Further, the development of the automobile industry would in turn lead to the expansion or establishment of ancillary and feeder industries. The need for the development of road transport and of the connected automobile industry has to be viewed in this perspective and due emphasis laid on their promotion and development.

The implementation of the Fourth Plan road programmes of the metropolitan cities of Bombay, Calcutta, Delhi and Madras should be speeded up. Studies should be made of the transportation and traffic problems, of some of the other growing cities like Bangalore, Hyderabad, Ahmedabad, Kanpur and Poona.

It is essential for attaining the objective of self-reliance as also for increasing our earnings of foreign exchange that a much larger proportion of our overseas trade should be carried in Indian bottoms. Viewed from several angles including the growth of coastal shipping, the development of ancillary industries, the manufacture of various items and the considerable volume of employment generation, the development of ship-building industry is of importance.

We feel that long-term programmes of developing the ship-building and repair facilities in our country should be undertaken.

(i) It is necessary that cargo handling facilities at the ports and haulage and transport facilities in the port areas, etc., are provided and expanded sufficiently.

(ii) Sufficient outlay also requires to be provided for the development of intermediate and minor ports so that the establishment of industries in the several areas served by such ports is facilitated.

(i) The Inland Water Transport Committee had made a number of recommendations relating to the improvement of production of ship-building yards, evolving standard designs of hulls and propelling machinery, the deepening and widening of certain canals, channel conservancy, etc. We understand that some of these recommendations remain to be implemented. We feel that early consideration should be given to the remaining recommendations of the Committee.

(ii) The question of establishment of suitable organisations in the riverine states should be taken up so as to speed up the pace of progress of the schemes recommended by that Committee.

(iii) We also suggest that some pilot studies may be undertaken by suitable organisations regarding the social cost-benefit aspect of the development of inland water transport in different regions.

The tourist industry, if developed adequately, can increase employment considerably and have a stimulating effect on a wide range of industries and tertiary activities, particularly in the services sector. The provision of 32,800 rooms in approved hotels by the end of the Fifth Plan to cater to the requirements of the increased inflow of foreign tourists inside this country, which is expected to reach a figure of 8 lakhs per year by the end of the Fifth Plan, can provide considerable direct and indirect employment.

It is desirable also that suitable facilities and amenities be provided for the growth of internal tourism at a faster rate.

In view of the accepted policy of fulfilling the need based demands of the people and the expansion of literacy in rural areas, the expansion of postal and telecommunication services should receive adequate attention and a programme for the steady expansion, on a long-term basis, of these facilities to rural areas be adopted for implemedtation.

The programmes for the expansion of broadcasting and allied facilities will, besides creating employment opportunities, give considerable fillip to the further growth and expansion of industries manufacturing radio receivers, transistor sets, etc., and also to the development of the electronics industry in the country. Besides, a number of other facilities and services will also develop in the tertiary sector, for example, repair and overhaul facilities, sales, transportation, etc. All these activities are expected to have a multiplier effect on the generation of employment in these fields.

The expansion of family planning services will create jobs for the medical, para-medical and other non-technical including clerical personnel, etc. This programme should be co-ordinated with other programmes in the rural areas and with the social welfare programmes like maternal and child healh programmes, nutritional schemes, etc.

The pace of execution of the rural water supply schemes needs to be accelerated in view of the magnitude and urgency of the problem. The question of providing the basic need of potable water supply to all the villages in the problem areas, including difficult and scarcity areas and villages suffering from endamic diseases, should be accorded a higher priority and adequate provision made for covering such villages during the Fifth Plan. Such a programme would involve an estimated outlay of about Rs. 650 crores. The question of providing supplementary sources of water to the villages in other areas would also have to be taken thereafter.

By the end of the Fourth Plan, 1,274 towns with a population of 1.82 crores would still require to be provided with protected water supply involving an estimated outlay of Rs. 275 crores. Besides, the water supply schemes of many towns would require to be improved and modernised. All these programmes of water supply in the urban areas would generate considerable employment.

Apart from the provision of house sites for the landless labour in the rural areas, there is need for assisting the small and medium farmers and non-agricultural workers to improve their condition of living by constructing better houses. It is essential that a larger scale programme of construction of rural houses should be undertaken both by the Centre and State Governments during the succeeding years. There should be a phased programme of constructing about 2.92 million houses in the rural areas involving a total cost of Rs. 875 crores. Out of this amount, a sum of the order of Rs. 700 crores could be provided from their own resources by the persons constructing houses leaving a sum of the order of Rs. 175 crores to be provided by way of loans from the LIC, the rural housing finance corporations, commercial banks, etc.

It is desirable to plan for an increased level of house construction activities in the urban areas so as to prevent any deterioration of the position in this respect. We feel that the present rate of house construction in the urban area should be stepped up substantially say by 40 per cent involving an additional outlay of the order of Rs. 2,000 crores over the Fifth Plan period. With this additional investment it should be reasonably feasible to construct about 1.35 million additional houses. We suggest that out of this total number, the construction of 0.75 million units may be undertaken in the public sector through the agency of the state housing boards, etc. In this sector the bulk of the provision should be for the economically weaker sections and the low income groups, i.e. 4 lakh units for the economically weaker sections and 3 lakh units for the low income groups. The remaining 0.6 million units may be expected to be put up by the individuals and others in the private sector. The total investment for such a programme of 0.75 million units in the public sector may be of the order of Rs. 800 crores. On the other hand, the investment required for putting up 0.6 million units in the private sector would be of the order of Rs. 1,200 crores.

Such an expanded activity in the sphere of housing in urban as well rural areas would need a suitable administrative and organisational set up. For this purpose, the activities of the state housing boards would need to be extended to a larger number of cities and towns. In respect of rural areas we would reiterate our earlier suggestions made in the Interim Report for providing the necessary institutional and organisational framework.

Besides the rural housing finance corporations, the other government agencies and financial institutions like the LIC and the nationalised banks should make their contribution to such a programme.

We consider it of importance that the LIC should play a larger role in promoting rural housing. The resources of the Housing and Urban Development Corporations (HUDCO) will also have to be augmented.

We feel that to the extent justified by their administrative and personnel resourses, commercial banks should provide direct assistance to persons desiring to construct their own houses. They should also divert some of their resources for refinancing the housing finance activities of the proposed rural housing finance corporations.

The rural housing finance corporations through their own branches or with the assistance of various banking and cooperative institutions could promote suitable schemes for attracting long-term as well as medium-term savings from persons in the rural areas.

There is need for developing a large number of suitable house plans to meet the diverse requirements of the different sections of the people and the varying local conditions.

Steps should be taken to ensure adequate and timely supplies of essential building materials. Their production should also be stepped up. It is also necessary to take steps to maximise the use of materials which are produced or obtained locally and to reduce, as far as possible, the use of scarce materials like steel and cement.

One of the problems hindering the proper implementation of the Plan programmes is the lack of foresight and care in the preparation and selection of projects before the outlays and targets are fixed by the planners.

In view of the number of programmes in different sectors which will need to be dovetailed into each other both at the planning and the implementation stages, it is necessary that there should be co-ordination committees of the technical officers of various departments functioning effectively at the district level as well as similar committees composed of higher level officers functioning at the regional and/or state levels. We suggest that such district and/or state level committees should be established where these do not exist at present and the existing ones strengthened wherever necessary. The district level committees should be supported and assisted by a strong planning cell in drawing up an integrated plan and in the co-ordination of programmes in the course of implementation of the district level schemes, the working of the district level committees should be integrated with the functioning of the state co-ordination committees. The planning cells at the district level may, in the first instance, be established on a pilot basis in some districts. Planning cells at the headquarters or at the regional offices of the departments should undertake technical examination and scrutiny of some schemes at the district level and of the schemes concerning more than one district. They should be able to avail of the technical advice of such consultants as may be necessary.

To support the working of these co-ordination committees at the regional or state level, a committee of secretaries and important heads of departments should be set up.

Another major lacuna in the implementation of the Plan programmes is that the benefits of such programmes in general and even of the programmes intended for the weaker sections of the community, do not generally accrue to them in full measure, but flow largely to the more influential and better-off sections of the community.

As in the States of Maharashtra and Gujarat, in other States also suitable steps should be taken for the establishment of panchayati raj institutions where they have not been established, and for vesting them with necessary powers and responsibilities for the execution of rural development projects and employment-oriented schemes.

We feel that the weaker sections should be encouraged and assisted to form at the local level organisations which should be constituted entirely from amongst these weaker sections. They should be kept fully in the picture in the selection of schemes. The legally constituted democratic bodies should take special care to arrange for consultations with these organisations.

The maintenance and upkeep of capital works specially roads, canals, irrigation works, etc., is very important. At the stage of formulation of a scheme at either the state or central level, adequate provision should be made for the maintenance of the durable assests created by the schemes up to the end of the Plan period during which these are completed. Such funds should not be diverted to other programmes.

The agency which will be responsible for the proper maintenance of such assests in the subsequent period should be clearly specified and its express acceptance of such responsibility obtained before the work on a scheme is commenced. Steps should be taken to ensure that the necessary financial resources for meeting such expenditure are made available.

We recommend that at the time of sanctioning the projects, the full financial implications including the phasing of expenditure in subsequent years should be kept prominently in view and the number and relative priority of the projects to be taken up should be regulated according to the likely resources available in future years.

Preparatory work for the prior planning of the programmes to be taken up in the Fifth Plan should be initiated immediatly, especially for surveys of the resource potential and of the requirements of the areas concerned, the assessment of the feasibility of programmes, preparation of project reports, etc. Steps should also be taken from now on to estimate the manpower requirements and to spell out the antecedent steps needed to ensure their availability at the relevant time.

Strategies for employment generation : We are of the opinion that efforts should be made to bring about better harmonization of the incentives given by the state governments and that the major concessions to industries should be determined on principles agreed to at the national level, having due regard to the great need for promoting the establishment of new industries in the more backward states and regions.

An integrated approach to the problem of economic development of under-developed and backward areas has still to be worked out. Since such development of these areas requires also the building up of proper infrastructure, the present position regarding the use of incentives for promoting such development has involved a somewhat fargmented and less efficient use of scarce resources. A more purposeful, vigorous and co-ordinated policy in regard to incentives combined with action to build up infrastructure would, therefore, appear to be called for.

(i) The quantum of incentives has to be determined with reference to the needs and circumstances of the situation regarding the relative level of development of industries and it should be adequate for achieving the objective in view.

(ii) It appears desirable that while providing incentives for say the greater use of labour, certain disincentives should also be introduced against the greater use of capital, since such a combination of incentives and disincentives would tend to reduce their net impact on the revenue resources of the government.

(i) There has been a hidden subsidy in the loans at concessional rates of interest charged by the financial institutions. This subsidy should be done away with not only with reference to the large scale but also the small scale industries as it is likely to promole a greater use of capital and capital-intensive techniques. Where the resulting increased cost would adversely affect the development and welfare efforts, a subsidy could be given towards off-setting the increase in costs. In a few exceptional cases where the development of a particular industry is considered to be of vital importance on the ground of its potential contribution to the national economy and where a subsidy in another form would not be feasible, the financial institutions may be permitted to charge concessional rates of interest.

(ii) The abolition of such subsidy should not, however, be taken as affecting the existing scheme of concessions in interest rates on advances made by the nationalised banks to selected low income groups.

We are of the opinion that a relief on the basis of

the additional labour (above the level existing in the year prior to the commencement of the scheme) employed by the existing units and of the total labour employed by new units should be provided in the form of a tax rebate equal to a percentage of the tax payable which should be linked with the wage bill for additional labour employed with a suitable weightage for wages paid to the industrial workers.

We recommend that in the case of priority industries and of industrial units in backward areas, the units should be permitted to create a special investment reserve fund by transferring to it upto 30 per cent of their pretax profits, to be utilised in priority industries or other specified types of investment or for investment in selected backward areas.

We are inclined to agree with the view that a suitable system should be devised by the total depreciation allowed—whether it be called development rebate or additional depreciation allowance— should be adequate to cover the replacement cost of plant and machinery. We consider that a periodical mark-up of the value of plant and machinery by a suitable proportion is essential in the context of the rising prices of plant and machinery and a suitable system should be devised for this purpose with such necessary conditions and procedural details as may be prescribed.

In order to stimulate investment, the long-term capital gains arising from the sale or transfer of an asset should be exemped from the capital gains tax if the proceeds are invested in a new industrial undertaking.

(i) We feel that there is need for making determined and sustained efforts for extending promotional and technical facilities like common production centres, facilities for testing and quality control, training, production of proto-types, market information, preparation of design and project reports, etc., to other centres where a number of small units may exist and to ensure that they are made available to all the small scale units.

(ii) In the case of medium and large scale industries also, certain facilities like research and development activities, market research, quality control, pre-shipment inspection, etc., would be useful in accelerating their growth and maintaining their viability.

(i) We feel that an appropriate agency to promote the development of backward areas would be a separate organisation to be set up in different areas, which may be called the Regional Development Corporation. Such corporations should be responsible for selecting suitable regions where growth centres could be established and developed. Such development could also be undertaken around the existing industrial complexes. These corporations could be entrusted with the task of coordinating the activities of various authorities concerned. They should play an active role in the preparation of area development plans and co-ordinate the efforts of the agencies concerned. In the initial period certain ancillary facilities may be provided by them. Althoug the role of these corporations is generally expected to be that of planning and promotion, they may themselves play a direct entrepreneurial role for the removal of specific bottlenecks to area development.

(ii) In order to assist the state governments to set up such regional development corporation, the Government of India may consider providing some part of the seed capital, securing where necessary, the services of managerial and technical personnel and providing training facilities to them.

We recommend that there should be a periodical review of the position in the areas selected for development by regional development corporations.

(i) In our view the quantum of subsidy allowed to industries to be set up in backward areas should be increased further from 15 per cent to 20 per cent of the fixed capital.

(ii) At the same time it is necessary to take vigorous measures for the development of infrastructural facilities in the backward areas, since without such development the provision of capital grant alone would not provide adequate stimulus for the growth of industries.

The concession of a transport subsidy equal to 50 per cent of the cost of transport of both raw materials and finished goods for all new industrial units to be set up should be admissible in other difficult and inaccessible areas also, as it is admissible at present in the State of Jammu & Kashmir, Assam, etc.

A scheme of assistance for meeting the costs of movement of certain categories of skilled personnel somewhat on the lines of schemes adopted in other countries, restricted to certain areas having special features or to some categories of skilled personnel who may be in short supply in particular areas might be introduced on an experimental basis.

(i) In our view, industry should be encouraged to go in for double and triple shift working not only from the point of view of increased production but also from the point of view of increased employment.

(ii) The existing provisions in respect of depreciation allowance for the second and third shifts need to be reviewed for this purpose.

Industry should be encouraged to introduce multiple shift working by the grant of suitable fiscal and financial incentives with adequate safeguards to ensure that these benefits are properly linked to the increase in production and employment actually resulting from the additional shifts.

We consider that at the present stage a system of tax rebate related to the total value of exports made by an industrial unit or an export house should be allowed. We further feel that a system of import entitlement under which import licences are given to eligible exporters to import raw materials and other essential items required for the production of goods meant for export should also be adopted to promote the export of labour-intensive goods.

We consider that the policy of giving tax concessions in respect of export of specific items of labour-intensive industries such as products of handloom, handicrafts, etc., should be accepted and necessary fiscal, administrative and other measures taken in ports substantially.

Government should consider the possibility of offering facilities and concessions like credit to the prospective buyers abroad of our industrial machinery, equipment, etc., in order to improve the competitive position of our products.

The supply of essential raw materials at international prices to certain industries should be considered if it can place an industry in a better position to compete in the world markets and thereby to increase its exports substantially.

(i) We feel that there is a case for earmarking for export purposes a percentage larger than 5 per cent (which is being contemplated at present) of the production of non-priority industries which use substantial imports.

(ii) More effective measures should be taken to ensure that export obligations of the units in the priority list are, in fact, met.

Our aim should be to maximise the export of goods in as finished a form as possible and thereby to reduce to the minimum the exports of bulky raw materials and semi-processed goods. For this purpose it will be useful if the items of raw materials, minerals, etc., which would lend themselves to further processing or finishing at an economic cost and without impairing their export worthiness, could be identified and their production and processing organised with in the country.

We feel that adequate arrangements should be made for the proper maintenance and preservation of our historical and archaeological monuments and for the provision of necessary facilities for the tourists even though this may involve additional expenditure.

We feel that the hotel industry is still at a nascent stage of development and it would be necessary to foster and promote it at least for some time so that it could adequately butteress the growth of tourism in the country.

We feel that the hotel industry should be given fiscal incentives and tax concessions so as to enable it to meet the increased requirements of the tourist industry. For this purpose a tax concession on the lines of the tax rebate, and the extension of some of the benefits and facilities allowed to other priority industries, might be considered for this industry.

We consider that it is of importance that the question of providing some measure of insurance against loss of employment should be given a high priority and the feasibility of the introduction of a scheme on the basis recommended by the National Commission on Labour be examined as a matter of urgency.

In a situation of labour surplus in the country when the incidence of unemployment and under-employment is so high, wide prevalence of overtime working is socially undesirable. Definite steps should be taken, in our view, to encourage the recruitment of new labour rather than the engagement of the existing labour on overtime work in the industrial and tertiary sectors.

In our view it would be desirable to consider the suggestions relating to the reduction of the number of weekly working hours from 48 hours to 42 hours and the adoption of a seven-day week, after ascertaining the views of labour in this regard.

It is desirable to encourage the employment of women at least upto the level at which it has been prevailing hitherto by offering some incentives to those employers who maintain the ratio of women in their labour force at a prescribed level.

In order to secure a reasonably high rate of economic growth, it is necessary to restrict the growth of population effectively, and for this purpose the adoption of a well-concerted and positive programme of population planning is very essential.

(i) The national target of family planning provides, as mentioned in the Fourth Plan document, for the reduction of birth rate to 25 per thousand by 1980-81. As a matter of fact we should think in terms of bringing down this rate to a still lower level so that around the end of the 1980s, the size of the population becomes stabilised.

(ii) It is essential that vigorous and concerted efforts for the intensification and extension of the family planning programmes be made so that the national targets can be achieved.

We feel that the provisions regarding the circumstances in which induced abortions could be permissible should be further liberalised and they need not be limited only to the cases of grave injury to the physical and mental health of the pregnant woman.

One of the essential practical steps for the implementation of the family planning programmes in the rural areas would be the provision of the essential facilities like hospitals, health centres, medical and paramedical staff, and inputs.

For the success of the family planning programme, besides a well-knit and effective administrative organisation, there must be emphasis on basic research in reproductive biology, demography, communication and methods of evaluation. It would also be necessary to strengthen the data base in all these subjects. Further research would be needed for developing more efficacious contraceptive devices, etc.

An attack on this problem could take various forms besides the conventional methods of contraception and legalised abortion, e.g., postponement of the age of marriage, motivation of young men and women for longer abstontion from marriage and the creation of a proper socialatmosphere for this purpose, promotion of female education and literacy, measures for increased participation of women in economic activities, etc. In our social conditions, the minimum age of marriage could easily be raised to 21 for boys and 18 for girls from the existing levels of 18 for boys and 15 for girls.

While the spread of education, particularly among women, would no doubt have beneficial effects, a sustained effort at dissemination of information and instruction about population matters, proper motivation, provision of medical services, etc., would be required for a greater measure of success of the programme.

Some states have taken steps to introduce education on population in their school curricula. Efforts are, however, necessary for the adoption of such measures by other states also. Apart from the education on population imparted in the schools, arrangements are also needed to impart such training to those young men and women who have not been to school or who have since left school. Further, education on population should find a prominent place in adult literacy programmes.

Agriculture and allied activities

We argee broadly with the view of the Working Group on Agriculture that the approach to the programmes of development for the rural areas must be employment-oriented for the next Plan period and should include a massive programme of rural works encompassing irrigation, soil conservation, land reclamation and rural roads.

The scope for expansion of minor irrigation in a number of States is quite large. Such works could be taken up over an area of 15 million hectares during the Fifth Plan period.

In view of the limited potential for the expansion of irrigation works in some of the States like Rajasthan, Maharashtra, Haryana, Tamil Nadu, Gujarat and Madhya Pradesh, there is need for undertaking an intensive survey of the ground-water resources, especially in the arid and drought-prone regions of the country.

In view of the importance of irrigation, we recommend that effective steps be taken to extend the activities of ground-water surveys to all those areas of the country which are not, at present, covered by the surveys undertaken by the Central Ground-water Board and by the State Ground-water Boards. The existing organisations at the State level would need to be strengthened and equipped so as to undertake and complete ground-water survey within a reasonable period. In other States the need for setting up similar organisations with adequate staff and equipment should be examined on an urgency basis.

We feel that care would need to be taken to ensure the optimum utilisation of the water resources and all possible avoidance of wastage. The appropriate soil and water management of irrigated land would require a number of construction activities, the exact nature of which would differ from region to region. It may therefore be necessary to undertake detailed studies of the cost of land shaping and of construction of field channels and drainage works needed for making the land suitabe for cultivation once irrigation is available. We consider that adequate provision should be made for these items in all projects of minor irrigation.

In view of the employment potential during the construction phase of the programmes of soil conservation and land reclamation, we recommend that programmes of soil conservation over an area of 15 million hectares, and land reclamation over 5 million hectares be undertaken during the Fifth Plan period.

We feel that there is need for intensifying research in a number of alternative patterns of multiple cropping suited to the local conditions in the different regions. It would also be necessary to try out on a sufficient scale in the cultivators' fields the results of experiments being undertaken on crop rotations in the research institutions. A programme of bringing an area of 9 million hectares under multiple cropping should be undertaken during the Fifth plan period.

In view of the rising cost of draught animals and increased expenses on their maintenance especially for the small farmers and in the low rainfall areas, we feel that the state governments should assist and promote the development of custom services by setting up agro-service centres equipped with tractors in adequate numbers. It should be ensured that the services made available to the small and marginal farmers are timely and prompt and that undue preference is not shown to larger farmers. The possibility of such centres providing draught animals on hire to small and marginal farmers should also be explored.

(i) While we have no hesitation in suggesting programmes of energising tube-wells and pump-sets through the extension of rural electrification and of promoting the use of improved minor implements, we feel that the introduction of more sophisticated and highly mechanised equipment is likely to have considerable repercussions on the employment of labour on the farms and may in the long run lead to the displacement of labour on a sizable scale. On the other hand there is a keen demand from the farmers in some areas of the northern states for the use of sophisticated mechanised equipment to overcome the problems arising from the adoption of multiple cropping. In these circumstances we are of the view that a selective approach needs to be adopted in this matter and that any indiscriminate extension of mechanisation needs to be effectively discouraged. For the purpose of determining the proper type and level of mechanisation suitable for the conditions prevailing in each region, more detailed studies should be undertaken in different regions of the country.

(ii) In order to cater to the requirements of small farmers a good deal of local and adaptive research would be needed so as to evolve suitable designs for more efficient implements and for less expensive equipment.

We consider that two programmes should prove crucial for the low rainfall areas : first, the techniques for conservation and economic use of available water and soil moisture, and second, the evolution of a suitable cropping pattern for the particular conditions in each area. We recommend that high priority should be given to the intensification of research for evolving suitable crop varieties and suitable cropping patterns in the low rainfall areas. Additional programmes to provide supplementary sources of employment and income would also have to be thought of. These could include road construction, animal husbandry, setting up of small industries, etc.

The programme of extending milk production and dairying activities is eminently suited to serve the needs of the small and marginal farmers by providing them part-time occupation and supplementary income. The form of the organisations for undertaking such programmes would have to allow for considerable variations in the different States. Whatever be the form of the apex organisation, it is essential that the small and marginal farmers who will be the main participants in, as also the beneficiaries of, the programme should be organised on proper lines at the village and block levels. The Government should foster and promote this programme by providing financial assistance for the capital investment, creating the apex organisation and setting up suitable agencies at the village and block levels for undertaking milk production, collection, sale, etc.

In the development of poultry farming preference should be given to areas which have got facilities of communication and transport to large urban centres. The government propose to encourage the establishment of egg collection and marketing centres at Calcutta, Delhi, Bombay and Madras in the cooperative sector with facilities of cold storage. Such arrangements would also need to be made for the organised marketing of popultry products in other large cities and towns.

In piggery development some bacon factories are facing difficulties in the full utilisation of their installed capacity due partly to the shortage of quality pigs and partly to the lack of demand for piggery products. A larger availability of better quality pigs, better utilisation of the capacity of the piggery units and a higher output should result in a progressive reduction in the production costs and this may help improve the demand.

Sheep breeding could be developed profitably in the desert areas of Rajasthan and Gujarat as well as in the hill areas of Jammu and Kashmir, Himachal Pradesh and Uttar Pradesh. The sheep extension programme would have to be integrated with fodder development and the provision of greater veterinary facilities so that this occupation may expand in a big way with exotic varieties of sheep.

For augmenting the foreign exchange resources of the country as well as supplementing the protein content of our diet and for providing more employment particularly in the maritime States, it is essential that greater attention be paid to the development of marine fish resources. Steps could also be taken to exploit the availability of seaweed and algae for their protein content and iodine, and also for compost and fertiliser.

An important activity for the diversification of

agricultural practices of farmers with small and marginal holdings, especially on the periphery of the bigger towns, urban areas and growth centres is the cultivation of vegetables. There are however marketing problems which have to be faced. It would be necessary to develop more facilities for cold storage in and around major cities as also to organise the marketing of the produce by the formation of suitable organisations.

There is need for the extension of cultivation of apples, pears and stone fruits like apricots, plums, etc., in the mountainous and sub-mountainous regions of northern India. Greater stress would also be needed on aerial spraying of pesticides for crops like mangoes, bananas and citrus fruits.

Some studies have indicated that there is a wastage of nearly 30 per cent of the fruits and vegetables produced in the country while barely 0.5 per cent of the produce is processed by the processing units. Greater importance therefore would have to be given to the promotion of processing industries in the producing areas. Organisational arrangements would also have to be made for the collection of fruits from farms, their transportation, storage and processing at convenient centres as well as for their sale at competitive prices.

The fruit and vegetable processing industry is stated to be facing difficulties due to several factors, such as high costs of materials, high and fluctuating prices of sugar and heavy overheads. It is important to take remedial measures to enable the industry to become competitive in the world markets in which there is an increasing demand for tinned products.

There are other valuable crops including plantation crops like tea, coffee, etc. which are grown in the country and provide employment to large numbers of persons. As these plantation crops are highly labour-intensive, and in view of their importance as earners of foreign exchange, as also of the increasing demand for them within the country, there is need for increasing their production and extending their area to the extent feasible.

Cashew is another crop which is an important foreign exchange earner and employs a large number of persons in its processing industry. Owing to the cashew nut producing countries themselves taking to mechanised processing of cashew kernels, it is apprehended that our supply of imported raw nuts required for the processing industry would be seriously affected. Therefore for maintaining the current level of production in the cashew processing industry, and also that of our earnings of foreign exchange, it is desirable that the cultivation of good quality cashew nuts in the country should be promoted.

In order to meet the deficiency in the production of edible oils in the country, it is necessary to explore the possibilities of extending the area under oilseeds and to introduce the cultivation of other oilseeds like sunflower in the different States. The cultivation of sunflower can help increase the intensity of cropping, and provide additional employment as well as add to the income of the farmers.

Another oilseed, which is a good source of both oil and protein and can be used for the manufacture of various food items and for industrial purposes, is soyabean. There are, however, some constraints hampering the extension of cultivation of this crop which are likely to be overcome in the near future. It should then be possible to increase the coverage under this crop substantially. Some technical problems also exist in the processing of this oilseed which need to be removed early.

A crop which can enhance the farmers' incomes by inter-cropping with sugarcane, especially in the irrigated areas of the northern states, is sugarbeet. It can supplement the raw material requirements of sugar factories enabling them to continue their operations for a period of two to three months. The major problem in the extensions of sugarbeet cultivation is, however, the cost of equipment required to be erected in the existing factories for undertaking the manufacture of sugar from sugarbeet. This problem would need to be resolved.

An activity which has great scope for expansion and for providing employment to large numbers in the rural areas is the exploitation of our forest resources. We would endorse the suggestion of the National Commission on Agriculture that in order to meet the country's requirements of timber and pulpwood, a total area of 7·26 lakh hectares could be clear-felled and planted between 1974 and 1980 in the inaccessible hardwood forests and the mixed forests of valuable and low quality stands, and that in order to develop this area, the construction of forest roads would have to be taken up over a length of 7,260 kms. This would not only help in the proper maintenance of the country's forest wealth and the exploitation of its resources, but would also provide much needed employment in the primary, secondary and tertiary sectors.

A large sized programme of road construction has a great employment potential not only in the construction phase but also in the maintenance phase. We feel that a larger programme of construction of 'rural roads' than one lakh kilometres as suggested by our Working Group would be necessary during the Fifth Plan as an integral part of the entire road programme to be taken up in the country.

A programme for land colonisation over compact

areas of 1,500 to 2,000 acres has been suggested by Shri V.V. Giri, our President. Steps to collect data from the States in this connection have been initiated by the Ministry of Agriculture. We suggest that once the necessary information becomes available, the various aspects of this programme should be examined as early as possible with a view to considering its implementation on an experimental basis.

Industry

It may reasonably be inferred that the industrial sector as a whole provided additional employment of the order of 4 million only during the two decades from 1951 to 1970, comprising two million in the factory sector and two million in small establishments outside the factory sector. The growth of the factory sector has, however, indirectly generated substantial employment in the primary and tertiary sectors.

Larger employment opportunities in the industrial sector could be generated in the short-term by accelerating the rate of industrial growth through increased production from the existing unused capacities as well as through fresh production from new investments. In the long-term the employment potential could be increased by reshaping the pattern and structure of industrial development. A reorientation of the industrial development programmes would call for an accelerated development of the less capital-intensive small scale industries as far as it is technologically feasible.

Further orientation towards employment could be given by developing selected industries for which the necessary expertise, resources, etc., are indigenously available.

Larger employment opportunities could also be generated by adopting the types of technologies suitable for our labour-abundant economy. Care should be taken to see that the modern type of technology is not imported without reference to Indian conditions. In the selection of technology or in the modernisation of industry, the use of highly sophisticated or automated machinery should be discouraged.

(i) The dispersal of industries away from the metropolitan areas or other places of concentration is important from the point of view of the removal of regional imbalances and the wider diffusion of employment opportunities. It is necessary that suitable measures be taken to build up infrastructural facilities needed for industrial growth in less developed areas and to ensure that wherever possible industrial units are set up at locations away from the highly developed areas.

(ii) The location of large industrial units in a backward area may not by itself generate significant employment unless a systematic attempt is made side by side to promote the setting up of a large number of ancillary units around a big industrial unit. We feel that the development of ancillary units should be regarded as an important instrument for the creation of new employment opportunities. It should be made obligatory for the bigger units both in the public and the private sectors to promote the development of ancillary industries by farming out the production of components, parts, sub-assemblies, etc. to small scale units.

The continued functioning at the existing levels of traditional, village and small industries is of critical importance from the point of view of preventing the accentuation of the present unemployment situation. Steps will have to be taken to make these industries economically viable over a reasonable period of time by upgrading their technology, improving their marketability through the diversification of their products and improvement of designs, and giving them necessary institutional support.

It would be necessary to take suitable measures to solve the technological, financial and managerial problems of sick and closed units and of some small scale units which are in need of modernisation in order to maintain the health of these industries as well as their existing levels of employment.

To facilitate the process of absorption of those employed under short-term employment schemes as well as of some of the unemployed, into more permanent employment in the growing industrial sector and also in the tertiary sector, it would be necessary to impart training in crafts and services to some of these persons and to upgrade the skills of others in suitable cases.

Better utilisation of installed capacity would help accelerate the rate of industrial production with beneficial effects on employment and concomitant multiplier effects on other sectors of the economy.

There is an imperative need to keep careful watch in regard to the overall supply/demand position of critical raw materials like steel, non-ferrous metals, etc. over the next few years, to take timely and vigorous steps to augment the indigenous production of these materials by establishing additional capacity to the extent necessary, and to ensure that realistic import programmes are drawn up well in time to maintain their satisfactory availability in accordance with the rising level of industrial production. There is also a great need for taking suitable steps to prevent the mis-utilisation or diversion of such materials.

In the short-term, every effort will need to be made for better utilisation of the existing power capacity through proper maintenance, reduction in transmission losses and strengthening of the transmission system so as to facilitate the transfer of energy from surplus to deficit regions. A crash programme on these lines will need to be drawn up and implemented. In the long term, power capacity should be substantially augmented by suitable stages somewhat ahead of the growing demand and adequate arrangements made for an integrated operation of the power system by establishing regional load despatch stations.

The current deficiencies in the supply of railway wagons would need to be critically examined and remedial measures taken urgently. From the long-term point of view, transport planning would have to be more closely dovetailed and co-ordinated with the location of industrial projects and their transport needs.

It seems desirable that comprehensive studies of industries affected by demand constraints should be undertaken in order to identify the factors responsible for the current situation, to examine the possibilities of diversification and to work out integrated industry-wise programmes to remove the existing malaise.

An improvement in industrial relations would also contribute to better utilisation of installed capacity. One of the factors affecting industrial relations in the past has been the erosion of real wages through a steep rise in prices. It is therefore, of vital importance to stabilise prices or at least to slow down their high rate of increase. Another step in this direction may be to link the wages with the price level and with productivity. The development of better human relations at all levels in industry would also be a contributing factor in the better utilisation of capacity and in increased production. No efforts should, therefore, be spared to bring about conditions conducive to more harmonious industrial relations. It is desirable that suitable working arrangements be devised in time to avoid situations leading to lock-outs etc., as far as possible, and all efforts made to settle industrial disputes in an amicable and expeditious manner.

For fuller utilisation of installed capacity, Government decided in January, 1972 to give a blanket permission to 54 (subsequently raised to 65) critical industries to expand and diversify their production upto 100 per cent above their licensed capacity. We would suggest that the question of the allocating adequate raw materials to, and of relaxing the existing constraints, if any, on the installation of necessary balancing equipment in respect of, the units in such industries should be considered. We would further suggest that the question of extending this relaxation to other industries also should be considered.

In order to achieve higher production and employment with the same capital outlay, industries in general should be encouraged to take to two or three shift working.

We feel that in a capital-short economy, once industrial capacity has been created, whether authorised or unauthorised, it should be fully utilised to maximise production and employment. While offences against the law should be suitably dealt with, the nation should not deprive itself of the benefits of investments already made.

We are of the view that advance preparatory action and planning with detailed cost estimates and time schedules and material procurement for construction should be undertaken urgently for new projects likely to be included in the Fifth Plan. Further, it will also be necessary to have adequate arrangements to monitor the progress in the implementation of projects and to take timely corrective action in advance of difficulties likely to arise.

The industrial licensing policy and the role to be assigned to the public sector for particular period need to be announced well in advance and these need to remain stable over the period.

In order to provide incentive for investment in industries for the people, particularly the small investors, the introduction of a suitable scheme of tax concession to persons investing in the equity capital of new industries upto a certain specified limit should be considered. There is need for a fresh examination of the handicaps from which industrial securities suffer, with a view to their relaxation or removal.

More positive steps should, in our view, be taken to assist the new and medium entrepreneurs in a meaningful manner so that they may be enabled to implement the new industrial licences and bring new industrial capacity in use. The public financial institutions should strengthen their capabilities for providing assistance to these entrepreneurs in various forms, for example, by preparing feasibility reports etc.

A strategy for utilising the substantial financial and managerial resources existing in the larger industrial houses for a faster industrial growth in a manner calculated to subserve the overall national interest also needs to be evolved.

There is a need for extending to fresh investors of small and medium levels further support by nationalised banks and other financial institutions. For this purpose these institutions should, in our view, give preference to such enrtepreneurs by earmarking a suitable proportion of their total advances as also by allowing them better terms and conditions for these advances, with due regard to the priorities that may be decided by the government. There should also be a suitable scheme of differential rates of interest on advances to such entrepreneurs in accordance with these priorities.

We are of the view that a detailed examination of the various regulations and controls which affect industrial growth should be undertaken as early as possible and that a new approach is warranted in the matter of administration of various regulations and controls pertaining to industrial development. Broadly speaking, the objective should be to retain physical control only in critical areas involving deployment of large and scarce resources and to reduce substantially the time-lags in securing clearances to a project from numerous agencies. We feel that a detailed examination of these aspects should be undertaken so as to evolve appropriate policies and procedures well in advance of the commencement of the Fifth Plan.

We recommend that industrial programmes in the large scale sector should be confined by and large to those items in which there are compulsions of technology and scale, which have high employment linkage effects or where there is immediate need to augment the supply of mass consumption goods. The public sector also should participate in the production of critical and mass consumption items. There is also need for a co-ordinated programme which closely integrates the small scale units with the large scale industries in terms of backward and forward linkages.

In order that small scale units may gear their production to meet the current and future demands for the items reserved for this sector at competitive prices, it is imperative that adequate support measures are taken to ensure that the policy of reservation encourages the existing units to expand their production and induces new units to come up in these lines of production.

We would like to emphasise the need to give particular attention to the development of agro-industries in the future strategy for the promotion of small scale indusries.

There is an urgent need to step up substantially the coverage of the Rural Industries Projects Programme. To ensure their success such projects should be preferably developed around growth centres. They should also take up the production of non-traditional items for domestic consumption and export.

In order to assist in the establishment of ancillary units, it is desirable that all new industrial undertakings and the existing units which apply for substantial expansion should be compulsorily asked to farm out to small enterprises such of the components, spares, sub-assemblies, etc., as are capable of being manufactured in the small scale sector. Even in the matter of certain processing and finishing jobs, the large scale units need not be allowed to establish such facilities within their premises. The existing as well as new large scale enterprises should consciously foster the development of ancillary units by providing them technological guidance, common service facilities, esting facilities, etc., and also by encouraging qualified and experienced persons in their organisations to set up such units. The supply of raw materials to ancillary units should be ensured and they should be accorded necessary facilities and assistance in securing such materials including additional allocations by large scale units from their supplies.

Certain fiscal measures like sales tax and excise duties fall cumulatively on both the large scale and small scale units. Some scheme should be evolved to avoid the cumulative incidence of such fiscal measures.

There is need for a legal framework to govern the contractual arrangements between large units and ancillary units. The possibility of legislation for governing sub-contracting should, in our view, be examined by government.

For promoting small scale units around large industrial complexes it would be desirable to set up sub-contracting exchanges in different parts of the country on the pattern of the exchanges already functioning in Madras and Bombay.

To cut down delays in the grant of loans and advances to small scale units, there is need for greater co-ordination between the State Finance Corporations and the nationalised commercial banks. These agencies should also earmark additional funds for assistance to meet the higher requirements of this sector in the coming years.

In the matter of allocation of scarce raw materials to small scale units, we fully endorse the recommendations of the Balachandran Committee which should, in our view, be implemented without delay.

The possibility of setting up trade centres and retail outlets at important places by the organisations of small entrepreneurs, state small industries corporations, etc., to assist and promote the marketing of the products of the small scale units, needs to be carefully considered. Further, cooperative marketing agencies formed by small scale units themselves could also be encouraged.

We understand that a committee set up by the Ministry of Industrial Development in January, 1972 has made recommendations for enacting suitable legislation for small scale industries on matters such as restricted partnership, development of ancillary industries reservation of items, etc. We recommend that the suggestions made by this committee should be given consideration and necessary legislation in respect of these matters promoted at an early date.

The consultancy services for the small scale sector need to be substantially expanded and strengthened to fulfill its growing needs. We consider it desirable that project profiles should be made available at a nominal cost. It would also be essential to strengthen adequately the small industries services institutes (SISI) with qualified and experienced staff competent to provide detailed consultancy services.

We feel that the Appropriate Technology Cell already set up in the Ministry of Industrial Development should be strengthened and better equipped to discharge its responsibilities and functions. It should also have the responsibility of sponsoring research schemes in national laboratories and of generally stimulating research and development work in this important field. Further, it may be empowered to operate pilot projects and conduct field demonstrations.

Encouragement has also to be given in general to the development of indigenous technology. Adequate support should be given to the activities of the National Research Development Corporation, the Council of Scientific and Industrial Research and other similar organisations.

The existing socio-economic milieu is not altogether favourable for the growth of a spirit of initiative and enterprise among young people. The long-term problem is one of creating conditions for the growth of self-employment through an orientation of our educational programmes, particularly of the programmes of vocational education, and through changes in the social values and norms.

We reiterate the suggestions made in our Interim Report that in the matter of providing credit under the special credit schemes, the banks should take a broad and liberal view of the categories of persons to be eligible for assistance and should extend such credit to the entire range of self-employment field and that the terms of the loans should be made softer taking into consideration the requirements and limitations of such borrowers.

With a view to removing the stagnation from which the economies of the backward and rural areas suffer and providing opportunities for gainful employment to the people of these areas nearer their homes, it will be necessary to spread the establishment of industrial units in semi-urban and rural areas as also in the backward regions of states which are still undeveloped. In this connection we feel that in a case where an industrial licence is issued for setting up a unit in such areas, the entrepreneur should not normally be permitted to change its location to a large city or a more developed area.

(i) In order to create an impact on the development of the backward areas, the industries to be selected for being set up should be such as have an organic relationship with the economy and resources of the area and the necessary forward and backward linkages with other economic activities therein.

(ii) Institutions for providing consultancy and other services similar to those provided by the Kerala Industrial Technical Consultancy Organisation (KITCO) and the State Industrial and Investment Corporation of Maharashtra (SIICOM) should, in our view, be created for other backward areas also. We recommend, therefore, that the necessary institutional framework should be established for the provision of consultancy and other services to the small scale sector in the backward areas of all the states.

In view of the large scale employment being provided by the traditional village and cottage industries, we consider that institutional credit should be made available to them on liberal terms and on a more extensive scale taking into account their requirements. We feel that the concerned agencies should also take up on a basis of urgency programmes for the improvement of skills, designs and production techniques in these industries. In the meantime, measures of fiscal support in their present form should be continued and extended to the industries not yet covered.

In view of the large number of persons dependent on the handloom industry who are exposed to under-employment or may be thrown out of employment due to the difficulties in obtaining cotton and art silk yarn, we consider that remedial measures should be taken as a matter of urgency for ensuring a better supply of yarn to handloom weavers at reasonable prices.

It is felt that the basic concept of decentralisation of industries to the village and household levels and the creation of employment thereby should be extended to other industrial activities also instead of being confined to the traditional industries only. There is need, therefore, for an investigation as to how far some of the activities of the modern industrial sector could be decentralised to the village and household levels. A few pilot projects should be taken up thereafter.

(i) In our Interim Report we had suggested the setting up of an agency in the form of a separate corporation charged with the duty of overseeing the economic health of industries where closures have taken place or are apprehended, with a view to remedial and timely action being taken. We would like to reiterate our earlier suggestion for the setting up of such a corporation.

(ii) In the case of industries like textiles and sugar which employ a large number of workers, suitable steps for modernising the plant and machinery, where necessary, should be taken as a matter of urgency and other necessary steps also taken so that the closures resulting from the inefficient working of the units or due to old and worn out equipment may be avoided.

Education and Training

The total number of educated job-seekers registered with the employment exchanges as on 31st December, 1972 was 32.78 lakhs, which constituted nearly 48 per cent of the total number of registered job-seekers. This number was increasing at the average annual rate of 20.1 per cent from December, 1966 to December, 1971 and has registered a further increase of 42.8 per cent from the end of 1971 to the end of 1972. While the number of marticulate job-seekers has nearly tripled between 1966 and 1972, the number of under-graduate job-seekers has quadrupled and that of graduates has become six-fold during the same period.

With the target of 5.5 per cent economic growth envisaged in the Fifth Plan, the employment opportunities likely to be thrown up by the organised sector would fall short of the increasing supply of educated manpower. It would, therefore, be necessary to promote the rapid growth of unorganised sector of the economy so as to create more job opportunities for the educated unemployed as also to foster self-employment among them. For this, the quality and content of the educational courses also need to be oriented so that the products of educational institutions are more employable and can fulfil the requirements of both the organised and unorganised sectors.

A comprehensive and phased programme of additional enrolment may be formulated for the primary and middle stages of education with the objective of achieving by the end of the Fifth Plan 100 per cent enrolment of the children of the age group 6-11 and 75 per cent of those of the age-group 11-14. Besides helping in the implementation of the Constitutional directive, this programme would generate direct employment opportunities for nearly 1.50 lakh teachers, 1200 assistant inspectors of the primary schools and ministerial staff every year, in addition to the requirements for normal replacement.

One major difficulty in the way of effective implementation of the programme of universal elementary education is the problem of drop-outs. To tackle this problem, not only the quality of primary education needs to be improved but other remedial measures need to be adopted to provide relief and assistance to the children of poorer sections. In this connection improvement programmes such as the provision of mid-day meals, free supply of text books to the needy children and improvement in the quality of teachers have *inter alia* been suggested by the Education Commission. In addition, the condition of school buildings would need much improvement. A phased programme of construction of new school buildings should, wherever necessary, be undertaken. Another measure which can help in reducing the number of drop-outs is the adjustment of school terms and vacation periods and of the working hours of schools, specially in the rural areas.

The system of single-teacher schools should, in our opinion, be reviewed and the existing single-teacher schools converted wherever possible into multi-teacher schools. Besides improving the quality of education in such schools, this will offer more employment opportunities for teachers.

We are of the view that a phased programme of adult literacy should be undertaken so that within a period of 10 to 15 years illiteracy among adults could be practically removed from the country. To start with, it is suggested that a suitably phased programme be prepared for the Fifth Plan so that, at the annual rate of 10 million adults of the age group 15-44, at least 50 million such persons are covered. For making this programme a success, a comprehensive follow-up programme for the supply of literature and the establishment and maintenance of libraries for the neo-literates would also have to be initiated. During the Fifth Plan, the total expenditure on this programme is estimated to be of the order of Rs. 100 crores.

A few short-term measures that can help in easing the problem of the educated unemployed have been mentioned. These are :—

(i) Government should consider the need for some form of legislation which would ensure that every industry employs a number of engineers and technicians determined on the basis of its scale of manufacturing capacity, technical processes employed, total number of workers, etc.

(ii) We feel that instructions requiring the appointment of qualified engineers by the contractors undertaking works for Government departments and also prescribing the number of such engineers, should exist in all the states. These instructions would need to be enforced effectively.

It would be still better if qualified engineers are encouraged to take up Government works contracts either individually or on a cooperative basis.

(iii) Planning units for preparing the engineering designs and project reports may be created in appropriate departments, where these are not in existence.

(iv) Research and development activities in the country should be expanded substantially.

(v) There is a need to tap the unorganised sector of the economy, where great potential now exists for absorbing educated personnel. Suitable training and orientation programmes may be drawn up in each area for the local talent among the educated unemployed. With the introduction of new techniques in agriculture, the scope for opening new labour-intensive industries, repair and maintenance workshops, shops, and retail centres, etc. has widened. Such entrepreneurship should be encouraged by the Government through the provision of financial and other facilities.

(vi) The state governments should take the initiative in fostering and encouraging self-employment among engineers, technicians and the educated unemployed so that they may take advantage of the scheme of the Ministry of Industrial Development for providing financial assistance for the opening of small industries. It is suggested that the original objective of this scheme to provide encouragement and financial assistance to the educated unemployed may be kept in view and non-technical educated persons also may be encouraged and assisted to set up as self-employed persons in suitable industries.

It is suggested that the programmes of expansion of elementary education and of adult literacy and the other short-term measures should be so formulated that their benefits are equitably distributed among different regions, more emphasis being laid on rural and backward areas.

In order to improve the employability of its products, the present educational system needs to be revamped so as to make education job-oriented with a technical bias right from its elementary stage.

It is desirable to reorient the methodology of teaching in elementary classes so as to inculcate in the children from the very beginning those basic attitudes and personality traits which are the pre-requisities for employment preparation, employment adaptation and employment creation. A comprehensive programme of work-experience as recommended by the Education Commission will help in developing these basic attitudes and traits.

While general education with a programme of work experience may be allowed upto the tenth class, education in the higher classes should be made vocational in character by introducing diversified job-oriented courses. We are strongly of the view that a stage has been reached when the pace of vocationalisation of secondary education has to be speeded up with a view to attaining the target set by the Education Commission of diverting 50 per cent of students at the higher secondary stage, i.e., classes XI and XII, to vocational education.

The courses of vocational education should be such that at the end of the course, the product should in general be ready to fulfil the requirements of industrial and agricultural occupations. All programmes of vocationalisation should, however, be linked as far as possible with the local manpower needs and should be operated in close collaboration with the machinery for vocational guidance, the training centres in industry and the employers. In determining the requirements of the various categories of skilled persons, local skill surveys and studies of the employment situation should be carried out periodically in close collaboration with the employing agencies.

We strongly recommend that steps should be taken to bring about a transformation in the existing social milieu, norms and standards so that more young people are encouraged to go in for training for jobs and occupations involving manual work. Besides other measures, we suggest that scholarships and other concessions should be provided in schools to students taking up vocational education, and better emoluments and working conditions prescribed for jobs and occupations involving manual work. We are of the opinion that a lead in this matter should be taken by the public sector.

The rate of increase in enrolment at the stage of higher education has been substantially higher than at the primary and secondary stages where such rates of increase should normally be higher. A number of measures can be adopted to moderate the pace of expansion of higher education by providing alternative avenues for a number of students. Firstly, an extensive programme of vocationalisation should be adopted at the higher secondary stage. Secondly, it should be ensured that adequate standards are maintained in institutions at the secondary stage and that the public examination at the end of the higher secondary stage is of a reasonable and uniform standard. Thirdly, higher education also should be diversified so as to provide for vocational and professional courses both at the under-graduate and post-graduate levels.

While these measures should to some extent be helpful, a long-term remedy to the problem would lie in accelerating the economic development of the country and the all-round growth of the economy in general with the conscious and deliberate objective of employment generation.

The Committee feels that the existing rules regarding recruitment and the practices followed in the selection processes would need to be modified. Only the minimum qualifications necessary for the proper performance of the duties of a post should be prescribed, and university degrees should not be used as a filtering device in case of jobs where the qualifications prescribed are lower. In order that persons with necessary minimum qualifications may be encouraged to apply and be able to compete on fair terms without undue preference being given to those with higher qualifications, the desirability of reducing the age limit prescribed for appointment to various posts, with suitable adjustments for the transitional period, would need to be considered by the Government and other employing agencies. The selection procedures would need to be related more specifically to the job requirements and duties expected to be performed. Besides, arrangements for entry into educational institutions at multiple points should be provided to enable student-workers with lower qualifications to improve their qualifications and professional competence.

(i) We would suggest that at every stage of technical education beginning from craft training to post-graduate technical education programmes of practical training linked as far as possible to job requirements may be introduced as a part of the curriculum.

(ii) It is necessary to ensure that satisfactory arrangements are made with the active co-operation of the managements of industrial unit for the trainees of sandwich courses acquiring practical experience in the industry. Similar sandwich courses may be introduced with the assistance and co-operation of other industrial units in a larger number of technical institutions. The programme of training should be drawn up according to the requirements of the various sectors of the economy and it should be reviewed periodically by standing boards of technical education whose membership should include some higher level technical workers of industry.

(iii) Technical institutions should be encouraged to provide short-term training courses for upgrading the skills of the existing stock of technicians and teaching them allied trades.

Some measures/studies that should be undertaken to assist in the better implementation of the programme suggested have been indicated.

It is desirable to draw up suitable training programmes of short duration with a view to upgrading the skills of the educated persons and improving their capability for getting employment or being self-employed. Tne proprietors of small undertakings as well as prospective entrepreneurs could be given managerial training. Some training programmes of pre-vocational type would also be necessary for a larger number of persons with elementary education or drop-outs, so as to impart to them elementary skills for improving their employability and making them more useful for their parental occupations or other trades. After completing such training the trainees should be assisted to start their own enterprises in traditional and labour-intensive jobs. The ultimate objective should be to incorporate such training in the system of elementary education.

Short-term training schemes being run by the DGE&T for technical personnel may be reviewed and rationalised in view of the changing needs of the occupational pattern. For enabling some educated and qualified persons to avail of specific job opportunities suitable practical training in specific jobs in the organised sector could be provided. It is also necessary to arrange for the training of a larger number of such persons in a variety of skills.

Training facilities would need to be planned in accordance with the manpower requirements in specific categories of skills. These should generally be planned on the basis of local field surveys undertaken in respect of the manpower requirements in existing and emerging occupations. A suitable machinery must be established at the district level for conducting such surveys and for linking education and training progrnmmes with the findings of these surveys. For over-all coordination at the state level, a board or council may be set up with representatives from government department, industry, workers' unions, elected bodies, etc.

It is suggested that large sized industries having their own training programmes should choose trainees from those selected under the Stipendiary and National Apprenticeship Schemes and share a part of the expenditure on stipends. Some of the difficulties in the working of these schemes and a few corrective measures for their removal have been mentioned.

To make the training programmes effective, industry should be encouraged and persuaded to participate actively in the planning of such programmes and their implementation. It should, as far as possible, be made obligatory on their part to give a measure of preference to such trainees in regard to job opportunities in their own establishments.

Machinery for continuous appraisal

While the work relating to manpower planning and employment is spread over a number of agencies at the Centre, including in particular the Directorate General of Employment and Training, the Employment and Labour Division of the Planning Commission, the Employment and Manpower Cell in the Cabinet Secretariat, the Directorate of Manpower and the Ministry of Education, there is no central agency at present which is responsible for bringing together and collating such data and making a comprehensive study of the various aspects of the problems of manpower and employment. We feel that there is a need for establishing such a central agency so as to ensure co-ordination, undertake timely compilation and collation of all relevant information on the manpower and employment situation and make comprehensive analyses and studies of such information for the purpose of planning.

The functions of some of the existing agencies relate exclusively to manpower planning and employment generation which are separable from the main sphere of work and function of their parent organisations. The functions of such organisations can easily be transferred to a suitable apex organisation which might be entrusted with over-all responsibility in respect of manpower planning and employment.

While the responsibility for the collection of data on various aspects of education may continue to vest in the Ministry of Education, it is important that suitable arrangements should be made for ensuring the regular and timely flow of such data to the proposed apex organisation responsible for employment and manpower planning with a view of facilitating a comprehensive study of the available data for effective co-ordination of the programmes of the Ministry of Education and other agencies concerned with specialised education, and for the formulation of suitable policies for ensuring supply of the requisite personnel.

While the monitoring and assessment of sectoral programmes in relation to the employment aspect should primarily be the responsibility of the executive agencies implementing such programmes, the apex organisation should be supplied with the relevant data and the results of assessment by the implementing agency so as to facilitate the assessment of the overall employment situation as well as the effecting of such co-ordination and such adjustments of policies and programmes as may be necessary.

It is necessary that the question of suitably strengthening the data collecting agencies and making adjustments in their procedures should be kept under constant review by the department entrusted with the subject of statistics in consultation with all the agencies collecting such data and the apex organisation which would be entrusted with employment and manpower planning.

A sustained flow of relevant and timely information has to be ensured from the various agencies to the apex organisation entrusted with he responsibility for manpower planning.

There is need for setting up a suitable organisation (a) to ensure overall co-ordination among the agencies generating data, (b) to analyse the available data and to suggest changes from time to time in the system of collection of data and (c) to formulate practical policies and programmes pertaining to the planning of manpower and employment from time to time in the light of developments in the economy.

We feel that at the Centre as well as in the states, the agencies which deal directly and exclusively with the planning of manpower and employment should be merged to form a separate department of the Central Government and of the State Governments. In particular, at the national level, the Directorate General of Employment and Training, the Directorate of Manpower and the Employment and Manpower Cell in the Cabinet Secretariat should be merged to form a Department of Employment and Manpower Planning.

The implementation of programmes of self-employment sponsored by the Government and other agencies as well as the situation regading self-employment in the country from time to time should be continuously monitored by the appropriate agencies of the Government, and the Department of Employment and Manpower Planning at the Centre should exercise a co-ordinating role in the matter.

We feel that it is necessary that there should be a separate organisation at the national level with sufficient autonomy and authority which should devote itself exclusively to a comprehensive assessment and review of the employment situation on a continuous basis and provide guidance and advice to the various ministries of the Government and other agencies in their policies and functions in relation to the employment situation. We feel that besides the Department of Employment and Manpower Planning at the Centre, there should be a separate high power organisation with adequate authority. We, therefore, recommend that a National Commission on Employment and Manpower Planning should be established. The Commission should enjoy the requisite autonomy and be in a position to take up suo motu the consideration of any matter relating to its functions.

The proposed Commission may be a compact body consisting of a small number of members some of whom including the Chairman, should be full-time members.

The Commission should have, inter alia, the following functions :—

(a) to conduct periodical reviews of the situation pertaining to manpower, employment and unemployment indicating, where necessary, particular areas demanding attention;

(b) to make projections of labour force and different categories of manpower on the basis of available data and information with an adequate degree of disaggregation;

(c) to evaluate the situation regarding supply of and demad for manpower at different levels and the likely developments therein, both short-term and long-term, having regard to the changes in the general economic situation, production targets and other relevant factors;

(d) to advise the appropriate ministries or departments on policy matters and to make suggestions to them for the better implementations of programmes in various sectors affecting employment generation.

(i) The suggestions and recommendations made from time to time by the Commission should receive careful and prompt consideration by all ministries and agencies of the Central Government as well as by the State Governments and other organisations.

(ii) A Committee of secretaries of the Central Government under the chairmanship of the Cabinet Secretary should be entrusted with the responsibility of considering the major issues arising from the Commission's suggestion and recommendations and taking necessary decisions on administrative and policy matters for the guidance of the various ministries, departments and agencies of the Government.

We would suggest that Parliament may consider the desirability of constituting a committee somewhat on the lines of its existing financial committees. The proposed Department of Employment and Manpower Planning as well as the National Commission should submit periodical reports to this committee on the employment situation in the country in general. Also, the Central Government should take steps to place before this committee the annual reports on the activities of the Department and the Commission.

We consider that as a counterpart of the Department of Employment and Manpower Planning recommended by us at the Central level, there should be suitable organisations also at the state level. These organisations should have the same relationship with other state government departments as the Department of Employment and Manpower Planning would have with its sister departments at the Centre. However, it does not seem to be necessary to have at the state level an organisation similar to the National Commission recommended by us for being set up at the Centre.

The review and appraisal organisation in the departments and ministries dealing with various plan schemes and other measures concerned with employment generation should be strengthened so as to cover the aspect of employment generation in addition to the physical and financial aspects of the programmes. The arrangements in the department for the formulation and review of Plan programmes should also be strengthened for undertaking the analysis and appraisal of employment generation in their respective fields. The strengthening of such arrangements in the executive and appraisal agencies at the state level would also be necessary.

It appears necessary to strengthen and suitably equip some of the existing organisations dealing with the collection of data and the appraisal of the progress of various programmes. In particular, the following suggestions are made :—

(i) The Programme Evaluation Organisation of the Planning Commission should be geared to increase the coverage of its work. In particular, it should evaluate the development programmes as regards their effectiveness in respect of employment generation.

(ii) With the increased emphasis on manpower planning and employment it would be necessary to strengthen at the state level the state bureaux of economics and statistics which are specialised organisations equipped to deal with the subject of statistics for all sectors of the economy. Their technical services could thus be more effectively utilised for developing employment statistics and manpower data.

(iii) The statistical machinery charged with the collection of educational statistics, both at the Centre and in the states should be strengthened so that in addition to the collection of educational statistics for administrative purposes, it can also provide necessary data required for employment and manpower planning to the apex organisation at the Centre and to the state departments dealing with employment and manpower planning.

The Department of Employment and Manpower Planning should be adequately equipped and provided with sufficient funds at its disposal to undertake studies directly in those states and union territories where a sufficiently well equipped organisation for this purpose does not exist or cannot be established within a reasonable time. It should also be able to undertake such pilot studies and surveys in special fields as it may consider necessary, either directly or by assisting suitable research institutions or academic bodies.

Note of Dissent by Jyotirmoy Bosu, M.P.

In my resolution on unemployment which was responsible for constitution of this Committee in 1969, I tried to make clear certain things connected with unemployment and its growth in the country during different plan periods. Almost the entire House of Lok Sabha was with me and the ground on which I had withdrawn the resolution from being put to vote was something different from what the terms of reference of this committee are. The terms of reference of this committee have been considerably watered down and in fact certain issues have been dropped. The government took about 13 months to constitute the committee and even after that the committee hardly got prompt and sufficient attention from the government in the matter of getting its many of the requirements met. I think the committee could have submitted its report earlier had the government shown keenness in helping the committee in its enormous task. In actual fact it was after a lot of pressure I had to exert on the government that the committee came into being.

Here I must thank Sri B. Bhagawati, the Chairman of the Committee who had made untiring efforts to further the cause of the committee, and other members, panel members, advisers, executives and staff for their continuous hard and sincere efforts without which the job would have been far more difficult for us to conclude.

The final draft has recorded a number of improvements. But in spite of that things remained with which I cannot agree. These are basic differences relating to our "approach to the problem". Hence this note of dissent.

I would like to make my basic position clear and the issue may be presented in the following manner :

Full and productive employment for all able-bodied persons of employable age should be the objective of the country's employment policy. No doubt there is always a big difference between the objective and what is feasible. Now the question that arises is, whether the objective of full employment is realisable under our present socio-economic set up which is based predominantly on private ownership in the means of production, particularly, when more than 90 per cent means of production are outside the scope of state planning. To my mind it is not possible. In an economy which is based on capitalist mode of production and where the productive activities are carried on with the sole objective of maximising profit, it cannot cater to the needs of the welfare of the society as a whole. The capitalists cannot thrive and their profits cannot be maximised without the existence of a reserve army of unemployed which was described by late Karl Marx as "the Industrial Reserve Army". This unemployed band are used as a weapon by capitalists to depress the earnings of the wage labourers employed by them. Because their anxiety will be always to remain in an "employer's market". In their drive for maximum profit the capitalists constantly resort to rationalisation, modernisation, automation, mechanisation, market manipulation and other labour-saving devices and thus the process of replacing of human labour by machines and other artificial methods, is a continuous one. In this process more wage earners lose their jobs and swell the rank of the unemployed. This is the universal law of capitalist development and like all other laws it is subject to variation according to circumstances. Even in a rich capitalist, highly industrialised country like America, they have failed to solve the problem of unemployment which ranges from 5 to 12 per cent (I do not dispute it is not high) of the labour force. In India, which is a backward, poor and much exploited country, there cannot be an exception to this general law particularly when it has taken the capitalist path of development since independence. I shall be living in a "fools paradise" if I think that the problem of unemployment and underemployment could be solved, and full employment ensured in my country under the present socio-economic set up.

In our constitution "right to gainful work" has been enshrined, but in reality our unemployment has grown by leaps and bounds with the passing of time. This has grown at such an alarming rate that it is now sapping the very vitals of the country.

The realisation of the objective of full employment is possible only in a real socialist system where productive activity is thoroughly planned and carried on solely in the interests of the society as a whole. It has already been demonstrated in practice in various countries what socialism can achieve. Soviet Russia solved the problem of unemployment in the course of its very first Five Year Plan. In China, where the problem was no less acute than what it is in India, unemployment has been banished from the society. Similar is the case with other backward countries which have taken the socialist path of development. Although I must admit here that there may be some sort of frictional unemployment in these countries; but the problem in the main has been solved.

We are quite conscious of the fact that the committee have had to formulate their recommendations under different circumstances altogether and not under a desirable or "ideal" system. One should not draw a pessimistic picture from what has been stated above. According to us, even under the existing socio-economic system it is possible to generate greater employment opportunities which could go a long way in arresting the deterioration in our unemployment position. To attain this objective it is necessary to radically change our whole approach to planning, investment, employment policy, etc. But with regret I must mention here that the committee's recommendations have not gone very far in that regard. I find much sense in what Dr. Ashok Mitra has said that the recommendations are confined to traditional sphere and line of thinking.

The schemes recommended by the committee are more or less already there, as for example; Crash Programme on Rural and Urban employment, expansion of irrigation facilities with particular emphasis on small irrigation schemes, land reclamation, rural electrification, rural roads, rural housing, rural water supply and similar other labour-intensive industries.

The committee of course in their sincere effort urged the government to provide adequate funds for implementation of labour intensive schemes and these will undoubtedly receive all full suport. But these project implementations alone will not achieve the desired objective of employment generation, unless radical changes are brought in the present institutional set up. There, unfortunately, the committee have not made positive and firm recommendations.

The basic cause of growing unemployment and under-employment in India, according to us, is the predominant existence of private ownership in the means of production. The problem got aggravated during the last 25 years because of wrong economic and fiscal policies pursued by the present government, which has a particular class character. These motive-oriented policies of the government are continuing to consolidate and strengthen more and more every day, the position of the big business houses and rural rich on the one hand and causing shrinkage of employment and job opportunities on the other. The same fatal policies have led to the fall in the actual growth rate of our economy. Unfortunately the committee did not apply their mind to this aspect of the problem. In the absence of a firm and basic approach the recommendations of the committee are inclined to be little stereotyped in character.

I must point out the committee have not dealt with the phenomenal growth of foreign and Indian monopoly houses in terms of profits, assets, turn over and remittances in spite of the so called curbs imposed on them by the government through its "NEW" industrial licensing policy and formation of the Monopoly and Restrictive Trade Practices Commission. The Committee did not find it important enough to recommend imposition of any drastic curbs on the activities of the monopoly houses. Over and above, their recommendation on industry under Chapter VIII on regularisation of irregular increase in installed capacity, if implemented, will undoubtedly lead to the further strengthening of the position of the monopoly houses which will in its turn worsen the problem of urban unemployment. Similarly we in the committee did not consider it necessary in Chapter VII—"Agriculture" to recommend measures for curbing the growth of the rural rich who are equally creating difficulties in the way of providing productive employment to the rural surplus landless labour force.

One of the fundamental drawbacks of the planning in India is the absence of any provision for compulsory implementation of the schemes included in the plan. Even most modest targets set in the plan remained unfulfilled or unimplemented. The fate of the Crash Scheme for rural and urban developments should act as an eye-opener to all of us. Even the meagre fund earmarked for a particular project has been either kept unspent or is being diverted to some other low-priority unproductive projects. The fate of "the crash scheme for rural employment", introduced in 1970-71 with the object of providing employment to 1000 persons on an average per year in every district is a glaring example. This scheme was put into operation on the basis of 100 per cent grant of the Central Government, and with an annual allocation of Rs. 50 crores. Thus each district was allotted on an average Rs. 12.5 lakhs per annum. The study of the expenditure pattern reveals the following picture :

During 1971-72, 81 per cent of the total expenditure incurred in 13 states and 5 union territories relates to one item alone namely "construction of roads." The expenditure incurred on minor irrigation is only to the tune of 8.89 per cent. And on land reclamation it is as low as 1.6 per cent (source—36th report of the Estimates Committee—, fifth Lok Sabha 1972-73, page 65). Many other crash schemes have met with the same fate.

Under the circumstances there is no guarantee that

the Committee's recommendations on the employment generating schemes, even if accepted by the government, will be given effect to. The government, as seen by its past and present performances, will discharge its duties by setting a number of targets without sincerely meaning their implementation.

It should be remembered that the bulk of the productive activities are carried out in India as in many other capitalist countries, by private individuals and joint stock enterprises. The productive enterprises owned by the government account for not more than 6% of the net domestic product. (Source : Pocket book of economic information, 1971, published by the Ministry of Finance, Government of India). The accepted recommendations of the committee will not be implemented in letter and in spirit unless there is some form of compulsion including provision for penal action. It is equally and urgently necessary, along with that, to raise the public sector to the 'commanding heights' of our economy in the true sense of the term meaning, the vital sectors of our economic activities, including business operations of the foreign banks and other companies where there is foreign equity participation, have to be brought under the public sector.

The committee have recommended additional and new fiscal incentives to all entrepreneurs with a view to encourage them to set up industries in backward regions. Before making these recommendations it was necessary to have an assessment of past overall impact of the incentives that are already available. From the reports that we have, we do not find any break-through in this direction unfortunately.

During the last 3 years, out of a total number of about 247 industrial licences issued to 20 larger business houses and foreign companies, not more than 25 relate to setting up of industries in backward regions (Parliament replies).

The lending policy of the term financing institutions and nationalised banks is more or less meant to favour the metropolitan cities and large business houses.

From a recent study by the credit planning cell of the Reserve Bank of India on the state-wise and region-wise performance in deposit mobilisation and sector-wise credit disbursement and also expansion of bank branches by the public sector commercial banks between end-June, 1969 and end-June, 1972, it could be seen that the public sector banks have not generally so far operated in the manner they should have had in conforming with the basic declared objective of nationalisation. Even now, the priority sectors remain neglected. Pace of expansion of bank branches in the rural and unbanked areas for mopping up surplus resources and for agricultural credit facilities to the rural needy has slowed down in the last 2 years.

It is not enough to recognise in theory, the necessity for tackling the problem of unemployment and under-employment on a warfooting. It is also necessary to translate this theory into practice and with that objective in view the committee could have recommended measures for compulsory implementation of the plan schemes with provision for punishment in case of failure and non-implementation.

But unfortunately no such recommendation has been made.

In this connection I fully endorse the suggestion put forward by Dr. Ashok Mitra for creation of a "Central Employment Fund" with contributions from industrial employers in the private sector, rural rich, public sector undertakings, nationalised banks, financial institutions and Central and state budgets.

On Chapter VII "agriculture" there is not much of disagreement over the recommendations. But it must be mentiond that the committee's recommendations have amounted to 'putting the cart before the horse'. It is necessary to take drastic and honest measures for break through in agriculture, which is now stagnating. In other words, it is absolutely necessary to improve agriculture on a sustained basis by releasing the rural productive forces. Adequate employment opportunities could easily be generated in the rural areas through this measure alone and not through mechanical implementation of a number of schemes.

In our opinion the country's strategy for breaking the stagnation in agriculture should be the adoption of a programme of genuine radical land reforms in the interests of the peasantry and this should get first priority.

The land policy of the government has not been directed to bring effective and radical land reforms in the interests of the peasantry. It was mainly directed at some reforms in the existing land relations by transforming the feudal landlords into capitalist landlords. In this way the government expected that agricultural production would substantially improve and food problem thus solved. In this process a new class of rural rich has come into existence and this class now dominates the rural economy. This new rural rich has been mainly able to derive major benefits out of the rural development schemes of the government. As a result, social tension in the rural areas has increased and the economic position of the agricultural labourers and small farmers worsened.

Even the limited programme of land reform (like consolidation of holdings, tenancy reforms, ceiling on land holdings and distribution of surplus land among the agricultural labourers and poor peasants) included in the First Plan remains unimplemented to date.

The Planning Commission's task force on agrarian relations has come to the conclusion : "In the context of the socio-economic conditions prevailing in the rural areas of the country, no tangible progress can be expected in the field of land reforms in the absence of requisite political will. The sad truth is that this crucial factor has been wanting."

The task force's report goes on to say that in no sphere of public capacity since independence "has the hiatus between precept and practice, between policy pronouncements and actual execution has been as great as in the domain of land reforms."

Farming cooperative movement in India has not made any headway and most of the existing farming cooperative societies are controlled by the rural vested interests. It is bound to be so. Correct solution of the land problem is the main guarantee for a successful cooperative movement. The cooperative movement in the Peoples' Republic of China was successful simply because the government of that country drew up and implemented a scheme of radical land reforms in the interests of the peasantry.

Rapid growth of farming cooperative societies (which is possible only in the back-ground of a successful implementation of the policy of radical land reforms), is the only solution to the problem of growing fragmentation of holdings. Unfortunately the committee did not lay any emphasis on this important issue.

The need for a bigger Fifth Plan

One cannot deny the fact that one of the main causes of growing unemployment-under employment in the country is the low rate of growth in the country's national income, which in its turn should be attributed mainly to the low rate of capital formation. Capital formation is not only low, the rate of growth has fallen during the past few years.

Why this low rate of capital formation ? Our country, though under-developed, has no shortage of financial and natural resources. By resources we mean not simply visible financial resources. By this term we mean actual and potential and hidden 'economic surplus' which is lying with monopolists, big traders, speculators and the rural rich. The committee did not deal with the question of resources.

We feel, it is possible to invest 20-25% of the country's national income without imposing any curb on the current consumption of the overwhelming majority of the population. Of course, the conspicuous consumption by the very small richer section has to be drastically curbed.

Without a bigger Fifth Plan, it will not be possible to create adequate job opportunities. According to us, it is certainly possible (and desirable too) to raise the Fifth Plan outlay by at least 50% without imposition of any fresh burdens on the common people. It is even possible to lessen the burden on the common man and at the same time step up Fifth Plan outlay and investment.

For doing this it will be necessary to launch a ruthless attack on the urban and rural vested interests. But we do not think, the present government with its particular class character has got the political courage and plans to do that.

Other topics of interest

"Dimension of the problem."

The final draft is somewhat improvement upon the first one in that an attempt has been made to present an overall picture of unemployment and under-employment in the country.

We have no disagreement with the view that the "the estimate of unemployment should include the persons who are wholly unemployed as well as those who have work for less than 14 hours a week. On this basis, according to the final draft, the likely number of unemployed persons may reasonably be taken as 18.6 million including 8.9 million who are unemployed and 9.7 million who work for less than 14 hours a week and who may be treated on par with the unemployed. This will include 16.1 million persons in rural areas. (7.6 million males and 8.5 million females) and 2.5 million persons in urban areas." According to us the figure relating to urban unemployment is a gross under estimate. The survey conducted in various States will bear this out. We think a separate paragraph should be inserted in this chapter dealing with the problem of under-employment.

Total number of persons working less than 28 hours have been estimated by the committee at 27.2 million heads. These 27.2 million persons should be categorised as "severely underemployed". This will enable us to get an overall picture of the magnitude of the problem. Besides, the committee could have also made the following recommendation : viz.

That the Central Statistical Organisation should publish every year a white paper on the trends of employment, unemployment and under-employment, on the lines of yearly statements on national income estimates.

Now I come to Chapter on Education and Training "Causes of educated unemployment."

According to the report "a major factor has been the evergrowing rush for higher education, etc."

A major factor, according to the Education Commission's report and many other such reports, is the present system of education itself. The British rulers introduced the colonial educational system in India to recruit clerks for their colonial administration. The system introduced by the alien rulers remains more or less unchanged even after the 25 years of independence. There had been however very minor modifications here and there. Surprisingly enough this basic factor has not been mentioned in the report.

The recommendations with regard to higher education, we apprehend, will lead to curtailment and restriction of higher education. This, we oppose on principle. The Committee's recommendations are based on erroneous and lop-sided notion of so called "higher educational explosion" in India. The following table will speak for itself.

Students in Higher Educational Institutions

(per 1000 population in 1968)

1. China (mainland)	..	122
2. U.S.A.	..	37
3. Canada	..	23
4. U.S.S.R.	..	19
5. Philippines	..	16
6. Japan	..	15
7. Sweden	..	15
8. Netherlands	..	14
9. Australia	..	14
10. France	..	10
11. Poland	..	10
12. Italy	..	8
13. West Germany	..	7
14. Belgium	..	6
15. U.A.R.	..	6
16. Pakistan	..	3
17. India	..	2

Source—India, Pocket book of Economic information 1971 ; Government of India, Ministry of Finance, Department of Economic Affairs.

It can be seen from the table that India's rate of admission is lower than even Pakistan.

Qualitative improvement in higher education is certainly desirable and for that the present structure has to be radically changed and a new one brought into existence. Higher education in the field of art, culture, etc. must not be curtailed in the name of "quality".

Some Basic Issues

The committee have rejected the suggestion for unemployment relief. We wholly disagree with this. We do not lose sight of the fact that it is an enormous job to identify the persons who are genuinely unemployed. The financial commitment in connection with the implementation of the scheme is also considerable. Besides there will be causes of misuse and corruption. But on these grounds we cannot deny subsistence allowance to the unemployed. They are suffering not because of any fault of their own. The Government has to take the blame for adopting wrong development programmes and in keeping alive the out-dated socio-economic system as we find today in India. It is the bounden duty of the Government either to provide them witb suitable employment or in the alternative give them subsistence allowance so that they can survive. In almost all the countries of the world worth mentioning, the government takes care of the unemployed persons. We feel in India, too, the unemployed persons deserve equal treatment. We should have recommended in clear language the broad principle on the basis of which the government should work out a detailed scheme on this.

If the government has the mind to be good to these unemployed, the problem of funds can't stand on the way. We have to treat this whole thing as a war on poverty and unemployment. And when we fight a war we do not hinder our cause for want of money.

The recommendation for the creation of a special fund (unemployment subsistence fund) should have been given top priority. This could easily be created by a direct special levy on the concerns under the control of the 75 monopoly houses, large independent companies, as well as the foreign controlled companies. Nobody will deny that they are passing through very prosperous days. This special levy which may be called "unemployment subsistence levy" should be imposed on the rural rich also.

While the committee have generally expressed their opposition to automation and other labour-saving devices, it had recommended introduction of sophisticated technology and mechanised equipment in certain cases. This recommendation, in our opinion, will undoubtedly lead to misuse and backdoor automation and mechanisation. It was necessay to say categorically in the report that we are opposed to automation in principle. Even in advanced countries like the U.S.A. and the U.K. it has been seen that automation has led to displacement of human labour. In India, where we top in the world in unemployment and where the avenues of employment is severely limited, any kind of automation will only make a bad thing worse.

I am grateful to my colleagues in the committee for giving me the opportunity to submit this note of dissent.

(Sd.)
(Jyotirmoy Bosu)

2. Dr. Bishamber Das Marg,
NEW DELHI-1.

Minute of supplementation by Gautam Mathur

I. Preamble

While forwarding the Interim Report of this Committee to the Hon'ble Minister of Labour and Rehabilitation the Chairman had mentioned that we were addressing ourselves to some basic questions and eliciting the opinion of the groups on them. Since, that time a discussion on these has taken place within the Committee on a number of occasions, and it has also had the benefit of the report of the Groups with their annexures including one dealing with the special viewpoint which is known as the Long-Term Strategy Approach. The Committee has wide terms of reference regarding Long Term measures for promoting employment including changes in the industrial, fiscal, monetary and educational policy required for the purpose. In that context, in the Chapter on Basic Issues the Committee has considered some of the elements raised by the Long-Term Strategy Approach and incorporated them in the relevant section of the Chapter. In view of this a Minute of Supplementation on this approach written by the present signatory is included as part of the Report as the issues raised require to be given serious attention in the formulation of Government and National Policy, though the way the Strategy may be implemented, would require a considerable amount of further research. In its various recommendations on particular matters the Committee has tended to lean towards the principles of choice as enunciated in the Long-Term Strategy Approach as far as it may be practicable. But the present signatory has the feeling that the Committee will find it difficult to see its way to accepting the Approach in its entirety, and hence it has been necessary to write a separate note to present the viewpoint in its essential elements in an integrated manner. This note, therefore, presents the elements which are of a basic nature in the Long-Term Strategy Approach which, in the opinion of the signatory, ought to regulate the policy towards non-employment.

II. Growth and Employment

In the Strategy Approach the question of creation of employment opportunities is intimately linked to the Growth process. The question of employment is viewed as an essential part of the development process and a part of the plan, not outside it. As a matter of fact in the Strategy Approach there cannot be any activity outside a proper Plan of Development, for any increased level of work in any field either uses physical resources or produces them, and hence the level and composition of the National Product is effected. For a plan to be consistent, production must be at least approximately, according to its provisions.

The Strategy Approach rejects the viewpoint that employment should be created in jobs which do not form part of a proper National Plan which is to be in accord with the optimum strategy for the path to a state of development and gives effect to it in operational terms. It is the growth of the National Product in the appropriate directions as laid down in the proper plan which must alone create employment, and it is denied that jobs ought to be created in any way one can even though for unproductive purposes, under pressure of vocal or dormant demand. This is so because the problem of unemployment can be tackled through the Development Path alone. There are innumerable avenues of productive employment in the country where each person can contribute to the National Product forming a part of a proper plan rather than drawing a wage from various forms of mis-employment be it as a doorkeeper outside an executive's office or at a higher level, a Minister without adequate portfolio.

Efficiency in production must be the criterion for creating the jobs, and what it consists in, is the scope of a part of this minute, in so far as an efficient technique is one which forms a part of the Optimum Strategy obtained on the basis of minimising the time for obtaining the objective subject to the constraints. Giving jobs through some special programmes outside the strategy can only be the result of failure of effort to plan for development properly or shortfall in implementation. A plan should be flexible enough to allow introduction of alternative measures in case of shortfalls without affecting the structure of resources required elsewhere in the plan.

Secondly, the Strategy Approach denies the view that in conditions of existence of quite a large reserve of non-employed population, employment can be created in the long run without growth, or that there is a choice between growth and employment. It is known that in the Optimum Strategy pertaining to the existing conditions, one cannot get employment except through laying the foundations of an economy growing in an optimum manner, and, on the other hand, one cannot get the economy growing in the *right manner* without creating sizable employment. If there is any deviation from these two counterpart principles, then any stray employment offered is misemployment, while any odd investment created is misinvestment, both of which reduce the capacity of the economy to offer more employment to others, because the appropriate capital and consumption goods are not correspondingly built up, on the basis of which goods, future growth would be accelerated.

One cannot also create employment validly by techniques which yield so little product that a part of the wage has to be subsidised from some other industries. To put full employment as a short-term objective in an under-developed country is to condemn it to perpetual under-development, because this can be achieved only by techniques of production which have so low productivity per man that even the payment of a subsistence level wage is jeopardised. Such a course must be avoided, howsoever strong may be the demands for full employment by the non-employed members of the working force. The economy should draw into the organised sector of appropriate techniques (be they found to be of high or low degree of mechanisation) as many non-employed workers, full-time or part-time, as possible at the subsistence wage, while the rest should remain waiting in the traditional occupation drawing the same wage as they have done till hitherto. It is through this that fast rate of growth will be engendered for those non-employed workers to be brought into the pale of the organised sector as employed persons in the next few years.

A contravention of this principle by using too high a degree of mechanisation (for the economy as a whole) gives little employment now and little in the future because of the low rate of growth on account of the very high capital intensity per man. A contravention by using too low a degree of mechanisation (for the aggregate economy) yields no possibility of growth, and hence it may be that a high level of employment (though at a wage level below subsistence) may be achieved now, but in the future the situation cannot improve much, as growth is stultified. The optimum technique is the proper vehicle of growth, employment and social justice, and it lies in between these two extremes, but leaning towards a fairly low degree of mechanisation in the consumption sector, and consequently yielding a high employment-potential.

III. Long Term and Short Run

When we talk of Growth, it is meaningful to view the process of growth over a long period. All development has to have its sights fixed to a long-term objective and what is created in the short run is the initial instalment of a long-term path of development. Non-serious thinkers often close their eyes to the long-term by quoting Keynes out of context : "In the long run we are all dead". They laugh over the forty-year old joke and for them the matter ends there. They fail to understand that Keynes was, in this quip, getting impatient with laissez-faire economists who were recommending government inaction on the basis of a theory that, in the long-run, unemployment would be corrected by itself. The aphorism has no significance for a situation of planning where the economist is recommending immediate government action but the matter to be decided is whether the choice of investment is to be governed by consideration pertaining to a short time-horizon or a long one. In this context it is relevant to assert that though we die in the long run, as builders of our national economy we live for the long-run and, aim to create an economy wherein our children will have a better deal than what we have been able to enjoy. This is envisaged through planning with a long-term horizon. A series of short-range palliatives will not change the situation substantially and will take the country astray.

It is, therefore, desirable to distinguish the term "long-run" which signifies automatic equilibrium through the market mechanism without government intervention, and hence a mythical state which may never be reached, from "long-term" which signifies the long-range horizon for active government intervention through a plan of development to actuate activities to take place which would not automatically have occurred in a laissez-faire economy.

Take for example, the policy that we earn foreign exchange in the short-term by exporting iron ore. It looks an exceedingly attractive proposition for solving balance-of-payment problems. But a little bit of thought as regards its long-term effects would yield the result that if this is continued to be done we shall one day find that the iron ore reserves for our own needs have been depleted, and our further development is retarded. This is apart from the result that much more foreign exchange could be earned by converting the iron ore into steel, the steel into equipment, and the equipment into consumer goods which are required for the export market. We also avoid thereby the loss of foreign exchange in the short-term which is due to other countries importing our iron ore, making use of it for their own growth, converting it with a superior technology into equipment and goods which they sell to us at prices higher than those charged by Indian manufacturers, as also compete with us in the market of developing countries. Further it hits markets within the country also, because of the craze for imported goods which finds scope through partially successful pressure for liberalising certain types of unnecessary imports or goods smuggled into the country.

In terms of employment, there is a similar confusion between short-term measures and long-term measures. For instance there is a lot of effort regarding implementation of crash programmes. A crash programme should not, in spite of what its name signifies, refer to an unplanned and haphazard set of schemes. Ordinarily the schemes should be well thought-out in advance for various contingencies, so that they may be interlinked in an integrated manner with the growth process. They should be parts of a contingency plan and there should be no quality of 'crash' about the programme when it means only that it is implemented speedily. It should really comprise of a set of interlinked district plans which are to be as a whole speeded up to the limits of the physical feasibility and should provide employment through that process, whenever special needs arise. The schemes in a crash programme which are not a part of the plan, conflict with the long-run needs of development because of the random use of the resources. Speeding up a properly worked-out plan does not conflict with the long-term objectives because it brings its fulfilment nearer. Hence, the latter alone should be the vehicle of providing employment. According to the Strategy Approach an ill-worked out crash programme will not solve the problem of unemployment but a well-integrated plan only will substantially solve the problem of unemployment. If the schemes are outside the plan, the problem of unemployment cannot be solved by crash programmes of the uncoordinated sort wherein a road is built from nowhere to anywhere, or a couple of extra clerks are employed to fill up ledgers which should have been done anyhow by the already under-worked staff.

Let us examine another view which states that short-term employment may be increased through production of goods which show a high demand-potential. When we decide to allow production of goods on the basis of demand alone we come across goods which cater to the requirements of those who have high purchasing power. In the short-run the production of these goods creates employment, but in long-run it takes the economy away from the equalitarian structure (of reduction in disparities in consumption standards). It militates against social policy as well as employment policy, for it brings about a regime in which goods percolate from the top towards the middle income-groups in a very slow fashion, while the common men's requirements are not met.

It also generates an economy in which modernised consumer durables are given substantial proportion of investments. Many of these goods can be produced only through highly mechanised forms of production which offer very low employment per unit of capital investment. They set the pace of the economy as a low-employment economy. What is gained in terms of short-range employment through consumer luxuries is lost in terms of potentiality to give employment in the next period. We have got into this malaise of a low-employment economy by concentrating upon the short-run each time. The country can no longer afford to take short-range measures which do not form a part of the long-term-Optimum Development path.

The above attitude does not deny the importance of the short-term and the action necessary to be taken therein. But it is to be emphasised that the short-term ought not to exist by itself but should be treated only as a segment of a longer horizon to which pertains a well thought-out plan of development from the present conditions to the objective to be attained in the long-term. Each bit of the short term must take us forward along the chosen path towards that long-term objective and hence the achievement of the short-term becomes extremely important. It is because of this that the short term cannot be thought of except in the context of the long-term path. On the other hand, with changing circumstances (like technical knowledge improving) the long-term path has to be rechalked periodically, while for short-term shortfalls in implementation changes are required for adjustment purposes. These are the proper domain of short-term considerations for economic action.

This also does not mean that when there are employment opportunities for productive purposes using little of the scarce resources they may be left untapped in the short-term. What is to be stressed is that if these cater to the needs of the common man they ought not to be left untapped and should form a part of the long-term path of development, because they would thereby be able to cater to the demand for consumer necessaries which a rapid expansion of the capital-goods sector necessitates. The production of such of the goods as can be exported as handicrafts or works of skill should also form part of the plan and encouraged. Since the same services may be got from many types of goods, the types which substitute the use of the production of the heavy-investment sector by those in plentiful supply may also be allowed to be covered by the plan (e.g. straw-curtains instead of air conditioners). There should be a provision in the plan itself for tapping of the potentials at the district level and the plan at that level ought to be flexible enough to make provision for the commodities which do not require scarce resources and are produced out of the enthusiasm of the local people.

We can, therefore, state that our sights fixed on the long-term objective and eyes both on the long and the short period will indicate investment plans for the present period which take us nearer to the target. Our eyes scanning only for feet make us oblivious that we are nearing the edge of a cliff. The tremendous inflationary pressures which an ill thought-out crash programme can generate in the economy, through unproductive investment, would push it to the brink of an economic disaster.

IV. Unemployment and Non-employment

In the literature of development economics an important distinction is made between unemployment which refers to people who were in employment previously and have been driven out on account of a depression in economic activity and the state of non-employment where in a large mass of people were never in appropriate employment and are to be drawn into it. If the figures as collected by various surveys are to be heeded they show too low a degree of lack of employment to be meaningful. The definition of lack of employment as used in these surveys itself needs to be revised, for people may be in jobs which provide them too little even for subsistence, or they may get paid employment for too few days in the year. The Committee has very properly rejected these definitions and has taken the poverty line as a more reasonable measure with social meaning of lack of employment providing even subsistence. In the present minute, an even wider definition is adopted, termed "non-employment" as referring firsty to the people who do not get subsistence wage whether occupied or not and secondly to those who do get it but not through using the more efficient set of mutually non-inferior techniques. In the two categories together are all the non-employed. It signifies that if one were wanting to shift to the most efficient set of mutually non-inferior techniques from the individual inferior techniques largely used at present, there would be no labour bottleneck to the shift to the extent of existence of non-payment. The degree of non-employment, therefore, reflects the magnitude of the task of development ahead and the degree of deprivation of the mass of our population at the present from what is attainable.

The most efficient set of mutually non-inferior and non-superior techniques are the set of techniques of both low and high degrees of mechanisation (arranged as what is termed a production function connecting capital intensity per man employed to productivity). Herein no technique is inferior to another on the criteria of productivity per unit of capital and per unit of labour, being satisfied simultaneously. Hence, techniques where output-capital ratio is high but output per man is low get high marks on one count though low on the other, are not, therefore, inferior to techniques where labour productivity is high but capital productivity low. They are mutually non-inferior and hence non-superior. They are superior to all techniques wherein output per unit of capital and per unit of labour are both low, because then both the criteria are satisfied simultaneously.

These techniques form the set of mutually non-superior and non-inferior techniques depicted as an Efficient-Production-Set or the production function mentioned above. Employment outside these is termed as employpment. To be given a job within this set, but in the subset of appropriate techniques chosen on the criterion of national benefit may be called 'True Employment'. During the path of development to the objective, people are to be gathered from the regions of inferior techniques in the sphere of non-employment and non-True-employment to the fold of superior techniques in the sphere of True Employment.

At the end of the path of development the appropriate techniques may be different from the path and hence by the time we have finished traversing the path of development and enter the state of development all the population must be truly employed in the "golden-age" technique as described in the literature pertaining to the work of Professor Joan Robinson in his book "Accumulation of Capital" written eighteen years back. This concept has been taken by the present signatory as the long-run objective of growth in analysis conducted since that time.

The problem of lack of employment is thus a long-term problem of lack of True-employment rather than a short-term one of too many people chasing too few jobs. It spans the whole Development Path and is solved by ending the state of under-development altogether. Provision of jobs without reference to this path is a short-run palliative and will not solve the problem of lack of employment. Consequently, if we have to look at the problems of Unemployment we cannot escape the problem of looking to the structure of Development Path and its objective as a whole.

This can be done through the framework of Strategies of Development, rather than merely Strategies of Employment-creation.

V. Objective of Development

The objective of long-term development taken as the

attainment of golden age refers to a state wherein all the working population then existing will have been given employment in the technique which gives steady growth at continued full employment at a highest standard of living technically feasible and rising according to the full utilisation of scientific advances. The composition of the packet of the standard of living at the objective of development is given by moral choice of the constituent individuals whether they would prefer to have largely material goods or cultural goods. But the potentiality of the economy will be to give goods of either composition, to prevent the situation where people in advanced countries enjoying higher standards of material well being, laud the great spiritual benefits accruing to the rest of mankind by the lack of these goods for the latter. If austerity in living will be chosen for the long run, it will be the choice of that generation based upon its will, not forced on them for lack of capital-equipment capacity to produce the material or cultural goods whichever they will demand.

Hence, in the long-run, for the economy to be able to give this choice, the capital stock of the country has to be very high, specially in the basic industries which provide equipment for themselves, for the newer forms of technology and for whatever type of consumer goods which the society may then want. The derived objective then becomes to accumulate the stock of capital in basic industries as much as possible.

It may be asked as to why we should worry about building up the capital stock of basic industries when the general standard of living is below what would be considered as a reasonable subsitence level if they were employed. The Central Legislature of a country is composed of members who represent the interest of the people of the country as a whole. In this function, it is submitted that emphasis must be placed on the interest of the future people of the country as well as the present, for it is only on this basis that nation and economies are built up. It is for this reason that our Parliament has committed itself to a policy of priority for heavy investment reflecting our national commitment to the future generation.

For more than a century and a quarter we have been in the process of slow development. If the commitment to rapid development had been undertaken a hundred years back, we would have been, by this time, economically one of the front-ranking countries. However, due to the lack of commitment by the Government then in power, our growth of infra-structure and basic industries suffered, so that although we had a College of Civil Engineering many years before the establishment of M.I.T., in the U.S.A., we have been left for behind in technology, though we started planning railroad construction a century and a quarter back, our present network is rudimentary for a large country generating the traffic attendant upon an industrial devolution. Our commitment to the present generation is to give it a subsistence standard as a minimum fot all the members who can be absorbed in employment in the optimum strategy, but it could not go beyond that till an adequate stock of capital has been built up in our basic industries. A hundred years back the decision rested with the foreign government. Now the decision lies with us and let us not be accused by the generation a hundred years hence that we left the pursuit of the future for the gains of the present beyond the level which necessity dicttates as subsistence. There will be plenty of opportunities twentyfive years hence to let off steam a little bit after a spell of the Austerity economy. By a gradual rise of the standard of living after near-full employment is achieved, the rigour of the capital-accumulation economy in the Development Path may be some-what alleviated through phased rises in consumer necessaries for all.

Various strategies by which accumulation of requisite stock of capital could be attained, can be framed with regard to the type of goods which they stress. The one which is likely to reach the objective in least time subject to the constraints on the path is to be selected as the optimum strategy.

VI. The Choice of Goods

There are two basic choices which must be made if the economy is to achieve true employment which, as we have stated, can come only from hastening the growth process in a proper manner. The first is what type of goods must an economy manufacture in the consumer-goods sector and the second is the degree of mechanisation for producing these. In some cases these are inter-related, for if cotton clothing is to be encouraged then there is a choice of technique through production of cotton by use of tractors or ploughs, but for terylene there is no alteranative to the use of highly-mechanised processes for the production of its basic material. The choice between production of modernised luxury goods and consumer necessaries cannot be escaped, because to the extent to which the former draw upon the resources of the Heavy-Investment Sector, the growth of the latter is restrained, because the essential Heavy-Investment materials which consumption necessaries require are shifted to luxury production (e.g. steel for drinking water pipes in rural areas is diverted to construction of superb residential colonies in suburbs of towns).

The possible strategies are divided into two types

on the basis of the choice of consumption goods. In the first case, the choice flows from the Doctrine of Percolation whereby modernised luxury commodities are manufactured for the benefit of the top income-level of the population and it is expected that their use may percolate downwards as capacity expands. But it has been noticed that this process must necessarily be thwarted for two main reasons.

Firstly, fresh investment goes into ever newer types of products which the high income-groups keep on voting to themselves. Thus they get promoted from earthenware coolers to ice-boxes, from there to refrigerators and thence onwards to the deep freeze, rather than simple earthen-ware coolers with drinking water sources being rapidly diffused and new investment substantially flowing into them.

Secondly, the productive capacity rising does not necessarily lead to economies, because, to achieve these economies large-scale factories with different techniques are required, which means a huge capital cost especially of scarce types of equipment. Hence, the cost may fall only slightly or may be higher than in other small-scale techniques, a phenomenon sometimes wrongly attributed to better quality but which may be observed as having been really caused by over-capitalisation. However, the income falls steeply as the market expands from the top, because of the highly-skew distribution. Hence, the market expands on the strength of high-level salesmanship, advertisement and the pressure of demonstration effect. This leads to shifting of expenditure from essential wants to inessential ones, and the attitudes of mind diverted from achievement of performance of one's work to achievement in acquisition of consumer durables and other essentials.

At the same time the techniques pertaining to modernised luxury-commodities being highly mechanised, and the volume of investment large in this sector and in sectors catering to its inputs, as a proportion of investment in manufacturing industry, the profit to wage ratio becomes high and the ratio of management-salary to wage bill of unskilled labour goes up, in spite of wages being above average in many of these industries. The whole process leads to increased disparities in income and through that further disparities in consumption in the absence of effective restraints on consumption. In this sense, a small portion of the working population drawing high salary, profit and wages above average helps in manufacturing the inessential goods which it consumes along with the other privileged sections of the society and the rest of the population keeps on watching this consumption taking place. But when the latter stretches its hand to purchase these goods, it finds them much beyond the capacity of the common man to buy. A so-called glass curtain separates them from the possibility of consuming that which others are seen to be enjoying.

The social tensions caused by the Glass-Curtain Economy have enormously deleterious effects. It makes the effort at work for the poorest operative seem to be irksome rather than creating joy in the application of effort. Interest in the work is also lost by those who no longer accept as an act of God the fact that widely disparate rewards are seen to be given per unit intensity of human effort, because those engaged in back-breaking traditional labour get much less than those tending equipment in conditions of ease. This also explains the phenomenon of demand for higher emoluments at all levels, as also the paradox that some unemployed people are not willing to take up regular productive employment at the subsistence wage but are working for short cuts through sinecure jobs like those of peons, or applying their ingenuity or luck to illegal transactions to gambling, lotteries and stakes. The entrepreneurship also shifts its character from the long-term risk-takers (who are supposed to be the captains of industries and on whom depends the justification for the temporary continuance of the capitalist system during the age of transition towards an egalitarian society) and becomes a band of short-term profit-earners and speculators. To get rich quick and to enjoy the fruits of high living becomes the matto of the society, and is confirmed by economists who call these the incentive to effort for the "take off". But it is not realised that for purposes of rapid development in a plan regime, the whole structure of our society gets vitiated by the picture which the Glass-Curtain Economy establishes. Apart from diversion of resources to inessential wants and fancy goods, the highly mechanised forms of production in this sector and the low rate of growth which it imposes on the economy as a whole results in continued non-employment for the rest of the economy for a very long span of time, if not possibly, on a permanent basis.

One cannot recommend the creation of employment through industries belonging to the Glass-Curtain Economy, for that employment is illusory in terms of the alternative employment foregone. Thus a tape-recorder factory may use up scarce types of physical capital to the extent of half a crore of rupees and a corresponding figure of scarce human capital, and the employment it may offer may be to a hundred workers direct or to two hundred including ancillary purposes. Increasingly, to secure a large chunk of allocations in the Fifth Plan, the manufacturers or the departments of industries at the State level and the Central level, are making out the case for the highly mechanised modern luxury-commodities to be actively encouraged, either on the basis of extra employment they will offer or by trying to show they are necessaries of a functional nature or are useful for education, or for family planning or rural uplift while it is well known that though these attributes may be true to a certain extent, the decisive factor for the goods to be produced depends upon the demand created by the entertainment or such other elitist value they may possess, and the employment created will be microscopic in relation to the opportunities lost through not making an alternative use of the scarce capital in less-mechanised techniques.

One can also countenance extension of this type of production through creation of demand for the goods through advertisement. The neo-classical economist stresses on savings but allows free inroads into its implementation through the process of advertisement which is more persuasive than the national call to austerity in consumption. Till the Advertisement Economy exists, and grows with better techniques of mass media, marketing etc., for the creation of more wants by psychological appeals, effort of the Government for a savings campaign is a losing activity. The strong appeal to consume more must, in the minds of the public, win out against the feeble attempt at the appeal to consume less. A reversal of the strength of these two appeals is essential to undo the ravages, which the Glass-Curtain Economy is bringing into our total economy and society.

Because of this, one must change over fundamentally from the procedure of asking how many jobs can be created in what industry and adding up for total employment. Employment created through the Glass-Curtain Industries and activities is dearly bought. It destroys employment opportunities multi-fold elsewhere. It also nullifies the attempt of the Government as has been accepted in the Fifth Plan Approach to give social and economic justice to the common man.

It having been decided that the Doctrine of percolation hitherto followed by our economic system cannot bring the target of long-run development and employment nearer, nor can it yield social justice, we turn to the Doctrine of Permeation, which is the alternative choice regarding method of diffusion of consumer goods for improvement in the standard of living.

According to this Doctrine, the consumer-goods sector of the economy concentrates on producing the goods which the employed workers require at subsistence. The idea is, as enunciated as a moral dictum by Professor Richard Khan in his Jerusalem Lectures about fifteen years back, that the standard of living ought not to be raised for the fortunate few who happen to be employed, while non-employment lasts and until the whole population has been brought into the net of employment. Till that time all increase in consumption-goods production ought to be more equitably distributed through greater employment. Only after near-full-employment is achieved can a moral case be built for gradual rise of standard of living beyond subsistence and there also the interests of the long-term growth may restrain the rise.

After full employment is achieved, whether the real wage may or may not be raised will depend upon the choice of Parliament, for reaching the state of full development early or allowing better living standards gradually. In any case the rise howsoever gradual will be through permeation of the economy with goods which all will consume rather than selected goods for the top-most income brackets. Hence, such an economy will not get to producing what nowadays may be described as luxury articles, until the time accumulation of capital has gone upto such a height that there is productive capacity for these goods to be given to all. Barring advance action in preparation of next phase so that changes are not abrupt, for the whole of the present phase it envisages the formation of a society in the meantime, which has equaliterian structure of consumption, through fast expansion of consumer necessaries. The rate of growth is initially very high in this economy as the wage is at subsistence, and technical improvements keep on taking place in the most efficient set of mutually non-inferior, non-superior techniques available to be embodied in physical capital. The rate of capital accumulation will, therefore, remain high in such a case. Only after enough capital has been accumulated to satisfy the requirements of consumption for everyone at the targeted standard of living, does not allow the actual standard of living to rise fast and the rate of accumulation to drop from the high level of the path of development to the lower level of equilibrium rate of growth as a developed country.

The planning authority in the regime of permeation, all the time chooses the consumer goods which are to be produced and takes measures to ensure that they are produced in the right quantum to satisfy the requirements of all in employment at the standard prescribed for efficiency, and of the rest at the minimum requirements for existence. The choice is a technical choice as regards nutritional and clothing standards etc., and is made by the democratic state not by the producer. Such an economy chooses the goods and equipment for producing them not by the pressure exerted by the producers that such and such products are "good for you", nor by the consumer that "we want such and such goods", but by the needs as envisaged by the

Democratic State.

The principle of democracy which envisages equality of voting rights for everybody is thus extended to the market. Hence, either there is equal distribution of income and wealth, or the principles of consumers' sovereignty is exercised through the choice of the representatives of the consumers elected to, Parliament and action taken through direct controls or fiscal instruments to enforce the choice. It cannot be allowed to be exercised by the individual consumers in an unfettered manner when inequality of purchasing power allows some individuals to cast more votes than others for certain commodities, thus violating the extension of the democratic principle to the field of consumers' choice in the market. The distortion in the composition of the consumer goods produced comes about because one of the essential principles of democracy of 'one man one vote' is not extended to the economic field.

There are other reasons also by which misinvestment is encouraged. Thus it is suggested sometimes that a rural housing programme is desirable for employment-creation because it will tap the financial resources of the farmer who has recently become rich. From the point of view of national benefit a rural mansion built for the new-rich farmer with a holding near the ceilings level is of very little value as a national asset. If the employment is to be created productively, it ought to be creating the infra-structure in the rural areas and not through allocations of physical materials in the rural housing programmes for the richer farmers. When one talks of housing in the rural areas one should first of all talk of investment in the worst parts of the village habitations and some minimum degree of shelter for the poorer farmer rather than for the richer one. In that case the linking of that programme with the wealth of the richer farmer gets us nowhere, for the poor farmers' housing schemes will have to be subsidised on government expense and the richer farmer's wealth does not automatically get mobilised for that purpose. Thus adherence to Classical Public Finance to "mop up financial resources" results in the distortion of investment in this and many other cases.

The structure, of the economy operating under the Doctrine of Permeation also envisages that demand cannot be left to determine the choice of the goods to be produced. Hence, the Democratic State takes up the right to determine what will not be produced, so that the top decile among unequal consumers will not assert their sovereignty against the class of consumers as a whole. What measures are taken towards it depends upon the political structure and the type of the economy. But let it be clearly understood that a mixed economy operating in a democracy is as much subject to the principle of choice of goods by the State, as an entirely socialist economy would be. The difference lies in the instruments of implementation to get the desired results through the private and public sectors, not in the purpose to be achieved.

Such an economy envisages the withdrawal of the right to advertise and to create wants where none existed. It cannot allow the continuance of the present state of affairs whereby two major policies of a conflicting nature are simultaneously being followed by the system, so that we have a powerful Advertisement Drive to consume more taking place through private as well as public sector auspices and mass media at the same time as a Savings Drive which is quite ineffective relatively in its appeal to consume less. We cannot expect the propensity to consume to be low in such a set-up. Under the Doctrine of Permeation the drive to consume less will not lose the game all the time to the drive for consuming more. Hence, persuasive advertisement in the press, on the air, screen and on the road-side and in buildings are all to be curbed. Informative advertisement as to where such and such goods in the priority sectors can be found, may be permitted, but great care must be exercised that it does not deteriorate into Persuasive Advertisement for the non-priority goods.

For such a purpose it is not much use pointing out that it would be impracticable to demarcate the line between the two types of advertisements. Such a criticism is being made even with respect to the line between essential and inessential goods quite often. But it should not be forgotten that the social laws are all the time making and enforcing fine distinctions. How is the line drawn between a "nice drawing" and an "immature depiction", between "good taste" and "bad manners", between 'libel' and 'fair criticism', between 'literature' and 'pornography'? Yet it is done every day by art critics, followers of social etiquette, editors, censors, courts, etc. So also, it can be easily determined whether the use of sex appeal for selling quality cigarettes can by any stretch of imagination relate to informative publicity for the priority sectors of the Austerity economy. Persuasive advertisement can be stopped without harming the flow of free information for industrial production of goods belonging to the optimum strategy and their equipment, if the authorities so wish and take action with a will.

It may be asked as to what is to be done with the industries already established or producing luxury commodities. The answer would be two-fold.

Firstly, the industry should be made export-oriented,

and even if it has to be subsidised for holding its purposes of competitiveness, there is a gain for the nation in foreign exchange for the subsidy will be in rupees. Secondly, the remaining product should be used for common consumption, for instance, the refrigerators in hospitals and laboratories, car as public vehicle, etc. To equate the position of those who already have these goods and those who would have bought them and they are now denied because of change in social policies, the consumer durables with the individuals may be requisitioned and taken for public purposes for which a rental should be paid to the owners.

It is undeniable that administrative problems for such actions would be enormously difficult to solve, but methods do exist of solving them. In conditions of stress other democracies have used the administrative sanctions for similar purposes. A firm state, if it is worth its name, ought to be able to solve these problems. If it is not possible to surmount the administrative sanctions in the structure of socio-political economy which we have, then let us be clear that in that case the society will have to choose between giving up the system of planning dedicated to equalitarian policy or the political structure itself. A society which allows itself to be dictated to by smugglers and black-marketeers and cannot change the situation will, in any case, collapse one day under the strain of the depradations inflicted upon it by the parasitic elements.

VII. Non-Inflationary Growth

In the working of the Doctrine of Permeation, the consumer goods necessary having been decided, the next choice to be made is the choice of techniques of production. For this purpose we have to choose between alternatives, each generating a strategy because the profile of production and the framework of the economy from the present time till the common objective of all strategies is reached is different for each type of technique used which generates the corresponding strategy.

In each case, growth is to be non-inflationary in the sense that real inflation would not arise wherein prices rise faster than money wages. This is brought about through investment in equipment and other inputs of consumer-goods production along with the equipment already existing being at a level sufficient for supplying the total requirements of consumption goods of the employed population. In such a situation, if the money wages are constant, so also will the prices be stable and vice versa. Hence, any other type of investment which does not enhance the production of consumption necessaries and only create the requirements, waits upon the expansion of investment in consumer goods so that the surplus created there may be used for catering to the requirements created in the consumer-goods sector itself and other outside investments or expenditure. The investment in goods which are not consumption goods can be planned only in a complementary manner with investment in consumption goods. The position of investment in nonconsumption items is like that of a guest in a Mess Hall who can validly gain entry only when accompanied by a member and when not more than, say, two guests come with the member (which in this case is amount of investment in consumption goods). The entry of the former without the appropriate quantum of the latter in a plan contravenes the rule of non-inflationary growth. As long as the correct ratio is maintained between the Inflation-Dampening and Inflation-Creating expenditure growth will be non-inflationary and there will be no shortages. It is the attempt by planners to make the non-consumption-goods investment gate crash into the system when unattended by Investment in Consumption necessaries that creates the bottlenecks, shortages and rise of prices, by upsetting the balance between investment in consumer necessaries (which are anti-inflationary) and other expenditures which are pro-inflationary.

In our monetary policy we have been under the substantial influence of the Classical Public Finance by which essential investments suffer from the bottleneck of finance, in the unfounded fear that inflation would be caused by providing finances beyond the current and the capital receipts of the government.

The main point which is brought out on the raising of resources overlooks the fundamental aspects of the situation that the resources at the national level are the physical resources and not the financial resources. If a certain set of projects interlinked together on the basis of present physical endowments including natural resources, equipment and skills, is physically feasible, then there must be a feasible financial counterpart of that. For projects to be physically feasible there must be the natural endowments, equipment and skills available, as well as the consumption goods for operatives who are engaged in completing the projects or those who are going to require goods, as workers operating the project when it is ready. Hence a huge programme of adding to the necessaries of consumption is an essential pre-requisite of any set of feasible projects.

The balance between the programmes which increase consumption of necessaries in a short time in relation to the projects of longer duration and other projects is referred to as Balanced Allocation Ratio. If the Planning Framework fails in putting investment allocations according to this ratio, there is bound to be expectation of inflation occurring. In this system, contro of inflation lies in the physical allocations themselves. This process liberates the planning of activities from the artificial constraint of financial resources, because for this expenditure in the Balanced Allocation Ratio the source of how finances are raised is immaterial regarding creation of inflation.

The conditions for non-inflationary provision of finance is unlimited quantum may be listed as follows :—

(i) The programme of quick-yielding nature for production of necessaries to be in such ratio with longer gestation projects that the surplus created in the former sector off-sets the pressure of demand for consumer necessaries generated in the other.

(ii) The technique used should have as high a surplus for re-investment as technology allows at a given capital intensity, and must not be an inferior technique for that capital intensity, after allowing for value of capital for the notional value of scarce types of capital whose actual price is low (e.g. foreign exchange).

(iii) The inputs should stress conservation of scarce resources (foreign exchange, steel and other products of Heavy Sector), if the production is outside the Heavy-Investment Sector, and techniques are available.

(iv) There should be linkage and coordination with other activities in the same field inside or outside the unit of development in keeping with the Area Development Plan.

(v) There should be feasibility in physical terms, e.g. the availability of raw material or possibility for it to be raised through quick investment, the existence of under-employment in that area or an active policy of labour immigration, etc.

(vi) The goods selected should be consumption necessaries or their equipment of a low degree of mechanisation or infra-structural facilities.

(vii) If the scheme is in the private sector with firms operated by the self-employed, it tends to encourage the miniature or small scale of production.

Under these seven conditions, the project can be immediately financed by deficit financing without fear of inflation. It is for spending on activities related to Defence or the Long-gestation projects or Consumption expenditure of government (e.g. the implementation of awards of the Pay Commission, or paying for huge secretariat buildings, military parades) or for making heavy-capital goods that the government has to be worried about financial resources through taxation, because of these expenditure some are highly necessary while others are unnecessary but all are of inflation-creating nature. We have, on the one hand, investments like Defence which create demand for necessaries through expenditure incurred but do not automatically increase the supply of necessaries of consumption. In technical terms this is equivalent to having a gestation lag as large as infinity as regards their capacity to generate product for the civilian sector of the economy. There ought to be, therefore, a balance between Inflation-Creating Investments and Inflation-Dampening Investments, so that the fear of inflation is not there whatever the way finances are raised. This particular attitude serves the link of physical planning and employment creation from the way finances are raised, and hence abandons the system of artificial restraint of financial resources which curb the fruitful investments.

The above does not imply that one lacks consciousness of the fact that creation of employment in a productive manner requires investments which will impose a burden on certain sections of the community. But it is not merely the financial burden of paying taxes which is the important aspect here but of denying to the upper-consumption groups of the community access to certain goods. It is the revenue from tax on advertisement and commercial broadcasting which men used for employment-creation generates sufficient productive employment, but the stoppage of further investment in television altogether, and utilisation of those resource for electric generators which will help lifting of underground water up in small villages where provision of water supply for irrigation or even for drinking is lacking.

It is not merely the resources raised by taxing occupants in luxury hotels which has to put a burden on the upper-consumption group, but the resources set free for the nation by not building any further luxury hotels for use by our countrymen. It is not the tax revenue from sale of luxury goods but the reduction of investment in such goods which are being sold which sets free resources of a physical nature to be utilised for productive-employment schemes which are of benefit to the lower-consumption classes in society. It is through this deprivation that the burden of higher employment ought to be imposed upon the higher consumption-groups. If the higher consumption groups continue to have access to goods varying from luxury limousines, hotels, restaurants, palatial residences or refrigerators, tape-recorders, decolam furniture, television sets, travel by Jumbo Jets etc., to terylene cloth and cosmetics, then what is the burden which is being borne by the higher-consumption-groups for the purposes of employment generation ? The burden of providing employment is not that some of their assets are being raked off through taxes, for that is no burden at all if the comforts which are being created, beyond the functional requirements, continue to proliferate among the richer classes, while the lower middle classes and the poorer sections of the community are not able to get even adequate nourishment for the purpose of efficient work, and their families are deprived of minimum clothing, shelter, and opportunities for training for productive jobs.

Hence, in the remaining year of the Fourth Plan the creation of infrastructure in about a thousand selected Growth Centres in the country, is essential for the provision of necessaries of consumption to the lowest income-groups. As the techniques used therein will be of low capital intensity, they will create employment as a necessary part of the plan of production. This will aim at rapidly increasing requirements of wage goods for subsistence for the weakest sections of the population. They will also serve partly the framework of securing the longer-term requirements of the infrastructure of growth in the Heavy-Investment Sector. All this will be attempted, moreover, without inflationary consequence, because the physical allocations would be done with the Balanced Allocation Ratio in the view. Social justice would be achieved, and the burden of this employment creation will then fall on the high consumption groups not merely through higher taxation on investments, production and sale of these goods but the diversion of physical resources of investment away from inessential goods which is taking away a big chunk of our industrial investment which ought to be going into Heavy-Investments for the future benefit or equipment for consumption necessaries of a low degree of mechanisation (and of a nature which conserves scarce capital). In such a situation deficit financing carried to any extent is free from danger of inflation, and a programme resulting in employment creation through Balanced Allocation Ratio does not have to be scuttled for lack of finance.

In a proper plan we shall have to determine the Balanced Allocation Ratio from the technological data of inputs and productivity coefficients and the gestation period of production alongwith real wage rate and consumption propensity of entrepreneurs. A considerable amount of research would be required for it, though the approximations could be done on basis of existing data. We shall then know that, say, Rs. 100 crore of investment in long-gestation projects can be added only if, say, Rs. 50 crores has been invested in, additionally, for the production of consumer necessaries. If the latter part is missing, the former can enter only by upsetting the balance and causing inflation all round. The Balanced Allocation Ratio is one of the most important parameters of economic planning but is not used in our planning structure, even approximately, as a yardstick.

In each strategy this yardstick would be different, as the technology used would be different. But sticking to the composition of investment according to this yardstick is most important for the strategy concerned. Under such a regime, real inflation cannot arise in the economy whether financial resources are raised through deficit financing or through taxation. In case of an imbalance in this, inflation must arise and taxation would be ineffective in curbing it purely through taking away a certain quantum of funds from the public for this burden may fall on investment and not on consumption or it may fall substantially on those buying consumer necessaries. Inflation has been caused in our economy in the past by never paying attention to allocations for investment according to the Balanced Allocation Ratio, while deficit financing has been accused of it each time, a situation as unreasonable as would exist if defective signalling equipments are responsible for railway accidents while the engine drivers were to get blamed for them repeatedly.

In a regime of non-inflationary growth with Balanced-Allocation Ratio, deficit financing would be available to any extent that physical feasibility allows for production of consumption necessaries through the techniques with high output to capital ratios. However, budgetary discipline will be maintained in a stronger measure—not as regards balancing the budget, but in respect of balancing the allocations. Any expenditure proposed to be incurred will have to be carefully scrutinised for its inflation-creating or dampening potential, and if it belongs to the former group it will have to be shown to be absolutely necessary (which scrutiny will apply even to various types of defence expenditure to determine which ones are inessential).

VIII. Choice of Strategy

Among the strategies of non-inflationary growth stressing consumer necessaries in the initial phases for reaching the objective of development, we take two main possibilities depending upon the technique to be used.

The first strategy uses the technique which advanced countries used for the production of necessaries like foodgrains and cotton cloth. They are highly-mechanised techniques and use the products of the Heavy-Industries Sector. The product per man employed is high in these techniques but capital is more than proportionately higher than in the less-mechanised techniques. In addition, the scarce type of capital owing its origin to the Heavy-Industries Sector is even higher in proportion than capital in general, which attribute would be shown to be an even more accentuated form if the correct notional value of scarce capital content were used. In general such techniques exhibit high profit to wage ratio when general wages are at subsistence level, while they create a distribution of income unfavourable to social justice.

They also create little employment per unit of capital in the aggregate (even if we include ancillary and servicing industries). They are viable because they create little employment for otherwise, with capital costs being so high in these techniques, if total wage bills were also to be high in this economy, it would be using a highly inefficient technique. The argument that tractors do not displace labour because of the supplementary employment in tractor manufacture, servicing, repairs, ancillary services, etc., is entirely fallacious, for when aggregate capital intensity is high, for a given investment definitely less employment will be offered. There is no point in comparing the situation with an advanced country to say that they have near-full employment in spite of capital intensity being high; for scarce type of equipment is the bottleneck for us while it is not so for them, and our criterion has to be measurement of employment potential per unit of bottleneck good valued according to its real value of alternatively more socially productive uses.

The argument against this strategy stems basically from the effect on long-run growth through the leakage of the products of the Heavy-Industries Sector to consumer-oriented production. To the traditional economist who uses simplistic models without differentiation between heavy and other types of investment, this technique seems to yield potentiality of future growth through the high rate of surplus to wages. But this does not mean high rate growth, for capital productivity is low because of capital intensity being too high. It does not also lead to high rate of growth of the Heavy-Industries Sector which is the key to the future growth of the economy.

The second strategy is based upon the use of the less-mechanised techniques for the consumption-good sector. Its rationale is, that for the attainment of the desired objective of the maximum accumulation of the Heavy-equipment and ancillary investment, the rate of growth of this sector should be kept as high as is compatible with technology and the needs of inputs of consumer necessaries. The Heavy-Industries Sector include all industries necessary for the self-reproduction of that sector with consumption goods used by the workers and equipment of their manufacture excluded. Thus it includes Steel, Metals Mining, Heavy Engineering, Machine tools, Transport, Colleges for Engineering and Managerial Skills, etc. But it does not include fertilisers because the criterion of ours is not whether the factory looks Heavy (as is the Planning Commission's criterion) but whether technologically it falls in the sector of re-production of the Heavy-Industries, or is derived from them, and is direct input in consumption-oriented industries. Many more industries would be included in the Heavy-Industries Sector, like paper, but only to the extent that it is necessary as packing, writing and drawing material for the Heavy-Industries while paper used for providing cartons for ice creams would not be a part of the Heavy-Industries Sector. If the consumption sector needs of these industries are minimised and substituted by the techniques conserving the use of Heavy-Sector resources, the investment flowing into many of these might have to be reduced to be only upto the minimum level which sustains the work of the rest of that sector. In such a case investment, though employment creating, in five-star hotel, construction would only be allowed to the extent that it caters to the actual foreign tourist traffic through demand which is not bolstered up by use by the executives and officials and tourists of our own country.

Now with the techniques of low degree of mechanisation used in this strategy in the consumption-good sector, we know that they are likely to be of such a character that they conserve the resources of the Heavy-Industries Sector and hence do not draw away the resources of that sector to any sizable extent towards consumption. Hence, the leakage out of the Heavy-Industries Sector being low, the plough back of its products within itself would be very high. The internal relation of processes in the sector are so worked out as to ensure demand and supply equality yielding a non-bottleneck and maximum rate of growth equilibrium of the Heavy-Industries Sector. Hence, no dearth of demand for steel and other products of the Heavy-Industries Sector ever arises, nor is there ever a shortage within the sector. For the essential uses of its product outside that sector, for example for the minimum amount of steel etc., required for the techniques conserving the input of the Heavy-Industries Sector also there would be no shortage. But for all other uses there would be created conditions of extreme scarcity and non-availability of the products of the Heavy-Investment Sector. Thus the pricing policy of controlling the maximum price of these products may be replaced by establishing a floor price and for consumption necessaries bought by workers in this sector a ceiling price.

The Heavy-Industries Sector may use the most

advanced and sophisticated techniques alongside the less-mechanised methods. Where superior techniques are available in the Heavy-Industries Sector and are highly mechanised, they should have preference over employment-creating but inferior techniques because the former increase the rate of growth of the Heavy-Industries Sector. But the same is not true for the Cousumption-good Sector, for it may happen that a seemingly superior technique uses so much of the resources of the Heavy-Industries Sector per unit of output of consumption-good, that the rate of growth of Heavy-Industries Sector is reduced because of the diversion of its products from that sector's own use.

A combination of techniques of different degrees of mechanisation in the Heavy-Industries Sector along with the techniques conserving the use of products of the Heavy-Industries Sector in the consumption-sector create a number of effects which give the due profile to this strategy as one generating Growth with Social justice.

Firstly, the stress on high rate of feed back of the products within the Heavy-Industries Sector itself creates the conditions for the benefit of long-run growth.

The emphasis on the use of techniques in the Consumption-good sector which conserve the product of the Heavy-Industries Sector ensure the minimum leakage of the products outside that sector and yet give scope for social justice. This is done, firstly, through the ample supply of necessary consumption-goods for the requirements created by the workers and in the consumption-good sector and the Heavy-Industries Sector. The price and wage stability is induced by this.

Secondly, the use of low degree of mechanisation is this production yields social justice through employment-creating techniques (which bear on their shoulder the burden of fast growth of the Heavy-Industries Sector rather than conflicting with their growth).

Thirdly, social justice is achieved through the techniques having a low profit to wage ratio and the distribution of income in favour of social justice which purely Fiscal Policy has failed in achieving hitherto.

Fourthly, these techniques are usually of the miniature scale, and some times of small and medium scale. Rarely will they be of large scale. Hence, the conditions which encourage monopolism in the market are absent in this picture and social justice is achieved through prevention of concentration of economic power and the encouragement of the very small producer.

Fifthly, social justice is achieved though the techniques which can be diffused in the countryside through the organisation of integrated programmes of Growth Centres. They do not require the expansion of metropolitan centres and their use may reverse the trend of mammoth urban growth with its undesirable social, regional and economic consequences.

The second strategy is the natural vehicle of the policy of the Priority to Heavy Investment, because it alows the rapid expansion of that sector to be achieved without the burden of inflation or cut in the consumption standards. This is made possible by the provision of consumption necessaries in balanced ratio with the demand created by the Heavy Industries Sector. In the first strategy considered earlier which used highly-mechanised techniques for consumption necessaries, the priority to Heavy Investment is either low (or if a higher degree of priority is imposed then the flow of resqurces to the consumption sector in the form of Heavy-Industries Sector's products would be reduced and hence quantity of investment would fall in the consumption-good sector leading to shortages in supply of necessary consumption goods). Hence priority to the Heavy-Industries Sector cannot be achieved through the first strategy but only through the second one. On this account we shall call the second strategy Heavy-Investment Strategy and the first one Mechanised Consumption-machinery Strategy, for the second strategy emphasise growth of Heavy Industries, while the first one stresses the growth of mechanised equipment for consumption goods.

It may be noticed that the act of diluting the Heavy-Investment Strategy by mixing it with Mechanised Consumption Machinery Strategy to that extent draws the resources of the economy further away from priority to Heavy Investment. The more is the dilution the less the priority to Heavy Investment, and the interest of the long-run suffers while less also is social justice, so the interest of the short-run suffer.

Now we may analyse our own economic policy of the last twenty-two years in the context of the framework of the strategies. The avowed national policy was enunciated by the late Prime Minister Nehru as Priority to Heavy Investment. Its means of implementation ought to have been through the Heavy Investment Strategy. But economic analysis had not at that time reached the stage of its having been worked out in the form of strategies. What came to be worked out was the Mahalanobis Two-sector Model which can be recognised to be a faithful reproduction of the first type of strategy and hence basically of the character of anti-priority to Heavy Investment and anti-social justice.

In fair tribute to Professor Mahalanobis it ought to be stated that he sought to mitigate the anti-social justice elements in his Two Sector Model by introducing another two sectors which were for creation of employment. But the key word is "mitigation" for the amendment was of a marginal nature. The addition of two sectors were annexures to the main technique used in the two sector model, while the methodology followed in the two-sector model remained the basic one. Even the leakage of the products of the Heavy Industries Sector to the consumption sector did not fall with the introduction of the employment-creating techniques; and hence the concept of use of employment-creating, low-degree-of-mechanisation techniques in their true elements as techniques conserving the products of the Heavy-Industries Sector was alien to the Mahalanobis Four Sector Model as it was worked out. There was no optimisation of the ploughback within the Heavy-Industries Sector for priority to Heavy Investment to be achieved, for in that case techniques conserving the products of the Heavy Industries Sector would have won the day and driven out of his Four-Sector Model, the second sector altogether composed of mechanised consumption-good-machinery technique. The Second Five Year Plan following the Mahalanobis Four-Sector Model also was, therefore, not a plan for priority to Heavy-Investment at all and its structure was quite different from the frameworks which could have given this priority. It was a mixture of the two strategies described by us, heavily weighted towards the strategies affixing low priority both to the Heavy-Industries Sector and to the social justice element. Our Planning has, since then, been basically anti-growth and anti-social justice in its basic structure, although they have been claimed to be pro-growth, pro-Heavy Investment and pro-social justice.

The Second Plan and the subsequent ones, in their working did not even confine themselves to the state of dilution described as mixture of the two strategies. The Mahalanobis Model did not specifically envisage huge investment in luxury consumption. It felt the field open for both types of consumption goods and investments as it talked in terms of average income rising. In the actual working of the model, the pressure from various directions stressed the implementation to be not in the form of emphasis on strategies of consumer-necessaries under the Doctrine of Permeation but in the form of the Doctrine of Percolation, and the substantial injection of elements of the Luxury consumption-goods strategy came about.

The priority to Heavy-Investment was later on even dropped from the list of pronouncements. The policy as it came to be implemented was, therefore, not merely of low priority to Heavy-Investment and of low element of social justice, but as we have stressed the whole atmosphere became one of the nature of anti-priority to Heavy-Industries and anti-social-justice. Hence, it is more appropriate to describe the mixture of strategies as in the Third and the Fourth plans by the term environmental pollution rather than dilution, when the country was in the early stages of development and there was quite a large degree of non-employment. It is this analysis of policy in the form of implementation which gives us the true picture of what has happened during the last twenty two years of planning. The Government and the Nation have been unwittingly caught in the system which has generated the pressures.

The general idea among members of the public and of some economists has been that the Mahalanobis Model was a model of priority to Heavy Investment. The strategy approach shows that it was just the reverse, because priority for Heavy Investment in that model could only be introduced by infringing the constraint of non-inflationary growth, for the larger is the proportion of heavy investment products which are to be devoted to Heavy-Industries Sector's further growth, the less is available for the consumption goods sector and hence the supply of necessaries must get adversely affected leading to a cut in real wages. Such a method of priority is entirely unacceptable, and, hence, the Mahalanobis Model was ineligible to be considered as a means of implementation of the policy for Priority to Heavy Investment. The failure of planning based upon the Mahalanobis Model has not been a failure of planning or of priority to Heavy Investment, for the proper strategy relevant to that end (i.e. Heavy-Investment Strategy) has never been tried, and did not ever form a part of the theoretical framework behind the planning action of the Government.

It is no use for those responsible for plan evaluations putting the blame for the past mistakes merely on implementation and making the framers of past plans escape responsibility for the wrong framework used by saying that we have already tried the policy of Priority to Heavy Investment, and its advocacy is nothing new, and why it did not work is well known to the Government and other economists as bottlenecks of implementation or limitations imposed by considerations of social justice like inflationary pressures etc. It is submitted that the furtherence of priority to Heavy Investment through the only strategy relevant to it was never tried and is neither well known to the economists in general nor had the Government in the past accepted it in principle even. It is only now that for Fifth Plan if the objective of self-reliance, employment generation and the common man's necessaries are translated into allocations, then something close to the Heavy-Investment Strategy would have to be followed, for this strategy is not only compatible with the Fifth Plan objective, but a necessary means of their implementation.

A reversal of the policy of the Third and Fourth Plan is being thought of now for the Fifth Plan with a welcome renewed emphasis on priority to Heavy-Investment Sector and on consumer necessaries. But without a change in the existing policy towards luxury consumption goods there is no indication that these industries will cease suddenly to draw physical resources of the economy from other spheres and unless that is stopped by some devices, the pronouncement of a priority of Heavy Investment will not again prove effective.

Further, all the time rapid increase in degree of mechanisation is going on in the consumption-goods sector which the Fifth Plan would have to keep in strict check. In the sphere of agriculture (which is very much the sector for creation of employment opportunities) the trend if allowed free play would be dangerous. Under the pressure of demand by some agriculturists, tractorisation is being pushed for becoming a part of the policy of some State Governments and the Central Government. The primary pressure for tractorisation comes from a similar lobby which has been opposing ceilings on land holdings on the basis of higher productive yields. Eight important matters have been confused by the protagonists of tractorisation.

Firstly, the productivity which needs to be increased is not per man but per unit of land and per unit of capital. There is little difference in the productivity per acre through tractorisation compared to the situation where sufficient additional ploughing is done by the less-mechanised methods in irrigated lands, and as regards the productivity per unit of capital, while it becomes still lower if it is measured with respect to the scarce types of capital (using resources of the Heavy-Industries Sector or foreign exchange, and skilled human capital).

Secondly, the displacement of labour is denied by the mechanisationists on the ground of a higher employment in ancillary occupations. This is not the proper method of evaluating employment potentials of techniques of various degrees of mechanisation. Tractors are only one example of a mechanised process for consumer-good production. If one takes the total quantum of highly mechanised equipment and finds out as to what amount of alternative employment it would have created in the economy with less-capital-intensive methods, the mechanised equipment would definitely be labour-saving. We cannot befool ourselves by believing that ancillary occupations cause more employment generation, for were it correct that tractors are as employment generating as the improved ploughs, they would be having very low productivity per man-employed in the aggregate and yet they would be more highly capitalised. Hence, they would form a fit case for being actively discouraged as a highly inefficient and inferior technique.

Thirdly, tractors are said to get rid of back-breaking work. If this is the objective then they will succeed in doing so for only a very small proportion of the agricultural population because of the high capital intensity. One has to build up enough capacity of the Heavy-Industries Sector to get sufficient tractors to replace all the ploughs and remove back-breaking work for all rather than for the fortunate few who can afford the tractors or facilities which the tractor custom-service stations can provide.

Fourthly, the cost of the tractor is not merely the rupee cost but the quantum of Heavy-Investment foregone. With ploughs we shall have steel ploughed back into steel production. With tractors we shall get the same total tonnage of foodgrains in ten years but perhaps four steel mills less than with ploughs. The cost in terms of our future capacity to grow is tremendous.

Fifthly, tractors are supposed to speed up operations and make three crops possible. It is not understood why such huge investment should go into the third crop in advanced regions when a much lesser amount investment in backward regions through providing irrigation or other inputs converts half-crop into two-crop land.

Sixthly, tractors are supposed to combat the local shortage of labour. This argument is not acceptable in planning for the country as a whole, for mobility of labour ought to be encouraged from other parts of the country. At the present, some of the more affluent areas resent the influx of labour from the less affluent areas as it goes against the sentiments of the parochial mentality. The Rules for Regional Preference for employment may not be in legislated forms everywhere, but they are no less real as sociological bottlenecks in the more affluent parts of the country in debarring free immigration of labour and evening out regional disparties.

Seventhly, wages are higher where tractors are introduced. This tendency is a sure way of creating wider disparities among workers in the agricultural fields and also a more unfavourable distribution of income because incomes are less diffused in a mechanised agricultural economy.

Eighthly, agriculture is the largest field for giving employment. If tractors are encouraged then one will have the pattern of production in which employment generation will be severely curtailed and the present situation will be worsened as regards unemployment among agricultural labourers. The same goes for dairying and milk products as regards their handling, processing, packaging and vending in all of which occupations mechanisation is being introduced rapidly in the economy with the usual reasons of efficiency, rapidity, cleanliness, reliability of quality, confidence in the big producers etc.

Under the conditions of increase of mechanisation the policy for the Fifth Plan as enunciated by the Planning Commission both as regards self-reliance and priority to Heavy Industries will remain in the field of pronouncements rather than implementation, because the strategy of production is unmistakably Mechanised Consumption good machinery Strategy which cannot yield priority to Heavy Investment nor, consequently, self-reliance, nor social justice. It is for this reason important to understand that through the objective of the Fifth Plan would be best served by adopting the Heavy-Investment strategy, yet the action of the Government departments geared to the earlier plans are in a different regime altogether and it would be expected that we might get ultimately the Mechanised consumption-good machinery Strategy in a much more reinforced fashion than in the last seventeen years. With that policy we may as well say farewell to the hope of either priority to Heavy Industries for self-reliance or employment and social justice. To escape from this conclusion one will have to lay down that use of large tractors and similar equipment is permissible only for reclaiming land or where bullocks are not available and either their services or of small tractors cannot be provided under the Agro-Service Centres under Growth Centre programmes from the Government stud farms with custom-hiring source for the really small farmer. Similarly safeguards would have to be used for preventing extension of mechanisation in the production of cloth.

The structure of the remaining portion of the Fourth Plan and the proposed Fifth Plan has to be geared towards reversal of the trend of the last seventeen years. Firstly, the strategy has to shift from the Doctrine of Percolation to Doctrine of Permeation in which the luxury consumption goods have no place and under which condition of austerity one may validly ask the working class to restrain demands for rise of standard of living to allow higher accumulation to take place. It will require also an economy wherein advertisement for purpose of expanding a market for persuading potential consumers to buy some product has no place.

Secondly, the strategy has to shift from one using highly Mechanised Consumption-good Machinery to one using a very low degree of mechanisation. Hence, employment generation has to be inbuilt into the structure itself through a low capital-intensity per unit of labour or high labour intensity per unit of capital in the Consumption-good sector.

Thirdly, the feeding back of the physical products of the Heavy Investment Sector into activities of that sector itself has to be rapidly stepped up within the next ten-fifteen years from one fourth to two thirds or so. This will also be employment creating due to rapid expansion of this sector, and this would be made possible only by the second action of shifting to a lower degree of mechanisation so that the leakage of the products of the Heavy Industries Sector to the Consumption-Goods Sector are minimised for fulfilling the requirements of necessaries of consumption for the workers employed in the former sector, in production of consumption necessaries and in the equipment for their manufacture with techniques conserving the products of the Heavy-Industries Sector.

Hence, when we talk of growth and employment the proper type of growth for employment creation and longterm development is, as we have seen, in techniques which, in the Heavy Investment Sector create employment through the fast expansion of that sector, and which in the Consumption-goods sector create employment through the use of processes of production which conserve Heavy Investment resources also happen to be employment creating per unit of investment of scarce types of equipment. These are quite different from techniques which will come about by purely following a policy of employment generation. There is a vast difference between saying that "a proper pursuit of growth leads to social justice", and attempting to maintain that, "pursuit of social justice is possible as an alternative to growth". Those economists who have attacked growth and stressed social justice alone have hardly had any concept of the proper pursuit of growth through the Heavy-Investment strategy and do not also have any idea how social justice will come about in the absence of rapid growth of employment opportunities.

IX. Implementation In a Firm State

Having decided the basic question of the choice of consumer goods, and of investment goods (dependent upon the choice of degree of mechanisation), and consequently the optimum strategy of development, we can now turn our minds to choosing the instruments through which the strategy is to be implemented. For this purpose we have to take as given the political structure which we have chosen, i.e., democracy, and the national policy objective of achieving an egalitarian state. Towards the latter objective, the present period is a state of transition, and has to be planned as such. It is, therefore, to be understood that the instruments for policy which are open to us pertain to the state of transition rather than to the long-term objective. Considerable difficulty is caused by confusing the two and thinking that we can apply the methods pertaining to the objective state when one is merely on the path towards it.

One can, of course, choose a political structure appropriate to the egalitarian state, and carry it into effect immediately. It is undeniable, that this will give the State the strength and the power to use the fiatory instruments, and through them there would be little difficulty in achieving the allocations which the optimum strategy requires. Thus, in such an economy it would be only necessary to order that a fresh engineering graduate would report for duty at the bottom of a coal mine by next Friday, and there would be no question of the person not following the order. Similarly, physical resources would flow out of terylene into cotton clothing, should it be so decreed, without anyone daring to disregard the edict. But a fiatory economy requires a Hard State wherein the directions are carried out without question, howsoever keen may have been the discussions and the controversies before a decision is taken. In a Soft State there is little difficulty in evading the implementation by a section of the population, and in effect there is one law for the poor and the powerless, and another for the influential or the rich. The very large number of underpaid officials makes it easier for those who can afford to pay gratuities to flout the edicts. There is a desire for increasing the standard of living to as high a level as people with corresponding rank in the private sector enjoy. This is evinced by even the more well-paid officials.

Hence, the Glass Curtain Economy coupled with the Soft State makes it easier for some of the rich persons in the community to secure favourable decisions even at the level of officers who are not ill-paid. The consideration offered is not in all cases illegal, for a social convention may exist that rewards are given in devious and indirect forms, or there may be merely an expectancy without an actual contract (for instance, that the person in authority concerned will be looked after well after his retirement, by the parties concerned).

The straight and honest officer in such a situation finds himself in a forlorn state and an object of derision. The political interference at the implementation stage creates further complications, as also the break-up of the rules of the administration regarding the limitation of access to authorities for complaints without proper channels. All these go towards breaking up the morale of the civil administration. The structure as it has evolved during the last few years is such that we have been engaged in almost destroying the capacity of the civil administration to act as an effective instrument of implementation. The Hard State also requires that the public, the govenment and the civil service are committed to the same basic set of ideals as regards its essential elements. This is also not the case in the present state of our administrative and political structure. We are in a Soft State, whereas we would like to think that we are in a Hard State and can consequently take measures which flow easily out of the latter sort of structure of administration.

To be a Hard State requires so many onerous conditions that it may be considered to be beyond the scarce administrative capacity available in the country at the moment, for creating those conditions themselves requires a long process of transition and effort. However, it should be well understood that a Soft State without a considerable reform of its administrative structure would find it extremely difficult to undertake a proper plan of development in which allocations are governed by the optimum strategy and not by the wishes of producers and consumers, as also powerful interests from abroad bringing pressures upon the government and the people in various ways.

Hence, though we might think that it is difficult to convert the body politic into a Hard State, it is the opinion of the present signatory that we shall find it not only feasible, but necessary, to convert its present system of governance into one belonging to the category of semi-hard, or the Firm State. In this state one does not require the public in general to be controlled, but it only requires that the very small proportion of population engaged in government administration and that of public-sector bodies will from top to bottom, conform to a strict code of discipline. If the country cannot keep the public officials in check, it is futile to think that in such a situation any plan of achievement of socialist objectives or of proper development can be successfully implemented.

The Firm State rests upon three foundations. Firstly, it uses the inducive instruments rather than the fiatory ones. Secondly, it relies on a strong Field Organisation for purposes of providing facilities for the plan to be completed in an integrated manner, and for inspecting that the benefits obtained on the basis of inducements to perform certain acts are rightly earned through actual performance, in the manner indicated. Thus if stainless steel quota is to be obtained for making surgical instruments by a small-scale firm, the field organisation will help both in obtaining the allocation and in ensuring that the allotment is not then sold by under-hand deals for making stainless-steel utensils in "black" plants. Thirdly, the Central Government will take up a strong position in relation to the choice of goods and equipment as well as methods of implementation and toning up the efficiency as well as the morale of the civil administration. It will also have a more unitary system of government with larger number of smaller states and ones which are more responsible to achieving the Central Government's objectives. It will also take up powers to solve the inter-state disputes on boundaries and water etc. more expeditiously as also settle disputes of individuals with the State on land acquisition etc. summarily but with adequate justice. It will also ensure that states may not be able to adopt policies whereby they may flout the Central Policy as regards National Development.

The hopeful possibility of the Firm State rests upon the assumption that though it is possible for a mass of individuals to conceal their incomes and wealth without collusion with government officials, because no information-system exists about individual transactions, their indexing and analysis, yet it is not possible to put up a factory (or a plant within the factory) producing a disapproved commodity without the whole set of officials belonging to the local inspectorate colluding with the erring member of the public. Whereas the Glass Curtain Economy and Advertisement Economy go on tempting the officers to break the code of discipline all the time, the type of Austerity Economy which the optimum strategy of development described earlier indicates, helps in one respect to make the civil administrators at all levels to conform to the code of discipline, for very little is to be gained in terms of consumption standards by overstepping the bounds of rectitude.

In the matter of the organisational structure of the economy, it is assumed that on the path of transition to an egalitarian economy, private enterprise in some forms would be continuing to exist. Having taken the decision as to the forms in which it may be allowed, the economy is not to be a mere mixture of private and public forms of enterprise, having two different value-systems coexisting. The concept of the mixed economy is not of two separate economies co-existing or a simple mixture of the two, just as the state of youth is not an average of the characteristics of children and middle-age people, but a separate state altogether with its own attributes, specific problems, and methods of dealing with them. For this reason, the system of public and private enterprise co-existing in a Firm State will not be termed as a mixed economy, but called a "Composite Economy".

In this system that part of private enterprise which is allowed to be included the Composite Economy is not treated as on sufference but an element at the age of transition, and there is no indecision and uncertainty about its role for the various phases of the transition path or what is expected of it in the phase unlike the present state when the Government speaks with two voices regarding the role of public and private enterprises, as also ambiguity regarding that part of the private sector which is not in the concentration ring. It would be clear from the very beginning that concentration of economic power in the hands of monopoly enterprise would not form a part of the Composite Economy. The managerial skills possessed by this form of enterprise would be placed at the disposal of the joint sector with the government having in its hands the reins of management. The smaller scale of enterprise is to be allowed to flourish provided they are in the priority sectors, and the government will give facilities to it both through creation of infra-structure, training facilities for its operatives, financial supports, quality control organisations, distribution centres etc. All operatives in public and private sectors must understand that the aim is an egalitarian society and the path of transition is towards attaining it. Production of refrigerators would not thus be an approved activity merely because it is proposed to be undertaken by a government company. The priority laid down by the planning authorities will be adhered to by both the sectors, and questions of alleged interference with sovereignty of producer's choice as regards the choice of goods or of equipment by the planning authority as regards what is included in the priority sectors will not be brought up. The vertical control system operates in this regard both for the public and the private sectors. It is within this sphere that choice is exercised, for the horizontal control system of checks and balances and price mechanism, the market, and the optimum profit rate. Hence Persuasive Advertisement would be discouraged in the Composite Economy, nor would a good be included in the priority sector merely because there is demand for it, for instance automobiles except as parts of the public transport system, or room air-conditioners for private use or office except for hospitals and laboratories. The feasibility studies undertaken for loans from the banking and other financial institutions would assess the potentiality of using available inputs to produce products which are required by the priority industries of the economy rather than the fact that they are demanded by those who can afford to buy them.

Both sectors must be made to follow the same code

of discipline, for otherwise the working of the public sector becomes vitiated by the sea of private enterprise around it with different practices. Wasteful use of resources is an infliction of damages upon the nation's capacity to grow, and would be penalised whether it is in the public sector or in the private sector, and one would not hear the argument in the Composite Economy that as long as the private sector makes profit it is efficient irrespective of how wasteful has been the use of resources. Hence the government would take steps to ensure that the rate of profit is assessed after taking into consideration the criteria of efficiency from the national point of view. For this purpose it would seek to change the market rates of profit by the actuative instruments at its command so that the priorities and efficiencies of allocations are maintained after inefficient use of resources has been penalised in the private and public sectors both.

X. Actuative Instruments

The instruments of a fiatory nature when they are used in either the Soft State or the Firm State do not always achieve their objective. The model followed by the plan as we have seen, was in itself inadequate and could not be expected to achieve the objectives. But superimposed upon that has been inadequate instruments of implementation. In addition there has been a lack of determination to seek the translation of the objectives into reality. All these taken together confirm the realisation that one ought not to have ever wondered why planning has not delivered the goods which we wanted over the last twenty-two years. Due to these combined causes, poverty is still widespread, unemployment is acute (as measured by definitions which are economically and socially meaningful), there is skew-distribution of holdings, the concentration of economic power in industry is growing, the price level is rising, the production in certain essential fields is lagging behind (leading to higher money wages being demanded by organised workers who have often to use methods of protest which affect production), while luxury consumption is still going on in spite of the shortage of essentials.

These phenomena, as we have seen, are basically caused by the wrong strategies of development which the country undertook (Luxury-goods Strategy in practice and Mechanised Consumption-good Machinery Strategy in theory) although national policy was Priority to Heavy Investment which, if it had been implemented through the Heavy Investment strategy, we would have secured economic growth and social justice and avoided many of the above manifestations.

To implement it, efficient instruments of inducive nature would have to be used. It is the purpose of this section to describe them.

The inducive instruments are divided into two categories. First of all they are Persuasixe and, secondly Actuative. In the Persuasive instruments comes the field of education which includes mass media. It also includes the means of indoctrination used by governments whether democratic or directed. For the long-run persuation by educational enlightenment is the strongest form by which one can be sure that certain modes of action will be followed, for it is difficult for a person to break the model code dinned deep into his sub-conscious by constant repetition from various sources, especially if it is based on logic and not merely on faith. From long-term commitment to the cause of development and for conformity to the code of discipline and social values which an Austerity Economy requires, there is no more powerful instrument than educational enlightenment. The educational system instils into its constituents the desirability to following codes of behaviour based upon methods of analysis which tend to set the mind free from superstition and unscientific thought. This element of education is necessary for development and has been used in the past whether it be to preserve the status quo or to maintain a revolution. This should not only form part of education in schools but also in Adult Functional Educational courses.

In the Actuative Instruments we have the combination of Penal and Incentive instruments. The rationale is that incentive by itself does not work, but first of all putting a penalty of wrong conduct is indulged in and then giving incentive for right conduct, acts as a powerful instrument because the differential between the right and wrong conduct becomes very large in that case. It also acts on the principle that an open door to the desired cool ante-room to a hall which is on fire and is undesirable to be in, is a better way of including a person to go to the desired place rather than just as an open door to the cool ante-room without the urgency imported in the situation by the fire in the hall, or alternatively, a fire in the hall without an open door. Tax incentives follow the policy of the open door, and taxation for revenue is of the nature of the hall on fire with a closed door.

The main Actuative Instruments for inducing the Private sector to conform to the required allocations under conditions of a Firm State are Monetary Policy and Fiscal Policy. They are to be supplemented by the work of the Public Sector in the Composite Economy, such as direct provision of facilities, infrastructure and environment for growth.

The incentive part of the Actuative Instruments is provided largely by monetary policy. With an inspectorate or field organisation as has been mentioned earlier as an integral portion of the Firm State, one can implement a policy of differential interest rates with easy accessibility, at low interest rates, for the small producers in the priority industries as defined by the optimum strategy. The policy is possible on account of acceptance of the theory mentioned earlier that deficit financing is not by itself inflationary, but how money is spent governs its pro-inflationary or anti-inflationary character. The rationale is, that for industrialisation progressing fast, the price level of necessaries for workers has to be kept under control, for otherwise a wage-price spiral which is an economically meaningless occurrence ensues. For this purpose basically the price of food-grains and cloth has to be kept low. This is compatible with raising profitability in this activity for purpose of attracting more resources into it, on the guarantee that prices of input are to be kept very low. Hence, the rate of interest is to be kept low provided the technique used is low capital intensity derived from the Heavy-Industries Sector. This will avoid over-capitalisation while keeping the rate of interest low so as to induce investment to be high in the priority lines.

The programme of non-inflationary growth and social justice cannot be implemented unless the doctrine of deficit financing being inflationary by itself and irrespective of the proportion in which funds are spent on various types of activities is completely thrown overboard. Both the sectors and self reproducing Heavy Investments may not flow into them on its own account in an economy where profitability is the criterion and is found to be high in inessential lines where the effective demand is always high because purchasing power is always high and we are in a regime where it can be freely exercised. As the production of necessaries consumed by the common man may not be the most profitable activity, a policy of loans at low interest rates for the producers of essential inputs for the farmers and operators of cottage industries may be necessary. It will, therefore, be dependent upon the provision of finance which does not depend upon the budgetary constraints, and is essential for maintaining profitability when the price of the product is to be kept low so that the inflation may not hit the working class in industry and agriculture.

At the present, we fail to provide finance at the proper time, and consequently get into an inflationary situation. When the wages and the cost of material rise, higher amount of finance is needed for more projects. The more urgent need not also be the most economically important expenditures. Hence, many highly important economic schemes get less investment or are shelved causing dislocation in the field of production and making implementation of the Plan impossible as bottlenecks arising at one place cut down production in the whole line of interlinked activities. The rise of prices in the economy as a whole leads to demand for higher wages by the government servants. These are resisted for a while but ultimately either through settlement of a strike or by awards of commissions at least a partial restoration of the real wage is affected. The acceptance by government of these rises can at that time come only from deficit financing. The Finance Ministry is then ready to increase the quantity of money but this time for an expenditure which is inflation creating, whereas it did not originally do it for inflation-dampening expenditure. The upsetting of the Balance of Allocations in the wrong direction must necessarily be inflationary. Because in the last step it was associated with deficit financing, the latter is held responsible and hanged for it and the Finance Ministry gets further scared of providing finances at the right time to the right schemes. The price level, therefore, continues to rise and distortions in the Plan keep on taking place.

The economists who look for slow rate of growth in lack of savings have caught the stick at the wrong end altogether. What is required is not savings but firstly curtailment of consumption and there is vast difference between the two, for one may buy a savings certificate through postponing investment in digging a well rather than cutting out a marriage feast. Secondly, what is required is investment of the right sort. Finances for that are not provided at the right time under the Doctrine of Restriction of Deficit Financing (irrespective of its complexion of the mode of spending for purposes of inflation-dampening investment) under the ungrounded fear that it will be inflationary which grips the classical economist and the administrator, and does not allow the Ministry of Finance to play its true role in development.

The Classical Public Finance as at present ruling the work of the government in all spheres renders the role of the government in development insignificant. As regards monetary policy because deficit financing is considered inflationary, direct help to miniature scale of production in necessaries and their equipment is kept at a low level, though a massive programme is required therein. If financial help to industries is to depend upon the principle of their capacity to repay, then there cannot be a subsidy element in the provision of the finances. Such help will, therefore, continue to be given in general, to high profit industries and to borrowers who are "Creditworthy" or guaranteed to be so by men of wealth who sometimes rake a commission for certifying the return of the loan. For high-profit industries to be helped there is no difficulty for the demand potential to be shown. The goods produced will, therefore, be heavily weighted towards the requirements of the rich from whom there is no lack of demand. The borrowers will also be predominantly among the wealthy or their proteges who are guaranteed by them.

For purposes of showing that a lot is being done for social justice, some of these rules will be relaxed in specific cases as show-window cases, but by and large the pattern will be against social justice, and bank nationalisation by itself would make no change in curbing production of the Glass-Curtain Economy. Deficit Financing of a sizable character has to be a firm tenet of policy and not an apology if price level is to be contained through production of necessaries and social justice is to be achieved through production of the common man's goods by the common man. We have hardly any monetary instruments of an Inductive Nature in our hands if Classical Public Finance continues to rule monetary policy. The Paleo-economics has deprived our government of a powerful incentive facility as part of the Actuative Instruments in a composite Economy.

XI. Allocative Efficiency of Taxes

Monetary Policy by which deficit financing would be permissible to any extent as long as the schemes of the total plan conform to the balanced allocation ratios between the feasible quick-yielding projects for necessaries and for all the other expenditures, sets free the instruments of taxation from merely serving the purpose of revenue raising to being an instrument of allocation. Taxation can then be used for the social purpose of allocating resources in the manner required by the optimum strategies and the social objectives to be achieved on the path of development as an Acuative Instrument pertaining to the Composite Economy in a Firm State. For this purpose the efficiency of tax is never to be judged by its yield, but by its success in shifting physical resources from inessential to essential uses as described in the optimum strategy. Hence, we have to search for taxes which have got a large allocative-efficiency rather than merely high revenue-yield.

The allocative efficiency in a composite state depends upon how individuals and firms are made to change their lines of investment from what the market now dictates in response to high purchasing power of a few, into what the market would dictate after the taxes have been levied and the profitability changed. The taxes in which the rates have to be changed by a very high percentage in order to achieve a small change in the rate of profit of the industry are termed as condenser taxes and in the reverse case magnifier taxes. Under the classical-doctrine of yield as a benefit of a tax in relation to the administrative cost of collection, the tax most popular with the government would be the Indirect Taxes. Yet from the point of view of decreasing the profitability of an investment they are ineffective. The reason is that the population is stratified into various consumption groups. For each consumption group the set of goods pertaining to it seem to be a necessity, and the goods pertaining to the higher consumption bracket are the luxuries. Hence, when the excise duty or sale tax or customs duty on a commodity rises, the demand for that is affected only as regards the persons in the lower consumption bracket who were looking forward to buying it. The demand of the persons in higher brackets remains intact for the commodity and they would be willing to pay for it at much higher prices also. In a country of the size with which we are dealing, 10% of the households is a market as large as one million, and hence demand is substantially there for everything this section wishes to buy. The increase of Indirect Taxes on gas stoves would indeed cut down the demand of the lower division clerk for it, but that of senior officers is unaffected unless the rate of tax is raised tremendously, while no feasible sales-tax rate hits the person at the top consumption-bracket sufficiently as regards his purchase of this and many other commodities.

Hence, for the goods the demand and the profitability remains high, so the goods continue to be good candidates for further investments and further loans by the government financing agencies basing their decisions on Feasibility Reports, and more investment is continued in these lines in spite of the complaint regarding the crippling and crushing burden of tax on the industry. The burden is easily passed on to those consumers who have the wherewithal to pay for these, or those on the margin who cannot really afford the commodity, but who (under social conventions of the Glass-Curtain Economy) are obliged to succumb to the Demonstration effect to prevent a loss of face in social circles, and hence have to curtail consumption in more desirable fields, for example purchase of books and journals or education of children, health, nutrition etc. The Indirect Taxes are thus Condenser Taxes, for their allocative efficiency for a unit percentage change in the tax rate is very low. Unless the burden rises as the consumption-group rises, the demand for the commodity from the upper strata remains high and the rate of profit remains high, in line. The Indirect Taxes unfavourably discriminate between the consumption of the rich and the less rich as regards each commodity, and violate the principle of economic democracy wherein the voting power for demand of goods must not be exercised unequally.

The use of Condenser Taxes for the purpose of changing allocation by reducing the rate of profit in essential industries is a crude instrument for a fine task. It is to be likened to the use of garden shears for performing an appendix operation.

When we come to the Direct Tax system, we find that the Income-Tax is capable of being progressive and hence is an improvement on the Indirect Tax System. In a tax system wedded to revenue raising, the Indirect Taxes will be the popular ones with the government. In a modern tax system dedicated to its function as an allocative mechanism the Direct Taxes would be the most important taxes. Shift of emphasis from the Indirect Tax to Direct Tax System is a condition for use of taxation as an Actuative Instrument in an economic democracy.

However, when we come to the Direct Tax system we find that the Income Tax does not discriminate between consumption and investment which form the constituents of income. It falls on both in the same manner while what is required is to treat two unequally in order to shift the resources from consumption to investment. Income Tax as a form of Direct Tax is also a Condenser Tax, and hence not a powerful Actuative Instrument. This is so for three reasons.

Firstly, it penalises investment and consumption equally and therefore acts like a spray which makes the plant as well as weeds wither. An addition to the tax rate on the other hand does not penalise the two constituents equally for it tends to fall more on investment than on consumption which is just what one would like to avoid in a Development-Oriented Austerity Economy.

Secondly, it has the property that rate of progressiveness tapers off at higher income slabs. Thus the rate of progressiveness for individuals rises very fast at lower income levels and as high income brackets it slows down because of the constraint of 99% maximum marginal rate of tax. The slowing down of the rate of progression is not easily visible because it gets hidden in the Finance Act through increased widening of the slabs for every five-ten per cent or so rise in marginal rates at higher income levels, whereas the slabs are Rs. 5,000 at the lower income level while the marginal rate jumps up by leaps and bounds in the lower ranges of the tax base. For firms it is at a flat rate.

Thirdly, in the Income Tax there is an inbuilt mechanism for encouraging evasion through the incentive to show one's assets in the name of less well-to-do relations and fictitious persons. For purposes of changing allocations, therefore, the Income Tax has little utility. It is like using the bread knife for the appendix operation which, though it is an improvement on the garden shears, is still hardly the instrument for the purpose for which it is required.

XII. Magnifier Allocative Taxes

The Direct Tax which ought to be used for encouraging employment through higher investment ought to discriminate against inessential consumption in relation to investment. This tax would be the Direct Consumption tax, a variant of which is the Expenditure Tax proposed eighteen years back by Professor Nicholas Kaldor in his book with that title. It hits at consumption and not at investment on three counts. Firstly, the tax exempts investment and falls directly on consumption.

Secondly, it can be progressively progressive, for marginal rates are no longer bound by the constraint of 99% which is so in the Income Tax System by its nature.

Thirdly, the tax has an inbuilt incentive to declare investments in the assessee's own name to earn the exemption and hence declared assets would form a larger and larger proportion of the total assets for an assessee as time goes by. Hence, evasion through transfer of assets, which is a very larger element in concealment of income, would be checked. The psychology would be to dictate that one would rather declare an asset and get immediate relief from a very high marginal rate of taxation (say, three or four hundred per cent) rather than pay this certain high tax penalty now by not showing all the investments in one's own name and reap an uncertain benefits later on. The Consumption Tax is not a Condenser Tax but a Magnifier Tax with powerful means to check consumption. Great as are the advantages of the Consumption Tax, it can still be likened only to a pen-knife for the appendix operation better than bread-knife (Income Tax) and a considerable improvement on the garden shears (Excise Duty), the still not the perfect surgical instrument for getting rid of inessential investments and consumption in the economy.

To perform the function of allocative instruments the tax must be capable of three further tasks. Firstly, it must take into account the fact that the Kaldorian Tax System acts only from the side of cutting down demand for consumption good by the assessees. Now in an economy where there is a parallel economy operating, it discriminates in favour of those who spend from undeclared income and the dread of the penalty of the tax at progressively progressive rates does not touch them at all. Hence, it cuts down the consumption of the more honest consumer while the demand remains high from the less honest consumer. This militates against the principle of equality in an economic democracy. It also keeps the demand for consumer luxuries high, and the rate of profit still remains sufficiently high for investment resources to flow into this sector from elsewhere. The tax as allocative instrument should not merely depend upon the demand for consumption luxuries to be cut out but must also apply the breaks from the supply side. The goods which are not approved must simply be unavailable in the market. Hence the tax must curtail supply through investments being penalised in the undesired lines.

Secondly, it must discriminate between different types of investments which the Consumption Tax does not do when it gives blanket encouragement to investment without specifying what type of investment deserves to earn it. The allocative tax must be like a horticultural operation which is not only able to discriminate between the plant and the weed like a weed-killing spray but also between the stalk and the fruit like techniques of grafting (as differentiated from the use of some fertilizers which help the growth of stalk and fruit and weed together).

Thirdly, the system of Magnifier Allocative Taxation must discriminate between different sources of income. Investment needs encouragement which a Consumption Tax gives in any case, but human effort requires more encouragement. Hence, the differential treatment of earned and unearned income is a fundamental aspect of a tax system and must be introduced in the tax. Also income earned from priority industries should be treated differently from income earned from non-priority ones as regards scarce skills and equipment are concerned to prevent scarce talents and physical resources from moving into non-priority lines with higher profits and high capacity to pay more. This will tend to shift scarce resources and scarce manpower skills into the priority sectors. This discrimination of source of income is of an entirely different nature from the discrimination between investments, for the latter refers to how income is spent and the former to how it is earned. Income may be earned from a wrong source but used for investment in the right lines and the latter act deserves inducement irrespective of the former act, and clearly differentiated from it. It may be earned from a right source and invested aright in which case it deserves double encouragement. But if it is earned wrongly, mainly consumed and the small balance is invested wrongly, three separate economic sins are committed and ought to be penalised separately.

Fourthly, the system must discriminate between the form of organisation so that large scale and monopolistic industries are put in a position of economic disfavour in relation to the smaller scales and more competitive industries. The income earned from miniature scale (investment of less than Rs. 10,000) is to be given the most favourable differential treatment, to encourage self-employed entrepreneurs, and more employment-creating techniques which are associated with the low capital intensity which miniature scale necessitates.

The Disparity Tax proposed five years back performs all these functions which Kaldorian Consumption Tax and the Income Tax do not. It is a powerful Allocative Tax, and termed, therefore, Magnifier Tax. With this tax in use, allocations would go into the desired lines even when we have an economy based upon the Private Sector. It harnesses the Private Sector in the Composite Economy to social needs and still uses the rate of profit mechanism rather than merely more exhortations to national duties. But it tilts the rate of profit substantially through fiscal action from the positive differential as at present in favour of the luxury-good industries, towards this differential in favour of the production of necessaries, and towards other right forms of investment and organisation. The tax system is used herein as an Actuative Instrument of an Inducive nature in a Firm State rather than Fiatory Instrument being used for allocation, which cannot work except in a Hard State.

The Disparity-Tax System consists in, first of all, finding out all the receipts of an individual through income, capital transaction and borrowings. The source of income is then ascertained and the amount scaled upwards according to the deviation from priority industries and optimum techniques of production and right form of organisation etc. This is a penal provision corresponding to lighting a fire in the hall with an open door. Income derived from the Heavy-Investment Sector, from production of consumer necessaries and their equipment with techniques which conserve Heavy-Investment resources would be scaled down forming an incentive instrument. Thus employment creation, the common man's need and long-term growth are all given incentives.

The national income thus derived, the assessee is next asked to present details of all investments which he has done. Each is allotted a scaling-up factor if it is in the approved (i.e. priority) lines, and a scaling-down factor if in an unapproved line. The former is an incentive instrument, and the latter a fiscal instrument. The two together indicate the tax to be an Actuative Instrument. The National Investment is thus ascertained by aggregating for all investments scaled up or down. The notional investment is deducted from the notional income and the residue is the base for the tax, as Notional Consumption. On the slab to which it belongs the tax is assessed on the basis of a scheduled constructed upon the principle of progressively progressive rise for higher and higher consumption brackets. In this there is no constraint of a hundred per cent maximum marginal tax and tax rates may be many hundred per cent. The tax assessed gets a rebate according to a schedule, if payment is made in terms of essential commodities or shares of firms within the concentrationing.

The person who acts according to the priorities of developments, who earn aright and invests aright, and who consumes little, receives the favour of the tax authorities and pays little tax. He has already paid his dues to the nation in helping to build up the economy in priority lines when all the market forces are inducing the individuals to deviate from these lines. The Fiscal Policy is attuned to steering clear the barge of the optimum economy through the great storm of market forces which threaten to overwhelm in any moment. But if the correct instrument is followed, the ship will go across unscathed as properly designed and piloted wooden sailing boats go across even the roaring forties. At the moment we are engaged in crossing the troubled waters of market forces and desires of the higher income groups, but have no sails designed to help us, nor is the boat specially constructed for crossing the rough oceans of development.

The Income Tax System has, therefore, to be converted into Disparity-Tax System which administratively presents no great difficulty because it deals with only two or three systematic schedules of approvals and disapprovals in place of the highly-complicated Income Tax Act which gives haphazard relief at scores of places.

The Wealth Tax has also to be converted into a Concentration Tax whereby firms owning more than, say, one crore of rupees capital would be subject to tax on their gross assets which are directly or indirectly controlled by one firm. This tax may be paid in the form of converting assets, to the extent of amount of the tax assessed, into ownership of the Joint Sector with clear government management.

It is denied that the Private Sector has access to management skills which the government does not have. The question is not one of availability but of the administrative structure. The skills exist in the country and can be shifted to the Public Sector if there are incentives for it and disincentive for their moving to private firms at very much higher employments. This can easily be rectified by the Disparity and Concentration Taxes.

But the real question is that a development-oriented economy requires in the Public Sector methods of administration and recruitment and criteria of efficiency which are widely different from the ones used in the present-day bureaucratic system, and whether the reorganisation of the administrative system can easily be made. Unless this is done, attracting personnel from the private sector does not fulfil the needs of society. If they are to be employed in the Public Sector to make profits for the enterprise then they will straightway start looking for avenues like Jumbo Jets, Refrigerators, Tape-Recorders and TV sets, or raising the charges for the essential services or goods produced (as the Railways and Airlines do under similar pressures).

The Disparity Tax is to be made applicable to Agricultural Incomes also for there could be a case for giving preferential treatment for those engaged in agricultural production but their spending would be treated in the same manner as those engaged in other priority industries. The Tax is meant to apply to Hindu Joint Families and religious trusts also. It also would apply to firms so that the incentives to boost up expenditure (as is prevalent in the present tax based upon preference Revenue and Expenditure) is converted to a disincentive. Thus the inessential consumption of firms would also be curbed and so also their size. The large scale usually uses the higher degree of mechanisation and yields a higher profit to wage ration. Irrespective of the degree of mechanisation, it also creates inequalities directly by the quantum of profits controlled by one group. The demand for luxuries comes basically from the inequalities of individuals and firms. This would be curbed at the source by achieving a more favourable distribution of income through production being encouraged by the Disparity-and-Concentration-Tax System in the smaller scales of production, specially the miniature scales.

This then is the surgeon's scalpel which we have been searching, as the fine instrument attuned to performing the delicate task attributed to it and not a crude instrument which harms more than it benefits. This can be in our hands through the slight appropriate administrative changes in tax administration necessary, with the tax authorities assisted by the Field Organisation to implement the objectives of the Plan. Comfared to this which can be available to the government as an efficient allocative mechanism, we have nowadays, under the pressure of Classical Public Finance, the revenue yielding taxes which are Condenser Taxes. With these being relief upon by the government there is little allocative mechanism in its hands.

During the last twenty-two years of Planning we have been trying to achieve the goals of development and social justice with hardly any instrument in our hands for if deficit financing under a Balanced Allocation Ratio and a Magnifier Allocative Tax System are ruled out the Actuative Instruments of Allocation pertaining to a Composite Economy are taken out of hands. Fiatory Instruments do not work in a State which is not a Hard State, for the dread of Atomic Bombs is ineffective for a rural economy. Paleo-economics has provided Condenser Taxes and the dictum of curbing of government expenditure on essential production till revenue is raised through high-yielding tax varieties (or borrowing from the public obtained at anti-investment rates of interests).

Classical Public Finance has thus given toy arrows in the hands of the Government. The builders of economic democracy in our Government with their enthusiasm to achieve growth and social justice are thus left defenceless and unarmed to go into battle against poverty. Little wonder that spectacular achievements in the sphere of attaining our objectives of proper types of growth and social justice have been absent in our system of planning. The remedy is to shift to a system of planning as pertinent to a Firm State in a Composite Economy functioning as an economic democracy where possession of wealth does not mean possession of purchasing power because of the penalties attached both the exercise of Consumer and Producer's sovereignty. The Plan regime cannot recognise any sovereignty except that of the State. The moment we are governed by the other sovereignties the Plan regime disappears, and it is only the outwards semblance of planning which remains with us. We must strive to put planning on a really firm footing in the country.

The problem of unemployment is not that of providing employment by itself but of the crisis in planning. This Minute is, therefore, written in order to reinforce the desire of the Committee to bring the basic issues facing national policies before the Government and Parliament. These refer to the framework itself and hence ought to relate to National Policy irrespective of differences of Political Parties.

Sd/-
(Gautam Mathur)

Note of Dissent by Dr. Ashok Mitra

I seek the indulgence of my colleages to append this note to the Committee's Report. The Committee's various recommendations in the preceding pages are by and large a compendium, I am afraid, of conventional wisdom, and mainly stress the need for enlarging the scale of official endeavours in various directions for redressing the burden of unemployment and under-employment. The implicit assumption is that employment creation is essentially a function of (a) the allocation of investment funds, and (b) the quality of organisation. A number of suggestions have been offered so that significant improvements could take place with respect to these.

The problem, as I see it, is however not one of parametric values. Even before one can discuss the issue of allocation of investment funds, one must refer to the fact of paucity of investible resources. And if the rate of capital formation in the economy is lagging behind, the underlying reasons may have to be sought in the social and political structure itself; exhortations on the desirability—or, for that matter, prescriptions regarding the modality—of raising this rate may by itself be of little avail. Similarly, if the pattern of expenditure in the Government sector has currently a particular orientation—for example, if provision for the maintenance of law and order is considered to be of greater importance than outlay for the relief of the unemployed—, any reordering of priorities cannot be effected in isolation of the basic political philosophy which informs the running of administration. If, despite the apparent soundness of schemes drawn up with the object of creating more jobs, at the operational level things go awry, it may be because of the political and social constraints that are at work; no amount of well-intentioned essay-writing would induce any additional purposiveness to the task of employment creation in case this cuts across the interests of entrenched groups.

It may therefore, not be altogether meaningful to indicate in any great detail those aspects of the Committee's recommendations in regard to which I have reservations. The problem is scarcely one of formulating an optimum frame of measures; it lies elsewhere—in the inertia and rigidities of the system. In what follows, I have contented myself by indicating the general directions along which pressures, I feel, have to be applied if the hopes and demands of the unemployed and under-employed masses are to be satisfied, even to a limited extent, in the near future.

Let me begin by referring to the demand voiced in certain quarters for the incorporation of a Constitutional guarantee to provide gainful work to all able-bodied citizens of the country. There is wide-spread political clamour for the right to work being enshrined in the directive principles of the Constitution and for full employment being declared explicitly as one of the major goals of public policy. Nothing more concrete is called for here beyond the passage of a Constitutional amendment; given the context, conceivably all political parties would support the measure. But, at the level of reality, the situation would perhaps remain much the same. The Constitution had directed that within a period of ten years from its commencement, children up to the age of 14 be provided with free and compulsory education. That stipulation has fallen by the wayside. A specific mention in the Constitution of the right to work and acknowledgement of full employment as one of the central objectives of public policy are unlikely to set any new rivers on fire. A dichotomy between official declarations and actual results obtained is by now taken for granted by nearly everybody, including, one suspects, Government agencies themselves. The course of history in the post-Independence period leaves one with little doubt that the authorities are stirred to effective action on an issue only when the consequence of passivity is reckoned to be far-reaching for the polity. In the matter of creation of employment opportunities too, it is only the acute danger of continued drift is recognised that one could look forward to a major overhaul of official policies and actions. Till that threshold is reached, resolutions and declarations of intents are likely to be of scant significance, for attempts to reach the declared goals would conflict with the interests of those on whom the authorities lean for political support.

This is the major reason for my inability to work up an excess of enthusiasm towards attempts to derive precise quantitative measurements of underemployment and unemployment in the different sectors of the economy. It is hardly the case that once the backlog of unemployment for a sector or region is known with exactitude, remedial measures would immediately follow. Till as long as the structural problems have not been squarely faced, it would be tantamount to skill fetishism to dilate upon the dimensional aspects of the phenomenon of unemployment. It is little solace to the deprived ones to be told that they are so many, or that the factors responsible for their plight are such and such, unless a genuine intent to correct the situation is evident in the appropriate quarters.

Besides, in the Indian mileu, the concept of employment itself has a certain vagueness about it. There are more or less standardised measures for assessing the degree of employment characterising a given unit of labour in an organised industrial sector. These however tend to get blurred as one moves away from the sphere of organised industry and enters the arena of rural employment, or employment in the so-called services sector. While it may be possible, under certain circumstances, to have well-defined concepts of wage employment, precision is necessarily missing from the various notions of self-employment. The concept of wage employment, it is certainly arguable, fast loses its immaculateness in the agricultural sector. A fair body of opinion will also assert that, for a large part of the Indian economy, the problem of employment creation basically hinges upon a wider diffusion of income opportunities. Provided the rate of economic growth is accelerated and, simultaneously, a range of reforms is pushed through to remove the institutional impediments standing in the way of a wider diffusion of incomes, the problem of unemployment and under-employment, it would be maintained, would lose its sting.

At the level of formalism, one may still want to force the authorities into accepting the principle of full employment for each and all. However, given the as yet inchoate character of several segments of the Indian economy, there will be scope for disagreement on the empirical correlates of the expression. A mere reiteration of the goal is by itself therefore unlikely to help matters. From the operational point of view, the most substantive part of the task, I feel, is to analyse the principal socio-political factors inhibiting the growth of employment opportunities and to enumerate the specific measures through which these difficulties could be taken care of.

Whatever else may or may not be said, the overriding cause for the slow rate of growth of employment opportunities is the slow rate of growth of the economy itself, during the past two-and-a-half decades, more particularly, in the more recent years. This slackening pace of economic growth has been a pervasive phenomenon, embracing both agriculture and industry, and in turn affecting the other sectors. Irrespective of whether the choice of technology during the period was optimal or otherwise given the inherently skewed distribution of asset-holdings, the halting rate of general economic growth could not but have led to a sluggish rate of expansion in employment opportunities.

The ultimate solution to the problem of general stagnation is intensified capital formation. Diverse views may be held over the pattern of allocation of aggregate investment which could bring about the optimum balance between growth of output and growth of employment. But there can hardly be any controversy over the need to increase, across the board, the rate of capital formation. If external resources are not taken into account the key task here is to raise the level of domestic savings. In this context, the possibility of coaxing additional savings through deficit financing may be discussed; some sympathy may also be expressed for the point of view that, since the authorities are not deterred from indulging in deficit financing to meet additional outlays for distinctly non-productive ventures there should be no qualms felt in recommending similar modes of financing for projects which hold promise of increased output and job opportunities within a reasonable period. But this would be in the nature of compounding a felony. Non-productive outlays would not be cut back merely because this Committee make certain recommendations. Under the circumstances, and given the administrative limitations and institutional biases, any attempt to force savings through credit creation is bound to give rise to indiscriminate price spiralling; this would tilt the structure of income discrimination further against the weaker sections and further shift the direction of private investments from productive to speculative ventures.

There can be ground for debate whether the bulk of fresh savings should be channelised to capital formation through the public sector or whether a significant portion be earmarked for private investment. This is however an issue of a second-order genre. It is the desirability of pushing up the national rate of savings which calls for prior acceptance. A major breakthrough needs to be achieved in agriculture, particularly that segment of it which is dominated by relatively prosperous farmers who produce for the market and enjoy surplus earnings. We now maintain in this country two dissociated regimes of savings and taxation. In the non-agricultural sector, savings perhaps exceed 15 per cent of income and taxes, as a proportion of income, are as high as 25 per cent. In contrast, in the agricultural sector, the level of taxation is unlikely to be more than 7 per cent of income; and the rate of savings is still less. Even taking into account savings directly invested in agriculture, aggregate savings in the sector, there is little doubt, has lagged way behind potentialities. The inordinately uneven structure of land distribution and the high concentration of the benefits of the so-called New Technology in the top fractile groups among agricultural earners have, if anything, aggravated this trend. The classical model of growth postulates an initial generation of savings in the farm sector; it is these savings which are subsequently transferred elsewhere in the economy for purposes of capital formation. In view of the political circumstances obtaining, even if it is conceded that no net transfer of resources away from agriculture to the other sectors need take place here, one may still maintain that, in the overall, agriculture should at least be self-reliant and should not depend upon resources generated in the other sectors, as is currently the case. A major institutional reform therefore ought to be directed towards reorganising the structure of agriculture, including the fiscal apparatus pertaining to it, so as to ensure that a larger flow of savings is forced out of the affluent groups. And it might indeed follow that once the affluent sections among the agricultural community are made to pay higher taxes, the rest of the economy too feel persuaded to move to a higher plateau of national endeavour.

One should have no illusion that voluntary measures by themselves would succeed in raising the level of farm savings, or in influencing the deployment of such savings along socially desirable directions. The instrumentality of taxation must necessarily play a major role here, and the underlying political issues have to be tackled. An incidental advantage stemming from more intensive agricultural taxation, as recognised by the Committee, is that it might force the pace of both land reforms and improvement in productivity, and thus reinforce the direct measures for employment creation. The increased burden of taxation could force the big landowners to dispose of some excess land at the margin, just as it might also induce greater productive activity where there is an urge to maintain the magnitude of net returns; in either event, employment is likely to expand.

The reluctance on the part of the authorities to add to the fiscal burden on the richer sections of the farming community has been made evident by a number of recent instances. Although several months have now elapsed since the Committee on Taxation of Agricultural Wealth and Income submitted its Report, not one meaningful step has been taken to process its recommendations. It is therefore futile to talk of a syndrome of higher savings leading to higher rates of capital formation leading to higher levels of economic activity generating higher levels of employment. The political pre-conditions for this are still lacking. An air of total unreality, I am afraid, thus attaches to the various proposals set forth in the Committee's Report seeking the deployment of substantially augmented funds for schemes intended to generate employment.

But even assuming that agriculture is cajoled into yielding a larger surplus, which in turn pushes up the level of savings in the other sectors of the economy, a host of other structural problems would still persist. Official endeavours for employment creation have concentrated on a familiar set of measures. These are the special and ad hoc schemes for providing short-term job opportunities for rural as well as urban youth, schemes for marginal farmers and agricultural labourers and plans and projects for assisting small farmers. There are also such ancillary programmes as rural works schemes for chronically drought affected areas and special schemes to provide employment to the educated unemployed. In addition, the banks and other financial institutions have been instructed to set up special proposals to advance credit for fostering self-employment. In the private industrial sphere, a number of fiscal and other incentives are available for promoting growth in the backward regions and in the small-scale sector, and which could be expected to have an impact on employment.

The broad thrust of the recommendations made by my colleagues is to enlarge the scale of operations of all such schemes, to have a vastly expanded base of outlays, to have, in other words, very much more of the same. Must not one take cognisance of the hard facts as they are? By now all of us should be well aware of what has been happening with the officially sponsored schemes over the years. Fiscal and monetary appropriations are scarcely enough. If the general mileau, the social structure, the political hinterland is each marked by a particular bias, the administration of the various employment schemes cannot but be affected by it. Funds intended for creating jobs for the landless and unemployed agricultural labourers have thus been diverted for other purposes, schemes for ameliorating the lot of the small farmers have lagged behind because basic inputs have not been made available, credit earmarked for impoverished cultivators or artisans at subsidised rates has remained undisbursed because of palpably impossible financial conditions imposed upon the latter, facilities reserved for small enterprises and backward regions have been diverted elsewhere on the basis of semantic pleas encouraged by the administrative hierarchy. A larger allotment of financial resources cannot alter the face of these realities. What is necessary is organisational overhaut at all levels and layers of the administration, an eradication of caste and class biases in the articulation of policies and programmes at the operational level, and a suspension of political predilections and animosities in the implementation of employment schemes. These changes are unlikely to come on their own. Where radical solutions are ruled out, one must think of instrumentalities within the existing polity which could force the authorities to move toward the direction of the institutional reforms referred to here.

Schemes for creating additional employment opportunities, referred to above, fall on the whole into three clear-cut types: those supported through budgetary measures, those dependent upon accommodation from the banking system, and, finally those heavily leaning upon subsidy-induced private industrial initiative*. True, total monetary provisions under these schemes are at present hopelessly inadequate to meet the requirements of the situation. A major plank in employment policy, there can be little doubt, ought to be to enlarge the scale of investments and ensure that the pattern of investment is optimally tilted toward the goal of employment generation. Even the limited outlays proposed under the various employment schemes have however not been fully utilised in recent years. Two principal deficiencies in the implementation of these schemes stand out. First, the actual expenditure has fallen considerably short, sometimes by as much as 80 per cent, of the intended target; second, whatever activities are undertaken under the schemes are confined usually to the top fractile groups among the unemployed, that is, to those who are on or about the so called poverty line, and the abysmally poor tend to be left out in the cold. Both deficiencies indicate an organisational lacuna which is as much an outcome of straightforward inefficiency as, let me add, of the institutional and social biases affecting the system.

The Committee's emphasis on ameliorating the conditions of those who are below the 'poverty line' is merely paying homage to current fashion. What is of much greater relevance is a concerted effort to provide work and income to the most under-privileged groups among them, a task the significance of which has been altogether missed out.

Moreover, under the existing arrangements, no opportunity cost attaches to any failure to fulfil the target of creating additional job opportunities. As far as the Government's involvement through the fiscal system is concerned, no further accountability than accountability to the legislature can of course exist in

---

* It could be argued that I am under-emphasising the role of massive public works based on direct mobilisation of labour for creating additional employment opportunities. But our experience with such programmes, wherever attempted, has been uniformly disappointing. And the reasons for this failure are well known. The effective implementation of socially oriented schemes of employment in the country depends upon the quality and dedication of rural leadership. Where the latter is given by sectarian biases direct physical mobilisation of labour becomes an unrealisable goal, or becomes the alibi for diverting associated public fund for the furtherance of private purposes.

the formal sense. Where the Government possesses a comfortable majority in Parliament, there can be no danger of any fall from grace even despite continuous failures to reach the set goals. Year in and year out, the number of new jobs created, whether under the Crash Schemes or under the SFDA programme or under the Scheme for marginal farmers and agricultural labourers, has fallen frighteningly short of the target announced with fanfare at the beginning of the fiscal year. As the year has ended, the usual, routinised explanations have been proffered for the failures, and the matter has seemingly closed there. Even with goodwill and good intentions at the top of the political and administrative hierarchy, organisational and socio-political bottlenecks at other levels can indeed stifle efforts towards creation of new employment opportunities. The point at issue is whether anything concrete is being done to eliminate the difficulties standing in the way. The presence of goodwill in the 'right' quarters is hardly enough. Where intentions are not backed up by adequate institutional measures, failure is foredoomed, for failure remains built into the system.

A similar fate has overtaken schemes for employment generation in the banking sector. From time to time, the banks have been urged to develop the necessary organisation and skills for promoting self-employment schemes and for providing financial accommodation to the weaker sections. But the authorities have been reluctant to set specific, time-bound targets for the banks and have been equally reluctant to assign notional targets of achievement for individual areas or zones. Here too, there is no dearth of ex post commiseration over the fact that not enough jobs are being created, but not enough stress is laid on the parallel fact that, given their inherited structural biases and the particular political pressures currently being brought to bear upon them, it would be impossible for the banks to fulfil the prescribed objectives. The banks, in turn, are aware that no particular stigma would be attributed to them in case the indicated goals are not attained.

In the private industrial sector too, while the Government have rules and procedures for encouraging the movement of investment to backward regions and for the creation of labour-intensive activities, in effect little has been done. Each of the procedures and norms has been reduced to a ritual, and apparently there is no serious effort in any quarters to translate them into reality.

The unemployed and the under-employed are therefore left to their own devices. From time to time, they are exhorted to take recourse to "self-employment" schemes, for which the financial institutions and other official and quasi-official agencies are supposed to offer special facilities. It is seemingly nobody's particular responsibility if these facilities are not actually forthcoming, and if no perceptible improvement takes place in the unemployment situation. It is a rather breath-taking instance of the lack of social ethics when the onus of obtaining gainful employment is transferred to the unemployed themselves, and the authorities merely observe from the sidelines.

Cannot one think of a penal instrument which, even within the present social and political framework, would compel the authorities to approach the task of employment creation with a greater degree of earnestness than what has been discerned till now ? In this connection, one may suggest for consideration the establishment of a Special Employment Fund to which compulsory contributions from the budget, the banking sector and the corporate sector could flow on a regular basis. Under the kind of arrangement I have in mind, at the beginning of each fiscal year, the Government would be enjoined to transfer the resources it intends to spend during the year on various schemes for employment creation to this Special Fund. Similarly, each bank or fiscal institution too would be asked to deposit with this Fund, at the beginning of the fiscal year, the financial resources which it was supposed to set aside for the promotion of new employment activities. Finally, a cess should be levied on organised industry at a rate, say, of two or three per cent of the average turnover of the preceding three years, and the proceeds of the cess transferred to the Employment Fund at the beginning of each fiscal year. In the course of the year, the Government agencies, the banks as well as organised industrial units would be able to draw from the Fund agreed sums, in accordance with specified norms, whenever projects involving fresh employment opportunities are being organised under their auspices. In case, however, there is a failure at the end of the year to reach the stipulated target by any of the agencies, the left-over resources would not revert to either the Government, or the banking sector, or the industrial units. These resources would stay with the Special Fund, which would use them to provide unemployment assistance to those who have registered themselves as unemployed in urban and rural areas, and who have remained involuntarily unemployed during the year. The necessary organisational under-pinning would have to be carefully worked out for ensuring that unemployment assistance is provided in an equitous and effective manner and with a minimum of leakage. If the organisation is not well-knit, there is a danger of resources from the Employment Fund being extensively misused. But it still depends upon whether the order of misuse of resources from the Fund is likely to be any greater than what it is at present under the various employment schemes. While the details of the organisation framework of the Employment Fund may wait, it seems reasonable to suggest that, at both the apex and the local levels, its administration should be reposed in the hands of a committee of which at least one-half of the membership would consist of elected representatives of the unemployed themselves.

The rationale of setting up such an Unemployment Fund is twofold. First, the awareness that a failure to fulfil the employment targets assigned to them would involve a measure of penalty could induce the corporate sector, the banks as well as Government agencies to a greater degree of effort to push through the necessary structural changes, the absence of which is largely responsible for the current failures. There is at present no cost attached to not carrying out the reforms, and the institutions and agencies are under no compulsion to change their attitudes and norms. Once, however, a monetary cost is chalked up against a failure to attain the targets, the banks, the Government agencies and the corporate units would be forced to initiate the necessary measures. If political factors stand in the way of implementing the called-for reforms, at least the opportunity cost of being swayed by a particular political consideration would be clearly spelled out in monetary terms.

The second point of attraction of a Central Employment Fund is that the social responsibility for the creation of employment opportunities would now be formally ascribed. If avenues for new job opportunities do not open up in an adequate manner, the fault for that does not lie with the unemployed, nor with the employed workers, but with those who take the basic economic decisions pertaining to the growth and distribution of incomes and assets in society. If, year in and year out, economic activities do not reach a level where at least some individuals are additionally absorbed in employment, under the existing arrangements, no responsibility for this failure attaches to anywhere, and everybody goes scot free. It is necessary that the Government and the richer sections of the community are made to admit their responsibility for looking after the unemployed and under-employed. At present, the vast mass of the unemployed are a burden on their friends and relations, who mostly belong to the acutely poverty-ridden social groups. There is, even today, a certain social fund which takes care of the unemployed, but to which no contribution is made either by the Government or the affluent classes. The unemployed generally spring from the families of small farmers, small artisans and the impoverished urban middle class, it is from out of the income of the latter that the unemployed are currently being maintained. Equity demands that the responsibility for looking after the unemployed is more directly assigned to those who are in a position to bear it better. It is only when the Government as well as the upper echelons in society are forced to become aware that there is a cost involved in not pushing through the institutional and social reforms necessary for facilitating additional employment that they would take up the obligatory task of social engineering with greater seriousness. Till that day dawns, the problem of unemployment will remain with us.

One feels tempted to end this note by generalising the plea for a Central Employment Fund, to be supported by fiscal receipts, for providing assistance to those groups of registered unemployed to whom society is unable to provide work. There seems little point in arguing that such kind of unemployment assistance, which may not immediately be matched by productive activity, spell danger for the economy. If society is unable to organise economic activities of the productive kind wherein the unemployed and under-employed could be gainfully absorbed, it would then be both cruel and immoral to deny them a minimum wherewithal for survival. Unemployment assistance at the rate of Rs. 500 per annum to, for exmple, 10 million individuals may of course amount to an annual outlay of Rs. 500 crores, but, then, the nation deploys more than three times as much for the maintenance of the defence services, which does not directly contribute to material output either. If ensuring the security of the nation is the primary consideration, it can indeed be argued that there could be no greater threat to the security of a nation than the existence of a massive magnitude, spilling into millions, of the unemployed and the under-employed.

Sd/-

(Ashok Mitra)

New Delhi,

May 15, 1973

INDIA, STUDY GROUP ON THE DEVELOPMENT OF THE PRESCHOOL CHILD, 1970—REPORT

New Delhi, Ministry of Education and Social Welfare, 1972. 100p.

Convener : Smt. Mina Swaminathan

Members : Shri M. C. Nanavatty ; Smt. Kitty Shiva Rao ; Dr. (Smt.) Margaret Khalakdina ; Dr. (Kum.) C. Nayar ; Kum. J. Jamuna Bai ; Dr. (Smt.) Chitra Naik ; Dr. (Smt.) Rajammal Devadas ; Dr. (Smt.) R. Muralidharan ; Dr. O. P. Ghai ; Shri Anil Bordia ; Smt. Champalakshmi Venkatachalam.

Member-Secretary : Shri J. P. Naik

APPOINTMENT

At its 35th Meeting held at New Delhi in May 1970, the Central Advisory Board of Education considered the services provided at present and those needed for the pre-school child and made the following recommendations in Resolution No. XVIII : "The Board recognises the significance of preprimary education and commends the proposal to try out pilot projects by mobilizing local community resources, especially in rural areas."

Accordingly the Ministry of Education and the Department of Social Welfare jointly set up a Study Group.

TERMS OF REFERENCE

To examine the question and to prepare a programme of action for the development of the preschool child through the mobilisation of local resources, especially in rural areas.

CONTENTS

Introduction ; Need, Significance and Objectives ; Existing Services ; Plan of Action ; Operational Models; Training of Personnel ; Equipment and Literature ; Research and Evaluation ; Administration ; Local Community Participation ; An Appeal ; Summary of Recommendations ; Appendices from I to IX.

RECOMMENDATIONS

Need and Significance

Integrated services combining education, health, nutrition and welfare are essential for the total development of the preschool child and should receive high priority and adequate resources.

Objective

The objective of such services should be to promote the optimum physical, mental, emotional and social development of the preschool child.

The different agencies concerned should make concerted and coordinated efforts to provide these services.

Collection of Data

Basic data collected at regular intervals are essential for a proper planning, implementation and evaluation of programmes for the preschool child. The Department of Social Welfare may be designated and adequately equipped to collect and publish this data annually.

Special Features that Need Emphasis

In drawing up a programme of services for the preschool population, special attention needs to be given to the vulnerable groups of children, remedying imbalances in the distribution of services, coordination among the agencies involved in the programme, expansion and reorientation of the training programmes and provision of guidance and supervision.

The New Approach

Strategies that would help in undertaking a sizable programme within the limited resources available include mobilising community support and involvement, employing local women in rural areas, part-time employment of educated women and students, maximum utilisation of existing institutions and facilities, and adoption of a variety of models.

Targets

About one million children in the age-group 3-5 are covered at present by existing services. A reasonable and feasible target of enrolment would be to cover 10 per cent or 5 million children by 1981, *i.e.*, one million more children by 1973-74 and a further 3 million by 1981, priority being given to children from the vulnerable sections of the population, *i.e.*, children from the urban slums, tribal areas and under-privileged groups in rural areas.

Need for Variety and Experimentation

(a) Flexibility and response to the needs of each situation are essential to maximise the benefits of the programme. A variety of operational models has been suggested which may be adapted to each situation in the most advantageous manner possible. These include the Comprehensive Day-Care Centre mainly for urban slums, half-day Balwadis, first stage centres, Anganwadis mainly for rural areas, and Primary school-based Centres.

(b) The special needs, difficulties and circumstances of the tribal areas call for an unorthodox approach and increased accent on community participation.

During the initial period (1972-74) greater emphasis will have to be placed on the low cost models. In the subsequent seven-year period, the improvement in the position expected regarding resources and trained personnel will facilitate the adoption of a larger proportion of the more comprehensive and hence costlier models.

Training of Personnel

The training and orientation of various categories of workers is essential for the success of the programme and should be accorded high priority. An adequate training programme of good quality should be designed for all categories of workers. It will also be necessary to create three new categories of workers : the part-time worker, the local woman worker and the supervisor.

The special features of the training programme recommended include : (1) alterations of the primary teacher training curriculum so as to bring primary and preschool education closer together ; (2) modification of the primary training course so as to bring it in line with the course for the Balsevikas ; (3) provision of new training courses for all categories of workers, including sandwich type courses and vacation and orientation courses ; (4) orientation towards urban, rural and tribal environments ; and (5) integration of extension, training and research in all training units.

Equipment

Provision of suitable and adequate play and educational equipment is essential for the success of the scheme. Scales of equipment have been suggested for the different models striking a mean between the optimum desirable and maximum possible. The State and local community should both contribute to provide these.

A variety of methods should be adopted to provide the necessary equipment, including mass production, local fabrication, class room improvisation, collection of folk toys, etc., and contributions of simple furnishings by the local community. Assistance should be given to institutions to establish prototype design units and display centres.

Literature

The existing literature on the subject being meagre, immediate steps should be taken to produce the needed literature for teachers, teacher-trainees, teacher educators, supervisors, administrators and planners, the community and the children themselves.

Research and Evaluation

Special emphasis should be laid on the development of appropriate programmes of research.

A programme of evaluation should be built into the different programmes recommended in the report, and should be the continuous responsibility of the supervisory staff and of the agencies at the district, State and national levels.

Administration

Implementation of a comprehensive programme of the kind detailed in this report requires a strong administrative machinery at all levels—national, State, district and local (rural and urban).

National Level ; (a) In order to ensure a strong and effective central machinery for the coordination of the programmes at the national level, a National Committee for the Preschool Child should be set up under the Chairmanship of the Union Minister for Education & Social Welfare. A Directorate for Preschool Programmes will look after the effective implementation of the decisions of the Committee.

State Level : (b) The department which would be responsible for the administration of this scheme at the State level will differ from State to State. Where more than one department is involved, a suitable coordinating machinery will need to be created. A full-time officer of appropriate status will have to be made responsible for the programme.

District Level : (c) The district being the most appropriate administrative unit for effective coordination in the field, a suitable coordinating committee should be set up with representatives from various agencies engaged in schemes of child welfare. A full-time officer of the status of a district officer and working directly under the Collector should look after the implementation of the programme.

Local Bodies—Rural : (d) Supervisors placed under the control of Zila Parishad or Panchayat Samiti should be provided facilities of transport to enable them to function effectively.

Local Bodies—Urban : (e) A Standing Committee of the municipal authority concerned should supervise the programme in urban areas. A special officer should be entrusted with the execution of the programme.

Estimated Costs

The total cost on the programme during 1972-74 will be Rs. 23.2 crores (Rs. 19 crores recurring and Rs. 4.2 crores non-recurring). This will involve an additional expenditure of Rs. 17.6 crores over and above what is already budgetted for nutrition programmes.

Local Community Participation

The maximum amount of community participation should be mobilised for the development of the preschool child. Such participation would include contribution in cash and kind, contribution in terms of voluntary services, and contribution towards buildings, equipment, and feeding programmes. Well-to-do communities should also extend support to those less advantageously placed. In addition, local bodies should explore all avenues to raise resources for preschool child services.

At the field level, all the programmes for the preschool child should be coordinated and implemented by a single field worker so as to convey the idea of integrated services to the community.

INDIA, COMMITTEE ON TECHNICAL CONSULTANCY SERVICES, 1970—REPORT

Delhi, Manager of Publications, 1971. 125p.

airman : Shri S. G. Barve

Members : Dr. A. Nagaraja Rao; Shri K. L. Ghei; Shri K. B. Rao; Shri P. C. Kapoor; Shri G. Jankiram; Shri R. P. Sinha; Dr. K. R. Chakravorty; Dr. K. S. Chari.

Member - Secretary : Shri Hari Bhushan.

(In March 1966 Shri K. L. Ghei expired; Shri T. Swaminathan, Secretary, Defence Supplies was appointed in his place but he had to leave, in order to take over as Economic Ambassador at Brussels. Subsequently the Committee received another shock through the sudden demise of Shri S. G. Barve. In addition, certain other changes in the posts held by the members of the Committee occurred as a result of which the Committee was re-organised in April 1967 as shown below :—)

Chairman : Shri M. S. Thacker

Members : Shri K. B. Rao; Dr. B. D. Kalelkar; Shri Ajit Mazoomdar; Shri G. Jankiram; Shri R. P. Sinha; Dr. K. R. Chakravorty; Dr. K. S. Chari; Shri R. M. Sharangpani.

Member-Secretary : Hari Bhushan

(Subsequently, Shri M. S. Thacker relinquished charge as Member of the Planning Commission, Shri Ajit Mazoomdar went on a long period assignment to a foreign country and Shri Hari Bhushan joined the Department of Iron & Steel. Accordingly the Committee had to be re-constituted in February 1970, as follows :—)

Chairman : Shri R. Venkataraman

Members : Shri K. B. Rao; Dr. B. D. Kalelkar; Shri K. D. N. Singh; Shri R. P. Sinha; Shri G. Jankiram; Dr. K. R. Chakravorty; Dr. K. S. Chari; Shri R. M. Sharangpani; Shri Hari Bhushan; Shri M. Satyapal.

Secretary : Shri N. N. Agrawal

TERMS OF REFERENCE

(i) To suggest the general type of organisational matters for the technical consultancy establishments which will be suitable for our conditions;

(ii) To recommend suitable measures to expedite the establishment of technical consultancy services to the requisite extent in country;

(iii) To advise on the pattern of technical collaboration or association, which may be necessary for drawing on foreign technical know-how to the required extent;

(iv) To assess the extent and types of technical consultancy services required to meet the country's needs during the Fourth Plan Period and subsequent years;

(v) To assess the existing facilities available in the country, in both the public and private sectors, and locate the gaps to be filled; and

(vi) To advise on the measures to be taken to fill the gap.

CONTENTS

Introduction; Nature and Types of Services of Technical Consultants; Regulation of the Profession; Conditions of Engagement and Scales of Fees; Measures for the Promotion of Indigenous Consultancy Services; Requirements of Consultancy and Engineering Services; Export of Consultancy Services; Main Conclusions and Recommendations; Appendixes I and II.

RECOMMENDATIONS

Technical Services

The services rendered by technical consultants can be classified into (1) Project Planning, (2) Project Designing, (3) Project Implementation, and (4) Project Evaluation. The professional engineers undertaking technical services can be broadly categorised as (a) consulting engineers, (b) process engineers, and (c) contracting engineers.

Consulting Engineers : Consulting engineers primarily undertake the planning and implementation of the projects. The process employed and the basic data for the process are generally obtained from the process engineers. Divergent views were expressed before the Committee regarding the definition of a consulting engineer. One view was that the consulting engineers should be 'independent' with no financial or commercial interests in manufacturing or contracting unit. The 'independent' consulting engineer could generally evaluate the comparative merits and select best of the available processes and equipment for his client. His judgement was not likely to get influenced so that the client stood to gain. Another view was that consulting engineers could be part of or 'associates' of equipment/product manufacturers, contractors or process suppliers. A consulting organisation 'associated' with a manufacturer could offer turn-key projects with guarantees of construction, time, costs, and performance and, therefore, more appropriate to the present stage of our development.

Process Engineers : These firms are sellers of the basic process and know-how and render an important service to the projects. They specialise in particular processes and cater, by and large, to the requirements of a section of a plant and have a complementary role. Their services can be obtained directly by the client or through the overall consultant, except in those rare cases where it is possible to engage the process suppliers and plant designers wholly to the exclusion of the other groups.

Contracting Engineers : They undertake the construction and erection of plants, based on the design and engineering done by the consulting/process engineers. It was suggested to the Committee that the role of contracting engineers should be recognised in view of their overall responsibility and the 'turn-key' project concept.

After taking into account the various views, the Committee has come to the following conclusions :—

(i) Consulting engineers may be grouped into two categories—(a) 'independent consultants' and (b) 'associated consultants'. Both types of consulting engineers have developed in India. They are helping in construction of indigenous projects, exports of consultancy services and turn-key projects. There appears to be need to disturb the existing pattern, although with the growth of a larger number of competing equipment and product manufacturers, the independent consulting engineers will grow and gain in importance.

(ii) The consulting engineers who form part of or are associated with any contracting organisation or manufacturer of product or equipment, should specify their status clearly so that the client knows their interests beforehand.

(iii) There is wide scope for the growth of process and equipment design organisations whose efforts are complementary to those of consulting engineers.

(iv) The manufacturers of equipment should strengthen their research and design cells and concentrate their efforts more on product design and development.

(v) The consulting as well as the contracting engineers are essential for setting up of projects and both should be given due recognition.

Regulation of the Profession

Engineering services have taken roots in this country during the last ten-fifteen years and time is now opportune to place them on sound footing. There was general agreement that in order to develop this profession on healthy lines and to avoid undesirable elements/practices, there should be an All-India Institution(s)/Association(s) on the lines of the Indian Institute of Chartered Accountants to lay down proper standards of education, experience, capability, capacity etc. There could be one All-India Institution/Association to represent both the 'independent' and 'associated' consultants; or else, there might be two such institutions/associations to represent the two types of consultants separately.

The proposed Institution(s)/Association(s) should prepare a Code of Conduct which should be followed by all practising consulting engineers. After examining the different standards/codes of conduct followed in other countries, the Committee was of the view that it was not advisable to adopt in entirety the U.K., U.S., Japan or any other foreign model. After taking due account of the developments in India, the objective of the proposed Code should be to encourage growth of consultancy services on sound lines, to make the services efficient, reliable and internationally competitive. The Code should also promote good relations beween the consultants, contractors and project owners.

The proposed All India Institution(s)/Association(s) will be useful particularly in respect of following :—

(i) Being an All India Organisation(s) with Government recognition, it will be able to lay high standards of discipline for the members.

(ii) Its standing will inspire confidence of the clients in its members.

(iii) It would more effectively represent the interests of the profession before Government and the public.

(iv) The unhealthy and self-defeating spectacle of rival claims by different bodies claiming to represent the same interests would be avoided.

(v) It would undertake, on behalf of its members, an examination of major projects planned for the future in order to identify the extent to which work could be assigned to its members.

(vi) It would provide an effective forum through which its members could advantageously consult each other on matters of common interest.

(vii) It would serve as the centre for documentation of information on consultancy and projects and thus it will be the store-house of least techniques and processes known to Indian consultants.

It is too early to establish such an Institution(s)/Association(s) by an Act of Parliament and to enforce its regulations through law. A start should be made initially by organising the proposed Institution(s)/Association(s) on voluntary basis and the Government recognising the Institution(s)/Association(s). After a few years of its working and in the light of experience gained, legislation could be undertaken to make it a legal entity parallel to the Institute of Chartered Accountants.

In order to expedite the formation of the proposed Institution(s)/Association(s) and to deal with other related problems, the Government should set up a broad-based "Panel of Experts" headed by a senior official of the Government of India with representatives of consultancy organisations of both categories (independent and associated), process and design engineers, contracting engineers, product and equipment manufacturers in the private and public sectors and Government Departments dealing with consultancy services and projects in one form or the other, with the following terms of reference :

(i) To decide whether there should be only one All-India Institution/Association to represent all types of Consultancy Organisations or there should be two—one to represent "independent" consulting engineers and the other for 'associated' consulting organisations.

(ii) To decide whether any one of the existing All-India Institution(s)/Association(s) should be recognised for this purpose or else a new organisation(s) set up.

(iii) To prepare the Constitution of the proposed Institution(s)/Association(s).

(iv) To set up and arrange registration of the proposed Association(s)/Institution(s) under the Societies Act of 1886 and recognition by the Government.

(v) To prepare guidelines for the appointment of consultants and fixation of their fees and other terms and conditions of their contract.

Conditions of Engagement

The Committee agreed with the view that engagement of consultants and fixing of their fees should be in accordance with the international practices adjusted to the Indian conditions. Price cutting and competitive bids should be avoided. Contracts should be awarded to the consultants based on their capability and experience and reasonableness of the bids. The consultants should follow the same standards and practices as are observed by the medical practitioners and Chartered Accountants. The method of calling tenders for appointment of consultants should be used only sparingly. Negotiations for striking a proper bargain cannot be ruled out. The quality of performance of a job would depend more on the competence and reputation of the consultant.

The proposed Institution(s)/Association(s) of the Consulting Engineers when set up could undertake to introduce guidelines and standards—(as drafted by the Experts Panel) amongst the consulting engineers. The Institution(s)/Association(s) should also prepare model contract forms for consultancy. Keeping all the factors in view, the Committee arrived at the following conclusions :

(i) Import of process know-how and equipment design should preferably be through consulting/process engineers. This would avoid the need to import the same know-how repeatedly, ensure quicker implementation and lower expenditure of foreign exchange.

(ii) This should not, however, tie the consultants and process engineers to a particular know-how, technology or process in a permanent or static way. The consultants and process engineers should keep themselves up-to-date and give up their interest in technologies and processes in which they hold rights in favour of latest and most up-to-date know-how. Client's interest in avoiding obsolescence has to be safeguarded.

(iii) In order to broad-base the industrial structure of the country and introduce latest know-how, import of new and improved processes and technologies for manufacture of the same product should be permitted when there is a demonstrable advantage in doing so.

(iv) Import of know-how and process designs should be as far as possible on non-exclusive basis.

(v) Import of package deals and turn-key jobs should not ordinarily be permitted.

(vi) Product and equipment manufacturers may not be precluded from acquiring the know-how and process designs from foreign countries to keep themselves up-to-date subject to the conditions that it is not on exclusive basis and it does not involve expenditure on machinery and equipment which can be fabricated within the country.

(vii) Facilities of foreign exchange for import of literature and for studies and re-orientation in foreign countries should be given to the Indian consultancy and process design organisations to enable them to acquire up-to-date knowledge.

(viii) The banks in India should regard consultancy and process design work as a regular business and offer advances on merits for meeting working capital requirements.

(ix) Proper liaison should be established between the Research Laboratories, Equipment and product manufacturers, Consultancy and Process Design Organisations. This will help to quicken the implementation and commercial use of the results of indigenous research, design and development.

The Committee noted the latest policy framework within which consultancy organisations with foreign collaboration are permitted to be set up in India. While such collaborations need not be discouraged, the uidelines provided and the powers already enjoyed by Government can be suitably used for ensuring that the country is progressively enabled to take up consultancy work for its own development, that knowledge and experience accumulates and that as little work as possible is contracted to outsiders. The guidelines could be enlarged to advantage on the basis of the following :—

(i) Collaboration between Indian Consultancy firms and foreign consultancy firms may be encouraged on the basis of specific projects in preference to foreign consultancy firms opening branches here.

(ii) Where Indian consultancy organisations or those with foreign collaboration already exist and do not have sufficient work load, new units in the same field with foreign collaboration should not be allowed except when they perform work on jobs to be put up outside India.

(iii) Foreign exchange should not generally be spent for feasibility studies.

(iv) The main work of compilation of data and designing of the plant and equipment must be done within the country, if necessary, by inducting assistance from foreign experts.

The Committee feels that in order to encourage the development of indigenous consultancy services, some fiscal reliefs are necessary. The following measures would go a long way in ameliorating the financial hardships faced by the consultancy organisations and would help their steady growth :—

(i) The banks should grant loans on easier terms to enable engineering organisations to meet their working capital needs. Consultancy and process engineering should be treated on par with other industries for purposes of bank loans.

(ii) The rate of income-tax for consultancy work should be lower than that applicable to other corporate bodies.

(iii) Income-tax should be levied on the average income of the past three years.

(iv) Indian Consultancy Organisations should be permitted to create special tax free reserve funds (like development reserves) from earnings during good periods to help them tide over occasional lean periods.

(v) Tax rebates should be permitted on fees received by indigenous organisations for passing on the available know-how.

Requirements of Consultancy Services

The consultancy charges vary from 5 to 15 per cent depending on the type of projects, specialisation involved etc. and on an average, such costs could be placed at 10 per cent of the project costs. The investments during the Fourth and subsequent Plans will provide ample work to indigenous consulting/process engineers.

The Committee feels that given suitable opportunities, Indian consultancy organisations would not be hindered by inadequacy of personnel. Apart from recruiting highly experienced and skilled personnel from within the country, efforts have to be made to get back the migrated Indian personnel working abroad by offering suitable assignments and conditions for work.

The Committee recognises that there are some gaps in consultancy and engineering services to be covered. The position in this respect is as follows :—

(i) **Process know-how** : Where there are restrictions to pass on the know-how to others in collaboration agreements, difficulties arise in dispersing the know-how and import from competitive sources for new projects becomes necessary. For some sophisticated industries not yet established in India, there are gaps in indigenously available process know-how. In such cases, foreign assistance has to be obtained which should preferably be on non-restrictive basis.

(ii) **Detailed engineering** : Once know-how details become available, the detailed designing and engineering of a plant could be satisfactorily undertaken by Indian consultancy organisations. With the increase in indigenous content of projects made possible, there is need for utilising indigenous capacity for detailed engineering designs for which the use of foreign consultants as supervisors may still be necessary.

(iii) **Procurement and Inspection** : In special cases where the process know-how has to be obtained from abroad for the first time, the help of a few foreign personnel for supervision, may be necessary.

(iv) **Start-up and performance guarantees** : Local consultants who have taken part in plant design may be capable of supervising the start-up and helping to achieve the performance guarantee. Wherever necessary, services of personnel from similar plants in operation or of foreign experts could be availed of.

(v) **Product and equipment design** : There is an imbalance between product design and production capacities in a large number of industries. The Committee feels that the main efforts required for correcting this imbalance should come from the plant manufacturers themselves. It would be better if the large design offices created along with various plants in both public and private sectors, are used more for product design and development. This would also result in reduction in their preoccupation with project design work which is mainly the function of consulting engineers.

The Committee reviewed the observations and recommendations made by a Study Group on industries in which foreign technical assistance was no longer considered necessary and suggests that, as a first step, use of foreign consultancy services with regard to the listed industries need not be allowed. This list should be periodically reviewed. Renewal of foreign collaboration agreements are resorted to on the plea of expansion and taking up the production of a new model or product. This often results in neglect of own effort to improve product design and process know-how. Extensions of collaboration agreements should be permitted in exceptional cases only.

Apart from the gaps in respect of functions, the gaps in certain specific sectors have also been studied which are summarised in the following paragraphs.

Power

Hydro Stations : The Central Water and Power Commission and the State Electricity Boards are well equipped to carry out all the work needed for planning and setting up of hydro electricity stations. A number of consultancy organisations both in the public and private sectors render engineering services in this field.

Thermal Stations : The Committee found that the existing consultancy organisations within the country would be adequate to take up the work involved in the setting up of thermal power stations in future.

Water and Power Development Consultancy Services (India) Limited has been set up in 1969 to provide engineering and related technical consultancy services for development of water resources, irrigation and drainage, electricity, flood control, etc.

Heavy Electrical Units at Bhopal and Hardwar are producing various types of equipment needed for electricity projects but depend upon their collaborators for securing design engineering for the equipment. The Research and Development Organisation for Electrical Industry (RDOEI) has been set up to prepare project reports, and to undertake consultancy and design work in electrical fields.

Telecommunications

The Telecommunications Research Centre undertakes design of telecommunication equipment and systems required by the P & T. All the designs evolved so far are without any foreign collaboration for know-how. The Research and Development Department of the P & T is also carrying out design and development work for specialised equipment for defence, railways and other users. Telephone equipment of different types and grades are now being manufactured in India without foreign collaboration. There are, however, various electronic components, such as, parmalloy laminations, mylar capacitors, integrated circuits, etc. for which India will have to import the necessary know-how.

Railways

The Research, Designs, and Standards Organisation under the Railway Board is well equipped to undertake consultancy services, import substitution, engineering services, preparation of designs and standards. RDSO is also rendering services for export of railway equipment as also for railway installations in some of the underdeveloped countries. India is more or less self-sufficient in all railway projects.

Ports

The country is not self-sufficient in providing consultancy services for the working and development of ports in India. In case of bigger ports and special problems, foreign consultants and engineers are employed.

Iron and Steel Plants

Some foreign assistance might be required in the detailed design and engineering for the main equipment. Steps have to be taken to develop these capacities quickly. Collaboration agreements would be necessary for L.D. Converters, similar to the ones now entered into by the Heavy Engineering Corporation for blast furnaces, coke ovens and concast plants. The CEDB should be strengthened to undertake work in fields in which India is not self-sufficient.

The Committee feels that the major equipment manufacturers could enter into licence agreements in selected fields with proper agencies in developed countries. The deficiency could be filled by :

(i) Liberal arrangements for taking up process know-how from abroad.

(ii) The existing heavy engineering firms or consultants should enter into technical collaboration with their counterparts abroad to obtain their research, development and designs for specialised and sophisticated equipment.

(iii) Strengthening of the heavy engineering units particularly, the H.E.C. by having design cells attached to them for designing specialised equipment for steel plant.

(iv) Strengthening of the CEDB which could in course of time undertake to work on lines in which India is still not self-reliant.

Aluminium

The NIDC has emerged as a fully equipped consultancy organisation in this field, with their taking up the Korba and Koyna Aluminium projects. The Committee understands that for the development of facilities for process know-how, an organisation in the nature of Aluminium Research Institute is proposed to be developed with the existing facilities in the National Metallurgical Laboratory as the nucleus. The Committee would urge that steps be taken early to fill this gap to ensure near self-sufficiency.

Coal Mining

There is no single indigenous organisation which can completely cover the technical consultancy services for the coal mining projects through organisations like NCDC, Sofra Mines (India) Ltd., and Civil and Mining Engineering Consultants can undertake the bulk of the consultancy work. In addition a few organisations like the Garden-reach Workshop, Mining and Allied Machinery Corporation, Heavy Engineering Corporation and Heatly and Gresham have developed sufficient design competency in selected fields.

The Planning and Development Division of the National Coal Development Corporation has now gained sufficient know-how and experience even for deep mines, and can undertake preparation of feasibility and project reports for future mines. Some of the deficiencies of the design and development cell of the NCDC could be supplemented by the MAMC. The consultancy services in the field of coal mining covered by the indigenous organisations need the following assistance :

(i) They have to be supplemented in the design engineering field by indigenous manufacturers of mining equipment, particularly MAMC.

(ii) In specialised fields, such as, new ventilation standards, hydraulic pneumatic stowing, introduction of new coal face mechanisation and support, development of very deep mines etc., the services of foreign experts should be allowed for a few years till expertise in these fields is built up.

Adequate facilities exist for working out the design parameters of coal washeries. Similarly, all the equipment required for coal-washeries can be procured from within the country.

Mining—other than Coal

Geology and Exploration : The Committee noted that expertise and facilities exist in the country for ground geophysical and geo-chemical surveys, mapping, surface and underground drilling, exploratory mining and ore appraisals. There are, however, no facilities to carry out air-borne geo-physical surveys. It is desirable to build up technical competence in the field.

Comprehensive geological investigations and appraisals of copper, lead, zinc, and iron ore deposits and development of large mines can now be carried out by Geological Survey of India and NMDC. In specific cases, however, if the services of expert drilling contractors from abroad are utilised, proper standards in ore drilling and sustained high rate of ore recovery could be built-up.

Mining

NMDC has built up considerable expertise for preparation of feasibility studies, choice of mining systems, mine layout development and operational know-how. The area in which foreign assistance would be required is in respect of up-to-date shaft sinking and tunnelling technique. Our engineers could be sent abroad for training.

Beneficiation

NMDC have so far utilised the services of foreign consultants for the project concept, lay out etc. of ore crushing, scruning, washing and loading plants for the Bailadila iron ore project. The know-how in the country for the beneficiation of iron ore fines by jigging or other methods is limited and it is necessary to have large scale tests *outside the country* and our plants designed accordingly. In the area of detailed engineering, good progress has been made by the Indian consultancy firms but there are gaps which have to be filled early.

Metallurgy

Process know-how is required in cases like flash smelting of copper concentrates, hydro-metallurgical techniques. In such cases, patents could preferably be obtained instead of taking them on the basis of tied credits and associated foreign consultancy with restrictive uses. In the field of procurement series and construction work, India know-how is sufficiently developed and use of foreign consultants should not be necessary.

Fertilisers

Complete consultancy services for the setting up of a fertiliser plant are now available indigenously. With the acquisition of know-how for ammonia, urea, ICI steam reforming process, Prayon phosphoric acid process and central Prayon hemi hydrate phospheric acid process, the Planning & Development Division of the Fertiliser Corporation of India and the FACT Engineering and Design Organisation (FEDO) of the Fertilisers and Chemicals Travancore Ltd. can take up new projects on 'turn-key' basis. In order to keep pace with the advanced technology, a good deal of research and pilot plant studies will be necessary.

Petroleum Refining and Petro-Chemical Industries

Apart from Engineers India Ltd., a public sector organisation set up to provide the necessary consultancy services in this field, other private consultancy organisations are also building up expertise for speedy and fuller development of indigenous know-how. The Committee is of the view that Indian organisations should be engaged as the prime consultant for all future refineries. Arrangements may also have to be made for close link-up of the experience gained by such organisations and problems covered by the Indian Institute of Petroleum.

(i) **Process know-how** : Initial purchases of process know-how with no restriction on repetitive use is desirable in petroleum refining and petro-chemicals. This could be done by either IOC or indigenous consultancy organisations.

(ii) **Process Design** : Once the process know-kow is obtained, the process design work should be taken up by indigenous design engineers. The services of foreign experts should be permitted where necessary.

Very little progress has been made to build up the necessary facilities for process design in the field of petro-chemicals. This needs urgent attention. Incentives for development of such facilities on desired lines may be considered.

(iii) **Detailed Engineering** : The detailed engineering can all be done in the country on the basis of process designs. Specialist assistance may be required in areas like (a) Design of thermally rated heat-exchanges ; (b) Design of distillation trays and columns ; and (c) Refinery heaters and furnaces.

(iv) **Shop Drawings** : Normally such drawings are prepared by the manufacturers of equipments themselves. Assistance may, however, have to be rendered by the consultancy organisations in view of inadequate drawing office facilities with some of the manufacturers.

The Committee studied the remaining industries, like heavy inorganic chemicals, sugar, cement and paper and found that the consultancy services in the country were more or less adequate.

The Committee has tried to identify areas where India has gained self-sufficiency and where the imports of consultancy services, process know-how, shop designs, detailed engineering were necessary. This does not, however, purport to be true for all times. Fields in which presently there is self-sufficiency may require imports of process know-how and consultancy services in view of new technological developments in foreign countries. On the contrary, fields in which presently there is need for import, India may acquire self-sufficiency with the research and technological developments being accomplished in the country. The proposed All-India Institution(s)/Association(s) of Consulting Engineers should prepare annually an authentic document indicating fields in which the country has gained self-sufficiency and gaps that still exist where imports are necessary.

On the basis of the Five Year Plans, the proposed Institution(s)/Association(s) may prepare a programme for developing consultancy and process engineering services needed for projects included in the plant.

For effective utilisation of the consultancy services available in the country, the proposed Institution(s)/Association(s) should arrange from time to time meetings of consulting/process engineers, contractors, equipment manufacturers, project owners/promoters, D.G.T.D., C.S.I.R. and other Research Organisations.

Exports

The development of consultancy and engineering services in this country is of recent origin, and primarily directed to import substitution. In several fields, India has built up capacities and gained experience which can be utilised to render engineering services to other developing countries.

India has an advantage over the more developed countries in providing consultancy services and undertaking 'turnkey' contracts in the neighbouring countries either for building up infra-structural facilities or for establishing industrial projects by virtue of her experience under similar conditions. India has reached self-sufficiency stage in respect of buildings, structurals, roads, bridges, rail transport, irrigation, power and telecomunication. She can establish complete projects of consumer industries like textiles, sugar, cement, paper, oil, food products, soap, cosmetics, leather, wool, beverages, alcoholic preparations and similar products, as also many types of mechanical, chemical metallurgical and mining industries. Projects could be set up with varying capacities to suit local demand. Further, the comparatively low cost of Indian engineering services is in advantage over the advanced countries.

India can render technical and organisational assistance to all developing countries in establishing small-scale industries with latest industrial technology and to undertake manufacture of various sophisticated items like radios, T.V. sets, automobile parts, colours, pigments etc.

In order to build up the exports of consultancy and engineering services from India, the Committee recommends the following lines of action :

(i) Conducting pre-investment surveys and preparation of pre-feasibility reports would be a distinct advantage for securing consultancy contracts in foreign countries.

(ii) Advance knowledge and information of the National Plants and the projects selected for execution will make consultancy organisations and equipment manufacturers ready with their bids to compete.

(iii) For meeting the requirements of package deals for turn-key jobs, Consortia of Consltants, process and design engineers and suppliers of equipment should be organised.

(iv) It may become necessary for the Indian consultancy organisations to go in for partnerships with reputed organisations in other countries and/or to accept sub-contracts from international firms.

(v) The proposed Institution(s)/Association(s) may bring out a Directory giving the names and fields of services of all consulting/process engineers, equipment manufacturers and contracting organisations in India and forward its copies to the Embassies in foreign countries.

(vi) Registration with the International Organisations like World Bank, UNIDO Asian Bank etc. would enable Indian consultancy firms to obtain consultancy jobs allotted on global basis.

(vii) In the interests of export of technical services and industrial equipment, credit facilities may have to be extended to developing countries which are short of foreign exchange and lack financial and other resources.

(viii) The banks may undertake to finance complete projects involving turn-key jobs and payments for contracts over long periods.

(ix) A Foreign Projects Development Fund may be created by the proposed Institution(s)/Association(s) for undertaking studies and establishing close contacts in foreign countries.

INDIA, COMMITTEE ON PRE-SCHOOL CHILDREN FEEDING PROGRAMMES, 1970—REPORT

Delhi, Manager of Publications, 1972, 125p.

Chairman : Shri T. R. Jayaraman

Members : Dr. N. A. Agha; Shri R. Subramanian; (replaced by Shri G. C. N. Chahal); Shri O. K. Moorthy; Dr. K. Bagchi (replaced by Shri R. Karnad).

Member - Convener : Shri K.V. Natarajan

APPOINTMENT

A suggestion was made in a meeting of the Nutrition Coordination Group Presided by Member (Agriculture), Shri B. Venkatappaiah on October 28, 1970 to constitute a Committee on Pre-School Feeding Programmes. The Coordination Group has considered various aspects of nutrition feeding programmes. It was proposed that an integrated picture of all feeding programmes catering to pre-school children should be obtained. Accordingly, the Planning Commission constituted the Committee on Pre-School Children Feeding Programmes Vide its Office Memorandum No. 20-4 (1)/70-Agri Dated December 5, 1970.

TERMS OF REFERENCE

(i) A close examination of the pre-school feeding programmes undertaken as part of the mid-day meals programme in order to dovetail them suitably with pre-school feeding programmes of the Social Welfare Department;

(ii) Suggesting ways and means of combining of the two programmes of the Department of Social Welfare to cover the age group of 0-6 years; and

(iii) Suggesting appropriate coordination between pre-school feeding programmes of the Department of Social Welfare and that of the Department of Education.

CONTENTS

Introduction; Pre-School Feeding Programme of other Departments and Policy Issues; Progress reporting on Nutrition Feeding Programmes; Research and Development; Transport for and Administration of Feeding Programmes; Coordination and Evaluation; Summary of Recommendations; Annexures from I to VIII.

RECOMMENDATIONS

Pre-School Children in Mid-Day Meals Programme

While 0-6 year is considered as the pre-school period, nearly 15-20 per cent of the age-group 5-6 years may already be in school though the compulsory school going age is six years. In streamlining feeding programmes, for pre-school children it is advisable to avoid catering for this group by two sets of feeding programmes. This can be ensured by confining pre-school children feeding programmes to age group 0-5 years, if the age group 5-6 years is covered in the mid-day meals scheme.

In certain States, Panchayat Raj institutions in rural areas and municipalities and corporations in urban areas are administering school feeding programme. In Madhya Pradesh the programme is confined to tribal schools. It appears advisable in the interest of mid-day meals programme that administration of the programme should rest with a single department in each State.

Assuming the number of feeding days in a year as 200 about Rs. 24.0 crores would be required in respect of food commodities for 119 lakh children now covered under the programme at the rate of 10 paise per meal per day. At present the States are spending about Rs. 6.4 crores on the programme. If the programme were to be self-supporting, the additional outlay required would be about Rs. 18 crores excluding expenditure on transport and distribution of foodstuffs.

The States were urged to consider large-scale schemes to utilize land attached to schools more intensively with the help of State Agriculture Departments.

Such an effort is yet to make an impact on feeding programmes. It should be intensified.

Increased community participation is essential for placing the mid-day meals schemes on a permanent footing. Participation of parents is also equally essential in a programme of this magnitude. If mahila samitis/mahila mandals are strengthened in each State, it may be possible to execute this programme at least partially through them in a period of 5—10 years. Panchayati Raj institutions can provide overall supervision in the implementation of the mid-day meals programme. State level nutrition coordination committee can also give leadership and guidance. If mahila mandals can take over the execution of the programme, the teacher will be relieved of the burden of cooking which is at present generally his responsibility.

In States like Punjab and Haryana, we noticed children of age group 4-5 years voluntarily visiting the schools which are also feeding centres. It is obvious that there is scope for arranging regular pre-school classes for such children. The Committee was glad to hear that the Union Social Welfare Department has a scheme under consideration for attaching balwadis to primary schools. When the proposal is put into operation, about one million children of pre-school age now attending school feeding centres can receive pre-school education and health service apart from the benefit of nutrition. We would, therefore, urge implementation of the new scheme expeditiously.

The number of feeding days generally ranges from 200-220. The National Institute of Nutrition is of the view that the number of feeding days in a year should be at least 250 to have the desired impact on the children. We suggest that this norm should be generally adopted.

We have considered the desirability of retaining the pre-school feeding component in the mid-day meals programme for school children. There are certain advantages in such an arrangement. The addition of the pre-school children to school children beneficiaries helps in improving economies of scale in terms of storage capacity, cooking time, etc.

The pre-school segment of mid-day meals programme of coordinated with the programmes of feeding of the Social Welfare Department, without much difficulty. In any village or town where there is a primary school and a centre for special nutritional feeding programme of the Department of Social Welfare, all the pre-school children should be fed at the latter centre.

The health and educational aspects of the programme are not always receiving the importance they deserve. The additional advantage of educating the pre-school child available in this programme should not be overlooked. It is necessary to inculcate the principles of nutrition both among the beneficiaries and the functionaries. From this point of view, we would recommend that demonstration feeding centres should be opened in schools in each state, fully equipped with model kitchens, utensils, etc., and adequate supply of drinking water. The existing facilities available for imparting nutrition education through mobile food and extension units of the Union Department of Food as well as through the demonstration feeding of the Applied Nutrition Programme and Composite Nutrition Programme conducted by the Union Department of the Community Development should also be fully utilised for the purpose.

Pre-School Feeding Programme of other Departments and Policy Issues

The major programme of the Department of Social Welfare relating to children of the age group 0—6 years in tribal areas and urban slums are administered by the State Governments directly. The other programme of nutrition feeding is organised through balwadis by certain All India bodies. We suggest speedy integration of these two programmes of the Department of Social Welfare.

The following suggestions may improve implementation of Special Nutrition Programme :

(i) immunisation programme for children and supply of drinking water should be adequately provided;

(ii) in the rural areas including tribal regions, the village school or the Panchayat Ghar could be utilised outside their normal working hours. There are plan programmes both in the Central and State Sectors which promote construction of school buildings, structures for mahila mandals, panchayat ghars and the like. Priority for locating these new buildings should be accorded taking into account the location of feeding programmes;

(iii) organisational machinery at ground level will have to be evolved to implement the programme without interruption;

(iv) effective supervision, guidance and follow-up at different levels will have to be ensured for this programme; and

(v) one of the weakest aspects of feeding programmes currently in operation is nutrition education. We noticed that even officers of the block level in some States were not aware of the educational aspects of the feeding programmes. There appears to be good case for imparting regular training in health, hygiene and nutrition education aspects to staff employed at different levels in feeding programmes.

In certain centres, the people resented immunisation being combined with feeding programmes. In such places, the State Government would have to take up the immunisation in a phased manner.

The question whether we should recommend a single administrative set up to deal with various pre-school feeding programmes in Government of India, has been examined. Taking into account various factors, an overall integration of pre-school feeding programmes does not appear to be attractive.

The Committee would like to recommend provision of sufficient manpower for cleaning all the food material at central kitchens before it is cooked.

One of the neglected but effective programmes with good potential is the use of locally produced food material for use in feeding programmes. If the country undertakes feeding programmes for pre-school children, pregnant women and lactating mothers on a large scale in the near future, as part of a general strategy of nutrition development, more attention will have to be devoted to enhance availability of locally produced foods for use in feeding programmes.

Modern bread used in feeding programme of Social Welfare Department in slum areas in Bangalore city is being supplied to the Government Dairy from where along with the bread, MILTONE produced in the dairy is sent out through the Dairy's usual channels of distribution to the distribution centres. Such innovations will have to be attempted in our view on a wider scale in various places.

In view of the difficulties of field level functionaries in maintaining accounts continuous efforts are needed in rationalising and simplifying feeding accounts. The attempt should be to evolve simple and easily understandable set of proformae. For this purpose assistance of experts of accounting procedures may be obtained.

The two schemes of Social Welfare Department supplemented by outright grants have been availed of with greater enthusiasm by State Governments than other programmes such as the Composite Nutrition Programme for Women and children and the mid-day meals programme for school children. The administration and transport costs for running these programmes are fully borne by State Governments. If special Nutrition Programme is extended to cover rural areas, there is a possibility of State Governments availing of the advantageous terms of central assistance of this programme and consequently shifting the beneficiaries from the pre-school component of mid-day meals to this programme. We would, therefore, recommend that Special Nutrition Programme should confine itself in future to the age group 0—5 years only if in any locality, the mid-day meals programme caters to the age group of 5—6 years.

Wherever any programme calls for a benchmark survey, the funds for the purpose should be provided in the initial sanction of the scheme itself and technically competent persons should be requisitioned to undertake baseline studies of anthropometric measurements and other important data as baseline.

Progress Reporting on Nutrition Feeding Programmes

The question, whether or not, it is necessary to collect progress reports on a monthly basis or more frequently was considered by us. It may not be necessary to collect information on a daily or a monthly basis. It is adequate if reports on nutrition feeding schemes are furnished to Government of India either quarterly or half yearly.

Various supplemental feeding programmes are being implemented by Departments of Education and Social Welfare at the Centre. We may have to move gradually to set up certain uniform standards and patterns for progress reporting on all feeding schemes. It would be meaningful to adopt the number of 'child days' or 'woman days' on which feeding was carried out as the unit for progress reporting. The concept of child days has been evolved by a simple process of multiplication of the number of beneficiaries by the number of days they were fed.

The proforma should be simple and should contain columns showing number of beneficiaries, feeding days, quantity of food supplied, type of food served and cost of food supplied per child per day. The existing proforma used for collecting progress reports on the Special Nutrition Programme in tribal and slum areas given in Annexure III may be considered for adoption.

It is necessary to set up a small centre for collection of data relating to various nutrition feeding schemes, preferably at the block level. Each feeding centre, would furnish information to the block preferably once a month to such a centre. Each block may be provided with one assistant, to coordinate this information and forward to state headquarters. Such a centre may function as part of the administrative machinery of the community development block level. The scheme could be financed by the Government of India during its operation in the first five years.

The progress reports received from the block will have to be examined at state level and discrepancies rectified before sending them to Government of India. A qualitative appraisal of the progress of each schemes should also accompany the consolidated statements from the state after they have been examined by the state level Nutrition Coordination Committee. One of the functions that we envisage for the State Committee is to evaluate the progress reports on nutrition pro- grammes from time to time.

At present, delays in submission of progress reports ranges from three to twelve months. It is necessary that progress reposts should be furnished in time not only for a periodical appraisal of the schemes, but also for modifications if necessary in their implementation.

Research and Development

Nutrition education is a weak link in the pre-school feeding programmes. To ensure healthy growth of the child, research in and development of nutrition feeding should be taken up on an extensive scale. Such research effort should encompass not only nutritional variables but socio-economic and socio-psychological variable relating to eating habits.

An area of research which requires priority is the communication of right ideas on hygiene, environmental sanitation and malnutrition to the mother and the child. We suggest that operating departments should set apart funds for research programmes relating to their fields in their annual budgets.

The Agricultural production plan should be oriented towards ensuring supply of adequate and sufficiently nutritive food for the child. In any such effort, both local research and local finance will play an important role. The effort should be to meet all costs of feeding programmes not so much in the shape of cash as of commodities locally grown and contributed for use in the programme.

Research has to be organised in small units such as a district or a group of districts. Two essential requirements of such research would be compactness and homogeneity of agroclimatic conditions. Institutions best suited to organise such areawise research are agricultural universities and national institutes of research like the National Institute of Nutrition, Central Food Technological Research Institute and Indian Agricultural Research Institute. Such research should lead to self-reliance in nutritional programmes.

Considerable experimentation and research needs to be done in existing pre-cooked or other suitably processed and nutritious foods which would be easy to transport and find ready acceptance with the child.

Existing feeding programmes for pre-school children, tend to serve more as a 'substitute' than as a 'supplement' to regular meals. The implications of such a development domestic, social and financial would have to be studied and solution found.

Patterns of consumption for specific age groups, communities, regions are not readily available. Data are limited on well balanced diets using locally available low cost foods. Department of Food of Union Ministry of Agriculture will shortly commence a research programme for linear programming of low cost nutritious foods. There is considerable scope for such research effort in future.

The operational difficulties of "take home" feeding have to be studied and it has to be assessed whether cost of such feeding would bear comparison with conventional centre-based feeding programmes.

There are programmes for expansion of production of MILTONE in the Fourth Plan of Union Department of Food. We would welcome such expansion so that the slender fresh milk resources of the country are extended in order to feed the pre-school child in various parts of the country.

It is necessary that locations of centres for feeding programmes of several departments and agencies of Government are not too widely dispersed. Feeding programmes in rural areas to the extent, it is feasible, should be located close to each other so that the results of efforts made in the local production of nutritious foods could be shared by all concerned. Similarly, State farms in such cluster areas could play a significant role in production and propagation of soyabean and other protein rich crops. A link has therefore to be forged between state farms and local efforts directed towards feeding programmes.

Transport for and Administration of Feeding Programme

Inadequate storage facilities have led to deterioration of foodstuffs used. We suggest, therefore, a phased programme for building godowns all over the country as part of the integrated programmes of nutrition in the five year plans.

It is necessary that problems of storage and delivery of food materials for feeding programmes in tribal areas are socially gone into and efforts made to solve them expeditiously.

It was noticed that owing to inadequate storage facilities, class rooms were being used for storage, thereby affecting normal work. Funds now being made available under crash scheme for rural employment could be utilised for building storage in schools.

The programme of administration of feeding materials should be handled by the bulk user department in each State. We would like to emphasise that the transport and distribution should remain the responsibility of a single Department in each State.

Coordination and Evaluation

The success of the programmes of supplemental feeding will depend on the effectiveness of machinery in State, not only for implementation of individual programmes but for their integration and coordination. For this purpose, the Planning Commission has recommended constitution of a Coordination Committee in each State. We suggest that the States which have not set up Coordination Committees should constitute such Committees early. It will be necessary for these Committees to meet at least once a quarter. Similar Committees may be set up at district level.

We envisage the following functions for State Level Coordination Committees for Nutrition :

(i) to work out as far as possible uniform pattern of procurement, storage and distribution of foodstuffs;

(ii) to avoid overlapping in setting up feeding centres and in coverage of beneficiaries;

(iii) to lay down guidelines for effective supervision and implementation of feeding programme by coordinating the functions and responsibilities of field staff presently appointed under different agencies;

(iv) to work out in-service training programme from time to time for field staff as well as for voluntary organisations involved in implementation of feeding programmes;

(v) to organise conferences and seminars from time to time on pre-school children feeding programmes;

(vi) to prescribe proforma and obtain quarterly reports, regarding progress and to evaluate them from time to time; and

(vii) to examine evaluation reports on feeding programmes and take quick decisions on them.

It is estimated that in the Fourth Five Year Plan, the outlay on supplementary feeding programmes would be of the order of Rs. 300 crores, including the cost of food material used and expenses on administration and transport. It is, therefore, necessary that planning and implementing agencies and departments at the Centre and States should know from time to time the impact of such feeding programmes on beneficiaries as well as on the community.

Evaluation can be broadly classified into two types : (a) internal evaluation and (b) independent evaluation. Internal evaluation, however, cannot replace objective assessment and evaluation by an independent agency. We recommend that an evaluation unit should be set up at the Centre for continuous evaluation of supplemental feeding programmes. Representatives of departments implementing these schemes as well as experts in the field will have to be associated with such a Centre not only to direct evaluation studies from time to time but also to review the reports and recommend action on them. It will also be necessary to formulate appropriate yardsticks for evaluation which are reliable and valid and at the same time simple and easily applicable to field conditions.

Apart from the agency for evaluation that we have recommended, universities and research institutions should be persuaded to undertake *ad hoc* studies on different aspects of feeding programmes.

CHAIRMAN INDEX

INDEX